AF605897

ALUMNAE THEATRE COMPANY

Nonprofessionalizing Theatre in Canada

Alumnae Theatre Company

Nonprofessionalizing Theatre in Canada

ROBIN C. WHITTAKER

UNIVERSITY OF TORONTO PRESS
Toronto Buffalo London

© University of Toronto Press 2024
Toronto Buffalo London
utorontopress.com
Printed in the USA

ISBN 978-1-4875-4826-1 (cloth) ISBN 978-1-4875-4829-2 (EPUB)
ISBN 978-1-4875-4830-8 (PDF)

Library and Archives Canada Cataloguing in Publication

Title: Alumnae Theatre Company : nonprofessionalizing theatre in Canada / Robin C. Whittaker.
Names: Whittaker, Robin, 1976– author.
Description: Includes bibliographical references and index.
Identifiers: Canadiana (print) 20240386108 | Canadiana (ebook) 20240386167 |
ISBN 9781487548261 (cloth) | ISBN 9781487548292 (EPUB) | ISBN 9781487548308 (PDF)
Subjects: LCSH: Alumnae Theatre Company – History. | LCSH: Amateur theater – Ontario – Toronto – History. | LCSH: Women in the theater – Ontario – Toronto – History.
Classification: LCC PN3169.C32 T67 2024 | DDC 792.02/2209713541 – dc23

Cover design: Alexa Love
Cover image: David Gardner

We wish to acknowledge the land on which the University of Toronto Press operates. This land is the traditional territory of the Wendat, the Anishnaabeg, the Haudenosaunee, the Métis, and the Mississaugas of the Credit First Nation.

This book has been published with the help of a grant from the Federation for the Humanities and Social Sciences, through the Awards to Scholarly Publications Program, using funds provided by the Social Sciences and Humanities Research Council of Canada.

University of Toronto Press acknowledges the financial support of the Government of Canada, the Canada Council for the Arts, and the Ontario Arts Council, an agency of the Government of Ontario, for its publishing activities.

Canada Council for the Arts
Conseil des Arts du Canada

Funded by the Government of Canada
Financé par le gouvernement du Canada
Canada

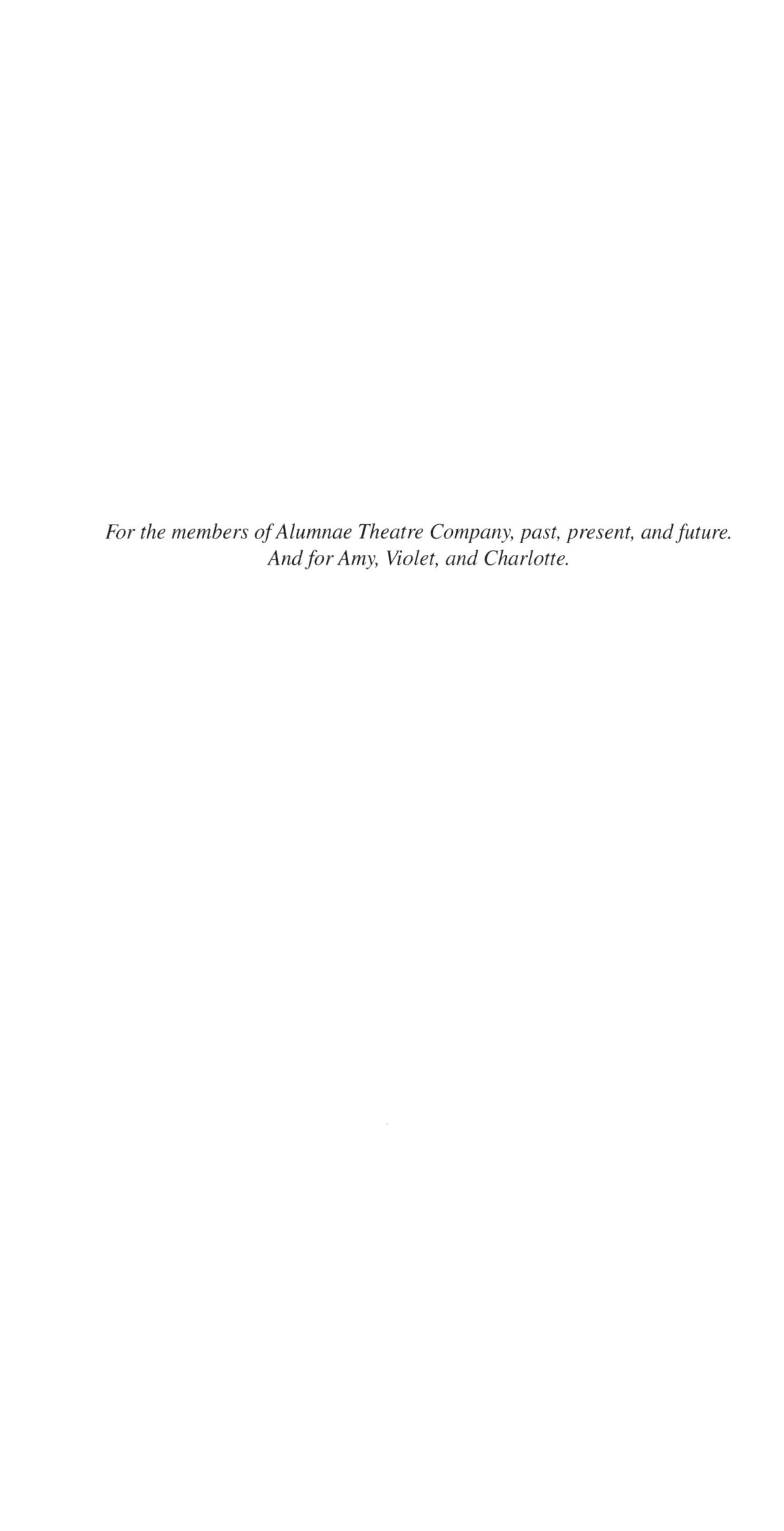

For the members of Alumnae Theatre Company, past, present, and future.
And for Amy, Violet, and Charlotte.

Contents

Illustrations

Preface

At the one-hundredth annual general meeting of Alumnae Theatre Company on 24 June 2018, club president Brenda Darling addressed the audience by enumerating a busy centennial season, one that had been officially acknowledged by Canada's prime minister, Ontario's premier, Ontario's Minister of Tourism, Culture and Sport, and Toronto's mayor. As had become typical of Alumnae's annual output, the season featured three mainstage productions, fifteen short plays at the New Ideas Festival, three full-length works at the FireWorks Festival, many monthly New Play Development Group meetings, various bimonthly member meetings, and half a dozen Next Stage Readings, as well as three-session Writers' Intensives, Write Now, Big Ideas, Doors Open Toronto, training and development workshops, a members' seasonal pot luck, opening night catering, a bimonthly newsletter, and "$60,000 worth of rentals."[1] The centennial also precipitated a new Aboriginal Land Acknowledgment,[2] a catered season launch gala, a fundraising campaign, an online auction, an audience program selling ads, new lobby furniture and manikins,[3] merchandising, and a host of policy and building upgrades. The exceptional "Ladies of the Alum"[4] were busier than ever.

Notwithstanding all of this activity, a year later a feature article by Sadaf Ahsan appeared in the *National Post* declaring that Alumnae had "become somewhat forgotten in Canadian stage circles" and "could use a siren to gain attention." Wrote Ahsan: "Later, when I reach out to a number of theatre experts, at least a dozen admit to not being familiar with Alumnae or much of its story. That seems unusual for a group with as much history as Alumnae's. Maybe it's because, since its founding in 1918 by University of Toronto graduates, the company has been moved around like furniture that doesn't quite fit a room."[5]

We will get to the moving of spaces and furniture in due course. For now, I wish to ask: How has a theatre company, very much producing full seasons of theatre in Canada's largest urban centre, achieved a century of longevity, yet found itself forgotten by contemporary scholars and journalists? How has it stayed relevant decade after decade as funding mechanisms, training practices, personnel, the profession, and the arts sector have changed? What does the creative ecology owe this long-standing, women-run theatre company and its founding daughters? In this book, I am interested in the discursive structures that give birth to the creative impulse to produce theatre, and in the moments at which urban companies like Alumnae reject the strictures of disciplinary professionalization in order to address the immediate, definable needs and goals of arts-interested citizens.

For more than one hundred years, Alumnae – or "*the* Alumnae" as members affectionately call themselves – have produced theatre at several locations across Toronto on lands that are the traditional territory of many nations, including the Mississaugas of the Credit, the Anishnabeg, the Chippewa, the Haudenosaunee, and the Wendat peoples. Since 1972, the furniture has fit the rooms at Toronto's repurposed Firehall No. 4. But also since that year, the idea of valuing amateur theatre practices has become far less stable. With the growth of professionalization and unionization in Canadian theatre, that idea has faded to the point that most drama, theatre, and performance scholars, as well as critics – the few who remain – ignore it completely. The field of nonprofessionalizing, participatory theatre has evolved from being nearly the only place to involve local talent (during the Little Theatre Movement in Canada's interwar years), to the best place to provide local talent with opportunities to engage with new and experimental work (after the Second World War), to an environment in which ideological and financial barriers have gradually denied professionalizing artists who join unions access to nonprofessionalizing practice (in the mid- and late twentieth century), to a site of near complete discursive obscurity today. Alumnae have succeeded better than most at navigating this shifting, professionalizing terrain, but they have also fallen victim to its machinations. As training conservatories became gatekeepers to Canada's professional stages, starting in earnest with the National Theatre School in 1960 and appearing in Toronto and across the country in the decades that followed, experience gained in nonprofessionalizing theatre companies like Alumnae lost educational and social capital, and as a consequence, emerging artists lost interest in those companies. Concurrently, as women increasingly entered professions, they often had less time for group-organized leisure pursuits with multiweek timelines. And audiences, for their part, preferred to spend their limited time and money on weeknights and evenings encountering professionalized activities. In a very real general sense, that is the history of a century of cultural practices under modern capitalism. Alumnae Theatre Company is a case study of a venue that confronted this trajectory.

An important element of feminist scholarship has sought to reconstruct women's experience using available, documented traces. The question of *why* this process of reconstruction has become necessary is itself essential to the field. In the case of Alumnae's many generations of educated women, part of the answer is both obvious and complex: as "amateur" artists, however professionally minded, they have eluded the attention of researchers, despite an extraordinary record of introducing Toronto to new and contemporary plays. In this study, whenever possible, I have attempted to incorporate a multitude of voices, especially those of the Alumnae members themselves. This polyvocality seeks to foreground Alumnae's women-centred management across the decades. I have also drawn extensively from theatre criticism, particularly reviews and commentary, that is contemporary to the practices studied in order to draw attention to how critical thought has evolved across those same decades. I have also brought to the fore relevant scholarly discourses about Canadian theatre over the past century. Taken together, the words of Alumnae's practitioners and the critics who encountered them help narrativize the story and impact of Alumnae Theatre Company in the context of Canadian drama, theatre, and performance studies.

Alumnae members have attempted several times to write their own history. The plethora of press releases and history brochures generated by Alumnae since 1945, and the occasional features about the company in the daily papers, amount to a series of fragmented narratives from year to year. The idea of a "book or booklet" about Alumnae was first suggested by long-time member Pamela Terry Beckwith in the mid-1990s and was taken up by then-president Sheila MacDonald Tait, who called for interested members to contact her to help "with interviews, research, and writing."[6] Around this time, Alumnae archivist Catherine Spence began putting out calls to the members to submit to her any archival material they had for Alumnae's collections. Later, it was suggested that a graduate student be brought in to undertake the "History project" and that Alumnae's erstwhile Priddle Memorial Scholarship Fund be used towards this purpose (an idea that was rejected because the fund had been established specifically to support training in technical theatre skills). By 2000, the idea of "creating an oral history" of Alumnae was being floated to the board, and board member Naomi Hunter volunteered for the task.[7] Hunter prepared to "interview and record older Alumnae members and friends, including Herbert Whittaker."[8] Inspired by a retrospective that Alumnae presented at an open house on 21 April 2001, members Helen Dunlop and Barbara Barnett began "discussing creating a book about Alumnae's History."[9] Francess Halpenny then took up the idea with Dunlop and presented a perspective that was "enthusiastically approved" by the board of directors.[10] Halpenny astutely wrote in her prospectus:

> The history of this company is a history of people, of playing spaces, of plays. It is a history of women who have acted, produced, been backstage crew, run the box office and managed the club finances. It is a history of friends – friends in theatre. Few groups have lasted this long and the history will try to explore why. The narrative will tell a story, both lively and serious. It will record successes but also setbacks. It will make use of anecdote and reminiscence to give the personal touches such a narrative needs. There will be spotlights on productions that represent key moments in Alumnae's story. That story will be, finally, a contribution to the history of theatre in Canada.[11]

She interviewed Herbert Whittaker, Cicely Thomson, Pamela Terry, Molly Thom, Esther Hocking, and David Gardner.[12] Dunlop reported in June 2002 that the project had "become a much larger undertaking than any of us realized when we began but we have been encouraged by the enthusiasm expressed by everyone we have reached."[13] They approached the University of Toronto for a research assistant to be paid by the government for a year.[14] They also retained a local writer to continue the project, who, unfortunately, had to abandon it. In 2005, I approached Alumnae for the first time with an interest in including them in my dissertation on nonprofessionalizing theatre practices in Canada, which I completed in 2009. In a sense, much of my research over the past two decades has sought to capture all of these aspirations in the context of drama, theatre, and performance studies, with the purpose of addressing liminal spaces and glaring lacunae. This book on Alumnae Theatre Company within a drama, theatre, and performance studies context does just that.

Acknowledgments

Two decades ago I emailed Alumnae Theatre Company asking if I could access any archival material they might have with the hope of fashioning an essay for a "Theatrical Documents" course taught by John Astington at the University of Toronto's Centre for Drama, Theatre, and Performance Studies (then the Graduate Centre for Study of Drama) as part of my doctoral studies. The result was a meeting with Alumnae luminaries Catherine Spence, Francess Halpenny, and Helen Dunlop at Helen's apartment. They happily agreed. And they asked if I was interested in writing a book about Alumnae. When I said it would have to be a scholarly, peer-reviewed assessment of the company, and not a "fond reminiscience," Francess said she would have it no other way. Over the next five years, the essay grew into a chapter in my dissertation on amateur theatre practices in Canada. That chapter formed the kernel of this study.

Catherine Spence, Alumnae's (volunteer) theatre manager and archivist, made this research possible. For two decades she granted me permission to access Alumnae's bountiful in-house collections. She also aided in scanning images and working through permissions. She made it possible for this examination of Alumnae's first century to be set in print. Before Catherine, Agatha Leonard collected Alumnae's materials from the 1920s to the 1980s, encouraging generations of members to submit their documents so that she could preserve them from one theatre space to the next. This is how histories are collected: persistent hands, manila envelopes, and metal filing cabinets.

Generous Alumnae members and former members took the time to be interviewed: Jane Carnwath, PJ Hammond, Shelagh Kareda, Martha Mann, Catherine Spence, Margaret Spence (with her husband Michael, Alumnae's building manager and technical director for many decades), Anne Tait, and Molly Thom. Shelagh, whose connection to Alumnae is as a former member and also through both her late mother Alison and her late husband Urjo, was particularly kind in engaging me in many conversations about Alumnae. I am saddened that this book did not make it to print in time for Francess, Helen, Martha, and Michael to see it.

For two decades, James McKinnon (who introduced me to Edmonton's nonprofessionalizing theatre, Walterdale Playhouse) and Barry Freeman have been among countless colleagues and friends at the Canadian Association for Theatre Research who provided feedback when I presented papers and engaged in "hallway chats" on Alumnae. I am grateful to my dissertation committee: Bruce Barton, Alan Filewod, and Heather Murray, and external examiner Anne Nothof.

Many generous colleagues and friends supported this book, including several who read early chapter drafts and the manuscript proposal: Kristi Allain, Matthew Hayes, Jessica Riley, Anne Nothof, and Nick Thran. Michael Dawson and Catherine Gidney at St. Thomas University gave particular collegial support and encouragement. Chris Saad, St. Thomas's technical director, kindly helped me understand mid-century theatre lighting equipment and estimate the dimensions of a 1918 stage from a photograph.

The Canadian Association for Theatre Research (CATR), an organization constitutive of many close colleagues, has been instrumental in the development of various threads of research pursued in this study. At CATR, I have presented nearly a dozen papers related to nonprofessionalizing performance practices over the past twenty years and received essential feedback from many colleagues that is represented, in one way or another, in these pages. For these opportunities, I am boundlessly thankful and humbled

I am indebted to the two enthusiastic peer review readers of this manuscript. Some of the most encouraging words I have heard about this project came from them. I am very grateful to the University of Toronto Press, editor Mark Thompson, copy editor Matthew Kudelka, and the UTP staff for their diligent work on the book.

The process of obtaining image permissions was fairly smooth. My thanks to Andrea Gordon and her colleagues at The Canadian Press's Licensing Department for promptly helping secure permission to print the whimsical *Globe and Mail* "Off-College St." map. Indeed, Andrea was a wellspring of information on how to strategize securing image permissions. I am also indebted to Jessie A. and her colleagues in the Special Collections Department at the Toronto Reference Library for digitally reproducing the two photographs of the auditorium at the old Toronto Conservatory of Music. I am also grateful to Marnee Gamble at the University of Toronto archives for guidance on Hart House Theatre permissions. Julie Grahame, representing the Yousuf Karsh estate, granted permission to use one of Karsh's photographs, and Dr. Martha Fleming kindly provided permission to reproduce her father Allan Fleming's show poster.

I am indebted to Stephanie Dotto for generating the alt.text and extended descriptions for the images that enhance this book's accessibility as well as for indexing the book, and to research assistant Hillary Shields, who digitized about 8,000 of 22,000 archival documents used to prepare this study, making it possible for me to write a book about a Toronto theatre company while living in Fredericton.

This book has been published with the help of a grant from the Federation for the Humanities and Social Sciences, through the Awards to Scholarly Publications Program, using funds provided by the Social Sciences and Humanities Research Council of Canada. I am grateful to St. Thomas University and its Senate Research Committee for recommending this book's manuscript for the Wallace and Margaret McCain Course Release Award and the STU Scholarly Book Publishing Grant, which afforded me time to complete captioning and proofreading, as well as money to generate alt text, extended descriptions, and indexing. Over the years the committee also approved a series of research and travel grants for me to work in Alumnae's collections and to present conference papers.

My father Brian and my late mother Marlene taught me that writing is vital. Both my father and my stepmother Marieken have supported my every step back in Toronto. Years ago, my grade eight teacher Mr. Maslan instilled in me a fearlessness of the over-forty-page-paper.

And finally, but really *imprimis*, my wife Amy and my daughters Violet and Charlotte have shown a world of patience, wonderment, and curiosity while I navigated all of the work of this book. To them I am boundlessly grateful.

Abbreviations

Alumnae	Dramatic Club of the University College Alumnae Association, University Alumnae Dramatic Club, the Coach House Theatre, the Firehall Theatre, Alumnae Theatre Company
CBC	Canadian Broadcasting Corporation
CODL	Central Ontario Drama League
DDF	Dominion Drama Festival
UADC	University Alumnae Dramatic Club
UC	University College
UCAA	University College Alumnae Association
WDC	Women's Dramatic Club of University College

ALUMNAE THEATRE COMPANY

Nonprofessionalizing Theatre in Canada

Alumnae Theatre Company, Alterity, and the Idea of Nonprofessionalizing Theatre

On 12 February 1918, three days ahead of opening night, the *Toronto Telegram* announced:

> DEBUT OF NEW DRAMATIC CLUB
> Four former presidents of the University Undergraduate Dramatic Club are members of the new organization formed by the University College Alumnae Association, which makes its histrionic debut this week on behalf of the University Base Hospital. They are the Misses Edna Bach, Isobel Cassidy, Marjorie Fraser, and Mrs. Lotton [*sic*: Laughton]; while the remainder of the cast, which will present the initial offering, *The Blue Stockings*, includes the Misses Erskine Keys, Mona Clark, Jessie Reade, Helen Stewart, Norma Mortimer and Margaret Boyle, president of the new club.[1]

Enthusiasm was calculated. It was reported that the 25¢ and 50¢ tickets[2] sold at the registrar's office[3] were "disappearing like hot cakes so no time ought to be lost."[4] Two days before opening, the front page of the *Varsity*, U of T's undergraduate student newspaper, declared that it "promises to be a Great Success – Full of Human Nature."[5] And hours before curtain at the 400-seat Conservatory Music Hall, the *Varsity*'s front page insisted, "You can't afford to miss *Bluestockings*."[6]

Thus, on the evenings of Friday and Saturday, 15 and 16 February 1918, audiences filled the Music Hall for a "very clever translation" of Molière's *Les Femmes Savantes*. From the "sympathetic"[7] and "big audience,"[8] "warm applause greeted the varied sallies of wit."[9] The *Varsity* declared the production a "distinct triumph," which the "appreciative applause of the audience confirmed." Moreover, the "stage stetting was most artistic, and the costuming admirably suited to the period in which the play was written."[10] The Toronto daily the *Globe* remarked that verisimilitude in all aspects of the staging was approached, although perhaps not entirely achieved: "The stage setting was capital, carrying out the eighteenth century [*sic*] period of the play very effectively. The dresses of the actors and actresses were also very handsome and in keeping, and, if a word of criticism must be offered, were rather better than the make-up of the players, but this is a defect that can easily be remedied before to-night's performance."[11]

No images of the set survive; however, contemporary photographs of the auditorium suggest that for it to be so convincing, the set must have been substantial, given that the stage was about 30 feet wide downstage, 20 feet wide upstage, and 30 feet deep. During that era, set painters were retained from the famed Arts and Letters Club, so it may very

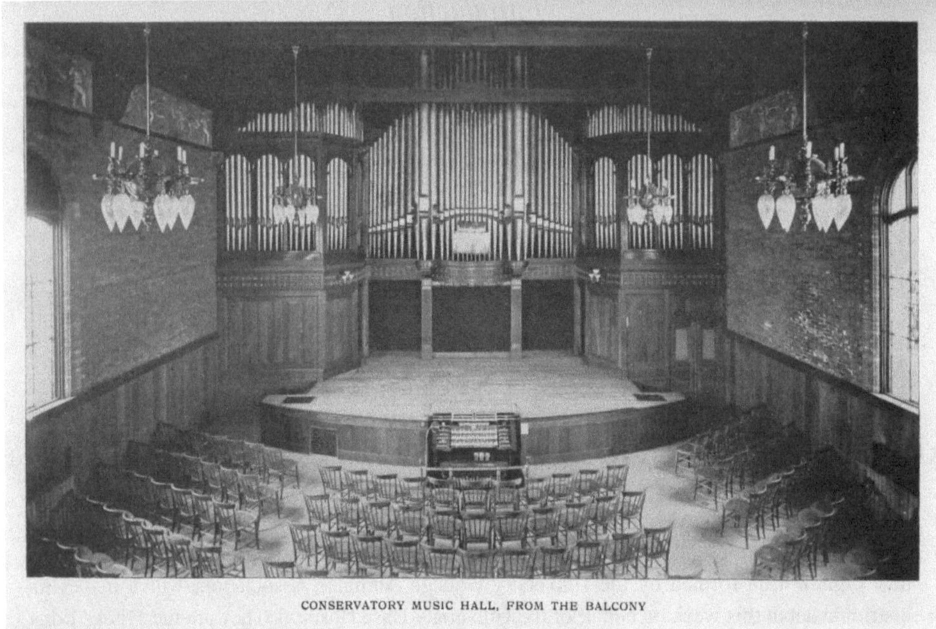

CONSERVATORY MUSIC HALL, FROM THE BALCONY

Figure 0.1. Conservatory Music Hall, view from balcony. Alumnae staged their first production, Moliére's *Les Femmes Savantes*, in the Music Hall at the Toronto Conservatory of Music in February 1918. *Toronto Conservatory Yearbook* (1918). Courtesy of Toronto Public Library.

well be that the "most artistic" setting was composed of flats painted by trained and accomplished hands.

The *Varsity* praised the cast. Edna Bach's Henriette, "by her wholesome charm, captured the sympathy of the audience in the first scene, and held it throughout the play." Norma Mortimer's triple performance of the Notary, Valet, and Lackey "provoked much merriment."[12] Isobel Cassidy's Chrysale, played by Molière himself in the play's 1672 Paris premiere, gave "scope for her powers"[13] and, surely, "to those who have witnessed her former success in similar roles, no comment is necessary." There was Mona Clark's "amusing" performance of Armande, Mary Laughton's "cleverly portrayed" Philaminte, and Isabel Jones's "interesting"[14] interpretation of Belise. Dr. Frank Home Kirkpatrick, the respected oratory instructor from the Toronto Conservatory School of Expression, directed the cast of eleven.[15] In presenting *The Bluestockings*, Molière's wry satire on women and education, these women were using their theatre talents to raise funds for the University of Toronto's University Base Hospital. A theatre group run by determined women was in this way born into a world at war.

The UCAA Dramatic Club – the group that produced the play – was bringing Molière's seventeenth-century play to a Canadian city that at the time was losing thousands of its husbands and sons in Europe. In the winter of 1918 the impact of mandated conscription and the progress of women's suffrage were unmistakable. A palpable, even political, realization must have entered audience members' imaginations as they regarded the all-female

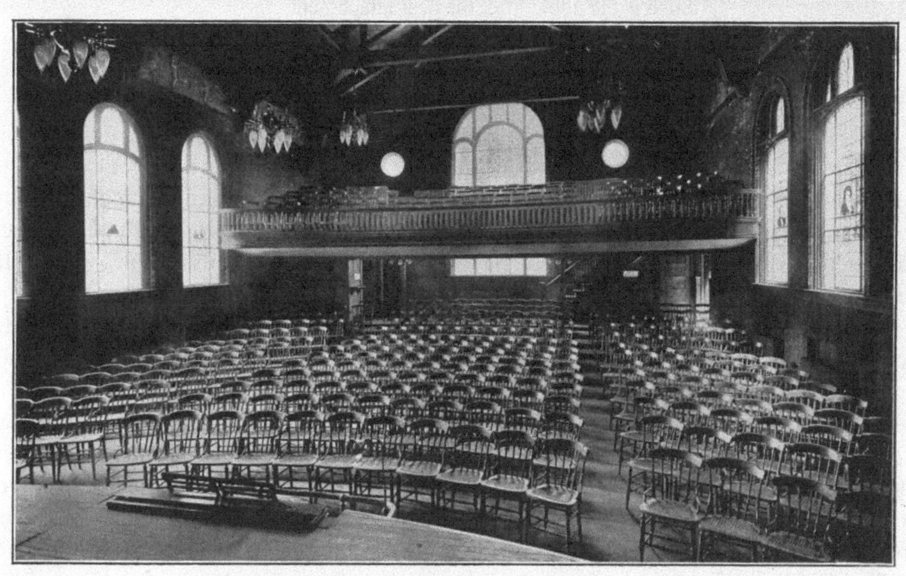

Figure 0.2. Conservatory Music Hall, view from stage. Auditorium of the Music Hall at the Toronto Conservatory of Music where Alumnae staged their first play, Moliére's *Les Femmes Savantes*, in February 1918. *Toronto Conservatory Yearbook* (1918). Courtesy of Toronto Public Library.

cast and heard, at the play's outset, a young Armande scolding her sister Henriette for her "vulgar plan" to marry:

> Lift up your thoughts and hopes to higher things,
> And train your taste to care for nobler pleasures;
> So, treating sense and substance with contempt,
> Devote yourself to mind alone, as we do.
> You have our mother for your perfect model,
> Whom all men honour with the name of learned;
> Try, then, like me, to prove yourself her daughter;
> Aspire to show a like intelligence,
> And learn to feel those raptures exquisite
> Which love of study pours through every vein.
> Nay, scorn to be the slave of some mere man,
> Be wedded, sister, to philosophy
> That lifts us far above mankind, and gives
> The reason sovereign lordship and control
> Over our brutish parts, whose gross desires
> Debase us to the level of the beasts.

Such is the noble love, the dear attachment
That ought to fill each moment of our lives.
Those lower cares so many women covet
Appear to me most wretched pettiness.

Armande attempts to convince her sister that she should apply her intellect to studious pursuits and abjure "lower cares" for "higher things." She should join with philosophy, not live for "some mere man." And she should "prove" herself worthy of her mother. Armande has chosen education and the "nobler pleasures" of philosophy above the patriarchal edicts and gendered expectations of her time, and she wishes her sister would do the same. In the context of families broken by international conflict, what the Toronto audience saw was their educated daughters publicly performing the choice of self-edification over traditional family responsibilities. They were not pining for absent love in times of war but seeking endless knowledge. Nor were they submitting to what Henriette, moments earlier, termed a "blameless life"[16] of marriage. On stage they performed characters who debated established norms. They were implicating themselves in new visions of the future where they could be active agents of social good and artistic influence. The fact that five of them played the play's male characters further performed alternative futures for women pursuing (conventionally) male roles in society. In the century to come these women and their successors would perform imagined worlds on many stages to raise capital for new buildings, new plays, new performance styles, and new talent. These University of Toronto graduates were *les femmes savantes* performing the emerging place of intellectualism and entertainment for women in a new society.

Born into the modern professional classes at the turn of the twentieth century, the founding daughters of Alumnae Theatre had fathers who were judges, lawyers, physicians, professors, architects, military officers, members of the clergy, and in one case a sea captain. Some had mothers whose names were prominent in the society pages or in charity and education circles. Many had attended private girls' schools like Bishop Strachan, Havergal College, and Glen Mawr (located where the University of Toronto's graduate residence now stands) and later involved themselves in events and fundraisers for these alma maters, as they would for the UCAA. At the University of Toronto, most of them developed leadership skills as members of undergraduate societies like the UC Women's Dramatic Club, the UC Women's Literary Society (where they organized lectures on drama and other literary subjects[17] and presented short plays), the UC Women's Athletic Association,[18] the Alliance Française,[19] and various sororities. Some made calculated use of their education, pursuing notable careers as lawyers, professors, social workers, teachers, editors, librarians, and secretaries. Some married doctors, lawyers, and artists. Others never wed, possibly because of their vigorous commitment to their own education and professional careers; possibly because of a lack of men on the homefront during and after the war; possibly because of a personal disinterest in entering into a relationship with a man; and almost certainly because of a newly articulated feminism that drove their lives, work, and theatre practice (see Appendix I).

As young women in the 1920s and 1930s, they remained avid readers of literature, especially plays, attended professional touring productions at Toronto's Royal Alexandra Theatre, and travelled to see shows in London and New York. Francess Halpenny, the influential editor of the University of Toronto Press and Alumnae's longest-serving member to date, explained that through the UCAA Dramatic Club they "built connections with the little theatre of Hart House and they had many links with the Arts and Letters Club ... They themselves sold tickets and sponsored Theatre Nights, a necessity that had an influence on repertoire."[20] Halpenny's words resonate with those of scholar Kym Bird, who describes the Canadian women who wrote plays in the decades before the UCAA Dramatic Club: "Educated, often well-married, employed in the professions [with] opportunity, instruction and moxie ... They were white, often middle and upper class of Anglo- and Irish-descent, and identified with the cultural elite of their societ[y]." Where Bird sees "gender oppression"[21] as a motivating factor in early women playwrights' work, Halpenny locates Alumnae's "moxie" in their education, connections, savvy work ethic, and strong interest in experiencing theatre on and off campus. Similarly, prominent member Molly Thom characterized the group's beginnings in the context of "women's liberation," for this was a time when "women were being emancipated and they wanted to do their own thing."[22] Many early Alumnae members found local celebrity working not only with Alumnae, but also with other groups like Hart House Theatre's Players Club, the Arts and Letters Club, the Dickens Fellowship, the Toronto Public Library's Drama Club, the New Theatre of the Margaret Eaton School, and the Playwrights Studio Group.

The Bluestockings was the first production by the women-run group now known as Alumnae Theatre Company. A prescient choice in name and content, the play provides an insightful touchstone for the company's ethos. Its premise serves as an analogy for the purposes, programming, space, and local and national distinctions that "Alumnae" have sought for most of their existence. Flexible from one decade to the next, yet committed to their chosen path, Toronto's learned ladies have produced timely, literate, intellectual, popular, and often politically informed plays, from Ancient Greek tragedy to world premieres. As philanthropic alumnae, they helped raise money for university infrastructure and community organizations; as new play purveyors, they helped lead the local surge towards a "national theatre" by presenting world premieres by Canadian writers; and today, they continue to nurture emerging writers of one-act and full-length plays. They have sold out theatres of various sizes and shapes even as critical standards and interests have changed and Canadian theatre has become professionalized. Devoted to quality theatre productions, the women of Alumnae were, and often still are, educated, middle-class career women in an industry notorious for keeping women out of leadership roles.[23] They have provided experience to generations of theatre artists and administrators and have influenced a long succession of Toronto theatre companies and audiences. Mentors, role models, and even landladies to mid-century stage stars and theatre founders, Alumnae's members have contributed to setting theatre standards. They are surely what Armande aspires her sister to be.

Toronto's *Femmes Savantes*

Alumnae Theatre Company is North America's longest-running women-led theatre company and Canada's second-longest-running theatre company (after Ottawa Little Theatre).[24] Although they built a series of intimate "Coach House" theatres in Toronto between 1957 and 1969, and were the only theatre company in Toronto to own their own space between 1962 and 1969,[25] Alumnae are identifiable today by their historic Edwardian-style firehall-turned-theatre-complex at 70 Berkeley Street at Adelaide Street in Toronto's post-industrial

Figure 0.3. Alumnae Theatre Company's Firehall Theatre in 2010. Since 1972, Alumnae's home has been in an Edwardian-style firehall on the corner of Berkeley and Adelaide streets. It was built in 1871 and renovated by renowned Canadian architect Ron Thom for their use as theatre and administrative spaces. Photo Credit: Robin C. Whittaker.

Corktown neighbourhood. As a not-for-profit theatre, they are known primarily for their commitment to developing and producing new full-length and one-act plays through two annual new play festivals, as well as for doing second Toronto runs of Canadian plays. They have produced plays for public audiences since 1918 (except for three years during the Second World War, when they performed private theatricals at club meetings, read plays for future productions, knitted military items, and, in the case of a few members, performed in troop shows across Ontario). They have managed their finances by balancing production aspirations with membership, box office, and rental income. They have never depended on government operating grants, a fact that has afforded them freedom of choice in programming. Their embrace of nonprofessionalizing, participatory labour is made possible by "immense volunteer assistance."[26]

But what most clearly sets Alumnae apart from other theatre companies is that all members – as has been true since the company's founding in 1918 – are women. In fact, until the Second World War, members were exclusively female graduates of the University of Toronto's University College. In later years, after the war until the late-1980s, members could be female graduates of any post-secondary institution.[27] Today, the club accepts any woman who wishes to contribute either through an Active Membership (i.e., she participates on- or off-stage) or through a Supporting or Senior Supporting Membership (i.e., she pays a higher fee but is not expected to participate directly in productions or administration). Men participate in productions or work on regular maintenance of the theatre as guests of the company. Thus, for more than a century, it has been women who have made all of the company's programming and administrative decisions. As Halpenny explained in 1968, the "composition may seem odd to men when they first encounter the group, but they soon seem to adapt themselves to what is, after all, rather an attractive situation in which participation does not mean responsibility."[28]

Alumnae's members have always all been women, quite intentionally so. Yet Alumnae both are and are not a feminist theatre company. The reasons for their success and endurance reside within this paradox: the companionship is *female*, yet the goals are not always deliberately *feminist*. Alumnae's women have always led their theatre with foresight and adaptability in the context of companionship, common objectives, and an interest in serving the broadest audience demographics. The companionship arises from a nonprofessionalizing theatre environment that relies on a desire to be present among others with shared objectives and the skills and interest to accomplish them, as opposed to doing the work to sustain a livelihood. In "Theatre, Performance, and the Amateur Turn," Nadine Holdsworth and her colleagues observe that amateur theatres lay bare the "practice of sociability" and "build the foundations for and reinforce social bonds."[29] But whereas these in themselves are not exclusively feminist experiences, Alumnae's members often reflect on how their particular practice of sociable theatre is experienced from a woman's perspective. After the Second World War, Halpenny wrote that

> on many occasions people have marveled that such a small group of women could work together harmoniously for so many years and have sought an explanation. No doubt there are many reasons. A lack of "professional" jealousy, a willingness to accept criticism cheerfully, and a dislike of bickering and malicious gossip would certainly be contributory causes, but in the writer's opinion there are two main reasons for the unity of the Club. There are two bonds which hold the members together and they are bonds not easily loosed. The first is an unshakable love of the theatre and the second is a virtue supposedly reserved for the male sex – real friendship.[30]

Seventy-two years later, long-time member Margaret Spence called Alumnae "one of my core friendships in Toronto. Probably *the* core friendship. My girls are both members … I don't know that I particularly encourage them. They've come along by themselves … My friends have become their friends regardless of the age."[31] Through theatre, Alumnae provide a unique space for female collaboration that is often intergenerational.[32] Taken together, their words serve as both a description of Alumnae's theatre practice and a prescription for a feminist theatre practice developed long before the city offered a dedicated feminist theatre.

Alumnae have attracted and retained women members for various reasons. PJ Hammond, a past president, treasurer, executive producer, and influential member from the late 1990s to 2014, said that it was the "quality of work and the commitment" that brought her back: "We all do what we have to do. And we do it together … And we do it well."[33] For director Jane Carnwath, who first worked for them in the late 1950s, Alumnae has long been a place to forge connections on multiple fronts, especially since her return to the company in the mid-1970s:

> We became very connected both socially and artistically. It was kind of home. It became, it still is, a home … I get to do stuff I really love to do. That's mainly it. I get to direct really wonderful plays. And have people to work with who are top costume designers and set designers who really know their craft. I love that cooperative kind of work. We're doing a team thing … If you can get a team that works the way you want to work there's nothing like it. You help share the vision. You know, you just put the rest of your life aside.[34]

This connection between the theatre as "work" and the theatre as a "home" has remained a constant across successive Alumnae generations. Taking the work seriously, coming back to work with friends, and inviting new women into the company are part of what sets Alumnae apart from other theatre groups.

The interests of Alumnae members have guided company choices since the First World War–era suffragist movement, through the women's liberation movement and second-wave feminism of the 1960s and 1970s and the third-wave feminism of the 1990s, right to the present day. In her study of the American Little Theatre Movement, Dorothy Chansky writes that the success of women in early twentieth-century amateur theatre was often used to reinscribe the binary "paid / outside / professional / successful (male)" on the one hand and "unpaid / local / amateur / inexperienced (female)"[35] on the other. But Alumnae have always leveraged the nexus of their nonprofessionalizing status and their all-female status to their advantage, proudly applying both to the cause of programming freedom. At times their play selection has clearly had a feminist bent, as in the 1930s and 1940s when they produced short plays by women involved with the women-founded Playwrights Studio Group in Toronto, and in the late 1960s through the 1980s, when they adapted literary works from women's perspectives for staged readings. Being a women-run company has made them stand out in Toronto's theatre ecology since their self-reflexive production of *The Bluestockings*, and they have repeatedly used this unique position to their advantage.

Yet Alumnae cannot be classified strictly as a feminist theatre company. Indeed, most of their productions do not meet the criteria for feminist theatre as articulated, for example, by Michelle MacArthur: "approaches to theatre creation and production that reflect a commitment to feminism(s) and to change, whether personal, socio-political, or artistic."[36] In many ways, their historical trajectory operates outside of feminist discourse, even though it serves that discourse from time to time. The company's early and mid-century leaders tended to reject the notion that theirs was a feminist theatre company; instead, they viewed their play programming as broadly modern, classical, avant-garde, or whatever was not being produced in the city at a given time. It was not until a relatively brief moment in the 1970s, and then more thoroughly in the new millennium, that Alumnae overtly sold their productions, and eventually their seasons, on the basis that the company was run by women. Yet even then, rarely have members publicly characterized this position as a feminist one. Certainly, Alumnae were producing theatre in a society growing increasingly attuned to women's voices. In their introduction to *Feminist History in Canada*, Catherine Carstairs and Nancy Janovicek observe that much early scholarship on women in Canada was nationalist in focus, writing women into a story of Canada in which space was offered for suffragist reform, women in professions and workplaces, and the "experience of motherhood and child rearing." Later, the focus expanded to consider how leisure and culture are gendered.[37] In seeking to uncover the "networks between women and women's organizations [that] remain largely hidden," Catherine Gidney focuses on early twentieth-century tensions between the maternal feminism espoused by non-academic professional women at the University of Toronto and women's struggle for equal rights. She thus illuminates a context for a number of markers that guide the present study, including club and society participation, female friendships and networks, social responsibility, and formal education, each of which became central to women's experiences following first-wave feminism's gains in the early twentieth century and would later endure critique under the second-wave feminism of the 1960s through the 1980s. Like Gidney's "ambiguous feminists, transitional figures, interwar feminists, or women involved in activities with 'feminist outcomes,'"[38] Alumnae's women, as this study shows, found pleasure and a sense of accomplishment in their theatre pursuits, as well as a means to exercise free will, all of this – usually – without signalling feminist intentions. A great many of their outputs might be read productively as feminist gains during a "period of quiescence,"[39] to use Nancy Forestell's phrase, but Alumnae members have not framed their work as such, and this study honours this self-positioning. Alumnae members carried their undergraduate responsibilities as educated and engaged young women from the campus to their own theatre buildings in the community, but not overtly in the cause of feminism.

In the 1970s, the feminist movement in Canada began to influence women who were seeking to produce theatre that reflected their own interests. Companies like Winnipeg's Nellie McClung Theatre (founded in 1968), Toronto's Redlight Theatre (1974), Montreal's Théâtre Expérimental des Femmes (1979), and Toronto's Nightwood Theatre[40] (1979), as well as Nightwood's short-lived Toronto antecedents, the Women Theatre and the Toronto Feminist Theatre Troupe, were or are characterized by their feminist artists and artistic output. Certainly, as a form of "consciousness-raising"[41] and solidarity in the context of feminism's impactful second wave, a handful of Alumnae press releases and posters began framing some of their productions as speaking to "any even fractionally liberated woman" (for Clare Boothe's *The Women* in 1973), as foregrounding the "role of women in society [with] different needs and very different perceptions of their roles" (for Carol Bolt's *Shelter* in 1974), and as articulating "what it means to be a woman today" (for Marie-Claire Blais and her collaborators' *A Clash of Symbols* in 1979). Some Alumnae productions, like these, questioned male dominance in the workplace, public sphere, political arena, and home, as well as in women's personal lives. But even in the 1970s, at the height of second-wave feminism,[42] these plays were the exception in Alumnae's season brochures, produced alongside Restoration comedies and works of phallocentric realism that paid no heed to feminist voices and at times even undermined them.

For most of their first century, Alumnae members did not seek to be identified as feminist theatre producers. As MacArthur asserts, "feminist theatre," publicized as such, has historically led to negative reviews that impact box office sales and reputations; this in turn has led to audiences predominantly made up of women, negative perceptions of the artists, and negative ways in which company histories are recorded.[43] Alumnae members, since their founding, have plainly sought to avoid such repercussions. Because they are a nonprofessionalizing theatre company, and thus ineligible for government operating grants, Alumnae have always relied on positive word-of-mouth, notably from influential reviewers, to generate box office income. One might argue that theatre productions led by women are inherently feminist statements, but Alumnae members have never made that statement themselves.

This complex relationship to feminism remains true for Alumnae today. Their current mandate states that they are "dedicated to the production of adventurous theatre not readily seen elsewhere and to skill development of women in theatre. We seek to be reflective of the diversity of Toronto on our stage and in our organization."[44] This is a revision of their previously expressed threefold mandate "to produce works that offer strong roles for women; to produce works that are not often seen in Toronto; and to produce works that are written by Canadians."[45] As both iterations demonstrate, providing experiences to women is central to their programming, as a means to ensure that members remain engaged. But Alumnae have not created and produced theatre solely by and for women, and the plays they produce do not expound exclusively feminist perspectives.[46] Rather, Alumnae are a women-run theatre company that has produced every genre and style of theatre they deem to have literary, cultural, or political value, all the while involving men as actors, directors, designers, and technical support. They produce plays created by a range of playwrights and collaborators meant to attract the broadest theatre-going audiences.

Alumnae's play selection process has not changed significantly since the 1930s. Working under a board of directors (formerly the executive), who are all elected at an annual general meeting of the company membership, the programming committee (formerly the playreading committee) sources, reads, and selects plays for production. Over their first one hundred years, Alumnae produced nearly 600 plays, as well as hundreds of original short performances through their New Ideas Festival (founded in 1988). In recent years, they have produced three full-length shows each season in their 138-seat Mainstage theatre and two new play festivals in their 80-seat attic Studio theatre. Excluding staged readings and New Ideas one-act premieres, they have produced at least fifty-eight world premieres (including fourteen full-length plays developed since 2013 through their FireWorks Festival of new plays), six North American premieres, twenty-seven Canadian premieres, and fifty-three Toronto premieres. The amount of volunteer labour required is remarkable. For example, during the 2015–16 season about 100 of Alumnae's 130 members contributed to 278 positions across all of their productions; non-production Alumnae events that season required another seventy-five members. In their 2017–18 centennial season, Alumnae reached a membership of 178, an all-time high for the club. Every year Alumnae also hosts various theatre workshops for members and the general public. They also rent their facilities to a variety of groups, including other theatre companies (twenty-one different groups during the 2015–16 season alone).[47]

When spoken of today, nonprofessionalizing theatres are often described in terms of their contributions to the profession. In this regard, Alumnae have been providing early experience to theatre artists and administrators who later enter the theatre, film, and radio professions. Over the years, most of these artists have been men, given that twentieth-century plays were written mainly by men writing about male experiences staged through male characters (perhaps ironically, the women-led Alumnae once held the record for the most acting awards received by men in the Dominion Drama Festival's Central Ontario Region Festival[48]). A list of Alumnae participants reveals some of the well-known professional artists who have been involved with Alumnae. Notable directors and theatre educators include Jennifer Brewin, Marigold Charlesworth, Pamela (Terry) Beckwith (a long-time Alumnae member), Karen Glahn, Molly (Golby) Thom (also a long-time Alumnae member), Kelly Thornton, Leonard Crainford, Robert Gill, Martin Hunter, Henry Kaplan, Leon Major, Jordan Merkur, E.G. Sterndale Bennett, Edgar Stone, and Herbert Whittaker. Along with Whittaker, two other theatre critics have directed for Alumnae: E.G. Wanger (1950) and Urjo Kareda (1972). Several theatre administrators honed their skills at Alumnae before moving on to their profession, including Mallory Gilbert and Shelagh Kareda (Hewitt).

The long list of notable Alumnae-involved actors includes Barbara (Allen) Barnett, Maggie Bassett, Eleanor (Norton) Beecroft (an influential long-time Alumnae member),

Martha Burns, Suzanne Finlay, Beatrice Lennard, Diane Polley (deeply involved with Alumnae in the 1960s and early 1970s), Sue Miner, Kate Reid, Naomi Snieckus, Wendy Thatcher, Severn Thompson, Andrew Allen,[49] W.E.S. Briggs,[50] Chris Britton, Mark Brownell, Raymond Card, Brent Carver, John Colicos, Hume Cronyn, Richard Easton, Don Ewer, Ted Follows, Ronald Hartmann, William Hutt, David Gardner, Gordon Jocelyn, Geza Kovaks, Uriel Luft, George Luscombe, George McGowan, Patrick McManus, Peter Mews, W.S. Milne,[51] William Needles, Stephen Ouimette, Michael Polley, Donald Sutherland, Jovanni Sy, and Hugh Webster. Poet Dennis Lee acted in an Alumnae play and, briefly, rented a flat from them with Tarragon's founder Bill Glassco when Alumnae were landladies for a three-unit residence in the 1960s.

Other prominent women were involved with Alumnae. Anne Mirvish briefly joined Alumnae after her husband Ed saved the Royal Alexandra Theatre from demolition in 1963 on his way to becoming a renowned theatre impresario. Other prominent Canadian men who participated in Alumnae productions include Eric Aldwinkle (the war artist), W.A. Atkinson (later of Ottawa Little Theatre), Murray Bonnycastle, John Buchan (producer, casting director, and Diane Polley's son), Dudley Doughty, Norman Green, Frank Hemingway, Wallace House, H.E. Hitchman, Brendon Mulholland, George Patton, Rai Purdy, Stewart Reburn (the figure skater), Frank Rostance, and Percy Schutte.

Several Canadian playwrights have had their works premiered by Alumnae, including Shirley Barrie, Carol Bolt, Patricia Joudry, Carol Shields, Anne Tait (a long-time Alumnae member as well as casting agent and screenwriter), John Coulter, James Reaney (twice), Wilfred Watson, and Norman Williams; most of these writers worked closely with Alumnae to develop their scripts before production (see chapter 7). Alumnae's influence on the entertainment industry is demonstrable. But the focus of this study is Alumnae Theatre Company itself.

Since their first appearance in 1918 as the Dramatic Club of the University College Alumnae Association, formed for the purpose of raising money for the war effort, Alumnae Theatre Company have repeatedly captured the attention of Toronto's, and at times Canada's, theatre-going public. Their longevity stems from the fact that since the days of the modernist Little Theatre Movement they have produced theatre at a consistently high level, with an eye for audience and member interest, in genres and styles that other groups have not embraced. Thus, this study doubles as a macrohistorical long view of the rise, impact, and wane of nonprofessionalizing theatre. It describes how the possibilities for organized participatory theatre have changed over the past century in the emerging context of a specializing, professionalizing theatre ecology; it does so by investigating those aspects of Alumnae that have held steady for more than a century and by tracing the impulses for alterity that characterize theatre work. By examining what makes Alumnae unique, including their membership, trend-setting programming, and perseverance, this study demonstrates how theatre companies find their niches and affect their cities.

Moreover, by offering a nonprofessionalizing theatre company as a case study for examining modern, contemporary, radical, and new play practices, this study challenges received boundaries of theatre scholarship and practice as they have emerged over the last 100 years. It draws from primary sources both internal and public, revisits commentary written by theatre critics and other journalists, and includes the author's interviews with influential company members in order to foreground the voices of the women who have led the company from one decade to the next, as well as those who have admired and critiqued them. Secondary sources in the field are used to contextualize Alumnae's activity,

Figure 0.4. (*left*) Diane Buchan [Polley] as Sara Melody and (*right*) Molly Thom as Deborah in Alumnae's production of Eugene O'Neill's *A Touch of the Poet* in March 1965. Directed by Herbert Whittaker with costumes by Margaret MacAulay and Martha Southgate. Photo Credit: John Reeves. Courtesy of Alumnae Theatre Company.

practice, and influence. This methodology provides insights into how one nonprofessionalizing company has meaningfully impacted its city's theatre ecology, and how critics, scholars, and practitioners have changed their diction and tone regarding amateur practices and female artists as theatre in Canada has professionalized.

As Nicholson and colleagues have observed, the "way that amateur companies select, programme, and curate a season for themselves reveals much about a company's self-construction, and how the group is thinking about the tastes and expectations of its regular and potential audiences."[52] Following this introduction to Alumnae and nonprofessionalizing theatre practices, Part I traces Alumnae's history and programming choices through three distinct eras: their university years contributing to campus philanthropy at Hart House Theatre and the UC Women's Union during the rise, height, and wane of the Little Theatre Movement; their mid-century modern and radical "Coach House" programming for loyal, "intellectual" audiences; and their Firehall years, during which popular programming and increasingly cumbersome administrative demands in a competitive entertainment market have challenged their reputation for aesthetic alterity. Part II revisits these eras by focusing on four dominant perspectives on Alumnae's influence and ongoing legacy: the ways in which Alumnae's theatre buildings have impacted their programming and reputation; the importance of festival competition to Alumnae's work and the importance of this work to their city, their region, and Canada; Alumnae's long-standing position as an influential producer of new plays; and Alumnae's relationship, both supportive and antagonistic, to an emerging theatre profession. The study concludes by tethering Alumnae's alterity to contemporary critical notions of the nonprofessionalizing theatre practitioner as "counter-cultural figure,"[53] while urging scholars and practitioners alike not to take for granted the values and possibilities of contemporary nonprofessionalizing theatre. Appendices offer biographies of Alumnae's influential early women and a detailed production history of the company.

The Politics of Nonprofessionalizing Theatre

In an effort to clarify Alumnae's position in Toronto's theatre ecology, a membership flyer from 1980 explained: "While encouraging professionalism and welcoming the assistance and participation of professionals, the Club is primarily non-professional. We all volunteer our skills." While emphasizing the company's professionalism through the decades, members have, by turns, adopted and rejected familiar labels such as "non-professional" and "volunteer," as well as "community," "semi-professional, " and "amateur" theatre. These different labels reflect a given leadership's nuanced perspectives on their work as well as changing terminologies over time. They afford flexibility when encountering emerging casting and hiring conditions, thus providing opportunities to a range of interested practitioners even while filling gaps in the city's theatre programming. These changes also exemplify a truism about arts vocabulary: the profession tends towards regulation and definition; those operating outside of the profession tend towards multiplicity.

However, these terms do not satisfactorily describe theatre companies like Alumnae. For example, the long-held negative connotations of the term "amateur" do not fit well with much of Alumnae's output, and company members reject it outright. Moreover, although they produce theatre largely in an unpaid capacity, Alumnae pay certain participants on certain productions, as when they occasionally retain Canadian Actors' Equity Association members to direct or act, or when they "profit share" among cast and crew members in their New Ideas Festival. Here, I concur with Michael Dobson that contemporary theatre practices often make use of the "permeable boundary" between professional and nonprofessionalizing activity in which the producer, director, and an actor or two are paid, but others are unpaid,[54] as is the case with Alumnae once or twice a season.

As for the label "community theatre," many Alumnae members consider the term limiting because they regard Alumnae as serving the broader Toronto area, as opposed to their immediate neighbourhood. They see Alumnae's programming as challenging and informed and therefore antithetical to conventional community theatre fare.[55] Moreover, to borrow from Colin Bell and Howard Newby, the term "community" itself is fraught and often weaponized as a utopian "God word" in front of which we abase ourselves even as we look back toward a nostalgic "organic solidarity"[56] that may never have existed. As an indicator of nostalgia, "community" shares with "amateur" the pervasive stereotype that it was best when it was in the past. Thus, I have rejected "community theatre" in this context because "community" is a complex structure that can mean less, or more, than what Alumnae represents.

The term "semi-professional" may be more helpful in that it avoids many of the negative connotations of "amateur." However, emerging theatre companies sometimes adopt the term before they turn professional, so it is misleading when applied to Alumnae. It also inaccurately suggests that the company is a fraction of the value of a professional company. In all, none of these terms encapsulate Alumnae's complex and dynamic relationships to their theatre ecology or to the profession.

It should be acknowledged that much scholarship in recent years, particularly from the UK, steadfastly retains the word "amateur" to label practitioners and companies like Alumnae that do not operate within the profession. The term is most often defined as a "person who takes part in a particular activity purely for pleasure or interest rather than as a professional,"[57] but its denotation of unwaged practices and the connotations of inferior product inevitably generate aesthetic meanings, financial implications, and disciplinary conflicts that do not accurately reflect the work of Alumnae and their comparators. Here I diverge from those who argue that the term "amateur" is "only belittling if it is used pejoratively" and that "euphemisms or substitutes risk undermining the creativity of amateur participants and undervaluing an important part of cultural life."[58] I respect the choice as it pertains to theatre in the UK, where "amateur" seems not to have fallen so far out of favour as it has in Canada. This lexical disjuncture reveals underlying differences in the North American context, not the least of which are the UK's strong national amateur theatre organizations and numerous nationally funded studies that bolster the cultural and economic capital, as well as the interconnectivity, of amateur theatre practices. But here in Canada, since the demise of the Dominion Drama Festival in the early 1970s, these companies have received very little organized attention beyond scattered provincial initiatives offering professionally led workshops. This, despite widespread (if largely uncharted) engagement with these practices today. Furthermore, whereas in the UK many theatre companies call *themselves* "amateur," in Canada, companies like Alumnae reject the term because of its negative connotations.

This does not mean, as David Gilbert and colleagues wryly warn, that "there is no such thing as the amateur" if "given another name."[59] I certainly do not mean to entirely jettison a word that has gained so much traction (even if today the wheels are spinning). The person or thing does not disappear when a new term emerges. "Amateur" may still best describe certain practices in other contexts. For example, in his consideration of "fancy dress" as a performative amateur pursuit, Stephen Knott lists the "amateur's quasi-commitment to performance, making and choosing the right or 'appropriate' outfit" that suggests "participation, engagement and the desire to inhabit a different persona, but in a partial or slight way."[60] But "quasi-commitment" and a "partial or slight way," although they certainly conform to inherited understandings of "amateur," hardly describe the activities of long-standing companies like Alumnae. The distinction is significant if we are to understand how such companies are to be positioned and valued in their respective theatre ecologies.

Given these slippages, I refer to Alumnae as a "nonprofessionalizing" theatre company. The term intentionally disrupts inherited vocabularies that have fallen victim to negative or misleading connotations. The term "nonprofessionalizing" emphasizes the alterity of Alumnae's practices relative to those of the established profession of the day while maintaining a key element of dynamism (with the present participle) that nods towards their repeated refusal over the decades to turn professional. The term can also be applied to comparable companies that have emerged since the 1910s. Along with Ottawa Little Theatre (founded in 1913) and Alumnae, these include Regina Little Theatre (founded in 1927), Victoria's Langham Court Theatre (1927), and Halifax's Theatre Arts Guild (1931).[61] As Canada's longest-running theatre companies, they emerged before a theatre profession had taken hold in their cities and have thrived alongside them. I contend that the term "nonprofessionalizing" goes some distance in generating new perspectives on increasingly misunderstood practices. These companies have not failed because they cannot turn professional; they have succeeded for so long because they have repeatedly rejected the profession, even while supporting it.

Above are listed dozens of professionalizing artists who have worked with Alumnae. But nonprofessionalizing theatres also benefit the profession in ways other than providing experience to future professional artists. In the British context, Nicholson and colleagues have noted that these theatres are significant producers of professional playwrights' work, helping through the sheer volume of productions to make writing careers possible for many professional playwrights.[62] As an extension, royalty agreements with rights holders and royalty distribution companies like Samuel French and Dramatist Play Services benefit greatly from payments from nonprofessionalizing theatres. Some professional companies make income from renting to nonprofessionalizing groups. And nonprofessionalizing groups often hire professional artists to facilitate workshops. Moreover, audiences that attend nonprofessionalizing theatre companies often become interested in seeing more theatre and spending their money on professional companies.[63] And in Canada in recent years, the Canada Council for the Arts has offered funding to professional organizations that provide nonprofessionalizing theatre artists with workshop and performance space, thus benefiting not only the community but also the profile of the professional organizations that are eligible to hold the grant. However, Holdsworth and colleagues rightly critique this notion that nonprofessionalizing activity is justified based on what it can do for the profession: "Within this idea of the creative economy, creativity is valued when it is operationalized for explicitly economic benefits and outcomes. It is perhaps not surprising that amateur creativity has not been valued or recognized within this rubric, except as a training ground for future employment."[64] It is important to remember that whether or not Alumnae's artists and administrators eventually plan to enter the profession, in the moment they participate with the company their work has artistic value to themselves, the company, their audiences, and theatre practice broadly. One's work at a nonprofessionalizing theatre is of immense importance not only to potential future employment, but also to theatre generally *while that work is being done*.

Nevertheless, a limited view of nonprofessionalizing theatre has persisted, largely because of a utilitarian narrative propagated across capitalist domains, including in academe. Despite Alumnae's achievements and contributions, there is virtually no scholarship on them; the same can be said about most nonprofessionalizing companies. Halpenny wrote an entry on the "University Alumnae Dramatic Club" (the group's name in the mid-twentieth century) for *The Oxford Companion to Canadian Theatre*;[65] Ann Saddlemyer and Richard Plant's edited essay collection *Later Stages* makes several passing references to Alumnae;[66] and one moment in Alumnae's history involving the New Play Society is afforded a paragraph in Paula Sperdakos's biography of Dora Mavor Moore.[67] Curiously, Martin L. Friedland's *The University of Toronto: A History* makes no mention of Alumnae, despite their popularity on campus during Hart House Theatre's early years and their patriotic and infrastructure fundraising accomplishments for the university in the interwar years.[68]

Indeed, until very recently nonprofessionalizing theatre companies have received limited scholarly attention relative to their professional counterparts. Certainly, the field is awash in how-to publications, notably the many theatre manuals published at the height of the Little Theatre Movement, as well as fond reminiscences penned by hired authors providing histories of theatre companies from their participants' perspectives.[69] But with the rise of digital media in recent years, more and more nonprofessionalizing voices in all corners of arts and culture, particularly online, are being heard and taken seriously. For theatre and performance studies this is encouraging, for it allows for more diverse performance-related perspectives. After all, nonprofessionalizing practitioners have been performing for millennia.

The present "amateur turn"[70] is now leading to the development of more rigorous approaches to researching nonprofessionalizing theatre. For example, in recent years international scholars have formed the group Research into Amateur Performance and Private Theatricals (RAPPT), out of which have emerged a series of theatre and performance studies conferences, special journal issues, and book-length studies. Nicholson and colleagues' *The Ecologies of Amateur Theatre*, Michael Dobson's *Shakespeare and Amateur Performance*, and Nicholas Ridout's *Passionate Amateurs* began approaching nonprofessionalizing practices in meaningful ways with insightful and flexible perspectives.[71] Special issues of the journals *Nineteenth Century Theatre and Film*, *Contemporary Theatre Review*, and *Performance Research* have collected a variety of approaches to diverse examples of amateur performance over the past two hundred years.[72] The most recent of these, a special issue of *Performance Research* titled "On Amateurs," collected seventeen articles and a manifesto to "explore the geographies and histories of amateur performance, think through the nature and limits of the idea of the amateur in different cultural contexts and help us to develop a new vocabulary to understand the complexity and nuances of amateur performance."[73] Although these volumes focus mainly, albeit not exclusively, on the British context, much of their broader thought can illuminate other theatre ecologies, including those in North America.

Given the lack of scholarly publications on nonprofessionalizing theatre, this study relies largely on extant primary sources to construct a history of Alumnae, their contexts, and their legacies. Michael Dobson observes that amateur performance often "leaves more diffuse and scattered traces"[74] than professional performance, and Nicholson and colleagues describe the paucity of archived nonprofessionalizing theatre materials at British museums and libraries. This dearth "privileges the professional sector,"[75] raises questions about what is considered "'authorized heritage,'" and "blights vernacular creativity in general."[76] In Canada, where there has been no bricks-and-mortar national theatre museum, the neglect is even more pronounced.[77] But Nicholson and colleagues note that nonprofessionalizing theatre companies often "maintain fulsome archives"[78] and on-site displays that preserve their heritage. Fortunately, it has been my experience that this is especially true in Canada.

For this study I have relied heavily on two types of primary sources. The first are documents produced by Alumnae members themselves, such as meeting minutes, brief internal histories and production lists, newsletters, correspondence, and half-a-dozen filing cabinets worth of production files; the second are various print media such as articles, previews, reviews, features, and advertisements. I have consulted these with the dual purpose of reframing Alumnae within received local and national histories and reframing nonprofessionalizing practices within theatre and performance studies. But I am also cognizant that many of these materials – especially the often stunning show posters, production photographs, play programs, season brochures, and costume and set designs – are of essential value to the wider population and might be made more widely viewable as part of both an "authorized heritage" and a people's history in an archive or museum.[79] I am thus grateful to Alumnae for providing me access to their extensive private collection, and pleased that this collection transcends Dobson's "scattered traces."

In determining a starting point from which to approach Alumnae's sheer quantity of productions over a century, my research relied in the first place on a production history list started by company members over the decades. But after extensive searches of newspaper notices and reviews, it became clear that Alumnae had on record less than half of their own past productions from their pre-Firehall days. Newspaper articles are integral not only to an understanding of what shows Alumnae have produced, but also to a broader understanding of their place in Toronto's and Canada's theatre ecology. Brief (one- to seven-page) microhistorical documents produced by the company from time to time, for reasons that include providing information to the media for anniversaries and preserving company heritage, are helpful in tracing past activities that members prioritize, and I have tried to emphasize them as such. But discrepancies arise between these microhistories, in part replicated from previous microhistories, when they are inconsistent with information found in external sources. Moreover, certain events yield much greater documentation than others due to their weighted importance at the time; for example, Alumnae's public Hart House Theatre productions tend to yield more preserved documentation than their invitational UC Women's Union plays, partly underscoring a gender bias in theatre production histories given that Hart House was a men-only building during the years that Alumnae produced plays there. Other factors include inconsistent company record-collecting and, for example, the fact that in the late 1930s the University of Toronto Archives stopped methodically preserving all press clippings related to university events and issues, including those mentioning in detail the UCAA Dramatic Club and its individual members. This study's historiographic process is influenced not only by what is told but also by what is not or cannot be told. We must therefore be aware of how the documents on which it is grounded shape the possibilities and limitations of our understanding of Alumnae, nonprofessionalizing theatre, and theatre and performance studies broadly.

Importantly, as Nicholson and colleagues have noted in the UK context, private collections provide evidence not only of nonprofessionalizing theatres' pasts but also of "broad social shifts."[80] Thus, a century of changes in programming trends and aesthetics in Western theatre, and the reasons for them, are evident in Alumnae's collection. But so too are innovations in theatre design (sets, costumes, hair, make-up, lighting, sound, projection, and video), audience outreach (production photography, playbills, and "bios"), publicity and advertising (newspapers, radio, posters, internet, social media, and blogs[81]), writing technologies (handwriting, typewriters, telegrams, mimeographs, photocopiers, fax machines, computer printers, and emails), document storage practices (notebooks, scrapbooks, albums, binders, duotangs, file folders, hard drives, and cloud storage), and fundraising strategies (teas, dinners, mailouts, garage sales, and silent auctions). In this sense, a theatre company's archive provides a diachronic material history of developments in theatre and, conversely, a diachronic theatrical history of cultural materials.

"Why would you want to study all the bad theatre?," a professor in graduate school once asked me. Having myself served as artistic director at a nonprofessionalizing theatre, I know first-hand from the focus and creativity we put into the work that there is more to nonprofessionalizing labour than dilettantism and hobbyism. Gilbert and colleagues assert that "the amateur resists the notion that professionalization is a narrative of progress. The slick professional represents the taste of the dominant social group while the amateur exposes how value is created through mastery of a craft. The amateur resists the commodification of talent. A skillful performance is still skillful even if it does not have an exchange value."[82]

The omission of nonprofessionalizing theatre by scholars and theatre professionals alike is a political omission. It is based on assumptions about class, gender, race, and aesthetics. Jennifer Beth Spiegel argues that the "amateur creative process at once reinforces and challenges organizations of cultural life." The times and spaces of nonprofessionalizing practices are defined by capitalist labour even as they perform a space outside of its edicts. There is something deeply resistant in choosing to commit one's training and labour to an unpaid craft beyond one's employment, as when professional engineers in their day jobs apply their electrics or building expertise to nonprofessionalizing theatre pursuits in evenings and on weekends. They perform unpaid labour to the audience, a *tromp l'oeil* in which you blink and you are paying for a product; blink again and you are paying for a "purer" experience of *amore*. Says Spiegal, "reaching beyond the limits of official economies, each performance nuances love differently."[83] By focusing on the "processes of making"[84] as a core function of nonprofessionalizing production, this study makes clear that in play selection and in theatre administration, Alumnae members approach their work with professionalism. Far from sidestepping aesthetic judgments as to the quality, or *qualities*, of nonprofessionalizing work, I deem professionalism in both process and product as intrinsic to Alumnae's ongoing legacy.

In 1904, American philosopher Bliss Perry saw specialization and the "professional spirit" as necessary products of modernization that require careful scrutiny. They had not been "carried too far" yet, but the potential was there and the amateur spirit might go some distance in reining them in for the sake of an America set to become a "nation of professionals." He argued that moral ideals must accompany commercial dominance, and that

> personal enthusiasm, the individual initiative, the boundless zest, of the American amateur must penetrate, illuminate, idealize the brute force, the irresistible on-sweeping mass, of our vast industrial democracy …
>
> There are already here and there amateurs without amateurishness, professionals untainted by professionalism … This union of strict professional training with that free outlook upon life, that human curiosity and eagerness, which are the best endowment of the amateur.[85]

The nonprofessionalizing artist adhering to professionalism sees their work as a passion, not simply the product of industrialized labour. In this way, they prevent the designation of "professional" from being an empty signifier pleading for special acknowledgment in the name of subjective quality and at the expense of quality of life. In the heat of early twentieth-century industrialization, Perry's writing warned that the "pure" professional is not the ideal towards which one ought to aspire. He believed that one should aim for a combination of professional and amateur traits in one's work. His warning echoes true today in the vacuous nine-to-five employment experienced by millions.

The term "amateur" has received such debased treatment that for some, today, it is difficult to take seriously as a practice that is worthy of our time or entertainment dollars. Despite Perry's optimism, today's amateurs are often viewed as "awkward"[86] and self-serving, as Sonja Kuftinec writes, "conjuring scenes of Mickey Rooney and Judy Garland rummaging through Granny's trunk in the barn, puttin' on a show."[87] The stereotype offers up amateur performance as "unquestionably shoddy and tied up in cultural imaginings of underserving prima donnas, tired repertoires, and shaky sets."[88] The thought of an amateur aesthetic might insinuate a "mythic version of amateur performance as catastrophically transgressing professional standards and norms."[89] Indeed, professional artists may weaponize the amateur stereotype "as a political tactic."[90] In labour discourse, amateurism echoes the "dilettantism of the idle aristocrat" or the "aspirational middle-class, available only to those with time and money to spare."[91] Gilbert and colleagues observe that "experts were trained, rational, qualified, and this excluded amateur."[92] Holdsworth and colleagues argue that "being 'amateur' is always caught up in relation to being 'not-amateur,' as what is amateur, vernacular, or everyday is produced in relation to the cultural value of 'not-amateur' creativity. In contemporary cultural contexts, being an 'amateur' and the cultural practices of amateur creativity are by and large pejoratively devalued through their relation to the professional, subsidized art world and their neglect by cultural policy."[93]

Owing in part to this neglect by cultural policy, a lexical disjuncture transported the amateur from "entrepreneurial" to "ineffectual" over half a century. Claire Cochrane notes that a "semantic shift in the deployment of the word 'amateur' [has developed where] 'Professional' now carries with it connotations of ultra-competence. The amateur is non-professional and by implication incompetent."[94] This shift means that amateur performance suffers "persistent inattention among scholars"[95] and a "disjunctive representation … in the cultural imaginary." The reasons for this shift, as I discuss further on, are closely connected to the increased professionalization of capitalist labour over the past century. I agree with Gilbert and colleagues that "it is time to rethink how amateur expertise redistributes political orthodoxies about knowledge."[96]

Jonathan Pitches, following Caroline Hamilton, asserts, perhaps radically, that "amateurism and professionalism are not best defined in counterpoint to one another … as this leads to the, frankly, silly conclusion that an amateur willfully avoids payment for their activities and a professional, by definition, doesn't like what they do for a living."[97] For Gilbert and colleagues, amateur practitioners are, more variously, "experts, enthusiasts, gift-givers, show-offs, connoisseurs, dabblers, perfectionists, hobbyists, dilettantes."[98] Established nonprofessionalizing theatre companies like Alumnae, as well as university and college drama clubs, culturally diverse secular and non-secular groups, and outdoor (and outsized) contemporary passion plays, comprise the majority of theatre participation in the Western world. Such forms of "serious leisure,"[99] to borrow from sociologist Robert A. Stebbings, position nonprofessionalizing theatre companies between a stratified profession and scattered groups of hobbyists.

In order to generate a more productive vocabulary that acknowledges the complex relationships between professional and nonprofessionalizing practices, we can turn to Robert Hutchison and Andrew Feist's 1991 study for the UK's Policy Studies Institute in which they review a broad range of amateur participation in the arts. They conclude that "rather than a clear amateur/professional divide, there is a complex professional-amateur spectrum of ambition, accomplishment and activity." This spectrum, they argue, is more in line with the "forever changing … social and economic bases of arts activity." They offer sub-spectra for eight signifying elements in terms of which any artist's or artistic group's practice may be measured: income from arts employment (negative – all), training (self – fully professional), artistic aspirations (unimportant – high), time allocated (hobby – full-time), status of the art form in society (not serious – considered a professional occupation), experience (limited – considerable), content and style (derivative – original), and general approach (recreational – creative and business-like). They explain that any "serious practitioner" can be placed somewhere along these spectrums and that this placement changes over the life course.[100] Their spectra provide a useful perspective from which the theatre practice of individuals and companies can be studied because they free the researcher from the inherited terminology that traps the discourse in a static and reductive amateur/professional binary. They provide a dynamic model of professionalization that acknowledges that a practitioner's or a company's status can change across multiple spectra over time. By troubling the static binary, this approach opens up space for a deeper understanding of how nonprofessionalizing theatres operate and contribute to a broad theatre ecology.

The term "nonprofessionalizing" refers to a dynamic (not static) practice that is, in significant ways, tethered to an emerging profession yet radically alternative to it. It is flexible diachronically and synchronically, like the various practices it describes, depending on how a profession is defined and disciplined in a given moment (e.g., by for-profit touring companies, by income-for-livelihood, or by a disciplining professional association such as Actors' Equity). The term "nonprofessionalizing theatre" refers to a theatre company that rejects giving over its core operations and productions to professional affiliation. It acknowledges a company's choice *not* to professionalize its practices for reasons that may include camaraderie, programming flexibility, finances, and members' desire to practise in flexible hours outside of their careers, studies, or family time.[101] In the past, nonprofessionalizing theatre practices have adapted to fill the gaps that the profession cannot as well as the gaps that the profession creates, particularly in terms of programming, community building, experience, and participatory enjoyment. Nonprofessionalizing theatre practices are therefore the majority of theatre practices. Importantly, "nonprofessionalizing" seeks to rewire our thinking about "value," "quality," and aesthetics – something that the term "amateur" fails to do because it is so often wilfully elided with "amateurishness."

A (Selective) History of Nonprofessionalizing Theatre before Alumnae

A "totalizing perspective"[102] on nonprofessionalizing theatre is inconceivable. The word "amateur" first entered the English lexicon in the late eighteenth century.[103] As Judith Hawley explains, "'amateur' meant lover of the arts. It is related to the term 'virtuoso,' which conveyed very positive associations of expertise, taste, broad-mindedness and interests across the arts. Moreover, it meant a connoisseur or collector, that is, an expert *consumer* rather than a performer, producer, or active participant in the theatre." Because Georgian amateurs were usually upper-class elites, their craft was to be held to a high standard and thus the term amateur was "not used as the antonym for professional nor to imply inferior artistic standards."[104] "Amateur" was not strictly applied to theatre as a formal designation until the mid-nineteenth century.[105] So it is for both etymological and socio-historical reasons that applying the term to theatre activity across the centuries risks anachronism.

That said, familiar distinctions between what we might refer to as professional and amateur theatre began to emerge during the medieval period. As Glynn Wickham describes, performers detached short "Interludes" from liturgical and worship dramas, which they performed at churches or at their masters' halls, in order to tour them. At first these players received a voluntary largesse, but by the late thirteenth century this became a requisite payment as finances grew inextricably connected to more elaborate performances. These neoprofessional players earned payment in a precommercial era. Conversely, by the early sixteenth century those who stayed closer to their church or master, both literally and figuratively, came to be defined and treated as what we might call "amateurs" today. Frequency and versatility of performance distinguished neoprofessional players from those who were increasingly viewed (accurately or not) as less valuable to the art because they did not pursue sustained effort or income. Because those who acted in Interludes, like the players in *Hamlet*, were still indentured to their masters, they may have earned a sizeable income from touring performances, but they were not professional actors as we define them, even as they committed to a "way of life." Wickham muses that the income of a neoprofessional player was likely no less erratic than that of a typical Actors' Equity member in the 1970s;[106] we might extend this musing to today's theatre ecology as well. From this nascent, yet today still ubiquitous, dichotomy, a concept of "professional" begins to come into focus, with "amateur" as the varied remainder. Yet where "amateur" lacks specificity, it finds flexibility, a trait modern companies like Alumnae have used to their advantage.

The sixteenth- and seventeenth-century Elizabethan and Jacobean troupes run by professional actors/theatre-owners like the famed Richard Burbage began to dominate the public consciousness[107] and form the notion of an identifiable theatre profession. Around the same time, British amateur theatricals were being presented on ships, in schools, and in private homes, where they offered some of the same plays presented elsewhere by professional troupes. Amateur theatre was frequently employed as a tool for colonization. As Dobson describes, the first recorded production of a Shakespeare play outside of Europe was also the first recorded Shakespeare production by an amateur group: a shipboard theatrical in September 1607 off the coast of what is now Sierra Leone.[108] In the eighteenth century, following the Restoration, playhouses grew and private theatricals came into vogue among those who could afford to put on theatre in their homes or barns. Georgian theatricals in the eighteenth century grew out of country-house masques and, as Hawley describes, often "adopted the repertoire and imitated the conventions of the professional theatre."[109]

Simultaneously, in British North America in the eighteenth and nineteenth centuries, amateur garrison theatricals performed by British army officers marked amateur performance as men's activity. That included men performing as women, as had been ubiquitous in Renaissance England. But these performances diminished with the gradual dismantling of the garrison military structure, and by the late nineteenth century women entering education and training institutions began taking the lead in various amateur theatre practices in Canada's post-Confederation university towns. The majority of amateur theatre moved from the activity of officers outside of their regular duties for the purpose of entertaining (and pacifying) citizens of garrison towns, to the activity of women outside of the home for the purpose of elocution training and raising money for charity. In garrison and university theatricals, the primary aim was not theatre for art's sake, but the calculated use of theatre as a social service. This is the performance lineage from which the Dramatic Club of the University College Alumnae Association emerged.[110]

In the nineteenth and early twentieth centuries, theatre managers in England and America toured complex professional productions across Canada by railway. Large playhouses seating 1,000–2,000 people were built to accommodate these productions. Prominent among Toronto venues were the Princess Theatre (1880–1930, the first building in Toronto to be electrified, later torn down for the University Avenue extension), the Royal Alexandra Theatre (1907, still operating), the Gayety Theatre (1909–27, a burlesque house, later the Victory Building), Loew's (1913, now the Elgin and Winter Garden Theatres), Shea's Hippodrome (1914, now the site of Nathan Phillips Square), the Imperial (1915, later the Palton in 1922, then the Rialto in 1925, then the Empire in the early 1950s, currently the Good Shepard Ministries), the Allen Theatre (1917, named the Tivoli in 1923, now the site of the Cambridge Suites Hotel), Loew's Uptown Theatre (1920, now the site of Uptown

Residences), and the Pantages (1920, now the Ed Mirvish Theatre). Torontonians, including Alumnae's early members and their families, experienced theatre and, later, film at these professional roadhouses and burlesque theatres.

Several of these theatres were devoted to hosting foreign touring shows from New York and London with their original casts, as well as a few Canadian resident stock companies. They occasionally offered travelogues, magicians, local operatic companies, and the famed Canadian Dumbells.[111] Their shows featured mainly foreign stars such as Maude Adams, Sarah Bernhardt, Sir Johnston Forbes-Robertson, E.H. Sothern, John Barrymore, Harley Granville Barker, Sir Herbert Beerbohm Tree, and Canadian expatriate Margaret Anglin.[112] They brought Toronto audiences the plays of Shakespeare, the jazz musicals of Irving Berlin and Al Jolson, musical comedies with chorus girls, vaudeville and burlesque performances, and melodramas. As arranged by student councils at the University of Toronto, these shows drew hundreds of university men to the stalls for "Theatre Nights." The First World War depleted the flow of touring companies as materials and rail lines were switched over to the war effort, but several small British and American stock companies still managed to entertain Torontonians by taking up residence at the surviving theatres. Producing mainly English drawing room comedies new to Toronto audiences by playwrights like Pinero, Lonsdale, and Galsworthy, these stock companies occasionally filled out their casts with "experienced local amateurs."[113] This was the theatre ecology into which Alumnae's early members, like Eleanor Norton Beecroft, who attended many such performances,[114] were born, and where they found inspiration for their theatre work.[115]

So pervasive was foreign domination of the theatre during these two decades, particularly by houses contracted by the powerful producers known as the New York Syndicate, that no local professional company, and therefore no professional school for theatre training, could be sustained in Toronto until after the First World War. Local theatre practice was nonprofessionalizing theatre practice, and it included elocution schools and the influential Arts and Letters Club. But the war afforded women increased experience in campus dramatic clubs while young men were overseas. Their do-it-yourself philosophy, cultivated during the war, would help drive local practice for decades. As Alumnae's publicity material declared shortly after their eightieth anniversary, "Long before there was a Toronto theatre scene, there was the Alumnae Theatre Club."[116]

Initially, much of the nonprofessionalizing theatre in the former British colonies was almost "purely social," and included private entertainments at churches, schools, and literary societies. In the UK around this time, three organizations "marked the rise of the amateur theatre sector as a *movement*": the National Amateur Operatic and Dramatic Association (NAODA), founded in 1899, the British Drama League (later the British Theatre Association), founded in 1919, and later, the Little Theatre Guild, which formed in 1946 among "building-based" amateur groups. Nicholson and colleagues have productively traced the British Little Theatre Movement back to the working classes who sought engagement with cultural activity and also, often, to emergent socialist discourse. Each theatre was a "beacon for local workers in the area," a place where "amateur creativity is not viewed as culturally marginal, but essential to the cultural ecology of reconstruction in post-First World War Britain."[117] This increasing popularity of nonprofessionalizing theatres in the UK began to inspire English Canadians to form their own theatre groups as the war generated interest in, and familiarity with, European art and literature. At the same time, young women educated in literature and the arts at Canadian universities began to find common interests and edification in theatre societies. Young British men and women immigrating to Canada with stage experience began establishing and performing in nonprofessionalizing groups. In urban centres across English Canada, the Little Theatre Movement began to develop.

Following the war, as men returned home to Canada, university campuses saw a marked increase in departmental and extracurricular theatre. Alumnae's origins are in one such campus theatre group, the University College Women's Dramatic Club. After the war, drama groups proliferated on the U of T campus. Popular musicals, comedies, and vaudeville began returning to venues like the Royal Alexandra, the Princess, the Allen, and the Gayety, but campus theatre was the most accessible student ticket in town. By February 1920, the *Varsity* student newspaper had a staff drama editor and no fewer than three drama reviewers listed on its masthead.[118]

Nonprofessionalizing performance practices in English Canada expanded exponentially after the war, serving as a locus for innovative theatre. The opening of U of T's state-of-the-art Hart House Theatre in 1919 drove Toronto's Little Theatres.[119] Chansky obvserves that across North America in the 1920s, as amateur theatre spread under the banner of the Little Theatre Movement, so too did studying and practising theatre in the education system. Drama education became largely the domain of women, who were trained and employed as high school drama teachers or elocution instructors. In Toronto in the first two decades of the twentieth century, the women undergraduates at U of T who would go on to found Alumnae were taught performance in the early manifestations of these environments for the dual purpose of self-improvement and social justice. Their performances raised money for patriotic purposes during the war and, later, for women's buildings and other on- and off-campus initiatives. Like teaching high school or post-secondary drama, starting a theatre group – particularly one that raised funds for social causes – was a "respectable endeavor for those from the social class that comprised most college students."[120] The education that Alumnae's early women acquired gave them the drive and the acumen for initiatives that would help constitute Toronto's theatre ecology before, and as, it professionalized.

PART I

History and Programming

Women have made Alumnae Theatre Company's programming decisions for more than 100 years. This fact sets Alumnae apart from all other theatre companies on the continent. From their first production in 1918, less than a year after the province of Ontario granted women the right to vote, through civil rights advances for women in the public sphere and in the professions, Alumnae's programming committees have chosen to stage challenging and appealing plays that Toronto rarely if ever sees. The four chapters in Part I examine Alumnae's programming choices and production conditions as well as the contexts in which they arose. By dividing Alumnae's work into four distinct periods – university, homefront and post-war, Coach House, and Firehall – I will show in the coming chapters how Alumnae's longevity has been largely the result of programming choices, production successes, and savvy awareness of their position in an ever-changing theatre ecology. Through literate, informed, and fearless choices, they have radically redefined their programming from one decade to the next. From British drawing room comedies in their early decades, to esoteric and absurdist modern dramas and Sunday evening dramatic readings curated by members, to political programming and new play development, Alumnae have at times led Toronto in theatre that rewards interest in familiar and radical literature and, increasingly, interest in new work. Critics like Herbert Whittaker, Nathan Cohen, and Urjo Kareda, steeped in dramatic literary traditions, chronicled Alumnae's formative transformations during the mid-twentieth century. They rewarded Alumnae's efforts with critical encouragement for their intentions and, when warranted, with praise for their accomplishments.

Chapter 1

The University Years: Founding Daughters and Their Philanthropic Little Theatre (1918–1939)

How were Alumnae's early members able to parlay their artistic and administrative talents into the foundations on which the company is built today? This chapter begins by tracing the founding daughters' pre-Alumnae theatre experience before detailing their fundraising efforts for campus women's spaces and the University Settlement, including popular "Theatre Nights." It then traces Alumnae's history of play programming at the forefront of Toronto's Little Theatre Movement. It argues that members' programming acumen contributed to the respect, and success, the company enjoyed in the theatre community; it garnered these in part *because* of the alterity and notoriety they generated as women thriving in a discipline in which male leadership was, and often still is, privileged. This chapter examines Alumnae's use of the UC Women's Union building, where, as UC alumnae, they had a degree of control in play production; by contrast, at Hart House Theatre their productions encountered politicized and gender-contested conditions. Here, as in all four chapters in Part I, the case studies record historic Alumnae productions and develop a picture of Alumnae's programming motivations, processes, critical reception, and impacts in their early years.

The Bluestockings was not simply a well-enjoyed, nearly defect-free production of a canonical play. It marked a point at which the growing talents of recent female graduates coalesced to serve their alumnae association's fundraising mandate.[1] It was also the first time the University College Alumnae Association had produced a play. Certainly, since its founding in November 1898, the UCAA had maintained a schedule of fundraising activities, holiday gatherings, receptions, bazaars, dances, campus advocacy events, regular member and executive meetings, invited lectures, and professional talks on topics such as journalism, advertising, insurance sales, and other increasingly popular careers for women.[2] But it had left theatre to its UC undergraduate counterparts: the Women's Dramatic Club (WDC), the Franco-British Aid Society, and the Women's Literary Society.

Indeed, many of Alumnae's early members "had made enviable records"[3] in annual performances with the WDC, firmly establishing it as one of the best amateur societies in Toronto during the First World War.[4] The WDC presented mainly Shakespearean comedies, led, first, by pioneering instructor Emma Scott Raff at the Margaret Eaton School of Literature and Expression from 1905 to 1911,[5] then by Dr. Frank Home Kirkpatrick at the Toronto Conservatory of Music from 1912 to 1918. WDC executives arranged for their plays' proceeds to be donated to "patriotic purposes,"[6] ranging from the University Overseas Companies to the Serbian Relief effort,[7] the Red Cross,[8] the "Varsity boys who are training in the University battalion,"[9] the Franco-British Aid Society,[10] and the University Base

Hospital. As students, their names became familiar throughout the city to their audiences and to readers of previews and reviews published in the *Varsity* and in the Toronto dailies: the *Mail*, the *Telegram*, and the *Globe*. According to the *Varsity*, by 1917 the WDC was comprised of "players … often competing almost with those of professional companies."[11]

In the months preceding *The Bluestockings,* several members of the cast rehearsed with two other groups: the Franco-British Aid Society and the Women's Literary Society. On 13 November 1917, for the Franco-British Aid Society, Isabel Jones appeared in front of a "large audience" at Foresters' Hall, adjacent to the campus, with future UCAA Dramatic Club members Marion Squair, Agnus Muldrew, Margaret Tytler, and Marguerite Phillips in a triple bill of Molière's 1665 comedy *L'Amour médecin*, Oliphant Down's 1914 fantasy *The Maker of Dreams*, and a third play titled *Call of France to War*, "arranged by"[12] Trinity College French lecturer Beatrice Embree.[13]

Then, on 5 January 1918, the UC Women's Literary Society executive hosted an "Alumnae Night" at the Women's Union Building at 85 St. George Street. The evening included Hermann Sudermann's one-act comedy *The Far-Away Princess* (possibly in the available 1909 translation by Grace Frank) featuring *Bluestockings* performers Margaret Boyle, Erskine Keys, and Norma Mortimer, along with future UCAA Dramatic Club performers Christina Cooper and Vera Robinson. Originally planned for 8 December, but "prevented by the weather,"[14] the evening gathered UC undergraduates and graduates together to strengthen bonds between female students and their alumnae association. Although Women's "Lit" students were accustomed to presenting at least one play each year, normally in service of their annual literary theme (that year, "modern literature"), it was novel for them to host a performance specifically for the UCAA. The *Varsity* characterized *The Far-Away Princess* as a lead-up to the following month's UCAA production of *The Bluestockings*, calling it "highly entertaining" and "cleverly given," and adding that the "undergraduates know now what good actresses the Alumnae Society has and many will attend [*The Bluestockings*]"[15] at the larger Conservatory Music Hall. Now populated with enterprising graduates with an interest in theatre as well as local name recognition and a record for contributing to pressing contemporary causes, the UCAA used *The Far-Away Princess* to signal theatrical performance as a new means of conducting business.

For the next two decades, the UCAA's thespians met as the "Dramatic Club of the University College Alumnae Association." As Francess Halpenny later explained, this "thoroughly unwieldy name was literally a descriptive one" that was intended to acknowledge their formal place within the UCAA. The UCAA provided the club with "support, both financial and moral,"[16] and the club provided the UCAA with a means to raise money for campus causes and to promote awareness of the value of female university graduates to local businesses and industries.[17] As formalized in 1922, the Dramatic Club's official policy[18] was to raise money for university projects led by the UCAA. The policy was adhered to until revenue was needed entirely for club activities beginning in 1940.[19]

The Dramatic Club raised money largely through ticket sales for their shows and conspicuous donations. Thus, when the *Varsity* concluded in its review of *The Bluestockings* that "altogether the success of the play reflects great credit on the Alumnae Association and on the distinguished patronage under which it was produced,"[20] it was pointing to the fact that the group's public roots lay with an educated and philanthropic university demographic. As was the custom, the patronesses attending *The Bluestockings* were announced in the local papers; they included Lady Falconer (YWCA president and wife of the university's president), Lady Walker, Mrs. Hutton, Miss Willson, Miss Wrong, Miss

Livingstone, Mrs. Bensley, Lady Eaton (wife of the department store heir Sir John Craig Eaton), Mrs. Pakenham, Mrs. Kirkpatrick (the director's wife), and the mothers of several cast members, including Mrs. Cassidy, Mrs. Boyle, and Mrs. Keys.[21] Proceeds went in aid of injured war veterans at the University of Toronto Base Hospital, recently established within the walls of the unfinished Hart House. Among the hundreds of playgoers attending *The Bluestockings*, as well as every UCAA Dramatic Club performance over the next two decades, were dignitaries who included lieutenant governors, university administrators and professors, sorority members, and "patronesses," whose names were confirmed at club executive meetings and listed in the daily papers whenever they brought groups or held pre-show dinner parties.

Thirteen months after *The Bluestockings* ran, the UCAA Dramatic Club presented its second play, *Trelawny of the Wells*.[22] Kirkpatrick directed Arthur Wing Pinero's showbiz classic about the height of the melodrama era in the 1860s for the UCAA Dramatic Club at the Conservatory Music Hall. Proceeds went to the University Alumni Memorial Fund[23] and would eventually be put towards the construction of the Soldier's Memorial Tower adjacent to Hart House, commemorating university members' lives lost in the war.[24] Pinero's work played to a large audience that included patronesses Lady Hearst (the wife of Ontario's premier), Lady Falconer, Mrs. Kirkpatrick, Mrs. Bach, Mrs. Bensley, Mrs. Groves, Miss Willson, Miss Wrong, and Miss Livingstone.[25] There was some question in the newspaper as to where to position the event: it was a campus production, yet it was not connected to a *student* club; it was Little Theatre fare, but the purpose of the production was to raise funds; and it was a play with twenty characters, but as with *The Bluestockings*, women played them all. Calling attention to the enduring novelty of the club's second all-woman cast, the *Globe* called the production a "very creditable one despite the fact that the parts were played entirely by ladies. The atmosphere of fifty years ago was well sustained through the performance, and presented an excellent study of life in the mid-Victorian days."[26] The "very clever" production earned abbreviated reviews of the cast in the *Telegram*'s "What Women Are Doing" section. The reviewer concluded that Mary Laughton's Rose Trelawny and Edna Norwich's Avonia Bunn were "charming," Christina Cooper's Miss Trafalger Gower was "excellent," Mabel Child's Tom Wrench and Erskine Keys's James Telfer were "also good,"[27] and Margaret Boyle's Ferdinand Gadd was "convincing."[28] The club's president from 1918 to 1924, Boyle reflected four decades later that "they were happy days" and that *Trelawny of the Wells* was a "splendid performance but it put us $125.00 in the hole. After that we nearly died, but recovered two years later when Hart House not only gave us inspiration, but offered lower theatre rental."[29]

Given that the production was a fundraising mechanism, this deficit may have been one reason why the following season, 1919-20, was the only peacetime theatre season in which Alumnae did not produce a play. But there may have been other reasons as well. For one, their director, Kirkpatrick, departed Toronto for a position at Columbia University,[30] leaving the club without a trusted director and, presumably, affordable access to the Conservatory Music Hall. There was also a uniquely complicated and increasingly diverse landscape for campus events. That fall, as men were settling back into campus life, and the campus was adjusting to having them back, there were more university sports being played and, consequently, covered in the *Varsity*. Students' "aesthetic development"[31] on campus was flourishing, with popular fortnightly organ recitals at the university's Convocation Hall, literary societies offering oratorical events and debates, and the formation of the Women's Press Association of the University of Toronto.

There was also a post-war renewal of interest in theatre, as evident in a brief note printed routinely in the *Varsity* starting in February 1920, asking, "Would all Dramatic Associations in the University wishing to have their productions reviewed in *The Varsity* send advance notices and tickets for their production to the Dramatic Editor."[32] Notices appeared for productions by the Victoria College Women's Dramatic Club, the UC Women's Literary Society, and a group of returned war veterans who collectively created the war-inspired show *The P.B.I.*[33] Lectures on drama were given throughout the year by professors and campus practitioners such as Hart House Theatre's Roy Mitchell, as well as by visiting speakers like playwright and poet William Butler Yeats, whose words inspired those keen on making Toronto a centre of production for the continent's burgeoning Little Theatre Movement.

Also, early in 1920 a flu "epidemic" struck the campus. It was not nearly as deadly as the "Spanish" flu pandemic that had shut down the city in October 1918, but the university administration was risk adverse. A campus-wide ban on social functions was put in place in January 1920 that was not lifted until the beginning of March (just before *The P.B.I.* ran). No UC classes were postponed, but other colleges and departments cancelled some classes, and dances were "called off" because, the *Varsity* reported, a "dance affords the greatest opportunities for the spread of the 'flu.'"[34] As if foreshadowing the public health concept of "flattening the curve" during the coronavirus pandemic a century later, the *Varsity* explained that "most of the members of the faculty have had the 'flu' but fortunately or unfortunately not all during the same period, so lectures still go on merrily without suspension."[35] But because of the ban, there were no university Theatre Nights.[36] These were the winter months during which Alumnae would have rehearsed and performed their annual play.

Fundraising for Women's Space and the University Settlement

By the end of the war, University College was experiencing startling changes. In the 1919–20 school year, nearly half of the then-record 1,030 students enrolled at UC were women.[37] With this increase in women's enrolment, the available spaces for them were no longer adequate. For example, the UC Women's Union at 85 St. George Street, where *The Far-Away Princess* had been staged, was insufficient and in disrepair (it had been obtained during the war from the UC men). A December 1918 *Varsity* editorial singled out the university's women graduates, setting out their material needs in a way that would define the conversation about campus women's spaces for a decade: "The Alumni have taken the first step towards raising funds and their example might be well followed by the Alumnae. An organized campaign for funds could be carried on by the Alumnae and undergraduate women … At the present time the need for additional women's residences, a new union and a gymnasium are pressing. Any one of these buildings might be erected as a memorial."[38]

The editorial went on to encourage women graduates to meet separately from the men. The gender imbalance could hardly be lost: the men's venue, Hart House, had been funded by a private Massey estate grant; the women's building was to be funded through the collective volunteer labour of women. Three months later, the UC Women's Undergraduate Association publication *The Rebel* observed that considering the post-war state of the existing women's spaces, the Women's Union and Queen's Hall, "when Hart House is open the material disparity may be on the side of the women." The editorial added that Hart House would be opening in the fall to "every man in the University," while the "women live in a perpetual state of over-crowding." It concluded by asserting that the "contrast between Hart House and the Union is certainly that of palace and hovel."[39] The UCAA set its fundraising sights on addressing this material disparity. The force of effort required to address it likely ensured that the UCAA women would not be combining their theatre-related energies with those of their male counterparts in the ways that other campus women's dramatic groups across the country would in the decade to come. While the men-only Hart House thrived, UCAA's labours were increasingly focused on women-centred practices and fundraising, notably at the expense of co-ed Alumni theatre adminstration.

The surge in campus activities at the outset of the 1919–20 season, followed by their sudden cessation due to the flu outbreak, sandwiched the UCAA Dramatic Club out of theatre production. But the resulting hiatus afforded the club time to pivot its fundraising efforts towards "new buildings for University College women,"[40] who, "having experienced all the discomforts of over-crowding[,] are unwilling that others coming after them should be similarly handicapped."[41] Relative to other colleges on campus, the building situation at UC was dire. Their "special grievance" was that the main building was shared between student common areas and the administrative offices used by the whole campus. The *Varsity* elaborated: "The only rooms in this building which are at all suitable for student gatherings are strongly stained with the awesome atmosphere of examinations, and their bare walls and scanty furnishings defy all but the most heroic efforts at camouflage. In such surroundings college spirit has little chance to thrive, and is only kept alive by the eternal vigilance of those who realize its significance." Because the men's accommodations were better equipped than the women's, the "first effort must be to provide women's buildings, with residences, dining-rooms, common rooms, committee rooms, a gymnasium, library and assembly hall, all on one site."[42] To these urgent reasons for erecting "permanent buildings" for women, an editorial added "overcrowding" as the "most obvious evil of the present situation."[43]

The UCAA made public its plans for an "agitation" for a UC women's space, one that would eventually include a theatre. The UCAA Building Fund Committee attracted several of its Dramatic Club's core theatre-makers, including Margaret Boyle, Marion Squair, Elspeth Wilson, and Agnes Muldrew, and this further decreased the likelihood that the club would be mounting a production that winter. The committee began collecting donations for an "up-to-date residence and a fully-equipped Union"[44] for UC women. It sought $400,000.00 from "friends of the college" and $95,000.00 from graduates, but only $5,000.00 from women undergraduates. As a *Varsity* piece noted, the "average student is not blessed with a superfluity of cash, but the need is great, and the war has shown us what can be done. There are four hundred and thirty-four women enrolled at present in University College and $5.00 a year for three years would more than cover our share."[45] Activities were added, including hosting speakers who discussed professions open to female college graduates.[46] The UCAA's "broad vision"[47] developed in the context of an improved co-educational environment. Concluded *Varsity*'s editors, the "interest of the men of University College is a foregone conclusion and we need not detail the benefits which will accrue to them."[48] The appeal worked. Within a month, students alone had contributed nearly $6,000.00.[49] The following year, the UCAA Dramatic Club returned to producing theatre, with the proceeds to go in aid of the UC Women's Building Fund. After production expenses, the club's Hart House Theatre production of Sheridan's *A Trip to Scarborough* in April 1921 raised several hundred dollars, and their Toronto premiere of A.A. Milne's *The Romantic Age* in April 1922 raised another $500.00.[50]

Then, three months after *The Romantic Age* ran, the university announced that it had purchased the late Senator Frederic Thomas Nicholls's property at 79 St. George Street and would be renovating it to serve for a new UC Women's Union. Today, the property is home to the Helen Gardiner Phelan Playhouse and is part of the Centre for Drama, Theatre and Performance Studies. After much debate, it was decided that the building's purchase price and the $100,000 required for renovations would not draw from the UCAA's Women's Building Fund because a provincial grant could be obtained instead.[51] The UCAA now pivoted its fundraising towards a new UC women's residence. They allocated Dramatic Club production income to this new cause from their subsequent Hart House Theatre shows – Davies's *A Single Man* in March 1923 ($100.00) and Hankin's *The Charity That Began at Home* in April 1924 ($200.00) – as well as one-acts mounted at the new UC Women's Union auditorium beginning in October 1923. Through their notoriety in the papers, these productions kept campus and public conversation going about the lack of women's space.[52]

The UCAA proved it could muster some of Toronto's wealthiest and best connected patrons and patronesses, in part through the performance of plays. It took until the next decade, but more than fifty years after UC began admitting female students, in October 1931 a new UC Women's Residence was completed. Designed by Royal Alexandra Theatre architect John Lyle and named Whitney Hall after its major donor,[53] it opened to 156 undergraduate women on lots 81, 83, and 85 of St. George Street (the old Women's Union). The *Varsity* reported that "it lacks the richness of the Hart House library, but it is quite inviting."[54] Featuring late Georgian architecture, the grounds offered "one of the finest gardens in the city with many rare species of vegetation."[55] Many of the amenities that had been sought for a decade had now been achieved thanks to what the university's chancellor, Sir William Mulock, referred to as the "pertinacity of women." Drama Club stalwart Agatha Leonard, now president of the UCAA, helped lay the cornerstone.[56] The UCAA had raised over $30,000, $25,000 of which went towards Whitney Hall's furnishings.[57] By November 1932, it had brought the amount to $40,000, with funds put towards the founding of an endowment library in Whitney Hall.[58] Moreover, with the new UC Women's Union, the UCAA Dramatic Club now had a more intimate venue than Hart House Theatre to stage one-act plays.

Campus women's buildings were not the only targets of UCAA Dramatic Club philanthropy. A few years before Whitney Hall was completed, the UCAA became a significant supporter of the University Settlement, which had been founded in 1910 by university president Sir Robert Falconer with graduates and other university members. By 1926 the settlement had moved to its current site, 23 Grange Road on what is now the OCAD University campus. It dealt with nearby areas of need and had connections to college chapters of the YWCA, as did some prominent members of the UCAA Dramatic Club, including Agnes Muldrew. By March 1941, the Second World War had increased the number of immigrants to Toronto, and more than 2,000 people were passing through its doors every week, "men, women, and children of 38 different nationalities from the district," according to the *Varsity*, who "gather and exchange views, acquire new leisure-time skills and find further enjoyment in life through recreation." For the 172 students and other volunteers that year, the settlement was a place to reach out to those in need and thereby "gain a wider sympathy and a keener insight into the actual results of our present-day social and economic forces."[59] As Cathy L. James notes in her study of the origins of Canadian settlements, the skills required to facilitate settlement activities were taught at the Toronto Conservatory of Expression and the Margaret Eaton School of Literature and Expression.[60] Those affiliated with these two schools, including many of Alumnae's founding members, who had performed with Ms. Scott Raff and Kirkpatrick through the WDC, were among those trained in settlement skills; they now contributed to settlement fundraising efforts while active with Alumnae. Settlements were among the "few institutions in the city to offer respectable, secular recreation to working-class women"[61] outside of church socials and theatre.[62]

The club's first effort to support the University Settlement involved a "cup and saucer shower"[63] to fund Settlement Christmas baskets, held at the new UC Women's Union in December 1927. Members sang carols and presented a "dramatic fairy tale" called *The Rim of the World*, reported by the *Globe* as "excellently played."[64] Further settlement donations on record came from club productions at Hart House Theatre. These included the Sierras' *Take Two from One* in January 1934 ($75.00), Campion's *Ladies in Waiting* in November 1935 ($256.60), Wood's *Charity Begins* in December 1936 ($200.00[65]), Act I of the Sierras' *The Cradle Song* in February 1937 ($200.00), and the world premiere of Coulter's *The Family Portrait* in November 1937 ($200.00). The club's November 1938 Hart House production of *Miss Black Sheep* ($205.00) was presented in part to support the Children's Little Theatre, which, according to the settlement, was "entirely dependent on your annual donation to us, and partly for class supplies."[66] The Club's last Settlement Night came in March 1940, when, despite not planning to present any further productions that season, members responded to an "emergency" request from the University Settlement, which was "in urgent need of money to carry on some of the special activities planned for this year."[67] Club president Margaret Ness reported that the settlement had "felt the loss of the Club's donation which it had unfortunately come to regard as annual."[68] The club decided to produce three one-act plays as a University Settlement Theatre Night, in this way raising $200.00 from $1.00 tickets and bringing the club's total settlement contribution over the years to $2,000. The settlement expressed its gratitude, saying that the funds were helpful, "especially in the field of children's theatre."[69]

Settlement philanthropy paled in comparison to a broader club scheme that ensured income for its own theatre purposes while benefiting other groups as well. Before the First World War, the popularity of student Theatre Nights was obvious, although bad student behaviour culminating in 1914 had made professional companies reticent to continue them.[70] Instead of students, who had proven to be unpredictable as audience members, the club sought out trusted community groups to sell discounted group tickets to. The purchasing group could then either distribute the discounted tickets to their members or sell them at an increased price, with the difference benefiting their own club or a charity of the club's choice. By 1930, the club's Hart House Theatre productions were popular enough that they could fill the theatre with multiple Theatre Nights during a run. Remarkably, in 1938, the *Telegram* reported of the UCAA Dramatic Club that "so popular has this organization become that Theatre Nights were taken for their annual production before the play had even been chosen."[71] Between 1930 and 1955, the club sold Theatre Nights to more than twenty-five different groups, including women's groups, nursing and hospital groups, school associations and alumni, and fraternities (the only student exception).[72]

Alumnae's November 1935 production of Campion's mystery play *Ladies in Waiting* at Hart House Theatre gives insight into the Theatre Nights scheme's efficacy. The first three performances of the run were Theatre Nights, which provided the club not only predictable income but also a month's worth of advance attention from the city's dailies, which listed those "entertaining before and after the event."[73] Financial statements show that the club sold each of the three sponsored nights at $150.00, their usual price during the 1930s, to

Figure 1.1. The cast and crew of Alumnae's December 1936 production of Ireland Wood's *Charity Begins*, a "University Settlement" production at Hart House Theatre. *(back row, left to right)* F.G. Venables (Henry), Christina Templeton (Emily), Dudley Doughty (Rodney), Erskine Keys (Daker), Agnes Muldrew (Mrs. Deveral), Bertram Stanley (Stage Manager), Eleanor Barton (Agnes), Mrs. Leslie Hunt (Alumnae President), Herbert Hale (Chief Electrician). *(front row, left to right)* Stuart Parker (Bobbie), Sheila Tisdale (Judith), Margaret Tytler (Catherine), Agatha Leonard (Prompter), Edgar Stone (Director), Mary Smart (Miss Case), Alison Ewart (Properties), Wentworth Walker (Asst. Stage Manager). Photograph by James & Son for Hart House Theatre (public domain). Courtesy of Alumnae Theatre Company. Gift to the author from Shelagh Kareda.

the Toronto Flying Club (opening), the Kappa Alpha Theta fraternity (Tuesday), and the Moulton College Alumnae (Wednesday). Thursday was the run's only "open" performance and was sold out by five seats beyond capacity in aid of the University Settlement. The three Theatre Nights were grand affairs, with two "entr'acte skits in front of the curtain,"[74] a fifteen-minute intermission "to give you time to visit the Sausage Bar" (according to the program) and, before the Toronto Flying Club Theatre Night, "many delightful parties." The Flying Club parties included a dinner at the Board of Trade, a second dinner at another site, a "coffee party" hosted by the Flying Club president and his wife, no less than three "after the theatre supper-parties," and a fourth after-theatre buffet supper, each at a separate location.[75] The guest lists for these were all published in the dailies.

Like the Toronto Flying Club's night, Moulton College's night was a hectic affair. The *Toronto Star* described the intermission: "Between acts the black and chromium sausage bar and the theatre lobby presented a friendly scene as members of the audience chatted about the play and speculated as to how it would turn out. Old friendships were renewed and college days reviewed." The *Star* described the outfits worn by the "pretty quartet of ushers" in even greater detail, as well as the decadent outfits worn by many of the notable Moulton alumnae in attendance.[76]

By selling Theatre Nights months in advance, the club could generate a degree of predictable income and publicity while reducing pressure on its members to sell tickets in the weeks while they were busy rehearsing. The club carried the scheme into the mid-1950s, until theatre companies with "professional competence"[77] (i.e., with dedicated marketing personnel) took up the strategy. By then, Theatre Nights had become less predictable to obtain, which made them too risky to build production budgets and season programming around. But for decades they served well as a fundraising mechanism, one that helped weave the club into the city's philanthropic fabric.[78]

Early Alumnae fundraising ventures engaged audiences beyond regular theatre-goers while increasing the club's renown. Before the Second World War, early performances raised more than $3,000.00 for various university projects, including the UC Women's Building Fund ($1,557.00 between 1922 and 1930), the carillon for the Memorial Tower ($150.00 from *Getting Married* in 1927), the UC Alumnae Scholarship Fund ($350.00 from *Pomander's Walk* in 1930), the University Settlement ($1,136.00 between 1934 and 1940),[79] and the University's Student Employment Bureau. During these first two decades, the club gathered Toronto's elite to generate income through Theatre Nights, individual ticket sales, and larger donations sociably arranged. Groups of skilled, articulate, and highly motivated UCAA Dramatic Club members managed this fundraising activity while producing popular plays within the Little Theatre Movement.

Intellectual Thespians, Jolly Groups, and Glorious Days

From their training and education at private schools and schools of expression to their numerous involvements in clubs and societies at University College, Alumnae's early women held deeply rooted, institutionalized, class-based assumptions that informed their programming choices. An example of Pierre Bourdieu's "history reproduced by education,"[80] the classic and modern plays they produced were well suited to finishing schools and the university as signs of higher learning, serving to educate the women who chose the plays as well as the audiences that attended them. Because their foundations were in student governance, Alumnae's women understood how to parlay administrative flexibility into programming variety and longevity. Like other Little Theatre practitioners, they often drew from close-knit bonds while sharing ideas with their community. As Dorothy Chansky writes of Little Theatre practitioners in the United States, since many "were in a position of some social influence (e.g., because they were writers, teachers, or monied), their work got public attention and eventually affected the thinking of many commercial theatre workers and audiences."[81] The choices that resulted from their early education influenced the idea of "modern" and "alternative" play production in Toronto.

In the thirty-nine years between their founding in 1918 and their move to their first Coach House Theatre in 1957, most of Alumnae's 149 plays were modern plays (113), with the most popular genre being modern comedies (51). Halpenny wrote that most were British comedies "in a light mode presented with taste and integrity."[82] They also produced Christmas plays (6), period comedies (5), revues (4), and various member-written and -performed skits, monologues, and variety shows (25). This programming is evidence of their extraordinary consistency across the decades when local theatre companies rarely lasted more than a few years. Their choices frequently filled gaps and even led the way for programming not found elsewhere in the city. These plays had often premiered in Europe or the United States just a few years before Alumnae's productions, making the group an important early interpreter of international plays in Toronto and eventually, by way of the Dominion Drama Festival, in Ontario and Canada. Moreover, Toronto theatres subsequently programmed these plays because Alumnae had made them known "commodities" and no longer "risky" ventures.

From the moment Alumnae produced their fourth play, *The Romantic Age*, in April 1922, their programming embraced certain facets of the sprawling Little Theatre Movements of Europe and the United States. One strong impact the Little Theatre Movement had on Western theatre had to do with its focus on thoughtful, not simply popular, playwriting and production. As playwright Constance D'Arcy MacKay explained in 1917, its informal tenets dated back to André Antoine's Théâtre Libre experiments in Paris in the 1880s. The plays prioritized a particular variety of programming, one that encompassed naturalism, Symbolism, verse drama, fantasy, and satire from a fresh, modern, middle-class perspective. Such programs had literary qualities, but they also turned to modern and abstract staging and lighting and a variety of stage shapes and usages. These plays could be one-act or full-length, and most of them were modern, although Little Theatres occasionally produced the classics as well. Compared to New York's Broadway or London's West End, they usually had low production costs.

Beyond programming, several operational facets characterized Little Theatres. They remained resident in their own cities and were not primarily touring groups. They were ensemble, even repertory, groups and to an extent each featured, according to MacKay, a "democracy of artists [wherein] each artist must be given an opportunity to reach his [*sic*] public." Some artists were professionals, some were "amateurs on the way toward being professionals" – that is, professionalizing – and some were nonprofessionalizing. The primary division between Little Theatre companies and other nonprofessionalizing groups was that unlike groups staging private theatricals for a "coterie of amateurs purely for the sake of the amusement derived," Little Theatre groups worked with intention and were judged by "theatre standards."[83]

This space of nonprofessionalizing theatre labour was gendered. Heather Murray has shown that during the first two decades of the twentieth century, Emma Scott Raff's Margaret Eaton School of Literature and Expression, with which a number of Alumnae's founding members gained early training and performance experience, was "classed in the category of 'amateur' rather than 'little' theatre" because of a "gender gap"[84] that separated the two terms and thus excluded women from the progressive discourse of Little Theatres in Canada. This, along with the fact that they did not have their own building during the height of the Little Theatre Movement, may explain why Alumnae have not been viewed by scholars as impacting theatre in Canada to the same extent as Canada's "flagship"[85] Little Theatre, Hart House Theatre. That said, Hart House Theatre helped boost Alumnae's visibility in the decades before the Second World War. Ultimately, Alumnae members' choice to keep their company nonprofessionalizing shielded them from the discrimination reserved for women who sought to enter the theatre profession in leadership roles as producers and directors.[86] By refusing to professionalize the company, Alumnae's women kept control of it.

Having read recent plays in acting editions, anthologies, and drama magazines, Alumnae's early members were aware of the most recent trends and innovations in English-speaking theatre. Perhaps uniquely, both public spectacles and private entertainments marked their interwar programming. Alumnae staged skits at closed club meetings at members' homes and one-act plays at the UC Women's Union for invited UCAA guests, although their primary concern was their annual Hart House production staged for broader campus, city, and regional audiences. Thus, from the outset Alumnae were positioned between their own amusement, their fealty to UCAA's fundraising projects, and their public audiences. These sometimes complimentary, sometimes conflicting loyalties defined them until they left the UCAA.

During the interwar years, the club's programming, production, and administrative choices were discussed at general and executive meetings held at members' houses one to three times a month according to need. At these meetings, members' engagements and marriages were formally acknowledged, as were departures from the club when members moved away or passed away; programming and financial details were discussed; popular Theatre Nights were settled on; and patrons and patronesses were confirmed for official post-show receptions. Following these administrative duties, members treated themselves to sandwiches (or sometimes full dinners), coffee, and amusing skits and playreadings. In these early years, the ebb and flow of membership was predicated on the number of drama-inclined women graduating from UC, many of whom had already gained experience with the co-ed UC Players Guild and Hart House Theatre Players Club. Some members hosted meetings more often than others. As an example, between September and December 1935, five members hosted meetings at their respective homes – Alison Ewart, Agatha Leonard (twice), Doris Shiell, Katherine Anglin (twice), and Margaret Tytler – with approximately fifteen members attending each meeting.[87]

On a Saturday or Sunday in May or June, an annual meeting would feature recreation, including tea and sunbathing (weather permitting), followed by executive reports, general business, and the confirmation of the members of the following year's executive. For example, as recorded in the minutes, Alumnae's June 1935 annual meeting took the form of a picnic featuring a "glorious day and a jolly group." Peggy McCready "produced a stew fit for the gods. Delicious fruits, scrumptious cakes and gallons of coffee followed. A serious evening followed in which much real business was accomplished to the accompaniment of much hearty laughter." Plays were read and royalties and costumes were considered, and the "ever present problem of how many men should we have in our plays arose." As recorded, the "picnic was adjourned at 11:30pm having begun at 3:30."[88] Another annual meeting, this one in May 1938, ended with the club putting together a modest evening of two one-act plays at the Erindale country home of president-elect Mary Evans, followed by refreshments. The two all-women plays were Kathleen Davey's comedy-drama *Unnatural Scene*, directed by Lorna Sheard, and Muriel and Sydney Box's backstage play *Slow Curtain*, directed by Agnes Muldrew, whose husband Edgar Stone "very kindly arranged the lights and curtains."[89] And in June 1944, at Alice Keys's home in Scarborough, a "long sightseeing tramp to the bluffs or sunbathing occupied the members until supper time," after which the entertainment included "three sets of 'Quizzes,'" Percy Corry's 1939 short play *Cupid Rampant*, a new monologue by Alice Keys, and performances of Alice Keys's monologues *The Picnic* and *The Plumber*.[90] These minutes suggest how much thought the women put into the club's programming and production and how they balanced it with pleasant camaraderie.

At meetings throughout each year, playreading committees were chosen, plays were pitched and debated, and directors were selected. As a retrospective article in the *Star* noted, "one of the first and founding principles of the company was that it should produce not only the little known masterpieces of the theatre world, but also the best contemporary plays from Broadway and London's West End."[91] Halpenny discussed the value of careful play selection in the early years: plays were to offer "good theatrical fare, if not particularly experimental, with special care for costuming, and they provided satisfaction and therefore enjoyment for the company in playing them, an important feature when almost everyone was performing as an amateur with other career responsibilities."[92] One of the club's unsigned history documents describes the play selection process and the intentions that had began to form in the interwar period:

> It all starts with the work of the Reading Committee whose members are constantly on the lookout for plays that suit the interests of the group – stimulating plays of good content and construction, worthy of the efforts which the Alumnae spends on production, that offer a good assortment of challenging women's roles but that will not present impossible problems in set construction, lighting and costumes. The reading Committee submits a report of the plays read to the Executive, then to the members as a whole. From this report a play is chosen. Then, when play, director and production dates are decided on, try-outs for roles begin. All members who are interested in reading for parts gather with the men reading for male roles, and from this group a cast is chosen by the director and rehearsals commence.[93]

Alumnae's members took play selection seriously, and first readings were conducted at the end of meetings. While there was not always unanimous agreement on play selection, members invariably found consensus.

Casting took into account personal and group fit for roles as well as interest, availability, and the broad participation of members. A handful of Alumnae actors, who were also active administrators with the club, appeared more frequently on stage than others. They became known in the dailies as "stars" of the local theatre community and included Margaret Boyle, Agatha Leonard, Agnes Muldrew Stone, and Margaret Tytler. Alumnae gradually built a "loyal audience,"[94] and box office income and theatre nights supported the club financially.[95] As with many nonprofessionalizing theatre companies, membership infers participation, though it does not always ensure it. In 1935, the *Star*'s influential critic Augustus Bridle noted Alumnae's recent world premiere of their member Katherine Anglin's new play *Boomerang* and her status as the group's president. He observed that other members were writing plays and that, moreover, "any member who fails to write or act in a play, or to help make costumes, or design scenics or look after 'props' is not a good member." He described Alumnae as "that society of high enthusiasts" and "this group of intellectual thespians."[96] This moment of insight into Alumnae's expectations and practices points to the imperative of past and present nonprofessionalizing theatres to consistently attract active members into their fold.

The processes for choosing a show's director depended in the first place on the venue. One-acts at the Women's Union were typically directed by club members: Margaret Tytler (three times), Margaret Boyle (twice), Agnes Muldrew Stone (twice), Eleanor Barton Woodside (twice), Katherine Anglin, Lorna Sheard, Francess Halpenny, and Jean Stewart. Hart House Theatre productions, including those mounted for the DDF regional festivals, were more technically elaborate, so not everyone could be expected to direct and design a full production there.[97] But a few Alumnae members did direct there, including Francess Halpenny (three times), Pamela Terry Beckwith (three), Margaret Boyle, Margaret Tytler, and Molly Golby Thom. Alumnae's list of male Hart House Theatre guest directors is a who's who of Toronto theatre at the time; they included Edgar Stone (eight times), Herbert Whittaker (five), E.G. Sterndale Bennett (four), H.E. Hitchman (three), William Needles (three; he would later make a career acting at the Stratford Festival of Canada), Frank Hemingway (twice), Henry Kaplan (twice), David Gardner, and Robert Gill (who rarely directed plays produced by companies other than Hart House Theatre's Players Club).[98]

The importance of finding qualified directors for Hart House Theatre productions was particularly evident during the early DDF years, when the festival was starting to influence programming and personnel decisions, as well as instil a competitive level of aesthetic choices for participating groups. Between April 1932 and October 1935, Alumnae tried without success to recruit a dependable director to manage their annual full-length play at the state-of-the-art Hart House Theatre. They had been pleased with Edgar Stone's direction of *Pomander Walk* (1930), *To Have the Honour* (1930), and *The Young Idea* (1932), but he was increasingly occupied with artistic director duties at Hart House Theatre and could not be counted on every season. By fall 1934, they had abandoned their futile search and decided to host a series of lecture meetings as a sort of "audition" for directors and an education in directing for themselves. As Alumnae secretary Genevre Campbell's meeting minutes describe in her impeccable handwriting, the "series was arranged that we might become familiar with the methods of various experts and so choose a director for the Hart House show and the Dominion Drama Festival."[99] The lecture series played out as follows: Edgar Stone at his Radio Hall at 12 Spadina Road (2 October), James Annand at an unnoted location (17 October), Dora Mavor Moore at a home on Spadina Road (23 October), Campbell McInnes at member Betty Green's home (6 November), and Bill Atkinson[100] at "the Barn," which was Alumnae's storage and occasional rehearsal space on Lonsdale Road (20 November). The series did not immediately achieve its purpose, but it did, reportedly, add entertainment to club meetings.

Over the course of this lecture series, in November 1934, members met to discuss their struggle to find a director. Soon after, they decided to invite Nancy Pyper, Hart House's new artistic director, who had replaced Stone in that capacity, to give a presentation to the club in June 1935 titled "What the Theatre Means to Me." After her talk, an "interesting discussion followed in which incidents about famous people and theatres were cited with increasing enthusiasm."[101] Then, at the same June meeting, after choosing a summer reading committee, Alumnae decided to ask Frank Hemingway to give the final lecture of the series in September 1935.[102]

At Agatha Leonard's house on Friday, 27 September 1935, a "red letter day in the life of the club" according to Campbell, Alumnae finally found their next Hart House director. Instead of giving a talk, Hemingway chose to direct a "reading production" of a play (title not recorded) "arising out of the minutes" and "directed the characters as they walked through their parts." This exercise, less a lecture than a demonstration, was taken seriously given the stakes of mounting a show for the Hart House stage. Campbell wrote that "from the very beginning, each member was impressed by his quiet manner and skill in producing something vital out of this weak skit. It was a very enjoyable evening." Hemingway was now the "unanimous choice"[103] to direct their next two Hart House productions: Cyril Campion's *Ladies in Waiting* in November 1935 and Oscar W. Firkins's *Empurpled Moors*

Figure 1.2. Directed by Hart House artistic director Edgar Stone with set design by Fr. (Frederick) C. Coates, Alumnae's production of Louis N. Parker's comedy *Pomander Walk* at Hart House Theatre in February 1930 featured (*left to right*) Ivor Lewis (Sir Antrobus), Eleanor Norton Beecroft (Pamela Poskett), Margaret Boyle Martin (Lucie Lachesnais), Pearl Gray (Marjolaine Lachesnais), Eleanor Barton Woodside (Ruth Pennymint), H.E. Hitchman, (*unknown*), (*unknown*), and Mary Smart (Annette). Photographed for Hart House Theatre (public domain). Courtesy of Alumnae Theatre Company.

for the DDF's regional festival in March 1936. Two other series lecturers, Edgar Stone and Lorna Sheard, would direct subsequent Alumnae productions. Hemingway's appointment raised the club's spirits and may also have helped attract new members. A note in the club's minutes praised him for his first rehearsals: "These were enjoyable to all taking part. Mr. Hemingway was always calm, composed and encouraging. He inspired such confidence that stage fright was reduced to a minimum. It is a privilege to work under such a director."[104]

At least in part due to Hemingway, that fall Alumnae's membership reached thirty-eight, its interwar peak. But as membership numbers increased, inexperienced members found that they were not finding sufficient involvement, or training, in company productions. In April 1936 it was suggested that small monthly productions be offered to give experience to more members and that Hemingway might be "informally approached"[105] to train them (although there is no evidence on record that he did so).

Conspicuous Private Performances at University College's Alternative Little Theatre

With the opening of the new UC Women's Union in January 1923, Alumnae and other UC groups were afforded a new space for informal gatherings and entertainments as well as formal meetings.[106] This conspicuous socializing was recorded in the dailies and the *Varsity*, with exhaustive accounts of the organizers, patronesses, and performers. The club's one-acts aligned with UC's long tradition of gathering together students, alumnae, faculty, and their families for tea, speeches, entertainment, and fundraising events. They also helped define Alumnae's now long-running mixture of meetings and social events characterized by self-generated performances.

The 1923–24 academic year was the first in which Alumnae presented multiple productions in a season (at both the Women's Union and Hart House). Productions at the Women's Union were not strictly speaking open to the public; rather, they were presented by "invitation" to the UC community, with donations to the cause of the day happily received. Many audience members must have recognized that in this sense, these productions echoed those of the original European Little Theatres that were "private clubs." This aspect gave them a mystique not shared by productions at Hart House Theatre.

In the Women's Union's 300-seat auditorium,[107] between the fall of 1923 and the winter of 1947, Alumnae produced twenty-eight evening invitational one-act plays, three of them during the venue's inaugural 1923–24 season. The first, part of an October 1923 meeting, was intended to be J.M. Barrie's 1910 comedy *The Twelve-Pound Look*, with the wives of UC faculty and the UC class of 1923 as guests of honour. But when Basil Morgan, who was to play the lead, took ill, they opted to present instead another Barrie one-act comedy, *Rosalind*, with UC Players' Guild student president Robert Finch agreeing to play the role of Charles with a week's notice. This marked the first time an Alumnae member, their president Margaret Boyle, was credited with directing for the club. Alumnae's Edna Norwich "revealed her wide experience and the versatility of her talent in the subtle interpretation"[108] of the actress Mrs. Beatrice Page. New club member Doris Dignum played the boarding house's landlady Dame Quickly "very well."

In February 1924, the UCAA "invited friends and others interested in amateur dramatics"[109] to an "At Home" at the Women's Union, where they produced *The Twelve-Pound Look* for an audience that was "very well entertained."[110] As was so often the case, Alumnae's choice of play was relevant to the times. The plot of *The Twelve-Pound Look* no doubt echoed some of the tensions felt by UC women graduates with respect to emerging post-war expectations in the workplace and in marriage: a man is about to be knighted when his ex-wife, who left him once she had earned the twelve pounds necessary to purchase a typewriter, responds to his ad for a typist to answer messages congratulating him on his achievements. Hinting at future programming spanning geography and genre, the evening's other two short plays were the first since *The Bluestockings* to be written by playwrights who were not British: the comedy *The Green Scarf* by K.S. Goodman (Chicago, USA) and *The Stronger* by August Strindberg (Sweden), whose work was enjoying renewed interest with Little Theatres on both sides of the Atlantic.

Alumnae's third and final Women's Union evening that season was their first production of a Canadian play: Merrill Denison's *Balm* in May 1924. *Balm* had had its world premiere nine months earlier at Hart House Theatre.[111] It has three female characters, one of them, fittingly, a settlement worker. The director was M.E. Allen, a 1904 UC graduate and Modern Languages and History teacher at the Collegiate Institute in Seaforth.[112] Alumnae's

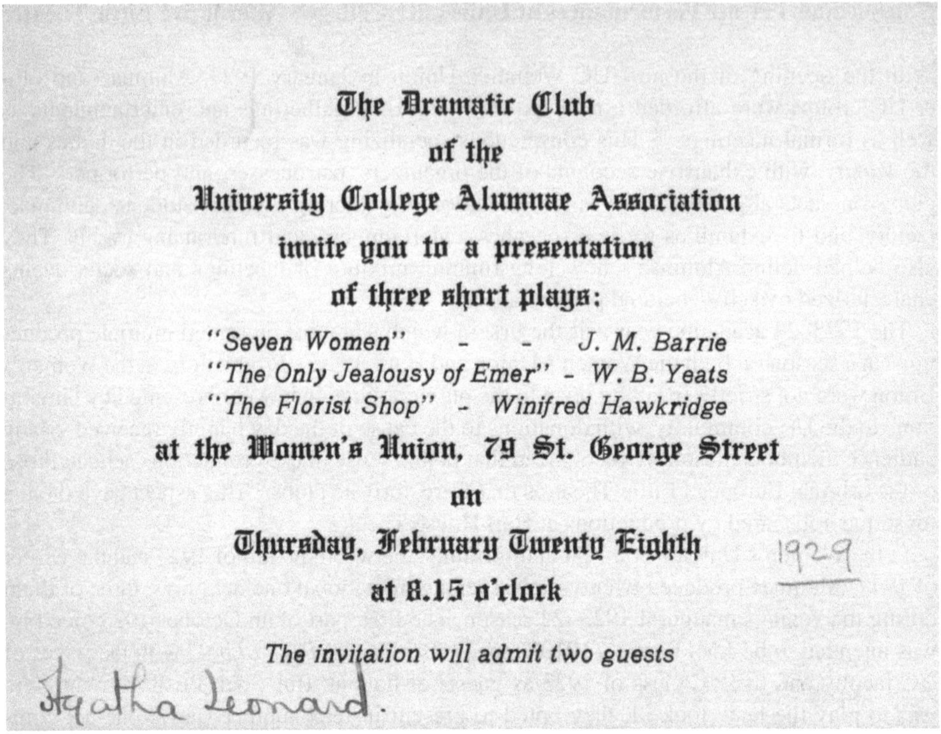

The Dramatic Club
of the
University College Alumnae Association
invite you to a presentation
of three short plays:

"Seven Women" - - J. M. Barrie
"The Only Jealousy of Emer" - W. B. Yeats
"The Florist Shop" - Winifred Hawkridge

at the Women's Union, 79 St. George Street
on
Thursday, February Twenty Eighth 1929
at 8.15 o'clock

The invitation will admit two guests

Agatha Leonard.

Figure 1.3. Invitation to one of Alumnae's many evenings of short plays in the 300-seat auditorium of the new UC Women's Union on St. George St. featuring three modern one-acts. Courtesy of Alumnae Theatre Company.

five one-acts over three evenings at the Women's Union that year were noteworthy not only for their value in attracting campus socialites and the correlated fundraising, but also because each had literary value that reflected the women's education as well as their awareness of current Little Theatre trends. The Women's Union quickly became known as the "alternate campus theatre"[113] to Hart House Theatre. Framed in the papers in this way, it was effectively the campus's second Little Theatre, programmed by women and featuring a range of important plays and playwrights. The Women's Union was the first of many "alternative theatre" spaces in which Alumnae flourished.

Importantly, the Women's Union provided Alumnae with some consistency and control over their productions. In January 1926, the *Varsity* announced that a bill of three one-act plays would be "tak[ing] the place of the Club's usual annual show in Hart House Theatre, which was not obtainable this year."[114] The three plays the Women's Union presented were Colin Campbell Clements's *Spring* (as collected in Clements's 1924 collection *Plays for Pagans*), J.A. Ferguson's *Campbell of Kilmhor*, and George Bernard Shaw's comedy *Overruled*. It is likely that when they were UC students, several Alumnae women had seen the Canadian premiere[115] of Shaw's four-hander at the Eaton School's Greek Theatre, directed by Hart House Theatre's first artistic director Roy Mitchell.[116]

Twelve months later the Women's Union produced three short plays, all comedies, first in their own venue and then remounting them at the Women's Art Association, which still stands at 23 Prince Arthur Street. This was the first time that Alumnae produced a play by a woman. Each of the three plays involved the theme of marriage, and each was directed by a club member: Margaret Boyle directed Alfred Sutro's *A Marriage Has Been Arranged*, Agnes Muldrew directed Mary Aldis's *Mrs. Pat and the Law*, and Margaret Tytler directed "by far the most finished production of the three," Angela Morris's *Dorinda Dares*, the stage version of a 1909 short story by Marjorie Bowen. The Women's Union performance, which "never flags,"[117] found a "large and enthusiastic audience in the auditorium,"[118] and the Women's Art Association performance played to about 150 people.[119]

At the Women's Union in November 1929, future CBC Radio drama producer and the first artistic director of the Shaw Festival, Andrew Allan, appeared in his Alumnae stage debut in Babette Hughes's late-1920s play about the early life of actor David Garrick titled *Three Players, a Fop, and a Duchess*. At the time, Allan was an undergraduate student[120] and assistant to the *Varsity*'s drama editor. His turn as Garrick, the *Varsity* noted, was "worthy of special mention." The comedy, set in 1743, was paired with Carl Glick's 1931 comedy *The Fourth Mrs. Phillips*. The *Varsity* declared that the plays "were not particularly good, but were rather well produced." There is no available record of who the director was, but the *Varsity* reported that the "directing of both plays was very capably done, though not especially difficult, and, as is not uncommon with one-acts, both plays had a certain unusualness of idea which in some measure compensated for dramatic weakness."[121]

Women-centred plays of note included Susan Glaspell's widely performed early feminist drama *Trifles*, presented in November 1931; Franz (Ferenc) Molnár's ten-minute celebrity comedy *A Matter of Husbands*, in which the character "Earnest Young Woman" demands that "Famous Actress" give her husband back and the latter explains how this can be done; and N. Hudson's 1915 "oriental" pantomime *The Shepherd in the Distance*, in which a Princess seeks out a Shepherd, who is rescued from a cruel Vizier by a goat. With these three plays, Alumnae presented female characters who had some agency over their fate. As the Great Depression began to grip North America, Alumnae increasingly turned to plays with female-dominant casts, even entirely female casts. This may have been in part because male actors were by then searching for paid work, or having to work more hours at their jobs for less income. Moreover, a number of Alumnae productions during these years were written or co-written by women, including world premieres by Alumnae member Katherine Anglin and Toronto playwrights Margaret Ness, Winifred Pilcher, and Mary Lowry Ross (see chapter 7). They also featured a number of plays by American and British women like Glaspell, Alice Gerstenberg, Doris Halman, Alice Pieratt, Winifred Hawkridge, and Winifred Stuckes Raffo.

Alumnae also offered Christmas performances featuring tableaux, nativity plays, and Bible stories. The first was an eleven-scene tableau "picturing the events of the first Christmas"[122] for the annual UC women undergraduates' Christmas party in December 1932. Invited guests included UC undergraduates and their parents, as well as faculty and their children. A year later, when Alumnae produced an Irish nativity play by Lady Gregory, directed by member Eleanor Barton Woodside, the event was referred to as the "Dean's party for UC women" and introduced by the Dean of Women Miss Ferguson, with the *Varsity* making note that the play was "particularly good in its tableaux effects" and that the "Dean's Christmas Party is becoming an important feature of UC social life."[123]

Staging Modern Comedies at Canada's Big Little Theatre

Alumnae's founding members were learned ladies in an emerging modern theatre scene. At the heart of their early play programming was their "annual production"[124] at Hart House Theatre. Following the departure of Kirpatrick from Toronto, Alumnae no longer had access to the Conservatory Music Hall. They needed a new performance venue that could generate maxium public exposure for their productions to achieve their fundraising goals. Thus, they began a long relationship with the new and innovative Hart House Theatre as their primary public performance venue. The original Little Theatres of Europe and America were often intimate store-front-sized spaces renovated to stage new plays; Hart House Theatre, by contrast, gave Toronto a nearly 500-seat[125] auditorium with a state-of-the-art proscenium stage that could feature creatively designed modern spectacles while training university students and local artists in acting and backstage craft. Hart House Theatre's programming and technical achievements defined its early years. There, the UCAA Dramatic Club staged large-cast shows that showcased their membership's talents and drew Toronto audiences to UCAA causes.

Construction began on Hart House a few years before most of Alumnae's founding women entered UC as undergraduates. By 1911, $125,000 in funding[126] had been assured by Vincent Massey, a twenty-five-year-old UC graduate and trustee of his family estate. The estate's original intentions for this "splendid gift" of "wisely-directed philanthropy" were set out in the *Varsity*: "It aims at furnishing the students with much-needed material accessories for the development of their physical, spiritual and social natures."[127] By 1913, it was reported that along with gymnasiums, reading and club rooms, and other amenities deemed essential to the development of modern young men, an "underground theatre" would be included in the plans for the building's "sub-basement," with its own "separate entrance." It would offer a 24-by-56-foot stage with "ladies' and gentlemen's dressing-rooms attached," as well as lighting "by an indirect system."[128] But construction was halted with the onset of war. The long delayed opening finally came on 11 November 1919, the first Armistice Day.

The theatre immediately surpassed technical expectations. As one of North America's best-equipped theatre spaces designed to create the most convincing naturalistic effects possible, the cultural jewel in the crown of the university's new gothic-style boys' club immediately impacted the theatre ecology of the campus, the city, and beyond. Said its first artistic director, Roy Mitchell, the "stage equipment is unequalled on the continent except by the Metropolitan Opera House in New York. The stage workmen's shops are as efficient as a clock. It is an ideal small theatre – almost perfect."[129] The material position of every drama club at the university was permanently altered by the completion of Hart House Theatre. The resident company that came to inhabit it, the Players Club, soon set the pace for Canada's Little Theatre Movement. Hart House Theatre provided campus groups with the technical capacity to realize their visions beyond what most spaces on the continent could manage. But it also presented challenges and disappointments. Almost immediately, Hart House Theatre was caught between its continental Little Theatre aspirations and students' expectations that it would be available for their own drama clubs. Hart House Theatre could not be for everyone; students were to be, at best, assistants.[130]

As a consequence, the organized presence of Alumnae members, *former students* all, in and around the new theatre was highly politicized. This was doubly true given the gender segregation at the time on the university campus, and in Hart House's policies in particular. The university and the Massey estate expressly intended Hart House to be solely for men. In his history of the university, Martin L. Friedland notes several occasions when "women's organizations were refused space" at Hart House.[131] Clearly, though, an exception was made for its theatre. Explained the *Varsity*: "In order that the theatre may be entirely set aside from the other activities of Hart House, and that women may be allowed entrance, there is a distinct passage way leading from the front of the building direct to the underground theatre. The entrance to this long and artistically-shaped passage is at the side of the main doorway on the southern side of the building."[132]

From the start, women participated in productions at Hart House Theatre, including student productions, using its "distinct passage way" to avoid contact with the rest of the men's club. Alumnae's presence at Hart House Theatre was as much about performing gendered space as it was about performing plays. For decades, they applied for and received an annual time slot in the theatre, producing at a consistently high level while sharing (non-student) actors with Hart House Theatre's troupe. For years, they may have been the only women's organization regularly active in Hart House.[133]

Alumnae's first Hart House Theatre production was a two-day, three-performance run of Richard Brinsley Sheridan's 1777 comedy *A Trip to Scarborough* in April 1921. Tickets sold for 75¢ and $1.00 at the door as well as at two booksellers: Tyrell's (King Street East and Victoria Street) and D.T. McAinsh & Co. (4 College Street).[134] The wife of Ontario's Lieutenant Governor Lionel Clarke brought a party to attend the production,[135] as did U of T president Robert Falconer and his wife.[136] Alumnae arranged with Hart House Theatre director Roy Mitchell to stage their third all-women production with twenty-one in the cast. With Kirkpatrick's departure from Toronto, the women directed the play themselves. Cast member Freda Waldon later remarked that "we made our own costumes and had no director other than the president, Margaret Tytler [*sic*: Alumnae documents indicate Margaret Boyle was president then], but Roy Mitchell helped us with at least one rehearsal."[137] Unfortunately, there is no evidence to reconstruct the extent of the director's contributions to the show, although both Margarets were in the cast, as Berinthia and Loveless respectively. Nor is there evidence beyond a note in the show's program – the first play program extant in Alumnae's collection – to expand on either Jocelyn Taylor's "stage settings" and her use of loaned T. Eaton Co. furniture for Sir Tunbell Clumsy's room in Acts IV and V, or the minuet "under the direction of" Miss Coventry with music provided by the Central Technical School Orchestra. The post-semester production dates meant that many students were no longer on campus to see it and that there was no *Varsity* review, for it came after the last publication date of the semester.

It seems that club members were lukewarm about Mitchell's limited rehearsal assistance. A handwritten note placed alongside the production's listing in Alumnae's collection reads succinctly: "Roy Mitchell who believed in dark gloomy lighting – for a comedy." More generously, Waldon said of Mitchell's presence that

> It was one of the thrills of my life that he said that I could act, but I must have overplayed badly. I scarcely recognized my part when I saw the play at the Malvern Festival [in England] later, but the star played Lord Foppington much as our star, Marguerite Phillips, had. Erskine Keys played the young hero [Tom Fashion] and I was her servant [Lory]. I think that most of the girls took the men's parts as well as women can and the women's parts were good.[138]

Alumnae's relationship with Mitchell was clearly complicated. Although his lighting choices were not to the club's liking on at least this occasion, his involvement was clearly an honour for some. And he did permit Alumnae to use Hart House Theatre, an arrangement that would last well after his departure.

Indeed, one might wish to find in Alumnae's early documents evidence of the influential spiritual and aesthetic philosophy known as "theosophy," which informed the "brilliant, charismatic"[139] Roy Mitchell's views of theatre in the context of Canada's Little Theatre Movement. Mitchell built Hart House Theatre's early reputation as one of the continent's most significant aesthetically experimental (as opposed to commercial) theatres on his theosophist ideals. His interpretation of theosophy, a "hybrid of various theologies, in particular Hinduism and Buddhism, peppered with a liberal dash of spiritualism" as selected and interpreted through Western colonial minds, informed his interest in connecting Hart House Theatre to, and in fact making it a leader of, Canada's emerging Little Theatre Movement. His rejection of commercial theatre was reinforced by his theosophy-informed "new expressionism."[140] His influence on local theatre practices across the country is often noted,[141] although rarely traced through the decades that followed because it was largely an influence on *nonprofessionalizing* practices.

Scott K. Duchesne situates Mitchell's formidable 1929 treatise *Creative Theatre* as Canada's only extended book-length study of modernist theatre theory, practice, and cultural analysis aimed at "spiritual communion and occult initiation for its pracitioners and its audience." But if the lone, dry comment by Alumnae's leadership about Mitchell's lighting input is an indication, it may have been his occult interests that turned them off his unconventional views. Their comment may also implicitly reference what Duchesne has described as Mitchell's vision of the "director and actor on his stage in purely conservative and masculinist terms [that] tended to reflect the presumed patriarchal structures" of society. This, in spite of the central role of women among early theosophists,[142] among whom their Russian founder Helena Blavatsky is counted.[143]

Did Mitchell permit Alumnae's women unique access to Hart House while devaluing the artistic practices of their female leadership? Given that Alumnae only mention Mitchell once in their documents, we can only speculate. In the 1920s, Alumnae were clearly more interested in philanthropy than theosophy. But they likely agreed with Mitchell (and with Hart House's overseer Vincent Massey[144]) in their focus on local theatre practices over foreign touring shows. Where they (and Massey) may have disagreed with Mitchell is on the relevance of theosophy (and darkly lit comedies) to their practices. Mitchell left Toronto after *A Trip to Scarborough* for the Drama School at Columbia University, the same university for which Kirkpatrick had departed,[145] and to start a new theatre company in New York. He later moved to the West Coast, where he lectured for the Theosophical Society.[146]

A Trip to Scarborough marked the start of a close and unique relationship between the two landmark institutions. It was the first of fifty-nine times that Alumnae made use of Hart House Theatre as a performance venue before moving into their first Coach House Theatre. After *A Trip to Scarborough*, the plays that Alumnae chose for their Hart House Theatre productions were almost all written in the twentieth century (two Oscar Wilde plays produced in the early 1950s are their only Hart House Theatre productions written before 1900). Remarkably, sixteen were world, Canadian, or Toronto premieres.[147]

Alumnae's first modern production at Hart House Theatre played to a "full house"[148] on its opening night and to nearly 800 people across three performances in April 1922. This

Figure 1.4. Drawn by influential Canadian actor and director David Gardner for Alumnae's October 1955 production of Anita Loos's comedy *Gigi*, this program cover is among some of the remarkable artwork held in Alumnae's collection. Gardner directed the Toronto premiere of Loos's successful Broadway adaptation of French writer Colette's 1944 novella for Alumnae at Hart House Theatre. It featured Molly Golby [Thom] in the titular role. Courtesy of Alumnae Theatre Company.

was the Toronto premiere of *The Romantic Age*, British author A.A. Milne's "comedy of love at first sight."[149] It was just eighteen months after its world premiere at the Comedy Theatre in London, England, and four years before Milne gained international recognition for his *Winnie-the-Pooh* books. They recruited a director who could manage a "major production"[150] at Hart House Theatre: the popular local actor A. Monro Grier, a lawyer affiliated with the university who was active with Hart House Theatre and the Arts and Letters Club.[151] They also addressed the issue of women playing men's roles – a practice that reviewers had previously disparaged – by casting men for the first time. As Halpenny later described, acting without men was "frustrating as well as boring" despite it being "perhaps appropriate to the suffragette mood of the times."[152] Moreover, they chose a play with a smaller cast than either *Trelawny of the Wells* or *A Trip to Scarborough*, possibly to address the increased competition for actors as the number of theatre groups grew on campus.[153]

The production helped put both Hart House Theatre and Alumnae on the map of Toronto's burgeoning Little Theatre Movement. In his review of the play, *Saturday Night*'s Hector

Figure 1.5. *The Romantic Age* was Alumnae's second production at Hart House Theatre (April 1922), their first that included men in the cast, and their first for which a photograph is extant in their collection. Most of the actors in the photograph are frozen, or nearly frozen, in tableau, in costumes and make-up, suggesting that it may be a posed rehearsal shot, on the forced perspective interior living room set from Acts I and III. (*left to right*) James H. Craig (Gervase Mallory), Margaret Boyle (Melisande), Margaret D. Tytler (Mary Knowle), A. Munro Grier (Henry Knowle), Christina A.C. Cooper [Templeton] (Alice), Marion R. Squair (Ern), Ivor R. Lewis (Gentleman Susan), Henry Button (Bobby Coote), and Agnes J. Muldrew [Stone] (Jane Bagot). It features furniture from Ridpath's Cabinet Shop.

The stamp of Toronto's James & Son Photographers appears on the back of the photograph. The Toronto Archives' description of the "William James family fonds" calls him Toronto's, and possibly Canada's, first "press photographer," or photojournalist, who sold his photographs to newspapers and magazines for $1 or $2 each. All three sons were photographers at some point, including Norman, who was a *Toronto Star* photographer for forty years. William almost certainly took this photograph of *The Romantic Age*. Hart House Theatre employed James & Son for other productions too. See, for example, Day, "Treading the Arduous Road to Eleusis," 197.

Hart House Theatre may have been responsible for engaging the photographer, but Alumnae likely believed the production to be of particular importance owing to their first use of men. That Alumnae preserved the photograph in their collections is evidence that they immediately recognized its significance; it also raises the question of why their previous Hart House show, *A Trip to Scarborough*, does not yield a preserved photograph in their collections. Photographed by James & Son Photographers for Hart House Theatre (public domain). Courtesy of Alumnae Theatre Company.

Charlesworth reflected bluntly that the "remarkable improvement in the standards of amateur acting which has taken place in Toronto since amateurs commenced to play pieces of real merit and distinction instead of trash, was notable in this performance. It was not, of course, entirely free from gaucheries, but it was vital and interesting, both in the matter of the personalities of the performers and the general standards of expression."[154]

Charlesworth's influential praise may have been enough to engage audiences in further Alumnae work. But this was also the third production of a Milne play in Toronto in recent months. Charlesworth raved that Milne was the "most gifted of the younger generation of British playwrights," that the play "enforces the idea that it is the plain and obvious realities of twentieth century existence that really count," and that the writing was "witty and delightful from first to last."[155] As was common in reviews of philanthropic shows, the *Globe*'s review was encouraging to the local company while quick to point out flaws in the foreign script. The *Globe* declared that the production "Delights Critical Audience with 'Action'" and "has some novel twists," although the "piece suffers rather from over writing. Some of the scenes would be greatly improved by the judicious application of the blue pencil." Even so, it was a "charming play, delightfully done. No other verdict could be passed upon the production," and the "playing does great credit" to Grier's directing as the "action progresses with certainty and the 'business' is conceived and carried out with deftness and finish." Margaret Boyle's Melisande, a young woman with romantic notions about finding her "knight," was "charmingly done"[156] and was "not only beautiful to the eye, but revealed genuine talent, especially in the changing moods of the final act."[157] Margaret Tytler's hypochondriac wife was "quite convincing"[158] as she "got real fun out of the role of the matchmaking Mrs. Knowle," while Marion Squair "played a yokel with piquant humour."[159] The *Globe* singled out two male guests: James J. Craig as the romantic hero "handles his whimsical speeches with considerable skill and feeling," and Ivor R. Lewis presented a "delightful character study"[160] as the peddler Gentleman Susan. Lewis would be involved in Alumnae and Hart House Theatre shows for many years. Grier also acted in the production, and Charlesworth applauded his "gracious touch that one does not often get in such roles, even in the best professional casts."[161] Grier would appear in two more Alumnae shows, although he would not direct for them again. The program for *The Romantic Age* included the note that the members of the UCAA "wish to thank the men of the cast for their co-operation," a nod to the men who had donated their time and talent to the production.

Indeed, several men had a singular impact on Alumnae's trajectory through their work on Alumnae's early Hart House Theatre productions. Wrote Halpenny, in the interwar years, "of all the men who have assisted the Alumnae Dramatic Club, Edgar Stone has made the greatest contribution. His unflagging interest, encouragement and direction stand as the greatest single asset on the Club's ledger."[162] Their "guide, philosopher, and director"[163] during those years, Stone had acted on the Hart House Theatre stage frequently since it opened and would serve as its artistic director from 1929 to 1934.

Stone's first connection with Alumnae on record came when he directed their March 1923 Hart House Theatre production, Hubert Henry Davies's 1911 four-act comedy *A Single Man*. It opened to a "large audience"[164] on opening night. Stone also played the titular lead role of Robin Worthington, who pursues Louise Parker, played by Christina Cooper, an "exuberant flapper girl who proves too great a strain on his middle-aged love of peace and quiet." A *Varsity* preview said that *A Single Man* was H.H. Davies's "best example of the comedy of everyday life," comparing it to Shaw's plays on the grounds that "there are occasionally other people besides Shaw who have ideas." However, the *Varsity*'s review appeared to dislike the play as much as it liked the production – a common pattern in reviews of the time. On the one hand, the "action is too mechanical to be convincing: one can see the strings which move the puppets. Nevertheless, it is bright, hangs together well, and is entertaining without being in the least original." On the other hand, the performances deserved the "most unqualified praise,"[165] included those by Agnes Muldrew (she would marry Stone in 1930[166]), Katherine Wells (whose Bertha Simms the *Varsity* considered "one of the hits of the production"[167]), and Agatha Leonard (her first involvement with the group). Along with Stone, the men in the cast included Raymond Card in his first of many Alumnae productions.[168]

Not until April 1924 was an Alumnae member fully credited with directing a Hart House Theatre production. Club president Margaret Boyle had directed Barrie's one-act *Rosalind* at the Women's Union three months earlier; now, fittingly, she was tasked with directing a 1906 four-act Edwardian "comedy for philanthropists" by Shaw's contemporary St. John Hankin, *The Charity That Began at Home*. Hankin's *The Cassilis Engagement* was familiar to Toronto audiences from a production by the Cameron Matthews Players the previous year. *Charity* featured Margaret Tytler as Lady Denison, who invites several of society's downtrodden and ne'er-do-wells to her country house to prove that the "less people deserve, the more we ought to help them. They need it more."[169] Scandal ensues, and Denison's daughter, played by Dorothy Stacey, announces she'll marry one of the guests.[170]

Attracting audiences was vital in order to pay the rent at Hart House Theatre, and this put Alumnae's programming acumen to a very public test. They had to balance a show's popularity with its quality (i.e., its ability to sell seats with its intellectual significance). This resulted in what Dorothy Chansky, in the American context, has called the "never static cultural field."[171] From their experience producing *The Romantic Age*, Alumnae learned that a premiere of a familiar playwright would lure curious Toronto audiences. So when they produced the Toronto premiere of Nobel Prize winner Joacinto Benavente's two-act modern seaport "satire of manners" *The Evil Doers of Good* (in a 1923 translation by J.G. Underhill) in February 1925, it was the third production of a play by Benavente in the city in the past year.[172] To leverage that playwright's recent notoriety, for the first time they put an advertisement in the *Globe*.[173] Cameo photographs of performers Dorothy Stacey, Margaret Boyle, Agnes Muldrew, and Doris Dignum appeared on the *Varsity*'s front page.[174]

Along with the playwright's fame, the play's theme was an important programming factor, particularly when they could advertise it as a good fit for the club. Having introduced the theme of marriage in their UC Women's Union one-acts in January 1927, Alumnae's third George Bernard Shaw production (and their first at Hart House Theatre) was Shaw's 1908 treatise on marriage and divorce, *Getting Married: A Disquisitory Play* in March 1927. Here they reportedly made "intelligent"[175] cuts to the script that made the "heart of the modernist tingle with elation."[176] Hart House Theatre was "thronged by an enthusiastic audience,"[177] and the set was "colourful and artistic, within the limitations of the realism of pre-war theatre."[178] It was the first of several plays directed for Alumnae by Hart House Theatre's "most able comedy actor,"[179] H.E. Hitchman. Again damning the script and praising the performance, the *Globe* reviewer said that the script's lines were "very apt to produce monotony, the dialogue being of a somewhat voluminous nature," while the production "would delight even the most exacting insofar as interpretation of the various roles is concerned." The cast, which signed a copy of the program still extant in Alumnae's collection, was "uniformly good"[180] and featured many actors "well known in amateur dramatic circles,"[181] including Agnes Muldrew, who "handled a long and difficult role with great credit to herself,"[182] in an Alumnae cast that was, for the first time, mostly men. Coversely, *Varsity* reviewer "N.P.H.B." wrote that while Shaw's drama was the "most vital thing in English literature of the last forty years," this performance was "almost adequate."[183]

Alumnae worked with some of the continent's best theatre designers and resources at Hart House Theatre. Among them was Hart House Theatre art director F.C. (Frederick) Coates, who designed and executed the set and lighting for Alumnae's November 1928 production of Somerset Maugham's 1919 three-act colonial comedy *Caesar's Wife*. H.E.

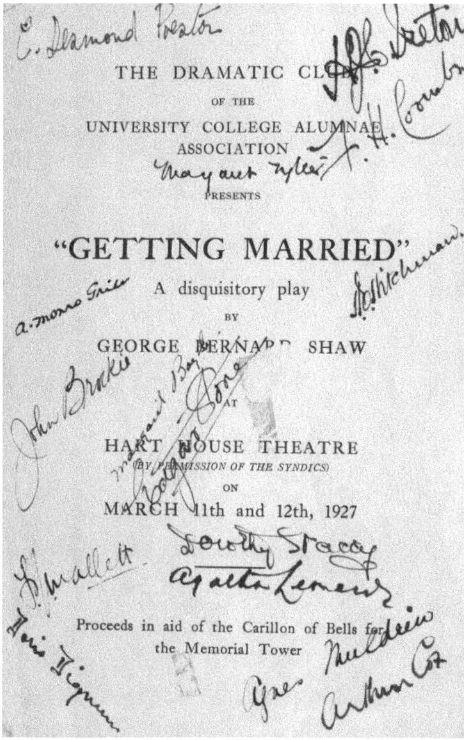

Figure 1.6. *Getting Married* program cover signed by cast. Alumnae's production of George Bernard Shaw's comedy *Getting Married: A Disquisitory Play* at Hart House Theatre in March 1927, directed by H.E. Hitchman, raised funds for the carillon in the Memorial Tower. It was the first Alumnae production that featured more men than women in the cast. Courtesy of Alumnae Theatre Company.

Hitchman returned to direct for Alumnae for the final time, although he would act in at least two more of their productions. The extant production photographs are almost ethereal, freezing in time actors in twenties-era costumes engulfed in Coates's clay-walled Cairo court interior. When *Star* writer Donald Jones viewed one of these photographs, kept at the Toronto Library, he commented that it "shows the high professional standards of [Alumnae's] productions even in the early days."[184] Alison Ewart as the "spring-like and virginal" twenty-something Violet, Agnes Muldrew as the "handsome"[185] forty-year-old Anne, Margaret Tytler as Mrs. Pritchard, and Marion Squair as the elderly Mrs. Appleby were the four women cast alongside eight men. More than 1,000 people attended the production over three performances.[186]

During Alumnae's early years, critics usually praised their (local) productions, even if they faulted the (foreign) scripts. *Varsity* reviewers in particular generally remained positive about the group's work, which had come to mean so much to the campus. Even when a production was not well received, it was generally understood to have been a worthwhile endeavour as a campus fundraiser. But P.A. Gardner forcefully reversed this tradition in March 1932 in his *Varsity* review of British sensation Noël Coward's first hit, the 1923

Figure 1.7. (*left*) Margaret Tytler (Mrs. Pritchard) and (*right*) Marion Squair (Mrs. Appleby) in Alumnae's production of Somerset Maugham's 1919 comedy *Caesar's Wife* at Hart House Theatre in November 1928. Hart House art director Fr. (Frederick) C. Coates's stage design and lighting placed the setting in the house of a British Consular Agent in Cairo, Egypt. According to the program, furniture was borrowed from the T. Eaton Company and "Eastern art objects" were from Araby on Yonge St. (across from what is presently the Mirvish's CAA Theatre). Photographed for Hart House Theatre (public domain). Courtesy of Alumnae Theatre Company.

comedy *The Young Idea*. Although directed by the respected Edgar Stone and featuring several of Alumnae's prominent actors in a "more worthwhile play than the Alumnae's last two choices" (Louis N. Parker's *Pomander Walk* and A.A. Milne's *To Have the Honour*), the production, said Gardner, was "most disappointing" and "far below their usual high standards." While praising Stone's "superior" direction "as regards movements" and his deft attention to pace, Gardner pointed to the mispronunciation of "-shire," as if rhyming with "higher" as evidence that the "English atmosphere was never successfully caught." Edna Norwich's "brilliant work" as Jennifer stood out as a "constant delight." However, the review was notable for its negative language describing several of the actors (none of whom were Alumnae mainstays), saying that one "has probably the most annoying voice I have ever heard on the legitimate stage," another was "earnest but awful," while a third was "painfully painstaking."[187] This choice of language for a reviewer of an Alumnae show was otherwise unheard of in those years.[188]

Figure 1.8. Members of the cast of Alumnae's production of Georgio and María Martínez Sierra's *Take Two from One*, produced by Alumnae at Hart House Theatre in January 1934 and directed by Lorna G. Rumball. Photographed for Hart House Theatre (public domain). Courtesy of Alumnae Theatre Company.

Alumnae required sufficient rehearsal time to mount full-length productions at Hart House Theatre. Their only surviving rehearsal schedule from before 1967 is from their January 1934 Canadian premiere of Gregorio and María Martínez Sierra's three-act farce *Take Two from One*, likely in the recent 1931 translation by Helen and Harley Granville Barker.[189] The typed schedule indicates that the cast's first rehearsal, for Act I, was held on Wednesday, 29 November 1934, from 7:00 to 9:00 p.m. They proceeded to rehearse on Mondays, Wednesdays, and Fridays until they accomplished a full run on 20 December. December 6 indicates a "7pm" rehearsal start at "grads hall" for Act I "Lines," with the following Friday and Monday used for Acts II and III lines respectively. They broke for the holidays, except for a "Whole Play" run on Wednesday, 27 December. They returned to their rehearsal pattern on 3 January, first entering Hart House Theatre to rehearse on 10 January and adding to their three-day-a-week schedule a dress rehearsal on Thursday, 18 January (initially scheduled to be a performance) before opening the next day at 8:30 p.m. This schedule is taped to the first extant Alumnae production script, which belonged to Jack Barber, their first credited stage manager. The script also shows rudimentary blocking notation and other marginalia, including the Hart House Theatre stage dimensions for Acts II and III (listed as 28 feet wide downstage, 15 feet wide upstage, and 13 feet deep at the centre line). Lorna G. Rumball[190] was paid $50.00 to direct the twenty-person cast. Because Act I is set on an ocean liner passing down the Red Sea, Canada Steamship Lines lent deckchairs and lifebelts for the production. Murray Bonnycastle painted the portrait appearing in the Madrid flat in Act II.[191]

When Alumnae produced a show featuring only female characters at Hart House Theatre in November 1935, critics objected. The Toronto premiere of Cyril Campion's "spine tingling mystery ending with the suicide of a lovely lady," *Ladies in Waiting*, was, in Halpenny's words, a "marked departure from the English drawing-room comedy which had been the Club's darling up to that time."[192] By this time, critics were paying more attention to product details, likely owing to the spotlight placed on performances produced for the Dominion Drama Festival Central Ontario Drama Region competition. The *Star*'s Augustus Bridle, who attended the second dress rehearsal and "sat from six until ten very nobly and saw half the show,"[193] provided questionably worded views of the process, calling director Frank Hemingway a "mere man"[194] with the "professional chore" of building up the mystery's suspense to intensive climax, with "only women as players." The problem, Bridle offered, was that it was "difficult [to get] a real dramatic chorus from voices often in the same key."[195] As if amplifying Bridle's critique two days later, M.K.H. wrote in the *Varsity* that the "voices of a feminine cast are rather a problem. Three acts of nine females in various degrees of excitement and hence of shrillness are apt to make one long for a certain alternating bass, purely by way of variety."[196] Still, Agnes Muldrew played the detective "with fine aplomb," while Agatha Leonard's Janet Garner was played "adroitly." Alison Ewart and Doris Shiell playing twin sisters were "as innocent as unborn babes," while Margaret Donald played the bride, Una Verity, "so well"[197]; concluded the *Varsity*, as a "matter of fact young woman confronted by a horrible situation she is good until she is called upon to drop the matter of factness." Margaret Tytler's servant "carried off what honours there were in the line of acting. Hers was a character part, and a difficult one, which was thoroughly convincing in its small way." M.K.H. clearly enjoyed neither the play nor the predictability of the mystery genre, stating that "to keep any tempo at all it frequently relied solely upon the interest of the audience as to the identity of the murderess. And even when this was revealed it comes too late, for by the time honoured method of eliminating those most suspected a choice lies between two aged and respectable servants and an equally innocent looking character who was, sure enough, guilty."[198]

Bridle concluded ambivalently that "except for rather too much speed in some lines, these excellent actors, capably directed, were able to keep the experts all guessing until the final bedroom scene. They all enjoyed the mystery as much as the audience did. And the play in some of its colour and action tableaus sometimes looked even better than it sounded." However, the costumes often clashed with Norm Nichol's "modern wallscapes."[199] That Alumnae sold out the run – thanks in part to an increased budget for publicity – suggests that Bridle's and M.K.H.'s negative views did not, at least, affect the box office.[200]

Alumnae's November 1949 program for their production of C.L. Anthony's *Autumn Crocus* reflected on the club's success in the context of the Little Theatre Movement:

> There have been changes through the years of course but there is a persistent loyalty which somehow subordinates the interests of an individual member to the interests of the Club as a whole and that leads to a very valuable kind of team-work and is perhaps the secret to the Club's long life.

> The changes which have taken place have been for the better and the development with the University Alumnae Dramatic Club has paralleled and perhaps been a part of the development of the Little Theatre in Ontario.

Here, however humbly, Alumnae were explicitly acknowledging that they had been part of the Little Theatre Movement. With two wars behind them, Alumnae could declare their *raison d'être* with confidence. Their early programming provides evidence that the popular Western theatre movement exerted notable influence over their production conditions and programming choices. Importantly, Alumnae had clearly influenced Toronto's Little Theatre, and Hart House Theatre, experience as well.

Chapter 2

Producing on the Homefront and in the Post-War Theatre Boom (1939–1957)

In a meeting of the UCAA Dramatic Club on Thursday, 7 September 1939, Agatha Leonard moved, seconded by Grace Stafford, that Jean Stewart, the club secretary, should write to the UCAA president "offering to co-operate in any war service work, either arranging entertainments or in any other way." On 10 September, Canada officially joined Britain in declaring war on the German Reich. Club members arranged to "meet fortnightly" thereafter.[1]

Alumnae began the war years with a robust thirty-four members,[2] led by Margaret Ness (president), Agnes Muldrew (vice-president), Agatha Leonard (treasurer), Jean Stewart (secretary), Alison Ewart (publicist), and Mary Evans (past president). Among their members, Erskine Keys and Edna (Bach) Norwich had participated in *The Bluestockings*, the club's founding wartime event. If Alumnae needed any reassurance that their good work could be set in the service of not only their campus but their country as well, Keys and Norwich could provide experienced and supportive voices. Of significance, 1939 was the year that Alumnae's longest-serving participant, Francess Halpenny, became a member. Having entered the club in a time of crisis, over the next eight decades Halpenny would become one of the company's strongest guiding voices.

This chapter assesses Alumnae members' contributions on the homefront during the Second World War. They produced one-acts, wrote entertaining skits, knitted for soldiers overseas, and performed in massive troop shows, including the famed "all-girl"[3] *Merry-Go-Round Revue*. It then describes how Alumnae gradually distanced themselves from the UCAA and moved towards producing theatre for themselves in the city's expanding post-war theatre ecology. After discussing select production case studies, the chapter looks at how Alumnae chose plays and guest directors. It also examines their off-campus production and design conditions and how they became a major theatre producer in the post-war years.

Skits, One-Acts, and "Briskly or Painfully"[4] Knitting

Within weeks of the war's outbreak, the Theatre Nights at Hart House Theatre that had served Alumnae so well proved "difficult to arrange." So "it was decided to cancel the Hart House performance"[5] and to notify Edgar Stone, who was to direct it. The war meant they could no longer produce major productions at Hart House Theatre; in addition, the DDF and its regional festivals had been put on hold. As historian Maria Tippet observes, the "demand for recruits robbed Little Theatres of their male actors."[6] But while many theatre groups across the country were forced to stop producing theatre entirely, Alumnae found ways to keep going, at least initially. They wasted no time developing one-acts, revues, short skits, and other entertainments to raise funds for the war effort.

The first Alumnae production during the war was a "special guest performance" of two one-act plays presented at the Dickens Fellowship Meeting at House Hart Theatre in November 1939. Margaret Tytler directed Muriel and Sydney Box's *Anti-Clockwise*; Dixon Wagner directed the Toronto premiere of the comedy *Green Eyes from Romany* by John Kirkpatrick. The evening reportedly "drew a large crowd." The *Globe and Mail* reported that *Anti-Clockwise* "proved a strong, virile vehicle for a capable cast, a bit gruesome at first, when the scene opens depicting a dead woman on a couch and a very frightened girl phoning for assistance." The all-woman cast included Dorothy Batchellor, whose "splendid acting … gave a realistic touch, in contrast to the calm, professional manner of Aileen O'Brien, playing the role of the doctor." *Green Eyes from Romany* "won great praise"; it was "difficult to differentiate among players all of whom were good." They included Eleanor Woodside, who "reminded one a little of the clever Gertrude Lawrence in *Susan and God*," and Helen Goulding, who happened to be renowned actor Raymond Massey's cousin. A music program followed. The evening raised funds for the Dickens Fellowship's annual Christmas tree, and those in attendance were reminded of the Dickens Fellowship's Christmas play and welfare work, including "taking groups of children to the matinée of their coming performance of *A Christmas Carol*."[7] It may have been in this spirit of giving that Wagner wrote with levity to treasurer Agatha Leonard returning $20.00 of his $25.00 director's fee for *Green Eyes from Romany*:

> It never came into my head that there was any fee or even the tiniest honorarium attached. Had I had any inkling of that, I should have been much more professional and worked you all to death – thereby probably spoiling the fun of the production. It was really a very enjoyable piece of work, as far as I was concerned, and I should like you to consider my small effort as a personal contribution to your work.

In a gesture of goodwill in times of war, citing the "expensive" cost of wool to make socks for the troops, Wagner kept only $5.00 of his fee, "to buy a bottle of Harps so that I can drink the health of all of you at Christmas. I think you would rather I did that than send you an exact *quid pro quo*."[8]

In December 1939 the University Women's Club hosted a "jolly Christmas party" at 80 Bloor Street West.[9] There, the UCAA Dramatic Club presented an evening of four short skits along with carols, music, and games led by master of ceremonies and club member Marion Hunter. The *Globe and Mail* described the performances as a "monologue" followed by skits titled *Air Raid Troubles*, *The Charity Bizarre*, and *The Royal Visit*. It is likely that Alumnae members wrote these works.[10] They would present them again throughout the war.

Adjoined to a regular UCAA meeting a month later, the second annual UCAA Dramatic Club revue (the first had been two years earlier) drew a "large and receptive audience" that reportedly "laughed and applauded uproariously throughout the evening." Again hosted by Hunter, who reportedly "gave away all the intimate back-stage secrets of the Club and set the gay and casual note on which the revue proceeded," the evening featured skits created by club members that humorously and creatively illuminated current political machinations. The first skit, *Pajamas for the Poles*, provided a "choral explanation of the European situation [and] brought current events up to the resignation of [the British government's

Mr. Leslie] Hore-Belisha." Subsequent skits included Eleanor Woodside as an "inquisitive brat after the manner of [Fanny Brice's radio character] Baby Snooks," Helen Goulding as Helen of Troy, Margaret Tytler and Jean Stewart discussing "fashion problems of the air raids" (surely the same *Air Raid Troubles* performed a month earlier), and a pre-intermission piece titled *For Amusement Only*. Part Two began with the "Bowery girls of the nineties in bewitching costumes and make-up." This was followed by a song (sung by Aileen O'Brien) and a dance; these were the "highlights of the evening." Then Margaret Tytler, "as an old Scottish woman, discussed with Genevra Campbell, the reasons why the Scots are no longer wearing kilts." Alice Keys "gave an indescribably funny interpretation of Mendelssohn's 'Spring Song' in dance"; after that, Agatha Leonard and Alison Ewart played a "large crowd of people cheering the King and Queen on the Royal Visit." The finale featured Dorothy Batcheller "singing a new version of 'Put on Your Old Grey Bonnet,'" which "presented a bright conglomeration of old Dramatic Club costumes and properties."[11] A reception followed. Alumnae's light-spirited skits show us how Club members' capacity for energetic fun and good humour could entertain both audiences and themselves, even in wartime. Financial records indicate that Edgar Stone was paid $25.00 for "assistance in producing" the revue.

With the national and regional festivals on hold, in the early 1940 the DDF's Central Ontario Region committee produced Toronto's first wartime revue, *Well of All Things!*, at Hart House Theatre, directed by E.G. Sterndale Bennett. It was part of the region's reported mandate to "continue dramatic activities despite the cancellation of the annual festival and at the same time to assist in whatever way possible Canada's war effort."[12] It was also the first time that the region's theatre groups "acted as a unit to sponsor a production."[13] The *Globe and Mail* reported that "dramatic groups, who for the past seven years have taken their drama in deadly earnest, running the gamut of Ibsen, Coward, Shakespeare and Canadian Playwrights, will this month put aside all competitive ambitions and join together in one big effort to aid war charities." *Well of All Things!* featured regional award–winning performers and groups from all seven years, including Alumnae members, with net proceeds "divided among a number of approved wartime charities."[14]

The twenty-two-act revue[15] opened to a "completely packed house" and "received an ovation from the enthusiastic first-nighters."[16] Opening night was sponsored by, and ticket costs were donated to, the Royal Canadian Air Force of Toronto Chapter, Imperial Order Daughters of the Empire." Opening night featured famed Toronto-born Spanish dancer Conchita Triana;[17] other artists included popular performer Jane Mallett and playwright John Coulter. Thelma Craig in the *Globe and Mail* described it as a "thoroughgoing success" that was "packed with pep and punch, comedy and character, timely hits and patriotic fervour." Craig went on with an enthusiasm that would have lifted the spirits of war-weary citizenry, describing a "full house that laughed until its sides were almost sore, and practically everyone of the great variety of numbers made its own creditable contribution."[18] The week of performances constituted the "pick of Toronto little theatre talent."[19] "Every performance was sold out, and the public were clamouring for tickets but were unable to get them."[20] All net proceeds for the week-long run went to "war work"[21]: Tuesday evening raised funds for the Toronto Scottish women's auxiliary;[22] Wednesday through Friday raised funds for the Active Service Canteen at 93 Yonge Street "operated by the Citizens' Committee for Troops in Training";[23] and Saturday benefited the Canadian Armoured Fighting Vehicle Corps."[24] Then, "at the request of Brigadier R.O. Alexander, who saw the revue twice," 500 troops from Exhibition Park attended a "special performance"[25] of *Well of All Things!* With thousands of people attending across the week, this was wartime fundraising writ large.

Among the talent were several prominent Alumnae members. The *Varsity* declared that Agatha Leonard and Alison Ewart provided "perhaps the funniest skit on the program"[26] by restaging a piece they had written, *A Day in May*, which was a "pageant in miniature of Five Reigns, from the time of the regency Rakes to a Canadian view of the Royal Parade"[27] (Alumnae referred to it in their notes as their previously performed *The Royal Visit*).[28] *University Monthly* asked its readers "who could possibly suspect that Alison Ewart and Agatha Leonard would win their spurs as comedians and bring down the house in their short turn … It surprised even themselves."[29] The publication *Gossip* hinted that "we know a man and his wife who went to Hart House three times last week just to see those two bring back the day the King and Queen came to Toronto."[30] As well, Agnes Muldrew, alongside Rita Weyman and Ivor Lewis, performed John Coulter's Irish comedy *Pigs*. In the *Star*, Rose MacDonald wrote that they "worked hard and with good measure of success … but somehow it took all the skill of these two outstanding talented players [Muldrew and Lewis] to make it quite come off."[31] Lewis was singled out by *Gossip* as still the "best contemporary actor in Canada to have found contentment in amateur theatre."[32] And Alumnae member Edna Norwich "would captivate another audience in a nostalgic song about the 'Gibson Girls,'" inspired by illustrator Charles Dana Gibson's famous version of the ideal American girl of the twentieth century. First-year Alumnae member Helen Goulding, "who just finished dancing her way through college in 1939 and picking up first class honours on the way," performed with her sister in *The First Dance*. Alumnae's Margaret Tytler managed properties for the *Revue*'s "fifty-odd performers." The *University Monthly* concluded: "It is very gratifying that among a cast picked from the best amateur players in Toronto there were so many from the Dramatic Club of the University College Alumnae Association."[33] Instead of languishing in wartime obscurity, Alumnae members were entertaining Torontonians on the homefront.[34]

Then in March 1940, in response to a request from the University Settlement, Alumnae presented three one-act plays at Hart House Theatre: Rachel Field's *The Londonderry Air* (1927), set in early-nineteenth-century England, directed by Sterndale Bennett; a translation of Romain Coolus's comedy *Love and Learning* (1900), set in Paris, directed by Edgar Stone; and Geoffrey Trease's *After the Tempest* (1938), set in the South Sea islands sometime in the future, directed by Percy Schutte. In her *Star* column "Over the Teacups," Claire Wallace offered a behind-the-scenes glimpse of the production that gave a sense of the culinary and costuming lengths Alumnae went to in producing the play:

> For the first time in her life Marion Squair Hunter has made bread … and she's appalled at the way it rises as she carries it daily home, across the campus to Hart House where it is "finished" on the stage in *Londonderry Air* … In the end her great dane "Cookie" gets the bread, but even he doesn't like it much. Helen Goulding in the same play makes cookies on the stage. Agnes Muldrew Stone, H.E. Hitchman, Agatha Leonard are in *Love and Learning* and at the moment are borrowing old family costumes. *After the Tempest*, the third play, is also causing costume trouble, since it is set on a desert island, twenty years from now. Just what they should wear, the actors don't know.[35]

As women producing theatre, Alumnae members attracted notice from prominent journalists like Wallace, who advocated for women in engaging ways.[36]

In April and May 1940, four meetings were held at various members' homes. The first two "were spent sewing on Pierrot costumes for the soldiers,"[37] although no reasons why were given. Also at these meetings, plans were made for a fall Hart House Theatre show, although this did not materialize. Their first annual meeting during wartime was held at past-president Mary Evans's suburban country home in Erindale (Mississauga) on Saturday, 8 June 1940, and opened with a few hours of leisure time: "In the afternoon swimming, sun-bathing and tea-drinking were the chief activities. Supper was served on the terrace, and concluded with a toast to Alison Ewart whose marriage to Albert Hewitt took place the following week."[38]

It is noteworthy that within a few months, Evans, who should have begun serving as past president, was no longer listed as a member. On Monday, 4 November 1940, president Margaret Ness reported the sad news that "flowers had been sent and a note of sympathy on the occasion of the funeral of Mary Evans, past president of the Club."[39] No cause of death was given.

Because of the war, documentation of Alumnae's activities in 1940–41 is sparse. It was clear by then that the fighting would not soon end. Membership slipped to twenty-eight, the first time it had been below thirty since 1933–34. At the season's first meeting a motion was passed "that in view of war time no flowers or gifts be sent to members. It was also moved by Agatha Leonard that fees be reduced to $1.00 – seconded by Edna Norwich."[40] That season, Alumnae produced only a handful of one-act plays as UCAA invitationals at the UC Women's Union, as well as a February 1941 production of Josephina Niggli's Mexico-set one-act comedy *Sunday Costs Five Pesos* at the UC Women's Union, which subsequently toured to Camp Borden for "delighted! troops."[41] The play's director, the popular Toronto playwright and friend of early club members, W.S. Milne, wrote to Alumnae's treasurer Edna Norwich upon receiving his director's fee: "I don't know when I directed a show that I enjoyed more, or in which I got more co-operation from the cast."[42] That cast featured Francess Halpenny in her first on-stage appearance for Alumnae.[43]

Club lore maintains that much of their members' time was spent at meetings knitting for the war effort and reading plays. Indeed, just nine days after Canada entered the war, the minutes record that Alumnae's "chief business of the evening was winding wool and setting up various socks."[44] The following Sunday, "knitting continued briskly or painfully as the case might be."[45] Financial records indicate that during the first year of hostilities, the club spent $22.65 on wool, with $19.39 of this amount received in contributions to their "Wool Fund." Knitting was in fact Alumnae's steadiest wartime activity. In the meeting minutes for May 1941, it is recorded that "all other warlike activities have been confined to knitting – of which there has been a good deal, for the Army Medical Corps, overseas,"[46] as organized by member Elspeth Wilson. An unsigned note in Alumnae's collections addressed to Wilson enumerates the "knitted articles received from your group" between 28 February 1940 and 27 May 1942: 114 pairs of socks, 57 sweaters, 21 pairs of mitts, 5 pairs of wristlets, 3 scarfs, and 3 helmets (presumably knitted head coverings worn within helmets). The note went on to list further donations: 31 pairs of socks, 1 scarf, and 1 sweater, for a total of 236 "knitted articles." Alumnae's formidable wartime textile output indicates that they were applying their task-oriented organizational skills to the war effort with considerable labour and success.

By the fall of 1941, membership was down to twenty-five as "club enthusiasm had dwindled." Halpenny recorded that at a "well-attended meeting" at Agnes Muldrew's home, the club "seemed eager to tackle something large and definite and so a three-act play was discussed." However, they decided that year that a "presentation in the Women's Union would be the safest proposition,"[47] although none came to pass until February 1942. That month, the members recalled their success with *Sunday Costs Five Pesos* at Camp Borden a year earlier, and the "matter of doing shows for the troops was raised. Agatha [Leonard] described her experience doing this type of show – something unsubtle, on the vulgar side, with pep and not much length, with loudness of voice an essential. It was suggested that we might prepare one or two skits with a view to performance at the canteen and that Sid [Sydney] Mulqueen be asked to inspect them first."[48] The club's friend Sid Mulqueen was already performing for troops as a dancer and was a dance colleague of Alumnae members Eleanor Barton and Constance Shiell.[49]

In March 1942 it was decided that because they had not found any existing skits of merit, Alumnae members would write their own. Alison Hewitt (formerly Ewart) and Agatha Leonard were already connected with the iconic *Merry-Go-Round Revue* by this point and suggested that they "would be interested in our effort and undertook to provide some of the youthful performance needed from its ranks." The immediate result, in April 1942, was an evening of eight skits that functioned as a *de facto* audition for the *Merry-Go-Round Revue*, performed "for Club and canteen people"[50] at the UC Women's Union. The evening featured Alumnae members with a number of non-members, directed by Billie (W.A.) Atkinson, with Agnes Muldrew as the master of ceremonies. Mary Bruck and Doris Stacey opened the evening with something called *Powder-room Pow-wow*; this was followed by a monologue called *The Plumber* by member Alice Keys about "father fixing the water-system,"[51] a song by Doris Stacey, a story by Francess Halpenny titled *Sadie Hoards*, a pantomime by Billie May Dinsmore and Mary Bruck with music by Helen Fisher, and Noël Coward's *Cats Cradle*, performed by Hewitt and Leonard. These were followed by member Isabelle Cleland's *Waiting for the Streetcar* "on the streetcar situation which seemed very amusing,"[52] featuring Dorothy Batcheller and Christina Templeton (presumably the "streetcar situation" referred to Toronto's emerging idea of having an "underground streetcar," that is, a subway, under Yonge Street). Another song by Stacey followed. The show ended with the "*pièce de resistance* of the evening," according to Alumnae notes. Although the title is lost, Jane Mallett and Frederic Manning of the much-loved Town Tonics presented the piece, written by member Margaret Ness. On the basis of this evening's efforts, Alice Keys was "asked to do her monologue *The Plumber* at the canteen with the famed *Merry-Go-Round Revue*. It was a great success."[53]

Membership Down, the Kamloops Corvette, and the *Merry-Go-Round Revue*

What is a theatre group when it is not producing theatre? As the club had feared, by the fall of 1942 its membership was down to nineteen, the lowest since before the 1926–27 season. Worse, among these paid-up members, many could not be active. In May 1942, they discussed what to program for the next season. Halpenny wrote at the time:

> It was felt that we had done nothing to enhance our reputation this year due to the inability to secure people with enough time to act and also to do backstage work. A motion was made by Eleanor Woodside, seconded by Francess Halpenny and passed by the club that we should not engage in such public performance for the duration. It was suggested that we concentrate on making our meetings next year really those of a dramatic club – reading plays, doing choral speaking, pantomime, skits. People were appointed to look after this angle – Doris Stacey, Jean Stewart, Eleanor Woodside, Dorothy Batcheller, Francess Halpenny.[54]

Members felt that they had spent too much time earlier in the year considering full-length plays and seeking a director and personnel to stage them. This had impeded their efforts as a dramatic club as the war persisted and membership numbers slipped. After the business of meeting concluded, in true Alumnae fashion they "adjourned for supper and skits."[55]

That fall, having "decided that no public performance should be given this year," club president Katherine Anglin proposed meeting every two weeks to knit, adding that meetings should start promptly and discuss business "without delay or interruption."[56] After nearly three years in which they had offered a dozen wartime theatre productions, in April 1942 they stopped producing theatre for public audiences. Except for a Christmas nativity play in December 1942, they would not start again until February 1946. Member-written entertainments at private club meetings continued, however.

Even so, club members found ways to redirect their philanthropic efforts. In the Little Theatre's spirit of self-edification, and to keep their spirits up, they met every second week, usually on Mondays, from 28 September through 26 October 1942 and then from 18 January through to 21 June 1943, reading a variety of plays to keep themselves up-to-date with new and popular work. These included many plays that would become canonical, as well as Broadway hits and lesser-known plays of interest, several of which Alumnae would produce after the war. All of the plays they set out to read during these years were contemporary, written just before or during the war, and were often found in curated play collections from licensers like Samuel French. It is likely that during the war it was difficult to receive plays by post from many sources other than major North American agents like Samuel French, and this inevitably affected what they considered for future productions. Several times in the fall, selections from multiple plays were read in the same meeting. By continuing to read plays they honed their taste in dramatic fare – evidence of the practical, forward thinking that would prepare them for the post-war theatre era.[57] While reading plays to themselves was no way to raise money, members could do so *while* working for the war effort in their ingrained spirit of philanthropy. They continued to roll bandages and to knit wool socks and other garments for the soldiers, and each spring, they purchased a $100.00 Canada Victory War Bond.

Moreover, in the fall of 1942, Toronto's Home Economics Association, founded in 1938, asked Alumnae to supply boxes for the "Kamloops" corvette, a Royal Canadian Navy ship that supplied other Allied ships in the Atlantic.[58] The executive's Ruth Home, Alumnae's "Kamloops Convenor," led efforts to gather supplies, at first by collecting books and magazines,[59] then widening the search to include games, candy, and cake, which were "especially wanted."[60] But as membership numbers were low, meeting attendance was minuscule, and only six members attended the meeting held on Sunday, 18 January 1943: Agnes Muldrew, Elspeth Wilson, Margaret Tytler, Florian Moore, Doris Stacey, and Katherine Anglin. They attempted to conduct some business, but little could be accomplished. They did, however, vote to put money towards repairing the club's spotlight, "which had been pronounced dangerous by an electrician"[61] (possibly during the December nativity play). The next five meetings only attracted between five and fourteen members.[62] In March 1943, and for the duration of the war, the club discussed the "inadequacy"[63] of their Kamloops collections and decided to target their work by alternating "magazines one month, and food the next."[64] They were also one of ten groups that sold raffle tickets for the Kamloops.

That year the club lost two more key members to the war effort. In November 1942, Christine Templeton was appointed vice-president to replace Francess Halpenny.[65] Halpenny, who had had a very busy theatre season with the club the previous year while starting out at the University of Toronto Press as a junior editor, left to work with the Royal Canadian Air Force in Torbay, Newfoundland, and then Summerside, PEI, as a meteorologist,[66] supporting the "anti-submarine patrol by tracking weather patterns in the North Atlantic Ocean."[67] She received as a present from the club a "leather money belt."[68] Soon after, Frances MacLellan was appointed secretary to replace Doris Stacey, who had left for Ottawa in January 1943 to join the civilian Directorate of Censorship within the Department of National War Services (founded in 1940),[69] whose task was to monitor information in the media, the post, and telegraphic communications.[70] Throughout 1942–43, Alumnae members continued to support the war effort while reading plays to one another for possible future productions.

Alumnae had been founded as a fundraising group. Now, with materials and skilled labour and being steered so strongly towards the war effort, they found themselves unable to produce plays. So they transferred their labour, material, and organizational skills to homefront endeavours. At regular meetings between 1943 and 1945, sometimes attended by as few as seven members,[71] they read plays,[72] continued to do a "certain amount of knitting," and made "several contributions to the Kamloops," including making a scrapbook for the Navy.[73] At one point they discussed producing two plays, one for the Home Economics Association's Kamloops drive and one for the UCAA, but it was felt that "so few members were available for acting and stage work that both projects, and even the Kamloops venture, would be impossible."[74] They did, however, decide to make their collections of skits given by the club "part of the nucleus of a permanent collection."[75] (If this was to include members' original skits, unfortunately none are kept in Alumnae's collections.) This is the first time that an archive, of sorts, is mentioned in extant Alumnae minutes, and suggests that members were growing aware of the importance of their work and very much wanted to continue and expand after the war, however small their present numbers. Expenses for the 1943–44 season included a $100.00 Government of Canada Victory Bond, the purchase of the Maxwell Anderson script *Eve of St. Mark* from Ryerson Press (which they read in June 1943), and 27¢ in stamps and phone calls. Their only income came from eleven members, each paying a $1.00 membership, and bank interest of 59¢, leaving the club with $77.19 in the bank.

The 1944-45 season found them facing a similar financial situation, and making similarly modest purchases, including Navy scrapbooks, $4.75 for fruitcake, and a $100.00 Victory Bond balanced by eleven paid memberships. Meeting attendance was "small, especially during the stormy winter months,"[76] and Christina Templeton's minutes lack the specificity of previous years, simply listing the names of members who hosted at their homes, the plays read, and other highlights without dates. As was the case for the past two years, many of the plays they read had war themes or were from Broadway. As had been the case since their founding, nearly all these plays had premiered in recent years.[77]

The club did not produce its own shows during these years; however, a few members performed in a mammoth "all-girl"[78] troop show that provided "hundreds of performances during the war."[79] In that show's first year, Agatha Leonard, Alison Hewitt, and Ruth Johnson were among a chorus of twelve involved in the *Merry-Go-Round Revue*. This was an all-woman, "well-paced, breezy variety program" intended for the troops, although it also sometimes played for civilian audiences at the Eaton Auditorium. The *Globe and Mail* described the twelve-person chorus as "attractive as well as efficient." Wearing "bright costumes ranging from per [*sic*], red and white for the opening, yellow and blue farmerette overalls, green velvet Aussie outfits, they danced difficult routines with smiling

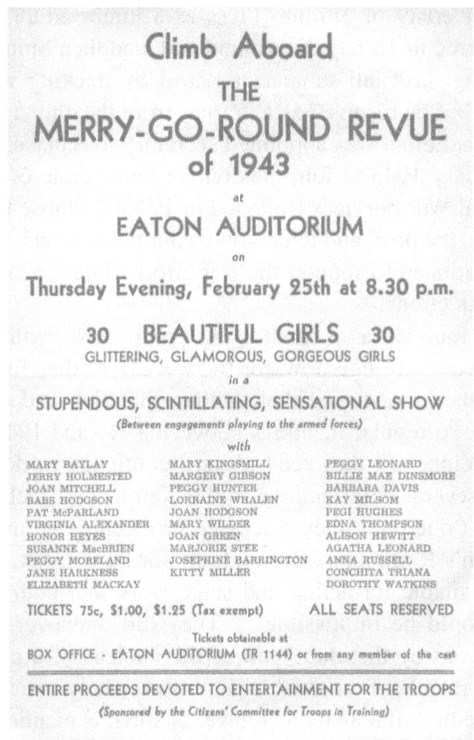

Figure 2.1. *Merry-Go-Round Revue* flyer. The *Merry-Go-Round Revue*, a thirty-woman troop show that toured Ontario army camps from 1941 to 1945, was directed by Lorna Sheard, Edgar Stone, and then Roly Young. It featured Alumnae members Agatha Leonard, Alison Hewitt, and Ruth Johnson. Leonard was also on the revue's programming team. Performances at the Eaton Auditorium financed the production each year. Courtesy of Alumnae Theatre Company.

nonchalance."[80] Leonard reportedly made 200 appearances in the *Revue*,[81] including skits with Joan Mitchell about a "mock radio program and a mother and child at the movies" that earned "plenty of laughs."[82] Leonard also sat on the "committee in charge of skits and arranging the programme."[83] Explained the *Globe and Mail*, "it isn't a professional show, but it has something that a lot of professional shows don't have. That's the enthusiasm, vigour and sparkle of 30 girls doing a good job for a good reason, putting everything they have into it, and getting a lot of fun out of it. The *Merry-Go-Round* is something to see."[84]

For five years, until 1945, the *Merry-Go-Round Revue* seasons started in mid-October and ran until June, preceded by six weeks of rehearsal. The women toured army camps across Ontario from Ottawa and Petawawa to London and St. Thomas (and once to Buffalo, New York). A two-night annual public performance at the Eaton Auditorium financed the production.[85] The show's flyer, red print on white, proclaimed: "Climb Aboard the *Merry-Go-Round Revue* of 1943 at Eaton Auditorium on Thursday Evening, February 25th at 8:30pm. 30 Beautiful Girls 30 Glittering, Glamorous, Gorgeous Girls in a Stupendous,

Scintillating, Sensational Show (Between engagements playing to the armed forces) … All seats reserved … Entire proceeds devoted to entertainment for the troops. (Sponsored by the Citizens' Committee for Troops in Training)." Tax-exempt tickets were 75¢, $1.00, and $1.25. It was the first time the club's members had been part of a show that overtly used sexuality to sell tickets, an indication of the predominantly male audiences the *Revue* sought to attract, as well as the changing times.

The initial Eaton Auditorium performance, along with a second show, netted $1,200.00, which was used to buy costumes and scenery for subsequent *Merry-Go-Round* performances. As the *Varsity* reported in a post-war article describing Leonard's work as a librarian at the university's medical school, the idea for the *Revue* had originated with several women at a badminton club discussing "what could be done in the way of entertainment for the boys. Someone suggested, 'Why not a revue?' 'Sure, – let's', another added. Right there and then they started a collection and netted $75.00. The presence of some American visitors helped."[86] Former Hart House Theatre artistic director Lorna Sheard was approached to direct it. Edgar Stone and then *Globe and Mail* theatre and film critic Roly Young took over as directors in subsequent years.[87] Some years later, the *Varsity* described Leonard and her involvement with the *Revue*:

> Had you been here during the war, you would have noticed her sitting on her bag every Thursday at 4:30pm in front of the Anatomy Building waiting for the bus to pick her up. Once a week the all-girl troupe did a show and once a month went for a week-end. Perhaps you caught her act when you were in the services, she played at Jarvis, Clinton, Newmarket and most of the camps in Ontario. Once, by special invitation from the mayor of Buffalo, she played at the Army Air Corps station. The girls staged their revues in any building that was handy at the time, ranging from converted boxing rings to hangars to drill halls.[88]

The *Varsity* article is significant in that it provides evidence of the theatre work that several Alumnae members did during the war, besides offering a glimpse of the sort of performances that people were attending on the homefront, and how often. More than one hundred women participated in the *Merry-Go-Round Revue* over its five years, and many of them found ongoing work in Canada's emerging radio industry because of it.

In the article, Leonard described a trip to and from a service-camp show in sub-zero temperatures. The bus had been borrowed from the Toronto Transit Commission. Already behind schedule, it stalled halfway up the first curve on Hamilton Mountain on the way to Jarvis, Ontario. The girls, who were "making-up their faces and legs and stepping into open-toed slippers," had to get out and push. Having surmounted the hill, the bus detoured "through a barnyard." They arrived at 10:30 p.m. for a show that was supposed to have started at 7:00 p.m. After the show, the girls ate steak dinners and ended up following a bulldozer on the highway, before a "breathtaking" ride down Hamilton Mountain; by then, the heat and the brakes had both failed, "leaving only the emergency [break]." By Leonard's account, she arrived home by 5:30 a.m., and "didn't bother going to bed since she had to be at the University by 8:45 a.m. Around this time, the Medical School was extra-busy since the courses had been telescoped to turn out more doctors"[89] during the war.

Club membership may have been eleven, but meeting attendance was even lower. Members were needed elsewhere, including beyond the city boundaries, and government-imposed gasoline restrictions limited car travel across the city. It was not until the club's June 1945 annual meeting, at Alice Keys's home in Scarborough, that an "easing of the gasoline restrictions since V-E day"[90] finally allowed all eleven members ("three carloads") to make the trip: president Jean Stewart, treasurer Florian Moore (who arrived after dinner), recording secretary Christina Templeton, corresponding secretary Elspeth Wilson, Margaret Ness, Alison Hewitt, Florrie Hunt, Margaret Tytler, Katherine Anglin, Agatha Leonard, and host Alice Keys with her guest Winnifred Redman.[91] When they arrived, the "cold and dull" weather precluded the planned picnic, forcing the members to "stay indoors by a roaring fire."[92] Here they approved the post-war executive: Agatha Leonard (president), Florrie Hunt (vice-president), Mary Smart (treasurer), Eleanor Woodside (secretary), and Jean Stewart (past president). It was decided to leave one position vacant until the fall, when "former members might return to town, and new members be admitted."[93] Leonard, among Alumnae's most consistently keen programming voices, proposed that they consider presenting an evening of plays in the fall in anticipation of attracting new members (they would not be able to offer a post-war production until February 1946). Florrie Hunt then presented Alice Keys's new sketch, *Thursday Night*, as a "telephone conversation with asides" in which Keys's mother and "one little friend" figured. Margaret Tytler presented a "very effective and moving performance" of a monologue called *The Old Actress*, which, they concluded, "should be repeated before a larger audience." Jean Stewart and Alison Hewitt presented *In the Midst of Life*, which had a "trick ending" and "gave Jean one of the 'jittery' roles she excels in." As the meeting concluded, they thanked outgoing president Jean Stewart, "who deserves great credit for holding the club together during the last two seasons."[94] By the September 1945 meeting at Leonard's home, seven of the now registered twenty-eight members were set to rebuild the club beyond philanthropy as an artistic force on an emerging Toronto theatre scene.[95]

A New Name beyond University College

During the 1930s and 1940s, Alumnae members took measures to extract themselves from University College. As with any nonprofessionalizing theatre company, membership plays a definitive role in maintaining the cast, crew, and administrative labour that produces theatre. With the women's building fundraising behind them and as the Depression wore on, they began rethinking their purposes. This was accelerated by a dip in membership in the 1935–36 season, by which time unemployment in Toronto had risen to 25 per cent and many women had become their families' primary breadwinners.[96]

During an executive meeting at Katherine Anglin's home in October 1936, ways to expand the membership were discussed. One strategy involved "associate members,"[97] specifically Sheila Tisdale, Dama Lumley, and Cecylia Long, whom Edgar Stone had cast in Alumnae's Radio Hall one-acts that month. It was proposed that non-UC graduates be cast in Alumnae shows when appropriate. The conversation was tabled until the next meeting two days later, when still another solution was proposed: Alison Hewitt moved and Margaret Tytler seconded "that the Club go on record as accepting at its own discretion members who are graduates of other Universities or faculties of the University of Toronto except the other arts colleges." President Florrie Hunt was "asked to advise"[98] the UCAA of this policy, which it approved.[99] The fee for Associate Members would be the same as for regular members – $2.50 (a reduction from the previous year's membership fee of $3.00).

Alumnae's identity as a theatre-producing entity was changing. No longer would club membership, and casting, be restricted to UC graduates. The club would now be open to women educated across the country. In addition to upholding their core philanthropic goals, they would attract and retain female participants from further afield who would serve their artistic goals in the new and increasingly competitive Dominion Drama Festival era. Regional and perhaps even national reputations were now at stake.

But this new vision did not succeed immediately. Alumnae attracted few women from other colleges. Why, after all, would a graduate of Victoria College, for example, want to join the Dramatic Club of the University College Alumnae Association? In the early 1940s, in the midst of knitting, skit writing, and play reading, and with no end in sight to the war, "heated discussion"[100] within the club ensued. Something had to be done to increase membership to the point that the club could finally resume producing full-length plays.

As Francess Halpenny recorded in May 1942 at the club's annual meeting, "the question of a re-organization of the Club with a view to acquiring new, active members was then discussed at length." Members considered three proposals:

1 Apply to the Alumnae Association for the right to accept associate members.
  (a) university graduates of any university [as members, not just as cast]
  (b) non-university graduates
2 Apply to the university for a charter for a club of members from
  (a) Toronto colleges
  (b) associate members from other universities
3 Dissolve present club and re-organize as a non-university group.

Inaction held no appeal for the ambitious club members. "Eventually," wrote Halpenny in meeting minutes, a motion was made by Jean Stewart, seconded by Agnes Muldrew, and passed with unanimous approval, "that the U.C.A.D.C. reorganize as a University Alumnae Dramatic Club" and "apply to the proper authorities for a club charter, the members to include alumnae of the University of Toronto with associate alumnae from other universities; and that a committee be appointed to approach said authorities and draw up a constitution for the club."[101] The committee appointed was Katherine Anglin, Eleanor Woodside, and Jean Stewart.

To separate from UC, Alumnae would need to set the bureaucracy in motion towards that end; they would also need to make it known that women from other colleges and beyond could now be members, and inspire them to join. Halpenny explained:

> During the discussion it was decided that a formal invitation be extended to the graduating years to join the club and that we should then bend every effort to secure those we felt would be most useful. It was decided, too, that it would be unwise for us to be committed to take so many members from each college or for the members of the executive to be distributed among the colleges.[102]

This was a complicated manoeuvre. So that it could take in non-UC graduates, the club voted unanimously to separate from the UCAA and to petition the university to allow it to accept members from across campus as well as "associate members" from other universities. Yet UC graduates would remain in control as the only women eligible to sit on its executive.

The letter the new committee had been deputized to write, signed by president Katherine Anglin, was the first step in the club's departure from the university. Anglin wrote to the university's president H.J. Cody:

> At its annual meeting the University College Dramatic Club discussed the question of Club membership. It was felt that there had not been enough recent graduates from the University College who were interested in dramatics to keep the club strong and flourishing.

We should therefore like very much to have your permission to change the name of our club to the University Alumnae Dramatic Club. This would enable us to draw our members from alumnae of the whole University instead of from University College alone and to accept associate members from other Universities as well.

We hope that this proposal will meet with your approval.

Respectfully yours,

Katherine B. Anglin.[103]

But would it work? It took president Cody less than a month to respond with measured approval:

I have spoken to Principle [Malcolm] Wallace of University College about your proposal and he will probably have a word with you about it. There does not seem to be any objection to the change you suggest. Possibly a strong club can be maintained only by widening the field of your selection.

With all good wishes,

Sincerely yours, H.J. Cody, President.[104]

Cody's "official goodwill" having been gained,[105] as well as that of principal Malcolm William Wallace by the end of the summer,[106] the new name "University Alumnae Dramatic Club" and a new purview were secured (each lasted until the late 1980s, except for a change in 1963 that added any current female university students, staff, and faculty as eligible for club membership[107]). Opening the club to women graduates of any university would help it gain members. However, all agreed that the club should maintain close ties with the UCAA and, in particular, maintain representation on its executive. They further agreed that while women members of the university's three arts colleges should be invited to participate in the club, "there could be no passing on of numbers by the executive." To sweeten the attraction, the word "associate" was dropped, so that "membership would be open to any eligible person."[108] This was a time in Canada of broad strokes and grand manoeuvres. Katherine Anglin and her contemporaries had developed a strong sense that the Dramatic Club had cultural value beyond UC itself. And they wanted that value, and the influence it promised, to endure beyond present predictions.

Letters were now sent to the other U of T colleges' alumnae associations informing them that their members were welcome to explore the new UADC. However, the responses were mixed. St. Hilda's president said she would inform her membership; other presidents claimed not to have received the letters. The "unnaturalness" of the war years was such that despite their official freedom from UC, the club made "no great strides … in becoming representative of the whole University."[109] It would take some time for them to attract committed theatre-minded graduates from other colleges, such as Martha Mann from the Ontario College of Art (for which they briefly considered "admitting membership to diploma courses that are affiliated with the University"[110]) and Molly Golby from Victoria College.

Unfortunately, despite attempts at collegiality, the Dramatic Club's formal departure somewhat chilled its relationship with UCAA. When a letter was sent informing the UCAA of the club's new status, it was read with confusion. Apparently, some UCAA members "had the impression that the Dramatic Club was ceasing operations." Anglin decided to say a few words at the next UCAA meeting to clear things up.[111] There was also the question of whether the club would present its annual UCAA evening of one-acts at the UC Women's Union. The UCAA's corresponding secretary, who had written to them expressing appreciation for the club's past theatre work, now wrote, perhaps pointedly, "We are eagerly looking forward to the time when we may once again enjoy your productions,"[112] and then added, "If the part of your group which is still active should feel that time permits you to produce a short skit, stunt, or review, we would be pleased to have it as a part of the programme at the Christmas or Spring meeting."[113] But club members decided they were "against doing one this year,"[114] perhaps concerned that performing *at* UC might further perpetuate the notion that they were still performing *for* UC.

After formally leaving the UCAA during the war, Alumnae performed only three more times in the UC Women's Union auditorium. The last of these was in February 1947, for a "drama night" featuring Alumnae members, the UC Glee Club, and Toronto "monologist"[115] Jane Mallet, hosted by the UCAA. By then, the UCAA had lost a valued fundraising arm. Alumnae may have outgrown the UCAA ideologically, but they did not yet have the membership to run far.

Programming Toronto's Post-War Theatre Boom

The war having ended, Alumnae's executive set out to rebuild their membership and resume producing theatre. By the time Francess Halpenny took over the club presidency from Agatha Leonard at the end of the 1945–46 season, the membership had returned to pre-war numbers – twenty-eight – as many familiar faces, and some new ones, returned to the club. There was much room for optimism as Alumnae rebuilt. Wrote Halpenny that season:

> Before the war the average annual membership of the Club was thirty-five to forty, the personnel varying from year to year. These women were of assorted ages, held together almost unconsciously by a small group who have been members for twenty years or more. By the time V.J. Day [Victory over Japan Day] finally rolled around eighteen active members remained, of whom twelve belong to the twenty-years-or-more class. As this small group of enthusiasts, which has been the nucleus of the club since its inception, is still in existence it is to be hoped, now that members are beginning to come home from the Services and from war jobs in other cities, that the Club will be able to expand once more, gather in the needed quota of young people and start production again.

Members like Patricia Godfrey and Grace Matthews had "graduated from the Alumnae to the professional theatre,"[116] but others remained, or returned from absence, to become increasingly active with Alumnae and other local theatres. Halpenny and Alumnae immediately set out to rebuild along these lines.

Within a year of the war's end, Toronto experienced a rapid explosion of theatre activity the likes of which it had not seen before. By the 1946–47 season, Toronto boasted "no less than seventeen dramatic and operatic groups" eager to bring live performance back to the city. There was also a growing desire for focused theatre training, and the Conservatory of Music sought to offer acting and stage technique classes. In the *Globe and Mail*, Colin Sabiston explained that "this community is revealing a strong urge toward dramatic and operatic expression which the commercial theatre alone is not satisfying" and that the large number of "active groups" and the large amount of "audience attention" these groups received was unique. Along with Alumnae, these groups included Hart House Theatre, the Earle Grey Players, the New Play Society, the Vagabond Players, the Belmont Group Theatre, the Comedy Theatre, the Plaquest Drama Guild, and the Haymakers (formerly Canada Players). The last four of these groups, along with Alumnae, were members of the Civic Theatre Association, established by *Globe and Mail* film and theatre critic Roly Young, in its second season. Sabiston divided the seventeen groups into three broad categories: "the professional but non-commercial, the quasi-academic, and the purely amateur." Interested in building a sustainable theatre ecology, Sabiston asserted that audiences had a responsibility, beyond simply financial, to develop local arts practices by developing "standards of public taste" and to "prevent mere preciousness from imposing itself upon the unwary." He argued that the burgeoning success of many of these groups could be attributed to the fact that they catered to a wide audience, "perhaps not great in numbers, but more representative of the community as a whole."[117]

Alumnae centred their efforts on the reopened Hart House Theatre, still regarded as an important theatre facility on the continent. Post-war Alumnae members would frequently act in and direct shows produced by other groups, including revived college and department clubs, as would more and more artists from other groups around the city; reciprocally, many men involved in other groups worked repeatedly with Alumnae. There was interest in building local Toronto theatre to a level it had never before attained. Alumnae would be a catalyst in this pursuit.

In the 1945–46 season, regular Alumnae executive meetings were publicized before or after the fact in the daily papers,[118] making the governance of the all-woman club conspicuous to those who kept up with Toronto's theatre and society pages. This helped keep the club visible among those who might consider joining. By 1953–54 their membership had ballooned to forty-nine, in large part because they had expanded their membership criteria beyond UC. But they were looking for more, in part because not all members were actively working on shows. They started their 1954–55 season with a pitch in the local papers and in the Central Ontario Drama League's September 1954 newsletter: "This group would be pleased to receive inquiries regarding membership from women graduates of universities in Canada and beyond, who are interested in acting, direction, stage design and construction, costume design and construction."[119] This particular pitch did not result in more members (they started the next season with two fewer), but it did add new members Helen Dunlop and Molly Golby, who would be among the club's most active and entrepreneurial leaders in the years ahead.

As meetings began drawing up to twenty-five members again,[120] Alumnae's social activities exceeded even pre-war levels. And without the UC Women's Union to host their private shows, they were using their annual meetings to produce more involved plays. For example, Alice Keys hosted the June 1948 annual meeting at her home, where, "as a startling innovation, husbands and a few guests were asked [to attend],"[121] an innovation that became an Alumnae tradition. There, members performed Philip Johnson's 1948 melodrama *Dark Brown*, directed by Elizabeth Mascall, as the "climax of the day."[122] Two years later, at a December 1951 meeting, because Christina Templeton could seat sixty people in her home,[123] Alumnae produced both Thornton Wilder's comic satire *The Queens of France* and Josephine Tey's (writing as Gordon Daviot's) *Three Mrs. Madderleys* as a "Christmas Invitational Evening," for which a "wonderful job" was done.[124] To support productions and keep spirits high, prominent members like Templeton hosted "entertainments" for Alumnae's casts, crews, and "ticketing committees"[125] before and during the run of shows, serving coffee and so forth. Like most other club initiatives, these were publicized through the "Social and Personal Notes" columns in the daily papers.

In the decade after the war, Alumnae offered both their fall productions and their spring DDF regional entries as well as their regional winning reprises at Hart House Theatre (see chapter 6). No longer having the use of the UC Women's Union, they also borrowed performance spaces in high schools, churches, and libraries for their one-acts (see chapter 5). They continued to focus on recent British and American plays, especially plays premiered in the 1930s and 1940s that had suffered shortened runs or lost out on subsequent productions because of the war. They returned to playwrights they had produced in the past like Susan Glaspell, Jacinto Benavente, Franz (Ferenc) Molnár, and George Bernard Shaw. But they also returned to playwrights they had read at their wartime meetings, such as Josephina Niggli, Ruth Gordon, Thornton Wilder, and Philip Johnson. And they added to their repertoire other prominent modern names like Oscar Wilde, T.S. Eliot, Christopher Fry, Jean Anouilh, and Ontario's own Robertson Davies. Moreover, playwrights increasingly wrote to Alumnae to make their plays known as they premiered more new plays, particularly by women (see chapter 7). The playreading committee, still responsible for recommending shows for production, kept detailed records of plays read and plays received.[126] Alumnae also started reflecting on their own production processes. At the end of the 1951–52 season, Francess Halpenny and Ruth Francis "originated an idea which would help members to understand and have a knowledge of the work that has to be done for a production." The idea met with an "enthusiastic"[127] response. It marked the start of Alumnae's first backstage production manual.

Halpenny's records of the playreading committee's work during the 1953–54 season provide evidence of the breadth of plays they considered and the sources that suggested them. Halpenny chaired the committee that season, which "read widely from various plays" from the catalogues of Samuel French and Dramatist Play Services. They continued to read through the summer. Aware of the value of keeping track of these plays, she reported that a "card index of plays is being kept."[128]

Alumnae also lit on several new directors for their post-war productions. In particular, lead *Globe and Mail* theatre critic Herbert Whittaker directed five plays for Alumnae in the decade after the Second World War, more than anyone else; E.G. Sterndale Bennett and Karen Glahn each directed four times for Alumnae. An examination of two of their annual Hart House Theatre productions, *Dear Octopus* in October 1951 and *The Heiress* in October 1952, sheds light on how Alumnae chose their directors at the time, often looking first to Whittaker.

Having achieved acclaim at the DDF finals with Whittaker's direction and design of Shaw's *In Good King Charles's Golden Days* in the spring of 1951 (see chapter 6), Alumnae, the "Prize dramatists,"[129] opened their next season with a Dodie Smith (aka C.L. Anthony) play, *Dear Octopus*, the polite 1938 English comedy about an English matriarch,[130] in October 1951 at Hart House Theatre. William Needles, the voice of John in the "long-lasting radio serial" *John and Judy*,[131] and future Stratford mainstay, directed the production. Needles had already directed Alumnae's Hart House Theatre productions of Dodie Smith's *Autumn Crocus* in November 1949 and Oscar Wilde's *The Importance of Being Earnest* in June 1950.

But Needles was not, in fact, Alumnae's first choice for director of the fall production. Alumnae president Barbara Barnett had phoned Whittaker in the summer and reported back that Whittaker, who had just directed *King Charles* for them, "does not believe in doing consecutive plays with the same group, but would be happy to do a Festival play or a June one." Barnett pitched to Whittaker some of Alumnae's choices, including Fry's *Venus*

Observed, Goetz's *The Heiress*, and Molnár's *Olympia*. But Whittaker "left the impression that he didn't want to decide anything immediately"; instead, he suggested that Keane's *Treasure Hunt* "would be an excellent play [for Alumnae]."[132] Barnett's August 1951 report gives insight into Whittaker's burgeoning relationship with the group. It reveals that Alumnae wished he would direct for them more often and were open to taking play suggestions from him, although they had the final word; conversely, he was happy to direct for them, but on some of his own terms, which no doubt took into account his position at the *Globe and Mail* and his desire to direct for other groups.[133]

Critics were pleased with Needles's "sound and warm production"[134] of *Dear Octopus*, which was "deftly directed" if "leisurely in pace."[135] As the wedding couple, Christina Templeton, "with rich natural charm and the confidence of long experience," and the "subdued, yet tender"[136] Robert Brodie, were "completely charming in their senility and put so much tenderness into their acting that the trivialities they have to say almost sound as if they made sense." Eleanor Beecroft was "delightful" and Marian Jones showed "fine sympathy and effective understatement."[137]

However, critics were not pleased with Alumnae's choice of play. They had chosen it over Clemence Dane's three-act *Cousin Muriel*, which Agatha Leonard's playreading committee had also recommended.[138] But E.G. Wanger, reviewing in the *Globe and Mail* in place of Whittaker, called the play a "hearty, well-dressed conversation piece that attempts to keep audiences suspended between laughter and tears, but on a few occasions brings them closer to yawning." The occasion of Dora and Charles's golden wedding celebration brings their children, grandchild, and in-laws together, but "most of the time is spent in nostalgic reminiscences about the good old days, after which each member gives a self-pitying account of his particular disappointments brought on by adult life."[139] Malcolm MacKinnon in the *Varsity* concluded that it "contains no evident plot, but rather a contrived series of conversations" that are too "shallow"[140] for the proven Alumnae company to bring to life.

Alumnae discussed *Dear Octopus*'s relatively poor ticket sales after the run, making note of their slow pre-show publicity, local competition from Sadler's Wells Ballet, which was visiting Toronto from the UK at the same time, and disappointing media coverage. It was suggested that Wanger's "poor review" in the *Globe and Mail* and the dearth of reviews in the other dailies may have been to blame. Ruth Francis drily suggested following up whenever complimentary tickets were given out "to make sure that we get someone to review the show and [find out] if it is the 'crime reporter.'"[141]

On another occasion, Alumnae wanted Whittaker to direct their October 1952 production of Ruth and August Goetz's 1947 play *The Heiress*, an adaptation of Henry James's novel *Washington Square*. A year earlier, Barnett had approached Whittaker to direct the play for the DDF regional festival. He was not interested, preferring instead to direct a Chekhov play. This raised the issue of "the difficulty of having too many men in the cast," and it was suggested that *Three Sisters* would be the "most appropriate [play] for the group." Members now suggested to Whittaker that he direct *The Heiress* for the June 1951 university convocation show at Hart House Theatre, hoping that he "could be persuaded to change his mind about Chekhov."[142] He could not be. By May, Alumnae was hoping to recruit Esse Ljunge to direct *The Heiress*. Ljunge had adjudicated the inaugural Central Ontario Drama League One-Act Festival in April 1951. But he was unavailable. Karen Glahn, who had already directed for Alumnae four times, was now suggested, but "it was felt that she might not be too good for pace."[143] Finally, over the summer, E.G. Sterndale

Bennett agreed to direct the show, his first for Alumnae in five years. The show flyers could announce him as the "Founder and Director of the Canadian Theatre School," which he had started in 1949 in Toronto (it would last until 1956[144]). He arranged for *The Heiress* to rehearse there.

The Heiress had been produced by another company the previous March at the DDF's Western Ontario Drama League regional festival, and it is likely that at least a few Alumnae members had seen it then.[145] It had already been a hit in New York and London,[146] and Theatre '49 would stage it in Toronto a few weeks after Alumnae's production[147] "in a loft on Brunswick Ave.," with the actors seeming to "surround" the audience in an arrangement that was "wonderfully intimate and usually fun."[148] For Alumnae it made a $938.26 profit over four Theatre Nights, a considerable improvement from *Dear Octopus* a year earlier.[149] This success was due in no small part to the media attention it attracted before and during the run. A preview piece in the *Globe and Mail* featured member Elizabeth (Betty) Gray, a social worker by day, and her costuming work. Gray, who had started costuming only a year before, would become a mainstay of Alumnae's more lavish productions in the coming years. She explained that for *The Heiress* she was using an 1859 *Peterson's Magazine* fashion guide, likely borrowed from fellow Alumnae member and fashion enthusiast Mary Smart,[150] as a reference for her designs. She noted that because the Hart House Theatre stage was at eye level, "if clothes are off the floor at all ... all you see is feet."[151]

The Heiress follows a woman who is blamed by her father for her mother's death in childbirth. Rose MacDonald in the *Telegram* said the play "could scarcely have been presented by an amateur group more intellectually disciplined and more effective in interpretation than [Alumnae]."[152] Hugh Thomson in the *Star* called it a "top-flight performance."[153] Whittaker in his *Globe and Mail* review declared that the production "justifies and enhances his [Sterndale Bennett's] reputation."[154] Malcolm Mackinnon in the *Varsity* said that the director had "guided the players ... with a sure and skillful hand into a production of uniform excellence."[155] In the lead role, Norma Edwards, who had recently moved to Toronto from Vancouver, was able to "build up a really tragic figure"[156] with "many vicissitudes" that gave her role "heart and soul."[157] Whittaker thought that Edwards gave "all the necessary facets of Catherine's character variety and skill" and at the end "sets the spine to tingling with her implacable decision."[158] Eleanor Beecroft played the aunt with "vigorous comic sense," and Ruth Johnson's Mrs. Montgomery was "one of the high points of the evening."[159] Set designer Roy Jackson provided a "calm, spacious setting ... with a great painting giving scale to the plum-coloured walls on which it hangs, and a staircase curving up into a dark hall." The director's "unusually accurate lighting" deserved "credit."[160] Elizabeth Gray's costumes provided "rich variety"[161] to a "splendid production."[162] In a meeting at the end of October, the club discussed entering *The Heiress* as their festival play, but voted not to (no reason was recorded).[163]

As the feature on Gray indicates, it was during these post-war years that Alumnae became known for their costuming acumen. They maintained a formidable wardrobe in Alison Hewitt's attic, and they drew increasing regional and national acclaim for their costumes. Talented seamstresses were attracted to Alumnae for the opportunities they offered at a time when training specifically for costume designers was rare. Members Betty Gray and Barbara McNabb took the lead on many of Alumnae's more complex costume shows. Gray and Judy Hill's costumes for Wilde's *A Woman of No Importance* in October

1954, for example, gained notice from critics, who judged them to be some of the most extravagant in Alumnae's history. Gray and Hill had needed assistance from five other members. An Alumnae history document from the time sheds light on their overall approach to costuming:

> The period of the play is approximately 1890, and there are six main feminine roles, each of the ladies requiring two costumes. The making of these was an exacting job, because period plays of this kind demand not only theatrical stylization but also the necessary chic of high society. High button boots from the attic [of Alison Hewitt] were pressed into service, and stays [fully boned bodices], to be laced tight about modern ladies not used to them, and petticoats. Bags were devised, and hats with graceful swirls of ostrich plumes. The evening gowns were magnificent, with tightly molded bodices and skirts with yards of train. Cloaks and gloves and fans were required. The dressing rooms during performance were filled to overflowing, not so much with actors as with what the actors wore. The men, also, were well taken care of (though in the case of some male garb costumes must be rented). Spats, canes, ties, shirts, waistcoats and gloves were but a few of the essentials here.[164]

Wrote Whittaker, the "production was most handsomely caparisoned, the dresses of the ladies being most splendid and a credit to Elizabeth Gray and Judy Hill who devised them."[165] On CJBC radio, Malcolm MacKinnon acknowledged this work, albeit not without some negative criticism: "[The] costumes obviously represented an immense amount of work. Individually most of them were quite handsome. Those that were not reflect, not upon the talents of their designers, but on the taste of Wilde's contemporaries. But neither did they unite to form a single picture … The Alumnae costumes, like the Alumnae players, appeared, not as a group, but singly."[166] It would be four years before Alumnae attempted another period costume piece, and another twenty-seven before they attempted another Wilde play – the same one – this time directed by Cecily Thomson, who had played Alice the maid.

In a typed but unsigned history document from 1956, written on the eve of their move to their first Coach House Theatre, Alumnae reflected on their first thirty-eight years: "All University Alumnae productions are worked on, from every angle, with great concentration, good taste, and ingenuity, and with the organization's whole heart and soul. Many observers have said it is fascinating to see this company in action when a major production is being lined up for performance." After listing several early productions and festival successes, they posited that their strength lay in their "ability to cope with the more thought-provoking side of drama – the side least probed by the majority of non-professional groups who tend, for the most part, to stress the latest Broadway or West End offerings." Alumnae cited *Star* critic Nathan Cohen as saying they were "holding high the banner of 'the playwright as thinker'" and described Herbert Whittaker as an "outstanding interpreter of the playwright as thinker" who had "joined forces with the company."[167] These programming aspects would continue to define the University Alumnae Dramatic Club for years to come.

Alumnae's success may have been possible in part because U of T had no interest in establishing a theatre training program at the time. Perhaps this allowed Alumnae to remain a key mentorship group for would-be theatre practitioners in the community, which in turn helped keep their ranks populated. It is arguable that elsewhere in the country, universities that established theatre training programs around this time were attracting students who were interested in pursuing theatre arts away from nonprofessionalizing groups.

Figure 2.2. (*left to right*) Christina Templeton (Lady Caroline Pontefract), Edith Orde Tuff (Mrs. Allonby), and Molly Golby [Thom] (Lady Stutfield) in Oscar Wilde's 1893 comedy *A Woman of No Importance*, produced by Alumnae in October 1954. Betty Gray and Barbara McNabb's lavish costumes for the play received much critical attention. Courtesy of Alumnae Theatre Company.

Alumnae's departure from University College to stand on their own, at a time when Toronto's theatre ecology was expanding rapidly, put a great deal of strain on the club. They would reap the benefits of autonomy but also suffer the consequences. One particularly detailed president's report by Eleanor Beecroft provides introspection on their work at the time. The 1954–55 season had been a difficult one, and Beecroft might have sounded alarmist had the club not just lived through it:

> Just this time last year we made the fatal error of saying, "Well, everything is set to have an easy production in the fall!" There followed loss of sketches, frantic efforts to extract our Director [Leonard Crainford] from London, England, a frenzied rehearsal programme and production set-up culminating in a *Woman of No Importance* competing with Hurricane Hazel [the closing night of Saturday, 16 October 1954].
>
> We emerged shaken, but uncowed, to dive once again into a more complicated session with *Uncle Vanya*. Your President most inconsiderately folded her hands and went into retirement for three months, leaving [first vice-president] Frances Jackson to handle the whole [CODL] Festival program, which she did admirably.[168]

Beecroft concluded: "May season 1955–56 be a successful one, and my very sincere thanks to every member of the Club for the support and loyalty I have had with me in the past year."[169]

The following June, in her last president's report, Beecroft acknowledged the work of Alumnae's committees:

> Commencing last summer, Christine Ward organized readings from the classics and has headed the reading committee. Her work has been splendid and constructive and I know just how much thought and study she has put into it, not that the Club may arrive at decisions in shorter times. Thank you so much, Christine …
>
> To Mary Smart for her many years most capably handling our frenzied finances. I stand in amazement and respect. I don't know how she's done it, but she's done it well.
>
> The loyalty and support of all the executive has been very heart warming. Cicely Thomson has been a grand Vice President and a most gracious hostess to us many times; Betty Gray as secretary has combined that thankless job most successfully with her directional duties with the CNIB; and Helen Dunlop as publicist has done remarkably fine work with the press.[170]

Beecroft's writing in these two season-end reports is remarkable for its reflective qualities, which tie together Alumnae's programming and production efforts in the early post-war era.

Chapter 3

The Coach House Years and Intellectual Modernism (1957–1972)

In April 2002, former Alumnae guest actor Blair Mascall addressed the company. In an invited speech he outlined some of his memories as the son of influential company member Elizabeth Mascall, whose guidance on the executive, on stage, and directing staged readings during the 1960s helped lead Alumnae's "Coach House" years:

> I still remember the constant hum of activity about the house throughout her term[s on the executive], as seasons were planned, meetings held, and crises faced. The Alum Ladies were a formidable group, not to be taken lightly. [Future Tarragon Theatre founder] Bill Glassco told me how terrified he was when he was asked to meet the Ladies in our house to discuss directing a production. The Alum years in our household were times of constant activity and excitement. I think my father was relieved when Mum finally stepped down, but I remember her years as being lively and exciting times for our household. I particularly remember assisting my father who acted as auctioneer at a function just before the Synagogue was closed, to sell off a lot of the stock. The Mascall family obtained one of the pews [benches] from the Synagogue, which remained part of the family home for decades.[1]

Theatre work is inevitably personal work, especially when it is unpaid, and few recognize this more than the families of those who give their time and space to it. Alumnae's Coach House years represent a shining example of skilled, nonprofessionalizing labour resulting in public creativity and acclaim.

This chapter examines Alumnae's membership and audience, as well as their administrative, programming, and production choices, between 1957 and 1972. It will show that this was the period – widely referred to by members as the "Coach House Theatre" years – during which Alumnae had their most profound impact on theatre programming in Toronto. During those years, their unique ability to cultivate new members and audiences and attract guest artists was combined with their uncanny sense for programming the "off-Bloor" and "off-College Street" plays that Toronto wanted to see. The modern, period, radical, and new plays they selected came to be their *raison d'être*. Challenging literary plays ideally suited to Alumnae's small stages came to reflect the "Coach House Program," and some of those plays would later be scaled up to fit their annual DDF entries at Hart House Theatre. At their four Coach House theatres – the first in an actual coach house, the next above a garage, then a synagogue, and finally a church – Alumnae produced world premieres by Canadians James Reaney, Wilfred Watson, Jack Richardson, and Rae Davis; the Canadian or Toronto premieres of Beckett, Pinter, Ionesco, Albee, Anouilh, Genet, Lorca, Frisch, Grass, and van Itallie; and new readings prepared by members Francess Halpenny, Molly Thom, and Anne Tait, among others. This programming alterity would inspire many of the Toronto theatre companies that followed.

Their transition away from the university, although fruitful, had not been easy. Francess Halpenny later explained that post-war Alumnae members,

> it had to be faced, were not really ticket-sellers able to contend with this competition – they preferred to give what time and energy and creativity they had to the plays themselves. They wanted also to be able to concentrate on the unusual plays which would benefit from the special contribution they felt they had to give: intelligent reading and a dedication to presenting the author's words directly and simply to the kind of audience that would be particularly interested.[2]

Without the UCAA, Alumnae were on their own. In the decade before 1957 they succeeded in addressing their post-war personnel deficiencies. Having separated from the shadow of the university after the war, they welcomed back old members and made good on their gamble that they could attract graduates from other universities.

By 1956, Alumnae's membership had increased fivefold since the end of the war, to fifty. Several of the founding daughters, now the "Old Guard," had remained very active even as a newer guard took over the club's day-to-day management. In his memoirs, Alumnae guest artist Martin Hunter describes Agatha Leonard, Christina Templeton, Margaret Tytler, and Eleanor Woodside as attending rehearsals "properly accoutered in hats and gloves and carrying purses," while "professional women" who had joined after the war, like Barbara (Allen) Barnett, Elizabeth Mascall, Elizabeth (Betty) Grey, Cicely Thompson, Pamela Terry (Beckwith), Helen Dunlop, Eileen Williams, Molly (Golby) Thom, Anne (Weldon) Tait, and Martha (Southgate) Mann took the lead onstage, backstage, and in administration. Francess Halpenny, writes Hunter, "though not always the president, was the acknowledged leader of the group."[3] New members came for the company's reputation and stayed for the rewarding work and companionship. Theatre historian Dennis W. Johnston writes that all were "tough-minded women"[4] managing a "mixture of aspiring professionals and middle-class, middle-aged theatre hobbyists in all areas of production."[5]

Alumnae's mid-century initiatives thrived in an atmosphere of female camaraderie. During the Coach House years, membership growth accelerated. By 1959, the club had more than eighty members.[6] In 1962, the year they moved into their third Coach House, the synagogue, they recorded a "bumper year" of thirty-seven new members, raising their total membership to 121. Since then it has rarely dropped below 100. As an indication of Toronto's growing theatre ecology and Alumnae's place in it, the increase included many new members moving to Toronto from out of town who wanted to be part of the city's theatre scene. Lorna F. Rogers, in the newly created position of "New Members Secretary," wrote that this increase "shows that our name and reputation has spread far beyond the borders of metropolitan Toronto. People want to act with us, they want the opportunity to work with us, whether it be onstage or backstage … Many had never had any previous experience with drama clubs, but they are willing to learn. Others had considerable acting experience." She concluded:

> If you see an unfamiliar face, talk to her. We all started out as new members once upon a time, and we all know how much we appreciated a smile and some words of welcome. Who knows, maybe the person you talk to might be your next leading lady, your producer, or costume mistress? … We're not a social club, except for cast parties and what follows this annual meeting. We're in this for the sheer love of it.

At least two thirds of the new members participated in some way in the 1963–64 season's shows "in one capacity or another."[7] This openness to attracting and retaining new members has always served Alumnae well.

Then, as now, Alumnae welcomed male assistance in producing the shows they wanted to produce. They wrote in 1961 that as a women-run company they had an "enviable record of co-operative effort without the storms and tosses almost traditional in theatrical groups. Of course, there has always been a loyal corps of husbands and friends standing by to help with carpentry and electricity and general advice. The men actors, for their part, seem to feel pleased to participate in the productions without any worries about administration."[8]

During the Coach House years, Alumnae served as a stepping stone for male theatre artists seeking to enter the profession who "[did] not have a chance to play elsewhere."[9] The company attracted emerging directors, who in turn attracted a "new group of guest actors, among them younger men who were getting their training at Hart House theatre [and who would later] try to establish professional theatre in Canada."[10] As president Molly Thom (formerly Molly Golby – she married architect Ron Thom in 1963) reported in 1963, the men "praised the organization of the Alum; they mentioned they appreciated the professional treatment that they received."[11] Alumnae's positive and often self-effacing relationship with their male artists, including theatre critic Herbert Whittaker, greatly enhanced their influence in the theatre world. Alumnae's association with theatre instructors like Robert Gill and E.G. Sterndale Bennett heightened that influence; all the while, their methodical approach to selecting plays made them a theatre company with which anyone in the city would want to work.

These years also brought mounting financial burdens for the club in terms of rents, mortgages, renovations, and production budgets. Meetings produced reams of minutes and executive reports as well as impassioned discussions that threatened to overshadow, at least in print, the recreational qualities that had characterized earlier club meetings. Nevertheless, as with many theatre companies, nonprofessionalizing or professionalized, the social aspects remained intrinsic. In September 1963, president Thom expressed her hope that "meetings would be more than mere business meetings," offering "opportunity for playreading, demonstrations of mime, *etc.*"[12] The 1967–68 season featured a return to post-meeting "playlets," echoing members' original skits of earlier years. As theatre technology advanced, general meetings sometimes included demonstrations of sound and lighting equipment organized by member Marilyn Turner.[13]

However, recreation at the spring annual meeting held at the home of a core member continued. After the meeting proper, refreshments were served and husbands and other men who had participated in the season arrived for the social portion of the afternoon and evening. Hunter described a typical annual meeting day: "In writing of the Alum I must not neglect the annual garden party, which took place each year in the spacious grounds of Cicely Thomson's house in Richmond Hill. The ladies convened in the early afternoon bearing vessels of potato salad, tomato aspic, and macaroni and cheese. They retired to the house for their annual meeting and we drones were bid to arrive at five o'clock for food and skits." Hunter listed himself along with John Beckwith, Harold Burke, Michael Polley, Rex Southgate, Michael Spence, Michael Tait, and Kenneth Wickes as Alumnae husbands or "perennial bachelors"[14] who frequently attended the parties. One annual meeting was capped off, according to the invitation, with an appearance by Robertson Davies.[15]

During these years, Alumnae's post-production parties achieved some renown among the Toronto theatre community. This led to a series of rules, including some that addressed the issue of gate crashers. In May 1963, it was reiterated that party guests could include "only cast, people who have worked on the show, members attending the theatre that night who particularly wanted to meet the cast, and invited guests." A particular concern was the cost of liquor, so a 50¢ guest fee was instituted.[16] Two years later it was decided that cast parties would be paid for from a show's production budget at 65¢ per person and that each member of the cast and crew could invite only one guest.[17] Then it was decided that an "older member of the Club should be in charge of the entertainment. This entertainment should be directed by someone specific and it should be rehearsed, changed, cut, *etc.*" Furthermore, members could bring husbands, fiancés, or steady boyfriends to the party, but not just anyone. The men invited could bring their wives, but if they were not married, they were to come alone. Halpenny suggested that a description of the annual party should be "drawn up and sent out accompanied by R.S.V.P. card to members and men affiliated with us."[18] In a very real sense, the organizing of a show's cast party became a production unto itself.

At their Coach House theatres, Alumnae served growing, educated, modern, urban theatre audiences interested in artistic developments within and beyond Canada's borders. These audiences were university students, faculty, alumni, artists, friends, and the members themselves. Members were strongly encouraged to attend Wednesday, Thursday, and Sunday performances because they traditionally had lower attendance,[19] thus making Friday and Saturday nights more available to the public. A "steady audience" from the university, recent immigrants to the city accustomed to "such 'special' theatre," and people who preferred the "new and the unusual" "gradually accepted" Alumnae's reinvention as the Coach House Theatre. They enjoyed the "intimacy of their relationship with the actors," and "soon a public began seeking out"[20] the Coach House Theatre. According to Thom, Alumnae's audiences were "academic people. We thought it was important to stay as close to the university as we could because we recognized that a lot of our audience came from the students and faculty and came from the downtown area. Also mothers and fathers, husbands and wives. In the 1950s and 1960s audiences stayed the same."[21] Martha Mann Southgate (she married actor Rex Southgate) adds: "All the continuing amateur theatres did have an audience. But there's no doubt Alumnae's audience was the most sophisticated and the most continuous. They were the devoted theatre-goers of Toronto."[22] By the spring of 1969, Alumnae could claim their Coach House Theatre shows received an average audience of 1,000 people.[23]

Coach House Programming at the Original Alternative Theatre Company

When Alumnae entered their Coach House years in 1957, there were only a handful of professional theatre companies in the city. The professionalized Jupiter Theatre had collapsed in 1954, but the fifty-year-old Royal Alexandra Theatre offered touring productions from

London and New York "as well as some entertainments of local origin." The professionalized Crest Theatre was into its third repertory season, and the Avenue Theatre offered new plays, produced mainly by the Dora Mavor Moore's professionalized New Play Society. Also, in an unusual move, the otherwise nonprofessionalizing Hart House Theatre hosted a commercial production called *Salad Days* as a side to its usual campus fare. But as Jack Karr wrote in the *Star*, the 1957–58 season looked like it would be far more "subdued." The Royal Alexandra featured a full season, and Hart House Theatre was back to focusing on campus productions, The Crest's financial woes led Karr to write that it "hopes to get the curtain up" on its season opener, while the Avenue had a "For Sale"[24] on its door. Nonprofessionalizing groups with which Alumnae compared themselves included Hart House Theatre's resident group and the Questers, led by Maurice Evans, which produced Canadian plays "almost exclusively."[25]

Alumnae began their Coach House years as one of only a few groups in the city publicizing a full season of theatre. But a programming format organized around Hart House Theatre productions was no longer the best approach for them to take because they were now losing important Theatre Night sponsorship to professional groups. Thus, they pivoted from an outdated Little Theatre programming model to a modern programming approach more attuned to recent developments in urban play-going. As past president Helen Dunlop told *Maclean's* magazine in reference to a common type of rental location, "now little theatre has left the church basement."[26] To set themselves apart, they offered programming that was "off the beaten track."[27] They argued that their "strength lies mainly in our ability to cope with the more thought-provoking side of drama – the side least probed by the majority of non-professional groups who tend, for the most part, to stress the latest Broadway or West End offerings."[28] Alumnae's "high literary standard"[29] and "informal connections" with U of T kept them in the public eye. As Johnston observes, until the rise of the 1970s alternative theatres, this programming made Alumnae the Toronto theatre that "produced the plays that theatre people wanted to see."[30]

Alumnae opened their first Coach House Theatre at 16 Huntley Street late in the 1956–57 season with Henrik Ibsen's 1896 four-act drama *John Gabriel Borkman* and Jean Anouilh's 1948 "wry and bitter comedy of love,"[31] *Ardèle*. With these two plays, as well as their next three – August Strindberg's *A Dream Play* (featuring a twenty-two-year-old Donald Sutherland as the Lawyer[32] whom the god Indra's daughter marries[33]), Samuel Beckett's *Waiting for Godot* (see chapter 6), and the world premiere of Norman Newton's *The Lion and the Unicorn* – Alumnae established their Coach House Theatre as a Toronto home for influential modern plays.

John Gabriel Borkman, directed by Christina Wade (who had directed Robertson Davies's one-act *Overlaid* for Alumnae three years earlier), did not receive much critical feedback: Rose MacDonald noted that Pamela Terry played "with conviction"[34] and Herbert Whittaker wrote that Wade set a gloomy mood too early, although "one can have only admiration for Mrs. Wade's handling of the huge play and its small cast."[35] The Canadian premiere of Anouilh's *Ardèle ou la Marguerite* (*The Cry of the Peacock*) received significantly more attention from critics, and offered a holdover performance due to audience demand.[36] Impressed by the young Gordon Johnson's recent direction of the Toronto premiere of Ionesco's *The Bald Soprano* "with a company of his fellow teachers"[37] at the Central Ontario Drama League one-act festival (Rose MacDonald called it a "crisp breeze"[38]), Alumnae retained him to direct Anouilh's *Ardèle*, with member Elizabeth Gray as producer. They used the production to raise funds to purchase a chair for the Stratford

Figure 3.1. Francess Halpenny (Ardèle) in Jean Anouilh's 1948 black comedy, *Ardèle ou la Marguerite* (produced on Broadway as *The Cry of the Peacock* in 1950). It was the play's Canadian premiere, and ran in June 1957 at their first Coach House Theatre, on Huntley Street. Courtesy of Alumnae Theatre Company.

Festival's new permanent theatre, opening a week later, by leaving a "conveniently placed bowl"[39] at the entrance to the Coach House and serving lemonade outside during intermissions. Halpenny later wrote that the "weather was kindly and the neighbours tolerant."[40]

Reviews for *Ardèle* were enthusiastic. Johnson's directing was "modest, intelligent in feeling."[41] Halpenny "shocks the house with her appearance"[42] as the General's wife, giving "her most distinguished performance to date – and she has been broadening and deepening her work markedly."[43] Elizabeth Mascall's Countess was "sensitively impatient with her life," and Molly Golby's "ingénue-no-longer"[44] was "made up beyond recognition for this unhappy creature"[45] and played "effectively." Whittaker concluded that it was, "on the whole, a fascinating and uncomfortable theatrical discourse, a must for the connoisseurs of theatre."[46] Writing in the *Sunday Telegram*, future *Star* critic Nathan Cohen concluded that the "really creditable thing is that the cast did not try to give their audiences a jolly evening, but an uncomfortable and agitating experience."[47]

Because their Coach House Theatre was a private club in a residential neighbourhood and not licensed[48] as an entertainment venue, Alumnae could not charge admission. This was technically true for all four of their Coach House Theatres (indeed, no admittance amount was even advertised until they moved into their third Coach House at the synagogue in 1962). Instead, admission was "by invitation only"[49] by phoning or writing to the appropriate member at her home (this was Pamela Terry Beckwith for the first two Coach House productions[50]). For box office income, Alumnae relied on a donation plate at the door. The system essentially prioritized Alumnae members, who were informed by early mail-out flyers, but was expanded to include the public, which could reserve tickets in advance.[51] This must have baffled at least some people who read about Toronto's newest playhouse in the dailies, although the exclusiveness of the performances was not always advertised.[52] This sometimes created confusion for box office volunteers, because the *Varsity*, for example, might report that admission was "free,"[53] but at the door the program would clarify that "one dollar per person in our bowl supports the productions of Coach House Theatre."

Having attended two plays at the new location, critics were poised to reflect on what this new programming in this new space meant to Toronto. Cohen declared Alumnae to be the "only noncommercial company in Toronto entitled to consistent critical attention."[54] Whittaker described Alumnae's "unique contribution to our theatrical life" as offering a "new play, a worthwhile revival or the presentation of a rare item of drama."[55] MacDonald wrote that with *Ardèle*, Alumnae "adds considerably to the debt owed this interesting amateur theatre group by sophisticated theatre-minded citizenry" and that over the years they had "guided attention to remarkably interesting plays. The group has not catered to the superficially popular taste."[56]

Alumnae sought to produce work that members had encountered as undergraduate students or come across on playreading committees. These were plays, they said, that "have aroused our own curiosity and that we hope will arouse yours."[57] If a play was finding critical acclaim in Europe or America for its contemporary insight before it had made its way across the Atlantic, or if it was on a university syllabus as representative of its time, it might be found at the Coach House Theatre. This included works from new Canadian and post-war European writers, "Art theatre movements," and later, radical British and American artists.[58] Alumnae described their "special contributions"[59] to the city's repertoire as founded upon "intelligent reading and a dedication to presenting the author's words directly and simply to the kind of audience that would be particularly interested."[60] Their explicit "intention" was to "present in an intimate theatre plays which would probably not be done in commercial theatre. [Our] firm belief that there is an audience for this type of theatre has not been disappointed."[61]

The playreading committee remained at the centre of Alumnae's play selection process. The ways in which it operated during the Coach House years were relatively consistent, with occasional fine-tuning. Martha Mann Southgate recalls that,

> We weren't told what to read. I was on this committee for some time. You were supposed to read plays that you thought might be of interest and then bring them to a meeting and talk about them. And if they were of general interest then everybody read them. And there was a further discussion, a serious one. [What we chose] depended on a lot of things. Who was going to direct it? Was it a play we could do physically? There wasn't much space for scenery in any of these [Coach Houses].
>
> I subscribed to two of the English theatre magazines and my mother used to give me the *New Yorker* a couple of weeks late [*laughs*]. And that was really how we found out about things. In both *Theatre Arts*, the American magazine, and *Plays and Players*, the texts were productions … You had to wait because they certainly didn't get them in the library very quickly in those days.[62]

As playreading committee chair for the 1961–62 season, Pamela Terry recommended an inclusive approach: plays under consideration would be read in whole or in part at general meetings so that the broader membership, including potential directors, could discover "material they weren't familiar with." This would also allow "new member actresses to be heard."[63]

Within a few years, members had developed a multi-pronged approach to Coach House season planning. Plays under consideration were divided into three categories: "classic or semi-classic," "Canadian," and "modern, not Canadian."[64] For each season they chose four or five "plays that an audience interested in exploring theatre would not be likely to see anywhere else in Toronto, productions deliberately kept simple and mounted on a tiny budget, attendance secured largely by means of a gradually increasing mailing list."[65] The restricted playing space and the limited seating meant that plays requiring small casts and simple sets were chosen out of necessity. Plays of the emerging modern theatre were especially suitable. Alumnae explained that "in 1957 the members decided they wished to be able to produce unusual plays of the past and present in a modest setting which would not demand the financial investment of even three nights in a large theatre, but which would on the other hand provide the experience of playing for a longer run."[66] These runs normally lasted five or six performances a week over two or three weeks and were often held over for up to two weeks more depending on audience demand. This scheduling afforded actors more performances to improve their skills in front of an audience than they would have, for example, at Hart House Theatre.[67]

In 1961, playreading committee chair Molly Golby contended that "what our audience comes to see obviously are new plays of the contemporary theatre and revivals of the classics – and in these two areas we have achieved our greatest artistic as well as financial success," in part because they were "written specifically for theatres much like our own." She continued:

> They are part of a movement extending and developing rapidly in Britain, Europe and now North America – surely the most exciting thing that has happened to the theatre in this century. These are the plays that have something to say about the world we live in and these are the plays our audience wants most to see. They ought to be done now while they are still fresh. It is our recommendation that we continue giving our audience these new plays as soon as they become available.

Conversely, she said, their "less successful" productions, both artistically and financially, were nineteenth- and early twentieth-century plays "written for stars" and for "large and well-equipped theatres." These latter plays, which included Shaw's *Major Barbara*, Chekhov's *A Country Scandal*, and O'Neill's *Mourning Becomes Electra*, Golby recommended Alumnae "abandon until we can be sure of a superlative cast and a practical and imaginative solution to their technical problems," concluding they "are not for us in this crucial point in our development."[68] Alumnae would choose to produce only the first two of these plays over the following five years.

Alumnae in its early Coach House years featured locally untested modern European works in the city's smallest theatre space.[69] This approach echoed the early naturalist experiments at European theatres like André Antoine's Théâtre Libre seventy years earlier (see chapter 5). But it was more often compared with New York's contemporary alternative theatre scene. With a nod to their three-block proximity to Toronto's Bloor/Yonge commercial district and referring to themselves as the "Coach House Theatre," they became known as Toronto's "first intimate theatre"[70] and "first off-Broadway"[71] or "off-College Street"[72] theatre. Within a decade they were praised as "one of the pioneers in the development of off-Bloor theatre."[73] They honed their public discourse with the notion of "Coach House programming," writing confidently that "members have one aim – to make a permanent home for Canadian experimental and classical theatre in Canada comparable to the Royal Court in London and the off-Broadway theatres in New York."[74] By the end of 1961, Alumnae's renown had found its way to the cruise ship publication *Ocean Times*, which proclaimed: "How that group of college girls maintained a dramatic society for 43 years, developing it through various phases until it became the first of Toronto's off-Broadway groups, is a story that commands admiration and respect."[75]

Alumnae's programming alterity quickly established a trend. It was during these years that they made plays by Beckett, Ionesco, Pinter, and their now-canonical contemporaries the "rage"[76] in Toronto, at which point other companies began mimicking their programming to capitalize on the popularity Alumnae had sown. In 1957, the Coach House program even inspired Toronto's professional Crest Theatre to briefly pivot its "Crest Theatre Club" towards producing non-commercial theatre like Alumnae.[77] Within a few years, wrote Lorna F. Rogers in her publicity report, nonprofessionalizing theatre groups were "springing up in Toronto like mushrooms, and they are putting on the type of program that once was solely our field – i.e. avant-garde, experimental type theatre and new Canadian plays. We cannot hope to maintain the space we once held in the papers merely by past reputation and our seniority. As a result, we are forced to be highly competitive."[78]

This sense of competition within Toronto's theatre ecology, which had only surfaced periodically in a given week or two in previous years, increasingly became the norm. In the first decade of Coach House programming, it manifested itself in terms of audience numbers as well as in struggles to obtain the rights to the kinds of plays Alumnae was already introducing to the city.[79] This competition would only deepen in the coming decades.

As with any theatre ecology, particularly an emerging one, critics are essential to articulating a theatre company's value to the public beyond self-promoted press releases. Within a few years of the Coach House program unfolding, *Maclean's* referred to Alumnae as the "best amateur theatre company in English-speaking Canada."[80] Whittaker wrote that Alumnae "recognized the nation's need and sought new writers" and that the plays they chose "were not all immediately popular but they were all immediately important."[81] Cohen praised them as a "model in every respect of what an amateur theatre organization should be. The members love the theatre devotedly and unselfishly. They are pace-setters for the entire Toronto theatrical community, with high standards of play choice and production and a purposeful artistic aim."[82] He went on to say that Alumnae's

> aim is to do plays – current, Canadian, and classical – because of their intrinsic merit, or because they have been neglected, or because they express the shifting winds of theatrical expression, or because their authors have something to say which they think deserves to be heard. The plays are not done to cash in on a prevailing fashion, or to beg comparison with professionals, or to win prizes in the Dominion Drama Festival, or simply to show off. In a very real sense, I would say, they are the best promoters we have of the larger idea of theatre.[83]

A year later, Cohen added: "In choice of plays and standard-raising, the UADC continues to set the pace for local theatre in Toronto."[84] Critics' recognition, Alumnae acknowledged, provided a "source of great encouragement to the Club where its high caliber presentations have been seen by large and responsive audiences"[85] and "allowed the choice of more unusual and more stimulating plays for director, actors, costume designers, and stage crew."[86]

Absurd Programming for a Modern City

As Molly Thom put it years later, the "post-war European theatre was producing some extremely puzzling fare – and we became curious about how playwrights like Samuel Beckett and Eugene Ionesco actually worked, were they stage worthy?"[87] Key to appreciating Alumnae's impact during their Coach House years is understanding their commitment to producing the modern plays that critic Martin Esslin in 1962 termed "theatre of the absurd." Beginning with Beckett's *Waiting for Godot* in November 1957 (see chapter 6), Alumnae produced thirteen theatre of the absurd plays at their Coach House theatres, eight of which were Toronto premieres and one of which was a world premiere (Robert Shirley's *Pi*). Of course, most of the sixty-eight modern plays produced at the Coach House theatres are not characterized as theatre of the absurd; several of these are discussed in Part II.

In the spring of 1959 at their second Coach House Theatre on Bedford Road, Alumnae presented two "gloriously absurd spoofs"[88] of "poetic expressionism"[89] by the "most controversial of modern European playwrights," Eugene Ionesco: the 1950 play *The Bald Soprano* and the 1951 play *The Lesson*. The Romanian writer was the "rage of Paris with his unusual dramas concerning the inability of people to communicate,"[90] and MacDonald warned that his plays were "not the sort of thing the literal-minded should be encouraged to attend."[91] The director for both was Gordon Johnson, who had introduced the city to Ionesco's plays some years earlier. Ionesco's plays were now the rage elsewhere in Canada as well: *Victimes du Devoir* appeared at the DDF finals later that May in a production by Québec's L'Atelier du Proscenium, and the York Community Theatre produced *The Bald Soprano* and *The Lesson* in Toronto later that May along with *Jack, or the Submission* and what was billed as the Canadian premiere of *The Chairs*.[92]

Whittaker considered Alumnae's evening an "intelligent, worthy introduction"[93] to Ionesco's work. MacDonald wrote that as a director, Johnson had a "light, firm touch affiliated with the Gallic temperament, also a predisposition to experimental theatre."[94] He showed "comprehension and resources" as a director of Ionesco's plays. Of the two, Whittaker preferred *The Lesson* as it had "more impact and a higher level of performance."[95] In it, Joanna Richardson's young girl showed "sympathy and simplicity"[96] and was "flower-like but tenacious and clever as the pupil," while Halpenny was "dark, powerful and earthy as the peasant woman." In a "virtuoso performance which combines high intelligence, emotion and extraordinary skill,"[97] Powell Jones "carried this macabre little effort almost single-handed and made it seem almost believable,"[98] and while he "sometimes forgot, too, that he was playing an older man,"[99] he acted "with brie and power."[100] David Peddie reported that *The Bald Soprano* "drew gales of laughter from the Coach House audience, as nonsequitor succeeded nonsense,"[101] and Whittaker felt that the cast "may lack the resources to go the whole way, but their effort was gallant and always amusing."[102] Whittaker put his finger on much of the confusion that local reviewers were finding with this production, comparing a play-goer coming upon an Ionesco play with someone "running into a cubist Picasso at the hobby show in the Country Fair."[103] Said Peddie, "by the time I had gone out for an intermission smoke, I couldn't help feeling – so what!"[104] In his memoirs, Martin Hunter credited Alumnae's *Waiting for Godot* and *The Lesson* as

Figure 3.2. Muriel Cuttell (Mrs. Smith) and Abe Roytenberg (Mr. Smith) in Alumnae's April 1959 production of Eugene Ionesco's 1951 play, *The Bald Soprano*, directed by Gordon Johnson, who was making a name for himself directing Theatre of the Absurd plays in Toronto. Courtesy of Alumnae Theatre Company.

introducing the theatre of the absurd to Toronto, establishing the club as a "serious player in Canadian theatre" and "lighting the way for the alternate theatres"[105] a decade later.

Seven months later, in December 1959, at the Bedford Road Coach House theatre, Herbert Whittaker directed and designed the second Toronto production[106] of Beckett's one-act play *Endgame* for Alumnae. That was less than three years after Beckett's original French version premiered at the Royal Court Theatre in London. In the *Varsity*, undergraduate student Warren Wilson, who had directed the Toronto premiere, explained: "One can say that the four characters are the last survivors of an atomic blast (and thus conveniently explain Hamm's blindness, his pathetic craving for pain-killer, and Nagg and Nell's ashbin residence), but one is immediately suspicious of perhaps oversimplifying the play's meaning. And on it goes."[107] Readers surely guessed that the upstart Wilson was trying to out-direct Whittaker with volleys of negative minutia that lasted half the review. He took this opportunity to question Whittaker's interpretation of Beckett, saying that Whittaker, like Beckett, is a "master of misdirection. He and his actors have ridden roughshod over the play, and the result is the longest hour and three quarters in theatrical history."[108] For Kenneth Johnson writing in the *Globe and Mail*, the production was "not to be recommended as light entertainment but as thought-provoking theatre it's well worth two hours."[109] The run was successful enough that it was held over two extra days and

Figure 3.3. Kenneth Wickes (Nagg) and Jacqueline White (Nell) in Alumnae's December 1959 production of Samuel Beckett's *Endgame*, directed and designed by *Globe and Mail* theatre critic Herbert Whittaker. Courtesy of Alumnae Theatre Company.

Alumnae had to turn people away at the door.[110] Production photographs reveal a stage design by Whittaker that convincingly serves the text with elegance and, according to Antony Ferry in the *Star*, "did the play more than generous justice."[111]

Reminiscent of the effects of Alumnae's *Waiting for Godot* two years earlier, *Endgame* generated public conversation. But this time it was not so much about what the play could mean, but rather whether there was value in a play that seemed so little concerned with conveying meaning at all. In the *Star*, Antony Ferry led his review by saying that *Endgame* was "on uneasy view at the Coach House theatre" and that Beckett was "modern drama's leading dispenser of gloom. Our pigmy society, having lost its right to appreciate true tragedy, has substituted despondency instead and made it, and Mr. Beckett, fashionable."[112] In response, and noting that Whittaker was in no position to give his own direction a "loud hurrah," a letter to the editor in the *Globe and Mail* argued from the position of a recent immigrant from England. Citing excellent experimental arts in Toronto that had surpassed her expectations, she wrote that the "quality of this current *Endgame* is one which critics in Europe as well as on this continent would like to achieve."[113] Oddly, the paper printed a response to this letter from Ferry in which he furthered his argument that Beckett, and indeed the Western world, was dispensing gloom in its poetry to an uneasy extent: "We are facing, with increasing malaise, a decade at the end of which Mr. Khrushchev has promised to see us buried. Our choice is clear cut. Either we find some positive and justifiable reason for continuing to exist, or we wallow in our society's unfortunate loss of dynamic and go under."[114] His point seemed to be that people needed the theatre to show them how to live and that Beckett's plays did not do this: "A theatre which does not serve this function in part, of helping people to understand life, is – in the 1960s – a theatre of self-indulgent decadence. Art is worthless unless it is useful."[115] This utilitarian view, with its long history of debate, seemed to drive the temporary critic, who clearly did not see what Beckett's work productively added to a post-war Western world that was grappling to find meaning in perennial threats and lives lost. It would take Esslin's seminal book three years later to interpret that which Ferry would, or could, not. Uriel Luft, who played Hamm, also contributed to the discussion, telling Lotta Dempsey in an interview in the *Star* that "all that has transpired of late – consciousness of the bomb and its power for destruction – has given us a sensitivity to the moment as we live it. *Endgame* has to do with some of the last of such moments."[116] The show received the most sustained negative criticism of any Alumnae production during their Coach House years from two reviewers, Wilson and Ferry, and became a locus for debate on the purpose and meaning of Beckett, the quality of Alumnae's production, and the work of the artist-critics Whittaker and Wilson.[117]

The 1961–62 Toronto theatre season exemplifies how Alumnae's experimental modern programming quickly became *de rigeuer* among professional theatre companies in the city. Two years after *Endgame* and the Ionesco one-acts, and concurrent with Alumnae's "An Evening of Moderns" readings in November 1961, the Crest Theatre presented a double bill of Beckett's *Krapps's Last Tape* and Albee's *The Zoo Story*, featuring past Alumnae guest artist William Needles and future *Beachcombers* star Bruno Gerussi, for whom the play was reportedly a "fine vehicle."[118] That same season, Jean Cocteau's *Intimate Relations* ran two weeks later at the Actors Theatre on Grenville Street,[119] Ionesco's *Rhinoceros* opened the Civic Square Theatre's first season that week,[120] and Michel de Ghelderode's *Pantagleize* ran at Hart House Theatre in February.[121] The influx gave *Varsity* reviewers the opportunity to write about these new modern works from an informed perspective influenced by a few years of Coach House programming and the recent writings of Martin Esslin.[122] Wrote campus modern theatre aficionado Warren Wilson, these playwrights "wish to restore theatricalism to the theatre, and have used as their mode not the Classical Greek Theatre, but the morality plays of the Middle Ages."[123] In the same issue, Peter Halsall and William Mitchell reviewed Ionesco's *Amedée, or How to Get Rid of It* at the Village Theatre, asking, "But what does it mean?"[124] The theatre of the absurd craze had hit Toronto, and Alumnae were its leading interpreters.

In February and March 1964, Alumnae, with whom "Toronto's best male actors count it an honour to play,"[125] produced the Toronto premiere of Harold Pinter's 1960 "horrifying and gripping and sometimes wildly comic piece"[126] *The Caretaker* at the synagogue Coach House Theatre, directed and designed by Herbert Whittaker. Alumnae had by then helped make Pinter a known commodity in Toronto theatre by presenting the city's first full production of a Pinter play, *The Room*, a year earlier;[127] it received critical praise for Whittaker's direction and the cast's performances. The film version ran in Toronto later that year.[128] The flyer for the show noted astutely of Pinter:

> It is possible to say that he has already won himself an important place among the playwrights of this century. His mastery of language, which has opened up a new dimension of English stage dialogue; the accuracy of his observation; the depth of his emotion; and above all, his ability to

Figure 3.4. (*left to right*) Don Ward (Aston), Donald Ewer (Davies), and Michael Barton [Polley] (Mick) in Alumnae's Toronto premiere of Harold Pinter's *The Caretaker*, directed and designed by Herbert Whittaker. The play's title is written on a scrim under Pinter's name. Courtesy of Alumnae Theatre Company.

> turn commonplace people and events into a profoundly poetical vision of universal validity justifies the very highest hopes for his future.

Alumnae's focus on intellectual discourse in their programming is particularly noticeable and prophetic here, where Pinter's language and "poetical vision" is foregrounded. Whittaker completely reconfigured the synagogue Coach House auditorium for the play. He moved the stage from the south end to the north end under the balcony, "capitalizing on the tin ceiling and the adjoining stairway to suggest a basement flat."[129] Explained the press release, this provided a proscenium presentation that "felt more suitable for the play than the open, apron stage employed in previous productions." It also allowed for a larger audience. Martha Mann Southgate and Margaret Spence created a "pop art" gauze curtain "with symbols of the play appliquéd on it" to mask the proscenium opening. In the *Star*, Arnold Rockman approved of the approach, writing that Whittaker's direction "ingeniously makes full use of the limited resources of the Coach House theatre."[130]

Alumnae advertised *The Caretaker* as boasting "one of the strongest casts in years." Broadway actor, Wayne and Schuster collaborator, and Actors' Equity member Donald

Ewer had just toured the play in the United States, playing Davies; Michael Barton (Polley), as Mick, had been in the Birmingham Repertory Company with Albert Finney and the popular television series *The Avengers* before moving to Canada two years earlier;[131] and Don Ward, as Aston, had just played in Alumnae's *Count Oederland* and the Village Playhouse's production of Arden's *Live Like Pigs*.[132] In the *Globe and Mail*, Ralph Hicklin called the three actors "as fine an ensemble as I've encountered in an Alumnae production."[133] Tony Advokaat wrote in the *Varsity* that the "acting throughout is sure and controlled, but really outstanding was Ward's soliloquy at the end of the second act."[134] Hicklin concluded that "whatever else it may be, *The Caretaker* is a powerful piece of offbeat theatre. What happens on the junk-cluttered stage of the Coach House is worthy of attention."[135] Advokaat went further than this: "All the productions at the Coach House in the past year have been of very high quality. *The Caretaker* is no exception and is well worth a visit."[136] A handwritten note on the back of a production photograph in Alumnae's collection echoes a comment made by Rose MacDonald in her column: Sir John Gielgud attended *The Caretaker* to see Ewer's performance.[137] It was Alumnae's most costly production that season, as well as their most profitable.[138] Uniquely, the production transferred to the Central Library Theatre the following November,[139] although with Ewer, not Alumnae, as producer.

A year later, with a clear mandate and a space of their own, Alumnae were taking production quality more seriously than ever before. Annual meeting minutes reported in June 1965 that outgoing president Molly Thom expressed

> concern about the artistic level of the productions of the past year; in only one case had the director used the stage simply but effectively, gaining his effects through good costumes and authentic props. In other cases directors had fallen into the old difficulty of creating a set that warred with the fixed stage and the existing facilities. Molly wondered what might be the cause of what was, in her opinion, an artistic decline. Could it be poor directors, over-ambition, too many shows in a season? She asked members to give the problem some thought.

It was the first time on record that an executive member had taken aim at the quality of the company's efforts. But it certainly fell in line with the general disappointment of the "big three critics" who attended "one opening only [while] *CJBC Reviews the Shows* 'hated us twice.'" Thom's recommendations were to continue the subscription series, "strive to simplify our stage sets," "continue to increase the power of the stage manager," and "attempt to vary our season with experimental efforts such as lectures, panels, demonstrations and the like."[140]

Importantly, the Coach House theatres provided a space where Alumnae could "keep backstage activities in-house at last."[141] With the goal of stabilizing production conditions, in 1965 Helen Dunlop recommended adding the positions of business manager and production manager to relieve the workloads long placed on the president and the treasurer.[142] The executive drew up brief descriptions of key duties wherein the business manager would be in charge of monitoring expenditures for each show, while the production manager would be in charge of making sure everyone understood their role and that "standards are maintained." There was some concern over the "recruiting of 'good men,'" and the executive noted that "we should eliminate those found to be difficult. A very strong S.M. is important."[143] Wardrobe mistress Martha Mann Southgate issued an edict to the membership mailing list "regarding wardrobe": "We cannot any longer afford to lend costumes; I am sorry, but this is a simple matter of economics. On the other hand, the rental scale is very low. Please do not take anything out!! We have had several unfortunate disappearances from the wardrobe lately. If any of you have Alumnae costumes at home would you please return them at once. Many thanks for your cooperation!"

Two years later, president Elizabeth Mascall reported that the general level of productions this past season was "better than the last."[144] The responsibilities inherent in building management had heightened the importance of managing volunteer labour. Disciplinary rules were laid out to ensure that the club produced the quality of shows expected of them. Rules for set and prop acquisition followed in 1970.[145]

Unfortunately, Alumnae's North American premiere of Jean-Paul Sartre's 1959 "relentless study of guilt and love in postwar Germany," *The Condemned of Altona*, in October 1965, would be remembered as one of the most tragic moments in the club's history. Don Ward, an advertising executive by day who had appeared in a number of Alumnae plays, died just a week before opening night while rehearsing the role of the Father. He was only forty-two. This led to the cancellation of the first two performances on Friday and Saturday evenings. The *Globe and Mail* reported that Ward "collapsed at rehearsal and died before arrival at hospital. He had had a heart attack while rehearsing."[146] In their announcement, Alumnae mourned that his death "has deprived all of us who knew him of his sensitive and gifted talents as an actor and of the warmth and generosity of his spirit as a friend … Don brought to his life, to his work in advertising and the theatre qualities of reliability, thoughtfulness and intuition which will long be remembered as cherished." Alumnae donated the opening night's proceeds to the Ontario Heart Fund in his memory. The director, Adam Ludwig, took over Ward's lead role. Ward had been scheduled to reprise his role in *The Caretaker* in Hamilton that season and to participate in more Alumnae plays. Whittaker wrote that "in his death, the University Alumnae Dramatic Club, which has had some of the leading Canadian actors playing with it as guest artists, lost one of its very best performers. Mr. Ward was of the generation which could not devote his full life to the theatre but his service to it was no spare-time hobby." Whittaker continued by linking Ward's death with Alumnae's purpose:

> When Sir John Gielgud complimented the Toronto actor on his achievement he was recognizing what many of us had, that only a person of rare gifts can play so beautifully, so completely. Don Ward was such a rare actor.
>
> Such a solemn occasion was not out of place at the Coach House, the former synagogue which sometimes seems to stand alone as a temple of serious drama in this town. The Sartre play was being given its first performance here, as so many other plays of significance are given their first showings at the Coach House.[147]

By tying the space to the occasion, Whittaker astutely made Ward's death stand as a symbol of Alumnae's thoughtful work. In practical terms, the misfortune compelled Alumnae's executive to consider the "possibility of having an understudy for each show," someone with a "bit part, a prompter, or the director,"[148] although this did not become commonplace.

Reading Plays to the City

The Coach House Theatre programming included thirty-five plays read publicly (at least fourteen of which had yet to be produced or read publicly in Toronto), as well as several member-only readings at club general meetings. Readings introduced at Alumnae's general meetings in 1967 built member interest in what would become a public Sunday evening reading series. Public readings – essentially an extension of Alumnae's private readings during the war – gave both new and older members the opportunity to take on central characters or to try their hand at directing. They were some of the first staged play readings in the city. When the plays were new, as process-oriented activities the readings prefigured the dramaturgical work that professional theatres later adopted as a means to receive feedback on new plays in development before committing to full productions (see chapter 7).

The idea of regular public Coach House Theatre readings dates back to Canada's centennial year; however, Alumnae's first public readings were held seven years earlier as a temporary solution for an overtaxed membership. In June 1961, Alumnae intended to open the next season with the world premiere of a play called *The Cupboard Orgy* by Donald Jack. Jack's play *The Canvas Barricade* had recently won a Stratford Playwriting Competition and was to be produced there that summer. Alumnae hoped to take advantage of Jack's popularity, but they were too occupied with finding their next Coach House and did not want "to dissipate our energies by attempting full-scale productions in rented quarters. It is demoralizing for the players and the audience."[149] Thus, in the fall of 1961, instead of a fall production, Alumnae offered a series of three one-night performances of one-act play readings titled "Seven Moderns: Three Evenings of Informal Platform Productions."

Molly Golby and her playreading committee wanted Alumnae to be the first to introduce Pinter to Toronto. This took some delicate negotiations with Pinter's agent, who apparently did not easily trust amateur theatres. He informed Golby that Pinter would visit Toronto and meet Alumnae himself between his trip to New York City to attend the Broadway premiere of *The Caretaker* and Alumnae's first planned reading date. Over the course of half a dozen letters, Golby assured the agent that their "fully amateur organization"[150] planned only readings and not fully staged productions.[151] He was suspicious at first but ultimately consented. Pinter himself did not make it after all, but Alumnae did introduce his work to Toronto with public readings of *The Applicant*, *The Black and White*, and *Last to Go*, along with plays by Beckett, Genet, N.F. Simpson, John Mortimer, and de Ghelderode.

All three evenings were presented at Trinity College's Convocation Hall, formerly its chapel, on Hoskin Avenue on the university campus, which had a seating capacity of 100.[152] The series' flyer was designed by Allan Fleming of the famed graphic design company Cooper and Beatty[153] (Fleming had designed the iconic "CN" logo for Canadian National Railway in 1960). Citing Beckett and Ionesco, the flyer declared:

> We know from past experience that there is one type of play in particular that you have always liked to see us do … Many of you became part of our regular audience [for which] you shared our enthusiasm for an important new voice in the theatre … Now, we have selected from this vigourous contemporary theatre a program of short plays by some of its most talented and talked-about writers. These plays do not depend on elaborate production for their impact, and we have been able to take advantage of this to devise a rather unusual production style.

For the first evening, only two actors were "dressed to character,"[154] as most of Alumnae's costumes and props were in storage. Lorna F. Rogers reported that publicity for the reading series, including the Fleming-designed flyer, gave the production a "fair amount of space in the papers and attracted good audiences."[155]

It is no longer common for public readings to be reviewed, but in the early 1960s coffee house poetry events were *en vogue*. Critical responses seemed to depend entirely on

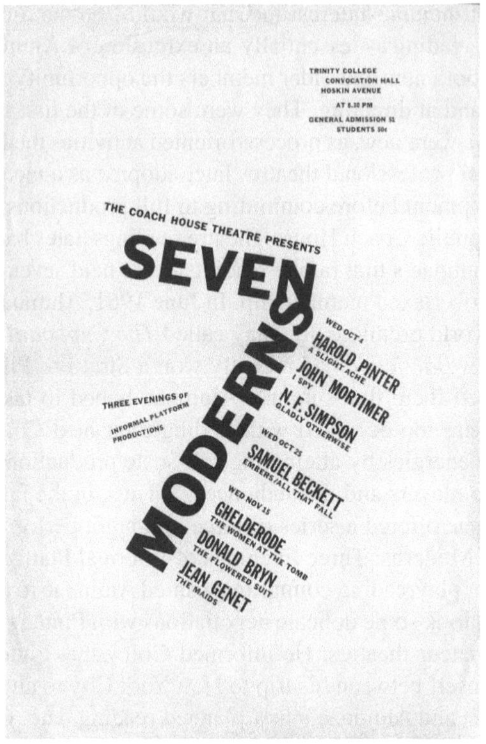

Figure 3.5. Alumnae promoted their "Seven Moderns" series with a flyer designed by Allan Fleming. Notably, Fleming, who was a typographic director for the Toronto typesetting firm Cooper and Beatty, also designed the iconic logo for Canadian National Railway in 1960. Courtesy of Alumnae Theatre Company, with permission of Martha Fleming.

who was reviewing and the extent to which the reviewer was keen to absorb the latest experimental modernism. Included among these critical voices were articulate undergraduate students in the new *Varsity Weekend Review* section, which gave space for multiple and lengthy reviews of theatre productions. Some of these student reviewers had already dug in on one side or the other of the modern theatre debate. Tony Robinow said Molly Golby introduced readings of works that "typify a new and exciting movement in British theatre"[156] initiated and influenced by Samuel Beckett and John Osborne. In the *Telegram*, MacDonald explained that the theme of the plays was "The Common Man" and that "each little piece was a gem of its genre, exquisitely satirical, often very funny." Pinter's sketches were "deftly played."[157]

Importantly, the readings gave several older Alumnae members the chance to publicly take on characters (script in hand) again. However, Robinow and MacDonald faulted several of the actors for their poor enunciation and low volume as they read their lines from books. He wrote that Agatha Leonard and Christina Templeton "managed, while remaining almost totally unintelligible, to establish distinct and extremely engaging characters." Pinter "was not fairly represented on Wednesday because of copyright difficulties"; even so, he enjoyed the "gloriously idiotic insouciance" of Tilda Stevens's Mrs. Brandywine;

her audibility, coming as it did after the Pinter sketches, he found "curiously reassuring." He concluded that the Alumnae women "have great enthusiasm for these modern plays and are enjoying their work very much. This sort of thing is catching, and one looks forward to the remaining two evenings in the series."[158]

Setting aside his stated general reservations about staged readings, David C. Humphreys in the *Varsity* three weeks later applauded Alumnae for choosing three plays for their second evening of readings that were "ideally suited to this medium."[159] Halpenny introduced them to a "capacity crowd."[160] In Beckett's *All That Fall*, Margaret Tytler as Mrs. Rooney "presented a dynamic performance within the limited means she had to work with." Her "good facial expressions transformed a mere script-reading into an interesting demonstration of exaggerated suffering."[161] Humphreys concluded that "one hopes that a change will come, that we will be delivered from a drama that derives its 'tragic' sense at the expense of man instead of his elevation … After Wednesday night, it is a cheering thought to reflect that when this change comes, as it surely must, a company of the calibre of the Coach House will have the resources to do the works justice."[162]

The less well-received final evening, introduced by Golby, "convincingly demonstrated the inefficacy of play readings," according to Jack Winter in the *Star*. The "apparent lack of rehearsal, perfunctory direction and inexperienced actors also contributed to the evening." Alison Cunningham's "voice – uncertainly pitched, breathy, uncontrolled and shrill – particularly suffered under the unnatural limitations of the reading. Both suffered equally from director Martin Hunter's inability to modulate their efforts."[163] Wrote Whittaker of the juxtaposition of the irreverent plays to the former chapel, the actors "try to summon the evil spirit of Jean Genet into this atmosphere. It is to Genet's credit (so little else is) that he braved the chapel atmosphere, the pure tones of the readers, the absence of stage action."[164] *The Maids* lasted 105 minutes as a reading and was thus "less suited"[165] to Alumnae's "'untrammelled' style of production."[166] Overall, Alumnae were pleased with the readings, noting that they and the university were still "steady and loyal friends."[167] The series had not been well attended due, they surmised, to "Toronto's active spring calendar."[168] And they might have reconsidered reading *The Maids* in its entirety.

Five years later, at a September 1966 general meeting at the synagogue Coach House, Molly Thom introduced a "dry run of a Sunday evening entertainment" that would eventually become an Alumnae tradition. It was the first of several prepared readings given that year that followed general meetings, this one of nine-year-old Daisy Ashford's famed 1890 novel *The Young Visiters*, "patterned after Victorian novels."[169] These post-meeting readings offered a "shop window" look at plays under consideration for a larger production; they might "lead to more creative work and more original [work],"[170] besides helping to develop and build a "stock of directors," given that more theatre companies were paying them.[171] Subsequent readings included Henry James's 1878 short story turned 1884 "unperformed"[172] full-length play *Daisy Miller* (November 1966), Jacobean plays by Webster and Beaumont and Fletcher, and writings by Samuel Johnson (January 1967). It was reported in June 1967 that membership support for the readings had been "disappointing, but the audience reaction had been so good it is planned to repeat it in the fall and have two other sets of readings."[173] Another general meeting reading was Ann Jellicoe's documentary drama *Shelley, or The Idealist* (April 1968), which they were considering for production. Also, member Phyllis Benvenuto produced an evening intended to contrast the Schiller and Maxwell Anderson treatments of Mary Stewart, Queen of the Scots (March 1969).

Having committed themselves to inviting the public to Sunday evening readings, for 1969–70 Alumnae offered a "subscription series" that included four readings at their new fifty-seat[174] Coach House Theatre on Maplewood Avenue. Although most of these readings were of new plays, they concluded their season with a reading of Jellicoe's *Shelley, or The Idealist: A Tragicomedy*, directed by Cicely Thomson over three Sundays in April 1970. Rehearsals were at a member's home on Lynwood Avenue and then at the Maplewood Avenue Coach House Theatre.[175]

On three Sundays in February 1972, Alumnae added political activism to their reading series. They presented dramatic readings, cut "quite ruthlessly" by director Diane Polley, of Daniel Berrigan's controversial 1971 "Off-Broadway Play of the Year," the "exceptional spiritual testament"[176] *The Trial of the Catonsville Nine*. Jesuit priest and activist Daniel Berrigan had crafted the play from transcripts of his own trial. The largely verbatim script (except for the narration) is a civil disobedience play about nine Catholics, including Berrigan, who were found guilty of burning 378 draft records with napalm at a Maryland government office on 17 May 1968. As the program noted, Daniel's brother Philip and six others went on trial in January 1972, just two weeks before Alumnae's dramatic reading, "charged with plotting to blow up government buildings" and kidnapping Henry Kissinger. That same month, Daniel was paroled due to ill health. Both brothers were nominated for the 1972 Nobel Peace Prize. This was the sort of radical political content that Alumnae were beginning to offer Toronto audiences.

In his review of the reading, newly appointed *Star* critic Urjo Kareda wrote that "for all the uneasiness of the actual production, the drama of the Berrigans is one to be seen, shared and committed to memory … *The Trial of the Catonsville Nine* is quite heart-stoppingly moving,"[177] a script so significant that "one simply cannot imagine it failing." But Kareda called Polley's production an "oddity" because she had chosen to stage it with stage lighting and actors moving around in costumes, although they "still cling, though not always, to their scripts." This "strangely inconsistent approach" resulted in the actors giving a "flat, almost colourless tone to their delivery," almost "tentative"; even so, he continued, this was "surprisingly useful, as it allows the words to become even more moving in their simplicity." Kareda also questioned whether so much should have been cut from the script, as "we could have used so much more of the evidence." And he wondered why Polley wove in "snatches of folk-songs and quotes from John Donne," which "works against the play's simplicity."[178] Kareda's review points to the fact that public readings, while a seemingly simple concept meant to foreground the text for an inquisitive audience, can easily be tipped towards performance by an enthusiastic director.

Back to Period Fare

Modern drama was the cornerstone of Alumnae's Coach House programming. But after opening their Huntley Street theatre, they also became known for offering period plays. During their fifteen years running the Coach House program, Alumnae produced eight period pieces (six comedies and two tragedies). These were memorable because of their lavish costumes drawn from Alumnae's enviable wardrobe and their informed attention to the language, and also because so few period pieces were being offered in Toronto at a time when highly lauded repertory productions were being staged by the Stratford Festival 150 kilometres to the west.

Figure 3.6. *A Scrap of Paper* production photograph. Members of the cast of Victorien Sardou's 1860 well-made comedy of intrigue, produced by Alumnae in June 1958. The production featured Martha Mann's set design, her first for Alumnae. Courtesy of Alumnae Theatre Company.

Alumnae's first Coach House period production was also their first show at the "experimental"[179] Bedford Road location in June 1958, at the tail end of their first full Coach House season: a play rarely seen outside of France at the time,[180] Victorien Sardou's 1860 comedy of intrigue, *A Scrap of Paper*, directed by theatre of the absurd aficionado Gordon Johnson. The impact of six months of *Waiting for Godot* performances by Alumnae had been great. A Central Ontario Drama League newsletter piece titled "The ladies no longer wear pants" declared that the Sardou play was "strictly for fun … lots of plot, no message, no controversy, just good entertainment."[181] It was the first Alumnae production designed by Martha Mann, an Ontario College of Art student who was "mad about theatre" and who "arrived to design sets and costumes, show after show."[182] As Whittaker put it in reference to the play's exposition: "An affectionate audience bore with the silliness of the play's plottings, then slowly became involved in that old, creaking Sardou magic … The audience started off thinking what a silly fellow this Frenchman was, to think that we could be amused by this, and wound up laughing delightedly as the plot took more and more farcical turns." Johnson's "makeshift" production with "simple" wardrobe and scenery avoided "burlesque" by keeping "credibility throughout." Leith Macdonald "sparkles brightly as the adventurous Suzanne" across from "gleeful adversary" Douglas Ney and Kenneth Wickes, "who delights as an avid butterfly-hunter." Whittaker concluded that "Alumnae offers an amusing studio evening to its invited guests and a chance to see what a now-unreadable

Figure 3.7. (*left*) Carole Purvis (Dorina) and (*right*) Judith Teague (Mrs. Sullen) in George Farquhar's Restoration comedy *The Beaux' Stratagem*, produced by Alumnae in October 1958. Courtesy of Alumnae Theatre Company.

play is like in action."[183] More than anything, *A Scrap of Paper* made clear that Alumnae would not be limiting their output to modern plays. They would also offer period pieces, like Sardou's melodrama, when no one else would.

The first of two busy Bedford Road seasons (of eight and five productions respectively) followed, starting in October 1958 with a "skillfully edited, certainly not emasculated"[184] production of George Farquhar's "saucy little"[185] 1707 Restoration comedy *The Beaux' Stratagem*, directed by Molly Golby, with two ten-minute intermissions. Golby and Mann designed the set, and Mann designed the lavish costumes. Reviews for the play were generally positive, if qualified. As *The Beaux' Stratagem*'s director, Golby achieved "speed" and "lightness," although the cramped loft space meant that "movement was restricted in a play that demands room for hijinks, flowing skirts and broad movement."[186] Judith Teague as Mrs. Sullen "snapped and simpered with great authority"[187] and was "delightfully vivacious, so does a great deal to keep the comedy buoyant,"[188] while Pamela Terry as Cherry was "pert and fetching"[189] and "reasonably virtuous" with "delightfully exuberant spirit."[190] For *Varsity* reviewer Marielaine Douglas, Powell Jones as Foigard was the "star of this production," who "glided [a]cross the stage with perfect control of movement."[191] Arthur Brydon in the *Globe and Mail* wrote that it was a "ponderous and somewhat talky production with a tedious exposition. But beneath the many words is some genuine humour which the occupants of the Coach House uncover with considerable

Figure 3.8. Robert Peace (Chrysale) and Eleanor Beecroft (Philaminte) in Molière's *Les Femmes Savantes*, directed in English by Leith MacDonald for Alumnae at the Art Gallery of Toronto (now the Art Gallery of Ontario) on 6 December 1961. The production's flyer read, "Molière's terse comedy on the dangers of a little learning." The Stratford Shakespeare Festival loaned the costumes and furniture to Alumnae for the one-evening performance. Courtesy of Alumnae Theatre Company.

facility."[192] For Rose MacDonald, it was "not the best the Alumnae has put on of recent seasons, but it's fun."[193]

In December 1961, nearly forty-four years after their inaugural performance, Toronto's learned ladies produced a seventy-five-minute version of Molière's *Les Femmes Savantes*, directed by Leith MacDonald and choreographed by club member Eleanor Stewart, with historical advice from UC French professor C.R. Parson. It was well-publicized as a "Wednesday Open Night" in the Sculpture Court of the Art Gallery of Toronto (now Ontario)[194] and included a gallery talk about painter Lawren Harris and a short film about glass making. According to the gallery's program, this "special performance" of a comedy about the "dangers of a little learning" was being presented to celebrate the gallery's Heritage of France exhibition of master paintings. By this point, most Alumnae members "felt that classics should be explored,"[195] although Molly Golby's playreading committee had recommended against them for the time being. But they could not pass up the opportunity to perform their first play in the gallery's Sculpture Garden, with a set designed by Russ Waller that placed the action "against a floodlighted tapestry." Whittaker's brief review of their dress rehearsal commended the "visual aspect"[196] of the show and also noted that acoustics would be improved when an audience filled the Court. Furniture was loaned from the gallery, costumes borrowed from the Stratford Festival's recent production of *Love's Labour's Lost*, wigs acquired from Maynard Robinson, curls accomplished by

Figure 3.9. Molly Golby [Thom] in the titular role of John Webster's 1613 tragedy *The Duchess of Malfi*, with Douglas Ney (Cardinal) and Bruce Evoy (Duke Ferdinand), directed by Gordon Johnson with costumes designed by Ronald Gilmore. Photo Credit: John Reeves. Courtesy of Alumnae Theatre Company.

Walter Wiegand, and antique spectacles procured from Braddock Optical Company. From the production, Alumnae's collections preserve several colour photographs and their first case of slides. These yield evidence of the quality of fabric used in the costumes and the sets, as well as the actors' clear focus.

Forward to Radical Play Programming

At the June 1967 annual meeting, president Elizabeth Mascall observed that a decade earlier, Alumnae's first Coach House Theatre "introduced a trail-blazing program. Now we are not alone, and perhaps we should shift our interest into the new lines in which theatre is travelling. This is something to think about in the coming years."[197] By the late 1960s, Alumnae's emphasis on modern theatre was beginning to age. Molly Thom contextualized the company as one that "has always held to a hard line of intellectualism and willingness to experiment in what is new in theatre."[198] Thus, Alumnae turned some of their attention towards politically radical contemporary plays.

Building on the success of their season-ending production of David Halliwell's rebellious 1965 play *Little Malcolm and His Struggle Against the Eunuchs* in the spring 1968,

Figure 3.10. Lawrence Schafer's set design for John Webster's *The Duchess of Malfi* was realized by Alumnae on their synagogue Coach House Theatre stage in January 1963. Courtesy of Alumnae Theatre Company.

Alumnae opened their fiftieth season in the fall of 1968 with the Toronto premiere of Megan Terry's 1966 anti-war play *Viet Rock (A Folk War Movie)* at the synagogue Coach House Theatre. Thom directed the production, which was billed as a "dramatic and musical revue from the new American theatre of improvisation." It was Alumnae's first sojourn into improv-based theatre.[199] The DDF and the Ontario Council for the Arts assisted by paying a member of the cast, David Clement of Toronto Workshop Productions (TWP), to conduct "improvisational sessions with interested Club members one evening a week" and to lead the cast in Laban Method physical exercises to support the play's "group action and improvisation."[200] This shift in thinking to take on the politically aware, improv-created *Viet Rock* was yet another moment in which the club showed itself capable of modifying their programming to embrace contemporary performance styles (and funding opportunities). That Agatha Leonard, an active company member since 1921, had presided over this shift as chair of the programming committee underscores how deeply such acumen was ingrained in Alumnae's ethos.

Alumnae's season pamphlet pitched the New Haven–premiered, New York–staged *Viet Rock* as a "challenging work from a new school of American theatre" and "very much a piece for our time, projecting many differing attitudes about this war – any war – in personal, domestic, military, and political terms. It is also a piece for our time in its form: a free and fluid

Figure 3.11. Members of the cast of Megan Terry's *Viet Rock*, promoted by Alumnae as "A dramatic & musical revue from the new American theatre of improvisation." The show ran in October and November 1968 at the synagogue Coach House Theatre. Courtesy of Alumnae Theatre Company.

structure of dramatic cartoons, parodies, mime, and music enacted by a company changing roles continuously as the theme is worked out." The casting notice added that the play was an "exceptional acting exercise." The *Globe and Mail*'s theatre listing described it as "Megan Terry's fragmentary look at the United States and its war."[201] The play had grown out of improvisation techniques developed by Nola Chilton, Joseph Chaiken, and Sam Shepard at New York City's Open Theatre. Written and designed to be produced at the Café La Mama Experimental Theatre, *Viet Rock* is an example of theatre drawn from television, newspapers, and "personal stories" by a generation, in Terry's words, trying to "deal with the bewilderment, shame, and confusion created by this war" and to "get at the essence of violence."[202]

Physical theatre styles were by then making their way onto the Toronto scene, and Alumnae were, once again, at the forefront of theatre developments. TWP had been using such techniques for years. But now, Terry's *Comings and Goings* theatre game, published in the same Simon and Schuster collection as *Viet Rock*, was playing that same month in the experimental hands of Ernest Schwarz, whose studio at 41 Collier Street was open to the public on weekends. He took his Michael Chekhov–inspired, improv-based event to Toronto libraries for children's audiences "of up to 100."[203]

The two Terry shows were in sharp contrast to Toronto's other theatre offerings that month: Hart House Theatre was running Thomas Middleton's *The Changeling*, directed by

Leon Major; Old Angelo's, a "three-hand revue by three bright youngsters" called *Watch the Birdie*; the Colonnade, Charles Dyer's *Staircase*; the Richview and Forest Hill Libraries, Schwartz's children's show *The Lion and the Lollipop*; the Royal Alexandra, *Anne of Green Gables* from PEI; the Belmont Theatre, Henry Livings's "light-hearted look at mechanized society"[204] called *Eh?*; and TWP, Peter Shaffer's *Black Comedy*.[205] However, a few productions did point to more political developments in theatre: the O'Keefe Centre was running *Hallelujah, Baby!*; the Playhouse Theatre on Bayview Avenue, a "Rock version of Shakespeare's *Twelfth Night*," "with hippies"[206]; and Trio Productions, Peter Weiss's famed *Marat-Sade* at Trinity Square.[207]

Future filmmaker Kaspars Dzeguze described Alumnae's offering in the *Varsity*'s double review of *Viet Rock* and the British film *The Charge of the Light Brigade*: five men and five women play multiple characters in a "birth-to-death cycle of the American male. Born, drafted, trained, airdropped into Vietnam, shot, and – home in a box." The intimacy of the theatre space deeply affected Dzeguze:

> It had an effect for a reason quite apart from the play or the actors: it was the first live theatre I had seen in a long time, and, after a steady diet of film, even the closeness of the actors (there are four rows of seats in the Coach House) threw me off balance.
>
> I felt jarred from the first moment the ten came on stage; these people had real, craggy faces; they walked and made noise. At times, I could hear them breathing. Often, I could see them straining to act. They looked and talked at me, and I didn't know whether to be offended that they acknowledged my presence. Film, after all, can unwind in an empty cinema, but actors play to people.[208]

Dzeguze's reflections are personal and affective, reminding us of theatre's unique ability to draw in the audience. Indeed, it is difficult to determine the degree to which his reactions were a result of the intimate Coach House space, or *Viet Rock*'s impact, or both.

Reviews were mixed and, like early reviews of Alumnae productions, were more critical of Terry's writing than of the performances themselves. Whittaker wrote that *Viet Rock* proved Terry had an "excellent ear for current speech, and her script, in the version used, was a compendium of popular U.S. catch-phrases," although it came across as "muted, generalized and full of sentiment" and therefore cast "doubt about Mrs. Terry's over-all achievement."[209] For Don Rubin in the *Star*, the play's "artistic merit" was in "direct relation to one's interest in histrionic techniques, in playwriting methodology and in that nasty real-life drama being staged half-a-world away. Some might consider that considerable. Me, I wonder." With obvious scepticism, Rubin described the play's original creation, which

> grew out of an experiment in which a group of actors worked together to answer such questions as "What is war?" "What is hate?" "What is love?" To find some answers, the actors reached into their own respective psyches and pulled out such plums as "mother," baby," "kill," "bomb" and so on. As new relationships presented themselves, as new situations and confrontations developed, Miss Terry watched with fascination. In time, she gave these situations a dash of form and a snatch of logic and from the potpourri emerged her play.

Rubin found her play's arguments "simplistic" and her words "rather pedestrian."[210] Contrasting *Viet Rock* with *Les Femmes Savantes* across Alumnae's fifty years, "R.H." in the *Telegram* declared, "I'll take Moliere over Terry any day," calling the latter's play "mushy, maudlin."[211] Reviewers noted that Alumnae had perhaps stepped out of their modern and period lanes, a point that might have been celebrated just a few years earlier but that now was grounds for critical reprimand because there was a greater variety of theatre companies regularly producing shows, including experimental ones. Regarding the directing and the paucity of familiar Alumnae faces in the cast, Whittaker observed that in "recruit[ing] a whole new company to master the multiple styles," Thom did "remarkably well, arriving at a beautifully integrated production."[212]

Viet Rock looked nothing like productions from Alumnae's first forty-nine years. The young performers were dressed in the non-descript dark sweaters, jeans, and patterned dresses of the day. They mimed rifles and other props in front of Ted Jackson's "sparse setting"[213] of scaffolding and contemporary art. In York University's *Excalibur* student newspaper, Herman Surkis described how the "actors lay on the stage in a circle, mumbling incoherent statements and words – 'Blood, gore. Love. Life. Shit' – *ad nauseum*. After which they leap up and play ring around the rosie for a few minutes and then literally fall into the first sketch."[214] Surkis concluded that considering that the "actors were all amateur, except for [Equity member David] Clement, they did an excellent job with the material at hand."[215] In describing the ensemble work, a first for Alumnae, Whittaker wrote that Thom's "scratch company of 10 is an impressively flexible unit. Girls and boys move easily through the various patterns of action, detaching themselves fleetingly to impersonate [the] various archetypes."[216] The choreography and movements were "often callisthenic, arty, or banal and messy."[217]

None of the critics believed that *Viet Rock* portended that improv was to be Alumnae's future focus. Whittaker posited that the choice of subject matter was the real problem. He questioned whether a Canadian audience "one remove" from the Vietnam War could see the play's immediacy, adding that, when the cast "moves out into the audience at the end, it is an encounter fraught with sympathy. (I am told that this is an action of alienation and accusation in the U.S. productions)."[218] Rubin, a New Yorker by birth, went further, writing that the same failure was true "everywhere else it has been presented – a curiosity piece for the avant-garde that is often interesting, but in total effect, almost non-existent."[219] R.H. concluded that Alumnae, "devoted to presenting plays that professional companies can't afford to take a risk on, must expect a certain number of clinkers. Count *Viet Rock* as one of them."[220] In their next press release, the company, as if to counter reviewers' scepticism of their programming choice, reported that *Viet Rock* played to 80 per cent houses and "turned a fair profit for the Club's coffers."

Because their Maplewood Coach House Theatre could not accommodate a large production, Alumnae ran their only full production of the fall of 1969 in November at the 225-seat Central Library Theatre: the Toronto premiere of Canadian George Ryga's "radical"[221] and Kafkaesque *The Ecstasy of Rita Joe*, directed and designed by Herbert Whittaker. By then, the national significance of Ryga's play was well known to Canadian audiences. It had been two years to the month since the Vancouver Playhouse staged, with much public debate, the world premiere of a play about what Dzeguze called a "fragile, eminently human vessel that sunders on the callousness of the city and its pavement-hard way of life, which is so different from the reserve's that Rita can't think straight, can't do anything right, and ends up time and again in court."[222] That year, *Rita Joe* received a reading on CBC radio, a production on CBC television, a French translation produced by Gratien Gélinas in Montreal, and opened the National Arts Centre in Ottawa. *Vancouver Province* critic Jamie Portman later acknowledged the play as having "altered the course of Canadian theatre," as having given "Canadian drama a credibility it had never achieved previously," and its November 1967 premiere in Vancouver as having been an "event of national importance."[223] Audiences wanted to experience Ryga's play first-hand. This was the sixties, a time when social justice was both a political and an artistic battleground. Whittaker stated in the Alumnae production's audition notice that the play "gives an impressionist view of the clash between two elements of society; the Indian [*sic*] heroine is confronted by white Canadian civilization." If Canadians had been resigned to ignore what was then called the "Indian issue," Ryga's play made them think twice, although it did not always provoke compassion.

Reviewers generally stated that Alumnae's production was a worthy attempt at social commentary, but that the script lacked substance. In the *Canadian Tribune*, under his pseudonym "Martin Stone," Communist writer and theatre artist Oscar Ryan wrote that the play "should be seen on every reservation and in every city ghetto. It is a cry for justice and a warning." He urged audiences from coast to coast to see the play and wrote that the "production comes alive with sensitive performances."[224] But there are few things that people find more uncomfortable than coming to grips with their country's great shame. Lorne Fienberg in the *Varsity*, while applauding the appearance of a new Canadian play that was generating attention, called it "nothing but an artificial, superficial and stereotyped presentation of the plight of the Canadian Indian" and a "melodrama" populated with "all kinds of cardboard people."[225]

For Cohen, *Rita Joe* was "pseudo-folk lore" weighed down by a "ridiculously inept" script. The first half of Cohen's review sought to clarify the play's social context by outlining an event that had occurred on the very day of Alumnae's opening: the Six Nations Confederacy declared their reserve near Brantford a "sovereign state."[226] Cohen conceded Ryga's "worthy intentions" but went on to say that the "story of Rita Joe and her boy friend, Jaimie Paul, is entitled to a much better script than Ryga provides with his Goldwaterite white magistrates, cretinous white settlement workers, sexually frustrated white school teachers," and so on. Ill-equipped to deal with a play that critiqued settler-colonial violences, Cohen failed to understand both the broad implications of the material and the non-naturalistic style of the play and the production. He concluded that although Alumnae

> is non-professional, on the whole its production standards have always been critically acceptable. Not this time ... From start to finish the whole affair has been directed by Herbert Whittaker with uncontrolled mawkishness, a condition reinforced by the cramped set design and stilted movements. There is no hint in his staging of a grasp of Rita Joe's predicament ... Adding further to the muddle, the show is under-rehearsed, and the cast last night had acute line trouble.[227]

Essentially, Cohen's words were true to his usual agenda, which was to balance cruelly honest criticism with words intended to prod Canadian theatre up the hill.

The cast did not fare much better in reviewers' estimations. Dzeguze cited the "weak performances" of most of the cast, save for Molly Thom, who "makes for a very energetic, emotional and appealing Rita Joe." In his first stage appearance,[228] then thirty-year-old Duke Redbird, who has since become an influential figure in First Nations literature in Canada, played Jaimie Paul. In a pre-show interview with Dzeguze, Redbird addressed accusations that the play's situations were too stereotypical; he also raised the question of cultural appropriation: "The issues in Rita Joe, for example, are several years out of date, simply because we've had good coverage of Indian problems by the

Figure 3.12. Molly Thom (Rita Joe) and Duke Redbird (Jaimie Paul) in Alumnae's Toronto premiere of George Ryga's *The Ecstasy of Rita Joe*, directed and designed by Herbert Whittaker. It ran in November 1969 at the Central Library Theatre. Photo Credit: Paul Newberry. Courtesy of Alumnae Theatre Company.

media ... But while Rita Joe is a good play, it's but superficial in its treatment of the problems. It's not written by an Indian. Therefore, I'd like to make my own films and plays, to express an Indian's view of the society that's been founded here by Western Europeans."[229]

In his review a few days later, however, Dzeguze concluded that Redbird was "unable to vary speech or actions" and that his character's "growing anger and disillusionment ... with the white man's perfidy never become apparent."[230] For Cohen, Redbird and Thom were "clearly unable to delineate their basic roles, let alone fill the large gaps in psychology, culture shock and yearnings left by the author."[231] Alumnae's foray into sociopolitical play production was finding mixed results.

These mixed sentiments carried over into the design elements. Dzeguze thought Whittaker's design was "very simple but effective,"[232] while Ryan thought his "staging could benefit from a greater use of Ted Pilkington's musical scene bridges and some accent of colour in the stark setting."[233] Fienberg, though, dismissed the set as "shabby and ineffective."[234] Dzeguze noted that an "interesting feature was the on-stage seating of all the players, whom the indirect lighting turned into eerie but familiar shapes reminiscent of the pop art plaster statues by George Segal."[235] That it was Alumnae who staged the

Figure 3.13. Director Herbert Whittaker rehearses Alumnae's Toronto premiere of George Ryga's *The Ecstasy of Rita Joe*. He holds the legal-sized pages of Ryga's script. Photo Credit: Paul Newberry. Courtesy of Alumnae Theatre Company.

Toronto premiere speaks to their savvy programming choices. They knew the play would garner broad attention, besides which, it was a good fit with their increasingly politicized programming interests.[236]

Rita Joe has since been studied, taught, and anthologized as a catalyst for modern Canadian playwriting. At the time, it also underscored Alumnae's willing engagement with the social justice movement. Toronto audiences were attending the Crest Theatre's *The Me Nobody Knows* (a "rock musical based on the poems and prose of ghetto children"[237]) and the Royal Alexandra Theatre's all-Canadian production of *Hair* in 1969 and its return engagement in the summer of 1971. But they were also attending Alumnae's productions of Terry's *Viet Rock*, David Halliwell's *Little Malcolm and His Struggle Against the Eunuchs*, Jean-Claude van Itallie's *America Hurrah*, and the variously authored *Collision Course*, as well as Alumnae's reading of Michael B. Polley's new play *The Song Is Far Away*, each of which helped to established the company as attuned to the activism of the day and as ready to introduce new ideas, and ways to stage those ideas, in Toronto.

Reflections on a Coach House Aesthetic

Following their first season at the synagogue Coach House Theatre, which featured no fewer than four Toronto premieres, fifteen club members on stage, and many more behind the scenes, Pamela Terry's 1963 programming report outlined some emerging pressures on the company:

> Of course, this first year back *has* been rough. We are continually being challenged, on all sides, to present not only interesting plays, without getting our toes stepped on by other theatre organizations that have recently started up; but also plays that will please everybody from the Canada Council through the reasonable request of Alum actresses for more and better acting parts, to the diversified likes of our audiences and the large appetites of our creditors. We are a shade self-conscious about the money-making side of the shows, as it is important now that each production net, ideally speaking, at least $500; at the same time, we don't wish to change or harm our policy in any basically threatening way. Polished productions are becoming the rule, whereas at [the former Coach Houses at] Huntley and Bedford, though polish was certainly aimed for, the smallness and innocence of our physical surroundings coupled with less financial pressure, made for – to my mind, at least – a rather more relaxed approach. We are becoming a bigger and more complex producing group than we perhaps anticipated when we started our first pocket theatre experiment in 1957. There is nothing alarming about this, really; we are just made more vitally aware of how important our Coach House work is in the challenge it presents to us to utilize energy, intelligence and talent to the utmost, still keeping our enthusiasm and enjoyment up to the usual high level.[238]

Running a space as their own theatre, publicizing it as such, and paying to populate it with plays meant new constellations of challenges for Alumnae. Increased competition, the struggle for funding, financial strains arising from material improvements to their buildings (see chapter 5), and the spectre of the company's previous successes frequently put pressure on the club. Those pressures would remain on the club permanently.

Towards the end of the Coach House years, approaches to selecting new plays had changed across Canada. Agatha Leonard remarked in 1968 that the

> current trend in modern professional repertory companies is to acquire an individual known as a dramaturge, whose job it is to scout for new plays, read and evaluate them, search for older plays which it may be timely to revive, and assist or advise in editing, adapting, or revising scripts of plays which are finally selected for what is hoped to be a successful season. In this club the dramaturge is the programme committee.

She went on to note that Alumnae's programming committee, like a dramaturge, assessed the "feasibility of producing, casting, and costuming the play within the resources of our company and theatre." Leonard here was signalling her awareness of the new theatrical language even while pointing out that Alumnae had decades earlier developed their own, collective version of the dramaturge, at least in terms of its literary manager aspects. She added that the programming committee had also "become adept at beating down the royalty rates" in a context in which plays available to amateur companies elsewhere were not available in Toronto "because Toronto is on the professional circuit and there are professional companies established here." This meant hours of correspondence by letter, telegram, and phone to secure rights – hours that sometimes came to naught.[239] At the end of Alumnae's fiftieth year (and her seventieth), Leonard asserted that having produced a variety of international plays from the 1960s, "though 50 years old, we are still mentally 'with it.'"[240]

In 1968, three members remained in the club from its founding in 1918: Christina (Cooper) Templeton, Margaret Tytler, and Marion (Squair) Hunter.[241] "Fifty years of producing plays is not to be sneezed at, as you all know," read an Alumnae membership letter to the "Ladies" introducing their "Golden Jubilee" year and selling subscriptions. Reflecting on the club's history and their university roots in the *University of Toronto Graduate* magazine, Halpenny observed that the "productions have their ups and downs artistically, of course. Choice of plays has its difficulties now that there are more companies in Toronto doing work that is somewhat similar."[242] Said Gordon Jocelyn in the *Montreal Gazette*, "if ever a theatre has given consistently interesting and serious attention to the demands of theatre, this is it. They have pulled some bloopers in their day, but at least nothing there is ever slap-dash."[243] Interviewed by Herbert Whittaker on the night of their Golden Jubilee party and invited preview performance of *Viet Rock*, Molly Thom focused on Alumnae's tradition of experiment and intellectualism: "I am cautiously optimistic … Our club is very strong right now. We have new members with good training and strong ideas, whose voices are beginning to be heard. Our club has always held to a hard line of intellectualism and a willingness to experiment in what is new theatre."[244]

Regrettably, Alumnae's planned celebrations for their fiftieth anniversary ran into challenges. They had planned a buffet supper at the Arts and Letters Club, but when they learned that the club could accommodate only 120 people, they were "forced to do some very quick and bitter arithmetic," according to president Margaret MacAuly. Instead, to their fiftieth anniversary celebration they invited only "large donors to the Building Fund, a few old hands in the membership to represent all the current members, past illustrious and founding members, and finally those gentlemen friends that covered us with glory in the past at CODL and DDF Festivals." Thus, the Annual Party at years' end would be "our second grand celebration and this will be free to members as well as this year's crop of gentleman helpers."[245] The Golden Jubilee Garden Party at the annual meeting was held at club secretary Joan Shaw's home and featured a "miniature casino," "mothers home cooking," and a "theatrical classic."[246] The party might have been merrier had Alumnae not learned that spring that their beloved Coach House Theatre property was to be expropriated by the city, marking the year as their last in the synagogue (see chapter 5).

Alumnae's Coach House years aligned with an important decade and a half for Toronto theatre. From the late 1950s to the early 1970s they helped prepare the ground for the city's theatre ecology by educating artists and audiences in dozens of recent plays while offering significant stage experience to women and men who were seeking to enter an emerging profession. As professional theatre began to take root in the city, Alumnae's Coach House program emphasized the types of shows that professional companies could not yet present. Their intellectual theatre served educated, modern audiences interested in both artistic developments outside of their borders and new plays locally written. Forced changes of location necessitated the sort of pared-down, intimate programming that Whittaker likened in his critical commentary to off-Broadway – a reminder that aesthetic creation cannot be divorced from economic necessity, even in nonprofessionalizing contexts. In these terms, Alumnae maintained sufficient continuity to preserve its public brand while using the economic capital it had accumulated after the war to deal with its changing circumstances. Their branding succeeded more often than it failed, in part because Alumnae found public advocates in influential critics like Whittaker and Cohen, who helped translate their

Figure 3.14. Alumnae's fiftieth anniversary featured their first three-fold season pamphlet, complete with a tear-away fold to mail in one's subscription. Adorning the pamphlet were images of gestures for the hands and feet indicative of Victorian acting technique. Courtesy of Alumnae Theatre Company.

intentions to curious audiences. Having attracted roughly 1,000 subscribers by the end of the Coach House years, Alumnae significantly shaped Toronto audience interests with the "relevant," the "thought-provoking," and the "new." They had moved into a small coach house because they needed space to store materials, as well as the capacity to control the scheduling of rehearsals and performances; that is, they needed more control over the means of production than Hart House Theatre could provide. But they were also watching trends, and they saw that theatrical modernism was moving into existential, absurd territory, with philosophical playwrights questioning the very notions of character and existence. Alumnae's material needs fit the movement they saw opening in front of them, and they moved towards the avant-garde of the time.

Their Coach House programming also marked a formal end to their association with the Little Theatre Movement. Having left Hart House Theatre as their primary physical and ideological venue, Alumnae would no longer be associated with what was, by the 1960s, an outdated movement to which less progressive companies still clung. Their move towards a new, trending, intellectual theatre took them through the avant-garde and into the politically radical. Alumnae's movement from one theatre space to another signalled a movement from one movement to another. Alumnae's next move, into their permanent home, would see this parallelism replaced with a different one: a historic company thriving in an historic building.

Chapter 4

The Firehall Years in Toronto's Expanding Theatre Ecology (1972–present)

Unquestionably, the most important dramatic event in Toronto next week is the opening of the Firehall Theatre [by] Toronto's oldest (54 years), fiercest, proudest theatrical company …

This is the group, more than any other, which has reworked Toronto's theatrical atmosphere …

Their achievements are legion. As a continuing, creative, productive force, the Alumnae have no equals. Their intelligent, visionary approach to program building is an object lesson. Over the half-century-and-a-bit of their existence, they have taken the first steps in so many directions …

How did they do it? Perhaps the Alumnae cannot be explained, only experienced; if you've never encountered them, you wouldn't believe it, but if you've worked with them, you'll scarcely forget it …

[They] represent a nest of seething egos which cannot be denied. The Alumnae is a stunning, startling example of a mass collective, unified will, modified by ambition, intelligence and the utter inability to understand rejections …

Can they continue in their status of superb amateurs when the market for good directors and actors is getting tighter? But I think that if anybody can face such very real worries sensibly and forcefully, it is the inspired madwomen of the Alumnae. They have done the theatre proud.[1]

– Urjo Kareda

More than a century after their inaugural production, Alumnae Theatre Company now resides in the old Firehall No. 4 at 70 Berkeley Street in Toronto's Corktown neighbourhood. They are now "custodians"[2] of a city heritage building as well as a century of theatre history. On Google Maps their tagline reads as follows: "Variety of dramatic productions staged by a long-running women-led company in a converted firehall." Unlike the move into their first Coach House theatre, which was voluntary, the move into the Firehall was forced on them when Toronto Hydro expropriated Alumnae's synagogue Coach House; had that not happened, Alumnae likely would have stayed on that property for years to come (see chapter 5). The move to the east-end Firehall conclusively disassociated the group geographically and ideologically from the U of T campus.

From one decade to the next, Alumnae have found themselves competing for public attention with an ever-growing number of Toronto theatre companies. In the early 1970s, Toronto's theatre ecology began to take on characteristics that are familiar to us today. Moving to the Firehall placed Alumnae in geographical and ideological proximity to the newly founded Toronto Free Theatre (now CanStage's Berkeley Street theatre) and to other new and professionalizing alternative theatre companies like Theatre Passe Muraille, Factory Lab Theatre (now Factory Theatre), and Tarragon Theatre. These companies were analogous to Alumnae with their commitment to staging local and Canadian plays that large venues like the St. Lawrence Centre and O'Keefe Centre almost never did. But unlike Alumnae, they sought to pay their artists and to focus almost exclusively on new Canadian works. Upon moving into the Firehall and with the coincidental emergence of the professionalizing alternative theatres, critics immediately ceased to regard Alumnae as a prominent alternative theatre, although Herbert Whittaker and Urjo Kareda relished reminding readers of their history of alterity, until they left the *Globe and Mail* and the *Star*, respectively, in 1975.

At the Firehall, Alumnae have continued to internalize the Janus-faced challenge of living up to past accomplishments while dealing with increased competition for members, volunteers, and audiences. In 1984, Alumnae president Victoria Santer, an advertising executive by day, told the *Star*, "We have to be more aggressive in a pond that has more big fish in it ... There is much more competition in the city's theatrical community in general."[3] With more theatres in the city and two theatre spaces to fill in the Firehall, audiences had become more difficult to attract. A decade later, treasurer Carol Palmer noted the club's steadily declining attendance and subscription list:

> We must recognize the constantly increasing availability of very good theatre in this city and the fairly static amount of money the theatergoing public is prepared to spend. So I think it only fair to ourselves to be pleased that we have been able to hold our own financially, retain our financial independence and know that we have enhanced our presence and reputation with a year of interesting plays, very well produced.[4]

Tension over competition for audiences had been, of course, a hallmark of Toronto's theatre ecology since the Second World War, provoking self-reflection about programming. Three years later, Palmer reported that although Alumnae operated at a profit for much of the 1980s, in the 1990s they operated at a loss and their net assets fell by nearly one third. She attributed this financial downturn to competition as well as a need to

> decide whether we are going to present plays we want to present or whether we are going to present plays that people want to see. Ideally, these two alternatives would produce the same result, but experience has shown us that that is not the case. Some decision, or preferably compromise, will have to be reached. I feel very strongly that some action or specific decision should be adopted for it would be a shame to let the Company drift in the direction it has been going.[5]

Palmer's suggestion that Alumnae might need to compromise their play selection principles for the sake of financial stability must have made many hearts sink. Here were the chilling thoughts that Alumnae needed to produce more commercial fare and that members were out of touch with the city's theatre audiences, or that the audiences were out of touch with the company, and that this conflict was visible on their financial ledger. This tension, sown by their move into the Firehall, has come to define the company for the past fifty years.

Even as they became known in the 1960s, as the Coach House Theatre – a synecdoche they actively promoted – Alumnae still kept as their official name: the University Alumnae Dramatic Club, or UADC. But after they moved into the Firehall in 1972, the Coach House name no longer made sense. A week before their Firehall grand opening, Kareda wrote that the "most awkward aspect of that company is the name … which hints at dilettantism, ingeniousness and pettiness, which have nothing whatever to do with the group's strengths and achievements." He recommended that the name "surely should be played down in the future."[6] But Alumnae were already doing that. When they sent out their first Firehall season publicity in June 1972, which Kareda had surely already read, they changed their public name from the "Coach House Theatre" to the "Firehall Theatre." Indeed, when Sid Adelman in the *Star* erroneously referred to the group as the "University Women's Alumnae," Molly Thom wrote to him with the correction that "henceforth the UADC, or the Ladies of the Alum, or the Aluminum Ladies, or the 'Women's Alumnae' would like to be known as THE FIREHALL THEATRE."[7] In aligning their name with their new building, Alumnae were seeking to rebrand once again. However, the name lasted only until the company "seized the occasion of its 60th anniversary to drop the Firehall title and put its own name in lights, at last,"[8] calling themselves "The Alumnae Theatre."[9] This was partly a response to the 1974 opening of the Second City comedy troupe's "Old Firehall Restaurant" a few blocks away at 110 Lombard Street, which "brought confusion in its wake" and the necessity of "redirecting"[10] each other's patrons. Moreover, the name The Alumnae Theatre had the benefit of vaulting them to the top of the newspapers' alphabetical theatre listings. Then, a decade later, it was decided that the name "University Alumnae Dramatic Club" would be replaced in "all publicity," where it had not been already, with "The Alumnae."[11] And in September 1991 they formally advised the city that they had changed their name to "Alumnae Theatre Company."[12] Five years later a draft membership information sheet read, "What is the Alumnae Theatre Company? It is a community of women dedicated to developing their theatrical talents and to producing adventurous high-quality theatre not readily seen elsewhere. The membership shares a love of theatre, a commitment to the production of good theatre, and a desire to explore and develop their individual talents."[13] Over their first eighty years, Alumnae produced a variety of official name changes and acquired many unofficial nicknames, including most current members' preferred moniker, "The Alumnae," as well as "The Alum" and, from Herbert Whittaker, "The Aluminum Ladies."[14] But the word "Alumnae" has remained constant.

This chapter examines Alumnae's programming at the Firehall since they moved in. It does so by studying changes in play selection, membership, production, administration, and building management practices while mapping their overall departure from programming alterity. It also considers changes in audience demographics and critics' reviewing practices at a time when members (and potential members) have been entering the workforce and volunteering in the community at increasing rates. Sarah Sharma's construction of "differential time"[15] is summoned to contextualize recent changes to work hours within the gig economy and its effects on volunteer time. Although Alumnae have moved towards more popular theatre fare, they still return to modern plays while aiming more than ever to introduce audiences to recent plays, often written by female playwrights, that serve their female members and a broad audience.

The Programming and the Critics

Alumnae's play programming remains the purview of the programming (formerly playreading) committee, whose members consider dozens of plays each season.[16] Joan Shaw's 1995 programming committee report described their communal play selection process. The report included the titles previously and currently proposed by members, "whom we expect to keep the season always at the backs of their minds and to feed us suggestions," as well as plays submitted by playwrights. The committee read and shared feedback on "likely prospects"[17] It then looked for a "theme of interest" and "dramatic impact," as well as for plays that would group well with other plays in the season and that would offer challenging and rewarding work for members.[18] During their centennial year, the programming committee sought pitches for the 101st season from the membership, the criteria being plays with casts of five or more actors (with about half of the roles for women) and with "public recognition to help bring in audiences."[19]

Alumnae's production output at the Firehall has been staggering. Between 1972 and their hundredth anniversary in 2018, they produced 305 Mainstage and Studio plays, as well as hundreds of world premieres at their New Ideas Festival, inaugurated in 1988. Not including their own world premieres, two thirds of these plays have been contemporary plays, demonstrating that Alumnae continue their commitment to producing plays that have had recent world premieres elsewhere. Another quarter of their plays have been modern plays from the first six decades of the twentieth century, echoing their Coach House ethos. Only about 5 per cent of their Firehall productions have been period pieces from the nineteenth century or earlier.

In the 1970s, Alumnae continued to distinguish themselves from other theatres by their programming choices, maintaining their "policy of presenting only plays of literary and theatrical merit to discerning audiences."[20] By the mid-1980s, however, their choices were echoing those of other nonprofessionalizing companies; in that regard, they were no longer the trend-setters they had once been. The playwrights produced most often at the Firehall before Alumnae's centiennial included Tom Stoppard (9), Alan Ayckbourn (6), Samuel Beckett (6), Tennessee Williams (6), Edward Albee (5), and Christopher Durang (4); Canadians George F. Walker (6), Shirley Barrie (4), Carol Shields (3), Judith Thompson (3), and Michel Tremblay (3); and Alumnae members Molly Thom (4 productions, 2 readings) and Francess Halpenny (2 productions, 4 readings). Most of these names were well known by the time Alumnae programmed their works, signalling a trend towards offering increasingly "familiar"[21] plays and playwrights. Remarkably, by 2018, thirty-seven Firehall plays, or around 15 per cent of Alumnae's Firehall plays, have been world premieres – and that is not counting New Ideas Festival shows.

During the 1970s, Alumnae continued to stage thought-provoking Coach House–style plays by Edward Albee, Christopher Fry, and Thornton Wilder while adding influential playwrights like Seán O'Casey, Peter Handke, Christopher Hampton, Lanford Wilson, Tom Stoppard, Václav Havel, Agatha Christie, and Canadian Timothy Findley. As Molly Thom told the *Ryersonian* student newspaper in 1975, their programming "usually leans toward plays that would not ordinarily be seen in other theatres but have literary importance."[22] Alumnae's programming of important contemporary writers during the 1970s aligned them with the new professionalizing alternative theatres and campus theatre groups as an important alternative to Toronto Arts Productions ("our most sumptuously-funded and equipped local theatre at the St. Lawrence Centre"[23]) as well as roadhouses like the O'Keefe Centre and the Royal Alexandra Theatre. Alumnae's flexibility and nearly wide-open programming variety made them one among, yet separate from – that is, "alternative" both *with* and *to* – what Urjo Kareda famously termed Toronto's burgeoning "alternative theatre."[24]

Figure 4.1. Members of the cast of Timberlake Wertenbaker's *The Love of the Nightingale*, produced by Alumnae in February and March 1992 at their Firehall theatre. The production was directed by Molly Thom, with costumes designed by Margaret Spence and set designed by Stan Sellen. Photo Credit: Susan Parker Munn. Courtesy of Alumnae Theatre Company.

At the Firehall, Alumnae shifted much of their programming towards plays by or about women. This was an obvious fit for the group and paralleled the politicized theatre they had cultivated in their later Coach House years. Works by Anne Hébert, Aphra Behn, Carol Bolt, Clare Booth Lace, Lillian Hellman, Beverley Simons, and members Francess Halpenny, Molly Thom, Juliana Saxton, and Anne Tait were ideally suited to the club's emerging identity as a company offering plays that were relevant to women's experiences. Supplementing these were post-Broadway commercial hits, political plays, and to a lesser extent the mid-century modern plays that had defined their Coach House years. In the 1990s, they also began to produce more local and national premieres of plays by edgy women playwrights like Timberlake Wertenbaker and Sarah Daniels. In February 1995, Alumnae's Toronto premiere of Marsha Norman's *Getting Out* ran as part of a public forum on "Women in Conflict with the Law" hosted by the Elizabeth Fry Society. Thus, Alumnae continued to reveal a discerning eye for bold public statements, reflecting their desire to offer Toronto audiences plays that represented the company's history and place.

The Firehall years have been remarkable for how Alumnae have pivoted towards more traditional "community theatre" programming – light comedies, thrillers, and the like. They have often framed this approach to programming as a balance. Club president Victoria

Santer told the *Star* in 1984 that "Neil Simon is a wonderful playwright, but even an awful production will still get a few laughs. We don't want to do work that doesn't really offer a challenge." Member Margaret Spence agreed at the time: "Perhaps we have been a bit riskier in the past, but we've always balanced it, for example, with Restoration comedies along with the avant-garde plays." Santer added: "We try to have a Canadian play, although we don't choose it just because it's Canadian … And we try to choose plays our audiences can't see elsewhere, either because they can't afford it, at a more expensive theatre … or because it hasn't been recently done."[25] In *Star* critic Vit Wagner's words, this "unique hybrid"[26] of "artistic daring" and "organizational skills and solid backing enjoyed by established community companies"[27] remains key to Alumnae's success. Alumnae are at their best when they stage important contemporary works by a variety of playwrights in a variety of styles. This speaks to the strength of the voices among their core members and to the fact that they are educated women capable of blending their knowledge of genres, trends, and traditions with marketing acumen.

Turning towards more commercially popular fare was not an easy choice. One year into her position as Alumnae's director of marketing and promotion in 2002, Tina McCulloch wrote in her report to the annual general meeting a remarkable observation regarding the company's place in Toronto's theatre ecology. Drawing together past and present situations, she argued that Alumnae needed to produce popular hits in order to set themselves apart:

> Some longtime Alumnae members seem to feel that by aggressively pursuing a larger audience (which they fear means producing hokey, done-to-death plays), we too are going soft and "selling out." I don't believe that. And even if I did, we cannot compare our situation now to the time when we were pretty much the only game in town when it came to theatre. Then, Alumnae could afford to program some obscure plays and experimental new works. Unfortunately we no longer have that luxury. Now we have lots of competition. Not only from the pros like CanStage, Tarragon, Factory, and the big-budget Mirvish extravaganzas, but community theatres like East Side Players, Amicus Productions, and the Village Players are all vying for the same people's time and money. WE NEED AN AUDIENCE! In order for us to survive, we must create a niche or "brand" for ourselves that appeals to a broad demographic; publicize and market that brand to our potential audience; and most importantly, ensure that they like what they see when they come here. I believe we can find an acceptable balance between art for art['] s sake and [that nasty word] commercialism.
>
> To that end, I hope Alumnae will continue to program accessible plays by well-known writers – the recognition factor is very important. At least one play per season should be a comedy – people like to be entertained – there's enough dark, gloomy stuff in the world; they don't need to pay to see it onstage. We need to carefully choose experienced directors who can deliver a quality production. And I will continue to be liberal with ticket-giveaways – at least until we're consistently selling out! Which I hope won't be long from now – we deliver great shows, and more people will soon know about them.[28]

McCulloch, of course, was not wrong: familiarity sells. But to those familiar with Alumnae's long production history, she must have sounded like she was describing another company. For decades, Alumnae had set themselves apart from other companies by being the one that could afford to take chances on strong plays no one else produced. Instead of introducing to Toronto the world's next Beckett, Pinter, or Quebec writer in translation, as they had done

Figure 4.2. Herbert Whittaker's colourful costume designs for Alumnae's production of Thornton Wilder's *A Life in the Sun*, which ran in November 1978. Whittaker also directed and designed the set for the production. Courtesy of Alumnae Theatre Company.

in the past, Alumnae, McCulloch argued, should pursue name recognition. They would no longer be pacesetters the way they once had been; instead, they would offer familiar fare. Her report set in words what in fact had been happening at the company since the late 1970s: Alumnae's programming was increasingly taking on the look of more traditional community theatres in order to attract broader, less theatre-savvy, audiences.

More than 110 people have directed on the Firehall's Mainstage and Studio theatres, not counting New Ideas plays. In 1985, program director Nan Hirst wrote to the membership about the process:

> If you would like to direct the play you suggest, let us know. We can't promise that you will be recommended as director of that or any play but you will certainly be the first to be considered. Keep in mind that those who have not directed for the Alumnae before usually do their first production in the studio (although the studio is *by no means* confined to new directors) and choose a play which can be adapted to the limitations of cast and production which the studio space imposes.[29]

Hirst's letter reveals that directing a production at Alumnae was considered an honour. In addition, a director could come from any corner of the membership (and beyond). This is clear from the names of those who have directed at the Firehall over the years. The most significant programming difference between the Firehall years and the Coach House years is that by far most of the Firehall directors have been Alumnae members. Excluding New Ideas Festival directors, Molly Thom (26), Mavis Hayman (16), Jane Carnwath (15), and Pamela Terry Beckwith (11) have directed more Firehall shows than anyone else; the next six most frequent directors are also all Alumnae members. Among male guest directors, Herbert Whittaker[30] (5), Paul Hardy (5), and David Savoy (4) have directed at the Firehall most frequently.

To renew their focus on directors and their connections with Toronto's theatre ecology, Alumnae created a Professional Director's Award in 1990. The broad intent of the award, which had been established for a director of "exceptional promise who shows their talents in an Alumnae production," was to "showcase new talent and form a bridge between amateur and professional theatre (the director must be actively connected with professional theatre), and to help create much needed opportunities for Toronto's young professionals to demonstrate their talents."[31] The hope was that the award would "attract better directors," adding that "presently the Company relies on volunteers who are often overworked." They hoped the award would "improve the quality of plays," attract more audiences, create a "new angle/direction for the theatre," provide new learning opportunities for club members, assist new directors (reportedly the idea had already "received approval in the theatre community"), foster a "display of female talent," allow "more ambitious projects," create "useful connections in the theatre community," attract outside funding, and provide some income.[32] When Jordan Merkur, recently graduated from York University and "one of the city's most talented young directors,"[33] directed Craig Lucas's *Reckless* for Alumnae in the spring of 1990, the company presented him with the inaugural award. Jeannette Lambermont won it for her direction of *The Trojan Women* in the spring of 1993. By offering the award to the director *before* the production (which had not been the case with Merkur's award), the director, they thought, might have the "time to devote concentrated effort to directing a play."[34]

The award began to redefine Alumnae's relationship to successive cohorts of directors, who would now be attracted (and paid) to work with Alumnae by receiving the award in the year before they directed a show. It also helped to draw renewed attention from the city's theatre critics. Within a few years, the award had become popular: eighteen directors applied for it in the 1994–95 season alone. Rebecca Cann won it to direct Bertolt Brecht and Kurt Weil's *Happy End* that November, and Linda Matassa won it the following season to direct Luigi Pirandello's *Six Characters in Search of an Author*. During the 1990s, the increasing number of professionalizing Equity members directing Alumnae productions through grants, some of whom won the award, helped raise Alumnae's profile and clarify their position in the city's theatre ecology. But because the award was contingent on outside funding, it did not last. Initially funded by the city through the Toronto Arts Council, it was later funded privately.[35] In 2000, Alumnae's board of directors sought to raise funds for the award again[36] before it disappeared entirely.

The directing award was a strategy for gaining publicity. Alumnae was finding it increasingly difficult to garner media attention; indeed, reviews all but dried up in the early 2000s. As journalist Sarah Hood wrote in the late 1980s, by the 1970s critics had begun treating Alumnae "like a poor relation of the professional companies."[37] When Whittaker and Kareda retired, the reviewers who replaced them assumed a different tone towards Alumnae, often driving a wedge between nonprofessionalizing groups and their professional counterparts. Alumnae now began programming Agatha Christie, Alan Ayckbourn, Hart and Kauffman, and other arguably popular community theatre fare. For example, although the *Globe and Mail* published a month's worth of listings for Alumnae's first Ayckbourn production, *Absurd Person Singular*, in October 1977, the paper did not review it (even though Alumnae paid guest director Marie Hopps with a Theatre Ontario grant[38]). The *Globe and Mail*'s listing even called it "yet another Alan Ayckbourn comedy"[39] because the Royal Alexandra Theatre had produced his most recent play, *Absent Friends*, a month earlier.[40] The *Varsity* also missed reviewing the production, claiming in its listings to not have enough space for a full review.[41] The critical vacuum left by the departures of Whittaker and Kareda and Alumnae's decision to program more stereotypical community theatre fare resulted in newspapers showing less interest in granting column space to Alumnae's offerings.

Certainly, the shift in tone towards nonprofessionalizing theatre, and the fall-off in critical attention to it, began after the war, a time when local professional theatre companies were growing in number. But the advent of professionalizing alternative theatres in the 1970s meant there were more productions than critics could review, which meant that nonprofessionalizing groups were often ignored. Moreover, there was a growing urge to compare Toronto companies to those in New York and London. And all theatre companies were now competing for column space with film and television. Newspaper reviews of Alumnae shows dried up to nearly nothing after Alumnae's production of Betty Lambert's screwball sex comedy *Sqrieux-de-Dieu* in October 1979.

The 1980s marked the end of critical attention towards nonprofessionalizing theatre in Toronto. Ray Conlogue, having settled in as the *Globe and Mail*'s theatre critic in the summer of 1979, wrote nothing about Alumnae's work until April 1982, when he reviewed their production of T.S. Eliot's *The Cocktail Party* because it was directed by his paper's "critic emeritus," Herbert Whittaker. Conlogue wrote that Whittaker "ably directed" the play with "assurance and style" and applauded frequent Alumnae guest actor and Equity member Michael Tait, along with the "amateurs who mostly possess more than 20 years of experience." He said that Whittaker "sometimes dons the mantle of director."[42] The *Varsity*, for its part, wrote that the "show will be a test for the director to practice what he preaches,"[43] as if the media had forgotten the award-winning director and designer's work. Conologue resurfaced again at the Firehall in April 1985 when Alumnae produced Michael Green's 1980 comedy of amateur stereotypes, *The Coarse Acting Show*. This gave Conlogue the opportunity to write, "Here, however, it is sometimes difficult to tell which fumbling is accidental and which is on purpose,"[44] before walking out at intermission to attend Factory Lab's Brave New Works festival.[45] *The Coarse Acting Show* may have given mainstream reviewers what they needed: confirmation that amateur groups produce amateur plays, and an excuse not to return to Alumnae again.

By the mid-1980s the dailies had stopped reviewing Alumnae altogether, publishing only listings and paid show advertisements.[46] Their publicist Ann Sargent lamented to *Toronto Theatre* magazine in 1988, "We have such a hard time getting people to come and review us."[47] Readers had to look to Toronto's alternative media for reviews of Alumnae productions, if they were reviewed at all. Pat Fisher's production report for Alumnae's 1984 offering of Warren Graves's *The Last Real Summer* in the Studio concluded that a "lack of publicity made for small audiences but as usual, momentum built and the final performance was sold out."[48] By the late 1990s, only *Now Magazine* and *eye weekly* were reviewing Alumnae shows; in the fall of 2000, *Now* seemed to "cut coverage,"[49] although denying it at the time.[50] At the June 2002 annual general meeting, executive producer PJ Hammond "urge[d] the entire membership to get behind [director of marketing and promotion Tina McCulloch] and help make the Alumnae a name in the Toronto Theatre community again."[51] By the 2010s, only online reviews were appearing, and even those with increasing irregularity.

The Moderns Maintained

Alumnae's first season at the Firehall featured four modern plays, one world premiere translation, and one reading. They opened "one of Toronto's most elegant intimate theatres"[52] with Seán O'Casey's 1926 "tragic-comic masterpiece of the Irish rebellion,"[53] *The Plough and the Stars*, in October 1972, directed and designed by member Patricia Carroll Brown. Seventeen years after the opening, Donald Jones wrote in his "Historical Toronto" column in the *Star*'s *Saturday Magazine* that it was "one of the most important 'opening nights' in Toronto's theatrical history."[54] Media coverage for *The Plough and the Stars* was significant across print, television, and radio. Mentioning patrons and patronesses in attendance in the daily papers may have been long been out of fashion, but the occasion called for a list of notable "first-nighters." *Globe and Mail* society columnist Zena Cherry listed the politicians: Toronto mayor William Dennison; East York mayor True Davidson; and several aldermen who had been influential in securing the firehall for Alumnae, including Horace Brown, William Kilbourn, and David Rotenberg. Also in attendance was Rev. Harry S.D. Robinson of the recently renovated Little Trinity Church and schoolhouse,[55] which Alumnae had nearly leased in 1969.[56] Toronto Free Theatre's John Palmer wrote to Molly Thom immediately after seeing the play to thank her for the invitation, saying, "I thoroughly enjoyed the production and must congratulate you on a literally splendid theatre – a beautiful job."[57] Telegrams were received from Francess Halpenny and Robertson Davies, who had to miss the production.

Although a press release stated that "its topicality is obvious," the inaugural play was a symbolically odd choice for a club so attuned to articulating their programming perspective to the public. There were no bluestockings performing *The Bluestockings*; nor was there a new Canadian play for this new Canadian theatre. Why did Alumnae not draw from their great strengths by opening their new home with a new play, a Canadian play, a play deeply important to their history, or a play otherwise meaningful to a new start in this new space? Perhaps Alumnae surmised that producing a modern Irish play from forty-six years earlier would provide an alternative to the alternative theatres emerging in Toronto.

In what is surely the most damning extant description of Alumnae and their production choices, in a piece titled "A new barn cannot stimulate creative juices of sacred cow," Frank Michael wrote in the *Canadian Jewish News* that for Alumnae, settling in the Firehall after what he (alone) called "50 years of makeshift meandering" illuminated that "with institutionalization comes ossification." He added that the "group's first production [at the Firehall] calls into question its whole *raison d'être* and raises the morbid spectre of a theatrical relic as quaint, ossified, and anachronistic as the 19th century firehall in which it is housed." With a nod towards the half-century distance between *The Plough and the Star*'s premiere and Alumnae's production, he added, a "play which drew first breath from the freshness of Irish amateurism suffocates in the stuffy atmosphere of drawing-room pretension in the Alumnae Club's production."[58] This was because, he surmised, Alumnae "cannot successfully compete for competent actors and directors with Toronto's increasing number of professional and semi-professional companies. The standard classics of modern drama are no longer its artistic preserve. To avoid ossification of an aging social clique, the

Figure 4.3. *(left)* Mavis Hayman (Mrs. Gogan) and *(right)* Morna Wales (Bessie Burgess) in rehearsal for Sean O'Casey's *The Plough and the Stars*, directed by Patricia Carroll Brown for Alumnae in October and November 1972. The play opened Alumnae's new Firehall theatre. Photo Credit: Linda Lewis. Courtesy of Alumnae Theatre Company.

Alumnae Club must revert to the role of pioneer and exercise its pronounced, finely-developed literary bent in presentation of the untried, the experimental, the controversial, and the undeservedly obscure."[59] Entombed within Michael's damning prose was his solution: Alumnae must go back to their proven cutting-edge roots. He was noting that Alumnae's celebrated moments had always come when they pushed boundaries with hitherto unseen plays. Of course, Alumnae would do all of this in the months and years following *The Plough and the Stars*, but the opening production had perplexed Michael, and surely many others.

Certainly, *The Plough and the Stars* is a highly political play and thus reflected Alumnae's interest at the time in offering plays of that ilk. More to the point, one Alumnae press release cited the "terrible struggle still with us," referencing the recent events of 30 January 1972 in Derry, Northern Ireland, that would come to be known as "Bloody Sunday." Although the play was written ten years after the "Easter Uprising" it depicts, Whittaker surmised that it "would likely still get a rough reception in certain parts of Ireland today," adding that it was a "rarely seen but important work of literary merit. But it also closely reflects the struggles which have broken out again in Ireland in our time, with the same heroics, the same bigotry

Figure 4.4. Ron Gilmore's costume design and fabric swatch for the character May Daniels, played in Alumnae's production by Beverley Miller, in George S. Kaufman and Moss Hart's *Once in a Lifetime*. It ran at Alumnae's Firehall theatre in November and December 1973. Courtesy of Alumnae Theatre Company.

and the same victims."[60] Oscar Ryan, under the pseudonym Martin Stone, wrote that the play by O'Casey, "who had been secretary of the Irish Citizen Army and a prisoner of the English during Easter Week,"[61] had a "poignant timeliness in view of the unresolved Irish conflict of our own day."[62]

The quality of the presentation also failed to impress critics. Despite Urjo Kareda's enthusiasm for Alumnae generally, and for their "lovely" new theatre in particular, he called the production a "considerably less invigorating event than might have been expected." As director, Brown offered an "unconvincing and lifeless production" that was a "dud"; it "consistently failed the test of truth: I could not believe in a moment of it" as it "struggled to simulate reality but never suggest it."[63] Nigel Spencer in *Toronto Theatre* wrote that the production failed to focus on the "*humanity* of these people, making them grittier, more hurting and more hurt."[64] Pamela Terry's daughter Robin Beckwith was "haunting" in her scenes as a "doomed Irish girl," but otherwise, the actors "strained to create an ambience without bothering to create identifiable human characters."[65] Whittaker concluded of the cast that "all of them failed to be always convincing, but none of them failed to be occasionally so."[66] He added that the production was "overshadowed here by the glory of Toronto's newest playhouse."[67]

But *The Plough and the Stars* was soon followed by plays more in line with Alumnae's cutting-edge mandate. About one quarter of Alumnae's productions at the Firehall have been "modern" plays premiered between 1900 and 1970. Alumnae produced most of these moderns before Toronto's influential Soulpepper Theatre emerged in 1998 with a mandate to offer modern classics to Toronto audiences, a clear indication that Alumnae's programming continued to echo their interest in staging plays that were not receiving attention at other theatres. These have included comedies, theatre of the absurd, and serious dramas by Samuel Beckett, Edward Albee, Tennessee Williams, and Noël Coward. In their second season at the Firehall, Alumnae produced George S. Kaufman and Moss Hart's 1930 comedy *Once in a Lifetime*, which featured "marvelous mad 1920s costumes by Ron Gilmore," according to the press release. Since the arrival of Soulpepper, Alumnae has returned to Coward, Williams, Albee, Christopher Fry, and James Reaney only occasionally. When doing so, they offer Toronto plays by known writers considered to be the best in the world at their craft.

Alumnae's first offering in the seventy-seat Studio theatre upstairs at the Firehall (at the time called "Stage Two") was a "considerably revised" dramatized reading of Anne Tait's[68] translation into modern English of the late fourteenth-century poem *Sir Gawain and the Green Knight*, which she had presented in the fall of 1969 at their "much plainer chapel,"[69] the Maplewood Coach House. The readings ran across the first two weekends in January 1973, directed by Anne Tait, with music of the time played on medieval instruments by the Toronto Consort, lyrics by Michael Tait, and medieval dances by the York Court Dancers. It was billed as a "tale of love and violence," "passionately moral – and wickedly comic," about a "beheading match" between a "great green horseman" and King Arthur's best knight, Sir Gawain. Anne Tait later recounted that the reading was "eminently suitable for that space with its beautiful arched ceiling, reminiscent of King Arthur's great hall in the play." Tapestries designed by Mary Kerr, of which both Whittaker and Kareda approved, were hung down the tower staircase.[70]

Critics were pleased with the new Studio space but once again disappointed with the choice and presentation of the work that launched it. Murray Pomerance in *The Walrus* described the Toronto Consort as "four young men who used strange old instruments to make sounds like elephant-sized kazoos or like mouse-sized kazoos or like pungent woodwinds sounded on an echo chamber."[71] In a review titled "New theatre is lovely but first play isn't," Kareda suggested that the script was more suited to be a ninety-minute radio drama and that the production was "limp and low on imagination," in part because the idea of staged readings had "now run out of impulse" despite, or in part because of, Alumnae's robust history of presenting them. He lamented that they had chosen such an "anti-theatrical" script to open such a "happy theatrical location," adding that the "stiff formality of what we see before us short-circuits our imaginative response." For Whittaker, the combination of reading, music, and dancing was confusing and took "no advantage of the natural setting of the new theatre."[72] Concluded Pomerance, the "audience gave the polite, lacey response the medieval can elicit when it is regarded as a relic."[73] At a time when Toronto's new alternative theatres were invigorating the city with new alternative works, a historic company staging stories of the past in a building of the past risked labelling Alumnae as Toronto's dated theatre.

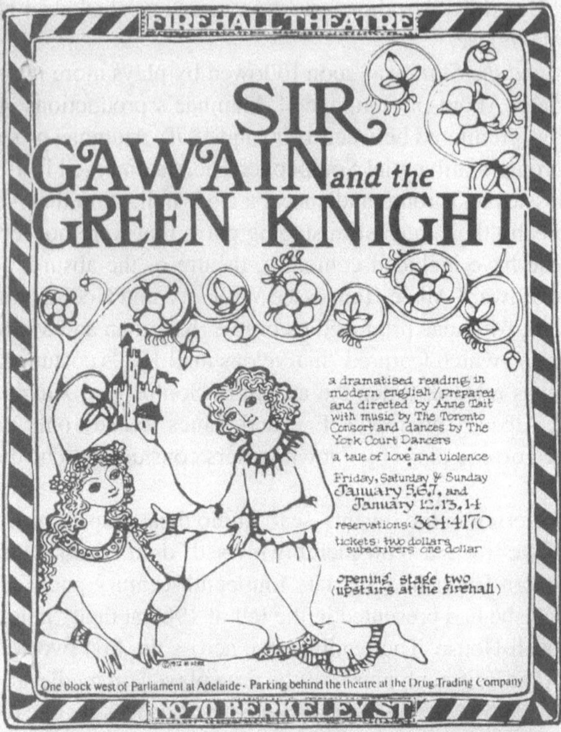

Figure 4.5. Mary Kerr's poster for *Sir Gawain and the Green Knight*, prepared and directed by Anne Tait for Alumnae as a "dramatised reading in modern english." Songs were composed by Garry Crighton, with lyrics by Anne's husband Michael Tait, and were performed by the Toronto Consort. Diane Polley was the show's House Manager. It ran in January 1973 at the Firehall theatre, four years after an earlier version was read at the Maplewood Coach House. Courtesy of Alumnae Theatre Company.

The remaining productions of the first Firehall season set a pattern Alumnae would follow for years: a world premiere of an English translation, an all-woman show from the 1930s, the Toronto premiere of two Edward Albee one-acts, and the North American premiere of a European modern.[74] They concluded the season in spring 1973 with the North American premiere of Maxim Gorky's 1914 play *The Zykovs*, adapted and directed by Thom and designed by Brian Arnott Associates. Arnott, a design consultant working for the first time in Toronto, had worked with the Royal Shakespeare Company and London's National Theatre. As Alumnae's press release proclaimed, he designed thirty-three trees for the show along with "massive cedar furniture designed and built in the Firehall workshops." Whittaker was pleased with this set, saying the production was a valuable introduction to Gorky,[75] although the acting was inconsistent. Kareda observed that it was "precisely the same" set that Timothy O'Brien had designed for the RSC's production of Gorky's *Enemies*. As the season ended, Kareda reflected that it had been a difficult year for Alumnae, who were "caught off-guard by the quite different demands of so auspicious a building." However, he believed *The Zykovs* provided "some evidence that the Firehall was

Figure 4.6. Terance Belleville in the titular role of Peter Handke's *Kaspar*, directed by Pamela Terry with costumes designed and executed by Eileen Williams at Alumnae's Firehall theatre in the fall of 1973. Photo Credit: John Bloom. Courtesy of Alumnae Theatre Company.

beginning to assume some authority" because the play "does at least move in the direction of the intelligent, thoughtful presentation which has been this organization's hallmark."[76]

"Long a force in harnessing Toronto to the avant-garde theatre,"[77] Alumnae enjoyed their first critical success at the Firehall at the outset of their second season with the English-language Canadian premiere[78] of Peter Handke's "major work,"[79] *Kaspar*. Directed by Pamela Terry, *Kaspar* received the positive response that Alumnae had grown accustomed to at their Coach Houses. Handke, an Austrian, had emerged as a master of language like Beckett, but with biting political nerve; Kareda called him a "self-styled, cultural revolutionary." Handke's inspiration was the historical Kaspar Hauser, a "savage child found in Nuremberg in 1828, terrified, wild, capable of speaking only a single sentence." (The word "Kaspar" echoes the German word for speech, "sprache," and the German word for clown or fool, *Kasper*.[80]) In Handke's treatment, Kaspar's "vocabulary has increased, but it is the tool of his enslavement … as Kaspar is initiated into the bourgeoise,"[81] wrote David McCaughna in the *Toronto Citizen*. Fresh in the minds of many at the time was the 1970 French film by director François Truffaunt, *The Wild Child* (*L'Enfant sauvage*), which told a similar story about a child in eighteenth-century France, as well as the Actor's Theatre production of Handke's one-act *Self-Accusation* in Toronto that summer.

Kareda found *Kaspar* an "amazing piece of theatre" that was "quite moving" and "persuasive."[82] McCaughna called it a "worthy mounting" that "captures forcefully the pathos of Kaspar's journey," adding that Alumnae had made better use of their "greatly increased space"[83] than they had the previous season. The monologue-style script featured six actors playing various aspects of Kaspar, as well as "haunting" masks designed by Joanna Jaciw that made Kaspar's "own open visage … hard to ignore."[84] Whittaker, perhaps baffled by the production, repeatedly wondered whether Handke was the new Beckett, concluding simply, "It was an evening."[85] Allan M. Gould of York University's Theatre Department wrote a letter to the editor in response to Whittaker's review: "Mr. Whittaker showed an embarrassing lack of understanding of this play."[86] He asserted that Alumnae had presented a "solid production of one of the most significant plays of the last decade."[87] Having an "undeniable way with the difficult and the obscure,"[88] Terry's direction was an "intelligent introduction to the play, without being the most vivid argument for its theatrical force," while meeting Handke "on close to his own terms."[89] Terry would direct eleven more plays for Alumnae, including challenging European works by Vaclav Havel (twice), Samuel Beckett, and Suzanne Finlay, as well as an Alumnae piece for Toronto's first Nuit Blanche festival in October 2006.[90]

When Alumnae "scored a coup again by being the first to mount"[91] a Toronto production of Harold Pinter's *Old Times* in 1974, Kareda commented that "in some ways, Toronto theatre has done such a good job of encouraging Canadian drama that we've rather fallen out of touch with what is happening elsewhere."[92] Reviewers observed that Pinter's plays had never received a professional production in the city, although there had been a number of amateur productions,[93] and "no amateur group in Toronto has been more active in championing Pinter than [Alumnae]."[94] Productions of plays like Leonid Andreyev's 1922 modern melodrama *He Who Gets Slapped* in 1977 continued Alumnae's record of offering European curiosities.

Alumnae's upstairs Studio production of four short Beckett plays – *Come and Go*, *Ohio Impromptu*, *Catastrophe*, and *Play* – in February 1987 brought Pamela Terry back to direct work by a writer who had helped define Alumnae's Coach House Theatre success three decades earlier (see chapter 6). Alumnae were among a number of Toronto theatres (including Toronto Free Theatre and Theatre Plus) offering a variety of Beckett plays in honour of his eightieth birthday. Alumnae's production involved a "good mixture of old and new faces," according to Catherine Spence's production report.

Confusion regarding Beckett's oblique writing was as apparent as it had been when Alumnae were the first to offer his plays to Toronto, but audiences now dealt with this confusion in a different way. In filled-out comment sheets left at the door after the show, audience members wrote everything from a "magnificent production," "flawlessly performed, and stunning to the imagination," to "What are you trying to do … confuse us?!?" and "Good acting. Empty stupid play." Times had changed, specifically the way in which theatre-goers viewed the use of their time. One person wrote, "I would like you to adopt the civilized practice of starting 20 minutes late, to accommodate people like me. Missed 1 1/2 plays. Otherwise I liked it very much." Another wrote, "I am speaking for myself and three others. We have been regular subscribers for six year[s]. This evening has been a complete waste of time. We have not understood any message and been totally bored. Next year we will subscribe to the downstairs only. I am very critical of whomever made this decision to present this drivel." Yet another wrote, "Fancy wasting your talent on such rubbish." No longer, it seems, was there the thrill of being confronted in the theatre by something unfamiliar and challenging and trying to work out the meaning of a play. By way of metacommentary, another audience member wrote, "Just reading the comments and it looks like many of your subscribers are of the 'dinner theatre mentality' – more's the pity." Two things had changed since their 1957 *Waiting for Godot* production (see chapter 6) that accounted for this variety of experiences: there was an Alumnae subscription series to snare audiences (for better or for worse), and there had been, for years, a dearth of attention to Alumnae in the papers. Without critics like Whittaker and Cohen consistently preparing subscribers for something different, the four Beckett plays had to speak for themselves to audiences not necessarily looking for a challenging evening of art. Unfortunately, Alumnae's press release for the show, which tied their Coach House Theatre *Waiting for Godot* production to the present Beckett offering, did not find a broader readership than the editors of the dailies, who did not print it or send to reviewers. Catherine Spence's production report noted that the average attendance was twenty-five of seventy-five possible seats; however, this overall low number included two sold-out evenings in the second week, leading her to conclude that it was a "most successful," "high quality production."

Contemporary and Period Plays

Most of the plays Alumnae have produced had their world premiere within a decade of the company presenting them. "Modern," of course, is a relative term, and from today's perspective it was during the 1970s that "modern" drama arguably found an end time. Whereas modern meant "contemporary" through the end of the 1960s, this study assigns the latter term to new plays that emerged in the 1970s. In that sense, two thirds of Alumnae's productions at the Firehall have been "contemporary" comedies, dramas, and adaptations by playwrights like Carol Shields, Sharon Pollock, Sarah Daniels, Judith Thompson, Tom Stoppard, Alan Ayckbourn, George F. Walker, Christopher Durang, Lanford Wilson, and Caryl Churchill, often produced within a decade of their world premiere. Critically praised productions of contemporary plays have included Margaret Edson's *Wit* in the fall of 2008, which *eye weekly* called one of Alumnae's "strongest pieces in years,"[95] and Judith Thompson's *Palace of the End*, staged in November 2009, just two years after it premiered down the street at CanStage.

In the 1980s, Alumnae largely turned away from political theatre in favour of lighter contemporary comedies. A jarring exception was Václav Havel's *Largo Desolato* (1984), translated from the Czech by Tom Stoppard and directed by Pamela Terry. It ran in the Studio from 14 November to 2 December 1989 during the Velvet Revolution, over the course of which the leaders of the Czech Communist Party resigned (on 24 November), one-party rule ended in Czechoslovakia, and the playwright Havel became the country's president. It was the only production of a Havel play in Toronto at the time and had been programmed with an eye to contemporary events. The result was a sold-out run.[96] (Ray Conlogue in the *Globe and Mail* only noted this success in a footnote in his review of a production of *Meet Me in St. Louis* in New York, after Alumnae's run.[97]) If Alumnae had relinquished their role as a politically astute theatre company, they temporarily regained it in Terry's hands with Havel's semi-autobiographical play about a human rights activist condemned for political dissent, presented at a time when communist governments were falling across Eastern Europe. The bluestockings could still produce relevant and radical theatre.[98]

Three months later, Alumnae programmed Carol Bolt's 1974 "Canadian classic"[99] *Red Emma: Queen of the Anarchists*, around the same time that an opera about anarchist

Figure 4.7. Dennis Horn's costume sketches for Alumnae's production of Sharon Pollock's mystery *Blood Relations* in October 1994. In 2006, Horn was nominated for the prestigious Siminovitch Prize for his body of work as a set and costume designer. Courtesy of Alumnae Theatre Company.

Emma Goldman was being developed for the Guelph Spring Festival.[100] In the communist *Canadian Tribune*, Brian Davis called Alumnae "probably the most stubbornly amateur theatre company in Canada. To call them amateurs is not to belittle them, however, for they are amateurs in the proudest sense of the word – people who are not motivated by money but do something for the sheer love and pleasure of it."[101] He declared the production, which marked the first time the play had been produced in Toronto since its premiere at Toronto Free Theatre sixteen years earlier – "worth seeing." Said Davis, "even when the actors' skills fail them, they manage to convey these passions with their intensity." In David Sinclair's hands, Alexander Berkman's dock speech "has a contemporary urgency about it."[102] Bolt herself "loved"[103] the production; in a letter to director Kerri MacDonald, she described it as "full of passion and spirit and fun, directed with intelligence and style."[104] In programming two revolutionary plays, *Largo Desolato* and *Red Emma*, Alumnae were making a political statement that other theatre companies in the city did not, or dared not, make at the time.

Alumnae's final show of the 1989–90 season, the Canadian premiere of postmodern American writer Craig Lucas's 1983 black comedy *Reckless*, also garnered unusually strong critical attention. It was a rare Alumnae co-production with the then five-year-old

Figure 4.8. Paul Markovich's set design for Alumnae's production of Carol Bolt's satirical collective musical docudrama *Red Emma: Queen of the Anarchists* in March and April 1990. Courtesy of Alumnae Theatre Company.

professional theatre company Eclectic Theatre Productions (ETP) and their artistic director Jordan Merkur; Alumnae were able to pay him to direct it through a Toronto Arts Council grant. What made the "elegant production"[105] unique was that it featured set designs by ETP members working with Alumnae producer Margaret Edgar.[106] The female lead was played by non-member Wendy Krekeler, a "recent theatre grad who plans to make a career on the professional stage."[107] It was a true co-production between Toronto's oldest company and one of its newest, with the former giving the latter space (the Firehall's Mainstage) and time (two weeks of tech rehearsals) that the latter could not otherwise have afforded. Edgar attributed the multiple interviews and reviews the production generated in print, radio, and television to Merkur's rising profile.[108] Conlogue and Kaplan enjoyed the production's comedy and its "clever"[109] set, although Alex Patterson in *Metropolis* expressed ambivalence about the play's refusal to adhere to naturalism, writing that the "only way to get this stuff past an audience is by sleight of hand: keep it moving along quickly enough that they don't have time to examine what they're being asked to swallow."[110]

Alumnae's greatest critical and financial success of the 1990s, if not of all their Firehall years to date, was their Toronto premiere of Carol Shield's *Thirteen Hands*, which ran in the spring of 1995. The play's director Molly Thom wrote in Alumnae's newsletter at

Figure 4.9. (*left to right*) Judy Darragh, Anne Harper, Barbara Barnett, and Esther Hockin of the "Martha Circle" in the Toronto premiere of Carol Shield's *Thirteen Hands* in May 1995. Shields won the Pulitzer Prize for Fiction for her novel *The Stone Diaries* that year, fuelling enthusiasm for Alumnae's extended run of her play. Photo Credit: Kerry Battersby. Courtesy of Alumnae Theatre Company.

the time: "Not since we opened the new theatre in 1972 has there been such excitement at an Alumnae opening. Surrounded by cameras and cables and major press (all the way from *Eye Weekly* [*sic*] to the *New York Times*), we waited in excruciating suspense to welcome Canada's Pulitzer Prize winner, Carol Shields, to the Toronto premiere of *Thirteen Hands*."[111] Shields had just won the Pulitzer for her novel *The Stone Diaries*, and Toronto could now celebrate by attending a play not so much about bridge, as Christopher Winsor wrote in *eye weekly*, but "about life's sometimes epic, most often banal, yet meaningful, parade through a community of 12 related women."[112] So popular was the run that Alumnae treasurer Carol Palmer reported that the production's financial success had created a "distortion"[113] because of its unprecedented five-digit revenue, three to four times higher than any other Alumnae production that season. Vit Wagner in the *Star* wrote that the group "hadn't seen this kind of excitement in a good long while."[114] This was clear from the critics, who had never before attended an Alumnae production in such numbers, revealing just how many reviewers there now were, even if they usually ignored Alumnae. But the media attention was not solely because of the playwright and the production. Alumnae's publicist Sally Szuster, who had worked with Theatre Passe Muraille, "pounded relentlessly on media doors" so that by the time *Thirteen Hands* opened, reported Thom in her year-end audience development report, "all her ships came sailing in." Thom went further, saying "Sally's success was a major step in legitimizing the work we do here and re-establishing the Alumnae as a significant player in the theatre community." Thom's audience development committee targeted high school drama teachers for all of their season shows and, for *Thirteen Hands* in particular, bridge clubs, who attended "in spades,"[115] with the hope they would return. Palmer even coached the cast in playing bridge.[116] They also added two-for-one Wednesdays, which were continued the following season. Notably, *Thirteen Hands* was the first moment in which multiple reviewers referred to Alumnae not as "amateur" but as "semi-professional."

Thirteen Hands became a crucible for celebrating Alumnae's invaluable position in Toronto theatre. According to critic Richard Ouzounian, Alumnae had been doing "straightforward productions of excellent plays that no one else in the city seems to be doing," and with *Thirteen Hands* they "hit the jackpot" with a "grand slam of a show."[117] Jon Kaplan called it the "best Alumnae show in several seasons."[118] In the 1990s, Alumnae often focused on plays by and about women, yet critics were amazed, and in one case angered, that Alumnae had scored the Toronto premiere. Wrote Winsor, with verve, "my only real bitch is much broader. What the hell are we doing giving a writer of Shields' stature a semi-pro, cash-starved Toronto premiere, however well-intentioned? Where are the big companies whose subscription base is the perfect audience for this show? Shame. No wonder established Can-lit figures rarely bother to write for the stage."[119] Ouzounian agreed, saying Alumnae "picked it over a year ago, for one reason only: they believed in it, and having seen it, so do I. The only perplexing thing is why Tarragon or Canadian Stage didn't have the foresight to program it. It's a thrilling evening of theatre."[120] For Winsor, Esther Hockin as Clara "turns in one of the finest performances I have seen in a long time. Period."[121] Wagner explained that Hockin "personifies that ability that some old people have to appear totally befuddled and marvelously astute, all at once."[122]

With the occasional exception, Alumnae have largely moved away from the period plays. At the Firehall they have produced only sixteen period plays, and between 1981 and 1995 they produced none. These are often complex plays to mount linguistically and in terms of costuming, providing a challenge that most companies cannot take on. However, Alumnae have the benefit of decades of accumulated wardrobe collections and continue to attract educated members interested in the classics. And although they are relatively few, Alumnae's period productions are often noticed because of their general rarity in the city.

Among the period plays with which Alumnae have been involved, the first production in over 400 years of *The York Cycle of Mystery Plays* was a landmark event. Over the first Saturday and Sunday of October 1977, U of T's Centre for Medieval Studies' Poculi Ludique Societas (PLS) produced the biblical "history of the world," from Creation to Last Judgment, in its entirety for the first time anywhere since 1548. Although the PLS had been producing medieval plays in Toronto and across North America for twelve years, their press release called *The York Cycle* the "high point" of their oeuvre. It featured all forty-seven plays in the cycle performed over twenty hours by various campus, church, and community groups, as well as other universities in Ontario, along with Syracuse and Cornell universities. More than 500 "amateurs, academics, and students of drama"[123] participated as if they were members of the medieval craft guilds producing in original conditions. For Alumnae, *The York Cycle* was something of a return to their early ties to U of T. The PLS, in conjunction with U of T's Graduate Centre for Study of Drama and the Records of Early English

Figure 4.10. Eleanor Aylesworth as Lady Teazle in Alumnae's April 1981 production of Richard Brinsley Sheridan's *The School for Scandal*, directed by Araby Lockhart and assisted by Francess Halpenny. Ron Gilmore designed the set and costumes. Photo Credit: Stephen M. Katz. Courtesy of Alumnae Theatre Company.

Drama (REED) project, provided the modern English texts, background materials, nine curtain-framed pageant wagons (including five farm wagons recently restored by PLS wainwright and stage manager K. Reed Needles), and assistance with costumes and properties.

The first thirty-three plays, including Alumnae's, ran on Saturday, 1 October. Alumnae chose to present the twenty-ninth pageant in the cycle, *The Trial before Caiaphas*, prepared and performed four centuries earlier by "two of the less prosperous guilds,"[124] the Bowers and the Flecchers, who "appropriately" would have provided "props, ropes and scourges."[125] Toronto Truck Theatre's Virginia Reh directed Alumnae's offering; she would return to direct a few Alumnae productions over the next decade. With plans to be staged on the one-storey harvest-gold "Dolphin Wagon," *The Trial before Caiaphas* was listed as starting at precisely 3:06 p.m. and running for nineteen minutes. However, "torrential rains" postponed many of the Saturday performances by several hours. Alumnae's performance was among those moved inside Convocation Hall, leading *Varsity* reviewer Therese Beoupre to lament that "it was almost a more oppressive environment for the festival atmosphere of the medieval cycle than any downpour would have been. The whole purpose of the play's revival – the creation of the pageant wagons' procession – was abandoned with the move inside." She suggested that the "Varsity hockey arena would have at least salvaged the

Figure 4.11. The cast of *The Trial before Caiaphas*, Alumnae's contribution to the University of Toronto's ambitious October 1977 production of *The York Cycle*. Courtesy of Alumnae Theatre Company.

dynamic staging of the cycle."[126] Moreover, because Alumnae's guest actor Garnet Truax, playing Malchus, was "due at another theatre" that evening, a member of the York Cycle Committee, Ben Gunter, "quickly learned and performed" his role.

The PLS again produced *The York Cycle* in June 1998, and Alumnae gave "support"[127] when Jennifer Parr directed *The Fall of the Angels* for the Vagabond Knight Company to open the cycle. Alumnae volunteers, audition and rehearsal space, and access to costumes and props were to be made available, as was season brochure advertising. In fact, the club had agreed to "accept the proposals of two members to support two York Cycle productions and advertise those productions in our Season Brochure, but that the Alumnae Theatre not commit any funds to these projects."[128] Francess Halpenny was to direct *Transfiguration* for Alumnae, but this did not come about. PLS itself offered the play instead.

The Audiences and the Membership

In their inaugural Firehall year, Alumnae's executive – Joan Shaw (president), Norma Clark (past president), Margaret Spence, Molly Thom, Diane Polley, Phyllis Benvenuto, Shelagh (Hewitt) Kareda, Agatha Leonard, and Mayvis Hayman[129] – navigated the company through the complications of enticing new and old members and audiences into a new building. The Firehall was a historic building that demanded attention from passers-by and visitors. It contained spaces for administration, storage, rehearsals, and a range of performance styles. There were two theatres: a midsize proscenium "Mainstage" and a smaller upstairs "Studio" they referred to in their 1976–77 press release as the "Firehall's own 'alternate theatre.'" In their sixtieth season they renamed the building "the Alumnae Theatre" and the Studio "the Betty Mascall Studio Theatre" to honour the passing of one of their influential leaders during the Coach House years. Now that they had two theatres, they were able to expand their Coach House programming, which previously had been centred on one small stage of their own, with a rented midsize venue, such as the Central Library Theatre, for larger shows. The Firehall gave them total scheduling and programming control over their own small and large stages.

Now that there were more theatres in Toronto appealing to more diverse audiences, Alumnae changed their approach to attracting and retaining both audiences and members. Their subscription numbers had fallen from between 600[130] and 1,000[131] in the 1970s to between 450 and 550[132] in the 1980s. By their hundredth anniversary, subscriptions were in the dozens. In an interview, Jane Carnwath described their current audiences as "mixed" in terms of their dedication to Alumnae:

> There is a very very small core of "The Faithful." They even sell a few subscriptions. But they're certainly not our biggest audience. It's usually driven not so much by "we're going to the Alumnae" as "we're going to see [a particular show]." And this I think is both a strength and a liability because each show has its own following. I think there's a tendency to silo each production just a bit. You get so into it, you get your group …The audience is often specific to the play, or the director, or the particular group that's doing it. Of course, that's not specific to the Alumnae. I would say it's hard to predict who our audience is going to be. We certainly market to groups who might have a particular interest in a production. And we have loyal followers, whether or not they subscribe.[133]

In framing audience outreach as navigating the tension between maintaining a loyal following and targeting shows to particular interest groups, Carnwath effectively alludes to Alumnae's new approach to carving out their new place in Toronto's theatre ecology: they now needed to reinvent their audience with each production. Their Coach House Theatre audiences, by sharp contrast, had been eager to try out anything the company produced.

However difficult Alumnae have found it to hold on to subscribers in recent decades, they have also found it "increasingly difficult to attract new members," despite having "one of the best theatre spaces in town" and "near professional standards."[134] During the Firehall years, membership has usually hovered between 120 and 150. The story of Alumnae at the Firehall has been, in significant part, a story of the ebbs and flows of volunteers' commitment to the significant administrative duties required to run the company and their building.

Nicholson and colleagues have theorized the relationship between work time and "free time" in our daily lives as it pertains to amateur theatre. "As a sociable activity," they observe, "the success of amateur theatre also depends on making time to take part." Drawing from Hannah Arendt, Theodore Adorno, and Sarah Sharma, among others, they argue that because theatre, as a leisure-time pursuit, "works under the pressure of time," nonprofessionalizing theatre is particularly susceptible to the effects of twentieth-century capitalism's "changing employment patterns"[135] in which time is valued most greatly when put towards consumption.[136] Underpinning this model are stereotyped notions about the value of nonprofessionalizing activity. Another factor has been the "politics of labour," which have marginalized nonprofessionalizing theatre and maintained "professional privilege" not only within theatre ecologies and the critical communities that review and research them but also among cultural policy-makers.[137] Fewer people spend their time reviewing and researching nonprofessionalizing theatre relative to professional theatre, and far fewer fund it.

As they moved into the Firehall, Alumnae needed to account for changing expectations of women in the workplace. Molly Thom went so far as to tell *Scene Changes* in 1978 that, ironically, the women's movement that had influenced Alumnae's first shows now threatened the company's existence.[138] Within two years of moving into the Firehall, the company was visiting other groups in search of new members.[139] In 1977, Thom worked on U of T's Sesquicentennial theatre season, even while, like many Alumnae women, she was looking for a day job for herself.[140] Said Thom, "Sixty years later, the women we used to count on for members are going into demanding full-time careers and can't give us the time we need."[141] This placed a strain on the nonprofessionalizing theatre model, in that members were expected to work on shows in evenings and on weekends even while maintaining their own jobs through the week. By the early 1980s, Alumnae described their members as "for the most part professional women – who contribute their time and tremendous effort on a purely voluntary basis."[142] By the 1990s, with a membership hovering around 130, annual membership turnover was around forty new members in, and forty short-term members out.[143]

The participatory principle continues to dominate executive discussions. But pleas from the executive to the membership to participate, especially offstage, are constant. Certainly, many long-standing Alumnae members have balanced their careers with their Alumnae participation, and many have balanced raising a new family as well. But women's careers and, importantly, their community involvement were now threatening Alumnae's participatory principle in new ways. In the fall of 1974, president Margaret Edgar wrote what she called "some worrisome thoughts" to the membership:

> Many of us joined in order to act. It is a fact, however, that for every woman's part on stage, there are often ten and more women working behind the scenes … Times have changed. Involvement not only at home but in jobs, community, education, all result in less involvement per person in the Club. One answer is to increase the membership from its present low figure of 80–90 paid members to 150–200. This can only mean fewer acting parts to go around, but at least we will have the bodies needed to mount shows we can be proud of.[144]

Edgar's thoughts were meant to energize those members who were not helping in one way or another with productions. But it also pointed to the central fact that many more women were now juggling jobs in addition to their home lives, so that theatre involvement was more difficult to incorporate into their activities. The following year, the *Globe and Mail* reported that Alumnae were experiencing "survival pains thanks, ironically, to the new state of femininity … Most of those committed and concerned women are out working and pursuing careers which leave them very little time for volunteer work, so the Firehall Theatre has to cope as well as it can."[145] This meant, for example, that for their fall 1974 production of Lanford Wilson's *Lemon Sky*, the producer had to be house manager and help with sets, sound, and lights while the two assistant stage managers took on the job of stage manager – a task with which they were not familiar. "This make-shift situation taxes everyone and contributes nothing to a fulfilling experience,"[146] wrote Edgar. Emphasizing how seriously the core members took their theatre work, she asked everyone to bring solutions to the next general meeting.

A decade later, the issue of participation continued to press. President Roz Heller called a general meeting in September 1986 on the issue of who was doing the production work. She wrote:

> I am very concerned about the Alum. For the past five or six years, certainly since I have been a member it has been difficult and at times impossible to get members to produce or crew a show and indeed, to serve on the Executive. My directors inform me that few members come out for auditions and the Front of House Manager has even had difficulty getting members to do Box Office for a night. All this summer when my Past President and I have asked, nay, begged members to fill executive positions the answer has been NO. Perhaps we are unrealistic in having seven shows a season? Perhaps we are choosing the wrong sort of shows? I need to know how you feel, to have your suggestions and ideas. In these changing times what does the Alum mean to you? What do you want for your $45 membership fee? … It is unacceptable to me to keep on expecting a handful of dedicated people to run this theatre.[147]

Five months later, executive member Jo Bruce listed between twenty and thirty-five production positions that needed to be filled in order for an Alumnae show to be produced, from producers, designers, and stage management to painters and costumers. She stated that the same people were doing most of the work: "If you are a member and acting in a production you should be prepared to participate in at least one other production as 'crew.'" She asked three remarkable questions: Should Alumnae institute a "performance fee" of $25 for men and women, with the option of women paying the membership fee instead "with its attendant benefits and responsibilities"? Should there be an initial women's audition for members only? And should "men be allowed to become associate members without voting privileges for a fee?"[148] These options, especially the first and third, would amount to a sea change for Alumnae if they were chosen. Administrative-minded women like Mallory Gilbert and Shelagh Kareda left Alumnae in the 1970s for careers in professional theatre. Alumnae were surely affected by an increasingly professionalized and monetized theatre industry, not only among performers but among technicians and administrators as well.

By the late 1980s, the place of nonprofessionalizing companies had changed to the extent that Alumnae now filled a new participatory niche in the theatre community. Publicist Ann Sargent described this niche to the *Star*'s Vit Wagner in 1987:

> There are just a lot of people around who know they aren't going to have a career in the theatre or may not even want to have a career in theatre … But they love theatre and they love being involved. They want to act, direct, do set designs or learn technical theatre … It may not be at the level of professional theatre, but I think it's a good calibre … And I think we take a lot of risks.[149]

The emphasis in Alumnae's public discourse had pivoted from providing pre-professional experience to providing paraprofessional experience alongside professional companies. This was one way to recognize the value of nonprofessionalizing theatre as a "leisure" pursuit within the capitalist market.

At the 2002 annual general meeting, executive producer PJ Hammond could state that when contacting members to work on shows, she made

> 70 phone calls, and received 33 replies (less than half even acknowledged my effort!). Of these replies, 21 were able to help with box office or bar. I needed 44 people. The lack of results makes it difficult to spend the time calling people begging. Why should I waste my time begging if the majority won't even give me 2 hours of help? We have had suggestions, but we need to devise a plan and carry it through. All departments, all members should be involved in solving this problem. It is worthy of each person's full attention.[150]

Beyond the particular circumstances of 1986 and 2002, Heller's and Hammond's respective efforts indicate that Alumnae's capacity to produce was being threatened by low participation rates. For Hammond, Alumnae were an "organization that passes up. Delegates up. By the end of the four years [I was president] it was a struggle to fill positions on the board. They're telling you what they can't do."[151] It remains an ongoing concern that the club's core members take on more than their share of the work as unstaffed duties are delegated upward. The same struggle was evident during the Second World War as Alumnae disengaged from University College; since their move to the Firehall, the broader scope of the company's operations, including building maintenance, has made recruitment even more crucial as well as even more daunting.

Work patterns have shifted in the twenty-first century from "9 to 5" lifetime careers to a patchwork of jobs in a "gig economy." This, according to Nicholson and colleagues, may be affecting the "annual rhythm of amateur theatre."[152] The mindset resulting from short-term contracts and self-employment is not conducive to committing to a theatre company over the long haul. In the summer of 2019, journalist Sadaf Ahsan wrote in the *National Post* that Alumnae's houses were rarely full any more and that they were finding it increasingly difficult to recruit volunteer administrators. "Most young people who want to pursue theatre want to pursue a professional career," Thom told her, "and while they see the importance of starting here, the numbers don't look great. I don't know how to entice them. It's a question of money and marketing."[153] Active member Catherine Spence observes,

> There's a bit of a different volunteer culture now than there used to be when I started with the company [in the 1970s]. People used to devote large chunks of time and come in and work on more than one show. And now it's likely to be, "I'll come in and work on my friends' shows and go off and work on something else" … It's a way of building your resume in a way that people weren't thinking about in the seventies. People weren't thinking of going on and doing something else. There are a lot of people who self-produce [now] … The roots aren't as deep … I'm not saying people aren't committed, but it's a different kind of commitment.[154]

Over the years, Alumnae have often struggled to expand the number of members running the company, and the gig economy has heightened these challenges. What one generation may perceive as a lack of "loyalty" or a "self-centered quest," another sees as part of a "cultural shift"[155] in which all of one's work, be it professionalizing or nonprofessionalizing, is fluid. This means that the struggle to gain and retain active members has intensified. Rather than non-commitment or self-interest, changing work patterns may be the reason why members like Margaret and Michael Spence and their daughter Catherine, as well as Molly Thom, Jane Carnwath, and a handful of others, have been so deeply concerned about the company's operations; it may also explain, in part, why influential past members have left, including PJ Hammond, who says she dropped her membership in 2014. The reality is that some members work in the gig economy and work freelance (including those who are also students), others hold jobs with more traditional 9-to-5 hours, and others are retired or semi-retired. The experience of "work time" is very different between these groups, and as a result so is their experience of "free time" for nonprofessionalizing theatre.

One way to negotiate this "differential time,"[156] as Sarah Sharma puts it, or these different "time zones,"[157] to borrow playwright David Ives's metaphor, is to take scheduling of rehearsal and meeting times seriously. At nonprofessionalizing theatres this can result in what strikes some members as draconian control over their leisure hours, which in turn generates mutual hostility and a disincentive to return. For Carnwath, who has directed fifteen shows at the Firehall, it is a question of how you frame the production process for your cast:

> I'm very strict about attendance and promptness, which sometimes goes *this* way [*points down*]. Because they're not being paid. They have other commitments and you just have to acknowledge that. We talk through that … If you can't be here be sure we know in time to do something about it. And they're usually good about it. There's the odd one … You don't say things like, "I know we're a community theatre, but we have professional standards," because that's blahblahblah. You just try to show them that … I know other community theatres and some very fine directors who get caught with that a lot. You know, we do this for fun. And if it's not fun we don't come … You don't have to say very much … People who consider working with us usually have a pretty good idea of what we're looking for.[158]

Like many long-standing nonprofessionalizing companies in this country, Alumnae operate with a professionalism that is necessary for their continuance and that is, they hope, contagious.

One way to broaden Alumnae's volunteer base – an option raised by members cyclically over the years – would be to expand the membership to include men. Alumnae's unique position as a women-only theatre society has been debated since men were first cast as guest actors in 1922. In the fall of 2000, Alumnae's vice-president of membership, Dawn Williams, raised the question from a perspective the club had not yet considered: the "ethical and legal implications of a women-only group." It was decided to form a committee, conduct further research, and report to the membership, possibly proposing a change to the by-laws at the annual general meeting.[159] Reflecting on this conversation, PJ Hammond says that some members articulated that they felt safe knowing that "I can come to this membership meeting with my baby on my lap and everybody's fine with that and that would fundamentally change if it were opened up." There was a fear that if the company were open to men and it did not work out, they could not go backwards. Others, like Hammond, question both the ethics and the "feminist agenda" of an all-women club that relies on men to do much of the manual labour that makes the club function:

> I've always had a personal conflict with saying I'm part of an all-women's organization because if you can't have an all-men's organization you probably shouldn't have an all-women's organization too. [*laughs*] Little bit? And if we are embracing that this is women doing it, then let's fucking do it! A halfway point where we go, "Oh, but we need a man to build the set" is not fulfilling a feminist agenda. We are looking for plays by women and strong women characters, but then we're turning around and saying, "I can't hold a hammer." I've always had a conflict with that. [As a producer] I've had female lighting designers and female set designers. It's one of the things I've tried to do, but it's not one of the things the organization tries to do.

> It's a very producer-specific thing. And I have a conflict with that. I love the feminist agenda. But then we actually have to own the whole thing.

Hammond adds that in these respects, since the 1970s "we haven't really found a new identity." She wonders whether the women-only status may now make the company look like "snobs" in the eyes of the theatre community. She calls Alumnae's male guests "friends" because "male participation is so regular, it's not remarked upon." And she comments on the "stories I've heard from the ladies about the sixties when the women would meet in the livingroom and talk about what plays they were going to do while their husbands built sets in the garage. There was that time when the women came with their husbands as part of it." This is no longer that time. But, as Hammond notes, the relationship of the men to Alumnae have been affected by the changing positionality of women to privilege:

> We talk about our crisis in terms of volunteerism right now and how do we get people who have jobs and families and don't live nearby to commit to doing work that needs to be done all year long. And we were like, "Well women don't need a hobby to take them out of the house anymore." There's a sociological change that has happened that has affected the way that we run things … It's the women of Toronto, the women of *privilege* in Toronto. I'll add that. Because these were university-educated women who had houses and garages that their husbands worked in, *right*?[160]

As anyone who has tried to own property in Toronto in at least the past thirty years knows, a home with a garage, for any purpose, is increasingly difficult to afford. This is one economic reality that has fundamentally influenced the perspective of any woman who comes to Alumnae.

In the new century, Alumnae have also sought to diversify their membership and audience by attracting, in early 2000s parlance, "more members of other cultures."[161] They do this in part by liaising with other theatre groups in the city. In January 2001, the board decided that it was "Alumnae's policy to encourage colour-blind and gender-blind casting, as well as including people of differing abilities."[162] The following season, president Pat McCarthy told the board that her "main objective" that year would be to "improve on diversity," citing *Now* reviewer Jon Kaplan's urging of Alumnae to "start a trend in Toronto, to include actors of diverse backgrounds on our stage." Audition notices began to include a note on diversity,[163] and in November 2001, McCarthy reported to the board that there was a "'buzz' about the Alumnae and what it can do to promote diversity."[164] Today, however, Alumnae's membership remains largely homogenous, and, as Margaret Spence notes, it can still be a "struggle"[165] to cast non-white actors.

As Nicholson and colleagues note, there are often "difficulties that circulate around the issue of ethnic diversity" in amateur theatre that drive to the core of homogeneous memberships. Perhaps not surprisingly, given that their founders a century ago were British expats, military men and their families, and university graduates, long-standing nonprofessionalizing theatre companies in Canada that were once deeply occupied with nation-building and the Dominion Drama Festival often maintain programs and memberships that reflect the settler colonialism they once served. Efforts today to break the mould and attract a diverse membership often fail, further adding to negative stereotypes surrounding nonprofessionalizing companies. Moreover, there is a "Catch-22 logic" at play that if members of racially diverse communities do not come forward, "then they are not seen and this creates a perpetual cycle of non-representation and non-participation"[166] that can result in blaming the non-white communities for their disinterest. When addressing a lack of diversity by attempting to generate diverse programming, a company must seek out and welcome diverse participants who are not yet members; if they cannot be recruited, then the play cannot be produced and the attempt at representation fails (see *The Comfort Girl* discussion in chapter 7). The result is a reification of settler colonialism and increasingly negative public perceptions of the company.

Nevertheless, as Barry Freeman observes, following Alan Filewod, many nonprofessionalizing theatres in Canada are openly "culturally focused."[167] In this light, perhaps, we might ask whether Alumnae are among the nonprofessionalizing theatre companies that are best situated to produce English-language settler-colonial work, the way Nové divadlo produces theatre by and for the Czech and Slovak community. Is the entire notion of producing within the Eurocentric-model of Western theatre inherently homogeneous and thus unlikely to move companies like Alumnae from occasional representation to full-fledged diversity? Or do the freedoms in programming and casting actually position these companies to pivot to inclusion more easily than their professionalized counterparts? Conversations today about equity, diversity, and inclusion are already informing the work that many of these companies do, just as is happening in other sectors.

Heading into Alumnae's centennial year, vice-president of membership Liz Best reported that of the club's 178 members, the highest in Alumnae's history, 134 were "active" in productions, owing to a volunteer program in which "active members are expected to contribute at least 20 hours of volunteer service in pre-determined areas, also known as, 'the jobs that are so darn hard to fill.'"[168] Perhaps the increase reflected the thrill of the centennial; even so, only rarely does a membership report fail to lament a lack of volunteerism among paying members in areas other than acting.

Even when membership and volunteerism flag, end-of-year work and play functions continue to be central to the club's internal identity. Well into the 1970s, the annual party featured skits[169] written by Alumnae members and their friends that were sometimes spoofs on recent productions (such as the *Power of Darkness* send up called *The Towering Darkness*[170]), along with "dinner, drinks, dramatic and musical merriment."[171] Member Cicely Thomson was still hosting the annual meeting and party at her home on Major MacKenzie Drive well into the late 1980s, forty years after her first appearance on an Alumnae stage.[172] Since then, the work of their meetings has been cleaved from the festivities of the annual party as their building has consumed more administrative time. By 2000, the question was being raised at board meetings as to whether the cast and crew of the past year's production should even receive invitations to the annual general meeting (it was decided that year that due to "budget restrictions," they would not, although they were still "welcome to attend"[173]). Not overtly inviting the membership to their own annual meeting amounted to an historic confession of the bureaucratic weight placed on the club after eighty years.

PART II

Perspectives

The four chapters in Part II revisit defining perspectives from Alumnae's first 100 years: theatre spaces, festivals and nationhood, new play production, and the emergent professionalizing era. These perspectives have defined Alumnae's private operations, public notoriety, and legacy from their first production at the Toronto Conservatory of Music raising money for the war effort, to their first world premiere, to their own centennial celebration. All theatre companies, whether nonprofessionalizing or professionalized, have dealt with elements from each of these perspectives, and scholars have studied each from various positions, although almost exclusively in professionalizing contexts. But because of their longevity, notoriety, and extensive archival collections, Alumnae provide us with a rare opportunity to reassess the value of nonprofessionalizing theatre practices to our understanding of culture spaces, nationalizing endeavours, artistic creation, and the professionalization of cultural activities.

Chapter 5

A "Distinct Passage Way"[1]: Theatre Spaces

The day after Alumnae Theatre Company opened their Edwardian firehall to the public, Urjo Kareda described the space:

> The entrance and lounge areas are particularly handsome, with the beautiful wallpaper, the elegant wood paneling and the subtle attention to detail. There is a special grace in the images of this building's past, in time-stopped photos of firemen, touching displays of old equipment. Here, we feel, is a civilized, authoritative environment for theatre-going.[2]

At Alumnae's Firehall Theatre the heroism of the first responders of Toronto's past meets the trappings of gentrified Toronto entertainment. Alumnae members curated the modern theatre lobby with William Morris wallpaper and the fire equipment of horse-drawn days to set the company's tone for decades to come. Places are not static but dynamic; they hold memories and rearrangements invoked through choices in architecture and art. Both proprietors and borrowers of space, Alumnae have built their reputation in relation to the buildings they have inhabited. At the Firehall, Alumnae benefits from an inferred symmetry between their historic building and their historic company. They capitalize on the commingled histories of a heroic city service and participatory entertainment whenever audiences cross their threshold.

In the section of *City Stages* titled "The Edifice Complex," Michael McKinnie observes that "performance space was coded in the late 1960s Canada as the architectural expression of artistic ossification and social privilege."[3] He is referring here to buildings with brutalist architecture, like Toronto's St. Lawrence Centre, linking them to similar theatre edifices in Winnipeg, Ottawa, and elsewhere that gained a reputation for their cold concrete exteriors irrespective of the vibrancy of the art within. In contrast, architect Ron Thom's design for Alumnae's Firehall Theatre created a warm, modern look that revered the histories of the building *and* its resident company, setting them in dialogue with other Toronto theatres, especially those that had also emerged around that time.

Alumnae now had two theatre spaces in one building, each designed to draw the audience into the same intellectual, physical, and communal space as the artists: a Mainstage space ideal for medium-sized casts and traditional stagings, and a smaller Studio space for new and experimental performances, workshops, and staged readings. Alumnae could now present "mainstream" proscenium plays on their main floor and "underground" radical incursions in their attic, a physical and ideological dualism unavailable to monostage theatre companies.

This chapter reflects on Alumnae's theatre spaces and associated locations, renovations, and negotiations. It demonstrates that over the decades, each of Alumnae's theatre buildings has helped define their programming and reputation by influencing the size, shape, and atmosphere of the plays they produce. The story of Alumnae's migrations across Toronto says as much about how they find ways to adapt as it does about how the city values the theatre they produce. For example, whenever Alumnae moved Coach House Theatre homes between 1956 and 1972, they generated public anticipation because, uniquely, women were finding buildings for theatre, and because, for so long, other companies could not afford their own spaces. This chapter traces Alumnae's use and management of, and impact on, the spaces and places they have inhabited and the contexts in which their property acquisitions emerged. From large public venues and large-cast plays, to small venues and small-cast plays, to a historic firehall showcasing a historic company, a significant part of Alumnae's identity and success has involved their relationship to the spaces they have transformed.

Over their first century, Alumnae presented their productions at thirty venues within, and fifteen venues outside of, downtown and midtown Toronto. They also produced plays and skits at members' homes after general and annual meetings. Geographically, the majority of their productions have been offered within a cartographic box loosely bounded by Eglinton Avenue to the north, Parliament Street to the east, Front Street to the south, and Bathurst Street to the west. In no small part, their longevity can be attributed to the places they have chosen to produce theatre. From April 1921 to the Second World War, most of Alumnae's full-length plays were produced at the popular Hart House Theatre (fifty-nine), and their invited one-acts and revues at the University College Women's Union (thirty). After uncoupling themselves from the UCAA during the Second World War, as intellectual nomads they sought off-campus spaces for their one-acts (because they no longer used the UC Women's Union) and for remounts of their Hart House Theatre regional festival entries.

Like other mid-century independent theatre companies, Alumnae also produced shows at community venues such as churches (First Unitarian Church, Parish Hall at Christ Church in Deer Park, St. Alban's Cathedral parish hall, Grace Church-on-the-Hill, St. James–Bond United Church, the Parish Hall of the Church of the Messiah), clubs (Women's Art Association,[4] Hamilton Players Guild, the Arts and Letters Club), and private and community auditoriums (Eaton Auditorium, Margaret Eaton Hall, CBC's Radio Hall, the auditorium of the Toronto Public Library, Erindale Community Hall). They remounted their festival shows at high schools (Central Technical School, Etobicoke HS, Forest Hill Collegiate, Leaside HS, Northern Vocational School) and the Garden City Theatre at the Vineland Festival in Ontario's Niagara region. And they sent their festival-winning shows to the DDF finals at Ottawa Little Theatre, the London Grand Theatre, the St. Charles University Auditorium in Sherbrooke, Quebec, the Queen Elizabeth High School Auditorium in Halifax, the Queen Elizabeth Theatre in Vancouver, and the Royal Theatre in Victoria. They even toured a wartime play to Camp Borden. These varied locations helped Alumnae build early audiences and media recognition throughout Toronto and beyond. The work of rescaling their shows to different-sized spaces that were far less equipped in terms of theatre technology than Hart House Theatre required Alumnae's early women to gain proficiency as stage managers and crew who understood how to run a variety of early lighting and sound equipment, or to make up for an absence thereof. At larger venues, sometimes they worked with men who were stage managers with electrics training, but at smaller

Alumnae Theatre Company Locations (1918–present)

Alumnae's Own Performance Spaces

1. Coach House #1 (16 Huntley St.)
2. Coach House #2 (200 Bedford Rd.)
3. Coach House #3 (151 Huron St.)
4. Coach House #4 (10 Maplewood Ave.)
5. Firehall (70 Berkeley St.)

Other Main Performance Spaces

1. Toronto Conservatory of Music (College St. and University Ave.)
2. Hart House Theatre (7 Hart House Cir.)
3. UC Women's Union (79 St. George St.)
4. Central Library Theatre (20 St. George St.)

Other Performance Spaces

1. Old UC Women's Union (85 St. George St.)
2. Women's Art Association (23 Prince Arthur Ave.)
3. First Unitarian Church (216 Jarvis St.)
4. Parish Hall, Christ Church, Deer Park (1570 Yonge St.)
5. Eaton Auditorium (444 Yonge. St.)
6. Margaret Eaton Hall (21 McGill St.)
7. St. Alban's Cathedral Parish Hall (100 Howland Ave.)
8. Northern Vocational School Auditorium (851 Mt. Pleasant Rd.)
9. Radio Hall (12 Spadina Ave.)
10. Grace Church-on-the-Hill (300 Lonsdale Rd.)
11. Parish Hall of the Church of the Messiah (240 Avenue Rd.)
12. Arts and Letters Club (14 Elm St.)
13. Forest Hill Collegiate Auditorium (730 Eglington Ave. W.)
14. Central Technical High School (725 Bathurst St.)
15. St. James-Bond United Church (1066 Avenue Rd.)
16. Leaside High School (200 Hanna Rd.)
17. King Edward Hotel Hunting Room (37 King St. E.)
18. Trinity College's Convocation Hall (6 Hoskin Ave.)
19. Art Gallery of Toronto Sculpture Court (317 Dundas St. W.)
20. Grenville Street Playhouse (23 Grenville St.)
21. Colonnade Theatre (131 Bloor St. W.)

Alumnae's Own Non-Theatre Building

1. Unused 'Coach House' (62 Birch St.)
2. Residential Rental Property (42 Cecil St.)

Rehearsal and Storage Borrowed

1. Storage Barn (Lonsdale Rd.)
2. Hewitt's Attic (Willcocks St.)
3. Library Staff House (222 College St.)
4. United Empire Loyalists (30 Prince Arthur Ave.)
5. Rehearsal Coach House (159 Cumberland St.)

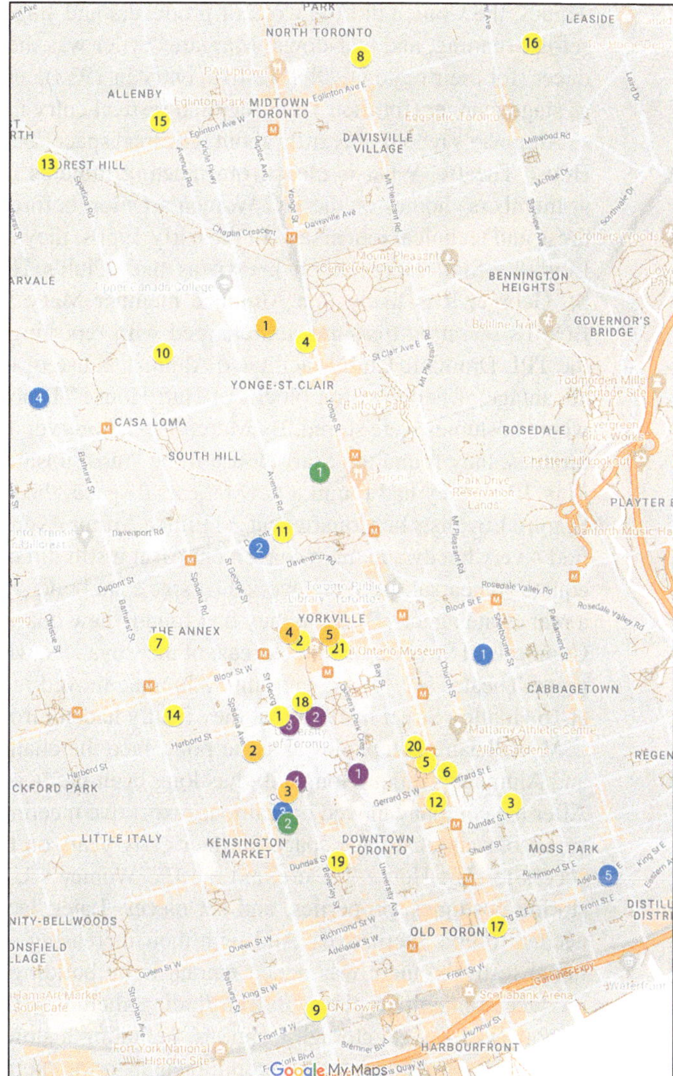

Figure 5.1. Map showing the Toronto locations with which Alumnae have been associated, including performance and storage spaces.

venues, the women did the work of producers and stage managers charged with a show's set-up, running, and tear-down. Margaret Tytler was the first club member listed as a producer (for their regional DDF festival entry in 1933), and Alison Ewart was the first listed as stage manger (for their DDF regional festival entry in 1934).

Alumnae's records say little about rehearsal spaces before they acquired their first Coach House Theatre. What is clear from meeting minutes is that scheduled rehearsals began at members' homes or the UC Women's Union before moving to a particular venue for dress and technical rehearsals. In the early 1950s, they rehearsed at the Toronto Reference Library's Staff House, then known as the "Club's House," on College Street west of St. George. It is likely that Alumnae member Mary Smart, who was both the Library Board's secretary-treasurer and charged with reporting to that board on the activities of the TPL Dramatic Club,[5] facilitated Alumnae's use of the Staff House. It had the distinct advantage of being within blocks of Hart House Theatre and Alison Hewitt's home attic, where costumes were stored. By March 1953, however, for reasons unexplained in meeting minutes, they found the Staff House to be "most unsatisfactory this year."[6] By the end of May 1954, they had found a new rehearsal space, the Governor Simcoe Branch's United Empire Loyalists headquarters at 30 Prince Arthur Avenue, which they "considered quite a find – very handy and most convenient." But it still did not satisfy their overall need for adequate "rehearsal space and workshop space" to build sets and costumes, so they contacted a real estate agent.[7] By June they had found "new quarters"[8] in a coach house behind 159 Cumberland Street, a few blocks east of the Loyalists, which they could share with the local group Theatre '49.[9] It was not until Alumnae moved into their first Coach House Theatre at 16 Huntley Street in 1957 that they finally had control over their own rehearsal space.

Most theatre companies at some point face the challenge of finding sufficient storage, and Alumnae's unique longevity has long been predicated on finding workable solutions. After the company moved off campus, executive meetings were largely taken up with conversations about storage space. In their early years on the U of T campus, they had some access to Hart House Theatre and the UC Women's Union when it came to making and storing costumes, properties, and set pieces. Later, lacking access to these spaces, they needed to find alternatives. And with their increasing successes at DDF regional and national festivals, there was added emphasis on building and saving the right materials to produce competitive plays. Before finding their first Coach House Theatre, they rented or borrowed several storage locations, including a storage barn on Lonsdale Road in the Forest Hill neighbourhood for building and storing their flats, furniture, and other sets and props;[10] member Mary Evans's house, where scenery and props apparently continued to be stored two years after her death in the early 1940s; the UC Women's Union basement;[11] the Toronto Reference Library's Staff House; the United Empire Loyalists' house; and the above-mentioned coach house on Cumberland Avenue.

Company lore has it that at some point before 1939, member Alison Hewitt began storing Alumnae's costumes in her attic office space on Willcocks St. (where the university's Sydney Smith building is now located). Hewitt's house was ideal for storing Alumnae's costumes, being within blocks of both Hart House Theatre and the UC Women's Union.[12] The club had agreed that she should "take full charge of the costumes kept at her house, as it was difficult for anyone else to look after them."[13] The unfinished attic was accessible through the room that became her daughter Shelagh's bedroom. Five or six times a year, Alumnae members went through her bedroom at night to get costumes (Shelagh admits to sneaking up to play with them as a child).[14] In January 1943, the executive discussed the viability of continuing to store costumes in her attic.[15] They decided to catalogue the items under executive member Ruth Home’s supervision[16] and discussed moving them to either the Women’s Union or St. Alban’s Parish Hall.[17] Nothing came of this, however.

In the fall of 1951, Hewitt raised the issue of fire insurance for the costumes stored in her attic and the set pieces stored in the Lonsdale barn. It was reported that insurance for her attic would be an expensive proposition at $23.00 per year; Mary Rose offered to find another rate, but it seems that nothing came of this. It was further noted that the contents of the barn “might not be an insurable risk.” Hewitt asked for volunteers to help sort additions to the costume collection, and Mary Smart, Ruth Johnson, and Margaret Tytler obliged. A party was organized to go to the barn with Hewitt’s husband’s truck “to evaluate all the flats and their condition” and to remove two trunks that were “cluttering up the barn.”[18] Within a month, Hewitt’s husband had looked into insurance. He believed that $23.00 was too high,[19] and Alumnae agreed. With no decision on insurance, Hewitt dryly “suggested that no one should smoke in the attic.”[20] Future conversations about the attic and the barn focused on the need for volunteers to help organize both.[21]

The next issue Hewitt raised was that “there was not enough equipment to store the costumes adequately.” So Alumnae agreed to purchase additional casters and racks. She then suggested shelves to replace “about 50–60 boxes piled around the room,” which “touched off a fairly lengthy discussion on the prospect of using apple boxes for shelves.” She then recommended that they “start a collection of small properties,” and Mary Smart “offered to work on a card index of properties.”[22] Storage was still a talking point two years later, when Betty Gray reported that “there are many costumes around at the homes of various members, but since there is no heat in the attic there is not much point in going over in the very cold weather”; she made arrangement to meet with Hewitt about it a few days later.[23]

Concurrently, Christina Templeton reported that she had been searching for an alternative to the Lonsdale barn,[24] which was falling into increasing disfavour among members. It had “long been considered inadequate for building sets, and the club members have searched in vain for a larger place.” Moreover, the barn’s owner, Mrs. Dick, had just raised the rent, “so it is hoped that a new location can be found by fall.” They maintained that the “ideal arrangement would be to have rooms for rehearsals and the making of costumes in the same building. Don’t pass by possibilities because they seem too big; it may be feasible to share the premises with another dramatic club.”[25] Thus, in early fall of 1954, Alumnae put out a call for a new storage location. Reflecting the mores of the time, in her “Person to Person” column in the *Globe and Mail*, Lotta Dempsey ended a piece about how one “could describe the typical beautiful Canadian girl”[26] by saying: “Canadian girls also enjoy play-acting. And one of them has asked our help on a problem faced by the group with which she is associated … If anyone has a large room or two (warehouse type) with wide entrance and high ceiling at very low rental (or *gratis*) Eleanor Beecroft … would love to hear. After 3:30pm.”[27] In the meantime, to manage cleanup it was decided that every member should “devote one day every three weeks toward the barn.”[28] As Alumnae continued to accumulate both a reputation and production materials, other groups approached them regularly to offer or ask to rent items.[29] Rentals would be an ongoing concern for Alumnae, particularly when they began managing their own theatre and storage spaces in the decades to come.

Lofty “Coach House” Plans in the City’s Smallest Theatre

Besides rehearsal and storage spaces, Alumnae have rented, leased, or owned seven properties, all since 1956. Of these, they turned five into performance spaces, including four “Coach House Theatres” on Huntley Street (5 productions), Bedford Road (13), Huron Street (41), and Maplewood Avenue (13), and the firehall where they currently reside (more than 300 productions as well as New Ideas Festival shows). They have also owned two other properties: a house on Birch Avenue intended for use as a Coach House Theatre, and a residential rental property on Cecil Street adjacent to the Huron Street Coach House Theatre. On the one hand, moving theatre spaces helped draw a substantial audience base from across the city by bringing fresh eyes in different neighbourhoods to their shows; on the other, moving added repeated administrative stress that periodically threatened their ability to produce plays.

For years after they left the UCAA, the company produced in a range of buildings. They soon began seeking a more permanent location. Across the 1953–54 season, during which they produced a demanding schedule with half-a-dozen shows at four different venues, ongoing rehearsal and storage concerns intensified Alumnae's search for a space of their own. In September the St. James–Bond United Church on Avenue Road arose as a possible venue.[30] The church had a playing space fifteen to eighteen feet deep and around twenty-two feet wide with lights overhead, curtains, and an audience capacity of about 350. Within a month, they had secured it and voted to make it their "experimental theatre" for an "arena style play."[31] They considered several plays for a December production, presumably to test out the space.[32] However, there is no clear record that the "Christmas Invitational" evening went through. They did, however, produce two one-acts there in May 1954. At their season-end annual meeting held at Cecily Thomson's home, the club again discussed performing shows in a smaller venue. Second vice-president Barbara McNabb's report on "studio performances" described "plans for a Nativity play at the Church, with the Club members as the chief actors, with children from the church helping in the cast," and the church paying a director. However, concerns were raised because the "Club would really be expected to do [backstage and design] production work," which would be difficult at that time of year because preparation for the regional festival production would be starting up. They voted that the executive "negotiate with"[33] the church; in the end, they decided not to perform there again.

In its thirty-seventh year, Alumnae finally found a theatre of their own when their rental offer on a coach house at 16 Huntley Street in Toronto's Upper Jarvis neighbourhood was accepted in the spring of 1955. They put half[34] of the $1,000.00 first-place prize money they had won at the 1956 DDF finals for Patricia Joudry's *Teach Me How to Cry* towards the "nest egg"[35] that renovated the space. Eleanor Beecroft's president's report that year called the months that led up to the rental "perhaps the most unsettled period" in their history:

> The atomic tests of the Yucca Flats have been nothing as compared to the trials we have endured in our efforts to find a home …
>
> Having built our sets for some years at … Lonsdale Rd … under difficulties – we had to find a new home. Many homes were [sought by] telephoning, walking, inspecting … by the Executive, until we found the most suitable place to house our efforts was on Adelaide Street – at $50 per month. After [a time] we were forced to admit that our budget could not stand the strain and again we were looking for a home.
>
> After much the same procedure … we were able to rent a wonderful coach house on Huntley St., with quarters for construction work and also rehearsal space. A four-roomed apartment above has been rented [by the owner] and the income from it should ease the strain on our finances.[36]

The coach house finally provided space for set storage and building as well as for auditions, rehearsals, and, of course, performances.[37] Centrally located southeast of Bloor and Jarvis streets, its main building was Woodsworth House, the headquarters for the Co-operative

Commonwealth Federation's (CCF's) Ontario section. Previously, the coach house had been the shared home of *The Canadian Forum* magazine and the Book Service (later called the Old Favorites Book Shop). Upstairs in the coach house was an apartment the landlord rented out, but downstairs was sufficient for a small theatre. It was a significant moment in the club's history: For the first time they were both play producers and building managers. The coach house afforded Alumnae the ability to control how and when they produced plays.

It would take two years[38] to transform the two-storey brick[39] building into a "miniature theatre."[40] By June 1955 it was clear that a "house committee"[41] was needed to focus efforts on painting and cleaning, which members Ruth James and Ruth Francis were already working on. All members were expected to give "full cooperation."[42] They commissioned Alumnae guest actor and CBC set designer[43] Russ Waller to "draw up plans" that would cost less than $100.00[44] to realize. Under the supervision of member Molly Golby (later Molly Thom), whose day job was typographic design,[45] Alumnae members and their friends executed Waller's designs, renovating one of the coach house's rooms to make an intimate thirty-five-seat "pocket theatre"[46] with a fourteen-by-eight-foot stage under a (notably low) seven-foot ceiling.[47] Having more than four people on stage was "extremely crowded." Waller designed a "lighting system out of tomato juice cans."[48] In her final president's report in June 1956, Eleanor Beecroft acknowledged the house committee: "Only those who have scrutinized floors and painted walls and hauled flats about can really appreciate how much we owe them."[49]

Once organized, the Coach House Theatre's first use was for set building. For the first time, Alumnae had control over their theatre designs and the shape of the space. This led to deeper thoughts about how to approach design, as articulated at the time in a four-page company history document, likely mailed out to members:

> The design of the play's settings is often undertaken by the director, or if not by him, by an independent designer interested in the work of the Alumnae. The company has its construction headquarters in a centrally located coach house, and stores there all material for this work. With rehearsals under way (first at the coach house before the noise of set construction begins, and then either at members' homes or rented quarters), properties and furniture being tracked down, and costumes started, the Alumnae sets up a Committee to work on scenery. These ladies, blue jean clad, build with boards, cloth, nails, and paint the walls, doors, windows, steps and levels of the stage setting. They make real the designer's sketches. The Alumnae has interested a staunch group of men who share with the company the responsibility of set construction. The Stage Manager, in charge of the technical side of production, is usually a man.
>
> On average, all these activities prior to performance take up about six or seven weeks of time. The great assembling comes at dress rehearsal when scenery, lighting, properties, furniture, costumes, sound effects and actors are joined together to produce the total effect of a play in performance.[50]

Besides providing a space for performance, the coach house rental was a means of easing the complicated process of creating and storing materials like set pieces while providing early- and late-schedule rehearsal space. Ruth Jones kept the coach house committee focused on its task so that a year later the theatre was "in order."[51]

The first Coach House Theatre production, in March 1957, played well on Alumnae's diminutive stage: Henrik Ibsen's drama *John Gabriel Borkman*, about a banker who has served time for misspending public money and is now cloistered in his home while his daughters scheme to bring honour back to the family name. Herbert Whittaker described the new stage as being of "postage-stamp proportions. But those few feet of space were enough to house the half-dozen major characters of Ibsen's drama, which looked no less titanic for being so confined."[52] Under the low ceiling, Rex Southgate was a "towering figure"[53] in the titular role. The novelty of the smallest theatre in Toronto drew crowds.

Yet the Coach House Theatre was far from an ideal performance venue. In the small space, three women created stage effects for the show.[54] Former Alumnae designer Martha Mann Southgate recalled how Alumnae solved the problem of an upstairs sound effect in the small building:

> Because it starts with Borkman walking around, and they couldn't get a decent sound recording of steps overhead, every night for the performance the man who lived upstairs in the top part of what had been the hay barn for the Coach House ... would be John Gabriel Borkman walking up and down upstairs for the whole first act of the play. One of my favourite Alumnae moments ... The person who was renting the top was a funny Englishman. It was a coach house so the bottom part, where the theatre was, was where the carriages were and the horses. And the top part was the barn where the hay and the feed was kept. And it had been converted long since into a very interesting but very tiny apartment. [The Englishman] was very involved eventually with the Alumnae. He actually married an Alumnae member. He was persuaded that he could walk around for half an hour upstairs making a lot of noise.[55]

Moreover, as one Alumnae document records, there was "no means of crossing over behind the stage, so that anyone who had to make an exit stage right, and then enter stage left, had to go out of the door on one side, run around behind the building, and come in the door on the other side."[56] Adds Molly Thom, once inside the front door there was a "dash past the flats storage, through the dressing room and back onstage."[57]

The lack of backstage crossover resulted in some awkward interactions in the neighbourhood during their June 1957 production of Anouilh's *Ardèle*. During the third act, which takes place at night, the "inhabitants of Huntley Street were treated to the strange spectacle of figures flitting in and out of #16, clad only in Victorian nightgowns."[58] Described Francess Halpenny, who played the General's wife, the "poor mad soul, appeared in a nightdress of the nineties, and, since there was no other way to get from one side of the stage to the other, each evening flitted back and forth outside under the trees calling like a peacock."[59] Thom explains that Halpenny's character was "called upon to shriek 'Léon' from offstage, which meant in our case from outside the back door. What the neighbours must have thought of this figure in a billowing Victorian nightgown standing in the garden screaming into the night can only be imagined."[60] Furthermore, from the apartment above a ringing telephone interrupted performances, as did the "musical sound of water being let out of a bathtub." But Alumnae spun the space's shortcomings in a positive light: "Despite these inconveniences, there was one big advantage in the presence of that apartment. When a play required a character to call from upstairs off-stage, or, as in August Strindberg's *A Dream Play* in October 1957, from Heaven above, the actor could actually go upstairs and speak through the heating vents in the floor of the apartment."[61] The trials of their Coach House Theatre buildings would haunt Alumnae for more than a decade, and their ability to creatively solve these trials would define their reputation as inventive women in creative urban spaces.

Meanwhile, the fire department "took a dim view of the premises,"[62] and the landlord wanted to use the building for other ventures. After just five productions, a move to

Figure 5.2. (*left to right*) Doris Stacey (Miss Ella Rentheim), David Bedard (Erhardt Borkman), Rex Southgate (John Gabriel Borkman), and Pamela Terry (Gunhild Borkman) in Alumnae's production of Henrik Ibsen's *John Gabriel Borkman* in March 1957. It was the company's first "Coach House" play. Courtesy of Alumnae Theatre Company.

a new location was necessary. In January 1958, reviewers announced that Alumnae's world premiere of Newton's *The Lion and the Unicorn* would be the last play presented at the Huntley Street Coach House Theatre.[63] Once again, Alumnae were looking for a new home. "Perhaps the standards of production have not always been as high as the ladies' taste," wrote Whittaker, "but each production has been treated honestly and intelligently. And where else could a serious Toronto playgoer see such a collection of plays?"[64] Both the 16 Huntley Street house and its coach house were later demolished for a high-rise apartment.[65]

At the end of May 1958, as they were returning from the DDF finals with the Festival Plaque for best production in English for *Waiting for Godot*, the "adventurous"[66] Alumnae announced[67] that they had rented upstairs loft space above a garage "devoted to a little light manufacturing" at 200 Bedford Road, in the northeast part of Toronto's Annex neighbourhood. The "inventive, industrious group of ladies" transformed the loft into a "most intimate studio theatre with better seating and playing conditions than they had previously"[68] and with more room backstage. The new Coach House Theatre – Alumnae kept the moniker to maintain name recognition with the company and its programming – had room for fifty-eight seats. "It leaves a good deal to be desired from the outside and is not nearly as colourful as our old coach house," Thom told the *Star* at the time, "but we've managed to fix up the inside pretty well."[69]

Like the Huntley Street location, the Bedford Road site was not licensed as an entertainment venue. So audience members phoned ahead for an invitation; admission was free, but they were expected to make a donation. As might be expected, this was not a foolproof plan for generating income, and the *Star* reported that within a year, university students "arrived, ignored the plate and took their seats. Theatre officials found it embarrassing but with rent bills staring them in the face, approached the freeloaders. Contributions were eventually wrung out of even the hardened hearts."[70]

Alumnae's tenure on Bedford Road did not last long either. At the time, they had nearly seventy members[71] and a mailing list numbering over 1,000 subscribers.[72] While they were presenting William Congreve's *The Way of the World* in February 1960, their landlord told them they were "being disposed"[73] from the Bedford Road property, "forced to leave" because a "fellow tenant ... wanted to expand his business."[74] Explained Halpenny, the "proprietors of the garage found the Coach House a somewhat odd tenant, and a move had again to be made."[75] Their last production on Bedford Road, the Toronto premiere of Henri de Motherlant's *Queen after Death*, closed the first week of May 1960.

Having attracted a following, and wanting to place themselves "beyond the reach of landlords and fire marshals,"[76] the club, "urged on by its friends," decided to "take its courage in its hands"[77] and raise enough money to purchase its own theatre. Alumnae would be the only company in Toronto at the time to own their own theatre. The idea was to present four or five productions a year and rent out space for the remaining time to "other organizations for meetings, concerts, or other theatrical productions."[78] They immediately set their eyes on a "long, narrow lot"[79] at 62 Birch Avenue near Yonge Street, "centrally located"[80] opposite Summerhill subway station, with nearby parking. By March 1960,[81] they had purchased the lot for $9,000.00, largely raised from members' donations.[82] Herbert Agnew, an architect and "tireless artistic consultant and professional advisor"[83] for the club, donated a design for a ninety-four-seat theatre.[84] Alumnae started fundraising again, this time for themselves. That meant writing letters, twisting arms, and begging.[85] They planned to start building by the spring of 1961.[86] However, they had not yet raised enough funds to do so, even after adding the net profits[87] from their 1960–61 season.

With an executive led by president Helen Dunlop and a fundraising campaign chaired by a well-connected friend of the club, Vida Peene,[88] Alumnae launched an ambitious plan to raise $65,000 ($9,000.00 for the land, $47,500 for the building, $8,500 for the stage equipment).[89] Peene's Building Fund Committee was comprised of club members Agatha Leonard and Francess Halpenny along with a "committee of good friends,"[90] including past Alumnae guest director Edgar Stone.[91] In early 1961, Alumnae incorporated with the province[92] and began collecting tax-deductible donations from the public. They promised that donors of $100 or more would be called "Founding Members" with "special recognition" of gifts of $500 and $1,000 and above. They explained:

> It is the hope of the company to have a new home which will be permanent, in which they can present the same theatrical fare as they have been offering in recent years. The building will be simple but functional for the purposes of the productions. There will be workshop and storage facilities. The price of admission has always been modest at the Coach House and it is hoped that a ticket will cost no more than $1.50. It is worthy of note that in its forty years of operation the Club accounts have always been "in the black," even if only by a modest amount.[93]

Contrast all this with the opening of the O'Keefe Centre a year earlier, in October 1960. In the *Globe and Mail*, Whittaker derided the O'Keefe: "[Alumnae's new theatre will be] as important in its own modest way as the spacious one that opened last October … [Alumnae's] ladies are determined that [their new theatre] will be self-supporting. Can the 3,200-seat O'Keefe Centre say the same?"[94] A committed core of members had run Alumnae responsibly for more than four decades, and they intended to keep doing so with the enhanced recognition of owning their own space. Halpenny later attributed this sound management to "rigorous control of ambitions and steady recognition of sensible aims."[95] Whittaker did his part by ending his piece, aptly titled "The Bluestockings have a blueprint," by saying that Alumnae had been an "important contributor to the theatre scene of Canada for 43 years. It must be helped to continue that contribution."[96]

While they strategized the procurement of a new performance space, Alumnae borrowed space around the city. They produced their 1960–61 season out of the Central Library Theatre[97] at College and St. George Streets (later the Robert Gill Theatre of the university's Centre for Drama, Theatre and Performance Studies), next to the Library Staff House, where they had once held rehearsals. It was the first year that the Central Library Theatre operated as a rental space for local companies, and Alumnae were among the first to use it. Then the Red Barn Theatre took it over, at which point Alumnae announced in a flyer to their subscribers that "we have promised you a new Coach House Theatre in the 61–62 season, and we are bending every effort to deliver it on schedule! In the meantime, even though our flats are in storage and our costumes in packing boxes, we ourselves can still be on stage." (At the time, Eleanor Woodside's garage was used as storage, although it would need to be cleaned out before Labour Day "when the Woodsides acquired a second car."[98])

Alumnae were now the legal owners of 62 Birch Avenue,[99] but as Dunlop, now past president, reported, expenses were proving to be very high.[100] They were at a crossroads. The executive noted that with just $7,868 in the building fund, "no decision [should] be made until Nov. 15th when we have heard from [the] foundation. A strong possibility that we might have to go back to rented premises on a good lease." It was suggested that they look into two possible spaces to rent: the vacated studio of the York Community Theatre, which had just "folded,"[101] and the library theatre, which they had rented the previous season. Dunlop investigated the former possibility and Lorna Rogers the latter.[102] By November they had raised just under $11,000 for the building fund from the membership and the public; business donations were "not as good."[103] They ran their 1961–62 season of one-act modern readings out of the Trinity College's Convocation Hall.

By the spring of 1962, it was clear that they would be unable to raise enough funds to make Birch Avenue feasible,[104] and they began to wonder whether the narrow[105] property warranted such an enormous investment. Its size was far from ideal, and it seemed foolish to sink all that money into something so restrictive. As Alumnae's theatre manager with "no theatre to manage," Thom concluded, "Obviously we must look elsewhere."[106] It was now five years since they had opened their first show in a Coach House Theatre and a year and a half since their last show. The ramifications were serious for club morale, audience retention, and public profile. Playreading committee chair Pamela Terry noted bluntly:

> Older Club members are champing at the bit, with vivid memories of organized Coach House fare, and long to get started again. Our audiences have naturally disintegrated, with no assurance of where and when we may pop up next. And new theatre groups have started up doing our kind of plays which may weaken our comeback. New members to the Alumnae are no

> doubt in a state of bewilderment most of the time. For in lieu of joining an actively producing theatre group of high standard (which we are, primarily) they must, at the moment, bear with our "if-maybe-perhaps" policy of enforced homelessness.[107]

Terry even wondered whether her committee should be reading plays if there was no "stable assurance"[108] of a space in which to produced them.

From "Vagrants"[109] to a Synagogue Home

Heading into 1962 with the Birch Avenue financial plans in stagnation, the executive began exploring a new option for their next Coach House Theatre. In January, secretary Marilyn Turner wrote in her minutes: "Theatre – synagogue – asking price $37,000 – 1950[s] [sold for] 30,000 – will prob. take 31,500 … attractions – plumbing, heating."[110] Alumnae's real estate agent (the mother of member Patricia Carroll Brown) had found[111] an Orthodox synagogue[112] for sale on the northeast corner of Huron and Cecil Streets, a block south of College Street and the university campus. Alumnae estimated that if converted into a theatre, the synagogue would generate income of $4,620 per year and incur expenses of $2,970. It was worth exploring. The executive prepared a brief on the synagogue for the membership. By March, the membership had passed motions to sell, or at least mortgage, 62 Birch Avenue to empower the executive to "make an offer of purchase" on the synagogue property, and to approach Herbert Agnew for a design.[113] Agnew agreed to design the new theatre and lobby for $2,300; Russ Waller submitted three sketches for a possible stage. It was agreed to use the synagogue's existing benches for seating. Agnew estimated the total renovation costs at $7,500,[114] although this amount ballooned to $10,000 by the end of May.[115] The Birch Avenue location would need to be "cleaned before being put up for sale";[116] also, two windows would need to be installed and some flats moved. Difficulties arose: Alumnae's initial offers for the synagogue were rejected, and only three parties had responded to their Birch Street ad in the *Telegram*.[117] An increase in the synagogue down payment was considered if the Birch property could be sold immediately.

Producing theatre without a home was taking a toll on show attendance, and concern continued to swell that a season without a space was draining interest from members and audiences. Their 1961–62 season of moderns and their Art Gallery of Toronto showing of Molière's *Les Femmes Savantes* "kept at least a feel of production."[118] But without a predictable location, they were getting lost in the events listings. Reported publicity director Lorna Rogers,

> unfortunately, one can't force the entertainment editors to give as much free space as one would want. Several times I was asked about our plans for building our own theatre, but was unable to comply simply because we have been in such a state of flux. This indicates that people are still very interested in our activities. Once we have something concrete to tell them, we shall be in the public eye once more. All going well, our publicity program will be stepped up considerably once we have a place to call our own.[119]

Without their own theatre, Alumnae's own members were not even attending their shows at a rate they should, let alone paying their annual dues.[120]

A "stalemate ensued for several months, with the men of our Committee advising patience until the owners turned our way."[121] In May 1962, members passed a motion directing the executive to purchase the synagogue and sell Birch Avenue, "contingent upon approval of building fund committee." They stressed the immediate need to find at least $2,000 more for the synagogue purchase.[122] Club president Eileen Williams wrote to the membership, "We are almost in sight of our goal and with a special effort now can undoubtedly reach it." She was "anxious that all members should feel it and respond to it."[123] Proving to be the club's most vigorous salesperson, Thom put it this way:

> If every active member of this Club could get $30 from someone, we'd have more than enough. I urge you all to rack your brains for new sources of money and make it your personal and individual responsibility to go out and find it ... Without a theatre next fall, this Club, which has endured for 43 years through every kind of crisis, will be dead. I want very much to have a theatre to manage next year.

Thom also thanked "that devoted band of men who stand by us through every emergency."[124] Williams emphasized that other Toronto theatre spaces were "disappearing," noting that Centre Stage was "becoming [a] subway," the Grenville Street Playhouse was "reverting to storage," and the Central Library was "booked for [the] season by the Red Barn." It was "urgent" for Alumnae to be in their "own quarters, working, and winning new members and our audience." She "reaffirmed the desire to see the Club in action once more with each member participating in some significant way in at least two of the five yearly productions." She concluded with an appeal to members to contribute to the property fund so that they could purchase the synagogue.[125] Thom reported that "these have been anxious times for us all – on occasion, faith and hope have been strained almost to the breaking point. But we must believe in the future, we must assume that we can complete the transaction and be in operation again next fall."[126]

Their efforts paid off. Alumnae took possession of the synagogue and the adjacent residential property on Monday, 16 July 1962, paying $32,000 with a $8,500 down payment[127] from the building fund. Income from the sale of Birch Avenue, when it occurred, would go towards renovations.[128] Members met on 19 July to vote for the "changing of the club house"[129] from 62 Birch Avenue to the 42 Cecil Street house location, as the synagogue did not yet have a separate street address.[130] Alumnae finally owned a theatre.[131] Wrote the executive to its ninety members in capital letters: "Every member must be prepared to assist in a position of responsibility to ensure that our Coach House Theatre is in tip-top shape for our first production." The message continued: "For 43 years we have been 'vagrants,' wandering from rented halls, to Hart House, to our own rented quarters ... Our dream has become a reality. From here on it's up to each and every member to work hard so that we will have a theatre to be proud of, so that we can show our subscribers and audience that we weren't shooting for a star."[132] Added Williams two months later, the coming season would be "crucial, we must succeed. We have a good program, we will need whole hearted support in work and attendance."[133] Unfortunately, by December 1962, for the first time in their history, Alumnae reported that they were in debt as a result of a higher than expected construction bill[134] and the fact that it would take another three months for the Birch Avenue property to sell.[135]

Rabbi Moses (Morris) Langner, a Sephardic Hasidic Jew from Galicia, Spain, founded the synagogue in 1924[136] as a home to the Chevra Mishnayes[137] (Congregation of the Mishna). He was the first Hasidic Rabbi to settle in Canada and is considered the "'godfather' of Canadian Hasidism because most Canadian Hasidic leaders either followed him to Canada or married into his family." A descendant of one of the first pupils of the founder of Hasidism, Moses lived in the adjacent 42 Cecil Street house.[138] His son Isaac succeeded his father as the synagogue's rabbi. But the congregation had dwindled greatly even as the number of synagogues in the area grew, prompting its closure[139] and sale in 1954. As Thom recalls when she first explored it, "paint was peeling off the walls, strips of tin were hanging from the ceiling or crunching underfoot, there was dust and filth everywhere."[140] Said Whittaker, the "interior was bleak and tiny but it had possibilities."[141]

Alumnae listed the synagogue's advantages as a theatre space: the building was self-contained, "big enough, attractive, will not bother people"; it was close enough to the university, the TTC, and restaurants; and the $2,940-per-year income from the property made it an "investment [that] would ultimately be less than Birch Ave." The disadvantages included a dearth of available parking and the need for a new furnace and repairs to the plumbing. Moreover, the synagogue was zoned as residential, so "our prospects rest in being a private club."[142] Alumnae would bear the burden of being residential landlords, but as a private club they would have a "free hand in renovation," for according to the "zoning man," the "activities of a private club [were] no one else's concern."[143] The synagogue was in a state of "charmed disrepair,"[144] "big and barnlike," and a "real challenge to the imagination of the Club and its advisers."[145] Curiously, for a time the *mezuzah* remained on the door and the Rabbi continued services on Saturday mornings[146] in front of Alumnae's sets,[147] although the congregation had dwindled to the required minimum number of ten.[148]

There was an extensive list of renovations to accomplish in order to transform the synagogue into Alumnae's new Coach House Theatre. Thus began "Operation Conversion."[149] The building had a "flexible"[150] auditorium space, thirty-five by forty-eight feet, with a two-storey ceiling that allowed lights to be hung from a gallery that wrapped around its one long and two short sides. Although there was no basement in the synagogue itself, there was a courtyard with a small basement underneath connecting it to the house. The lobby, which needed new flooring, was "tiny in the extreme"[151] and divided from the main auditorium by a screen comprised of panels alternately painted a rich brown and ivory.

Agnew's theatre design called for ninety-four seats "around three sides of an open, Stratford-style [thrust] stage."[152] The stage in the "wide, shallow building"[153] could be "made into a variety of shapes and sizes."[154] The colour scheme was brown and ivory, with the stage wall painted a light, neutral taupe. Rust velvet drapes ran along the north and south walls of the theatre, and two windows were blocked out. With the audience seated on three sides on five benches downstage and two on each side,[155] "no one is too far from the centre of action."[156] Initially the plan was to use the synagogue's own long oak benches, but several of them "were too bad to use"[157] so Anne Tait was empowered to buy seventeen benches that she saw were being sold by a nearby synagogue[158] for $60.[159] For added comfort, Alumnae decorated the benches with "rust coloured"[160] cushions they already owned.[161] Nathan Cohen later noted that for the audience, "visibility is fair, since the benches are all at floor level. What you see is partially determined by the height of the person ahead of you and the angle of your distance from a pillar at the front of either side of the stage. The general interior atmosphere is, at the moment, somewhat austere."[162] After one production, Alumnae raised the back row's benches to improve visibility.[163] Stairs rose from both sides of the stage[164] to the three-sided balcony,[165] where the synagogue's women used to sit.[166] There, a workshop area and dressing rooms were built along with pipes to hang costumes, storage for flats and properties, and, on the south end of the balcony, space for the lighting board. Because the balcony, "painted ivory, with gold detailing,[167] was open to the auditorium, a "vow of silence" was imposed: "move a chair or whisper during a performance and you were dead."[168] Outside signage would have to be installed, the exterior painted, and an "attractive front" created with cobblestones, brick, or asphalt.[169] Williams referred to it as an "attractive design and promised to carry on worthily the tradition of the Coach House Theatre."[170]

To do this work the executive put out a call to the members in the summer of 1962 for paint and building supplies, "wholesale, cut rate or for free," adding: "Come on members – it's time for some teamwork. There's a brand new playhouse on the Toronto theatre map – let's show them what we can do."[171] A letter from Williams to friends of the Coach House Theatre announced that the "audience will rejoice in a proper foyer and attractive washrooms" located downstairs.[172]

Happily, the residential property was already rented out when Alumnae purchased it. It was a semi-detached house with three flats, two bathrooms, and a large, "chaotic" basement. It was home to a "lady on first floor [who] acts as janitor and collects rents (gets rebate)."[173] The intention was that the house would provide much-needed rental income to offset theatre production expenses. However, for several years it was an expense, and, as Thom describes, it made them "slum landlords to a generation of impoverished university students."[174] By late October 1962, the house required "serious" attention (meeting minutes reported hyperbolically that the "house was falling down"[175]). In mid-November, the city's Department of Buildings issued Alumnae a notice that they would need to "repair and point up deteriorated brickwork"[176] and repair the "defective roof"[177] on the house, as well as attend to several other important but relatively "minor"[178] maintenance issues. Throughout the winter, tenants frequently complained that their apartments were cold, so radiators were fixed and heaters were purchased. Most of this work was completed by June 1963; some remained, because a contractor "went away for a weekend. And, apparently, never came back."[179] Alumnae now had all the management concerns of landlords. Meetings were filled with residential building management issues.

Then there was the question of training club members to run their new theatre. The executive planned a three-night workshop to acquaint members with its workings.[180] The instruction included "how to run the lights and sound system, manage the backstage and front of house, so that, allowing for the inevitable minor catastrophes, our shows should be able to run in a smooth, professional manner. We are trying to present you with an operation which will provide creative satisfaction for every member of the club."[181] Providing invaluable assistance in the new theatre during this time was Michael Spence, noted as a supervisor in charge of Alumnae stage building (with Lew Preston), stage lighting (with Arthur Davies and Bill Cuttell), and house lighting.[182] Michael was thanked enthusiastically at the end-of-year meeting as a "compendium of expert knowledge in every conceivable subject and heartiness in the face of adversity."[183] His father had even made a model of the new coach house that was "admired by everyone."[184] By the end of the year, Margaret Spence, Michael's wife and soon-to-be active Alumnae costume designer, was volunteering backstage as well.[185]

When Alumnae opened the synagogue Coach House Theatre with James Reaney's *The Easter Egg* in November 1962, they were finally "self-supporting."[186] Stated one company document at the time, "members have one aim – to make a permanent home for Canadian and experimental ["and classical" was inserted in pencil] theatre in Canada comparable to the Royal Court in London and the off Broadway theatres in New York."[187] Halpenny

Figure 5.3. (*back*) Allison Roach and Judith Ramsay with (*front*) Barbara Walker painting Alumnae's new "Coach House Theatre" in the synagogue at Huron and Cecil Streets. Courtesy of Alumnae Theatre Company.

told the *Star*, "We wanted a place where we could do new plays and show new writers to a necessarily small but interested audience."[188] *The Easter Egg*'s first three nights were for "donors only"[189] to thank them for giving money to the new theatre; their names were featured on a plaque in the lobby.[190] Tickets went for $1.50 and, importantly, because Alumnae were running a private "theatre Club," anyone who attended a play at the new Coach House Theatre was technically a club "member" for that moment, so a record of all attendees' names was kept.[191] The show's flyer explained that the "Coach House Theatre is one of the activities of its sponsoring body, the University Alumnae Dramatic Club, and admittance to it will be by associate membership in the Club."

Critics were animated in their anticipation. For Whittaker, the new Coach House Theatre augured the "promise of good things to come, things that will enrich our theatre generally."[192] Cohen compared it to other theatre spaces in the city and the region: "It's not as opulent and leviathan as the "O'Keefe Centre; not as atmospheric and acoustically fine as the Royal Alexandra; not as much an entertainment place as the Crest; not as intimate and comfortable as the Central Library playhouse; not as picturesque and festive as the Stratford theatre."[193] However, he contextualized the importance of the "semi-professional but altogether excellent"[194] Alumnae to Toronto:

Figure 5.4. The nearly complete auditorium at Alumnae's synagogue Coach House, *circa* October 1962. Inspired by the Stratford Festival's thrust stage built in the previous decade, the auditorium featured benches arranged in a "V" shape meeting at the downstage apex of the stage with a balcony behind and above the benches. Courtesy of Alumnae Theatre Company.

> Little by little, and in sudden spurts, the number of legitimate theatres in Toronto is increasing. We have acquired two new playhouses in the tail's end of the year. Sometime next season, a third will open its doors …
>
> The Coach House gives us something we have never had: a permanent experimental workshop where what is very modern in drama, and very old, and what is new, can be presented regularly and without any of the risks that make commercial theatre so timid an institution. The record of the University Alumnae is proof positive that the Coach House will be an important force in Toronto's theatre life.[195]

Going further, and with the aid of an accompanying caricature map of Alumnae's new neighbourhood, Whittaker described the new Coach House Theatre as one among several "off-College St." theatre buildings that included the Central Library Theatre, Theatre in the Dell, the Village Playhouse, the Bohemian Embassy, the Grenville Street Theatre, and the "most historical" of the bunch, Hart House Theatre. As responses to Toronto's commercial theatres, the off-College Street theatres were "brave ventures" with "one thing in common: the certain uncertainty of their future." Collectively, and a decade before the

Figure 5.5. When the *Globe and Mail*'s theatre critic Herbert Whittaker wrote about what he termed the "Off-College St." theatres in November 1962, his piece was accompanied by this whimsical caricature map of the "off-College St. theatres." Along with Alumnae's Coach House Theatre at their synagogue location (*bottom left*), the theatres are (*clockwise from top left*) the Central Library Theatre, Hart House Theatre, the Bohemian Embassy, the Grenville St. Theatre, the Village Playhouse, and Theatre in the Dell. Courtesy of the *Globe and Mail* (public domain).

"alternative theatres" emerged, they had the potential to offer "healthy and determined"[196] homegrown theatre.

Offering a concluding note to the last, anxious, two years, and perhaps echoing the gendered self-effacement that had characterized Alumnae's early women, Thom reported at the June 1963 annual meeting that regarding the synagogue, they had been looking at a

> buy it or perish proposition. Our theatre identity was more precious to us than our money and holding our courage tightly by both hands we completed the purchase in July. The months that followed required more than courage from the Club and its friends – they required ingenuity, co-operation, and backbreaking labour as we pooled our small talents and big ideas to build our theatre. The Club must be forever grateful to its hardworking and enthusiastic members and more especially to unqualified generosity of the talented men who quite assumed the major burden of the task.

She added her view that "this year there has been a higher level of professionalism in the backstage operation than in either of the former Coach Houses." And she encouraged future directors and designers to "exploit" the flexibility of their new stage and to "have the courage to tear the place apart and stand it on end."[197] Lorna Rogers wrote in her publicity report that the "Coach House is already becoming a familiar landmark to Toronto's little theatre audiences," recognizable by "those shiny red doors"[198] opening onto Huron Street.

Rethinking the Coach House Theatre and an "Honourable Retreat"

After their first season in the synagogue, with a membership numbering ninety,[199] Alumnae sought to improve how the theatre ran. Members Lorna Rogers and Joan Shaw cleared out the remainder of Alumnae's properties from Pamela Terry's basement[200] while Martha Mann agreed to take over as wardrobe mistress with a "plan to weed out and catalogue costumes."[201] Costumes were covered with plastic and hung in the Coach House's basement after years of being kept in boxes.[202] The organization of the costumes made it simpler "to see what we had and to rent out far more than in the past."[203] Mann requested that no one access costumes without consulting her first,[204] later recommending that that the costumes, "now in danger of being destroyed because of damp,"[205] should be moved into the back room of the first floor flat of the rental house to make it into a "costume workroom."[206] In the theatre, the heating, roof, storage, and noise from walking on the balcony were priorities.[207] The "Spence team" organized the storage of flats, platforms, and spare lumber around the theatre based on size, and Michael Spence made a tool chest.[208]

The rental house, instead of paying for their productions, continued to be a financial drain, as did renovations to the theatre. Over the next two years, they increased income by fixing budgets and target revenue for each show, raising ticket prices, devising a new rental fee structure for the theatre (and advertising it on campus, in the Central Ontario Drama League Newsletter, and in the Faculty of Music's Edward Johnson Building), renting out more costumes, properties, and set pieces, applying for capital grants, increasing donations, and reminding all members to "get audiences."[209] By the end of the 1964–65 season, they had paid off half of the mortgage and the taxes from house receipts.[210]

Owning a theatre at a time when improvements in theatre lighting and sound equipment were becoming available to even small theatres meant more design opportunities and steeper learning curves. To improve members' familiarity with the theatre and its equipment, a January 1964 general meeting focused on the following: the theatre's floor plan, a revised production manual handed out by new theatre manager Anne Tait, the duties of the stage manager in "organizing work parties meticulously and at least a week in advance,"[211] and the "why and how of lighting."[212] This last point included a detailed demonstration of Fresnel and ellipsoidal spotlights, given by Barbara Macallum. They also sought to upgrade their stage management practices. Member Margaret Hamilton demonstrated sound editing and cueing,[213] including the "problems and pressures of the sound technician."[214] Much of Alumnae's sound editing was done on a "superb" sound system that Sol Mandlsohn, founder of Bay Bloor Radio, lent to Alumnae, although the time-consuming editing process required planning and practice. Hamilton's demonstration was noted for its effectiveness, despite being given without a tape recorder (someone had forgotten to bring it). Unfortunately, the meeting was not well attended by new members. They concluded that "we tried to cover too much information in too short a time."[215]

After two seasons, members pushed for further improvements to make the company run more effectively. Importantly, they reconsidered the shape of the theatre. The space had "enjoyed a greater flexibility than any other theatre in town [as] its stage platform was moved to suit each type of play." Members like Thom praised the theatre's flexibility, and Alumnae were "celebrated for the variety of their experiments in dramatic form."[216]

However, repeated stage conversions were taxing volunteers, who needed to focus on realizing the set designs as well as on reconfiguring the stage between productions. The current layout was not ideal for their productions, nor did it best reflect the building itself, occasionally disorienting the audience.[217] Assistant theatre manager Helen Carscallen now argued for one stage and more ingenious uses of it: "The question arises about the value of this very changeable stage. If a theatre is in a very real sense known by its stage, would the energy used to determine the shape and position of the stage for each show be used just as effectively or more so in employing the facilities of a more permanent structure which would necessarily be more elaborate and complete?"[218]

Molly Thom proposed a redesign of the theatre "that met with approval." It included sketches by her husband Ronald Thom, architect of Massey College and Trent University, "probably assisted by his family." His design called for an "open affixed stage with angle seating."[219] Intended to give the "building more unity and balance,"[220] the design affixed the stage to one location on the west side of the building, "thrusting forward into the audience," to provide a predicable "new and permanent look"[221] for directors, designers, and producers to plan each show. The refurbishment added "cedar walls, a somber, grey stage and bright panels around its balcony."[222] This "completely new approach to over-all production" better focused Alumnae's time and energy from one production to the next. In addition to changes to the stage, the Thoms proposed a "dark, rich grey"[223] or brown[224] paint colour for the interior of the theatre because the current colour "lacked mystery and gave it a boxy effect."[225] This would "keep the eyes of the audiences from travelling up to the high ceiling of the theatre and … throw into high relief the costumes on the stage. Elsewhere in the theatre, the audience is surrounded by deep, vivid colours of stained glass – blues, greens and purples—to give an intimate atmosphere." Audience seating was placed in "V-formation, using the oak benches."[226] The plan was "understood to be experimental; if it is satisfactory, it will be continued."[227] When the remodelled theatre[228] was completed for the first show of the 1964–65 season (at a cost of $1,200[229]), Alumnae deemed it an "unqualified success"[230] resulting in "enthusiastic"[231] reaction from members, audiences, and reviewers alike.

In October 1964, Ron Thom designed the set for the first production on the secured stage: Luigi Pirandello's *The Emperor*. He sought to maximize the use of his new configuration, while Ron Gilmore's costumes designs incorporated the space's "vivid colours of stained glass."[232] But Whittaker was ambivalent about the Thoms' redesign. Although it "made a handsome and appropriate setting for *The Emperor*," the "new arrangement commits the Coach House to an open stage, for the audience sits around Stratford-style. Electing for a permanent back wall, it dooms the Alumnae to play forever without a centre entrance, unlike Stratford. Considering the Alumnae has always prided itself on variety of choice, Thom may have done the theatre group a limited service, no matter how handsome the effect."[233] Whittaker, who had directed the Toronto premiere of Harold Pinter's *The Caretaker* for Alumnae in a significant rearrangement of the space eight months earlier, clearly mourned the loss of previous design flexibility.

The new stage also created, or revealed, tensions within the club. Their fall 1964 production of *The Doctors of Philosophy* had to be put off by a week owing to "difficulties attendant on this show"[234] within the company. These difficulties apparently stemmed from miscommunications among director and long-time member Cecily Thomson, producers Celia Armitage and Frances Jackson, stage manager Kay Martin, and the executive concerning how the new fixed stage might, and might not, be used and how and when production activities could be decided. Although precise details of the tension do not survive,

Thomson wrote to the executive with her suggestions for improvement, and the executive wrote back to say “they would be implemented wherever they applied to future productions.”[235] Furthermore, the executive decided to have Rex Southgate address the membership at the next general meeting about the work of the stage manager, believing that many of the duties and decisions of Alumnae’s show producers would be better handled by their stage managers instead.[236] Thus, the executive confirmed that the producer would “become more of a business manager”[237] contacting workers and “generally oversee[ing] operations as official representatives of the Club,”[238] while the stage manager would be the “authority on all technical matters” and the “disciplinary authority of both actors and crew.”[239] As stage technology specialized and accepted theatre practices professionalized, Alumnae updated their own procedures to reflect these changes. Front-of-house staff were given “celluloid tags marked COACH HOUSE THEATRE to identify them as theatre officials.” And although it had apparently already been a rule in the recent past, new members were provided with keys to the theatre (an announcement made to this effect at the June 1965 annual meeting “brought wails from new members who had never heard of this rule”[240]).

Concurrently, Alumnae were fully immersed in residential building management. All three units in the rental property were now occupied most of the time, with the third-floor tenant receiving a rent reduction for custodial services. (The exception was the first-floor tenant, who did not appear able to pay her rent, a point underscored in October 1963 when her husband died and she remarried and moved out without paying what she owed[241]). Then, in the summer of 1964, the Muddy York Theatre Club – organized by future Tarragon Theatre founder Bill Glassco with Bob Hamlin and poet Dennis Lee[242] – rented the house’s first-floor flat for $100[243] (solving an issue with a tenant who was not paying her rent) and the theatre for $650[244] to produce Thornton Wilder’s *The Matchmaker* and Anton Chekhov’s *The Seagull*.[245] They further agreed to pay the phone bill and raise the audience benches off the ground to partly attend to heating issues.[246] However, by the end of the summer it was reported that though “Muddy Yorkers” had paid their rent,[247] they had left both the house and the theatre “in poor condition.”[248] Then, a flea infestation, apparently from a stray cat,[249] took over the flat after the Muddy Yorkers left, requiring a call to the exterminators.[250] Following several repairs across the next year, Lorna Rogers, now property manager, reported that by June 1965, “no. 42 [Cecil St.] is now in pretty good shape.” However, she concluded that “we sometimes have trouble extracting rent payments on time – most of the tenants seem to be at various levels of bare subsistence. The house has certainly not proved to be the moneymaker we hoped it would be.”[251] Alumnae were now different sorts of community benefactors, having moved from supporting campus women’s spaces and the university settlement, to providing accommodation to Toronto renters living month to month, all while producing theatre.

During the 1965–66 season, “by some sort of minor miracle,”[252] the house’s rent payments were up to date. As it turned out, the new building provided a “most marvelous place for cast parties – lots of room, it’s handy, and no need to worry if you spill your ashes on the floor!”[253] But that season also saw further challenges, characterized by ten days in March during which the insurance company threatened to pull the house’s fire insurance unless the electrics were upgraded and the house properly maintained. Especially dangerous were light bulbs and paper lampshades hung from coat hangers by the tenants. Wrote Rogers humorously:

> There are probably some of you, new to the Club, who have walked past the faded façade of the house on the corner and noticed the overflowing garbage pails, the peeling paint and sparse grass. You may, indeed, have seen one or two rather shady looking characters hanging

> about. And during the casual perusal, you may have wondered what Alderman June Marks [known then for her judicial probe into Toronto's housing conditions] would say if this Charles Addams [creator of the Addams Family cartoons] creation ever came to her attention.
>
> Normally we try to play down the fact, but every year at this time comes the sordid revelation – no. 42 Cecil Street belongs to us. And in all likelihood, those "characters" are our tenants. As landlady of this establishment, I wish to state that, appearances to the contrary, no. 42 has never looked better, at least internally. It has been a year fraught with crises and at times there seemed to be more drama concerning the house than ever took place on the stage of the theatre.

The house may have "never looked better," but it also made no money for Alumnae that year. Along with the insurance-mandated upgrades, the house's issues included an "old refrigerator tossed out on the roof, [which] has been retrieved and is now in use as a bookcase"; the necessity of "employing a cleaning lady" (at $2.00 an hour for 40 hours in one month); an infestation of cockroaches necessitating, again, fumigation; and pigeons in the eaves. The "dream" of using the house's first floor "for a green room and costume storage"[254] was still far distant. Michael and Margaret Spence recall that when Margaret was theatre manager she would periodically check in on the house. At one time, she

> opened the door and all the walls in one room were completely black. [The tenant had] offered to paint the room himself if Alumnae bought the paint. He wanted black paint and he just painted everything: the ceiling, the walls. And there was a blue light. And the word love, L-O-V-E, on the staircase going up to the room. We didn't ask any questions about what was going on inside.

Margaret adds that there were the "old gaffers that used to sit in the sun outside the theatre. And one time one of the girls had forgotten her key to get into the theatre. And they said, 'listen, if you go in the house next door and you go through the basement downstairs you can get to the theatre.' [*laughs*] You could!"[255] Building security remained on the executive's agenda throughout their time at the synagogue.

Despite the challenges associated with the house, by the fall of 1966, Alumnae's production successes had brought in 566 theatre subscriptions and their bank balance had ballooned from $78 in September[256] to $4,300 by November[257] (with heating pipe insulation still to be paid for[258]). There was much discussion about learning an array of construction skills that would save them a "great fat fee"[259] for repairs, especially carpentry, including "how to build from working drawings, how to estimate costs, which materials are best to use how."[260] In 1968, they applied to the City and received an address for the theatre, 151 Huron Street, and sought a number and mailbox for the door.[261] But security was still an issue. There had been several break-ins during rehearsals for Jack Cunningham's *Aperitif* that led them to install bolts and change the locks on the door. A neighbour gave them the house number of "two of the plague of junior burglars,"[262] and the Youth Bureau, staffed "almost entirely by women"[263] since its inception in 1958, "tracked down culprits to a total of ten," resulting in a few articles[264] being returned. Margaret Spence further reported that "we cannot get theft insurance in that neighbourhood" and that their fire policy of $415 might be lost if the break-ins continued. President Elizabeth Mascall reminded members to lock the theatre using the new locks.[265]

Alumnae started the 1968–69 season, their fiftieth year, primed to celebrate as Toronto's longest-running theatre company. Over six seasons at the synagogue Coach House, they had presented forty-one plays, kept within budget, renovated the theatre, purchased their own sound and lighting equipment, introduced a subscription season, added dramatic readings, and grown their audience as well as, "we hope, our reputation and standard of production" while continuing to produce the "kind of plays in which we are interested."[266]

But by early spring of 1969 there was "news of great import concerning our new home."[267] On formal Alumnae letterhead, president Margaret MacAulay wrote to friends of the Coach House: "It is with regret that we must tell you that this is our last season in the present Coach House. Though it is not our wish, we must sell our present property and we have, therefore, been searching for a new home … But this chapter of the Club's life has been lively, happy and satisfying, and for this we owe you, our friends, our warm gratitude."[268]

The reason for the sudden forced move was that Toronto Hydro was expropriating the house and the synagogue properties to build a substation to "meet increased service needs in the area."[269] Due to university expansion[270] and new high-rise apartments, the City needed to do cabling work to feed the neighbourhood, and the theatre and house corner lots were the ideal location.[271] Alumnae had left the university for the city to serve their own needs only to have the City claim their property twelve years later to serve the university.

By the "crucial" April 1969 general meeting, plans for an auction were being made. Wrote MacAulay, "We have been jolted out of our old rut, for a time at least. This is our Club – what are we going to do? Where are we going? Please be prepared to speak your mind." They planned for the auction to follow the annual general meeting; on offer would be "pews [benches], pew [bench] cushions, assorted properties *etc.* to the highest bidder. Gentlemen, and ladies, friends who wish to bid may do so." With dry wit, MacAulay added, "Following the auction, the wake as promised will be held," quoting from Shakespeare's *As You Like It*: "Let us make an honourable retreat; though not with bag and baggage, yet with scrip and scrippage."[272] Molly Thom later reflected that this was "just before the time when ordinary citizens understood how to exert their rights; a year or two later, we could and no doubt would have mounted an aggressive campaign to retain the property as one of the city's valued cultural institutions. Instead, we settled for what at the time seemed a substantial sum of money."[273] But Michael Spence notes that the house, in particular, was deteriorating and, "frankly, Hydro came along at the right time."[274] Although Alumnae had imagined themselves ladies of their own domain when they went from renters to owners, frequent reminders that both theatre and house were still subject to municipal regulations culminated in the ultimate claim on their property.

Having been forced from their synagogue theatre, Alumnae quickly rented a small brick church as their next Coach House Theatre at 10 Maplewood Avenue off Vaughan Road, two blocks north of St. Clair Avenue. No strangers to converting buildings into theatres, they accomplished the necessary renovations over the summer of 1969,[275] creating a fifty-five-movable-seat[276] theatre, which was ready by October for readings and Sunday evening studio presentations. In February 1970, members met to officially change the "club house" from 42 Cecil Street to 10 Maplewood Avenue.[277] Of the $82,000 they received from the City as compensation for the synagogue,[278] they used $18,000[279] to purchase the Maplewood property in the spring of 1969, eventually spending another $4,000 in renovations and investing the remaining $60,000.[280] They also added a staircase to the lobby for $1,000, as well as carpeting, risers, a platform, a lighting grid, and lobby chandelier.[281] The *Star*'s Urjo Kareda later wrote that it was an "almost irresistibly attractive home for intimate, low-key productions."[282]

During their housewarming general meeting at the cramped Maplewood quarters, Alumnae announced "many planned productions"[283] for the season. Even so, they were already searching for a more suitable and permanent theatre. "Young toddlers in tow," president Norma Clark and building committee chair Molly Thom began their search "downtown in the old warehouse district, where there were many attractive large empty buildings." This prompted a "number of near misses"[284] until they lit upon the Enoch Turner Schoolhouse, on Trinity Street off King Street East, a Gothic Revival-style building dating back to 1848. It is Toronto's oldest schoolhouse building and is owned by the adjacent Little Trinity Anglican Church. It had fallen into disrepair, for the congregation was occupied with restoring the church, which had been gutted by fire in 1961. Despite its condition, it was a fairly active venue, and its wardens, seeking help for its repair and preservation,[285] found a number of suitors, including the Beta Sigma Phi sorority[286] and Alumnae, who quickly took the lead among them. The *Telegram* reported in October 1969 that to "minimize the cost to the taxpayer plans are afoot to transform the schoolhouse into a little theatre [for Alumnae, who are] ready to enter into a long lease and to meet some of the costs of refurbishing the interior."[287] However, by April 1970 the opportunity had, "unfortunately, fallen through."[288] Thom later recalled that Little Trinity Church was "reluctant to dislodge a neighbourhood bugle band which had been guaranteed one evening a week to practice."[289] The membership met in April to consider other ways forward.[290]

Continuing their search, Alumnae joined a "consortium" that included an engineering firm and an architecture firm, which "drew up plans for the large building complex"[291] at 24 Berkeley Street, built by the Consumer's Gas Corporation in 1887.[292] That building later became Toronto Free Theatre and the Canadian Stage Company's Berkeley Street location. However, this opportunity was also lost when a demolition contractor "snatched the property"[293] from them.[294] Alumnae also looked at the buildings that Young People's Theatre and Theatre Passe Muraille later claimed. As time passed, "real estate prices were moving up," said Thom, and "our Hydro settlement no longer appeared quite so substantial."[295]

Firehall Dreams and "Radical Chic"[296]

At the outset of the 1970s, theatre in Toronto was between epochs. The professionalizing Crest, with its long-held supremacy over the city's theatre scene, had disappeared in 1966, but the "alternative" theatres had not yet hit their stride. Jim Garrard and his fledgling Theatre Passe Muraille were producing theatre at the church at 11 Trinity Square (echoing Alumnae's church Coach House), and Ken Gass's Factory Lab (later Factory Theatre) arose in the summer of 1970 above a garage on Dupont Street (echoing Alumnae's second Coach House above a Bedford Road garage). The Graduate Drama Centre's Glen Morris Studio, Hart House Theatre, the Central Library Theatre, and numerous campus dramatic clubs were presenting Alumnae's style of rare and compelling modern plays of interest to students, faculty, and the community. These helped offset the touring fare offered by what one *Varsity* writer referred to as the "hinterlands"[297] – that is, the O'Keefe Centre, the St. Lawrence Centre, and the Royal Alexandra Theatre.

With the schoolhouse opportunity behind them, Alumnae turned their attention to a new prospect for a permanent home in Toronto's Corktown neighbourhood. Clark and Thom learned in February 1970 that the City's 1905-built Firehall No. 4 at Berkeley and Adelaide streets, two blocks north of the future Toronto Free Theatre building, was to be vacated by

Figure 5.6. Toronto's Firehall No. 4 at Berkeley and Adelaide Streets in Toronto's Corktown neighbourhood decades before Alumnae moved in. Photograph by James Victor Salmon, January/February 1952. Courtesy of Toronto Public Library (public domain).

June[298] because a new firehall had been built just one block to the southwest, on Princess and Front streets. Thom would recall that she and Clark "walked in as the firemen were packing up. They gave us a tour and told us something of the history of the building."[299]

The location had been home to a firehall since 1851, when part of an earlier building was used as a stable and blacksmith shop and for storing the firemen's old hand engine. In 1859, a new hall was built; in 1871, it was remodelled to accommodate a steam engine, stables, and a hose tower.[300] Famed architect A. Frank Wickson designed the present Edwardian-style firehall in 1905, accommodating the move from horse-drawn to mechanized fire engines.[301] The building's eye-catching exterior features a two-storey arched window, large stone quoins, and a tall hose tower.[302] Along with the 1887-built firehall at 110 Lombard Street,[303] it is one of two extant original downtown Toronto firehalls.[304] When Clark and Thom came upon it, wrote Alumnae, the firehall looked "abandoned and forgotten: its windows are boarded, its brick is a dirty red."[305]

Pursuing the firehall turned into an ordeal. City officials began receiving offers of purchase in the fall of 1969.[306] Read one Alumnae press release, Clark and Thom's "initiation into the world of participatory democracy is a story in itself, at once amusing, frustrating and involving"[307]; Halpenny later referred to "much complex and interesting negotiations."[308] By October, the City Planning Board had determined that although the Lombard Street firehall

Figure 5.7. A sketch of Toronto's Firehall No. 4 after it was remodelled in 1871. "Duke St." is now called "Adelaide St." Courtesy of Alumnae Theatre Company.

had "historic and architectural significance" and could be used as a fire department museum, the City should not retain the Berkeley firehall unless a City department wanted it. Within two weeks, I.B. Forrest, the (aptly named) Commissioner for the City's Parks and Recreation Department, recommended that the Berkeley firehall be demolished and the property turned into a "sitting-out park"; he later recommended that a "children's playground"[309] be added. When the City's property commissioner told Clark and Thom that the City had handed the Berkeley Street firehall to the Parks and Recreation Committee in March on the assumption that the building would be torn down to create a parkette,[310] Clark told Thom, "We don't need the property commissioner, we need a politician! Who do we know?"[311]

Thom had a "vague family connection with a junior alderman" (and future mayor), John Sewell, who used to deliver her papers. When she phoned his constituency office, Thom recalls, it was he who "picked up the phone on the second ring, listened attentively to my proposition, and recommended that we make a presentation to the City's executive committee."[312] In the meantime, Parks and Recreation received word that the Fire Department had "no further use" for the firehall, the Toronto Historical Board "declined to accept" it and concurred with the plan for a parkette, the City Property Department reported on its physical condition, and a private citizen inquired about purchasing or leasing it.[313]

As in all things theatre, timing is everything. There had been a trend over the previous decade towards protecting Toronto's historic buildings. Elsewhere in the city, old firehalls were being torn down, but others were being repurposed.[314] The fight over preserving the Royal Alexandra Theatre, old City Hall, Union Station, the Lombard Street firehall[315] (whose rehabilitation as the original location of the Second City Comedy Club a few years later would affect Alumnae), and others had touched off a movement.[316] Moreover, local residents had "invested considerably" in refurbishing the Corktown neighbourhood. The worn-down workmen's cottages across from the Berkeley firehall had been "converted into town-houses, boutiques, and elegant offices."[317] Influential interior designer Klaus Nienkämper (who personally supported refurbishing the Berkeley firehall[318]) had converted the nineteenth-century-built J.H. Greenshields grocery store at 300 King Street at Berkeley Street into a "beautiful shop for contemporary furniture,"[319] still occupied by his company.[320] Alumnae argued that their plan was the "most desirable sort of urban renewal and we are convinced that No. 4 Fire Hall has also many years of usefulness ahead of it." Drawing members and audiences from across the city, it would "enhance the life of the street and the whole developing area"[321] as a "focal point."[322] Nonprofessionalizing theatres in Canada are not always associated with the two common reasons for government-sponsored arts initiatives – "regenerating areas of urban deprivation" and encouraging "cultural hotspots"[323] – but at the time the City was looking for a reliable occupant with capital, a history of reinventing buildings for public use, and the potential for longevity.

From March to June 1970, Clark and Thom, whom Urjo Kareda called "as persistent as they are charming,"[324] along with Alumnae's "legal mentor" (and stage lighting guru) Arthur Davies, petitioned the Parks Department to save the firehall, offering to spend between $80,000 and $90,000 of Alumnae's money, acquired largely from the expropriation of the synagogue, for renovation and restoration.[325] In July 1970, they met with City officials, arguing that with renovations the existing building would make an excellent 150-seat theatre. Clark asked the City's executive committee, "Why tear down a beautiful building to create a tiny park?"[326] The City's property commissioner noted that the building was in poor condition, with a leaky roof, cracked exterior walls and ceiling, some exposed electrical wiring, and a heating system that was about to break down.[327] He also characterized Alumnae's move to repurpose the building as a theatre as an "impassioned plea."[328] Thom reflects,

> Those were the days of political activism, of dynamic, noisy ratepayers' associations, when progressive and enlightened individuals took to civic politics with a vision of what the city could be. We hoped some of these reformers would support us. And we were not disappointed. [Alderman] Bill Kilbourn, who knew the theatre's work, leapt to his feet, eloquent in his support of our proposal and his praise for the Club's historic contribution to the City. But the enthusiasm of some of the older politicians, notably Horace Brown and Fred Beavis, was unexpected. We had hit a nerve, Toronto was not about to abandon yet another historic landmark, and the Committee voted to reconsider the fate of old Firehall No. 4.[329]

A remarkable public debate now arose. The day after the *Globe and Mail* reported on Clark's pitch, it ran a contrarian editorial titled "The park thieves." The piece cited "most experts" as saying there should be 5 acres of parkland for every 1,000 acres in a city and pointed out that Toronto was presently at only 3.4 acres. It tied Alumnae's plan together with that of noted Alderman Joseph Piccininni, who was petitioning the city to "buy a miniature display of Canada from a group in Niagara Falls and place it on an 11-acre site in High Park." The editorial concluded that "if Toronto needs still another theatre (and that is a very large if), then find a building or site not designated for park purposes. Stop the whittling."[330]

Unusual as the arts-versus-environment debate might seem, Alumnae appeared to be falling victim, however ironically, to a moment when more and more theatre companies were popping up in Toronto and when views of how to approach urban renewal in underdeveloped neighbourhoods were increasingly progressive. Yet the argument to preserve the firehall developed at an opportune time, as it aligned well with the contemporary debate over how to revitalize Toronto's urban landscape. Favoured at the time was the "preservation of old buildings in declining neighbourhoods as one of the prime means of preventing further decay."[331] Karl Jaffary, an alderman for the firehall's ward, responded to the *Globe* with a letter calling the editorial's two examples of park thievery "simplistic beyond the point of reason."[332] He argued that while part of the ward "needs parks," there were better locations for them, and that a "distinguished" group like Alumnae ought to use the "fine old building."[333] Another letter, by Alumnae member Morna Wales, challenged the editorial for presenting the club as an "aggressive group trying to steal parkland away from the poor people of downtown Toronto." She criticized the editorial for saying this would be a "new" theatre rather than a long-running group and for manufacturing a "'theatre versus park' controversy," which was the "kind of insidious trouble-making that I hate to see."[334] Others wrote that the City should increase its park space but that Alumnae's plan for the firehall was not the problem.[335]

At an October 1970 meeting, the City took up the firehall's fate as Parks and Recreation's "main item." Previously, politicians had argued that there were better examples of an old firehall in Toronto and that the Toronto Historical Board had said it was not "worth preserving as a public museum." However, over the summer, members of the Historical Board, having been swayed by architects, planners, and historians, "testified to the value of turning old civic buildings to new uses and thus helping to rehabilitate rundown areas." A private citizen proposed buying the building and renovating it into mixed residential and office space. Alumnae, for its part, proposed to lease the building from the City "at a nominal rent," and offered to spend $80,000 "on restoration immediately, to maintain the building in the future, and pay city taxes on it."[336]

Local residents and businesses added their views. Contradicting Parks and Recreation's earlier view that local residents would "benefit"[337] from a park, businesses that had worked on refurbishing the area supported preserving the firehall as an "architectural and historical entity"[338] in line with the recent and "successful"[339] restoration of the nearby St. Lawrence Market. Moreover, it was a high-traffic, polluted area unsuitable for a children's park,[340] which would be "totally of out character on this corner," given that the property stood between the "Men's Hostels and a wine store."[341] If it were a park, wrote one Alumnae plan supporter, "potential users would probably be those who go to the wine store at the corner of Berkeley and King, and it is most likely that this park would become their permanent summer residence"; it "would be an invitation to yet more out-of-work drunks."[342] Residents told the executive committee that "many gentlemen of the road" patronized the adjacent wine store and that the area's traffic was too high to be safe for children to play in a park there. Many argued that a small theatre would be an "ideal way to give their neighbourhood vitality in the evening hours," noting that for fifty years, Alumnae had given Toronto the "essential service of a fine, small theatre and a training ground for many of Canada's finest actors."[343] Alumnae member Pamela Campion felt "sure that there are all kinds of derelict property [*sic*] for you to tear down in that neighbourhood to make parkland,"[344] adding that this was her "plea from an actress who looks forward to acting in the No. 4 Fire Hall."[345] Alderman Fred Beavis noted that it was a "better way to invest the City's money in theatre than to spend large sums on major ventures such as the St. Lawrence Centre and its program."[346] Notably, Alumnae had never asked for the City's help before. Still, there remained some dissent, owing to a vague argument that "quite honestly theatrical groups are hard on the buildings they occupy," whereas the private citizen who wished to make the firehall into a "commercial industrial design establishment" was a "god-fearing, hardworking, responsible individual."[347]

On 1 October 1970 the Parks and Recreation Committee voted unanimously to instruct the City executive not to tear down the firehall because Alumnae's proposals were "viable and worthy of every consideration and represent financial responsibility,"[348] leaving it up to the City's executive and Alumnae to "work out the details."[349] The following day, the *Telegram* reported that the Berkeley Street firehall had been "saved from the wrecker's hammers or use as a furniture showroom … with a City parks and recreation committee move to turn it into a theatre."[350] Alumnae were on their way to inhabiting an impressive permanent home. The following week, the president of the Architectural Conservancy of Ontario, James Acland, wrote to the City's property commission with a detailed description of the building in his argument for refurbishment:

> The fire hall at the corner of Adelaide and Berkeley is a building designed with great imagination. The heavy pyramidal tower, gabled fronts, masonry quoins and hammered stone surrounds combine to a design of substantial power in a small compass. Certainly it is one of the most striking and able turn of the century buildings in the city.
>
> The brickwork and masonry is in splendid condition, and the structure is well suited to a variety of commercial functions: for example it could well be used for theatrical performances or as a drama school.
>
> Situated in the heart of Old Toronto, on a street where an entire terrace row of houses has been refurbished, this building could contribute to the rebirth and revival of downtown Toronto, to add interest and variety to our city.[351]

Acland's letter, which contradicts the Toronto Historical Board's initial assessment that the property was of no value to them, remains one of the great descriptions of the firehall. Seventeen days later, Alumnae announced to their membership: "CHEERS and more CHEERS!!! WE GOT THE FIREHALL!! Come and hear proposals, and give opinions re: the lease (now being negotiated), the renovations (Molly with blackboard), and generally rejoice!"[352]

But the negotiations were not over. In March 1971, the City's executive committee drew up the terms and conditions for a twenty-five-year lease between the City and the University Alumnae Dramatic Club, which would pay rent of $1 per year but also pay annual taxes of $6,400.[353] This tax bill, Thom wrote to alderman David Rotenberg on the executive committee, was "greatly inflated" compared to that of nearby properties. She also expressed concern over investing so much Alumnae capital in a building with only a twenty-five-year lease, suggesting instead that a City by-law be passed to waive the taxes and that the lease be extended to fifty years. She asserted to Rotenberg that the "advantages surely are mutual: we get a home, but the City gets one of its fine old firehalls saved from demolition and lovingly renovated without the expenditure of any public funds."[354] To alderman Thomas Wardle, chair of the Parks and Recreation Committee, she added that Alumnae had been led to expect a fifty-five- or even a ninety-nine-year lease and had been "truly led up the garden path,"[355] although "at one stroke the City could support the Arts and preserve a fine old building and both at no cost to the public purse."[356]

Alumnae's "complicated negotiations" with the City over the firehall had taken eighteen months. What the club called a "remarkable partnership" was finally reached in the summer of 1971, "ensuring the restoration and renovation of this building." The City agreed to the by-law as long as a Board of Management was appointed that included representation from the City and the club. The agreement in principle ensured that the "City's future rights to the property would be protected while providing the Club with some security of tenure in return for their considerable investment." The by-law gave Alumnae "control of the firehall through a Board of Management appointed by City Council."[357] Passed 5 August 1971, By-Law No. 181-71's purpose was "to provide for the maintenance and management of premises No. 70 Berkeley Street, Toronto, being the former Berkeley Street Fire Station, as a place of recreation and amusement and auditorium by a Board of Management to act on behalf of the Council and for the appointment of the members of such Board."[358] Declaring that the "omens are right" and that a "beginning has been made,"[359] Thom told Whittaker a year later that "we almost lost it several times. We only got it because we are such fighters."[360]

In November 1971, Alumnae publicly announced that they had secured the firehall and that they planned to start renovations before the New Year.[361] George Ono in the *Ryersonian* heralded the planned restoration as "preserving a small section of the inner city from complete assimilation into Toronto's rapid urban development."[362] Urjo Kareda wrote in his *Star* column, four months before directing Alumnae's final show at the Maplewood theatre, that the club "edged their project past several occasions of imminent collapse, surrounded by flurries of committees, phone calls, letters, personal deputations and pleadings." He called it an "extraordinary, unprecedented collaboration between a private artistic organization and the city."[363] Publishing just four days into its existence (following the collapse of its predecessor, the *Telegram*), the *Toronto Sun* printed a photograph of Clark discussing the planned renovations with Mayor William Dennison."[364] Thom later explained that although the City would not sell the building to Alumnae outright, "in exchange for one dollar, we became the custodians for fifty years, with our investment in renovations and restoration protected should the city decide to terminate the agreement."[365]

The year spanning July 1970 to July 1971 had been "filled with countless phone calls, letters to officials (municipal and provincial), personal interviews with members of Council, committee meetings followed by more phone calls and delegations." Alumnae explained that the "task was not easy and several times, the project was on the verge of collapse." The firehall agreement came about not just through the efforts of Clark, Thom, and other club members, but also because of support from local residents who spoke about how the theatre would help revitalize the neighbourhood. Others supported Alumnae as well, including "several well-known architects," the Toronto Historical Society,[366] and key politicians.[367]

Converting the firehall into a theatre was a monumental task. Ron Thom, described by Kareda as a "very distinguished"[368] architect, was tasked with designing and overseeing the firehall's extensive transformation into Alumnae's fifth theatre, assisted by Club friends Michael Spence and Les Japp. A building committee chaired by Molly Thom, with her expertise derived from previous Coach House renovations, and including Agatha Leonard (front of house), Martha Mann Southgate (stage), Eileen Williams (costumes), Margaret Spence (backstage), and Michael Spence (technical), wrote an early "Architectural Program" for the building in November 1970: "There is in the club an overwhelming desire for intimacy. If it were possible, and it certainly appears dubious and costly, we would wish to open up the entire ground floor, so that stage and auditorium are contained in a square running the full width of the building. The ideal for our purposes is a thrust stage in one corner encircled by the audience."[369]

This initial vision imagined the firehall as the next "Coach House," featuring a thrust stage reminiscent of their beloved synagogue. However, conceding that "we are prepared to forgo the fun of total flexibility"[370] in order to achieve greater efficiency, the committee allowed the thrust to be replaced with a proscenium stage. To that end, Ron Thom combined the former engine room and stables; the result was a well-equipped 154-seat theatre with seats donated by Famous Players. This required removing the part of the second floor[371] above the theatre that had been the firemen's bedroom, leaving space for a technical booth and rehearsal hall.[372] The dark-wood-panelled[373] Edwardian-style third floor was converted into a flexible, intimate Studio to continue the recent Coach House tradition of experimental productions and Sunday evening readings. Likely a billiard room for the firemen in the original design, the Studio preserved the firehall's "magnificent floor-to-ceiling curved, arched windows offering a beautiful view of the city,"[374] as well as the existing dark-wood panelling with "enormous timbers cross-braced to support the roof."[375] Said Molly Thom, "what intrigued Norma and me immediately was the third floor ... Here was exactly the kind of space to continue our Sunday evening readings. We were hooked."[376]

The tall tower used for drying the hoses was converted into stairs for audiences to access the Studio theatre.[377] The firehall's oak-panelled office and locker room were turned into a bar, and the new lobby walls were lined with William Morris wallpaper from Sandersons.[378] Ron Thom designed the bar, window seat, box office desk, stairwell, and thirty-foot lantern,[379] and Alumnae members and other volunteers built them with wood found around the building.[380] Recalls Molly Thom,

> I have a long memory, and after renovating three theatres, whenever I heard of anyone with any kind of special skill who had even the vaguest connection with the theatre, I would tuck that information away for future use. Now was the time to redeem every IOU, every hint of expertise, every offer of help. Morna Wales taught a team of women to strip years of thick discoloured varnish from the oak panelling in the lobby. [Guest actor] Ian Orr had boasted one night at a cast party about his prowess in hanging wallpaper, so he was given the daunting task of hanging the hand-printed William Morris wallpaper. Ron's contacts were invaluable. Illustrator Robert Montgomery did the graphics; Ed Cowan, who had connections with Famous Players, found us theatre seats which we refinished and reupholstered; Daryl Morgan built the huge lamp for the lower lobby; the acoustician working with Ron on the Shaw Festival Theatre rushed down the Sunday before opening to give advice and supervise the hanging of acoustic panels onstage. A supplier provided the carpeting at cost. And everywhere there were women painting, and sewing, and feeding and organizing the workers.[381]

Notably, Ron Thom's design preserved the brass pole used by the firefighters to get from the second floor to the engine room, as well as the original lockers in the lower lobby bar. The wooden staircase was replaced with concrete to adhere to fire code.[382] Included were "ample storage areas, workshops, wardrobe, backstage and lobby space."[383] The plans preserved and renewed the exterior, leaving it "virtually unchanged,"[384] although the original red doors[385] for the fire engines were converted into large glass windows[386] and a new audience entrance was added to the tower.[387] Windows throughout the building gave a "feeling of involvement with the surrounding inner city."[388] Club members volunteered their time towards interior decorating tasks and installing the seats.[389] By June 1972 the firehall's structural renovations were complete[390] and the Maplewood Avenue Coach House Theatre was officially sold.[391] Deftly citing the theatre versus parks battle in the pages of his own paper,

Figure 5.8. Architect Ron Thom's cross-section sketch of Alumnae's Firehall theatre showing (*top*) the attic Studio theatre, (*middle, left to right*) a small front lobby and the raked auditorium seating with stage, and (*bottom*) below-ground wardrobe storage, dressing rooms, and set storage. The top of the staircase, formerly the tower for drying fire hoses, is visible at the top left. Courtesy of Alumnae Theatre Company.

Whittaker wrote: "Today, the annual meeting, a traditional garden party for the Alumnae, will be held in a treeless area of Toronto, but one which shows definite marks of the best kind of urban renewal."[392] Led by Margaret Spence, members could begin backstage and workshop construction as well as the front-of-house finishing led by Molly Thom.[393]

The occasion of a historic company opening their new home in a historic building precipitated long-view thinking among journalists, with restoration and alterity as the theme. The refurbishing of buildings was *en vogue* and worthy of column space. With Alumnae preparing their new building for the public and Toronto Free Theatre down the street well into production, Marci McDonald penned a virtual walking tour of Berkeley Street on the front page of the *Star*'s entertainment section titled "The arts are rescuing a gray old hobo of a street." The full-page piece featured photographs of Molly and Ron Thom in front of Alumnae's "$100,000 Firehall Theatre"; Tom Hendry in the doorway of Toronto Free Theatre; a sign at the United Church of Canada (an old Methodist Church) reading "Berkeley Studio: Films, Radio, Television"; and a photograph of cosmetic surgeon Dr. Harold Silver on a stairway in his "lavish private castle, a four-floor bachelor's dream that looks out on a beflowered courtyard." In purple prose, McDonald detailed the "faded glory" and "uncertain fate" of Berkeley Street,

> where diesels shriek to a stop in front of the truck-wash and a crane hurls its rusty relict bundle of wrecked fenders through the air, wild deer once frisked and salmon leaped from long-lost

streams and Berkeley St. once housed the glittering salon and gardens of one of the most prominent citizens [farmer and public official Charles Coxwell Small] in the little settlement they came to call the City of Toronto.

Added to the two theatres were two film studios, the "beginnings of a boutique and restaurant complex," a gallery for artists, architects, designers, filmmakers, and "hip rich expatriate uptowners who've moved their drawing boards – and in some cases their living-rooms – downtown to Berkeley St." McDonald noted that none of this was due to philanthropists or changed zoning by-laws, but "sprung up on its own. Berkeley St. has suddenly become radical chic." Importantly, she also cited a city planner who "lamented the loss of yet another low-income neighbourhood – the fact that once the rich and artsy move in, the poor are pushed on in their endless search for yet another cheap roof."[394] McDonald was describing gentrification and, an example of the urban phenomenon Richard Florida has since defined as the "rise of the creative class."[395] Both Alumnae and Toronto Free were "pleased to be part of a recognized off-King Street theatre area."[396] Each had grown grassroots ideas that had their start with the theatre makers who ran them. Each also benefited from the federal government's LIP (Local Initiative Program) grants. In Alumnae's case, nonprofessionalizing theatres are not often associated with "'cool' or cutting-edge"[397] urbanity, but by taking their experimental history and relocating it to Berkeley Street, they were proving to be an exception. In matters of both theatre and real estate, Alumnae continued to be trendsetters.[398]

In unveiling their new Firehall Theatre to the public in October 1972 with Seán O'Casey's *The Plough and the Stars*, Alumnae threw a gala affair that for some must have echoed the relative opulence of the national Dominion Drama Festival finals. Mark McAllister wrote in the *Varsity* that "flocks of brightly dressed socialites seemed to enjoy exploring the spiffily renovated firehall and sampling the various exotic beverages before and afterwards, as much as the production itself."[399] Champagne was provided after the performance, which he suggested was a "formality quite superfluous with the alarming number of thoroughly bottled patrons about." Of the building, Kareda said that the entrance and lobby offered "more quaint and cozy lounge facilities than any other Toronto theatre,"[400] although he was disappointed in the Mainstage auditorium's design, which he found "somber, less imaginative; the performance area already seems too rigid and old-fashioned for future use. Acoustics last night were dodgy too, and the ear had to be constantly re adjusted for each individual speaker."[401] Perhaps in keeping with contemporary sentiments towards experimental spaces, he was more pleased with the upstairs Studio, which he called, when it opened two months later, the "building's real jewel, an ideal situation for intimate chamber plays" and "that happy theatrical location, a space which creates sense of anticipation."[402] Whittaker called the Studio "Toronto's latest chamber theatre [using] a fine timbered space under the eaves of the Firehall Theatre on Berkeley Street. Gothic, gabled, half chapel and half barn, it cries out to have some Ingmar Bergman tragedy or medieval morality play staged in it."[403]

Alumnae's historic building would demand a whole new level of administration. In the British context, Jane Milling puts into perspective the tensions inherent in running established amateur theatre companies. Amateur theatre, she writes, is a "hobby that has serious financial implications around its activities. There is a tension between the enjoyment of a hobby and the need for more business-like practices. You can't keep running what are in effect small businesses on the back of a fag packet."[404] Similarly, Francess Halpenny recorded that from the outset the firehall was a "joy to possess" but also a "challenge for the women who managed it. A large budget had to be met. How would younger members aiming to be professionals be accommodated?"[405]

Under Toronto City By-Law No. 191-71, which made Alumnae "custodians" of the firehall on the City's behalf, their use of the building was subject to a municipal lease agreement and related regulations. At the start, a management board was appointed, with at least five members, including club representatives and a city councillor nominated by the club.[406] This board "provides for the maintenance and management"[407] of the firehall and would operate it as a "place of recreation and amusement and auditorium," as well as their "club house." Alumnae were to be responsible for "alterations, renovations and improvements"[408] to the building in compliance with city by-laws. Then, as now, discussion was ongoing regarding building locks, bells, and buzzers with the aim of ensuring that members and rental groups had convenient access without compromising safety and security.[409] Upkeep, or what the theatre's long-time building manager and technical expert Michael Spence anthropomorphically called the "care and feeding of the building,"[410] became more time consuming and costly, as did the administration of said upkeep. In 1987, Alumnae's auditor suggested that the management board "be separated" from the executive, including with separate books.[411] By March 1987 the separation was in effect and details of respective responsibilities and budgets had been ironed out.[412] Alumnae's own by-laws were amended in June 1987.[413]

The firehall was immediately the envy of other arts groups, and rentals quickly became an important source of income,[414] positioning Alumnae as a sought-after host to theatre groups in the city. Groups like the influential Young People's Theatre, which did not have its current space until 1977, sometimes asked to book across a multi-year period;[415] others booked consistently over the Christmas holidays,[416] when the firehall spaces would otherwise go unused. Other groups, such as Mariposa and Ariel, rented in the 1980s at rates that needed to gradually increase, after much discussion, to pay for pressing capital upgrades.[417]

The question of to whom Alumnae should rent spaces has always been a matter of serious discussion. For example, in 1985 theatre manager Nola Wale was tasked with reviewing Alumnae's rental fees. She expressed concern that renting to those not close to the club, such as professional groups, risked reducing the rental transaction to a "landlord problem" if damages to the facilities resulted. Wale further noted that professional groups have access to government and private sector support that community groups do not.[418] For these reasons, she did not recommend renting to professional groups. At the June 2002 annual general meeting, in praise of the first year that the Toronto Irish Players began frequent rentals at the firehall, Angela Finlay's rental report noted that Alumnae should

> carefully choose the rentals we accept, both to protect our property and because audiences don't seem to differentiate between our Alumnae shows and rentals. For instance, if someone sees a substandard show here, they're going to tell their friends that they saw a bad show at the Alum the other night, and rarely make the distinction that the production company was not us! This damages our reputation and reduces potential audiences.[419]

It is through rentals in particular that Alumnae have directly served many of Toronto's performing arts activities at the cost of incalculable hours of volunteer administrative labour. Volunteer members continue to guide and accomplish this work, which constitutes a "unique format"[420] that is frequently honed and reapproached.[421]

To provide members with training in the use of the firehall, workshops and manuals remain central. Workshops often focus on backstage training in set construction, set painting, lighting, sound, front of house, and building security in order to familiarize members with the spaces.[422] One club seminar invitation in the fall of 1985 read, "Let's try to take the frustrations and the 're-inventing of the wheel' out of this year's productions."[423] Decades worth of revised manuals serve to clarify the responsibilities of directors, producers, designers, stage managers, and nearly everyone else working at the theatre. Shortly before taking over the firehall, Alumnae developed a "Manual of Production Procedures" because, as the manual introduced, "we are not a professional producing unit; but our public, and the people who work for us expect the standards and methods of the professional theatre. With organization, planning and thought we are able to provide them."[424] Written by Agatha Leonard in great detail, the manual covered the work of each member of the production team, from casting procedures to operating lighting equipment, to the producer's requirement to be familiar with Actors' Equity rules. This nineteen-page document would be revised and replaced several times.[425]

"This Is the Competitive Democracy of Amateur Drama"[1]: Festivals and Nationhood

There is still complete agreement in all quarters with the original aims of the festival – to encourage the best use of recreation by Canadians as individuals, and to implement the establishment of a Canadian theatre. By the latter we understand the development of dramatic art in which the genius of a whole nation's experience can be expressed. There have been differences of opinion, however, on the methods of realizing the aims. The theatre foyers bristle with such discussion. It is important to bear in mind that the winning of the trophy is a spur to effort, a means to an end, not the end in itself.[2]

– Pearl McCarthy on the Dominion Drama Festival

The development of theatre in Canada is marked by competition. From the early roadhouses that competed to attract foreign touring companies, to the interwar Little Theatres and post-war nonprofessionalizing companies that competed for awards at the Dominion Drama Festival (DDF) and its regional festivals, to post-war professionalizing companies that competed for audiences and prestige, to the rise of state funding that made professional theatres compete for operating and capital grants, to regional theatre awards, Fringe festival lotteries, and playwriting prizes, competition has always been core to the efforts of entrepreneurs and governments to raise awareness of theatre and shape the conditions for its support and expansion. One way or another, theatre competitions have been linked to culture-building projects at the national, regional, and community levels. This is particularly true of the DDF (under the patronage of Canada's governor general) and the work of the Canada Council (an arm's-length Crown corporation). Many competitions have also been professionalizing projects meant to publicly perform the professionalization of the nation and its cultural properties. The Earl Grey Musical and Dramatic Competitions (1907–11) and the much longer-lived DDF (1933–72) were viceregal contests at which amateur practitioners (however defined) won awards, shared experiences, and gauged their progress and degree of professionalization against that of their counterparts through a juried selection process and a public adjudication. Helen Nicholson and colleagues have observed that "festivals establish the habitus, the public culture of amateur theatre, not least the culture and ritual of putting creative practice under scrutiny and judgement via competitive processes designed to acknowledge talent and raise artistic standards."[3] Raising artistic standards was the goal of the DDF and its nonprofessionalizing participaints.

Many of Alumnae's most significant productions competed at the DDF's national festival, its feeder the Central Ontario Drama League (CODL) regional festival, and CODL's one-act festival. As Francess Halpenny observed, DDF productions forced "sights to be set higher"[4] for all who competed. Over thirty-five years, Alumnae eventually won every major DDF award.[5] These festivals helped Alumnae focus their efforts; it also brought them fame and earned them space on the country's front pages. And with the monetary rewards from their winnings, Alumnae were able to strike out from the University of Toronto campus for a theatre space of their own.

It may seem jarring today that nonprofessionalizing theatre could be viewed as "competitive" and "national." Certainly we are familiar with competitive youth drama festivals, but representations of adult nonprofessionalizing performance often yield notions of local narrow-mindedness and hobbyistic inferiority. In this regard, in "On Amateurs," David Gilbert and colleagues write that "the amateur is too often made to seem parochial, closed and insular and set against the spaces of professional performance. The spaces of the amateur are seen as small and often inadequate, particularly when compared to those of professional performance. A manifesto for amateurs rejects these associations. We need new geographies of and for the amateur." In delineating "geographies of and for the amateur," they go on to list a "wide variety of spaces" in which amateur companies work, arguing that they are often parts of "stretched networks"[6] across local and national spaces, some of which resemble Canada's DDF in its prime.

Many of Alumnae's most influential productions found success at regional and national DDF competitions. Their more successful productions were held over and remounted at Hart House Theatre and other venues across Toronto, as well as in the cities where the finals were held. Tens of thousands of people saw these productions and read front-page critical commentary about them. By tracking Alumnae's journey through the DDF years, I interrogate the paradox of nonprofessionalizing theatre as local and inferior, yet national and competitive. To do so, I draw from selected productions to show how Alumnae's DDF entries, including award-winning Toronto premieres of Patricia Joudry's *Teach Me How to Cry*, George Bernard Shaw's *In Good King Charles's Golden Days*, and Samuel Beckett's *Waiting for Godot*, connected them to Canada's nationalizing and professionalizing theatre project and an emerging national audience for theatre. This success placed Alumnae at the summit of Toronto's mid-century theatre scene and, periodically, Canada's as well. Through these competitions, Alumnae contributed to the idea of a "Canadian theatre," and this, reciprocally, fuelled their programming. Along the way, the chapter traces influential *Globe and Mail* theatre critic Herbert Whittaker's complex involvement with Alumnae as a guest director and designer for three national successes.

In her ubiquitous *Love and Whisky: The Story of the Dominion Drama Festival*, Betty Lee recounts that the DDF was born on Saturday, 29 October 1932, at a meeting hosted by the Governor General of Canada, the Earl of Bessborough, at Rideau Hall. For Bessborough, Vincent Massey, between international diplomatic duties, curated a national guest list of thriving Little Theatre leaders. Bessborough announced his plan to those in attendance: "Now that the Little Theatre has gained so strong a foothold in this country there is, without any doubt, a great opportunity for its development along national lines, with the ultimate objective of creating a national drama."[7] By bringing together theatre figureheads from across Canada, Bessborough and Massey hoped to surmount the twin obstacles of distance and regionalism and begin establishing a theatre profession. The stated goal was to raise the quality of theatre in both languages across the Dominion by way of competition, comparison, and mutual instruction.

The fourth week of April 1933 was chosen for the inaugural DDF, to be held in Ottawa, where the best productions in Canada, one from each province (and from three separate regions in the more populated province of Ontario), would compete for national honours. An article in the *Globe* explained, "It is hoped that the reading and acting of drama will be greatly encouraged by the festival, and that the various representative dramatic groups all over Canada will be united in a friendly rivalry."[8] Competitors were to include only "established amateur dramatic societies,"[9] which ultimately included all manner of institutions, including Little Theatres and guilds, church and library groups, high school classes, undergraduate student clubs, and university alumni associations.

Three days after the DDF's inaugural meeting, Edgar Stone – wearing the quadruple hats of DDF executive member, inaugural Central Ontario region chair,[10] Hart House Theatre director, and competing play director that would place him under scrutiny due to his extraordinary directing success during the festival's early years – told the *Varsity* that the new national festival was a "tremendous stride in the forming of a cultural background in Canada." He underscored the broad implications of the DDF, which would produce new talent, new groups, and an "interested and intelligent audience," each of which would "stir up an interest in the professional stage which is in great need of support." He added that the DDF would also "encourage a more intense study of drama in the schools where at present it is almost completely ignored."[11] U of T's campus theatre community, anchored by Hart House Theatre, was cautiously enthusiastic about the idea of the DDF as a vehicle for encouraging nonprofessionalizing groups and their Little Theatre Movement.[12] Said one fourth-year UC student, "Canadians are conservative and slow to make decisive steps, but I am sure such a movement is worthy of their support."[13]

Narratives about the DDF's influence on a burgeoning Canadian theatre ecology formed within a few years. Those narratives help clarify Alumnae's artistic and social position within the DDF. In 1936, regional adjudicator Allan Wade noted that the quality of plays was improving,[14] particularly in the Central Ontario region (Wade adjudicated all of the regional competitions that year). The *Star*'s Pearl McCarthy, following Wade, happily observed a "return to favour of the legitimate theatre, not alone by the quality of the [festival's] stage work but by this animated attitude of the audience. We saw reason in the suggestion that lack of a critical audience had been one factor in the decline of the stage's popularity. The central Ontario Region presented an acting stage and an active audience."[15]

Views on the cultivation of a national theatre emerged with vigour.[16] In its early years, some expressed concerns about the festival's shortcomings, including that it was growing so much that it might not be serving the strongest groups (which might be dragged down), or rural groups, which started without the city's material advantages and thus found themselves being declined entry.[17] Also, many felt the festival finals should not always be held in Ottawa because the "matrons and dowagers of the capital"[18] were not the only ones who deserved to see the "best drama Canada can provide."[19]

Moreover, charges of elitism emerged, including in the *Varsity*, which accused the Little Theatre Movement and its purveyors of being a "sophisticated artistic outlet for the socialites" that privileged dilettantism and their own "ridiculously poor" plays over arguably higher-quality student productions, which could not compete because the festival was routinely scheduled during exams.[20] That was a particular shame, the editorial noted, because many university students wanted to make theatre a career, and the festival would be an excellent step towards that goal. Where the editorial concluded that the DDF "cannot make any lasting contributions to Canadian culture if it is primarily a series of social functions not to be missed,"[21] Alumnae members perhaps felt called out, because the festival's social aspects, an extension of their philanthropy, were integral to their company. Given the concerns about too many entries, one wonders whether the choice to hold the festival when students could not compete was purposeful among those whose groups feared rejection.

The students' criticisms were never adequately addressed. However, the following year the finals were held away from Ottawa for the first time, at Winnipeg's Walker Theatre, and full-length plays competed. This reduced the number of plays overall from eighteen to twelve (those twelve having "survived a process of elimination"[22] over four months). The DDF began as, and remained, the purview of practitioners and audiences with leisure time as well as money to spend. Charges of elitism would continue to haunt the festival. A symptom of that elitism was the atmosphere of the DDF and its regional festivals, which quickly became at least as important as the art itself. Alumnae designer Martha Mann Southgate recalls the Toronto-area groups that competed and the atmosphere they inhabited:

> If you look at the CODL programs you'll see it was the same people year after year. There was a great rivalry among them between the various groups … I used to go and see the CODL festival for years. It was always the same six people competing for years, particularly the men because it was whomever was going to give them the best part. The DDF was a hugely important thing. It was very social as well, which was an aspect of it I always found kind of alarming – I mean only in that it was kind of an elite event. It was a very big deal. [If you went to the finals] you had to go to a different city. You had to get there. A week of plays. And a lot of partying. And the competition was very serious. People took what they were doing very seriously.[23]

This serious-but-light environment, the friendly rivalries, and the partying characterized the DDF and Alumnae's participation in it. If a national theatre was going to emerge from a competitive framework, it would happen within a (generally) congenial Canadian atmosphere. As this chapter investigates, Alumnae were occupied not only with the production of competitive plays but also with the social functions that attended them, thus playing their part in both competition and atmosphere.[24]

Performing the Local to the Nation from *Nine Till Six* to *The Cradle Song*

Each year in the 1930s, Alumnae produced a regional DDF offering at Hart House Theatre, which they would then, occasionally, produce at least once more by invitation later in the year. Alumnae's 1932–33 season was occupied with several full or partial showings of their first DDF regional entry, Aimée and Philip Stuart's 1930 drama *Nine Till Six*, directed by Alumnae member and the DDF Central Ontario region "Honourary Secretary" Margaret Tytler, with an all-female cast (their first in years). The production showcased core members of the club to a wide Toronto audience. The play, which was set in a London dressmaking shop and focused on the status of working women in a man's world, reflected pressing concerns for recent female graduates of UC in the early years of the Great Depression. The all-female play, which had had a Broadway run, was a good fit for Alumnae's first festival offering.[25] Alumnae opened their season with the play's third act at an "invite night" at the Women's Union in December 1932.[26] By March 1933 they were ready to present a full production at Toronto's Art Deco-styled, 1,275-seat Eaton Auditorium, with seventeen women in the cast,[27] before presenting the third act at the Toronto DDF regional feeder a week later[28] and a full production at Hart House Theatre as a Theatre Night for the Canadian Business and Professional Women's Club a week after that.[29]

Figure 6.1. Members of the cast of Alumnae's March 1935 Central Ontario Drama Region entry, Ethel van der Veer and Franklyn Bigelow's *As the Tumbrils Pass*, directed by W.S. Milne with costumes designed by Lillian Milne and executed by members of the Club. Photographed for Hart House Theatre (public domain). Courtesy of Alumnae Theatre Company.

Nine Till Six was prologue to Alumnae's four decades of involvement with Canada's largest and longest-running theatre festival. That inaugural year, they were one of nine groups presenting twelve plays at the regional competition.[30] *Saturday Night* editor B.K. Sandwell, who spoke as one of three festival adjudicators, said that Alumnae "did not quite succeed in 'putting over'"[31] the third act of *Nine Till Six*, and placed them outside the top four groups.[32] Their failure to move on to the finals in Ottawa was taken as a learning experience by club members. Even so, their all-women festival appearance had made a statement that challenged the male leadership in the movement to nationalize and professionalize Canadian theatre.

Alumnae stayed "on brand" with all-female casts at the next two annual Central Ontario regional festivals, offering Harold Bridhouse's social comedy *Smoke Screens* in March 1934, directed by club member Agatha Leonard, and Ethel Van Der Veer and Franklyn Bigelow's one-act French Revolution drama *As the Tumbrils Pass* in March 1935, directed by Toronto playwright and frequent Alumnae guest actor W.S. Milne, with period costumes designed by Lillian Milne (who would come to be very active as a costume designer in the city[33]). But like *Nine Till Six*, neither production fared well in the eyes of adjudicators Rupert Harvey and Malcolm Morley respectively.[34]

DOMINION DRAMA FESTIVAL

REGIONAL FESTIVAL AT TORONTO DATE 30, MARCH 1935.

NAME OF PLAY "AS THE TUMBRILS PASS" PRESENTED BY DRAMATIC CLUB OF THE UNIVERSITY COLLEGE ALUMNAE ASSOC.

CHARACTERS:	REMARKS:
Manon Moreau	Well characterised - needed expansion
Gervaise	Fairly good though rather over-declamatory
Gobemouche	Interesting
La Vicomtesse	Very fair - too placid in the situation
Citizeness Jurevant	Satisfactory
Citizeness Clapart	) Strong
La Tripère	) performances

ACTING (50 MARKS)	MARKS	REMARKS
Characterisation	13	On the conventional stage side of the French Revolution. The performance was straight forward. The characters played to themselves more than to the others on the stage. Individually their work was good - the team spirit was not always evident insasmuch as the characters did not listen well to each other. Set and costumes fairly good.
Variation of Tone	4	
Emphasis	4	
Gesture	3	
Movement	3	
TOTAL	27	
PRODUCTION AND STAGE PRESENTATION (50 MARKS)		
Interpretation	12	
Team Work	2	
Tempo	3	
Grouping	3	
Movement	2	
Sense of Climax	2	
Properties	3	
Stage Setting	3	
Lighting	2	
Costumes	2	
Make-Up	2	
TOTAL	36	
GRAND TOTAL	63	

Adjudicator. Malcolm Morley.

Figure 6.2. Adjudicator Malcolm Morley's form for Alumnae's production of *As the Tumbrils Pass* at the Central Ontario Regional Festival in March 1935. Courtesy of Alumnae Theatre Company.

Figure 6.3. (*left to right*) Christina Templeton (Tabitha), Alison Ewart (Anne Brontë), and Agnes Muldrew (Charlotte Brontë) in Oscar W. Firkins's *Empurpled Moors*, produced by Alumnae for the Central Ontario Regional Festival in March 1936. Photographed for Hart House Theatre (public domain). Courtesy of Alumnae Theatre Company.

The following fall, after influential critic Augustus Bridle objected to yet another all-women cast when they produced Cyril Campion's *Ladies in Waiting* at Hart House Theatre under Frank Hemingway's direction, Alumnae decided to change strategies. Having failed to reach the DDF finals in the competition's first three years, they chose for the 1936 regional festival Oscar W. Firkins's 1932 play about the Brontë sisters, *Empurpled Moors*,[35] with Hemingway directing. Among competing groups, which had ballooned to twenty,[36] Alumnae received somewhat more positive criticism than in previous years from regional adjudicator Allan Wade,[37] although he was reported to have exclaimed, "What a horrible title for a play!"[38] As a director himself, he confided that he "felt tempted to want to meddle with it." There was something more in it which might have been brought out, he felt, although he "felicitated the players on having brought out so much."[39] Alumnae had not yet managed to crack the top three and move on to the finals; perhaps they had been marked by then as one of the offending urban groups taking up space at the festival. If so, that was a mark that might become more difficult to weather if the number of competing groups continued to grow.

Alumnae's first four festival entries had not impressed. But starting with their fifth, the club would be counted among Toronto's most reliable annual contenders. At the February 1937 Central Ontario Region competition at Hart House Theatre, in front of a full house,

Figure 6.4. (*standing, left to right*) Erskine Keys (Sister Tornera), Christina Templeton (Sister Inez), Katherine Anglin (Monitor), Margaret Tytler (The Mistress of Novices), Florian Moore (Nun), Agnes Muldrew (The Prioress), Elspeth Wilson (Nun), Margaret Ness (Monitor), and Jean Hunnisett (Sister Sagrario); (*kneeling, left to right*) Agatha Leonard (Sister Joanna of the Cross), Alison Ewart (Sister Marcella), and Doris Shiell (Sister Mary of Jesus) in Alumnae's production of Gregorio Martínez Sierra's *Cradle Song*, which won the Bessborough Trophy in May 1937 for the Best Presentation in English (other than the winner) at the Dominion Drama Festival. Photographed for Hart House Theatre (public domain). Courtesy of Alumnae Theatre Company.

Alumnae earned third place – and a spot in the DDF finals in Ottawa – for their production of Act I of Gregorio and María Martínez Sierra's "touching"[40] play *The Cradle Song*, translated from the Spanish by John Garrett Underhill. Edgar Stone directed the production, which sent him to Ottawa for the fourth straight year.[41]

Among their interwar productions, Alumnae credited *The Cradle Song* as their "greatest achievement."[42] The cast of fourteen women and one man began rehearsals in January at Radio Hall, to which Stone had access.[43] The play concerns the sisters at the Convent of Enclosed Dominican Nuns in Spain, around 1911, and a baby girl who is left by an unmarried mother in a basket at their door. Augustus Bridle's review noted that the play had been performed at Toronto's Princess Theatre some years earlier and that Stone's choice to direct it amounted to the "most precarious director's job" because the "trick was to portray the austere life of a convent as humourized by humanism; to play casual comedy in a religious scene by means of skillful dialogue and speeches. The general effect was much like a musical pantomime." He went on to say that Alumnae "have never done anything else quite so delicately skillful in scenic art, atmosphere and character" and concluded that "so many people to direct in movements, dialogues and tableaux made this production one of the rare gems of art in any festival."[44] In granting it third place, adjudicator George de Warfaz said it was the "most touching of all plays"[45] and "a most lovely presentation" with a "beautiful job"[46] done on the "really exquisite"[47] "silver and black"[48] set and costumes that "took one's breath away."[49] Rose MacDonald reported that "so beautiful in its austerity, indeed, was this Dominican convent scene that when the curtains parted upon it the audience burst into spontaneous applause." The movements, she reported Warfaz as saying, were "full of life and grace." Agnes Muldrew's Prioress was "very distinguished,"[50] with "excellent" diction,[51] although some of the rest of the cast's speech was "a little too fast."[52] In an example of Alumnae's dedication to the socialite aspects of the festivals, they hosted a reception at the Women's Union for all groups participating in the festival two days before its opening, with university president H.J. Cody among those receiving. Then, upon hearing from Warfaz that they would be going to Ottawa, they held their celebration at Agatha Leonard's home.[53]

A note in Alumnae's meeting minutes ten months before *The Cradle Song* ran at the regional festival had stated that the following spring, "if we don't go to Ottawa,"[54] three one-act plays would be offered for an Alumnae invitational evening, one being their regional festival entry. This, as it turned out, was not necessary. Their first appearance at the DDF finals at the Ottawa Little Theatre, which had hosted the event in each of the previous years, was on 1 May 1937, the last day of the festival. Competing as the "Dramatic Club of the University College Alumnae Association," they won the award for best play in English, in a tie with the Strolling Players of Vancouver (who offered Rudolf Besier's *The Barretts of Wimpole Street*).[55] In his two-page report, DDF finals adjudicator Michel Saint-Denis said of *The Cradle Song* that "this has been for me in many ways the best production we have seen."[56] Along with the success of the lighting, the scenery, and the "team-work," he emphasized Stone's direction, in which "each time something happened, you had pleasure … all those things, perfectly right, beautifully correct." Like Warfaz, Saint-Denis singled out the acting of Stone's wife, Agnes Muldrew: "full of quality, full of feeling, full of balance, a charming smile, great dignity, and all that without falling into sentimentality or what I have called 'nobility' in the voice."[57] He noted that she and Alison Ewart were among the women he had to eliminate before giving the award for best performance by a woman in an English-language play to Gay Scrivener of the Strolling Players.

In contrast to a disappointment Warfaz had expressed with the Central Ontario regional offerings, Saint-Denis said of the national festival, "I go back with an extremely good impression. It is not so much the number of good productions as the quality of some of them. They show feeling for the stage itself and you would not find better in the professional theatre. Some of the actors know what acting means."[58] B.K. Sandwell astutely noted that *The Cradle Song* had "climbed up nearly to top-place after achieving a comparatively low position" at the regional festival because the "members of the cast had striven to cure certain defects that were apparent two months ago." He cited in particular Agatha Leonard's work in improving the delivery of a "key line," which had "faded out" in Toronto but was "so beautifully rendered at Ottawa … that it enthralled every listener."[59]

A series of celebratory social events followed. The day after their performance, Alumnae's cast and crew attended a reception at Rideau Hall, where Governor General Lord Tweedsmuir presented the trophy, to be shared with the Vancouver club.[60] The following week, Alumnae members attended two dinners at Eaton's Round Room: the first with

Figure 6.5. Alumnae's Award certificate for their production of Act I of Gregorio Martínez Sierra's *Cradle Song* at the 1937 Dominion Drama Festival. Courtesy of Alumnae Theatre Company.

the members of the Toronto Masquers[61] and the second with all three Toronto finalists, with Michel Saint-Denis as the guest of honour.[62] The UCAA then invited its drama club to a recognition dinner on 20 May and, eight months later, to another reception at the Women's Union dining room after Alumnae performed a "thirteen-act-revue"[63] at which the trophy they had won in Ottawa was displayed along with a picture of club members presented by Alumnae guest actor Frank Venables.[64] The *University Monthly* reported that the cast "had worked sometimes more than four nights a week all through the winter at rehearsals" and that "this is the highest honour that has come as yet to the Club, and it is an honour in which not only University College but the whole University has a part, for in Ottawa the players were known as 'the group from the University of Toronto.'"[65] These were local celebrations worthy of a top national competitor and definitive of the high-society culture that attended the DDF. Alumnae's breakthrough served as widespread confirmation that they were among Toronto's most influential theatre companies.

The win also confirmed Stone's directorial influence on the company and on Toronto theatre generally. With humility a decade later, Alumnae credited Stone with much of *The Cradle Song*'s success: "By din of tireless effort and inspiration close to genius, Edgar Stone transformed fourteen ordinary Club members into nuns, or reasonable facsimiles thereof and made a beautiful and convincing stage picture of Mother-love in a convent. In this production such a high standard was set for the Club that they have never since aspired to reach it."[66] It was the fifth play Stone had directed for Alumnae since his first in 1923. The overwhelmingly female cast must have suggested to the national audience that women were major influencers in Toronto theatre and in the Little Theatre Movement generally.[67]

Although they continued to participate without fail every year in the regional festival, Alumnae would not be sent to the national finals again until after the war. Their 1938 entry, Zoë Atkins's Pulitzer Prize–winning drama of two years earlier titled *The Old Maid* (based on an Edith Wharton novel), generated more off-stage controversy than artistic recognition; in the end, the club issued an apology to adjudicator Malcolm Morley for the conduct of one of their members.[68] And although their 1939 festival entry, *Short Circuit*, was a world premiere written by member Margaret Ness in a festival that featured no fewer than six Canadian plays (a record at the time for any DDF regional or national festival[69]), it went no further than *The Old Maid* in competition.[70]

However mixed their results in the festival's early years, Alumnae members were participating in a theatrical revolution. After the 1939 regional festival, in a piece titled "Amateur festival 'art democracy,'" the *Telegram* reflected on how far Ontario's theatre activity had come since the inception of the DDF, acknowledging the rise in participatory theatre and the effect of film on audiences. Toronto, it read,

> teems with actors learning a new art of expression. Ontario is full of them. Instead of the old-fashioned singing school and debating society, our towns, villages and townships have young people in plays with scenery, drapes, homemade costumes, self-made props, lights in all sorts of reflectors made of tin cans, or what have you?
>
> Movies have become schools of drama to thousands. The little-theatre movement extended long ago to the church basements, parish halls, libraries. The one most important feature in all the school-assembly halls built since 1910 was the stage and its equipment. Every secondary school has its groups of players. They have entered four or five plays at the Toronto Festivals since 1933 and there are two yearly secondary school festivals.[71]

The DDF's impact was significant. Bessborough's great dream of a Canadian national drama was taking hold. Across its first seven iterations, around 1,000 actors performed with forty groups under fifty different directors.[72] Although Ontario's regional festivals featured far more productions than those of other provinces, those productions could lose to stronger ones from elsewhere, leading the *Telegram* to conclude: "This is the competitive democracy of amateur drama."[73] In the *Globe and Mail*, Roly Young noted that at least three actors had competed in all seven pre-war festivals, including Alumnae's Alison Ewart and Margaret Tytler, along with Alumnae guest actor Eric Aldwinckle.[74] But unbeknownst to festival followers, 1939 would be the last chance for Europe's adjudicators to judge Canada's theatrical emergence for nearly a decade. The Second World War meant the cessation of the DDF and its regional festivals as personnel and resources were pivoted towards the war effort.

Years Ago, a Post-War Festival Success

During Alumnae's last two club meetings before hostilities ceased in 1945, the discussion turned to "the National Theatre." Alumnae members had attended several meetings at the Arts and Letters Club on the subject.[75] Alumnae president Jean Stewart reported that attendees were "mainly in favour of building on the existing foundations and reviving the [Dominion] Drama Festival."[76] Nevertheless, Alumnae's first post-war initiative, although they were involved in it for only one year, was to join *Globe and Mail* film and theatre critic Roly Young's short-lived (1945–49) Civic Theatre Association (CTA).[77] The CTA gained start-up financing from the last civilian showing of the *Merry-Go-Round* revue, which Young directed,[78] and effectively took the place of the Toronto-area DDF regional festival before it returned in 1947. As Anton Wagner recounts, about fourteen theatre groups, ten of them amateur, joined the CTA[79] to "discover whether more popular programming could significantly widen the limited audience base of amateur companies and thus rival commercial professional theatres like the Royal Alexandra."[80] Young hoped to entice both professional touring companies and Little Theatre groups (especially Hart House Theatre) so as to build a collective identity and an audience. His CTA vied for the income of the former and the social status of the latter. And he sought to alleviate Canada's loss of talent abroad[81] with an income-generating local festival.

Thus, after an uneventful fall in which Alumnae prepared to return to full public productions, in April 1946 they repurposed their winter Women's Union production of Philip Johnson's *Orange Blossoms* for the CTA's first drama festival at Toronto's Northern Vocational School. Young announced on opening night that the festival was not a "commercial proposition"[82] but rather an "interassociation clambake"[83] intended to give the participating groups a chance to present themselves after a decade of relatively low activity.[84] The program featured twelve competing plays from nine theatre and ballet groups. Having been ranked best among the festival's three opening-night plays, *Orange Blossoms* performed again on the final night. Adjudicator chair H. Napier Moore, the British-born Canadian editor of *Maclean's*, applauded the production's pace and Christina Templeton's performance as "uniformly good," although the cast struggled with the dialect.[85] W.A.D. in the *Globe and Mail* remarked that it was "of the same general excellence"[86] as the winner and runner-up plays.

On the surface it may seem odd that Alumnae, a group connected to the Little Theatre Movement – not to mention a group that would soon lead the way for modern theatre production in Toronto – would align themselves with an association dedicated to commercial, professionalizing theatre. But considering that Young followed Lawrence Mason and preceded Herbert Whittaker at the *Globe and Mail*, Alumnae were being savvy by aligning themselves with the tastes of an influential critic, as they would later do with Whittaker. They were seeking to raise their profile in order to expand their membership and build back audiences after the war. Young was one of Toronto's early critic-practitioners in that he not only wrote about theatre but also actively sought to make it happen.

When the DDF returned to the Central Ontario region, Alumnae offered Thornton Wilder's *The Happy Journey*, directed by Sterndale Bennett, on opening night of the festival at Hart House Theatre in February 1947.[87] It placed fifth; the other show that Sterndale Bennett directed went to the finals in London, Ontario.[88] The following year, in March, Alumnae's production of the first act of Broadway actress Ruth Gordon's autobiographical play *Years Ago* found greater success under the "gifted young director"[89] John Mantley. In the *Globe and Mail,* E.G. Wanger described the play as a "sort of dramatized high school diary. Like many of its predecessors, it isn't really a play at all – rather a reasonably funny dialogue around the question, whether young Ruth should become a physical culture teacher or actress."[90] Adjudicator Robert Stuart[91] praised Alumnae's work: "I laughed my fool head off. It was quite excellent … It is a comedy in which most of us found something of ourselves – or of some of our relations."[92] Alex McKee, "that reliable character actor"[93] and Toronto radio performer,[94] earned the regional festival's president's award for best performance by a male actor for his work as the father, while Alumnae member Barbara Allen earned runner-up for the best performance by a female actor in the autobiographical role of Ruth Gordon Jones. Future actor, director, and scholar David Gardner, still an undergraduate at Victoria University, was described as "excruciatingly funny in the role of an excessively shy young college boy trying to make a date."[95] *Years Ago* earned the Hugh Eayrs Trophy for best performance and was selected among fourteen productions[96] across Canada to travel to Ottawa for the DDF finals the next month.

After the war, the newly named Central Ontario Drama League (CODL) represented DDF activity in the region with a mandate that had now expanded beyond the festival. A new charter promoted in the festival program expressed CODL's aims: to "encourage, develop, and promote all arts and crafts of the university; to correlate the activities of individuals and organizations in the theatre throughout Central Ontario," with the regional drama festival as one of its "main activities";[97] and to cooperate with the Ontario government, including operating the Provincial Dramatic Library, which made plays available to dramatic groups throughout Ontario. But despite these well-viewed activities, reflections on the year's festival were mixed. Reviewers felt that productions were "necessarily uneven,"[98] largely because groups had not recovered from so many years off, and that there was a "wide gulf which separated its best from its less good performances," although it was a "brilliant affair," with "no one single group or clique dominat[ing] these audiences." Overall, while there was "evidence of potential community support for an emergent national theatre,"[99] Rose MacDonald called it "manifestly unfair"[100] that the DDF was now allowing professionals to compete at the festival. Along with the plays and competition, the debate over culture making kept the DDF in public view.

This was Alumnae's first finals appearance since their 1937 Bessborough-winning production of *The Cradle Song*.[101] Wrote Kay Rex in the *Globe and Mail*, "by train and bus they have been pouring into the capital which hasn't seen such a contest in 11 years."[102] In April 1948 at the Ottawa Little Theatre, Alumnae presented the first act of *Years Ago* at the DDF finals. Adjudicator Robert Speaight[103] remarked that it was a "splendid little comedy,"[104] and the *Globe and Mail* reported that the "audience laughed until it had tears in its eyes over the antics."[105] Speaight called McKee's performance "superb" and given with "complete assurance,"[106] although he thought the rest of the cast did not match his intensity.[107] He awarded the London Little Theatre the Bessborough Trophy, the "highest tribute to amateur and professional acting in Canada,"[108] for their production of Shaw's *Saint Joan*. Along with Allen and Gardner in Alumnae's production, other 1948 DDF participants who would become influential professional theatre artists included Joy Coghill, Douglas Rain, Amelia Hall, and John Colicos. That Alumnae had their first opportunity to sample some of the best post-war theatre in the country would surely burn in the minds of members Christina Templeton, Katherine Anglin, Francess Halpenny, and the others who made the trip. In Alumnae's "Summary of Year's Activities 1947–48," a note appears that the "party afterwards was strictly 'off the record.'" They opened their next season with the "money-maker"[109] *Years Ago*, the Canadian premiere of the full-length play.[110]

Curiously, set dressing became the theme of Alumnae's time in Ottawa that year. The cast arrived the day before the performance, but Mantley was there already, seeing the other plays. He reported back to the club in a telegraph: "Bring all set dressings and pictures you can find to clutter repeat clutter mantel sideboard curtains *etc* adjudicator has phobia about period atmospher [*sp*] criticized *Silver Chord* last night period nineteen fifteen for lack of effective atmosphere in knick knacks but approves ingenious use of curtains everything under control."[111]

Figure 6.6. (*left to right*) Barbara Allen (Ruth Gordon Jones), Beatrice Ramsay (Katherine Follett), and Elizabeth Rand (Anna Witham) in Alumnae's production of Ruth Gordon's *Years Ago* at the 1948 Dominion Drama Festival. Photographs for the 1948 festival, including this one, were taken by renowned Canadian photographer Yousuf Karsh. Courtesy of Alumnae Theatre Company and the Estate of Yousuf Karsh.

Given this forewarning, Alumnae should have brought an aspidistra to Ottawa. A curious piece published in the *Ottawa Citizen* the day of Alumnae's performance opened, "Has anybody in Ottawa got an aspidistra? Not the biggest in the world but one of a modest size – about 12 inches high."[112] Alumnae needed it for their set which, the article noted, "deals with a time when an aspidistra could be found in almost every home, however, modest." The article explained that Alumnae had arrived the night before by car but that their set had been shipped by train ahead of time and, "being Torontonians, none of them doubted but that bringing an aspidistra to the Capital city would be as foolish as carrying the proverbial coals to Newcastle. To their amazement so far, they haven't been able to scare one up."[113] The post-war media machine that followed the DDF for years was cutting its teeth on reporting on the minutiae of producing theatre, at once educating and entertaining the nation's readers. By that afternoon, Alumnae were rehearsing in the Ottawa Little Theatre for their evening performance,[114] presumably with perennial in hand.[115]

Remarkable production photographs remain from the Ottawa showing of *Years Ago*, courtesy of famed Ottawa-based photographer Yousuf Karsh. Captured under warm stage lighting, the photographs exhibit the play's personal relationships between Ruth Gordon

Jones (Barbara Allen) and the other characters, including her beau Fred Witmarsh (David Gardner), her father Clinton Jones (Alex McKee), her mother Annie Jones (Christina Templeton), and friends Katherine Follett (Beatrice Ramsay) and Anna Witham (Elizabeth Rand). Karsh's photographs provide little evidence of the cluttered design Mantley called for in his telegram, and Speaight made no mention of it in his adjudication.

Alumnae's next two CODL festival entries did not find the same success as *Years Ago*. In March 1949, regarding Norman Holland's "vignette of humble Irish life"[116] *The High-Backed Chair*, directed by Karen Glahn, Speaight, now regional adjudicator, praised Agatha Leonard's acting but added that the play missed its point, that no one in the cast sounded like an Irish villager,[117] and that the set was "a complete failure."[118] The following year, in March 1950, Alumnae presented Thomas Job's 1945 modern tragedy *Thérèse*, adapted from Emile Zola's *Thérèse Raquin*, a "tale of passion, murder and retribution"[119] directed by Henry Kaplan; but adjudicator Maxwell Wray[120] determined that the chairs were English, not French, that the cupboard was Canadian Victorian,[121] and that the "bastard period mirror" should not have been painted cream. MacDonald relayed in her review Wray's plea: "Was it impossible to find French furniture in Toronto? From the audience with unblushing aplomb came agreement that this was so."[122] However, Toronto's already infamous critic Nathan Cohen offered emphatic praise for Alumnae's production in his magazine, *The Critic*:

> From a truly critical viewpoint, the one show which blended art and entertainment, which was acted with understanding and dramatic skill, which was directed with honest awareness of its theme and potentialities, was *Thérèse*, presented by the University Alumnae Club. Henry Kaplan's direction artfully differentiated between pace and tempo, and tried, often successfully, to achieve variety of mood and sensation. William Needles brought an unusual gradation and subdued force to the part of the murderers' victim. The play was one you could enjoy and, at the same time, its value did not end with the formal curtain call. But *Thérèse* was not an amateur presentation![123]

This pronouncement is the first of Cohen's writings that appears in Alumnae's collections. Cohen had arrived in Toronto in 1945 and begun reviewing theatre in magazines and on radio. His criticism on the state of theatre in Canada was startlingly direct and judgmental, as were his reviews of the work of specific artists, gaining him a reputation for being overly harsh. Praise earned from Cohen was not taken lightly. Despite Cohen's approval, *Thérèse*, like *The High-Backed Chair*, did not rank high enough to be sent to the DDF finals.

King Charles's Days and *The Family Reunion* Expose Herbert Whittaker's Dual Role

On 16 March 1949, within months of arriving in Toronto from Montreal to find the CODL festival "in even better shape than the bilingual one I had left behind," theatre critic Herbert Whittaker wrote his first piece for the *Globe and Mail*. Three days later, he began to offer his kindly worded knowledge of theatre in Canada for the upcoming CODL festival. Owing to Whittaker's extensive experience and reputation "as both successful competitor and active executive member,"[124] he could already speak authoritatively in a way that previous theatre critics in Toronto could not.[125] His influential dual role as critic and artist (not to mention as a DDF governor) defined his extraordinary career trajectory and the trajectories of many mid-century Toronto theatre companies. Indeed, he did not review the 1950 CODL festival because he had directed and designed the set for the North Toronto Theatre Guild's production of Robertson Davies's *King Phoenix* for the competition. With reference to the recent Massey Commission report, to which Davies was a significant contributor, Whittaker coyly wrote that "like Royal commissions, the adjudicators are above criticism, until afterward."[126]

Whittaker directed and designed his first of many plays for Alumnae in February 1951 when they presented the Canadian premiere of George Bernard Shaw's "little known"[127] 1939 history lesson *In Good King Charles's Golden Days: A True History That Never Happened* at the Arts and Letters Club. It was Alumnae's first performance at that location and a preview of their planned festival entry.[128] Whittaker accepted Alumnae's offer to direct and chose Shaw's work,[129] which he had wanted to do in Montreal, thus beginning what would be a thirty-two-year directing and design relationship with Alumnae. Halpenny later credited Whittaker with inspiring the club to "try particularly ambitious plays for its Festival entries, at the same time setting for them sights in acting, costuming, and décor which challenged their best efforts."[130] In his "Showbusiness" column, Whittaker took a tongue-in-cheek tone when referring to his own play competing at CODL. Required to write about the festival as part of his job, but wanting to downplay the conflict of interest inherent in discussing it regularly in print media, he wrote about philosophical issues around whether awards should be given at all in DDF feeder festivals and musing about "our summary of the odds against the Women's Alumnae production of *In Good King Charles's Golden Days*, the Shaw play with which we find ourself associated this week."[131]

The production was both timely and ambitious. Shaw had died just four months earlier after taking a fall in his garden, slipping into a coma, and "sleeping the deep sleep of a tired man."[132] His death at ninety-four spawned nearly two dozen articles and letters to the editor in the *Globe and Mail* alone commemorating the accomplished life of a prolific writer. This production of one of his last plays, written for Barry Jackson's decade-long Malvern Festival in its last year, when Shaw was seventy-three, would prove to be among Alumnae's great successes. It begins in Isaac Newton's house in 1680, and relies less on dramatic action than on lively fictional dialogue between Newton's guests King Charles II and Charles's brother the Duke of York (later James II), the Quaker leader George Fox, three of Charles's mistresses, the Duchesses of Cleveland and Portsmouth, Nell Gwyn, and the portrait painter Sir Godfrey Kneller. It ends in conversation between Charles and Queen Katherine of Braganza, at the latter's apartment. A subsequent show program noted that "here is no costume piece full of fancied intrigue, romance and plotting. In fact, you won't find a plot in the whole play, but there is good talk, theatre talk, Shavian talk. And our modern theatre has produced few things to equal Mr. Shaw's talk."[133] Whittaker chose to cut the script, as well as to add a break in the middle of the very long first act to give the play two intermissions.[134] Because corsets were involved, Alumnae member Elizabeth Gray had the women wear them a week early to get used to the "iron curtains"[135] and what Lotta Dempsey referred to in the *Globe and Mail* as the "girdle gasps."[136] David Peddie's advice in the *Varsity* was that "if Mr. Whittaker, the director, can improve the stage groupings and movements (especially the King's entrance) the cast will probably become much less self-conscious and more relaxed."[137]

Alumnae's production gathered together male actors who would soon find success across North American stages and screens, including John Colicos, Ted Follows, Norman Moore, William Needles, and Ron Poffenroth (later Ronald Hartmann). The recent ability to cast professional actors in festival plays was a clear benefit to Alumnae's production and their promotion of it. Colicos, Needles, and Follows ranked among CODL competitors who earned their living from CBC radio and emerging professional theatre companies. Media response was overwhelmingly occupied with the performances of these men, directed by a prominent Toronto man, for a woman-run company. Alumnae would go on to exhibit astute decision-making by including men in their festival plays; this would serve them well in the mid-century's patriarchal adjudication culture.

When Alumnae took *King Charles* from the Arts and Letters Club to Hart House Theatre for CODL in March 1951 as the fourth of seven entries, it was an immediate hit for both the audience and adjudicator Robert. G. Newton.[138] On *CJBC* radio, Alex Barris reported that the "'best play was the University Alumnae …'"[139] Also on *CJBC* radio, Cohen concurred that no one attending the festival would have disagreed with his choice. The performance itself was riddled with interruptions of laughter, to the extent that in the second act the "audience applauded each member of the cast as they left the stage."[140] Newton remarked, "Here we have one of his [Shaw's] very last plays and I had to come all the way to Canada to see just how good a play it is."[141] He added that it was "produced with great sensitivity and care"[142] and that "we have been inclined to dismiss it as one of Shaw's lesser dramas. I myself have always regarded it as little more than a conversation piece. Until now, I never really appreciated what a good piece of theatre it could be."[143] Presented with "slick professionalism,"[144] *King Charles* won the Hugh Eayrs Trophy for best play, the design won best visual presentation, and John Colicos[145] won best actor as Charles. Newton praised Whittaker's "exquisite groupings"[146] during the long conversations and noted that the "lighting was expertly handled to bring out the richness of sets and costumes," although one opaque window in the set seemed out of place, reminding him of a New York hotel window.[147] Before the performance, in the spirit of festival gamesmanship, Whittaker received a "jumbo pink carnation" from the North Toronto Theatre Guild, for whom he had directed the previous year, with two cards attached. The first card wryly read, "To wish you good luck (but not too good)"; the second, "In Deepest Sympathy – alternative message – according to what the adjudicator says."[148] Fulfilling the prophecy of the former card, Newton selected *In Good King Charles's Golden Days* to compete at the DDF finals in London, Ontario.[149] Although perhaps not entirely in keeping with his famous support for emerging Canadian writers, Whittaker celebrated the win in his column, writing that Shaw "showed that he could write rings" around younger playwrights and, "without a vestige of plot to aid him, still provide a prize-winning play."[150]

From the skilled cast, Newton singled out Colicos as providing the "most remarkable performance" with his "realization of the pathos behind the light manner of the King that made his interpretation so outstanding. This pathos was the whole intention behind Shaw's gaily written lines." He added that Sheila Craig "gave a very gay and lively performance, although her voice perhaps did not quite measure up to the freedom of her movements." Marian Jones, as the Duchess of Cleveland, "hit on the idea of the part absolutely, but needed a little more vocal control – so important in a play that was very much a conversation piece."[151] Ruth Norris was "delightful, but a little too deliberate about her (French) accent."[152] Halpenny also struggled with her accent, although "she created moments of great tenderness in her scene with Charles." Templeton was "just the sort of housekeeper you would like to have," and Edith Orde Tuff, as the maid, "showed great charm and ease."[153]

In May 1951 at London's Grand Theatre, which reportedly boasted a 10,000-person subscriber list at the time,[154] Alumnae brought *King Charles* to the finals of what was then the "only national amateur drama festival in the world."[155] Of Alumnae's three-hour offering – the third play running at the festival that ran that long – adjudicator Jose Ruben[156] initially sighed and said, "No one could be as endless as Mr. George Bernard Shaw." Ruben ultimately praised the group for handling well the challenging scene between Charles and the Duke of York, saying it was "one which the actors never let drop for a second." Overall, the cast's performances were "very alive and colourful,"[157] and Ruben awarded Colicos the Henry Osborne Challenge Trophy for best male performance, presented to him by renowned London, Ontario-born actor Hume Cronyn. He also awarded Whittaker the Louis Jouvet Trophy, presented by Edgar Stone, for best-directed play (tied with the Welland Players' James A. Falconer for *Juno and the Paycock*). Regarding the directing, Cohen concluded that Whittaker's "achievement was that from these garrulous, non-theatrical materials he fashioned a piece of drama that made ideas the stuff of conflict and crisis."[158] Whittaker later reported that the acting award came as "something of a shock"[159] to Colicos because Ruben had not mentioned him during his adjudication. Jack Karr was less circumspect in his *Star* "Showplace" column, declaring that if the national festival is any indication, the "best actor in the country is John Colicos."[160] Speaking of the production in his trademark biting diction, Cohen concluded, "I've no doubt this play is not really worth doing; but I've no doubt either that of the eight entries in this feeble and unrewarding festival, the production of *Charles* was the most worthy."[161] Cohen's shot at the festival itself rang counter to the celebratory atmosphere that the organizers propagated and that most other members of the media echoed and embellished at the time. With Whittaker and an outstanding cast, Alumnae had achieved major recognition with Shaw's obscure play.

Although they would receive praise for their next CODL entry – Ferenc Molnár's comedy *Olympia*, which earned Douglas Ney the President's Award for Best Performance by an actor – it would take another year for them to earn another trip to the finals.[162] However, they did find another sort of commendation when Alumnae president Barbara Barnett read a letter to the membership in December 1951 informing the group of a planned DDF costume exhibit. Members Barbara McNabb and Elizabeth Gray volunteered to help.[163] McNabb assembled the Queen's and King's costumes from *King Charles*, a costume from their recent production of Oscar Wilde's *The Importance of Being Earnest*, and the boating costume from *Thérèse*.[164] By their June meeting they learned that two of the four costumes they had sent to the exhibit had won second prize in the form of a cheque, which was received with "enthusiastic clapping."[165]

"By all odds, the most ambitious amateur group in Toronto,"[166] Alumnae produced the Toronto premiere of T.S. Eliot's "highbrow" poetic piece *The Family Reunion* in February 1953 at the Arts and Letters Club, which was "crammed to capacity."[167] This was a warm-up performance prior to entering the production in the festival. Again, Whittaker directed and designed the set, while member Frances Jackson was put in charge of costumes that were "modern dress of a simplified kind."[168] Eliot's plays were finding numerous productions in England at the time.[169] The *Varsity*'s Malcolm MacKinnon described the challenge of performing his verse play, in doing so exemplifying Toronto's increasingly patronizing tone towards nonprofessionalizing groups: "For amateur actors, the task of speaking verses without resort to recitation is onerous indeed. To bring to life a verse play which has been repudiated by its author as deficient in character and plot approaches the impossible." Nevertheless, MacKinnon concluded that "as an instrument of impact of the fullness of Eliot's vision upon an expectant audience, Herbert Whittaker's forceful production is one of the most exciting pieces of theatre of this season," one that is "characterized by a fluidity of motion which creates pleasing stage pictures in all but the static opening scene." He added that Whittaker was doing "his best work with this group."[170] The set was a "sonnet of grey tones in classical harmony establishing at sight the mood of waiting,"[171] a "menacing and melancholy symphony in grey and black, whose strange angles and perspectives accentuate the feeling of standing on the threshold between reality and dream. It is only marred by two playfully stylized Greek columns whose frivolity seems strangely out of place!"[172]

Alumnae presented *The Family Reunion* at the CODL festival at Hart House Theatre in March 1953, competing against six other plays.[173] Apparently for the first time for any of their productions, they discussed filming parts of the dress rehearsal, but it was decided it would be "too expensive and too late to be of much help in the production itself."[174] Actor, producer, and author John Allen adjudicated the regional festivals, attending fifty-four plays across the country. Regarding Alumnae's production, Alex Barris reported that a "number of people present left with the vague impression that he [Allen] liked the production, but they weren't really sure because he didn't say whether he did or not."[175] In fact, Barris quoted Allen as saying, "I don't know quite what it needed," trailing off with "I can't quite analyze it right now, but …" Allen perceived a "slight sleepwalking quality," with actors lost in a "delicate submission to the poetry," even "acting mood instead of characters."[176] He could only conclude that Alumnae's offering was "quite an experience in the theatre."[177] Despite Allen's initial ambivalence, the production won the (new) Calvert trophy (sponsored by the whisky company to generate revenue for the DDF[178]) and a $100 cheque[179] for best play, the president's award for best actor for Richard Easton[180] (on his twentieth birthday[181]), and both best director and best visual presentation for Whittaker. Ironically, the women-run company now held the record for the most best male actor prizes at CODL,[182] leading the *Telegram*'s Margaret Aitken to comment that at Alumnae "men are merely tolerated because most plays have to have men and then they go and cop the prizes!" She added that Alumnae's win meant financial headaches because they now needed to find the money for fifteen cast members to travel to Victoria for the finals.[183] The same day that Aitken's piece ran, Alumnae met to discuss travel expenses. Member Katherine Anglin reported that CODL was providing $1,000 for those expenses, that the DDF was providing $350 and paying the hotel bill, and that a forthcoming performance at the Forest Hill Collegiate auditorium would earn about $250.[184] The following day, Lotta Dempsey added in the *Globe and Mail* that Alumnae's "trek west will be accompanied by half-a-freight car of scenery."[185]

In Victoria in May 1953, at the "invigorating and exciting"[186] DDF finals, on the sixty-by-thirty-five-foot stage[187] at the Royal Theatre, *The Family Reunion* competed for the $1,000 prize[188] Upon performing the play, they were immediately described as a "strong threat to take the [national] Calvert trophy."[189] Adjudicator Pierre Lefevre, familiar to Alumnae from the previous year's regional adjudication, called it a "magnificent performance. It was played as beautifully and as close to the thought of the author as one would ever hope to see it done. The play was on a higher level than any we have seen so far in this festival"[190] and "could hold its own against any company in any country."[191] He called Whittaker's directing "very distinguished,"[192] but added that some of the lighting changes "were not subtle enough, nor sufficiently keyed into the lines."[193] Easton, Lefevre said, gave the audience an "extremely distinguished performance."[194] *The Family Reunion* won the festival plaque for best English production excluding the festival winner, making it a "close second"[195] to Le Jeune Scene's production of Marcel Dubé's *Zone*, which Lefevre "hailed as the arrival of the new Québec drama."[196] Whittaker won the Louis Jouvet Challenge Trophy for best director and the Martha Allan Challenge Trophy for best set design. Alumnae won Montreal sculptor Sylvia Daoust's trophy, titled "Tragedy," for best production,[197] along with "The Festival Plaque," which is displayed at Alumnae Theatre to this day. Six of the fifteen Alumnae actors were "singled out for special mention," including Easton, whose work Lefevre described as a "brilliant, relaxed and imaginative – if somewhat romantic performance."[198] He commended the four-person chorus, featuring David Gardner, Rex Sevenoaks, Christine Templeton, and Ruth James: "Perhaps if the award could have been split, they would have had them."[199] In reference to the offerings by Alumnae and the Ottawa Little Theatre in particular, Lefevre was enthusiastic: "If a Canadian company can do that there is no point of talking about the future of the Canadian theatre. The future of the Canadian theatre is now."[200] In June at the annual CODL meeting, there were "no fewer than three parodies of the play – all of them funny,"[201] and Alumnae themed their own annual meeting to *The Family Reunion* with "several extremely successful skits"[202] about the "hazards of being adjudicated upon."[203] Alumnae's success at the DDF bolstered the group's confidence as much as it did their renown.

For Whittaker, the DDF adjudication of *The Family Reunion* provided a "brief hour of torture and glory." In his regular column he reflected on his nationally famous dual role of critic and director. Between the play's DDF performance and the awards presentations, he wrote:

> Listening to your entry being adjudicated and attempting, at the same time, to take down his comments for a newspaper report, provides an unusual experience, too. One is afraid to miss anything and also afraid that the swift pencil will next write down some devastating words. Happily, due to a splendid showing by the players of the University Alumnae Club of Toronto, the report of Mr. Lefevre's remarks on their presentation of *Family Reunion* contains no devastation. Indeed, we are somewhat amazed to say, it contains little that is not praise.[204]

Whittaker then proceeded to detail Lefevre's criticism of Whittaker's own show and to respond in print. Surely this marks an unusual moment in the discourse of Canadian theatre, but, having found himself on the west coast and on duty, he was compelled to report.[205] He concluded by saying that now he "can sink happily back into the audience side of the festival … with all the sympathy of someone who has been there himself, and survived."[206] Then, as if to put a more performative point on his dual role, shortly after returning from the festival, Whittaker penned in his column a fictional dialogue between himself as director and himself as interviewing critic on the topic of winning the Louis Jouvet Trophy.[207] The following month, perhaps having reached a pinnacle and internalized an uncomfortable conflict of interest, Whittaker informed Alumnae that he "prefers not to direct another Club Festival play"[208] – although he would again in two years.[209] Forty-six years later he recalled that *The Family Reunion* program he had kept was "one of my 'treasures,'" adding that among Alumnae's many achievements, "this one – because of its illustrious content and because of the link with both the University Alumnae Dramatic Club and the Dominion Drama Festival – deserves a place on its walls."[210]

Although Alumnae's production of Christopher Fry's *Venus Observed* at the 1954 CODL festival did not find "full realization of the play's potential,"[211] according to British adjudicator Graham Suter, and therefore did not move on to the finals, their 1955 entry of "one of Chekhov's moodier pieces,"[212] his 1899 five-act comedy *Uncle Vanya*, made history as the first DDF production to receive the repurposed (four years earlier[213]) Bessborough Trophy for a presentation of unusual merit of a classical play in the regional finals.[214] For Whittaker, who directed the production, the trophy "carries with it, not only the approbation of the moment, but a whole tradition of Canadian theatre. It is most welcome to the city."[215]

Alumnae's experience immediately following the Second World War mirrored that of theatre in English Canada generally. As theatre artists prepared themselves to work with the growing number of professional companies emerging across the country, the late 1940s and early 1950s saw the start of a transition from the dominance of the DDF to the eventual dominance of major professional companies like Stratford, Shaw, and the Canada Council–funded regional theatres. In a lengthy piece praising Vere Brabazon Ponsonby, the ninth earl of Bessborough, for founding the DDF, Whittaker wrote that although Bessborough's efforts did not directly lead to the founding of Canada's Stratford Festival, they did create a national festival that "kept Canadian theatre alive during the dark days," out of which, "to a degree, has emerged the growing professional theatre." Well entrenched in the maturation narrative that amateur theatre birthed professional theatre, Whittaker celebrated both. And in noting that the DDF now included both professional and amateur artists, he drew the line between them: "The principle connection between the two today lies in the development of actors. Up from the ranks of Lord Bessborough's amateurs come the actors who will play at Stratford, in Canadian Players' tours, in the repertory companies and in television *etc*."[216] This is what Alumnae president Eleanor Beecroft signalled in June 1956 when she reported to the membership that their *raison d'être* now included helping to professionalize actors for Canadian theatre, radio, and television.

Alumnae's *Teach Me How to Cry*, and How to Win

In a commentary about the state of theatre in Toronto during the 1955–56 season, Whittaker wrote that the club was a "women's group of university graduates which has distinguished itself in the past by its choice of plays. This time it has achieved something of a scoop."[217] In March 1956, Alumnae, "one of the most highly respected of the Little Theatre groups here,"[218] produced the Canadian premiere of Alberta/Montreal/Toronto writer Patricia Joudry's *Teach Me How to Cry* at Hart House Theatre, directed by fourth-year U of T student Leon Major.[219] This was Alumnae's annual "tryout"[220] performance before it entered the play in the CODL festival. Eleven months earlier, the play had had its world premier in a six-week run[221] at the "tiny"[222] off-Broadway Theatre de Lys (now the Lucille Lortel Theatre) in New York. Alumnae's program celebrated it as "what we believe to be the first original Canadian play to have a successful New York run," and as having received the "unanimous praise of New York drama critics."[223]

The *Star* described *Teach Me How to Cry* as "concerning a lonely boy and a lonely girl in a small town who find comfort in each other's companionship."[224] Joudry, Whittaker reported, attended rehearsals, declaring them "most stimulating"[225] and indicating that she found Suzanne Finlay a "more satisfactory leading woman than the one in the New York production."[226] Her writing showed "vividness," using "many bold symbols and a flow of dialogue which, although perhaps it may become overly effective [*sic*] at times, is nevertheless always clear in intention."[227] Rose MacDonald wrote that "dreary people, suffering from Chekhovian frustrations, are made interesting by the author and in the present instance, also through Leon Major's direction."[228] The production exceeded Jack Karr's expectations: "Technically, this is an amateur production and should be approached as such. But I have no hesitation in saying that, in a great many ways, I found it a superior piece of work to the one presented in New York's little Theatre de Lys last spring. Under Leon Major's direction, the alumnae players have been martialled into an emotional exercise in nostalgia and sentiment."[229]

Finlay showed "sensitive purpose"[230] and "brought both gentleness and spunk to her illustration of the torment of a kid who is tired of being treated like an odd-ball but hasn't yet learned the magic of asserting her own personality."[231] The cast included Phyllis Malcolm Stewart, who was "singularly touching"[232] and "weirdly pathetic as the girl's childish, bird-like mother,"[233] "ingénue"[234] Molly Golby, and George Luscombe (who later founded Toronto Workshop Productions). Les Lawrence, who won U of T's Ernest A. Dale Memorial Award for the "greatest contribution by a student to theatre,"[235] and Major co-designed the "impressionistic sets on two levels – to keep the narrative flowing through its many scenes."[236]

In advance of the April 1956 CODL festival, adjudicated by the DDF's first female regional adjudicator, Pamela Stirling,[237] telegraphs poured in to Alumnae, including well wishes from the club's treasurer Mary Smart, writing from Staten Island, and Edgar Stone and his wife Louise (Stone had remarried after Agnes Muldrew's death). The *Globe and Mail* printed a photograph featuring Finlay, Joudry, and Joudry's daughter holding her hundred-year-old doll that Finlay had used as a prop in the play.[238] When Stirling's adjudication of *Teach Me How to Cry*, the "most favourable"[239] play of the festival, was complete, she asked Joudry, who in her words "made this evening possible,"[240] to stand and take a bow. Noting that it was the "tenth original play she had seen in her tour of the country,"[241] Stirling declared, "I like the title. It has poetry and nostalgia. Whether we have a happy one or not, we always seem to regret our childhood."[242] She called it a "sensitive, intelligent, imaginative play"[243] and praised Major's direction for its "delicacy and feeling" as well as for its tempo "after a slow start."[244] U of T professor Dr. Richard Johnston's original musical score, she said, "stressed the mysterious element of the play." Finlay's performance had "great sincerity."[245] Alumnae won five of the nine festival awards: the Calvert Trophy and $100 for best production, the Lieutenant Governor Award for best Canadian play, the Samuel French Challenge Trophy for best presentation of a play by a Canadian, the Edgar Stone Challenge Trophy for direction, and for Finlay the President's Award for best actress. It was thus chosen among the eight plays to compete at the DDF finals at the St. Charles University Auditorium in Sherbrooke, Quebec.[246]

However, Stirling, the English-born actress from France, was "slightly disappointed"[247] with CODL's offerings overall. She had adjudicated sixty plays across the country and had been led to expect "great things"[248] from Toronto's festival, but it had not lived up to its reputation. She pointed out that the "standard of work" was no better than at several other festivals where groups "do not have the access to the professional theatre and professional advice that those in Toronto have."[249] She contended that what Canada needed were "stronger directors" to work with the "untrained, inexperienced actors."[250] Whittaker suggested that groups should seek out the funds to pay more experienced directors.[251]

Whittaker noted downsides to participating in the annual festival: He attributed production costs, including the difficulty in finding rehearsal space and selling tickets in Toronto, as a factor forcing groups to focus all of their resources on the annual festival production, thus limiting their actors' ability to gain extended experience and causing the groups to cast only their "favourites … whether they are suitable to the roles or not." Alumnae's breadth of talented women and reputation for attracting a range of men, Whittaker and Major included, set the company above others in the city. The director, Whittaker continued, must be the focus, even if shows are "staged in private homes to an audience of twenty or twenty-five people." He concluded that if there was no improvement, the festival should be shortened, compelling the "weaker companies back into the One-Act Festival."[252]

Teach Me How to Cry competed at the DDF finals in Sherbrooke in May 1956, but the road there proved difficult. First, a situation arose pitting Alumnae against the burgeoning Canadian music profession. According to an undated draft letter from Alumnae, the musicians' union now required them to use five musicians instead of the three who had played Dr. Johnston's original music, but CODL refused to pay the extra $120. To address the issue, Alumnae's draft letter indicated that owing to the extra expense, they would either use three musicians or "do without any musicians at all," adding that the situation was "nothing short of tragic"[253] because a Canadian composer had written original music for the production and this music had been integral to the winning production. Whittaker further reported that Alumnae were being forced to produce the play without Dr. Johnston's original score, thus putting the three musicians, all Royal Conservatory of Music students of his, out of work.[254]

Then, as reported in a subsequent CODL newsletter, the trip to Sherbrooke began with some confusion when Alumnae heard that the railway car transporting their scenery had been sent back to Montreal. They then discovered that the platforms for their set were "not forthcoming, and would have to be built." With the help of the festival stage manager and crew, the platforms were ready "by six o'clock on the day of the performance." The newsletter commented that Alumnae "have always been praised for the high degree of teamwork and organization which goes into their shows. Once again those qualities have brought new acclaim to the group, and a broad hint to other companies venturing into the highly intricate field of festival competition."[255] The CODL newsletter praised Alumnae's professionalism by noting their ingenuity.

During her adjudication, the French opera singer and film star Françoise Rosay called the cast back up to the stage, exclaiming,

> I have read this play two or three times. I read it this afternoon. I loved it. I saw it tonight and I loved it more. I am sure you loved it, too. It is a lovely play. It is poetic – that is the word? It is so moving, the story of that girl who has no father. She is not like everyone. The boy suffers a little differently, but he has a difficult time … A little girl suffers not because she has no father but because she is different from the others. The boy suffers because he is different from his parents, so moving … a lovely play.

Regarding Finlay, whom she brought "down to the footlights"[256] for her critique, Rosay said she was "very, very charming and very good," but "rather aggressive, a little bit too aggressive both with your mother and in a different way with that charming boy."[257]

Whittaker wrote that this DDF production was "one of the company's best, despite the physical and psychological circumstances" of Sherbrooke's much larger auditorium and the general pressure of the finals competition. Overcoming the auditorium's poor acoustics – what Whittaker called "part of the evil that architects have blithely inflicted upon the theatre in Canada"[258] – *Teach Me How to Cry* won the Calvert Trophy for best presentation, which, being taken from an "assiduously guarded suitcase,"[259] was presented to cast member and club president Eleanor Beecroft by Governor General Vincent Massey, along with the $1,000 prize, in front of 1,100 attendees.[260] Alumnae had competed in every CODL festival and had won every award except for the top prize, until now.[261]

A ball was held after the awards ceremony at the Willams Street Armoury, featuring a "Scottish piper from strongly French-Canadian Sherbrooke," who "piped a procession through the ballroom." Finlay was not present, having been asked to fly to London, England, "to take over"[262] Kate Reid's role in a production of N. Richard Nash's *The Rainmaker*.

Figure 6.7. Members of the cast and creative team of Alumnae's production of Patricia Joudry's *Teach Me How to Cry* with their Calvert Trophy for Best Presentation at the 1956 Dominion Drama Festival. (*left to right*) Alumnae President and actor Eleanor Beecroft, actor Helen Dunlop, and director, co-set designer, and fourth-year University of Toronto student Leon Major, are seated in the front row surrounding the trophy. Courtesy of Alumnae Theatre Company.

Before *Teach Me How to Cry* went to Sherbrooke, Major had agreed to be the resident summer director for the Garden Centre Theatre in Vineland, Ontario. There, he directed the same play in a June 1956 production that was "substantially the same." The three musicians (back with the production) and cast remained the same, with one exception: understudy Irena Mloszewska took over Finlay's lead role.[263] Meanwhile, Finlay had learned that British Equity would not accept her because she was, in fact, a US citizen born in Chicago. So, rather incongruously and at the last minute, British Equity went with American Geraldine Page, who had created the original Broadway role. Whittaker termed it a "dark week"[264] for Finlay.

The play was a great success in Vineland, and the "brilliant performances of the actors shone through." However, reviewer E.H. Lampard reported that on the first night, the "rowdy raucous audience" was a disaster:

> They howled with laughter where no humour was. They made remarks that were rude in the extreme, they shuffled feet and banged seats.
>
> We had to move to the side and rear to get away from them. Even then, they applauded boisterously at the end of each tender scene, utterly ruining the effect. In short, they virtually ruined

> the performance and we can only marvel that the players were able to keep their composure and play at all. We have never, in all our years of theatergoing, been so outraged by an unruly audience.[265]

That "largely teen-age and exuberant" first night audience, however, was in contrast to the audience for the second night, which, MacDonald reported, numbered more than 300 in the 400-seat auditorium. She noted the contrast between lead actresses, writing that Mloszewska "plays it more softly, with less determinedly defensive spirit." The set had been expanded for the Sherbrooke auditorium; at Vineland it was contracted, and a landscape backdrop replaced the two levels of the earlier design.[266] Major moved the scenes played on the higher back level to the downstage playing area "because of the height and the width of the stage." Mloszewska and Lawrence stayed on as part of Vineland's repertory company for the remainder of its summer season,[267] and the press, particularly the *Globe and Mail*, kept the play on its pages through to the fall.

A month later, Toronto mayor Nathan Phillips presented Alumnae with a silver tray with the cast members' names engraved on it while "expressing the City's appreciation of the group"[268] for their DDF win. Alumnae had brought local and national fame to Joudry's playwriting. In July 1958, *Teach Me How to Cry* opened in London's West End with a new title, *Noon Has No Shadows*, directed by Leon Major with an all-Canadian cast – a first for London's West End[269] – featuring a redeemed Suzanne Finlay reprising her role.[270] Alumnae had once again proven to be savvy programmers and career makers.[271]

In June 1956, Eleanor Beecroft gave her last report as club president after two extraordinary years that had seen her shake hands with the governor general, be part of Alumnae's local and national awards, and prepare the club for their Coach House Theatre era:

> Two years ago at the beginning of my term of office, I found myself rather frightened and a bit insecure, feeling that I had taken on a great deal in an attempt to guide the Alumnae through stormy theatrical seas to a safe harbor. Well – with the Calvert Award in our arms and the $1000 in the bank I can truthfully say that I feel very happy that we have reached a sound financial footing …
>
> In these two years we have won most of the major awards in the regional festivals, and the distinction of being given the Bessborough Trophy for outstanding presentation of a classical play in 1955 – and the Calvert Award this year.
>
> All these things have been achieved only by the untiring effort of the majority of members of the club to make our shows the perfect resolution of unselfish unified endeavour. The perfect example of this was the DDF show in Sherbrooke. I am absolutely convinced that everyone present at the festival both in the Hotel and at the St. Charles Auditorium was most impressed by that wonderful feeling of a team pulling together. At the beginning of rehearsals there had been some considerable friction, but by the time *Teach Me How to Cry* reached Hart House for the regional festival, we were all working together in harmony and this grew stronger the more we played.
>
> No one will ever know the mental and physical work that Francis Jackson as VP and producer put into four separate productions of this last show, and is still doing so for the fifth time [at Vineland]. Kay Anglin as assistant producer and property mistress was unerring – Christine Templeton with costumes, Barbara Waller on sound, Kay Thompson as assistant SM, Francess Halpenny on both properties and travelling organization. We should never have reached Sherbrooke if Fran had not planned everything so carefully. To these and all those who worked with

> them, my grateful thanks. To all the members of the casts and crews of the four productions in these two years, thank you for work well done.[272]

Teach Me How to Cry was a landmark production for the Club, and Beecroft recognized it. The DDF's $1,000 confirmed Alumnae's place among Toronto's most influential theatre companies. And also it enabled them to rent their first Coach House Theatre.

Waiting for Godot on the National Stage

"The University Alumnae Dramatic Club, a fully amateur organization, wishes to ask whether performing rights are available for Samuel Beckett's *Waiting for Godot* in November, 1957,"[273] read Doris N. Stacey's 27 June 1957 letter to the New York office of Dramatist Play Services. She added: "One of Toronto's leading drama critics recently said that ours was 'the only non-commercial group worthy of consistent critical attention.'"[274] Came the reply five days later: "I am glad to know of your interest in giving a possible production of *Waiting for Godot* in November; also to be able to inform you that the play is available to you for such production at that time. We will of course do everything within our power to bring the play within your financial reach since the seating capacity of your theatre is but 40."[275] Although *Godot* had already been heard in Toronto as a radio play (likely the Columbia Records version with Bert Lahr),[276] it had not yet been seen on stage. Alumnae's "elegant and moving"[277] stage premiere of the "intellectual vaudeville"[278] *Waiting for Godot* opened as the second production of Alumnae's first full Coach House Theatre season on 6 November 1957, directed by member Pamela Terry. They had missed producing the Canadian premiere of the English version by four months: UBC's Players' Club Alumni had produced it at the Frederic Wood Theatre on 28 June 1957,[279] while Stacey was still negotiating the royalities.

The "indomitable"[280] Alumnae had "finally brought"[281] Toronto its first Samuel Beckett play. After enjoying "lineups around the block,"[282] it was held over for a second week, then for a third.[283] Halpenny, the show's invitation manager, was kept busy as curious Torontonians flocked to the small space to catch their first glimpse of a Beckett play. Halpenny later called it a "legendary occasion."[284] It was Alumnae's most successful Huntley Street production, generating audience and media attention like few Toronto productions had. By the end of the season, it had gained near mythic status for a club that Terry's husband John Beckwith, the legendary Canadian composer, later described as a "serious-minded amateur society with a strong reputation."[285]

Some Alumnae members had read *Waiting for Godot* a year earlier, but Terry, who had never directed a play before,[286] was the only one in the club who, in her own words, "had a feeling for the play."[287] She later explained: "We decided to do the play because no other group in Toronto wanted to."[288] Beckwith recounts in his memoirs that she had been "moved by the dialogue" of friend James Reaney's poetry cycle, *A Suit of Nettles*, and approached Alumnae to do a reading of it, which resulted in her organizing and directing that reading. A year later she was "powerfully impressed"[289] reading *Waiting for Godot* and pitched directing it for the club. Although Terry and her husband had visited Paris about five years earlier,[290] Beckwith makes no mention in his memoirs of seeing, or even being aware of, the 1953 French-language world premiere of the play and its unusual style.

Figure 6.8. Alumnae's flyer for their Toronto premiere of *Waiting for Godot*. Although "1958" is penciled in the top left, this run of their production ran in November 1957 at their Huntley Street Coach House Theatre. Courtesy of Alumnae Theatre Company.

Although directed by a woman with an all-female crew, "who never for a moment regretted the choice of play,"[291] *Godot* featured an all-male cast "as the play requires."[292] Terry did, however, make cuts to the script. Rose MacDonald did not specify in her review exactly what was cut, but did say that Vladimir's "penciled-out earthy lines" were "played down."[293] Decades later, member PJ Hammond relayed the story that members of the original cast told her about the cuts:

> It was the first day of rehearsals with an all male cast and Pamela's directing. One of the first things that she says in the first rehearsal is, "The line at the top of page 26 will not be spoken." And everybody crosses it out without saying what the line is. It's the line, "What about hanging ourselves?" "Hmm. It'd give us an erection." They cut that line. A woman directing it. That line will not be spoken. In the 50s. What kind of magnificent woman was that in the room?[294]

For the first two weeks, rehearsals were held in the Beckwiths' living room in their Summerhill Gardens home overlooking the park.[295] A feature about their family in the *Telegram* a few years later, very much of its time, noted that while Terry rehearsed, her husband "baby sits"[296] their three kids.[297]

Waiting for Godot was received with a rare combination of immediate acclaim and amusing confusion. In a review accompanied by a fluid sketch by Lewis Parker of the four main characters, Whittaker wrote that Terry "tackled the work fearlessly, and with a pretty certain hand," and although the "production lacks something of richness," it presented a "surprisingly clear idea of a play that is never clear, or intended to be."[298] MacDonald wrote that Terry "more than fulfills expectations" and that "under her direction and with the sensitive accomplishment of the actors concerned, this strange, mystical tragic-comedy on thoughts of the sufferings of mankind and hope deferred, is of absorbing, deeply penetrating interest."[299] Powell Jones designed a set that was "simply suited to a stage nearly six times bigger than a bathroom."[300] Kenneth Wickes, a "newcomer" to the stage with "the Gift," gave a "wistful, poignant interpretation of Didi."[301] Fred Euringer,[302] the "dramatic stalwart"[303] and anthropology student[304] from the U of T's Victoria College, provided a "hardier performance" as Gogo. Ivor Jackson "rose to his acting best" as Pozzo, "stricken suddenly with blindness and bewildered in his pride." Jones, as the "sardonically named"[305] Lucky, "joggled about with a weird and alarming manner."[306] Reg Barnes, a high school student[307] and pupil of Toronto's influential theatre teacher Jack Medhurst,[308] gave a performance of the Boy that was "well done."[309]

Future journalist Cathie Breslin recounted the play's premise in the *Varsity*: "Roughly, *Waiting for Godot* is the story of two tramps of philosophic and psychotic bent, waiting for the one who never appears. If you want to be obvious you can call Godot a symbol of God; more abstrusely, you might call him the pre-Hellenic notion. The Good. One's as good as another – the point being, of course, that Godot never does put in an appearance." Breslin noted that the "biggest laughs came from the strangest lines, and they seemed to be more a matter of audience nerves than a credit to Mr. Beckett's wits." She sweepingly concluded that the "trouble with the whole mess is that it underlines the dangerous modern trend toward incoherence in art. I'm reluctant to call it dubious; I'd hate to call it bad, but I'm damned if I'll say it was good. Borrowing from Beckett again, we might see in the dead dog a symbol of the play, and in its plural version that oh-so-arty Toronto audience."[310]

Indeed, there was then, as now, a fascination with Beckett's curious play. Accompanying Alumnae's journeying production over the following months was public commentary about what the play meant. Whittaker introduced the Toronto premiere by calling it the "controversial *Waiting for Godot*."[311] A week later he repeated public comments about the play – "'It's about nothing!' and 'It's about everything!'" – adding that "people have stalked out of the theatre when it was playing in Paris, London and New York, but nobody has ignored it."[312] The next day, he wrote that in Alumnae's production "there is every reason to think it will be found equally controversial."[313]

MacDonald assured her readers that on Alumnae's opening night, "nobody left the little theatre on Huntley St. until the curtains finally came together." But, she added, "quite apparently members of this audience had definitely varying reactions to the play," citing those who found interest in the comedy and others who found that the play "mirrored to a degree their own feelings."[314] Whittaker himself offered that "Mr. Beckett is a miserable cuss, with an excellent ear for a sequiter. His view of life we deplore, but his ability to make bricks without straw is remarkable. He has the gift of creating mood, dramatic situation, even suspense, and he does it without recourse to the time-honoured use of narrative." Here, "man has gone further and for less reason" and

> we are convinced that Godot himself adds up to God – or, if you prefer, the hope in mankind which expresses itself in God. Man waits for God arguing with himself through the ages …

Figure 6.9. *(left to right)* Ivor Jackson (Pozzo), Powell Jones (Lucky), Fred Euringer (Estragon), and Kenneth Wickes (Vladimir) in Alumnae's Toronto premiere of Samuel Beckett's *Waiting for Godot* at their Huntley Street Coach House location, directed by Pamela Terry, with set design by Jones and costumes by Eleanor Beecroft. The production would go on to win the 1958 Dominion Drama Festival's plaque for best production in English (other than the winner); Wickes won best actor in a leading role. Photo Credit: Robert Muckleston. Courtesy of Alumnae Theatre Company.

> Pozzo and Lucky seem to represent the eternal "they" of life, the bullies and the victims, essentially each to the other. The boy who comes with the message from Godot? Well, if Mr. Beckett was not consciously using a pure soul as the prophet of the One awaited, he must surely have hit on this ancient symbol by accident.

Whittaker added that Terry "does not believe that Godot is God, which goes to show you."[315]

A month after the extended run closed, Whittaker reflected that in combination, the radio version of *Godot*, Alumnae's stage production, and the recent introduction of Eugene Ionesco's play *The Bald Soprano* at the CODL One-Acts made it the "big year of the intellectual vaudeville." He further surmised that because Ionesco's *The Chairs* and *The Lesson* were running in New York, and because Ionesco's *Amédée* and Beckett's *Endgame* were about to open there too, with producers who also own the Canadian rights, it was likely that Toronto's professional theatres were about to produce more plays in this style.[316] Whittaker was correct: In Toronto, Alumnae were leading the way.

Hart House Theatre's Robert Gill did not at first like the play, yet it was he who suggested that Alumnae make it their festival entry after he saw the November Coach House production.[317] Competing against five other groups chosen from eleven earlier in the year,[318] Alumnae offered *Waiting for Godot* at the nineteenth CODL festival at Hart House Theatre in March 1958. British regional adjudicator Richard West called it "full of Irish charm and whimsy" and praised Terry's "admirable use of silence."[319] Calling her "that little bombshell,"[320] he noted Terry's "fine use of depth in grouping, the excellent distribution of groups, and the cut and thrust of the dialogue."[321] West mused, "What does it all mean? Perhaps Godot is God; perhaps Pozzo and Lucky are the sins and tribulations of the world. But God is compassionate – and Godot beats little boys." He added that Lucky's "thinking" speech revealed Powell to be an "actor of the most accomplished skill." While he perceived some boredom among the audience, wondering how long they "would survive on the iron rations of the Beckett dialogue," he concluded that the production achieved the "cut and thrust"[322] of acting. Terry's "achievement in steering the ... actors through this plotless wasteland of a play"[323] earned Alumnae the "two top awards"[324]: Calvert Distillery's Challenge Trophy (and $100 cash prize) for the best presentation of a full-length play, and the Edgar Stone Trophy for Terry's direction. Given the directing trophy's criteria – "to be awarded for interpretation of the play and constructive leadership of the actors" – Terry, as a first-time director working with four men and a young boy, was an ideal recipient. All four men in the play received festival distinctions too: Fred Euringer and Kenneth Wickes received honourable mentions for lead acting, Powell Jones received honourable mention for best supporting actor, and Ivor Jackson received the President's Award for best performance by an actor (although not for his work in *Godot*, but for his lead role in another play at the festival, Nikolai Gogol's *The Marriage*, produced by the Richmond Hill Curtain Club).

In her column "Once over lightly," Mary Jukes interviewed Terry the week after her CODL win. She focused on how Terry balanced her family life with her theatre work, quoting her as saying, "I find it hard to get away during the day with three children under 5."[325] Jukes concluded that if Terry could raise "three children who are hardly more than babies, perhaps a five-man cast was somewhat of a cinch." Like other journalists at the time, Jukes infantilized Terry variously as a "mere slip of a girl" and an "elfin director" who "looks more like a teen-ager just past the bobby-sox age." She asked Terry if "directing a group of men had presented many problems, considering her inexperience, sex and age"[326]; Terry responded, professionally, that there had been no problems, in part because "I have always had a deep regard for Samuel Beckett and think I had some understanding of what he was trying to say."[327]

Terry had come to Toronto in 1949 as a UBC graduate (she had starred in several shows there and may have known that her *alma mater* had produced *Godot* mere months earlier) to study at the Canadian Theatre School under E.G. Sterndale Bennett, whom she called a "great influence in my life, he taught me so much."[328] She came with her high school sweetheart from Victoria, John Beckwith, who was studying music at the Royal Conservatory. They married in 1950 and "sailed for Paris the next day"[329] on Beckwith's Canadian Foundation Scholarship. In Paris, while Beckwith studied music under the famed teacher, composer, and conductor Nadia Boulanger,[330] Terry acted in Gertrude Stein's play *Yes Is for a Very Young Man*, an experience that sparked her interest in avant-garde theatre.[331] After a year and a half, they both performed in a tour across Germany and Austria with the US Occupation Forces' Special Services Branch for six months.[332]

She then returned to Toronto in 1953 to "become a mother"[333] while Beckwith joined the music faculty at the university and became one of Canada's best-known composers. Terry first joined Alumnae for the 1952–53 season and acted in several productions. She also directed for campus groups like the Trinity College Dramatic Society.[334] With Alumnae as her home base and *Waiting for Godot* as a catalyst, Terry became one of Toronto's most noted directors, introducing and interpreting the moderns to the city and receiving consistent acclaim.

"Already one of the most-played works of our time, despite its unusual structure,"[335] *Waiting for Godot* ran again at Hart House Theatre for one week in April 1958 "to give playing experience to the local festival winner, in the hope that it will be invited to the Dominion Drama Festival finals."[336] The run also "enabled larger Toronto audiences to see this amusing and highly controversial play"[337] and helped raise funds for a possible trip to the DDF finals in Halifax, pending the conclusion of West's cross-country regional adjudications. Whittaker attended and explained in his column that the cast was "playing smoothly and with confidence. The gaps in sequence have closed up, and there are very few passages in which they do not hold the full attention. Pamela Terry's production is in excellent shape, physically and in acting." He went on to say that Jones's Lucky was still the "outstanding performance" and a "real *tour de force*, remarkably poetic, clear and true." Wickes's Didi was "sensitive, humourous and expressive. And although it sadly lacks vocal variety, it is remarkably well sustained." Of this iteration, Whittaker concluded that it is a "performance worthy of the University Alumnae, and a tribute to this noble body's intelligence, selflessness and vision. It is worthy to represent this region if invited to Halifax. And we can't help wondering what the Maritimers will make of it."[338]

Alumnae's *Waiting for Godot* was creating a sensation in Toronto, and many were having fun applying its open references to various situations. Of the "no-plot play," the CODL newsletter observed that "even the sophisticated audiences of Toronto haven't quite sorted out the meaning Mr. Beckett never stated. It isn't easy, because everybody has a different idea and wants to tell you while you're trying to tell them." The CODL newsletter printed an interpretation by one Helen Arthurs, who proposed an alternative theological interpretation:

> Godot is the Messiah for whom mankind is still waiting … Pozzo is God – in the first act, the Old Testament Johovah [*sic*], vengeful, vain, desiring to be praised and appealed to, even fussy about his name … In the second act … he is a helpless god, cut off from man and ignored by him, no longer completely in command of his own church but now dependent on it … Lucky is the faithful church, the ministers and worshippers of God … In the second act the church, having lost its inspiration (the top hat: Vladimir becomes quite eloquent when wearing it) – clings to its servitude and with pitying love still tries to preserve its God. The Boy is the prophets, the forerunners of the Messiah … Vladimir and Estragon are body and soul, or the spiritual and reasoning mind versus the animal self.[339]

Her insightful critique, after just one viewing, is evidence of the clarity of Alumnae's production and Terry's direction. It also indicates the deep interest Beckett's play drew among Toronto's intellectual audiences.

Alumnae offered their DDF finals performance of *Waiting for Godot* on 15 May 1958 in Halifax's 1,280-seat Queen Elizabeth High School auditorium in front of Philip Hope-Wallace, who had adjudicated the finals in Toronto in 1949.[340] Alumnae had received $443

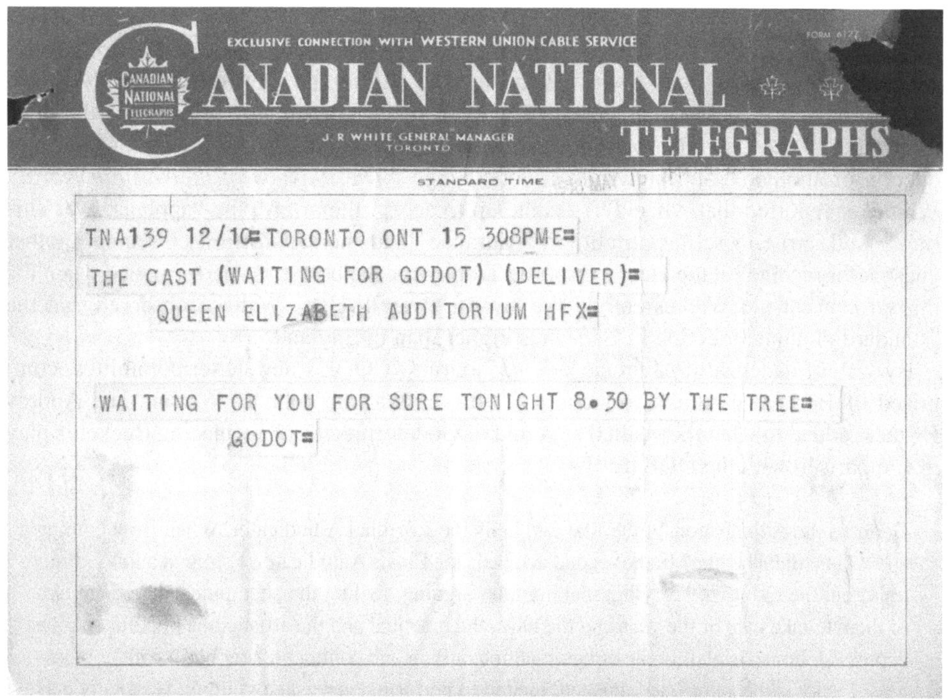

EXCLUSIVE CONNECTION WITH WESTERN UNION CABLE SERVICE

CANADIAN NATIONAL TELEGRAPHS

J. R. WHITE GENERAL MANAGER TORONTO

STANDARD TIME

TNA139 12/10=TORONTO ONT 15 308PME=

THE CAST (WAITING FOR GODOT) (DELIVER)=

QUEEN ELIZABETH AUDITORIUM HFX=

WAITING FOR YOU FOR SURE TONIGHT 8.30 BY THE TREE=

GODOT=

Figure 6.10. A supportive tongue-in-cheek telegraph addressed to the cast of Alumnae's production of *Waiting for Godot* at the 1958 Dominion Drama Festival at the Queen Elizabeth Auditorium in Halifax. The text reads: "WAITING FOR YOU FOR SURE TONIGHT 8.30 BY THE TREE =GODOT=. Courtesy of Alumnae Theatre Company.

from the DDF "to assist with travelling expenses"[341] for their sixth finals appearance. It was the first time they had brought an all-male cast to the finals.[342] Along with extensive national media coverage, the production attracted a flood of well wishes from home, a sign of the event's importance to supportive friends. Some were topically humorous, like the anonymous Toronto telegraph to the cast that read, "Waiting for you for sure tonight 8.30 by the tree =GODOT="[343]; another, from club president Barbara Barnett, declared "We are not beggars but even ten francs would be a help"[344]; Alumnae members left behind in Toronto looked to the script for their tidings, writing collectively: "Think pigs dance hogs make the gopher Godot oceans love"[345]; CODL's Kenneth Levinson wrote to Terry: "We too are waiting. CODL wishing you every success"[346]; and a telegram to Ivor Jackson read: "If Godot is luck may he be with you tonight."[347]

Again, acclaim and confusion attended the production. The *Halifax Mail-Star* reported that *Godot* played to a "responsive audience, but also a puzzled audience."[348] Hope-Wallace called it an "imaginative and sensitive" production of "one of the most awkward things for a competing group to try." He called Terry a "good director" and the costuming by Eleanor Beecroft "thoroughly professional,"[349] as was the make-up. He wrote that Wickes played "beautifully … with a thorough touch of professionalism,"[350] that Lucky's "grotesque dance"[351] was "splendidly executed,"[352] earning a "real standing ovation,"[353] and that Jackson's Pozzo was "better than any other production of the play."[354] Overall, it was a "significant success"[355] from, as Whittaker wryly concluded, "these mysterious ladies whom we never saw."[356] In front of DDF festival patron and Governor General Vincent Massey, Alumnae earned the Festival Plaque for the best production in English other than the winner of the Calvert Trophy (which went to BC's White Rock Players for their production of another Irish playwright's work, Singe's *The Playboy of the Western World*). Whittaker reported that when Terry came up to accept the award, the "applause was stirring." And, "true to selfless tradition," Alumnae "had the satisfaction of seeing another guest actor receive"[357] the Henry Osborne Trophy for the best male performance when the thirty-four-year-old Wickes earned the award. Overall, Hope-Wallace observed that the "standard of amateur acting in Canada is higher than in England."[358]

By way of cadenza to Alumnae's *Godot* journey, CODL's newsletter committee, comprised of Herbert Whittaker (of course), Vida E. Watson, John L. Watson, and Audrey Hozack, added to what they called a "round of Godoterpretation" by placing Beckett's play in comparison with the DDF itself:

> Godot is the Adjudicator. In the first act, he is the Regional Adjudicator. When is he coming and what will he be like? In the second act, he is the Finals Adjudicator. Estragon and Vladimir represent the Group – worrying, making talk, arguing, feeling the shoe pinch. There are two of them to take care of the yeas and the nays, the practical and the artistic, the hopeful and the depressed. Pozzo is plainly the director, at first bulling and confident, later blind with nervousness. Lucky is the actor – led, pushed, incited to perform, even asked to think. He finally gets laryngitis. All are waiting, losing hope but waiting for the Adjudicator who will recognize them, appreciate them, honour them. The indefinable place is the stage, different every time but always the same. The tree? That must be the drama itself. It provides identification. We hide behind it. We want to hang on it. With any luck it will put forth a few leaves for us.[359]

The End of a Festival Era

When Alumnae offered "Spain's leading modern poet and dramatist"[360] Frederico García Lorca's *Yerma* at the 1958 CODL festival, Beecroft received the L.C. Tobias award for best supporting actress, but the production went no further. It was widely agreed that the CODL festival had yielded sweepingly poor quality. Public dissatisfaction was reflected in Whittaker's comments at the festival's opening when he said, "Here, today, even a final festival seems less important in the face of the development of Stratford, the Crest and television."[361] By the end of the 1950s, professional performance in southern Ontario was verging on commonplace, and nonprofessionalizing groups were losing traction in the public imagination. A brief stage fire at Hart House Theatre during another company's performance was taken to be symbolic of the dissatisfaction – both its causes and its symptoms.[362]

Alumnae now returned to one-act play competition, entering Eugene Ionesco's *The Lesson* in the inaugural Ontario One-Act Festival in May 1959. Held in Kitchener, Ontario, at the Eastwood Collegiate Auditorium, and sponsored by the Kitchener-Waterloo Chamber of Commerce and the Western Ontario Drama League (WODL), the new festival encompassed the whole province. Out of eighteen plays chosen to compete from thirty-four entries across eleven Ontario communities, *The Lesson* won the $100 prize for best performance, best actor for Powell Jones, and best supporting actress for Joanna Richardson. Adjudicator and past Alumnae guest artist William Needles said that Jones "whisked through a maze of lines with extraordinary delicacy and great accuracy";[363] Richardson was "praised for the subtlety and depth of her performance."[364] As the winner of the festival, Alumnae presented *The Lesson* as a "special showing"[365] for attendees of a theatre conference convened with the DDF finals at the Hunting Room of Toronto's King Edward Hotel. Several CBC television producers asked Alumnae to stage it "for their benefit"[366] the following week.

Alumnae's 1961 CODL festival appearance would be their last full-length submission for six years. In February and March 1960 they staged, for the first time in Toronto in "many, many years,"[367] William Congreve's 1700 Restoration comedy *The Way of the World*, directed by Molly Golby. This marked the 300th anniversary of the restoration of Charles II and, appropriate to Alumnae, the 300th anniversary of women in English theatre.[368] Martha Mann's set design bore a "definitive"[369] relation to Restoration comedy and "miraculously opened up"[370] the small stage in the Bedford Street Coach House Theatre. Mann's wigs and Jennifer Cuttell's costumes were a "delight,"[371] with the latter being "bravely bright in the face of history's most difficult period." Whittaker deemed Congreve's play the "worst great play ever written," with a plot that "cannot be kept track of even with an IBM machine. It can be comprehended, but not followed." He then added, topically, that owing to the play's "greatness," one might conclude that the "plotless playwrights, like Beckett and Ionescu, may be not so far off (or out) as is claimed." Golby's direction was "remarkable"; the "pace and sparkle of the Congreve lines are sustained in a most professional fashion."[372]

To prepare the play for submission to the 1961 CODL festival and to launch the public portion of their fundraising campaign for a new Coach House Theatre, Alumnae revived their "highly successful"[373] *The Way of the World* in October 1960 at Hart House Theatre. More than half the cast were new for this iteration and, according to Whittaker, the "standard has, if anything, gone up."[374] The run sold out its first two nights.[375] Mann's set on the much larger stage was "overall a great success, not withstanding those handsome columns, stylishly finished off though they were, that did not go up the visible height of Hart House stage and therefore had nothing to 'support.' The effect was disconcerting." Halpenny gave a "smashing performance" that helped keep the pace up. MacDonald said the production was a "perfect example of what players of taste can do in creating impeccable effects with a lusty vocabulary."[376]

Alumnae offered Congreve's comedy at the 1961 CODL festival at Hart House Theatre in March 1961 with a cast somewhat different from the successful fall remount. Adjudicator Esse Ljungh, who had judged the 1947 CODL festival and the 1951 inaugural CODL one-act festival, took Alumnae to task for playing the piece "too broadly." In his view, Golby's directing made the first scene "static and declamatory"; moreover, the play was marred by some poor character groupings. He then "painstakingly went through the large cast,"[377] offering either negative or mixed reviews, although he allowed that Joan Shaw gave a "delightful performance" with "wit and charm."[378] In the end, Shaw earned best supporting actress, and Halpenny and Rex Sevenoaks earned honourable mentions for best actress and best supporting actor respectively. Noteworthy is that Ljungh "made history"[379] by awarding his wife the best director award for the Barn Players production of Edmund Morris's *The Wooden Dish*, which he also accounted one of the three top productions in the festival, "despite its lack of pace."[380] He awarded the Drao Players the winning trophy and $100 prize money for their visually stunning production of *Rashomon*.[381]

By the fall of 1961, Alumnae had established itself as one of Toronto's most successful DDF competitors. They had participated in every CODL, winning "every possible award,"[382] including acting, directing, design, new play production (see chapter 7), and best Canadian play. Seven times they had gone to the finals. But a number of hurdles now presented themselves: Alumnae were in the midst of procuring their third Coach House Theatre, and with fundraising efforts under way,[383] they lacked sufficient time, money, and personnel to mount a full festival production. Also, the late March 1962 date would, as it had before, coincide with student exams,[384] potentially impacting attendance at and income from the CODL performance, as well as potential remounts. Meanwhile, they were meeting with the Red Barn Players and the West End Players to discuss a summer stock season for Toronto's "better amateur groups,"[385] and the decision whether to join that effort had become "tied up"[386] with the question of whether they should continue to produce classics. That had become a point of contention among members in recent years, given the relative success of their modern programming. The decision to pass over the festival for the first time in the club's history was not an easy one. Members debated the situation, characterized in meeting minutes as "no money vs. tradition." Reaching no conclusion, they moved to raise the question at a second meeting.[387] Alumnae did not participate further in the summer stock conversation, nor did they participate in any CODL festival, full-length or one-act, that year or in the next three years.[388]

Alumnae returned to the full-length CODL festival in Canada's centennial year as one of twenty-seven CODL-affiliated companies involving about 700 people in Toronto alone. According to an article in the *Star*'s Leisure for Learning section, most of these groups did "everything from Shakespeare to original variety," although some offered more specialized fare. Most were using community centres and school auditoriums, although some, like Alumnae and Richmond Hill's Curtain Club, had their own stages.[389] Alumnae's entry, in March 1967, was a co-production with the Company of Pilgrims of the world premiere of Canadian Rae Davis's challenging and imaginative intermedial work *Daily News from the Whole World*. Director Pamela Terry was by then in the midst of a busy, but difficult, decade since her breakout work on *Waiting for Godot*, as her husband later wrote in his memoirs:

> The decade 1958–68 was a period of constant theatrical activity for her. She gained a reputation as a versatile director with imagination and drive, and as a stickler for discipline. Her work was regarded as professional in the sense of highly competent, though her fees were usually minimal. When looking for better pay and higher status through opportunities with the bigger companies, she experienced real prejudice as a woman in a field almost exclusively run by men. At this period there were virtually no female stage or film directors in the country. Managers extended a condescending pat on the back but no contracts. The Club [Alumnae] gave her strong support and an outlet for her ideas.[390]

As an extraordinary interpreter of poetic text, and as a woman in the traditionally male role of director, Terry was an unheralded trailblazer in Toronto theatre. She gravitated towards avant-garde plays, and *Daily News from the Whole World* was certainly that (see chapter 7).

The regional festival had a new format for the centennial year, Whittaker's "brainchild," wherein the DDF allowed only new Canadian-written plays to compete. A producer selected from each of the four Ontario regions was responsible for their region's play,[391] "thereby forcing the theatre groups in each region to share in the enterprise."[392] A committee comprised of Pamela Terry, Esse Ljungh, and chair Robert Gill selected the plays. The winner would go on to the DDF finals in Newfoundland in May to compete against five other plays; all five finalists would then play at Expo '67. Robertson Davies, the festival's adjudicator, told Whittaker that these were "plays which try to deal with problems in Canada in our time."[393] *Daily News from the Whole World* won the CODL festival's Centennial Production Award for the greatest backstage contributions by producer, stage manager, and crew. However, the production was "bypassed"[394] by Davies for acting awards. Beckwith, who composed music for the script, later wrote that Davies gave "bewildered comments" about the play: He "praised Pamela's direction,"[395] but, as Whittaker reported, he offered a "warning that the experimenters are not always right."[396] Instead, frequent Alumnae participant Martin Hunter won several accolades for *Out Flew the Web and Floated Wide*, his "vivid study of a Toronto Establishment family,"[397] taking home $1,000 from the Centennial Commission prize, the Lieutenant Governor's Medal as the author of the best Canadian play, and the Samuel French Trophy for best Canadian play in the festival. Perhaps festival audiences, and Davies in particular, were not as prepared to accept Davis's avant-garde work as they were Beckett's *Waiting for Godot* a decade earlier, even under Terry's guidance. One wonders what notoriety the DDF finals might have brought *Daily News from the Whole World* and Alumnae in the centennial year had Davies passed it forward, or had another adjudicator been at the helm. Terry would not direct for Alumnae again until 1971.

Davis's play was Alumnae's last entry in a regional festival that had influenced much of their programming for more than thirty years and that had boosted their local and national profile during the 1950s in particular. When the DDF was renamed Theatre Canada and its festivals were discontinued in 1972, organized attention to nonprofessionalzing practices became the purview of the provinces and Alumnae joined Theatre Ontario. With its inaugural mandate to "serv[e] and develop[] theatre throughout Ontario,"[398] that organization provided nonprofessionalizing groups like Alumnae with training and apprenticeship opportunities, workshops, the publication *Scene Changes*, audience development, and liaison with government and educational institutions. But no national platform. Canada's era of nationalizing and nonprofessionalizing festival competition was over, and, with that, so was the vehicle for Alumnae's national reputation.

Chapter 7

"No Cause for Alarm"[1]: New Plays

Alumnae were among the first theatre groups in Canada to commission and stage works by Canadian playwrights "long before it was fashionable to do so."[2] Their first world premieres were Katherine Anglin's *Boomerang* (1935), John Coulter's *The Family Portrait* (1937), Margaret Ness's *Short Circuit* (1939), and several member-written and -performed one-acts and skits before and during the Second World War. By 1963, playreading committee chair Pamela Terry could write to the Canada Council that Alumnae were making "every effort to seek out and perform Canadian material of merit; not out of a sense of grim duty, but because we found it stimulating – also rewarding when talented writers were happy to entrust their stage works to us, knowing they would be produced with considerable care and intelligence."[3] For most of Alumnae's existence, new play development and production has been among their most celebrated achievements. This places Alumnae alongside other of Canada's oldest theatre companies, all nonprofessionalizing, that have contributed significantly to the development and production of new plays. Those companies include Ottawa Little Theatre, which, since founding its groundbreaking National One-Act Playwriting Competition in 1937, has introduced new plays by dozens of career writers, including Robertson Davies, John Murrell, and Erika Ritter; and Edmonton's Walterdale Theatre, which has produced new plays since 1961 and run a juried new one-act play festival since 1988.[4]

This chapter traces Alumnae's long history of new play development and production. Using selected case studies of significant Alumnae world premieres, including John Coulter's *The Family Portrait*, James Reaney's *The Killdeer* and *The Easter Egg*, Carol Bolt's *Shelter*, and Linda Gaboriau's translation of *La nef des sorcièrs*, it analyses production conditions and critical reception, thus situating Alumnae as an important producer of new plays in Toronto's theatre ecology.

Alumnae today are known for three important new play initiatives that provide a "space for learning and development"[5]: the New Ideas Festival (since 1988), the members-only New Play Development group (since the early 2000s), and the Fireworks Festival (since 2007). New play development is what member Jane Carnwath calls Alumnae's "biggest contribution … New playwrights are getting more exposure elsewhere, but we actually work them through so by the time the script is production-ready it really is pretty close."[6] At their Firehall Theatre, Alumnae have produced thirty-seven Mainstage and Studio world premieres and hundreds of new short plays through the New Ideas Festival. And even before their move to the firehall in 1972, Alumnae had staged twenty-one world premieres and fifteen new play readings. Alumnae started early, at a time when new plays were rarely seen, or even encouraged, in Canada, and by the 1960s, they were leading the way in Toronto. They even attempted collective-creation methods when the form emerged in the late 1960s and early 1970s.

In Canada, new play production has always been a highly politicized venture and core to the "culture debate"[7] within which theatre is practised. In surveying prominent scholars' writings about Canadian nationalism and canonicity in order to apply these ideological forces to the study of new play creation in the 1990s and 2000s, Bruce Barton observes that

> There is no question that contemporary Canadian playwrights and dramaturgs work within both explicit and implicit traditions: ideological, political, cultural, and aesthetic. And it would be naïve to underestimate the overt and subtle operations of nationalism in the structures and processes of producing and non-producing theatre organizations – as in the public and private institutions and individuals that fund them. Yet these operations are rarely fully predictable, systematic, or stable.[8]

As Canada and its arts moved towards nationhood in the early twentieth century, new works of art were viewed as signs of independence from American and, to a lesser extent, British and European culture. This involved distancing Canada's theatre ecology from Broadway and the West End. Critics like Hector Charlesworth, B.K. Sandwell, and Lawrence Mason filled their newspaper columns with pro-Canadian encouragement across the arts. After the Second World War, Herbert Whittaker, Nathan Cohen, and Urjo Kareda did the same for theatre. What characterizes most of their writings is the strong belief that Canada must untether its play production from foreign ideologies and practices; put simply, Canadians must tell Canadian stories, and those stories must be produced and performed by Canadian citizens in Canada. The result will be a cultural economy that is nationalized in creation and scope, yet decentralized from the nation's capital in Ottawa – a regionalized "Canadian theatre." New plays will emerge from sundry locales both urban and rural, not from a centralized sense of a unified "Canadian voice." During the mid-twentieth century, a handful of playwrights were praised by audiences and critics, sometimes seemingly for simply showing up, as evidenced by the many DDF awards that flowed towards Canadian plays, their playwrights, and their producers. But while Alumnae and other nonprofessionalizing theatres have enthusiastically sought to offer new plays, often through the DDF, since the 1930s, it was not until the 1970s that new play development and production took flight in the professionalizing alternative theatres. Since that time, and particularly since the Fringe Festival phenomenon arrived in Canada in the early 1980s, new play production has been an integral part of many nonprofessionalizing and professional theatres.

New Comedies for the Interwar Years

Unfortunately, little evidence survives regarding Alumnae's early approaches to new play production. They were producing new plays well before the notions of "process," "workshopping," and "dramaturgy" took root. Playwrights generally presented the director with a script, and some changes might be made shortly before and during rehearsals. In the 1930s, when modern British and American comedies were the usual fare, Alumnae found mutual interests with the Playwrights Studio Group, which was Toronto's only organized group of playwrights at the time[9] and possibly the first playwriting organization in Canada.[10] At Hart House Theatre, that group's plays were attended by some of the same Toronto audiences that attended Alumnae plays, including members of the Arts and Letters Club, the Heliconian Club, the Women's Press Club, and various members of the press.[11] As women-led theatre groups, Alumnae and the Playwrights Studio Group shared actors and directors, gave a space for women's drama to find audiences, and imprinted the theatre work of women within the walls of the Hart House boys' club.[12]

Alumnae produced their first three world premieres in the 1930s. Two were one-acts written by members Katherine Anglin and Margaret Ness and performed at the UC Women's Union; the third was a full-length play by British ex-pat and rising star John Coulter, performed for the DDF regional festival at Hart House Theatre. Anglin's first play, *Boomerang*, premiered in January 1935, directed by Anglin herself. The evening was co-hosted by UC principal Malcolm Wallace, Alumnae president Doris Shiell, and active Alumnae member Alison Ewart (then president of the UC Alumnae Association).[13] Unfortunately, the script does not survive in Alumnae's collections, but the *University Monthly* magazine briefly described the eight-actor play as having a "scene laid in the lobby of any little theatre."[14] Six months later, Anglin met with an "interested group" of Alumnae members in the office of Hart House Theatre artistic director Nancy Pyper as Pyper read "bits" from both Anglin's new play *Tenth Anniversary* and another backstage-antics comedy, Hart and Kaufman's *Once in a Lifetime*; it was noted that Anglin's writing was "very much enjoyed."[15] *Star* critic Augustus Bridle wrote that Anglin's world premiere had sparked interest among Alumnae members in writing plays,[16] although after some discussion they chose not to offer one of Anglin's works-in-progress (it may have been *Boomerang* or *Tenth Anniversary*) for the next DDF regional festival.[17] Clear from all this is that Alumnae valued a member's new play and were ready to develop it. They viewed the invited UC Women's Union performance not as an end, but as a step forward for Anglin's writing. Indeed, it was followed by a development meeting with Pyper and possible consideration for a second production in front of a larger audience at Hart House Theatre for the DDF regional festival. That this process caught the eye of Bridle points to the importance that both Alumnae and the critic placed on new play development at the time.

Alumnae's next world premiere earned enough attention before opening that it cemented the idea in members' minds that they should attempt more new plays. An enthusiastic *Globe and Mail* review[18] of the published script of John Coulter's *The Family Portrait* led Alumnae to produce its world stage premiere with "enthusiastic approval";[19] thus, they booked the DDF's hottest Canadian playwright.[20] Coulter's play is about a son inspired to write a play about his family. The program explained that the "whole rumpus happens in Neill's kitchen-house in a back street of Belfast at the present time." Edgar Stone, who had had directing success in recent festivals, including Alumnae's award-winning production of *The Cradle Song* the previous year, directed it. Presented at Hart House Theatre in November 1937, with Coulter himself as assistant director, *The Family Portrait* opened to a "capacity house" that "applauded warmly" a play that was "typical Irish in its temperament, its humour and kindliness." But although the published text had been praised, its actual staging received a less enthusiastic response. Rose MacDonald in the *Telegram* reported that the dialogue was "smooth, natural and quick, but there is little action and the play tends to limp in the latter part of the second act and the beginning of the last act."[21]

The *Globe and Mail* said it dealt with "Irish tenement life in a rather routine way, with 'thin spots' and a somewhat shaky Act III, which badly needs rewriting." However, "good acting and directing did much to save the play."[22] MacDonald agreed, writing that Agnes Muldrew, now married to Stone, as the mother "carries the burden of the performance tenderly, passionately, angrily, and throughout excellently,"[23] with a "flexible art," in a "wonderfully interpreted role of emotional comedy" that "sets both tempo and temper for the entire cast."[24] Florian Moore's Jenny "was charming," and Christina Templeton performed the hymn-singing daughter "ably."[25] Margaret Tytler played the "furiously funny tailor's wife,"[26] making a paradoxically "unexciting but interesting family,"[27] with Donald Smith as the young son and Eric Aldwinckle[28] as the older son. Ivor Lewis, "as is customary with him, gave a remarkably expert acting performance but his articulation became somewhat muddled with the Irish brogue." Edna Starr Thompson's set design created a "realistically drab kitchen set."[29]

Coulter, Stone, and Alumnae had gained enough national attention at the DDF that Governor General Lord Tweedsmuir, a DDF Distinguished Patron, was pleased to accept Alumnae's invitation to attend the Thursday performance, though he would have to leave by 10:45 p.m. to catch the train for Montreal.[30] This was a unique honour for the club. One Alumnae history document records that his interest threw "everyone into a pleasant frenzy" and added "considerable prestige to the production."[31] Upon hearing of Tweedsmuir's affirmative response three weeks before the run, "Excitement reigned for the rest of the meeting."[32] Lady in Waiting Joan Pape immediately wrote to Alumnae on the governor general's "Train" letterhead that Tweedsmuir and his wife were "much impressed with the production."[33]

Perhaps building on the club's enthusiasm for new plays, Alumnae followed *The Family Portrait* two months later with their first revue at the UC Women's Union as part of the UCAA annual meeting. The revue offered thirteen short performances, including several monologues and short skits, most of them written by club members. Sixteen women participated – precisely half of that season's membership. The *Varsity* reported that the "popular numbers" included "The Prompt Corner" and "As Others Hear Us," the "latter being an exposé of what goes on when two women meet in a theatre lounge."[34] According to the extant one-page program, the entire club participated in the finale, titled "As We Wish We Were." No scripts survive. The revue evening, held twenty years after the club's founding, indicates that Alumnae members were now eager to create new work in the comedic vein, including skits about backstage antics based on their theatre experiences.

A year later at the UC Women's Union, Alumnae produced the world premiere of recent UC graduate Margaret Ness's one-act comedy *Short Circuit*, directed by CFRB radio personality Rai Purdy, as part of a double bill alongside Wilfred Grantham's historical drama *The Italian Woman*. At first, the playreading committee reported "some difficulty in finding plays, and getting sufficient members to take part"[35] in the evening. Ness, a former *Varsity* staff writer turned drama critic for *Saturday Night*, had written very few plays[36] as a UC Players' Guild playwright.[37] She was, however, an active member of the Playwrights Studio Group, where, mainly, she contributed "criticism and advice."[38] She had read *Short Circuit*'s first scene at an Alumnae meeting in September, receiving feedback,[39] before approaching them in January "with the scribbled manuscript." Described *University Monthly*, the "harassed play-reading committee at once recognized that here was a Heaven-sent piece of sure-fire comedy, with good characterization, several women's parts, and a plot that was guaranteed to short-circuit the audience." The actors performed "amid gales of laughter." They included recent UC graduate Aileen O'Brien, who, as the maid, "once and for all established her reputation as a comedy actress."[40]

"Favourably impressed"[41] by the warmly received world premiere, and cognizant that new Canadian works were finding encouragement and success at the DDF, in March 1939 Alumnae presented *Short Circuit* at the DDF regional festival. The *University Monthly* celebrated it as a "home-grown, made-in-University College achievement."[42] However, Thelma Craig in the *Globe and Mail* dismissed the "light little comedy"[43] as "quite entertaining but lack[ing] the finish both in the writing and presentation"[44] of the festival's stronger offerings. George Skillan, the regional adjudicator and an accomplished London actor, producer, theatre scholar, and teacher, said the "plot is fragile, but it was a very entertaining piece. I am sure it was not intended to be ambitious. On the whole most of the characters were pretty well developed."[45] Actor Edna Norwich, Skillan quipped, "should give more sauce to the goose and give her part fussier treatment."[46] Notably, reported *University Monthly*, "for the first time in several years, the Club assembled its own set (Margaret Tytler), shifted its own scenery (Agatha Leonard and Alison Ewart), and, with the invaluable advice and assistance of [Toronto Little Theatre stalwart] Murray Bonnycastle, decorated its own stage (the entire Club)."[47] *Short Circuit* earned from Skillan a third honourable mention for original Canadian play.[48] Aileen O'Brien and "all the ladies in this play"[49] earned honourable mention as well, although Ness's work was not selected to go on to the finals at the Grand Theatre in London, Ontario. Ness was elected Alumnae's president for the following year, and in November 1939, before the opening of Alumnae's first play that season, she would speak on "Plays and Play-Writing" as the author of "Practical Play Production for Canadian Schools and Communities."[50] Although Alumnae's collections do not contain a copy of *Short Circuit*, the play is listed in the "Selected List of Plays Produced" section in *University of Toronto Quarterly*,[51] a fine epitaph for Alumnae's early homegrown play.[52]

In February 1942, with the war now hampering large productions and script procurement, Alumnae responded to a UCAA request (while they were working towards leaving the UCAA) by presenting an evening of short plays at the UC Women's Union. The evening included another world premiere by a Playwrights Studio Group member,[53] Winifred Pilcher, called *It May Happen Here*. Alumnae recorded that it was "undoubtedly the snowiest day of the winter." "Despite a blizzard of near Russian intensity" that held up multiple actresses who were snowed in,[54] two hundred people attended, including several members of the UC graduating class of 1942.[55] Alumnae member Marion Squair Hunter was Mistress of Ceremonies "in her own inimitable style," a task she would take up frequently in the coming years. The plays were chosen "as an antidote to gloom" and ranged from "farce to comedy." "Those twin darlings of the Little Theatres, Tragedy and the Art Play, were completely ignored." Pilcher's play had a plot "built around the fact that, at the moment, domestic servants are rare and hard to get." Besides directing the play, member Jean Stewart "played with zest" the part of the maid "who interviews her prospective mistresses in her own kitchen rather than waste her valuable time going to them." The mistresses were played by Christina Templeton, "resplendent in mulberry velvet and sequins"; Elspeth Wilson, "pale and with only a year to live if she doesn't get help"; and Margaret Ness, "who due entirely to the fact that she lives beside Chorley Park, wins the dubious prize in the end."[56] The comedy was meant to distract the audience from the war's harsh realities and was well attended. These earlier premieres point to how the Little Theatre Movement brought local female voices to the stage. They also anticipated Alumnae's new focus on supporting the work of new playwrights.

The *Tiger*, *The Killdeer*, and Other New Plays from Known Writers

Over the next fourteen years, from the last years of the war until they moved into their synagogue Coach House Theatre, Alumnae produced only a few more world premieres. They were all one-act plays or brief skits; none were full-length works. There were several reasons for this. The war, of course, would not end for another three years. After that, Alumnae focused mainly on their annual regional festival entries, besides being consumed with finding a venue of their own. Also, they were burdened by the need to attract audiences to pay significant rental fees at Hart House Theatre and other venues around the city. As is often the refrain, the financial and reputational risks of producing new plays were too great. Nevertheless, writers like Lois Reynolds Kerr wrote to Alumnae hoping they would consider producing their plays.[57] Alumnae recognized that there were established writers interested in writing plays and that the emerging professional theatre companies were rarely producing them. It was with familiar writers that Alumnae soon built their reputation for premiering intellectual and experimental new plays.

In fact, it was a brief moment of panic that directed Alumnae back towards new play production. After "much summer reading," the playreading committee intended to enter George Bernard Shaw's *Heartbreak House* in the 1957 CODL festival, but the plan fell through when the licenser said the play was not available in Toronto "due to possible tour by an American production." Pressed for time to choose a January festival play to which they could give a trial run in November while preparing to open their first Coach House Theatre in the spring, it was "back to the libraries, out come the collections, once more through the files!" But then a telephone conversation with the "much-decorated young Canadian playwright" Norman Williams revealed that he was working on a new play. Explained a CODL newsletter, "within a few days," Alumnae president Francess Halpenny

> had got the play to the committee, passed it on to the director, attended a session between playwright and director in which further revisions were discussed and copies of the first act typed. Also Miss Halpenny organized the first meeting for casting. This all took high-powered work on the part of the Alumnae, but at the end of a week exactly they had the satisfaction of not only finding another play to do, but one which they found equally exciting: a first full-length work of a new Canadian playwright which offered the tremendous challenge of a first-time-ever production.[58]

The diligent work and professional attitude of Halpenny (among others) had saved the season. Choosing Williams's play meant they could build on the previous season's success of their Canadian premiere of Patricia Joudry's *Teach Me How to Cry*, which they called in the program a "source of pride." In November 1956 at Hart House Theatre, the "versatile and talented"[59] Alumnae presented the world premiere of *To Ride a Tiger*. Optimistically, Williams viewed the moment as a "nice time to be writing plays in Canada."[60] By then, he had found success with three of his one-acts at the previous two CODL one-act festivals.[61] By 1959, his collection of six short plays published by Copp Clark, *Worlds Apart*, had helped establish the Toronto-born playwright and "leading

Canadian author of radio drama"[62] as "one of the most promising playwrights to appear in the 1950s."[63]

However, Williams's orientalist writing approach would not be received well today. Peculiar and stylized, *To Ride a Tiger* is about China's Boxer Rebellion. According to the program, it "arose from his long fascination with the Orient and wide reading in its history." Steeped as it was in post-war curiosity about foreign lands, the play was received at the time as a learning opportunity and a design spectacle, although today it would be viewed as racist. Williams told the *Telegram*, "I have never been to China … But I have always been interested in that country, as a reader and as a collector. I have what might be called a feeling for the East. Writing a play is a rather lonely business but once it goes into production and so many people become interested in your play – well, I've never had so much fun in my life!" Publicity announced that the play, which had taken Williams "less than a year"[64] to write, had been adapted from the Chinese theatre. In her "Person to Person" column, Lotta Dempsey had questions: "So I called Mr. Williams. 'Come to coffee and tell me what a red-blooded young Canadian, a graduate of Eastern Commerce High and a business man, is doing writing a Chinese play.'"[65] His answer: "The time has come when the East is so vital to us we are going to have to reckon with Asia as never before. Too many of us have always seen the Orient in black and white; I have hoped to convey some of the shadings."[66] Dempsey explained that his curiosity "stemmed from seeing a good many moving pictures at a time when the Mysterious East *a la* Myrna Loy [the Montana-born film actress who often played Asian roles] was being portrayed 'in a welter of bad taste' all over the screen."[67] He went on: "As a child I used to burn incense and sprawl out on the living room floor to draw huge and grotesque heads of mandarins with long drooping mustaches in the best Hollywood tradition."[68]

Williams was still revising his play at the end of October. Herbert Whittaker, the play's director and set designer, was compelled to write in his column: "A playwright's work is never done, it would seem. Mr. Williams is steadily rewriting his play, one step ahead of the rehearsals."[69]

Set in the 1890s, in Peking's Forbidden City,[70] in the Manchu court of the Empress Dowager Tzu Hsi, the three-hour[71] play "sets the battle of wills for the Dowager and her clinging to statescraft of a dying era, against the efforts of the young idealistic Emperor Kwang Hsu with his sense of the future."[72] It is also, indirectly, the "story of the exodus from the imperial household, the destruction of the foreign legations by the Boxers." Whittaker's set was minimal, with a bare stage, as per "traditional Chinese theatre." An "authority in the University's department of Far Eastern Studies"[73] created Chinese symbols on banners. Throughout, a stagehand and his assistant give "amusing comments about the play and players"[74] while accomplishing set changes, thus "lending something of Shakespearean comedy relief."[75] In the *Star*, Jack Karr concluded that Whittaker's direction and design made the play "quaint, colourful and exotic."[76] A dozen wardrobe assistants supported Elizabeth Gray in creating thirty-six "of the world's most elaborate and luxurious" costumes in the three weeks before opening;[77] MacDonald called the costumes "imposing."[78] Almost uniformly, reviewers praised the show as "eminently satisfying to the eye, yet "too static for a plot constructed in accordance with Occidental theatre conventions," with language that was too "flowing" and "intellectual"[79] for Western theatre sensibilities. Williams's colonial orientalism met the reviewers' equally racist focus on the Western dichotomies of mind and emotion as they struggled to accept the aesthetics and contemporary politics of the play. Thus, the characters "present ideas walking rather than flesh and blood,"[80] and the "play remains as flat and unmoved as a garden pond" by simply retelling newspaper stories that vilify "Western commercial interests in China" as "Foreign Devils" with what David Peddie on *CJBC* radio called "naïve simplicity avoiding the actual facts of history."[81] Moreover, the director and cast were attempting an "unfamiliar style of acting" with the "heavily scented language of the Orient."[82] Unfortunately, not all members of the press could refrain from making racialized remarks that referred to facial features[83] and the pronunciation of the characters' names.[84]

To Ride a Tiger won several awards at the January 1957 CODL festival, although not the top Calvert Trophy, which would have sent it to the DDF finals in Edmonton.[85] Festival adjudicator Cecil Bellamy[86] found the Chinese setting to be "absolutely right" and the costumes to be "quite remarkable and quite lovely,"[87] although the lighting could have been "more experimental." He emphasized that Williams had "set a difficult task and the players have surmounted the hardships admirably well – admirably well."[88] But regarding the script, he could not tell which "side of the plot the author was on … The viewpoints were too evenly balanced." And he "regretted that the love story, which started out beautifully, died out later in the plot."[89] He wrote that Marian Stewart played the Empress "like a terrifying chairlady of a committee meeting."[90] As the best (and only) Canadian play in the CODL festival, it received the Lieutenant Governor's Award, and Alumnae won the Samuel French Challenge Trophy for best presentation of a Canadian play. Said Bellamy of the two Canadian play awards, "I think these awards are more worthwhile than any other. I am glad to see a young playwright who is not afraid to be experimental. I do congratulate him."[91] Additionally, Rex Southgate won the L.C. Tobias award for best supporting actor as the Grand Councillor Jung Lu. Three months later, Williams learned that among the six Canadian plays[92] across the thirteen regionals, his had won the DDF Executive Committee Award (and its $100 prize) for the best play written by a Canadian across all of the regional festivals. And Alumnae learned that they won the Sir Barry Jackson Trophy for the best presentation of a Canadian play across all regionals. Williams's fame continued that year at the CODL one-act festival in April 1957, which featured two of his plays, *Protest* and *The King Decides*, with *Protest* presented twice, among eight total entries, all of which were Canadian.[93] Alumnae had contributed to Williams's mid-century renown as an up-and-coming writer of note.

Three years later, Alumnae again produced the first full-length play of a familiar author, this time one that found interest among urban Canadians as a slice of nearby rural life. "If James Reaney continues to write plays, as he must, *The Killdeer* is likely to become an historic event – and perhaps even the most important one in contemporary Canadian arts and letters,"[94] wrote influential theatre artist and commentator Mavor Moore. It was the first play by University of Manitoba English professor James Reaney, who had won the Governor General's Award for poetry the previous spring.[95] Moore quickly championed the play, or at least the *idea* of the play, and affirmed Reaney to be a playwright of significance, later declaring that "when the history of Canadian theatre comes to be written, I should not be at all surprised to find *The Killdeer* listed as the first Canadian play of real consequence, and the first demonstration of genius among us."[96] Moore compared Reaney's ear for language with that of Irish playwright John Synge: "He has taken a regional dialect (southwestern Ontario), fed it through his own highly personal imagination, and produced a flexible, full-bodied idiom which no human being ever spoke but which all of us recognize at once. In brief, from our somewhat raw and sweet Canadian wine, someone has at last distilled an Aqua Vitae."[97] Taken together, Moore's statements verge on myth-making and amplify what were common reactions to the first play of the already "well-known Canadian poet,"[98] and possibly Canada's "most prolific literary figure"[99] at the time.

Running at the Bedford Road Coach House Theatre in January 1960, the "violent comedy"[100] was one of Alumnae's most significant world premieres, as well as an indication that Reaney had a promising future as a dramatist, even if the play itself was widely acknowledged, including by Moore, to be flawed. Encouraged by the play's director Pamela Terry,[101] who had gained national recognition for her direction of *Waiting for Godot* a few years earlier, Reaney wrote the play for Alumnae, who selected it for production "while still in *outline* form."[102] Set in what Reaney called an "idealized Stratford, Ontario,"[103] *The Killdeer* follows three small-town Ontario families related through "murder (several varieties), sexual deviation (likewise), love, hate, and greed."[104] For Whittaker, the play, like the law court it stages, "becomes a shambles"; Terry "has obviously done wonders in shaping the play to action, but has not gone far enough in using the knife."[105] MacDonald contended that the play's fourteen characters were too many,[106] while Nathan Cohen called it a "mass of unsorted ideas, story threads, poetic devices, literary and visual symbols, verse techniques, and emotional climaxes, all flung together in a tentative, disconnected stage patchwork." Among critics, Cohen was impressed the least, concluding that "this is not a play worth seeing for its presentation or acting or dramatic merits. The point is that if James Reaney interests you as a poet then *The Killdeer* will interest you as an example of his first attempt to discover the workings of a wholly unfamiliar medium."[107] But if critics agreed that the play was flawed, they could not agree on the remedy: Whittaker suggested dropping the trial scene at the end,[108] Cohen suggested staging the whole play in the courtroom.[109]

The *Varsity* published several pieces about the production, including a preview, a feature on Reaney, a review by Howard Adelman (later a founder of the student-run Rochdale College), a letter to the editor replying to Adelman's negative review, and a *Varsity* listing noting that the play was being held over for a third week and adding that "practically no one agreed with our reviewer's appraisal of it."[110] Adelman argued that "as a drama, the play lacks a central focus in either character, situation or theme," and that the "ever present evil in the form of sadism, homosexuality, gruesome murder and vicious gossip manifested in the majority of characters never really clashes with the innocency [*sic*] of youth."[111] One letter to the editor commended Alumnae's "excellent acting," although the play "never gets off the ground."[112] Another rebuked Adelman "in anger," defending Reaney's writing:

> That the speeches are beautifully speakable, taut, proportioned, almost carrying themselves, and a brilliant fusion of poetry and the plain Ontario voice, this seems to have missed his ear completely … There are few Canadian playwrights who can shape the individual scene as Mr. Reaney can, and none, perhaps, with a more sensitively accurate ear; none who can so riddle the ordinary with strangeness and terror and the extraordinary and still keep it in the honour and integrity of its commonness.[113]

The argument was not really about the major shortcomings of this first iteration of Reaney's first play, which critics agreed was flawed. It was about the value of hearing "Canadian diction" on stage, even if justified by blank verse, and encouraging writers to use more of it.

Borrowing from the inference that new playwrights slowly reveal their best work after multiple attempts, while trying to seduce Reaney into future playwriting, Whittaker concluded that *The Killdeer* "might be played in a cellar in Stratford during the festival as a piece of fringe Guignol. We wait with almost avid interest Mr. Reaney's next play. And the one after that."[114] Wrote Moore, the production "shows up flaws which I feel sure would plague a cast of our finest professionals. Miss [*sic*] Terry's direction is, in fact, perceptive and sensitive – her single serious weakness being a tendency to indulge Mr. Reaney's already dangerous tendency toward artiness for its own sake." But for Moore, the actors were too used to playing British and "classical" characters, and audiences were not used to hearing Canadian speech on stage. Like Arthur Miller in the United States and, later, Michel Tremblay in Quebec, Moore hoped that Reaney in Ontario could help lead actors with text so that "we stop copying and begin creating."[115] Nowhere was it clearer than with *The Killdeer* that Alumnae's greatest national value was in their play selection, a point repeatedly made by critics, who increasingly shamed contemporary professionalizing groups for their lack of programming ingenuity.

The spring of 1960 was to be the season of *The Killdeer*. As the "longest local contributor to the annual Festival,"[116] Alumnae entered *The Killdeer* in the CODL competition at Hart House Theatre, running in April 1960. After being asked to "cut down some of the excess crop of his imagination," Reaney reworked the play, particularly the "melodramatic trial sequence," so that it "made better sense."[117] Seven plays competed in front of the adjudicator, who was from Calgary: Dr. Betty Mitchell,[118] whose own productions had found many DDF successes and after whom the Calgary theatre awards have been named. Mitchell praised Terry: "I really cannot think of anything more wonderful for an author than to have a director of the perception and brilliance of this director."[119] The praise was especially meaningful given that Mitchell "confessed that when she read the play herself she did not understand how the lines could be spoken,"[120] adding that "tonight a director has made it clear"[121] with her "perception and brilliance."[122] John Beckwith's music also found "high praise" (Reaney and Beckwith had been friends since they were U of T students). *The Killdeer* won the Calvert Trophy and prize money for best play,[123] Terry won the Edgar Stone Challenge Trophy for direction,[124] the production won the Samuel French Trophy for best presentation of a Canadian play (it was the only one in the festival), and Martha Mann won the Hugh Eayrs Trophy for best visual presentation. Robin Smith and Robert Huber were given mentions for best actress and actor respectively.[125] Mitchell praised the festival overall for its "very superior plays.[126]

As the CODL winner, *The Killdeer* ran again at Hart House Theatre the following month. Anton Ferry encouraged *Star* readers to see the "expressionistic 'who dunnit,' gorged with verse and imagery, leading off with a fine first act … For anyone who didn't see this new play first time round, opportunity beckons with a mad demon glint." Reaney's imagination, said Ferry, "puts out shoots like a menacing tropical plant."[127] The added run allowed for refinements in rehearsal, on which Whittaker reported as if providing public dramaturgy. He noted that although the play "grows with seeing," Reaney's edits had cost it some of its local appeal and a new setting "made some of the playing awkward." He felt it "could still stand some cutting, but it no longer sags suddenly … and some of the side-revelations contain some of his best writing."[128] Under Terry, Alumnae reworked the production elements as well. Terry, wrote Moore,

> has already clarified the line of her production, and come close to making the last act work. There are still gaucheries in her staging, such as keeping the action too far upstage, and placing

> the witness-box in front of the judge in the trial; but she compensates for this by her obvious grasp of a complex work.
>
> The great thing is that the words Mr. Reaney has written for Miss Terry and her actors soar, spin, whirl and flash like nothing ever heard on our stage before.
>
> And he rips us open as people with a sort of jolly whimsy which may forever mark the end of the myth of the stolid, sober, inarticulate Canadian.[129]

This is how theatre mythology is born – from assertive writing in the dailies for all to consider. Like Urjo Kareda in the *Star* a decade later, Moore drew from experience to praise the unique voice of the "authentic Canadian," or at least the rural southern Ontarian. Twenty-three years after Alumnae premiered *The Family Portrait*, playwright John Coulter wrote to the *Globe and Mail* that Reaney's play was not realism. Rather, it "shares with the avant-garde plays of Beckett, Ionescu, Genet, and others" a concern with the "world that lies below surface appearances, the fantastic world of the subconscious. Its logic is the frightening (because wholly irrational) nonlogic of nightmare, in which all moral, ethical and other inhibitions of conscious behaviour are absent." Responding to those who wrote off the "Nightmare in Three Acts" because of its seemingly incoherent plot, Coulter aserted that it featured a "complex labyrinth of plot, compared to which the complexities of restoration costume drama were simplicity itself."[130]

Observed Ferry of *The Killdeer*, the "whole thing looks like setting sedate Vancouver on its ear."[131] Reaney's play completed its journey from the fifty-eight-seat Coach House on Bedford Road to the 2,800-seat Queen Elizabeth Auditorium in Vancouver for the DDF finals in May 1960.[132] As one of two Canadian plays (out of eight in total) competing in the finals, and one of fourteen Canadian plays across all of the regionals, *The Killdeer* provided "evidence" that a "completely Canadian play festival"[133] might be possible for Canada's forthcoming centennial. Agreeing with reviewers, adjudicator and *Manchester Guardian* drama critic Philip Hope-Wallace lauded the first act of Reaney's play but added that "it completely collapsed" into a "perfectly terrible"[134] courtroom scene in the third act. Reaney, he said, was too concerned with retrospective dialogue instead of present action;[135] even so, he commended his work as having the "stuff from which great drama can be made."[136] Terry's direction showed "absolute skill and precision," although the play's climax was lacking with "rather a frost at the end." Actors Francess Halpenny and Virginia MacLeod provided good comedy in the first scene, with "gorgeous" gossip. Martha Mann's set, he said, was "beautiful, its second act being one of the loveliest I have seen."[137] Despite the third act's "collapse," *The Killdeer* won five DDF awards, more than any other group in the finals: the Sir Barry Jackson Trophy for best production of a Canadian play, the Louis Jouvet Trophy for best direction (Terry), the new Massey Award for best playwright (Reaney), the *Saturday Night* plaque for best supporting actress (Virginia MacLeod), and the Martha Allan Trophy for best set design (Mann).

Six decades later, Mann recalled that her design win in Vancouver was "what started me, gave me a career,"[138] when the London Grand Theatre offered her a job a few weeks later.[139] She said of Reaney, "He was a madman, but he was very interesting to work with. He knew very little about the theatre. Virtually nothing. Including the construction of a play … It was a question of talking it through with him, saying this stage is sixteen feet wide and eight feet deep and we really can't do that and we have no money to do that." As if to confirm the prophecies of Moore and other critics, Mann added:

Figure 7.1. *(left to right)* Francess Halpenny (Vinnie Gardner) and Virginia MacLeod (Sally Budge) dance with paper sewing patterns in Alumnae's world premiere of James Reaney's *The Killdeer* in 1960, directed by Pamela Terry. Photo Credit: Kenn Orr. Courtesy of Alumnae Theatre Company.

> The version we worked on above the [Bedford Coach House] garage was very different from the one we did at the DDF. The original play has twenty characters in it, most of whom are totally irrelevant to what's going on or they had an amusing moment or something to do with the plot. He was very interested in playwriting because he came to a lot of performances … The plot in the first go around was truly incomprehensible and the actors just got up and did it and kind of hoped for the best. The second one we took to the DDF was tighter and a lot better play. And the third version was even better. The Alumnae did it [in April 2013 at the Firehall] and he had extensively rewritten it again, which I think is the best version. I think it's only got about eight characters by this time. Because they had done his plays at Stratford he had had a lot of opportunity to see how it worked.[140]

Through Terry, Alumnae had developed a process of dramaturgy with Reaney that resulted in significant changes to *The Killdeer* across five productions in five months. Critics publicly discussed many of these changes, particularly Whittaker owing to his close association with the club and his first-hand knowledge of directing and designing. Macmillan would publish *The Killdeer and Other Plays* in 1962, with Reaney dedicating the collection to Pamela Terry and John Beckwith. That book's dedication nodded to the couple's work

The Sir Barry Jackson
Challenge Trophy
for the Best Presentation of a Full length Play
written by a Canadian
awarded to
The University Alumnae
Dramatic Club of Toronto
for their presentation of
"The Killdeer"
by James Reaney

President
Dominion Drama Festival
Vancouver · British Columbia · Canada
The Twenty-First Day of May, Nineteen Hundred and Sixty

Figure 7.2. Alumnae's Award certificate for their Sir Barry Jackson trophy for the "Best Presentation of a Full length Play written by a Canadian" at the 1960 Dominion Drama Festival. Courtesy of Alumnae Theatre Company.

on *The Killdeer* and to their subsequent collaboration with Reaney on the opera *Night Blooming Cereus*, which Terry directed and for which Beckwith composed the music.[141]

New Plays at the Synagogue

When they moved into the synagogue Coach House Theatre in 1962, Alumnae saw an opportunity to associate the new location with new play creation. Francess Halpenny told the *Star* at the time, "We wanted a place where we could do new plays and show new writers to a necessarily small but interested audience."[142] In reference to the traditional notion that new plays are risky, she humbly added, "We don't have the professional polish. But we can do understanding presentations of new plays and give people a chance to see them."[143] Cohen agreed, writing that in Toronto, when it came to fostering new plays, "only one company shows any awareness of the need, and is doing anything about it."[144] He later reiterated that Alumnae were "doing infinitely more than the formally professional organizations in the cause of the Canadian playwright."[145] They continued to leverage the national and "impressive reputation"[146] they had gained from their Canadian premiere of Joudry's *Teach Me How to Cry* and their world premiere of *The Killdeer* by premiering more new Canadian works. No longer hampered by the unpredictability of renting space, particularly at Hart House Theatre, they could give new playwrights and their plays more time for development.

Throughout the 1960s, successive playreading committee chairs Molly Golby, Pamela Terry, Elizabeth Mascall, Agatha Leonard, and Shelagh Kareda generated reams of correspondence with writers interested in having Alumnae produce their plays. They received and read dozens of scripts and hundreds of inquiry letters from across Canada, and if the committee of the day was not interested in producing the play, they still replied to the author. For example, in advance of the 1967–68 season, marking both Canada's centennial and Alumnae's fiftieth anniversary, Alumnae had let it be known that they were interested in producing Canadian works. After receiving, reading, and reviewing submissions with her committee, Leonard replied to each playwright whose work they did not accept, commenting on the play's value and fit for the club, making recommendations that might lead to resubmission, or suggesting other groups whom she and her committee thought might consider it.[147] Corresponding playwrights included Elinore Siminovitch (whose husband later founded the coveted Siminovitch Prize in her honour), James Reaney, Herman Voaden, Michael Cook, Norman Williams, Wilfred Watson, George Ryga, Donald Jack, and, because Alumnae actively sought French-language plays to translate, the National Film Board's Jacques Bobet. Notices sent out by CODL and the DDF specifically encouraging new play entries and new playwriting awards (with or without funding) often accelerated Alumnae's search for new Coach House Theatre scripts, as did the selection of DDF adjudicators who were known for preferring new plays. And because theatre critics consistently encouraged new plays during the 1960s, it was almost always a good idea for nonprofessionalizing companies to seek out strong ones.

That said, encouraging new playwriting in the mid-twentieth century was profoundly challenging for a theatre company and was often unrewarding for the author as well. When playwright Donald Jack wrote to Nathan Cohen in 1964 saying that he was leaving Canada, "probably to England,"[148] because Canadian theatre "is a fraud"[149] and an "imitation fireplace giving out some light and colour, perhaps, but precious little warmth of self-discovery,"[150] Pamela Terry wrote a letter to Cohen stating her own view:

> It is alarming to me that Canadian theatre seems almost happy to get rid of those such as Stanley Mann, Donald Jack, Patricia Joudry, Joseph Schull, to mention a few; as if this country was somehow embarrassed to have them around. I wish we could cherish those playwrights we could, and should, have, without appearing stupidly partisan. But is there some conspiracy among us that is fiercely dedicated to the annihilation of anyone who writes, with some degree of talent, for the stage? We all have our various personal apathies, dislikes, and outright hatreds directed against playwrights of international reputation. Is it that, collectively, we can't tolerate anything Canadian but the best, and not being up to knowing what the best is, we end up by tolerating nothing?[151]

Terry's frustration was rooted in her view of how Canadian playwrights were treated generally, and in Alumnae's inability to procure as many good scripts as they could in particular. Golby had by then observed that while Alumnae had made a "vital contribution" to new play production, the quality of submissions was poor: "Whenever we can find promising scripts we intend to go on producing them. We must confess that we have been somewhat appalled by the calibre of Canadian scripts which have been submitted to us, and so we decided to go out and look for some ourselves." These searches included contacting James

Reaney and Donald Jack. Golby called for playwrights to "ally themselves" with Alumnae to "form a sort of minor league writers' theatre" because to "produce new playwrights is surely the most important function of any theatre, and every encouragement should be given to this ambitious project." Alumnae thus adopted a "general policy"[152] of producing new plays, which dovetailed with the nationalizing and professionalizing agenda for theatre in Canada. Because they did not pay their actors and crew, they could take some risk producing new plays while paying their playwrights.

In 1962, to introduce their new synagogue Coach House Theatre as a home for new plays, Alumnae, the "only non-professional company in Toronto whose work deserves constant critical attention,"[153] re-engaged Reaney, now on faculty at the University of Western Ontario, through Terry. After the messy, public development process with *The Killdeer*, Reaney promised Terry a "neat, tidy play"[154] written for Alumnae[155] a year in advance.[156] It was the fifth time in six years that Alumnae had offered a world premiere of a new play, and the first of three world premieres during their 1962–63 season. In November 1962, Alumnae previewed Reaney's *The Easter Egg*, a "play about resurrection,"[157] in Hamilton in the new 300-seat[158] Physical Sciences Auditorium as a McMaster University Students Union–sponsored event, rehearsing in the Coach House Theatre, "often with a background of hammers and swish of paintbrushes"[159] as members renovated their new theatre space. The McMaster students' council had invited Alumnae to bring a full-length play to their inaugural Arts Festival for one night "so that we might secure an adequate level of professional excellence."[160] Wrote Stewart Brown in his *Hamilton Spectator* review, "It's not every weekend you have a world premiere in your own physics lab!" Brown acknowledged that the space's "clinical traces (a long laboratory table)" had to be "hidden under a portable stage" for this "clinical play." With standing room only, "500 eyes peered down to watch"[161] the play.

"A curious mixture of pathos and farce," *The Easter Egg* follows a twenty-one-year-old stepson in a Quebec college town who, after witnessing his father's suicide, remains "mentally a six-year-old" until he becomes a "fairly responsible adult in the final moments."[162] The play's critical reception was ambivalent. Although Reaney wrote the play "specifically for the occasion"[163] of opening the synagogue Coach House Theatre, with the McMaster showing as a preview a week earlier, Whittaker determined that the Stratford-style "two-level stage makes an uncomfortable bow as the interior of one of those large old houses 'in the English part of Lower Canada.'" Whittaker concluded that *The Easter Egg* "may be best remembered as the first play of the new Coach House rather than the Coach House for it,"[164] while Ronald Evans in the *Telegram* more forcefully dismissed the play as "ludicrous in the extreme."[165] *The Easter Egg* was eventually published in 1972 in Reaney's collection *Masks of Childhood*.[166] A decade later, Alumnae approached Reaney again for a third collaboration; he replied in some detail that if commissioned he would love to work with Terry, his "favourite" director, and the group "a great deal beforehand before putting pen to paper."[167] However, nothing came of it.[168]

In May 1963, Alumnae produced a world premiere by another Governor General's Award–winning poet, Wilfred Watson. Directed and designed by Michael Tait, although his wife and Alumnae member Anne Weldon Tait was originally announced as the director, *The Trial of Corporal Adam: A Comedy in Verse* was Watson's second play, his first Toronto production, and the first of Alumnae's world premieres to have a script still extant in their collection. Terry's playreading committee initially read "with serious intent"[169] Watson's *Cockcrow and the Gulls*, which Terry reported had "received a fine production"[170] at the University of Alberta a year earlier. But they were "forced to exercise a sort of strange caution in plays programmed"; most likely, this means they were hesitant about *Cockcrow* because of its abstract content, given that they were still in their first season of "renewed operations"[171] at the synagogue. Moreover, Watson told Alumnae that a "writer like a mother always loves his latest offspring the most, and so I would, if asked to choose, rather have you do *Corporal Adam* than *Cockcrow* even."[172] Flyers announced that *Corporal Adam* was "specially commissioned by the Canada Council."[173]

By following a fall-and-redemption-of-mankind structure from a notably paradoxical point of view, Watson told Alumnae that he "tried to re-write *Everyman* – I see it as a pagan play written by a Christian author – as a Christian play written by a pagan author. Something else happened, of course, but that's how it started."[174] Perhaps as a consequence, reviews were ambivalent. Determining that it presented "mixed but not dull results,"[175] Whittaker saluted Watson "for daring such an eroded theme, and doing it so forcibly."[176] Wendy Michener in the *Star* called it a "web of words with more tension, structure and interaction of a literary than of a dramatic kind"[177] in a "creditable if rather humourless production."[178] Ron Evans in the *Telegram* applauded Michael Tait's direction as "vigorous, spacious and sometimes stunningly effective."[179] Celebrating *Corporal Adam* as the "Best New Play of the season"[180] (over Reaney's *The Easter Egg* and three other Toronto world premieres), Evans wrote that although the play had its faults, it was "not all creaking cant and dogma – or indeed, clacking verse, either. It has many vivid, inflammatory moments."[181] For this tribute, Alumnae wrote to Evans to express their "appreciation and pleasure."[182]

The run was plagued with both health and scheduling issues. Watson, an English professor at the University of Alberta and a collaborator of famed media scholar Marshall McLuhan, used his Canada Council writers grant[183] to fly to Toronto for opening night on 24 April. But he "flew back to Edmonton" to return again on May 1[184] when the opening was postponed after actor Don Ward was "forced to retire from the leading role"[185] due to an "illness"[186] from which he "collapsed under the strain of the strenuous role."[187] A few days before the opening, it was announced that director Michael Tait would be taking over for Ward. Tait was "delighted"[188] when Equity member James Peddie now took over the part, although Peddie soon after suffered a leg injury that cancelled two of the ten performances.[189] In addition, Tait was forced to take over John Watt's role as Death halfway through the run due to (expected) Stratford Festival commitments[190] that Herbert Whittaker had noted in his column the week before.[191]

Two months after the run, Watson wrote to Alumnae promising to attend to rewrites of the script in order to make "less possible the thing that, I know, really perturbed the reviews, the hint that here was an ANSWER." He then thanked Alumnae for their "intensely beautiful production," saying, "You promised me that the group would give *Corporal Adam* a sensitive and searching production, and you much more than kept your promise. I am extremely grateful both to you and to Michael Tait and his cast – despite their misfortune I thought that their best performances were moving and convincing in the extreme."[192] In 1989, *The Trial of Corporal Adam* was collected in *Wilfred Watson: Plays at the Iron Bridge, or The Autobiography of Tom Horror*.[193]

Over the next few years, as "one of the most venturesome of all dramatic groups in Ontario,"[194] Alumnae produced several world premieres. These included plays by American Jack Richardson; Ottawa's George G. Blackburn; and Quebec's Robert Shirley, Russell MacCallum, and Jacques Languirand, whose *Le Gibet* found its first English production, translated by Albert Bremel, in Alumnae's hands in May 1964.

Wrote Whittaker, in Canada's centennial year "at last the Canadian playwright is getting some attention."[195] In March 1967, Alumnae co-produced, with the Company of Pilgrims, the world premiere of a "bold and avant-garde script"[196] by "conceptual and literary"[197] artist Rae Davis titled *Daily News from the Whole World*.[198] Directed by Pamela Terry and staged at Hart House Theatre, it was Alumnae's last CODL festival entry (see chapter 6). Davis had taken her title from a line in Robert Lowell's 1963 poem "The Voyage," but the play was very much of the 1960s experimental theatre. Although they had long been staging world premieres and avant-garde works, Alumnae had not yet tackled a play of this style – or styles. Davis's approach was interdisciplinary, multisensory, and multimedia. Not interested in the "long psychological bit" about character, she saw her plays as happenings and, in the case of *Daily News*, a "trilogy of assemblages," in reference to its three parts, titled Transistor, Projector, and Dissector, "involving various actors balanced by extensive use of theatrical machinery, especially synchronized sound and lighting," according to the casting call. "Using Theatre of the Absurd techniques, each presents disjointed, unrelated fragments of humanity, responding to, or isolated by, the operation of modern communication techniques." In an interview with Whittaker, Davis added, "I'm also interested in the dance," citing Merce Cunningham and Charles Weidman. She went on:

> I'm also interested in the film gesture. I pore over books of old movies. I love Bette Davis movies and I've seen *Gone with the Wind* eleven times. I'm interested in television and I love newspapers … the things in rent columns and the want ads. I love cities. They are an ecstatic experience for me. I lived in New York for half a year when I graduated from Columbia University, walking all over, going to out-of-the-way places.[199]

An interdisciplinary artist in the extreme, Davis explained that "Transistor" was inspired by a TV picture of a boy walking in traffic listening to a transistor radio accompanied by hammering heard offstage.

Daily News was very much of its avant-garde, "happenings" time. Whittaker fought bravely to delineate the play's action in what read like random jottings:

> The archbishop is plainly forcing the masked bride through the marriage ceremony, undeterred by arrival of welders and policeman on motorcycle. The welders supply a dummy groom; music swells into Berlioz's *Symphonie Fantastique*. A cop places the bride in sacrificial position on his cycle.
>
> It is the most exciting image of a whole set, all equally incomprehensible as logical action.

And later,

> Petula Clark's "Downtown" blasted. A tramp emerges from a recognizable dustbin and is joined in nostalgia by a faded female. Their dreams don't coincide. Failure to communicate is not limited to kids, but they have advanced the condition – as Mrs. Davis points out on the other side of the stage. Here the Kid sits glued to a transistor.

Whittaker reported that Davis's trilogy "held the audience rapt in bafflement."[200]

Daily News helped signal a turn in Alumnae's programming. Their productions were beginning to reflect emerging theatrical experiments in style and form. When Davis responded to Agatha Leonard's request two months later for another "hitherto unproduced full-length Canadian play"[201] for the Coach House next season, she noted in her conclusion that Terry had done "a masterful job with [*Daily News*] as director,"[202] but that she was "disheartened that it did not get more exposure, even in that large hall [of Hart House Theatre], which was spatially unfriendly to the intimate feel of the play."[203] Mixed reviews and dismissive CODL adjudication from Robertson Davies left the potential impact of Davis's experimental new play in a miasma of what-ifs.

In the spring of 1967, Alumnae, having garnered a "well-earned reputation for excellence in these parts,"[204] received a grant from the DDF to pay for a director and a "hitherto unproduced" play in advance of Canada's centennial year. But they would need to choose a script from among the "masses of suggestions"[205] received by programming committee chair Agatha Leonard. President Elizabeth Mascall explained that the grant program helps the playwright "by giving him the chance to work with a professional director and to have the benefit of his advice in any revisions that may be necessary."[206] Leonard's committee read more than sixty scripts[207] that spring and summer, then forwarded three to Herbert Whittaker for his "final decision"[208] as the professional director and designer.[209] Although the centennial submission pool was fairly deep, the committee's notes were remarkably unanimous in their determination that Montreal playwright Jack Cunningham's "*Virginia Woolf*" play, as one committee member called it (he had submitted two plays),[210] probably had the best-written dialogue, despite a number of qualifications, particularly regarding the play's climax.[211]

Thus, the only full production of a world premiere given by Alumnae in their 1967–68 centennial season was so new that they publicized it in September simply as "New Canadian Play (title to be announced) by Jack Cunningham."[212] A letter to subscribers added that Cunningham's untitled play would be about "family conflict." The DDF award given by the Ontario Council for the Arts afforded Cunningham the opportunity to work with Whittaker on the script, including paying for script duplication and travel expenses.[213] Whittaker travelled to Montreal in September to discuss the play with Cunningham, writing to producer Margaret Spence that "ideas are churning as the Hearth Fire Keeps Burning,"[214] a reference to the play's working title of the moment, *Hearth Fire Burning*, before Cunningham returned it to his original title, *Aperitif*.[215] Cunningham, who had won a number of awards for his playwriting, including DDF awards in 1965 and 1966, had lived in Montreal most of his life but gone to NYU for theatre studies. An Alumnae press release noted that his plays had been staged across Canada (Montreal, London, and Vancouver) and in the United States. Mascall said of Cunningham that "obviously, he is a man of the theatre who will continue in the theatre, and it is gratifying that we can help a man like this."[216] Alumnae later described their new play productions as providing a "show window"[217] for new plays that "could make a contribution to Canadian theatre."[218]

Aperitif premiered at the synagogue Coach House Theatre in February 1968 and ran for sixteen days. Although the publicity preceding the opening was intense, with about a dozen differently focused press releases, the reviews were not kind to Cunningham's script, or to the production. The play's men had been cast with "great difficulty," in part because of Whittaker's busy schedule but also due to what Alumnae called "hard luck." Being "short on rehearsal time" (Cunningham had attended rehearsals), they were forced to postpone the opening by a week.[219] Writing in the *Globe and Mail*, Lawrence Stone determined that the "content seemed to be much ado about nothing," with relationships that were too "complex" and "self-involved."[220] Jim McPherson, in the *Telegram*, compared the show to a "rather tedious pastiche of leftover scenes from *Long Day's Journey into Night* and *Virginia*

Figure 7.3. *(on couch, top left)* Elizabeth Ward (Bea), *(leaning on table, top right)* Albert Hand (Alf), *(front, left to right)* Beverley Paul (Janice), Gary Shallenberg (Jerry), and Robert (R.H) Thomson (Jamie) in Jack Cunningham's *Aperitif*, directed by Herbert Whittaker for Alumnae in February 1968. Photo Credit: H. Robinson. Courtesy of Alumnae Theatre Company.

Woolf."[221] Cohen wryly went further: while watching the performance, he had played a game called "Spotting the Source," listing Edward Albee, T.S. Eliot, Harold Pinter, John Osborne, Noël Coward, Joe Orton, Sidney Howard, and Sophocles, "to mention a few," as playwrights on whom Cunningham had "baldly modeled himself."[222] Gordon Jocelyn, an occasional Alumnae guest actor, wrote in the *Montreal Gazette* that "no problem was presented, so nothing was solved,"[223] and that he "hoped they wouldn't all get together again for another 10 years."[224] The *Varsity*'s "K.K." could not be bothered to write a review, concluding in a backpage blurb that an "extensive review is unnecessary because *Aperitif* is a thoroughly genuine flop from its opening guzzle to its dying gasp … Since the play is bogged down with Britishisms and irrelevancies, the action moves ever so slowly."[225]

Reviewers noted that Whittaker's direction was generally "brisk,"[226] with a "fine ear for pace,"[227] which "aided the author in his apparent intention to keep the talk moving like greased lightning."[228] Jocelyn concluded that "little was said, but it was said with verve; and little was done, but it was done with style. Mr. Cunningham is not likely to get a more sympathetic production."[229] K.K. was not so kind, determining that the play was "amateurishly directed and clumsily acted. The stage itself was left barren a number of times. What more can be said of such a vague, sloppy, and physically distressing piece of drama?"[230] Cohen

Figure 7.4. Herbert Whittaker's set design sketch for *Aperitif*, with its early draft title *Hearth Fire Burning*. Courtesy of Alumnae Theatre Company.

concluded that Whittaker "has done much of his best work" for Alumnae, but here, "he has instructed the cast to walk, gesture, sit and stand like zombies, with their fists tightly clenched when possible and their faces absolutely blank. Or maybe I am giving them an underserved benefit, and they are incapable of better."[231] Not much else was said about the cast. Equity member Elizabeth Ward brought "vitality to her performance, alternating her storms with melancholy calm,"[232] while Robert Thomson (member Cicely Thomson's son, later known in his theatre career as R.H. Thomson) played the younger son Jamie with "sensitivity," although he "lapses into melodramatic prose."[233]

Whittaker's "rather bleak set" included a raked platform, a first for the Coach House.[234] Cohen described it as "evidently some kind of hall and drawing room. Severely simple and bare, it is so sharply angled at the rear that what little movement there is happens chiefly in the centre of the intimate open stage."[235] Jocelyn described the set as "ingeniously contrived to make his actors use the whole miniscule stage by setting up an obstacle course with a raked day-bed, a bar and an angled window that all jutted into the room."[236] Whittaker's sketch of his set design dated 23 November 1967, while the play was still called *Hearth Fire Burning*, is extant in Alumnae's collection, as is a copy of Cunningham's production script.

Alumnae's centennial world premiere was not a box office success," earning less than $600. Nevertheless, Cunningham reportedly told the club that it had been a "good experience" for him and that "he had got a much better production than he had expected and a great deal of help from H. Whittaker."[237] *Aperitif*'s mixed reception led to introspection among Leonard and her programming committee, which had been unanimously enthusiastic about the script. Although Leonard reported at season's end that the DDF would be providing Alumnae with another grant to premiere a Canadian play and that her committee was considering this option, it "was not felt to be good because of the lack of plays." Like other companies, Alumnae were concerned that while producing new Canadian plays was important, if the audiences did not come, they risked low box office income[238] and, worse, harming the very concept of new Canadian work in performance. They would not fully stage another world premiere for four years, when they offered member Anne Tait's "urgent, cohesive and vivid"[239] *Tonight: Bert Brecht*, directed by Tait with Beverly Miller, and produced by Mallory Gilbert (later to be Tarragon Theatre's founding theatre manager). Tait's work was Alumnae's only new play production at their Maplewood Avenue Coach House Theatre.

Sunday Evening New Play Readings

Since the interwar years, Alumnae members had held play readings at their club meetings; these were entertaining and also generated helpful dramaturgical feedback. Later, in November 1961, they presented public play readings as part of their series of moderns. These yielded one new play, Alumnae guest actor Donald Bryn's *The Flowered Suit*. At the time, *Varsity* reviewer Tony Robinow wrote with biting sarcasm that "whenever an audience is told that they are about to see an original play by a Canadian playwright … they brace themselves," adding parenthetically, "it's a mysterious fact that while other people just write plays, Canadians nearly always write 'original' plays."[240] In preparing to see an original Canadian play, Robinow said, audiences "probably, and with some justification, fear the worst. However, there was no cause for alarm on Wednesday [for Bryn's play]."[241] Jack Winter wrote in the *Star* that the play revealed Bryn's "mischievous wit and an amusing trick ending [that] combined to provide an enjoyable interlude. And apparently it is still possible to write a new Canadian play with no nationalistic pretensions!"[242] A Canadian play without nationalistic pretensions seemed to Winter to be original indeed.

Five years later, Molly Thom introduced regular Sunday evening readings for Coach House Theatre subscribers.[243] Although not exclusively for new plays, these became an important vehicle for receiving audience (and reviewer) feedback for scripts in development; they also provided experience to new directors. The same script could be publicly read and potentially reworked by the playwright across three consecutive Sundays, which were the "dark days" of Alumnae's full productions during a three-week run. The format found leaders in members Molly Thom, Elizabeth Mascall, Francess Halpenny, and Anne Tait, who were often offered the chance to have their scripts read again by other theatre companies, universities, and CBC radio. This inspired members Joan Shaw and Juliana Saxton to generate new works.

As a trial run for Sunday readings, Alumnae presented *A Centennial Tribute to the Ladies of the Canadian Frontier* on 2 April 1967 at the synagogue Coach House Theatre. By involving a number of members as readers under Thom and Mascall's guidance, the evening put a new spin on their tradition of presenting period fare; the writings added a nineteenth-century colonial Canadian flavour to the centennial year.[244] After seven months of weekday-evening readings of plays from various periods and in various styles during the 1966–67 season, Alumnae inaugurated their Sunday evening new play readings with *This Beggarly Wooden Country: A Centennial Tribute*, presented on three consecutive Sundays during their November to December 1967 run of Carl Sternheim's *The Underpants*. Advertised as a "bonus to our subscribing members" for a $1 charge, the two-part event revisited the *Centennial Tribute* with Thom's excerpts from the writings of Susanna Moodie,

Catherine Paar Traill, Anne Langton, and Anna Jameson in the first part and Mascall's *Sweet Songstress of Saskatchewan* in the second.[245]

Alumnae then put out a press release for two evenings of readings to be held in May 1968, *not* coinciding with a full production, to celebrate a "most enthusiastic response to our informal entertainments this season." The production this time was *The Matter of Arthur: A Panorama of the Great King Whom the Centuries Would Not Willingly Let Die*,[246] prepared by Halpenny. She based the reading on Alfred Lord Tennyson's poetic cycle *Idylls of the King*, "with a look behind to Mallory and Spenser and a look ahead to T.H. White."[247] Alumnae hailed their early readings as successes enjoyed by participants and audiences alike. They proved particularly useful for giving "more experience for younger members." They also required less commitment from everyone than a full production.[248]

Like *This Beggarly Wooden Country*, and *Pablo Neruda: Lives of the Poet* (which coincided with Neruda's Nobel Prize award in November 1971), new plays at Sunday readings were usually programmed to run concurrently with relevant local, national, and international events. This was true for the first of three readings prepared and directed by member Anne Tait in December 1968 titled *So Great a Sweetness: Yeats and Maud Gonne*. "Not so coincidentally,"[249] Toronto was having a mini-resurgence of interest in Irish theatre that fall, in particular a "boomlet of interest"[250] in Williams Butler Yeats. In December, U of T's St. Michael's College and the Centre for Study of Drama organized a conference on Theatre and Nationalism in twentieth-century Irish theatre that featured the popular culture and media scholar Marshall McLuhan, a well-regarded interpreter of James Joyce;[251] U of T's Drama Centre hosted the artistic director of Dublin's Abbey Theatre, Tomás MacAnna, and his production of Yeats's last play, *The Death of Cuchulain*, at their Studio theatre;[252] and Brown University's David Krause spoke on Seán O'Casey, Samuel Beckett, and an unpublished lecture by Yeats on Irish theatre in a non-public interuniversity lecture.[253] Anne Tait, a freelance writer and broadcaster who had been a script assistant in the CBC-TV Drama Department,[254] wrote *So Great a Sweetness* after taking a summer course on Yeats[255] while enrolled in graduate work in English at U of T.[256] Her professor, Robert O'Driscoll,[257] appeared in the cast along with Tait's husband Michael, who played Yeats.

So Great a Sweetness, the title of which comes from a line in Yeats's poem "Friends," is comprised of "selections from published autobiographies, diaries, letters and poems that show or comment on this tough but fruitful relationship"[258] between Yeats and Maude Gonne, founder of the Nationalist Society[259] and the "woman who for over 20 years gave Yeats the blues, out of which he squeezed his best love poetry." Tait borrowed her text from writings by Yeats, Gonne, Yeats's "platonic friend" Katherine Tynan, and his patron Lady Gregory to illuminate "each stage of the affair." In his review, York University professor Stan Fefferman said of the play's structure that "as the paths of these two people prepare to cross, you can't help think of the Titanic and the Iceberg." Describing the reading as if it was a more fulsome production, he wrote that the actors read while "perched in front of lecterns on highstools, carefully placed around the intimate apron stage of the Coach House"[260] under spotlights. Noting that Alumnae readings were for subscribing members only, Cohen wrote that the "rules for attendance at *So Great a Sweetness* preclude regular criticism. However Miss Tait clearly is still working on the exact form and pressure of her material. Certainly more definition is needed of the quiet intensity of Yeats' love for Miss Gonne, and the double shocks he receives when she rejects his proposal and later notifies him that she has married."[261] Fefferman concluded that Tait's script let the "flashy Maude Gonne upstage Yeats. You can't get Yeats's real toughness out of the tame gentlemanly prose of his autobiography, or out of an exchange of letters that show him hopelessly caught in the treads of Maude Gonne's juggernaut."[262] Fefferman also wanted more of Yeats's poems in Tait's script.

But Tait's conception of a "Maude Gonne juggernaut" fit more securely within the women-run company's theatre juggernaut. Like the readings assembled by Thom, Mascall, and Halpenny, Tait's script found further life, first as a revised set of Alumnae readings in March 1969, then as a CBC radio production in December 1969, a reading at Dublin's Abbey Theatre in August 1970, a showing at the Dublin Theatre Festival in 1975, and a revised and abridged 1982 script extant in Alumnae's collections.[263]

Tait returned to the format a year later, after Alumnae opened their Maplewood Avenue Coach House Theatre, preparing and directing a "delightful"[264] reading titled *Sir Gawain and the Green Knight*. It ran on three Sundays in October and November 1969, but not during the run of a larger production – they had deemed Maplewood to be generally unsuitable for a full show. This medieval romance in modern language was given the tagline "a deadly bargain / a game of love." Tait "prepared the script from both the original 14th-century text and the modern English translation, thereby retaining much of the original alliteration while devising a workable rhythm for the 20th-century actor."[265] The reading's flyer featured a medieval woodcut-style image of a knight on horseback with a thin dog keeping up and a castle in the background.

A week later, across three Sundays in November 1969, Mascall directed a dramatic reading of Michael B. Polley's new three-act play *The Song Is Far Away*. Publicity described it as dealing with the "explosive confrontation between a Radical Student and a University President with a revolutionary past," set in the "office of the President of a Canadian University today." Polley's play was very much of the times. The playreading committee called it a "combination of Forest Hill and Sir George Williams protests," referring to recent Toronto events. Ontario's fourteen universities were cracking down on campus protests with a "stringent 'get tough' policy for dealing with dissident faculty and students." The universities were calling for students or faculty engaging in "obstructive behaviour" to be "immediately suspended, expelled or dismissed."[266] The *Varsity*'s pages were filled that year with stories of dissent and retaliation on university campuses across the country.[267] Proclaimed one *Varsity* cover by way of a Captain America–style cartoon strip, "This is the day of the anti-hero – the age of the rebel and the dissenter!"[268] These real-life "radical"[269] interventions were reflected in Alumnae's recent programming, which included shows like *Little Malcolm and His Struggle against the Eunuchs*, *Viet Rock*, and *The Ecstasy of Rita Joe*, the latter of which Alumnae programmed concurrently with Polley's play. With an early line in the script spoken by the University President to the Dean, reading, "Your department is showing a film tomorrow called *The Militant Student*," Polley's play fell in line with this broad conversation. A copy of the script in a Duo-Tang is extant in Alumnae's collections.

In February and March 1971, a third reading arranged by Tait appeared during off nights of Alumnae's run of D.H. Lawrence's *The Widowing of Mrs. Holroyd*. It was Tait's new and "exhaustive criss-crossing of texts and quotations (all of them authentic)"[270] titled *D.H. Lawrence: Man and Demon*. The *Toronto Citizen*'s reviewer opined that Tait's script and Lawrence's play "together possess a strength which neither has alone."[271] Whittaker went further, wondering aloud whether Tait's script was Alumnae's "greater achievement"[272] over those weeks. By piecing together extracts from letters and other writings by Lawrence and his friends, including "incredible excerpts"[273] from the testimony at the 1959 obscenity trial (in which the publisher Penguin Books was found "not guilty" for publishing Lawrence's unabridged version of *Lady Chatterley's Lover*), Tait's script "captures great chunks (if not all) of that extraordinary character, his philosophy and his times."[274] Tait juxtaposed passages from Lawrence's novels with descriptions of his personal relationships to create a "fascinating study of a man trying to force his life to conform to a literary vision"[275] that he could not achieve. Much "more ambitious" than Tait's *So Great a Sweetness*, it involved five women and four men reading, accompanied by recorded music, including hymns such as "Stand Up Stand Up for Jesus," and slides showing Lawrence and his world, including images of rural 1920s England and Lawrence's own paintings, which depicted the "beauty and the ugliness" that affected Lawrence, according to the press release. But Cohen concluded that the music and slides "don't really contribute anything, chiefly because Miss Tait is still groping her way toward a thematic narrative line," and that the play "at the moment is a series of disconnected tableaux." The actors sat on stools and played multiple roles,[276] but, Whittaker asked, "How can an actress of flair like Molly Thom fail to rise to an occasion which invites her to play, in swift succession, Katherine Mansfield, Lady Ottoline Morrell, and Rebecca West?" Still, Andrea Rosnick was a "remarkable Frieda," and Michael Polley's Lawrence "never stood in the way of our understanding of that rare genius, and better than that, tied together many new insights."[277]

Readings gained traction among some members and guests interested in workshopping their new scripts, becoming an Alumnae tradition that lasted into the 1980s. But by the end of the 1960s, a script was not the only way to develop a new play.

Improvisation and Collective Creation

The Maplewood Coach House Theatre was not large enough[278] to accommodate most full productions, but it could host workshops in the emerging style of improvisation. Alumnae's first improv workshop, in November 1969, was intended to culminate in a new play staged over three Sundays in April 1970. But as with many improv-based creations, the process had an unexpected and unprecedented (for Alumnae) outcome.

Alumnae felt that the improvisational aspects of their production of Megan Terry's *Viet Rock* in the fall of 1968 had "engendered a great deal of enthusiasm" among club members and friends for creating their own play based on improv techniques.[279] Furthermore, their full-length winter production of *America Hurrah* and the five short plays collected as *Collision Course* that they presented thereafter had all been devised from improvisation.[280] Ultimately, members felt that *Viet Rock*'s shortcomings lay with the actors trying to make sense of a play that had been developed out of other people's improvisations, and that "to be, ourselves, the original improvisers of a play, would be a challenging and worth-while project in theatre." To that end, club president Margaret MacAulay applied for funding from the DDF's Professional Direction Committee to pay a guest playwright for a short play with low production costs created from improv techniques. This was ambitious new territory for the fifty-year-old company and spoke to Alumnae members' awareness of current trends. However, this initial approach led to tensions that Alumnae, for the first time in their history, could not overcome.

In Alumnae's application to the DDF, MacAulay noted that while improv-based theatre often centres on the actors, Alumnae's "tastes … are for literate, well-constructed plays." To generate an improvised play, they would seek a playwright with "acting and directing experience." They pitched Martin Hunter, who had acted and directed for Alumnae, won the CODL best Canadian play award in 1967, and was resident dramaturge at U of T's Drama Centre. MacAulay wrote that "Mr. Hunter has been intrigued, as have we, by the possibility of improvisational theatre and is willing to work with us on this project." The director would be member Joan Shaw, who had "extensive acting experience," including with Alumnae in *Viet Rock*. MacAulay requested a fee for Hunter as playwright and perhaps for Shaw as well, who "as a Club member, would not normally receive this." The plan was for club members and male guests to meet twice a week for improv work under Shaw's direction, with Hunter observing several sessions. Shaw would lead the actors on improvisations based on Hunter's theme or related situations, and then Hunter would "create his characters and play" from his observations without being "obliged to copy verbatim from the company." They would then select the cast from these sessions and rehearse regularly with a "theme, or possibly a plot," provided by Hunter.[281] The workshop received a grant of $800 from the DDF and the Ontario Council for the Arts to employ Hunter as "Dramatist."[282]

They sent out a call to members and subscribers in September 1969 for a workshop that would introduce the "techniques of improvisational theatre – physical and vocal control, methods for achieving concentration and unselfconsciousness, and group scene-building." Appealing to the participatory elements in Alumnae's orbit, they sought the "experienced, those who have never set foot on stage, men, women, and teenagers, all are welcome." Perhaps with a nod towards encouraging their adult members and guests, even those "who have previously decided it is not their cup of tea are urged to attend once and see. *We are all improvisors* and a good improvisational group session can be as much fun as a good cocktail party!" The announcement added that those not chosen for the project "may well decide to continue meeting with a new leader, possibly to pursue a project of their own. This is exactly the kind of creative spirit we hope to encourage." Through the planned public performance they were hoping to encourage other companies in the city to "attempt similar projects."[283]

Forty-seven participants attended the first improv session, many of them teenagers,[284] which became a bone of contention throughout the process. During the six sessions,[285] Hunter created an "outline of a script" and a cast was chosen that included some of the teenagers. What appeared on 30 November were eleven selected sketches drawn from "concentrated" improvised work. Hunter and Shaw explained the process to a "large audience" that included members, friends, and regular patrons.[286] MacAulay later described the talkback after the scene presentations as an "open discussion between the audience and the company of the form and value of improvised drama [which] showed that these were subjects of interest and disagreement among members and audience."[287]

But after the November presentation, the planned season-long process broke down due to scheduling pressures, creative conflicts, and, Alumnae had to admit, generational differences. In May, MacAulay was forced to report, with "regret," to the DDF that so many of the improv actors were involved in *America Hurrah* and *Collision Course* as actors and crew that a "made play" could not be offered by the end of the season. "Frankly," she continued, "our resources were not sufficient to our ambition."[288] In his published memoirs, Hunter would write that Shaw, whom he had known as an undergraduate actress, told him "I don't want you to write any more neurotic women characters."[289] As the "improvisations continued, the group rejected Hunter's outline of a play and elected to pursue its own course." Hunter informed MacAulay that he did not want a fee for the fall project.[290] He explained in his memoirs that he "enjoyed working with them and found much of what they did amusing. Joan was less impressed and declared the whole enterprise to be nothing but a pile of clichés. She was not entirely wrong. I told the Alumnae ladies that we had not been able to construct a play and told them to keep their thousand Canada Council dollars. Ah, the arrogance of the young."[291]

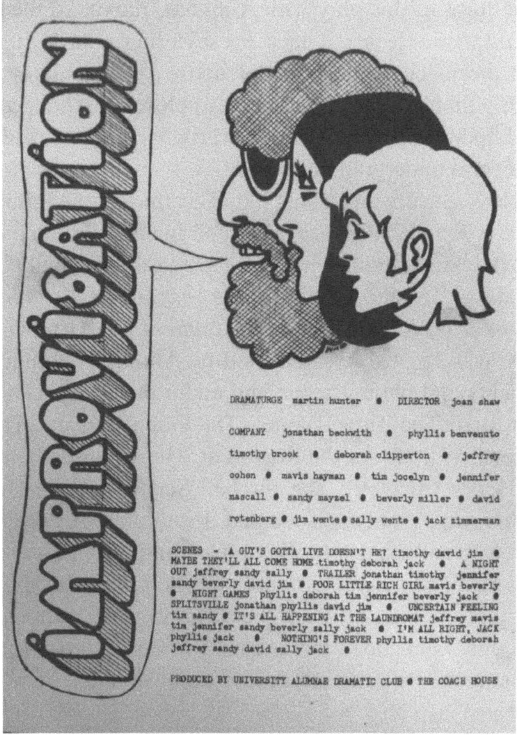

IMPROVISATION

DRAMATURGE martin hunter • DIRECTOR joan shaw

COMPANY jonathan beckwith • phyllis benvenuto timothy brook • deborah clipperton • jeffrey cohen • mavis hayman • tim jocelyn • jennifer mascall • sandy mayzel • beverly miller • david rotenberg • jim wente • sally wente • jack zimmerman

SCENES - A GUY'S GOTTA LIVE DOESN'T HE? timothy david jim • MAYBE THEY'LL ALL COME HOME timothy deborah jack • A NIGHT OUT jeffrey sandy sally • TRAILER jonathan timothy jennifer sandy beverly david jim • POOR LITTLE RICH GIRL mavis beverly • NIGHT GAMES phyllis deborah tim jennifer beverly jack • SPLITSVILLE jonathan phyllis david jim • UNCERTAIN FEELING tim sandy • IT'S ALL HAPPENING AT THE LAUNDROMAT jeffrey mavis tim jennifer sandy beverly sally jack • I'M ALL RIGHT, JACK phyllis jack • NOTHING'S FOREVER phyllis timothy deborah jeffrey sandy david sally jack •

PRODUCED BY UNIVERSITY ALUMNAE DRAMATIC CLUB • THE COACH HOUSE

Figure 7.5. The one-page program for Alumnae's experimental *Improvisation* variety show in November 1969 at their Maplewood Avenue Coach House. Courtesy of Alumnae Theatre Company.

MacAulay rejected any notion that the project had been a failure and was quick to blame the young non-member participants for the show's collapse. She said the teenagers were "enthusiastic" but that their lack of experience and unwillingness to "explore areas beyond their own immediate interests" challenged the process. She reported that the club found the teenagers to be "quite ruthless in their exclusion of the adults in the company" when, for example, "one actress with extensive improvisational and acting experience remarked that you had to fight to get in. A small illustration of the generation gap." The gap was ironic given that fifty years earlier, young women had founded Alumnae, although middle-aged women were now running it. She further concluded that it had been a mistake to assume that both a director and a playwright were needed, arguing that in this process they should be one in the same so that the actors could be "guided to a play rather than directed to a script." This distinction between the "play" and the "script" evidences the club's increasingly nuanced education in their craft. But they still had much to learn where improv was concerned, telling the DDF that "developing a play by improvisation alone appears to be impossible. The answer may well be a play by committee, with the director acting as chairman." Continuing on the generational theme, MacAulay concluded by musing that a "wider experience of life gives a broader base upon which to improvise, leading to a more interesting piece for the audience as well as the actor."[292]

Hunter, seeing no future for his play with Alumnae, reworked the material into a script called *Flowers of Paradise*. He set it in a Presbyterian church inspired by Alumnae's Maplewood building, produced it at the UC Playhouse at 79 St. George Street (formerly the Women's Union with which Alumnae had been so closely associated), and cast Alumnae members Francess Halpenny, Jackie White, Beverly Miller, Valerie Grabove, and Juliana Saxton, along with several undergraduates.[293]

Inspired by alternative theatre successes like Theatre Passe Muraille's *The Farm Show* and *1837: The Farmer's Revolt*, Alumnae tried their hand at a related improv-based collective creation format, the "docudrama," in May 1974 at the Firehall. Celebrating the 140th anniversary of the City of Toronto, *Muddy Little York, or an Examination of some of the History of the Town of York, including, amongst others, the Discovery of How the White House Got Its Name*, was created by a cast led by Alumnae member Juliana Saxton using historical documents and photographic and audio materials related to Toronto's early history. With scenes titled The Time Tunnel, The Grand Square, The War of 1812, The Elizabeth Russell Scene, Waiting for the Regiment, The Inhabitants of York, The Beautiful Vale of York (Mrs. Henry Chewett), The Firehall Scene, and The Grand Finale, *Muddy Little York* remains Alumnae's only self-created docudrama. A note from the playreading committee indicates early enthusiasm for Saxton leading the creation of a docudrama; they called it a "first rate" idea and a "good project" for the group that they would be "crazy to miss." Kareda noted that the Firehall itself "used to be along a thoroughfare which led to the Parliament Buildings," and added that the bar for this sort of project was high: "We've been spoiled for documentary drama in Toronto because much of what we've seen so far has been so good."[294]

As with their improv experiment, however, Alumnae's process for *Muddy Little York* was more compelling than the actual result. As a touchstone, Saxton provided the cast with information about the recent docudrama work of Stoke-on-Trent's Victoria Theatre. Perhaps having learned from Alumnae's past experience with improvisation, she underscored that Victoria Theatre plays "consist almost exclusively of documentary material entirely collated, edited and assembled" by director Peter Cheeseman and the "company as a group." She clarified that "no writer is allowed to make a script for the documentaries – nor are they the result of 'improvisation' by the actors." She also structured a ten-month creation process, putting out a call to the membership a year in advance seeking a

> group of interested bods who are prepared to research over the summer – books, documents, films, slides, pictures, music *etc. etc.* – to meet during the fall and winter to build the script and to rehearse intensively during April and perform in May.
>
> Docudrama is a group experience – everyone takes part in all the process – right through to performance – you must be prepared to *follow* and to *lead* – to have your "baby" thrown out if it inhibits the total dramatic event – to work *constructively* and *supportively* at all times – its frightening, chaotic, frustrating, but challenging and fun – if its neither of the latter two – we'll stop and go home!!
>
> No guarantees of success.
>
> No guarantees of anything.
>
> Trust me, trust yourself, trust the group.
>
> We are interested in interest
– daring
– courage.

Figure 7.6. John Illingworth and cast members of the world premiere of Alumnae's collectively created play *Muddy Little York*, produced at their Firehall theatre in May 1974, directed by Julia Saxton. Courtesy of Alumnae Theatre Company.

Saxton's call deftly signposted expectations by noting the requisite research, time, involvement, and collaboration. Would-be participants met at the end of June 1973 in the Drama Studio at U of T's Faculty of Education, with which Saxton was affiliated. Here she allocated "summer reading" in advance of the next meeting in September, at which they discussed the "theme, direction of thrust, point of view" as well as "areas of intensive reading." The group met again in January 1974 to frame the general scene division and structure of the play before gradually building the script over Thursdays in March and adding the "final audio-visual choices" in early April from photographs and other materials accumulated during the process. "Intensive rehearsals" began the following week and lasted throughout April. Thom, as publicity chair, wrote to local teachers emphasizing that *Muddy Little York* "will be both instructive and entertaining for young people studying the early history of Upper Canada."

But critics were not impressed with *Muddy Little York*. Kareda noted that despite Toronto's recent successes with the form, it is "tricky and not infallible."[295] Whittaker determined that the show performed Toronto's past and "shining present" "rather sketchily," although the "eager researchers rather than expert dramatizers" performed with "enthusiasm."[296] Kareda offered fewer qualifications, stating that the production offered too many lists and clichés and amounted to a "long, dull evening" that provided "depressing evidence of what happens when inspiration and imagination fail and when almost an entire company of actors seems lost beyond recovery."[297] Whittaker concluded, perhaps ironically given that Alumnae's previous creation was led by a playwright, that the "material gathered justifies a further refinement, perhaps with the help of a dramatist, and one hopes that the firehall will not shelve the program after its present run is over." Still, the eleven-person cast offered some highlights, including long-time member Cicely Thomson, who "brought the dancing mistress to life here."[298]

The Firehall Gives Us *Shelter*, *A Clash of Symbols*, and Two Festivals of Firsts

When they reopened the Firehall as their theatre in 1972, Alumnae continued to develop, read, and perform new scripts on Sunday evenings in their upstairs Studio theatre. For many, these became a "trademark"[299] of the company. But so many alternative theatres were taking up new play production in the 1970s that Alumnae could no longer use world premieres to distinguish their programming.[300] So they focused their new play production on women-centred work, capitalizing more than they had, to date, on their position as a women-only theatre group. This set them apart from the emerging male-led alternative theatres. But with the demise of the DDF, arm's-length new play development funding was now exclusive to professional theatre. By the 1980s, Alumnae had turned to established, popular plays to fill seats. Their new play output fell off drastically until the New Ideas Festival emerged in the late 1980s, at which time Alumnae redefined itself (again) as a producer of new works. Nevertheless, Alumnae did offer full stagings of several important world premieres during their first two decades in the Firehall. These included the first English-language translation of Québécoise playwright Anne Hébert's *Le Temps Sauvage* by member Elizabeth Mascall[301] and an adaptation of Leo Tolstoy's *The Power of Darkness* by Molly Thom.

Among the most significant of Alumnae's 1970s world premieres was "anti-establishment" playwright Carol Bolt's twelfth play,[302] *Shelter*, which ran at the Firehall in November and December 1974. The *Star*'s Metro section noted that an explosion at the ammonium nitrate plant across the street from the Firehall on the evening of 27 November meant that the audience was "treated to two performances,"[303] one of them through the theatre windows before curtain as firefighters battled the blaze. As Bolt's first play that was not based on documentary material – at the time, *Toronto Life* magazine called her "Canada's most prolific writer of docudrama"[304] – *Shelter* is a comedy that deals with five women, one of whom is the widow of a politician who herself goes into politics. It was a joint production between Alumnae, as producers, and Young People's Theatre (YPT), which contributed the services of director Eric Steiner,[305] and was assisted by an Ontario Arts Council grant through Theatre Ontario. The press release explained that YPT founder Susan Rubes had sought a "way to work on and develop new plays without the enormous financial commitment of a professional production," avoiding "overnight rewrites" on "tight rehearsal time." Bolt was active throughout rehearsals, changing lines as they went.[306] Artist Charles Pachter, whose controversial and eventually iconic[307] painting of Elizabeth II riding a moose was on exhibit at the new co-op gallery The Artery,[308] designed the "subtle, oddly suspended setting,"[309] while Alumnae Margaret Spence designed the costumes.[310]

Shelter brought Alumnae members together to produce a politically charged new play about women of the day. It was probably their greatest production success of the decade. Barb Shainbaum's *Varsity* review declared that "it's a pleasure to review an interesting play about women, and Canadian women at that, who aren't drowntrodden dramatizations of failures."[311] Kareda called it "one of the most interesting plays in a long time,"[312] celebrating it as a "big, lovely, delicious hit" and a "communal triumph" for Alumnae, YPT, and

Figure 7.7. (*left to right*) Phyllis Benvenuto (Jory), Helen Carscallan (Luel), Pixie Bigelow (Vicky), and Diane Polley (Win) in the world premiere of Carol Bolt's farce *Shelter* at Alumnae's Firehall theatre, November to December 1974, directed by Eric Steiner. Photo Credit: John Bloom. Courtesy of Alumnae Theatre Company.

director Eric Steiner, who led the "meticulously uproarious production." Said Kareda, Bolt wrote "that rarest of home-grown scripts, a truly funny, truly contemporary, truly Canadian comedy, hilarious, thorny, observant and absolutely explosive with wit." He added that Bolt's "approach to structure seems at times almost by free association, a looseness covered by the brilliant energy and risk-taking, intelligent heartlessness"[313] of Steiner's direction. Shainbaum praised Diane Polley, who "convincingly portrays the wisecracking and cynical Win," Colleen Wagner, who "touchingly" played the "overfriendly" Calla, Helen Carscallen, whose Luel was an "outrageously funny satiric target for misconstrued attitudes about political women, or just women in general," and Phyllis Benvenuto, who took the underdeveloped role of Jory and "gives us a Jory full of integrity, determination and genuine spunkiness."[314] (On this point, Bert Cowan on the radio program *Offstage Voices* said that the "basic flaw of the play is that we don't learn what she is idealistic about – only that she wants to change the world"[315]). Kareda concluded, "If there were any sense at all in Toronto runs, it would go on a lot longer."[316] Toronto Arts Productions offered Bolt's play a year later to great acclaim, again directed by Steiner.[317] Whittaker, of all critics, offered a more tempered review, saying it was a "little off balance." Because it was a "workshop production,"[318] the audience was invited to make suggestions after the show, and he hoped the play would be revisited after the run.

But as members of the then-six-decades-old theatre company could attest, the 1970s was a reactionary time for women's voices. Kaspars Dzeguze, now writing for the *Toronto Sun*, announced with 1970s misogyny that *Shelter* added "new colour to the political spectrum – parliament pink. This isn't the vaguely liberal-leftist shade you might expect, but a riotous comic colour produced at the giddy point where women and politics intersect ... Parliament pink will be the colour of those women's libbers, who think the play was meant to vindicate their position in the corridors of power."[319]

Dzeguze's sexist, urban-centric, and demeaning review described each character, variously, as a "whole circus, or play, in herself," a "fem-lib journalist," a "lightweight in this collection of 97-pound weaklings [and a] trouser romantic," someone who "should be enough to make dozens of professional media ladies shiver with embarrassment of its aptness," and "once housebroken, though, ... sure to make a fine candidate." Steiner, said Dzeguze, "might have used rather more discretion and rather less hysteria; matriarchs should appear strong and willful, ruled by themselves rather than by the hormone imbalances of old age."[320] Dzeguze's diatribe may indeed have echoed the expected opinions of the right-leaning *Sun*'s readership, but it did not do justice to the significance of either Bolt's play or Alumnae's production.

Among Alumnae's most remarkable world premieres was the English-language translation of *La nef des sorcières*. The play is a collection of eight monologues by seven prominent Quebec women: Marie-Claire Blais, Nicole Brossard, Marthe Blackburn, Odette Gagnon, Luce Guilbeault, Pol Pelletier, and France Theoret. The original French production premiered at Montreal's Theatre du Nouveau Monde in 1976 as part of International Women's Year. It staged what *Varsity* reviewer Robert Read called the "triumphs of individual women over the constraints and oppressions of their day to day lives."[321] Without the translation talents of member Elizabeth Mascall, who had died shortly after her translation of *Le Temps Sauvage* premiered during the Firehall's inaugural season, Alumnae commissioned Linda Gaboriau, already one of the country's most important translators of dramatic texts. Funds had been donated by member Maggie Bassett. The translation was "pre-published" in a Coach House Press "manuscript edition" (what they called "computer line-printer copies of work in progress"[322]) so that audiences could purchase the script after the performance. Director Molly Thom announced auditions with the notes "English title to come" and the "six actresses must be prepared to play with absolute candour and directness and risk." By its January 1979 run in the Studio, where "seating is sparse (so arrive early); the setting is sparser," the translation was titled *A Clash of Symbols*. It was billed as a "dramatic collage presented for the first time in English in Canada" in which "7 women from Quebec speak out on what it means to be a woman today."

Some reviewers helped navigate the play's feminism for Anglo-Toronto audiences. Robert Read said it was the "sort of theatre I recommend. All of the women are familiar to us; the performances are gutsy and honest."[323] In *The Newspaper*, Christopher Power wrote that the actresses performed monologues that were "not so much the blatant feminist statement but instead a female character study done in the context of an offensive male society." He reported that the script's "sheer power obviously lost nothing in the translation from the French, as was reflected by the many male members of the audience slinking out of the theatre immediately after the final applause."[324] However, the *Globe and Mail*'s Roy Conlogue was dismissive and apparently had no idea what, or who, he was watching. For him, "no amateur can hope to render"[325] this poetic text, apparently not even Alumnae members.[326]

From the moment that Alumnae opened the Firehall in 1972, there was considerably less space in Toronto's theatre ecology for them to continue their decades-long interest in new play production. Between *A Clash of Symbols* in 1979 and the first New Ideas Festival in 1988, Alumnae read or performed just over a dozen world premieres; after 1988, they reserved their world premieres almost exclusively for their New Ideas Festival, with only a few full-length exceptions. This remained true until they inaugurated the FireWorks Festival in 2013. Today, Alumnae may be best known as the producing company of the annual New Ideas Festival. Just over a decade into its existence, Halpenny referred to the festival as a "rite of spring in the studio space – it is a public showcase for writers, actors and directors and it is a success."[327] Toronto reviewers recognized it as "one of the key ways for authors to develop their plays."[328]

In the late 1980s, Molly Thom and emerging director Kerri MacDonald conceived of a festival of short new performances as an antidote to the administrative structuralism that had taken hold of the company, a product of inflation, competition for audiences, and the demands of managing their own vast, aging building. Years later, Thom explained that Alumnae had long been

> known as a theatre company where you could learn just about anything, and you could do just about anything you set your mind to … It seemed an infinitely flexible organization, whether by design or accident, always ready to encourage creativity and individual initiative. In the Coach House days from 1956 to 1969, after all, not much money was at stake, and the audience was always there. There was room to take a chance …
>
> The move to the Firehall in the 1970s brought escalating costs, and coincided with the explosion of professional theatre in Toronto. There was suddenly more competition. Alumnae audiences were not always as full as they had been. And more money was at stake. Inevitably, spontaneity began to give way to caution, and caution to structure.

She explained that as "committees sprang up" and formal processes emerged, "there was less and less room for impromptu choices." The Studio series became a fixed part of the subscription series and featured established playwrights. Experimentation and readings disappeared.[329] Sets were becoming more elaborate even while builders were increasingly difficult to find. And to direct a Studio production, she reflected, "you had to make an application, it had to be on the subscription list, it was all so formal and restrictive. We were longing for the days when there could be impulsive productions and things done on the spur of the moment – somebody with an idea!"[330] A new director had little opportunity to "try her hand," an experienced director had no place to try something new or experimental, and writers no longer had a supportive place to try their work. Alumnae had lost an important part of what had long defined them. Thom and MacDonald "groused and complained to each other" and then lobbied the executive to try a "modest program of new work."[331] What would soon be titled New Ideas Festival appeared one year before the Toronto Fringe Festival debuted in 1989.

Alumnae's 1987–88 brochure boldly announced the season's theme as "New Plays, New Discoveries," adding that it would include a "very special project at the close of the season – NEW IDEAS – a showcase for plays and new directors." The juried festival would allow members and non-members to experiment with new ideas not only in playwriting, but also in directing, performance, design, and technology. Dramaturgical mentorship would be central to all of this, and there would be workshops and talkback sessions to "encourage audience participation." A work could be presented "at any stage of its development – as script-in-hand reading or finished production."[332] New Ideas soon developed a "built-in audience," with several dozen actors and crew attending one another's works along with their friends and families. From the first day, written audience comments provided feedback for the plays and the festival, which eventually became a "financial boon"[333] for the company.

The inaugural New Ideas Festival was arranged in three separate programs running in May 1988, all free for members and subscribers. Following a juried submission process, six plays were mounted: four world premieres by members, one multimedia experiment, and two published one-acts staged by new directors. Among the offerings were a play by Colleen Williams called *Undergrowth*, featuring long-time member Cicely Thomson, and a play adapted by Colleen Williams from Alice Munro's writing called *Mrs. Cross and Mrs. Kidd*, directed by Pamela Terry. From there, the festival expanded quickly. New directors became interested in Alumnae again, and a number of members grew interested in writing. In 1996, for example, Alumnae received about 100 scripts, eight of the chosen directors were members, and the company was "overwhelmed"[334] by member and non-member auditioners. By 2001, the festival was known as a "place of intersection between many areas of the Toronto theatre community."[335] New works sometimes found new life after the festival.[336] An echo of Alumnae's DDF past, however unnoticed, the festival could generate broad enthusiasm for unproven work across a relatively broad and new-to-Alumnae audience demographic. It helped generate community recognition and company definition. For Alumnae's 2017–18 centennial season, the festival received 247 play submissions (up from 182 the previous year); 130 of these were Canadian, and just over half were from women. Clearly, Alumnae were on the national map (from Halifax to Victoria); indeed, they were on the international map as well (primarily the US). Of the fifteen plays chosen, only two were written by members, and five of the fifteen directors were members. In total, 135 people participated in the festival and 1,101 attended it.[337] Importantly, with the New Ideas Festival, Alumnae members who were also members of Actors' Equity and ACTRA could "take risks with new material without the pressures of self-producing," take on challenging and lead roles, and create "visibility"[338] with new audiences and artists. The purpose, radical in contemporary theatre, was to serve the practitioners and "not necessarily to entertain the audience" (although of course that was happening too). Although Thom warns that "regulations and structures are always threatening to intrude in the name of efficiency,"[339] the New Ideas Festival continues to serve its original purposes for its artists and Alumnae's membership.

Although many plays developed at the News Ideas Festival have gone on to new lives elsewhere, some have encountered complications. A full production of Roger Rudick's *Story of a Comfort Girl* had to be replaced at the last minute in the spring of 2001. The play had been read at the 2000 New Ideas Festival under Molly Thom's direction; Rudick and Alumnae then sought to develop the full-length world premiere. However, the board of directors heard concerns from the Asian acting community that the story,

> about Korean sex slaves held by the Japanese in World War II, was written by a non-Asian and will be directed by a non-Asian, and therefore will not be accurate. The Board agreed that these were legitimate reservations, and did not want to offend the Asian community. Therefore efforts will be made to include them in the production process. It was also pointed out that *Comfort Girl* is a workshop production, and as such, is still a work in progress.[340]

Thom had already expressed concern that the script would not be ready, so they moved it to the final slot that year.[341] She also assured board members that she was "quite open to having members of the Asian community join the production team" and that she "would welcome an Assistant Director or dramaturge." She added that she had already been in contact with members of the Asian community and "reported that no one has voiced any concerns to her."[342]

But there was an additional worry: none of the actors in the New Ideas production were Equity members, but six of the ten were ACTRA members and were "all in demand on television." Thom was to hold auditions for the others.[343] But as Alumnae attempted to adapt to a new Equity/ACTRA agreement in which ACTRA members were to be paid as Equity members (see chapter 8), they could no longer financially afford to cast ACTRA members in a workshop production that Thom felt required experienced performers to contribute to the presumably evolving script. Furthermore, Thom reported that the playwright did not want to workshop the play,[344] a concern echoed by executive producer PJ Hammond: "He definitely had his sights set bigger than us." Recalls Hammond, "And it was like, this isn't going to happen, we're not going to get a show out of this. So we cancelled it … I had to talk to a lot of people who said this is not going to work."[345]

Alumnae withdrew *Story of a Comfort Girl* just weeks before its run because it could not be cast with nine non-Equity Asian actors. A note in the program for the season's previous productions alerted patrons to the programming change: *Story of a Comfort Girl* would be replaced by *The Next Stage: Readings from the New Ideas Festival 2001*. The readings went on but reportedly had "attendance problems."[346] Rudick later published the work as a novel in 2012. More than forty years after Alumnae's world premiere of Williams's *To Ride a Tiger*, issues of ethnicity, authenticity, and staging had grown dramatically more salient. As with Alumnae's early improvisation experiment, the show did not go on.

In addition to the New Ideas Festival, Alumnae have done an extraordinary amount of new play development since the turn of the twenty-first century. In the early 2000s, the New Play Development (NPD) Group emerged within Alumnae, made up of "members who are playwrights, as well as a few who are interested in helping them."[347] They began meeting regularly to share and respond to one another's work, intending to eventually offer fully mounted shows. Initially, they hosted a forty-eight-hour playwriting challenge and selected several plays for reading; several of these were produced at the following New Ideas Festival. They also facilitated a monologue creation event with several group members. This initiative helped expand Alumnae's membership, particularly among playwrights and actors who "work sensitively with original material."[348] By Alumnae's centennial season, the NPD Group had about twelve members meeting monthly and was offering an annual Write Now weekend writing challenge, an annual non-juried readings event called Next Stage where ten new full-length plays by active Alumnae members were read, and the Big Ideas Festival where full-length plays were read and assessed with an eye for full production.[349] Then, after members expressed interest in a festival of full-length original plays,[350] in the fall of 2013, the FireWorks Festival emerged as an annual dramaturgical process and new play festival staged in the Studio. Plays are sometimes first tested in the New Ideas Festival or the NPD's Next Stage readings. Playwrights Shirley Barrie, Catherine Frid, and Chloë Whitehorn are among the women whose works have premiered at the FireWorks Festival. Now Alumnae run their FireWorks Festival in the fall and close their season in the spring with the New Ideas Festival, signalling that their commitment to new play production remains central to their purpose, with an impact on theatre in Toronto and beyond.

Chapter 8

"Pace-Setting and Ranging"[1]: A Nonprofessionalizing Theatre in the Professionalizing Era

[T]he activities of amateurs in the theatre have a serious side, and are not participated in merely in order to be sociable. Sociability does have a place in the amateur theatre, of course, and I do not wish to seem to slight the pleasure of working with generally congenial people who share one's interest and then of vocalizing interest and opinions over coffee and/or beer. Because we come to rehearsals and performance after a day's work, the element of relaxation and refreshment is a necessary one for us. In this, perhaps, we may have an advantage over professional working conditions which can sometimes seem not very adventurous or warm, but routine and even as cold as a summer theatre without a summer sun.[2]

– Francess Halpenny

On Saturday, 10 March 1928 an unaccredited *Telegram* review proclaimed that "last night's performance, though lacking the professional touch, lost little of the original sparkle." It referred to Alumnae's production of St. John Ervine's 1923 "witty and amusing comedy"[3] *Mary, Mary, Quite Contrary* at Hart House Theatre, which drew 752 people to three performances in two days. The review provides what may be the first use of the word "professional" to invoke a comparative value judgment against Alumnae. Notably, a (professional) Broadway[4] production of the play had toured to Toronto "some years ago."[5] Yet Alumnae's production had some "professional" attributes: They had paid Hart House Theatre's resident designer T. (Trevor) Tremain-Garstang $50 to design the set ($25 each for the Hinton Street garden and drawing room), and they had paid the director, the "much beloved"[6] "favourite"[7] Hart House Theatre actor H.E. Hitchman, $75. Although these payments obviously do not reconstitute Alumnae as a "professional" company, there was a professionalism to these actions that signalled a considered compensation for labour on the part of both Alumnae and Hart House Theatre. Those actions marked a key disruption of the static professional/nonprofessionalizing binary – a binary that was not uncommon at that time in that venue and is not unheard of today at many amateur theatres. Thus, if not backstage, where exactly was Alumnae's lack of "professional touch"? And why was it worth mentioning, apparently for the first time, for an Alumnae production?

The term "professional" took on various referents throughout Alumnae's first century. At the time of the *Telegram* review, the word best described foreign companies, like the Dublin Abbey Theatre Players and the Stratford-upon-Avon Festival players, that toured Canadian roadhouses, as well as a handful of resident stock companies who set up in

Toronto theatres for a season or so before disbanding.[8] Although Canadians like Tremain-Garstang occasionally found their way to professional Toronto stages (and backstages),[9] the companies that employed them were not locally formed and usually featured trained British and American artists as echoes of the theatre syndicate "star system" of the previous generation. It was in this context that *Mary, Mary, Quite Contrary* lacked the "professional touch" of touring foreign artists, some of whom produced modern plays similar to those that Alumnae produced at the time. Thus, the *Telegram*'s comment drew Alumnae's philanthropic goals into a modern age of theatre criticism. By comparing the quality of their production to that of professional groups, the review pulled Alumnae into a broader conversation about the value of the terms "professional" and "amateur" within a shifting theatre ecology.

Whereas one review might say a "professional touch" was lacking, others might say Alumnae compared favourably to professional productions. A year and a half after *Mary, Mary, Quite Contrary* ran, the *Varsity* called Alumnae "one of the most finished and expert amateur groups in the city" when they performed the Toronto premiere of A.A. Milne's 1924 reunion comedy *To Have the Honour*. Run in November 1930, the production was part of the university's annual homecoming festivities, which brought graduates back for the "annual struggle"[10] between the Queen's and U of T football teams. The game was followed by a recital featuring the recently erected carillon (partly funded by Alumnae's theatre productions), before the club fittingly performed *To Have the Honour*.[11] The *Globe* reviewer said the play "stood comparison very well" with one he had seen at the (professional) Liverpool Repertory Theatre in England. Still, the reviewer qualified his praise by citing the presence of one key amateurish trait: aside from "several lapses of memory, the cast acquitted itself with credit."[12]

Alumnae have navigated the professionalizing discourses of artists, critics, unions, and funding bodies in ways that have contributed greatly to their success and longevity. While faithfully remaining nonprofessionalizing, in the sense that members believe they should not give over their company to the theatre profession, their ongoing relationship with an emerging profession has always been as multifaceted as it is unavoidable. After the Second World War, the initial surge and steady growth of professional opportunities in theatre, radio, film, and television had a defining impact on Alumnae's membership. To parse their fraught relationship to the profession, this chapter examines several points of contact: DDF adjudicators' reflections on the "progress" of a "Canadian theatre," critical discourse in the press on the emerging profession and Alumnae's relationship to it, sporadic conflicts with professional companies, instances in which Alumnae have retained professional artists, dealings with the Canadian Actors' Equity Association, and challenging moments of self-reflection as membership and finances have been strained under theatre's professionalizing era.

Post-War Brushes with an Emerging Profession

The Dominion Drama Festival introduced a national network and annual schedule around which many of Canada's nonprofessionalizing theatres programmed their seasons. In 1933, along with the competitions themselves, the DDF and its regional feeder drama leagues began providing national and local encouragement for amateur groups through workshops and newsletters, while garnering front-page media attention for their member groups. Under the viceregal patronage of Governor General Lord Bessborough, the DDF intended to professionalize the country's theatre practices by nationalizing them through public competition, performance spectacle, and foreign (British and French colonial) adjudication. When the DDF dissolved into Theatre Canada in 1970, then closed completely in 1978, nonprofessionalizing groups were denied a nationwide platform. As DDF board member and participant playwright Robertson Davies brazenly observed, the DDF was an "artistic venture dedicated to destroying itself in the cause of art" in order to "bring about a better theatre, in the hands of professional artists, in which the amateurs would either have to relinquish their status, or go back to seats among the audience. This is what it achieved."[13] In Canada, unlike in the UK, nonprofessionalizing theatre ceased to be a national concern and was accepted instead merely as a localized phenomenon. However, many members of amateur companies who competed in the DDF did not "go back to seats among the audience" (although like their professional counterparts they were often also audience members); rather, like Alumnae, they continued producing ably in a nonprofessionalizing capacity.

The DDF's value in enabling affordable theatre outside of increasingly expensive professional ventures gained international attention. To open the 1951 DDF finals in London, Ontario, adjudicator Jose Ruben initiated a broad discussion about the value of nonprofessionalizing theatre practices when he addressed reporters:

> To me it is exciting … that tradesmen, lawyers, doctors, people who work hard all day, who are wobbling on their feet from fatigue, should be willing to come faithfully to rehearsals … The Little Theatre is our salvation; it is a school for both actor and public … The Little Theatre is independent; is not harnessed to huge financial interests … The production aspect is hopeless when to put on a play involves an investment of thousands of dollars.[14]

Throughout the festival, Ruben commented in a similar vein. "How vital are the efforts of the Little Theatre to the commercial theatre,"[15] he exclaimed while adjudicating on what the *London Free Press* termed the "greatest 'first night' in Canada's year."[16] He asserted the commonplace Latinate comparison that the only difference between professional and amateur was that one worked for money, the other for love.[17] On the final night of the festival, he returned to his theme: "Don't constantly underestimate your audiences as the commercial theatre does. Fresh materials interest audiences."[18] Fresh material would be a hallmark for Alumnae for years to come. Adding to Ruben's comments, the *London Free Press* ran an editorial situating the festival as a "matter of moment to the whole cultural scene in this country and across the border." The editorial also emphasized the challenges and sacrifices that nonprofessionalizing companies endured to compete nationally, saying this "vast movement" of "volunteer players, directors and stage crews" arrived "often at considerable personal cost in time and money."[19] This commitment to the craft, including its artistic and social aspects, publicly defined DDF competitors in Canadian newspapers. The comments made by Ruben and those printed in the *London Free Press* celebrated the idea and practice of nonprofessionalizing theatre in and of itself, not merely as a stepping stone or historic precursor to a profession.

From one decade to the next, newspapers normalized the idea of theatre beyond Broadway, the West End, and touring companies by putting the DDF competitions on the front pages of host-city and national papers. Local papers brimmed with photographs of festival participants dressed in their finery, stories of committee members who organized the festival at various stages, and interviews with actors, costumers, and other creative team members. The media also sought out those who had graced local stages in the past and now worked in professional theatre, film, and television, such as Hume Cronyn and Alexander Knox, both with London, Ontario, backgrounds relevant to the 1951 DDF finals. The DDF was an annual celebration of theatre and of those who practised it while "wobbling on their feet from fatigue" after their daily routines.

Theatre scholars have understood the mid-twentieth century as an era of converging and reactionary movements in Canada. Locally created theatre transitioned from the dominance of the amateur Little Theatre Movement and the amateur state-sponsored DDF to the dominance of the professional state-sponsored regional theatre movement and the professionalizing grassroots alternative theatre movement. Alan Filewod explains that this canonizing historical practice means that cyclically, theatre historians "rely on coherent movements to create the narrative structures of history and at the same time accept these movements as positive evidence of their narratives." But he rejects the connotation of a "historically coherent mass effort" in which movements "arise and disappear" like rock formations. Like Filewod, I see movements as "organizational strategies"[20] describing power structures that inform and result from the motivations of the practitioners, who respond to what came before. It is clear that Alumnae's members were well aware of how their own play programming informed, and responded to, the offerings of Toronto's emerging post-war professional companies. But movements also contain internal contradictions. Thus, although Alumnae shared the Little Theatre Movement's ethos of local education and experiment, they also troubled that movement by programming both popular and "alternative" plays; they remained adamantly "nonprofessionalizing" in operation, yet "professional" in outlook and approach; they were part of the Little Theatre Movement, yet they viewed their position in Toronto's theatre ecology more broadly.

During the 1950s and 1960s, Toronto theatre could not draw hard lines between its professional and nonprofessionalizing practices because many of its practitioners sought meaningful theatre experience wherever they could find it and whenever possible, regardless of pay. As a profession emerged, professionalizing companies sometimes sought to make connections with respected nonprofessionalizing companies like Alumnae, as when, at an October 1951 meeting, president Barbara Barnett read a letter from John Drainie of the barely one-month-old Jupiter Theatre asking "for any available actresses who would care to audition for them"[21] the next day; as Francis Jackson's minutes coyly recorded, "Needless to say, our 'stars' were at rehearsal that evening."[22] The next month, Barnett read another letter from the Jupiter Theatre announcing that they were offering courses in theatre make-up consisting of ten-and-a-half lessons for $20. Concurrently, executive member Marian Jones reported that she had received a "charming letter" from past Alumnae guest-turned-professional-artist Douglas Ney kindly "offering his services."[23] Emerging professionals sought to extract from, train, and offer talent to their nonprofessionalizing counterparts.

When the Stratford Festival opened on 13 July 1953 with Shakespeare's *Richard III*, followed by *All's Well That Ends Well*, it was a moment, Herbert Whittaker later noted, when "Canadian theatre took a major step into professionalism."[24] Importantly, nonprofessionalizing theatres contributed to that moment. When Tyrone Guthrie organized events the previous year to publicize the festival he had worked to found, Alumnae offered their support "immediately."[25] Of course, British luminaries Guthrie, Irene Worth, and Alec Guinness[26] were the main draws for the festival, but emerging Canadian talent appeared at Stratford that summer too. In fact, between the two inaugural casts playing under the famed tent appeared one woman and four men who had performed with Alumnae, among

Figure 8.1. *(left to right)* Eleanor Beecroft (Agatha Payne), Agatha Leonard (Lucy Amorest), and Barbara Barnett (May Beringer) in Alumnae's production of Rodney Ackland's *The Old Ladies* at Hart House Theatre in April 1954, directed by Robert Gill, with set design by Gill and Stanley Fillmore and costumes by Barbara McNabb, Nicky Fillmore, Marian Jones, and Margaret Tytler. Photo Credit: Robert Muckleston. Courtesy of Alumnae Theatre Company.

other companies, in the preceding decade. The sole former female Alumnae member acting in Stratford's first season was Beatrice Lennard, playing Diana in *All's Well* (she had acted with Alumnae in Thomas Job's *Thérèse* in 1950). The men were William Hutt as Brackenbury, Captain Blunt, and a French Minister of State in *All's Well* (he was in Wilde's *The Importance of Being Ernest* in 1950); William Needles as the First Murderer, Norfolk, and Renaldo (he had directed or acted in six recent Alumnae productions); Peter Mews as Bourchier, Exford, and a soldier in *All's Well* (he had appeared in Emerson's one-act *The Screen* for Alumnae in 1942); and Richard Easton as Vaughan and an extra in *All's Well* (he was fresh off his DDF success in Alumnae's *The Family Reunion* that year). Alumnae later celebrated Easton by noting that Guinness was so taken by his work at Stratford that he recommended him for further study in England before Easton toured with John Gielgud's company in *King Lear* and *Much Ado About Nothing*.[27]

Whittaker wrote extensively and with guarded optimism about the emergence of professional theatre groups during these years. Following Stratford's inaugural summer he found the "prospect of three professional companies" in Toronto to be "intriguing," wondering whether there was enough audience interest to support the new Crest Theatre in addition to the New Play Society and the Jupiter Theatre. He wrote that "every cultured person" thought the city should have this kind of activity, but the "chances are that three companies cannot exist side by side, each secure in a full subscription audience. But they can vie with each other for public attention, and healthy competition is an element which has been sadly lacking from the dramatic scene."[28] As an example of this growing competition, towards the end of the 1953–54 season, Whittaker noted that Alumnae's production of Rodney Ackland's *The Old Ladies* in April 1954 overlapped with the openings of Gershwin's *Porgy and Bess* at the Royal Alexandra and Eliot's *Murder in the Cathedral* at the Crest.[29] Borrowing from the DDF philosophy that competition breads improvement, Whittaker was applying this view to the profession.

A Fry Too Frequent

Despite these productive connections between professional and nonprofessionalizing groups, frictions also surfaced, especially around programming. At one point, the Crest Theatre, which would fold in 1966, was among other Toronto theatre companies that were making play programming a challenge because, as Molly Thom reported to Alumnae's executive, the Crest "kept rights tied up securely without making decisions."[30] As they do today, agents and play publishers often privileged professional companies over nonprofessionalizing companies when granting rights. But confusions can develop.

Perhaps the most telling example of Alumnae's relationship with Toronto's emerging theatre profession was the *Venus Observed* controversy, which pitted their production against that of Dora Mavor Moore's professionalizing New Play Society (NPS). In mid-September 1953,[31] Alumnae, the "prominent Little Theatre group,"[32] confirmed that they would open their season with the Toronto premiere of Christopher Fry's poetic 1950 autumnal comedy at Hart House Theatre in October 1953, directed by E.G. Sterndale Bennett.[33] Toronto's tastes in modern theatre were by then expanding beyond drawing room comedies, and Alumnae were part of this shift. T.S. Eliot had been popular the previous season, when Alumnae won the DDF finals' festival plaque for *The Family Reunion*; now Fry, the "most talked of English dramatist of this day,"[34] was *en vogue* too. Whittaker noted that the previous season had seen *The Lady's Not for Burning* produced at both the Museum Theatre and Hart House Theatre. Theatre-goers could also see *A Sleep of Prisoners* at St. Andrew's Church and *Ring Round the Moon* presented on campus by the Victoria College Drama Society.[35] By then, Ottawa's Canadian Repertory Company had produced *The Lady's Not for Burning* (in March 1953)[36] and another Ottawa company had produced *Venus Observed* (that April).[37] Ottawa Little Theatre would produce *A Phoenix Too Frequent* in their 1954–55 season.[38] This popularity had been sparked by a collection of Fry's plays published in early 1953 by W.H. Smith & Son and advertised and discussed in the daily papers.[39] In the 1953–54 season, Alumnae and NPS would produce Fry's *Venus Observed* back to back, and NPS's production would run at the same time as Jupiter Theatre's *Ring Round the Moon* at the Royal Alexandra. And previously, Hart House Theatre had produced Fry's *Boy with Cart* and *A Phoenix Too Frequent*, and *Thor with Angels* had seen a Toronto production as well. Whittaker jested, "What this town would seem to need are some more plays by Fry."[40]

It is worth tracing the path that led to Alumnae and NPS's *Venus Observed* duplication in order to delineate the parallel production conditions experienced by nonprofessionalizing and professional companies at the time. Paula Sperdakos concludes that Dora Mavor Moore did not learn that Alumnae also had the rights to the play until "well into NPS's rehearsals" that fall, at which point there was no turning back. Sperdakos explains that NPS originally secured the rights to *Ring Round the Moon* for a two-week slot starting 19 October 1953, even though Jupiter Theatre had secured the rights for the same play in that same slot. Moore had gone through the play's licensing company, whereas Jupiter had gone through the playwright's agent, and both professional companies had received the go-ahead. After some antagonism and expense,[41] and having already secured the venue, NPS decided to produce *Venus Observed* instead of *Ring Around the Moon*, in the same slot.[42] NPS was apparently unaware that Alumnae was producing *Venus Observed* in October too, even though Alumnae's season announcement had appeared in the *Globe and Mail* on the same day in September, and on the same page, as the announcement of NPS's production.[43] The public were catching on that there would be two productions of the same play by two respected Toronto companies, one nonprofessionalizing and one professional, in tandem with Juniper's production of a play by the same playwright, all within a week of one another.

Because Alumnae's production was first (and Toronto's first), it drew most of the Fry-related advance press. Whittaker navigated this situation with lines like, "But it is true that another group is doing *Ring Around the Moon* (for that matter another group is doing *Venus Observed*) at the same time that [director] Mr. [Guy] Verney and the New Play Society are exhibiting their *Venus Observed* … But we're not going to mention that other group right now for fear of further confusion."[44] Furthering the confusion, advertisements for NPS's production appeared in the papers before Alumnae's run.[45] When the week arrived for Whittaker to review NPS's *Venus Observed* and Jupiter's *Ring around the Moon* with the same opening night, he chose Jupiter's production because it was at the Royal Alexandra, a "professional house,"[46] whereas NPS's production was at the rented Museum Theatre.

But how did Alumnae's *Venus Observed* come to be? The idea of producing *Venus Observed* had been discussed at an Alumnae meeting two years earlier, in August 1951.[47] Alumnae president Barbara Barnett had tried to secure the rights, but they were unavailable because Laurence Olivier, who had commissioned the play from Fry and had directed and starred in its London premiere, was "expected to do it in New York."[48] The idea resurfaced again at a March 1953 meeting, but because only nine members were in attendance, "no decision was made beyond trying to get the rights for it in case we wanted it." However, as reported, having three copies on hand they moved on to "reading parts of the play and discussing it over coffee and pickled onions."[49] At the next meeting, it was reported that the rights for "non-professional groups" were unavailable. They immediately struck a new reading committee with Ruth Norris as chairperson to choose a director and a fall play they could also perform at the DDF regional festival in January.[50] Then in May, it was reported that the rights for *Venus Observed* had been released to Alumnae and "it was thought that this would be an excellent drawing card." The question of who would direct it was "discussed but not solved."[51] In June, Christina Templeton again reported the "all clear"[52] for the play's rights. In July, in a notice evidently missed by Moore (possibly because she was deeply involved in supporting the Stratford Festival's inaugural season that summer[53]), the *Globe and Mail* reported that the "rights to Christopher Fry's play, *Venus Observed*, have been secured by the University Alumnae Dramatic Society … Winners of this year's Central Ontario Drama Festival, the club will stage the play at Hart House Theatre on Oct. 12–15."[54] However "inadvertently,"[55] controversy ensued when NPS, "revived after two years' absence"[56] from producing a full season of plays, obtained the professional rights to *Venus Observed* for a two-week run starting the week after Alumnae's run. Moore told Whittaker that the duplication was a "disastrous experience."[57] Whittaker observed that amateur and stock companies producing in the city "draw on the same audience and limit the NPS choice."[58]

For Alumnae, there was also the question of location. Hart House Theatre informed Alumnae in February 1953 that the only dates available to them in the fall would be the week of 12 October, although it could not run on Friday or Saturday because UC had booked both evenings for its centennial celebrations.[59] Alumnae, on Margaret Tytler's suggestion, considered approaching UC about making an Alumnae show part of the festivities; however, it was decided in June 1953 not to pursue this.[60] Instead, they booked Hart House Theatre for a run earlier in the week (Tuesday through Thursday).

Alumnae's decision to produce *Venus Observed* was noteworthy, although not at all unusual, in that the play has more male roles than female roles. The press noted that those four female roles were "strong individualistic roles."[61] Pamela Terry, who had recently graduated from Sterndale Bennett's Canadian Theatre School, played the female lead Perpetua in her first show with Alumnae.[62] Reviews were mixed. Rose MacDonald reported that it opened a "little heavily and uncertainly, then consistently gained momentum."[63] The *Varsity*'s reviewer said the production was "enjoyable although it failed to capture all the fantasy of which the play is capable, mainly, I think because [of] the fact that the actors were frequently both inaudible and partially invisible, [which] blurred the brilliant adages of Fry's poetry."[64] Whittaker observed that in performing the play, in which phrases "hang in the mind like jewels," they needed to "uncover more of this brightness." He concluded that the production was "quite well cast, sensitively staged, nicely decorated and charmingly lit."[65] Terry was "gracefully winsome, achieving tenderness in her quiet moments and lightness in her gay ones,"[66] although she was "not quite as vivid as we thought she might be." Marian Jones, Francess Halpenny, and Ruth James "acquitted themselves gracefully."[67] Halpenny in particular was "warmly delightful"[68] and "played with clarity of intention."[69] But Sterndale Bennett needed to give the cast "one little more push and we'll enjoy it more."[70]

The costumes, created by Elizabeth Gray and several other Alumnae members in the games room of Gray's home, were described in a *Globe and Mail* feature. Most of the play's dresses were "cut from costumes used in previous presentations" with the costumers showing "remarkable imagination, skill and ingenuity both in the dyeing and recutting." The four women wore "cleverly designed clothes in lovely blending autumn shades." The designs and colours were inspired by the "autumnal" mood of the play as well as by the "floor-length modern dress"[71] of Stratford's recent *All's Well That Ends Well*.

Comparisons between the two productions of *Venus Observed* were inevitable. Sperdakos wrote that Moore "maintained that the Alumnae production was so bad that word of mouth kept theatre-goers away from her show, but it is possible that Toronto audiences had simply had enough of Fry." (The latter point, at least, was almost certainly valid. Halpenny told Sperdakos that ultimately, neither group should have produced the play.[72]) Here, Moore was hinting at the common sentiment that a professional production is more valuable than a nonprofessionalizing production and that if a choice ought to be made, the professional one should be favoured. But this was clearly not the case with *Venus Observed*. Alumnae received mixed reviews, whereas NPS was thoroughly panned in the *Varsity* for director Guy Verney's decision to modernize it, as well as for the performances. In her *Varsity* review, witheringly titled "More astronomy,"[73] Nancy S. Donnell called NPS's production "musical hall entertainment" where it should have been "poetic drama,"[74] adding that they worked (as they had before[75]) "under the unhappy conditions of the Museum Theatre's minute stage, which scarcely left them room to be impressive." NPS's actors delivered "every word of [the play] in prose" instead of poetry, and their appearance was "no more poetic than their speech." Because the characters were made to seem so "probable" in their twentieth-century costumes and "stance," Fry's jokes "became a puzzle instead of delight."[76] NPS lost $3,225 on their production, and for this, and for Alumnae's preceeding production, Moore blamed the director.[77] For their production, Alumnae's two Theatre Nights did well, but they reported poor ticket sales for their "own" night, with only 322 tickets sold.[78] Ultimately, *Venus Observed* was an "expensive show"[79] for Alumnae, earning only $93.42. The two productions surely pulled audiences away from each other.

As coda, as if three weeks of *Venus Observed* by two companies were not enough, Alumnae booked the production to run on 6 November 1953 at the newly opened Central Technical School theatre because the UCAA wanted a Theatre Night to raise money for scholarships.[80] For those unaware of the timeline, it may have seemed curious that Alumnae had booked two productions on either side of the NPS showing of the same play. Fortunately, the show's producer, Eileen Williams, reported to the executive that Sterndale Bennett had made some changes to the show.[81] This extraordinary few weeks of Fry ended with Mona Purser writing in her *Globe and Mail* column that Ted Scott, playing the boy in Alumnae's production, had to catch a train to Sudbury as he was cast in the Earle Grey Shakespearean Festival Company's *As You Like It* the next day.[82]

Funding a Few

The relationship between nonprofessionalizing theatre companies and their professionalizing counterparts was intensifying, due in part to several top-down government and arm's-length initiatives. The post-war emergence of professionalization and a golden age of festival competition were being spurred by the Royal Commission on National Development in the Arts, Letters, and Sciences, colloquially known as the Massey Commission, whose findings exposed the harsh realities facing those who sought to make a living in the theatre and whose efforts to address those realities contributed to enthusiasm for theatre's role in an emerging nation. Theatre was, in Whittaker's words, fighting an "economic struggle for existence." He articulated this struggle when, in March 1955, the Ontario government announced that it would exempt theatre companies from the provincial tax: "Now, at least, theatre people in this Province feel that their hard work to establish the drama here is not being opposed by the representatives of the Government but rather healthily approved and supported." This "fine gesture of enlightenment"[83] in Ontario amounted to more than just verbal encouragement; it provided some real relief. But it also exposed the bleak conditions that confronted professionalizing arts groups, which increasingly disparaged nonprofessionalizing groups like Alumnae because the latter did not seem to be sharing in the same struggle.

The federal government moved to support professional theatre at the national level as well. In 1957, the Canada Council for the Arts was founded as a means to give professional Canadian arts and culture a top-down, state-sponsored boost. As Mark Czarnecki explains, for theatre the council focused on creating large, multipurpose professional companies in each region of the country, following the example set by John Hirsch and Tom Hendry's Manitoba Theatre Centre in 1958. It then established financial incentives for these regional theatres to follow the "three C's"[84] of programming – classic, contemporary, and Canadian – through subscription-based season planning. But the effect was to lessen the likelihood that any Canadian, untried, or otherwise "experimental" play would be programmed.[85]

Adventuresome play programmers like Alumnae now became even more indispensable as the regional theatres stayed relatively conservative in their programming.

The founding of the Canada Council was a double-edged sword for groups like Alumnae. As Maria Tippett notes, the council's focus on supporting "professional" artistic practices meant that the amateur groups that had been "central figures" in the cultural conversation to that point were now "occupying a distinctly indifferent position." They had been "transformed," at least officially, "into consumers, rather than producers, of culture."[86] Professionalizing voices often weaponized this transformation to marginalize nonprofessionalizing artists. But this did not take into account, for example, that Alumnae programmed the three C's much more consistently than the regionals. Increasingly, whenever professional practices could be nurtured, there was a decline in positive commentary about nonprofessionalizing practices. The content and programming of the regionals was, with few exceptions, conservative and predictable for the first few decades of the Canada Council era as professional groups sought to ensure successful bottom lines in order to receive operating grants.

Sometimes it seemed as though the emerging profession negatively affected the quality of work done by nonprofessionalzing groups. When the 1956 DDF regional adjudicator Pamela Sterling remarked on her disappointment with the overall quality of Toronto's offerings, Whittaker, speaking from experience, suggested that it is "difficult not to relate the decline in the festival with the rise of the professional theatre." A major purpose of the DDF was to spawn professional theatre in Canada, and that plan was well enough on its way that talent was already draining away from DDF competitions and into professional ventures in Toronto. Whittaker noted that Canada was using its festival to professionalize, whereas in England, the "only other English-speaking country where drama festivals abound," there were more artists who were "unmistakably and proudly amateurs," and content to be so. According to Whittaker, the DDF eventually did not prevent those identifying as professional from competing because, in Canada,

> the difference is often infinitesimal and the one aspect of theatre still needs the other. But actors, newly "professional," often find it necessary to repudiate their amateur connections to prove their position.
>
> Perhaps this is what is happening to Toronto, that the better trained players can't and won't work in the festival now. As there is a tradition here that nobody is paid for a festival show (a tradition that doesn't exist in Montreal, for instance) this is quite understandable. All an actor can gain is a chance to do a role that he may never get on radio, in television or at one of the local legitimate houses. And to work on it long and hard.
>
> If that is what's happening here, the festival must accept the achievements it has so long worked toward, and go on with its business of being a training ground.

Allowing professional companies to compete, as the DDF's regional arm did in Montreal, gave actors, particularly those in radio, the chance to improve their live performance skills[87] even as it muddied the distinctions between "professional" and "amateur."

Critical Discourses on Professionalization

Herbert Whittaker opened his discussion of the forthcoming 1954–55 Toronto theatre season with a provocation: "Does [the] professional theatre flourish at the expense of the amateur theatre, which for so long held the fort in Canadian theatre? From the look of the advance schedule put forth by the Central Ontario Drama League this week, it does not."[88] He expressed concern that several Toronto-area nonprofessionalizing groups had chosen not to participate in the 1955 CODL festival. Given that more Canadian content was being presented by professionalizing companies, there might have been some worry that nonprofessionalizing theatre was in decline. But Whittaker went on to list the 1954–55 season of shows in the Toronto area, in effect celebrating the city's variety of fare. He ended by noting that Leonard Crainford, the former business manager of the Jupiter Theatre (which had dissolved in the winter of 1954[89]), was holding a CODL-sponsored course on directing starting on 5 October, "a move which can only be commended highly, proving as it does that the non-professional theatre is also aware of its responsibilities."[90] Like Urjo Kareda's discursive mythologies on Toronto's professionalizing alternative theatre companies in the 1970s, Whittaker's and Cohen's commentaries on resourceful nonprofessionalizing groups like Alumnae, and emerging professionalizing groups like NPS, Jupiter, and Crest, at once described and prescribed, for a generation of theatre-makers and theatre-goers, a perspective of contestation between nonprofessionalizing and professional theatre practices that has not been abandoned.

As was evident in Dora Mavor Moore's assessment of Alumnae when they produced the same play as her company, the post-war founding of a handful of professional groups changed the discourse surrounding the value of nonprofessionalizing companies. This was particularly notable among critics. Colin Sabiston in the *Globe and Mail* provided an early sign of this shift in tone in November 1947. Perhaps revealing a personal agenda to professionalize the post-war Toronto theatre scene, Sabiston wrote of the divide between nonprofessionalizing practices and commercial professionalized practices, saying that the "bane of amateurism, both that which is merely ambitious and that which seeks differentiation from the commercial theatre, too often is a descent into vulgarity, the former through not knowing, the latter by indulging in 'refrainments' instead of those refinements of technique which pertain to theatre and have no substitutes."[91] These harsh sentiments were relatively new to Toronto theatre, at least in print.

Seven years later, an anti-amateur distain had settled in among some critics. In a review of Alumnae's October 1954 production of Paul Dehn's new, "radically pruned,"[92] three-act adaptation of Oscar Wilde's 1893 comedy of morals *A Woman of No Importance*, Malcolm MacKinnon sweepingly declared on *CJBC* radio that "it is useless to instruct an amateur in intricate figures until he can follow a straight line. Most of [director Leonard] Crainford's cast need basic instruction in fundamental things like phrasing, stance and movement."[93] Moreover, MacKinnon challenged Alumnae's play selection and their nonprofessionalizing status in his review:

> No one expects the Alumnae Club to present a performance of professional caliber – although they have done so in *The Family Reunion* and *In Good King Charles's Golden Days*. But there is no good reason to attempt so difficult and unrewarding a play as *A Woman of No Importance* unless a group feels it has something definite to contribute – a new interpretation, an understanding of the style, or even particularly suitable players for the leading roles. The Alumnae group began with none of these and found but little in their rehearsals.[94]

In terms of intention and novelty, MacKinnon overlooked Alumnae's interest in producing Dehn's fresh version of the play, instead blaming his dislike of the production on his generalized notion of amateur theatre. Alumnae's program argued that in Dehn's much-distilled iteration, which featured, among its changes, a revised ending, the "best has been retained and most of the worst eliminated."

Dehn's adaptation of *A Woman of No Importance*, about an "illegitimate son accidentally bringing his long-separated mother and father into a meeting,"[95] had had a "successful"[96] run in London. However, while some reviewers thought it was the right thing for Alumnae to attempt the play, owing to the play's weaknesses there was little hope of success. Having seen the London production at the Savoy Theatre a "little more than a year ago," Jack Karr reported that it was "one of the handsomest plays we'd ever seen and one of the least interesting." Alumnae's production had not given him "much more enthusiasm for Mr. Wilde's simpering comedy-drama."[97] Whittaker agreed, saying that it had been "improved by surgery. Although not enough, perhaps."[98] MacDonald argued that it may be "said to be a play of no importance,"[99] although Alumnae "merit appreciation for showing us this so rarely-done play and thus enlarging local knowledge of Wilde's acted work."[100] For Nancy S. Donnell in the *Varsity*, that Alumnae "tackled it is good proof of their optimism; that they failed is equally good proof that even Homer nods. The difference in tedium between dialogues on the values of irresponsibility and monologues on the rewards of virtue is less than I had always imagined."[101] These general comments on Alumnae's production suggest that despite MacKinnon's sentiments, it was not Alumnae's nonprofessionalizing status *per se* that resulted in a weak performance, but rather the play itself. From around the end of 1959 on, Whittaker often reviewed Alumnae's plays near the end of their runs to prioritize his time for professional companies, but also to give Alumnae's cast and crew time to iron out early-run foibles.

But even as critics increasingly altered their language, Alumnae often fared well, particularly with regard to play selection. For example, Cohen concluded his review of their June 1959 Canadian premiere of James Merrill's "science fantasy of a sort," *The Immortal Husband*, by saying that it

> confirms that this fine company is an excellent test-tube for beginning and new actors in Toronto, and that it can be relied on for an unfailingly interesting program of plays. The UADC has the best amateur virtues – a love of theatre, a high and scrupulous standard of production and performance, and a genuine willingness to explore what's best in the theatre, both old and new. Would that we had more like it.[102]

Even when the quality of Alumnae's performances fell short, Toronto relied on their programming virtues. Moreover, a month earlier, when Alumnae produced, according to their advertising, an "evening of comedy and hocus pocus" with Ben Jonson's 1610 play *The Alchemist* in March 1959, Cohen was pleased that a work by Jonson was being staged in Toronto. Reviewing the play both in the *Star* and on *CJBC Views the Shows*, he was quick to note that these were "amateurs" "doing it with enthusiasm, intelligence and dramatic flair" and that Pamela Terry's direction revealed a "complete grasp of the theme. Within the crowded space of the club stage on the second floor of a Bedford Rd. factory, Jonson's fantastic-realistic fools and rascals enact their revels in spirited and carefully-managed fashion."[103] He concluded that "it is amateur theatre at its best, and in the best sense."[104] Whittaker agreed, noting that the "university is particularly interested in the production of the play which is on a number of undergraduate courses,"[105] adding that Jonson, "once literary dictator of London, has fallen into a long neglect. So we are (once again) grateful to the University Alumnae for reviving his rude and wiry satire."[106] Molly Golby's costumes were "marked by a good sense of period and witty intention."[107] Alumnae were professional in their astute programming choices, even if they were not a "professional" company. Reviewers' language routinely placed Alumnae above the city's other nonprofessionalizing companies, but only occasionally could they aspire to the professional standard set by the emerging discourse of professionalization.

An October 1960 piece by Whittaker continued the public conversation about professionalization. Titled "Remember amateurs? They're still around," he updated his readers on the state of professionalization in the city's theatre ecology. He suggested that "we are not so dependent on the amateur," but "we must not forget our old friends, for they have still many prizes for us. They can still venture, if they will, into fields where the commercial do not dare."[108] Whittaker's public voice was integral to framing Alumnae as more venturesome than Toronto's professional theatre companies. His argument allowed him to celebrate the emergence of professional theatre in Toronto while also celebrating experimentation and thoughtful programming. Likewise, while introducing the 1965–66 theatre season, Cohen wrote that the Coach House Theatre was

> the only place in the city where theatre-goers are steadily reminded of the larger purpose of the dramatic art.
>
> Here is an organization which is amateur in the exceptional and best sense, high in its production goals, pace-setting and ranging in its program. It provides a continuing opportunity to meet and appreciate the playwrights, modern and classical, whom our other companies will not or dare not or cannot perform – the Pinters and Becketts and Frisches, the Jonsons and Congreves and Websters. I have never gone to anything done by the group, contemporary, original, or traditional, and felt the evening totally wasted, however unsatisfactory the show turned out to be. I have never missed one of its shows without being aware that I have lost out in my theatrical education.[109]

Cohen's praise was as much a dare to the professional companies as an approval of Alumnae. In a sense, Cohen was using Alumnae to chide professional theatres for their overly cautious programming. Thus, when Cohen was not pleased with Alumnae's November 1965 production of William Congreve's *Love for Love*, he noted that Congreve's language was so difficult that "our professionals cannot do it. Why then demand it of our amateurs, however superior their aspirations?"[110] In Alumnae's hands, he said, there was no hint of an "intelligent and sympathetic rendering of the play's comic spirit."[111] Similarly, Whittaker agreed that Alumnae's efforts were not equal to those of past work, although he added that it was a "better representation of Congreve than most persons will get in the classroom or library."[112]

As DDF competitions faded into Theatre Canada, the 1970s saw a broad redefinition of the spirit and practice of theatre in the country. In his last month with the *Globe and Mail* in September 1975, channelling the participatory ethos that had characterized his commentary over the years, Whittaker asked, "Whatever happened to Little Theatre? It flourishes as ever, only its light doesn't shine so much these days from under the bushel of professional and semi-professional theatre that's landed on the Toronto scene in recent seasons. But not only Actors' Equity members like to act."[113] He warned that it was "still not advisable to draw any bold divisions" between professional and nonprofessionalizing practices, "despite the valiant efforts of a great many people to make the difference clear." He asked the provocative question, "In what other country, for instance, has management conspired to

Figure 8.2. (*left to right*) James Mainprize (Subtle), Patricia Carroll Browne (Dol Common) and Michael Tait (Face) in Alumnae's production of Ben Johnson's 1610 comedy *The Alchemist*, directed by Pamela Terry at Alumnae's Bedford Road Coach House in March 1959. Courtesy of Alumnae Theatre Company.

establish unions to prove professionalism?" He noted that although the nonprofessionalizing Toronto Truck Theatre had just lost the use of the Colonnade to the Actors Repertory group made up of Equity members, they were moving to Heliconian Hall. Moreover, the Central Library was opening a new season featuring Ionesco and Pinter plays, curiously resembling Alumnae's Coach House Theatre programming fifteen years earlier.[114] Professional companies were finally managing to produce plays that had gained Alumnae local, and sometimes national accolades.

In the late 1970s, a new set of Toronto critics began to articulate a redefined theatre ecology featuring a profession at its centre and nonprofessionalizing companies like Alumnae on the periphery. As Whittaker had warned years earlier, certainly the emerging profession threatened to drain the best artists from the nonprofessionalizing theatre companies. But the new reviewers no longer spoke about nonprofessionalizing theatre as inherently progressive and valuable, as Cohen, Whittaker, and Kareda had done so eloquently. When Whittaker retired and the *Globe and Mail*'s dance critic John Fraser took over as theatre critic, he quickly signalled that he was less willing than his predecessor to forgive the quality of a rare or previously unseen production. Fraser flatly dismissed Molly Thom's direction of Aphra Behn's rarely produced comedy *The Rover* in the spring of 1976, writing,

"Alas, but then most Restoration plots have left me perplexed … The plot progresses as knight's moves and, in any event, is largely irrelevant." In fact, Alumnae produced far fewer period pieces after Whittaker's departure from the *Globe and Mail*. In his review of John Guare's 1971 comedy *The House of Blue Leaves*, produced a month after *The Rover*, Fraser slightly altered his perspective on Alumnae by adding an element of "forgiveness," almost gratuitously. He differentiated the "solid professionalism"[115] of Equity member James B. Douglas and the "small parts handed out to highly enthusiastic and recently recruited thespians who have hardly a clue what to do on stage. The mix is inevitably disconcerting, but one comes to the firehall armed against it and fully prepared to forgive all if the production is interesting, which this one certainly is." But he concluded that Alumnae were "having a harder and harder time keeping this important theatre afloat. As a final production [of the season], *The House of Blue Leaves* is greatly to its credit."[116] It was as though Fraser was implicitly perceiving a disconnect between the impressive Firehall Theatre and Alumnae's nonprofessionalizing status. Readers could hardly miss the disconnect between Fraser's and Whittaker's views of nonprofessionalizing theatre.

The following fall, Fraser wrote of Alumnae's production of Agatha Christie's *Murder on the Nile*, directed by Pamela Terry, that Christie "can make an amusing evening of theatre that continues to sell well (especially good when you have problems getting people in the first place)." The programming choice disappointed Fraser, who concluded that "something as insubstantial and mediocre as this play is a departure for this admirable and venerable theatrical institution which has done so much to bring new drama to Toronto."[117] Similarly, four months later in his review of Alumnae's next mainstage production, Lillian Helman's 1934 drama *The Children's Hour*, Fraser wrote: "It was done with sincerity, which counts for something, and you get Lillian Hellman's gist, which counts for a lot more. Maybe that's all we can expect from the Firehall Theatre right now, but that doesn't sit very well with all the accomplishments of the past. C'mon guys! You can do better, I know you can."[118] Fraser's patronizing prose in calling out Alumnae's turn towards commercial fare surely began to wear on the experienced company, especially since he was left "perplexed" by uncommon period fare. Alumnae were increasingly stuck between their celebrated reputation for programming and an emerging narrative that nonprofessionalizing practice was a relic of the past. By 1977, the illustrious Alumnae were being referred to by Bryan Johnson in the *Globe and Mail* as "chronically uneven,"[119] without a hint of historical context.

Meanwhile, Gina Mallet arrived from New York to become the *Star*'s theatre critic after Urjo Kareda left the paper to become Robin Phillips's literary manager at the Stratford Festival. She opened her review of *The House of Blue Leaves* by saying that "comedy is not really fun, laughs and a nice warm feeling round the heart. On the contrary, it is ruthless, cruel and draining – at least the very best of it is." She expressed enthusiasm for Guare's play but determined that although Alumnae were "brave to choose to do it … the players are continually hampered by that plague of amateurs – a lack of pace."[120] And the following season, upon reviewing Alumnae's production of Arthur Wing Pinero's Victorian farce *The Schoolmistress*, Mallet concluded that Alumnae needed to "find the right context in which to present plays at this time."[121] In calling out Alumnae for drifting into fare that was either too commercial or, in her opinion, irrelevant, Mallet further drove in the wedge between professional and nonprofessionalizing theatre. From then on, rare was a review that missed noting that Alumnae were amateurs who could not be reviewed through the same lens as professionals.

This language was spreading. Even the student-run *Varsity*, so closely knit to Alumnae's origins, yet by definition a newspaper with a high turnover of writers, took up the discourse of "amateur" as the defining descriptor of Alumnae. In the fall of 1976, Jennifer Martin, reviewing *Murder on the Nile*, prepared her *Varsity* reader for her uncommon critical voice, even if arriving at the same conclusion:

> I've done enough non-union shows in Toronto to have developed a tolerant amusement toward reviewers from University newspapers. [They] would sometimes sum up all our weeks of effort with a wave of a hand and a cavalier phrase like "youthful exuberance." Worst of all was the dreaded adjective, "amateurish." To most people, amateurish reeks of tackiness and of high school so I would like to preface my comments about the Toronto Dramatic Alumnae's [*sic*] production of Agatha Christie's *Murder on the Nile* with an explanation.
>
> I see the essential difference between amateur theatre and professional theatre as being a matter of detail. Ideally, professional theatre is clean and polished while amateur theatre is careless and patchy.

She proceeded to note that Kay Griffin "wore the best costumes on the stage," that "Margaret Milne was a "lovely and competent actress," and that Robert Miller's sound design "created some wonderful atmosphere with his music and sound effects, but he should check volumes. The set and props were fine and had potential but were not finished properly. The faded and patchy walls in the observation gallery of the boat were an obvious paint job." She concluded that a "group of very talented people have pooled their wits and their resources, have not taken care of a lot of small details and have come up with exactly what I was writing about earlier – an amateurish production."[122] Following an occupation-bending preface and amid these and other "amateurish" vagaries, Martin fell into noting the same nonprofessionalizing stereotypes that were becoming the norm.

Two years later, when R. Read reviewed in the *Varsity* Molly Thom's second time directing Farquhar's Restoration comedy *The Beaux' Stratagem* for Alumnae, he described a performance aesthetic in which "Some of the actors (necessarily the males) may be professionals or aspiring such, but the actual production, the design, the direction, the delivery, has that theatre-in-your-spare-time enthusiasm." Moreover, the principal actors apparently "repeat entire sentences whenever they stumble on a word or forget a vowel sound."[123] Asta Baskevicius's *Varsity* review of Thom's direction of Tom Stoppard's *The Real Inspector Hound* and *After Magritte* in spring 1977 said of Alumnae that the "organization is prone to self-indulgent directing and extreme acting," although the "facial grimaces were kept under control after a shaky start." This further suggested that the era's critical discourse had congealed around Alumnae's nonprofessionalizing practice as a lost cause where quality was concerned. As if to expose this automaton reaction, at the end of the review Baskevicius celebrated the "detailed, highly directed acting" of the leads "backed by a strong cast." And, "as usual with UADC productions, costuming is thorough and sets well-done."[124]

Marigold Charlesworth and Her *Three Sisters*

To this day, like many nonprofessionalizing theatre companies, Alumnae occasionally pays guest professional directors, a move that continues to problematize the professional/amateur binary, particularly in the eyes of reviewers. In the fall of 1966, Alumnae staged *Three Sisters*, Anton Chekhov's 1901 "moving portrayal of provincial desires and frustrations," making use of a DDF grant that paid the influential Charlesworth to direct the production and design the lighting under the Ontario Arts Council (OAC) Training Plan, which sent at least nine theatre professionals to work with community theatres to give classes, hold seminars, and direct plays under a total budget of $30,000.[125] The use of a professional director by a nonprofessionalizing company in effect provides a crucible for gauging public sentiments around professionalizing and nonprofessionalizing practices. There was some nervousness among Alumnae members: it took some time for them to learn who the director was going to be, but when word came in mid-August that it would be Charlesworth, they reported that "fortunately"[126] she was happy with Alumnae's choice of play. The casting notice advertised the play as an "actor's dream," with an "excellent director and some of the best parts that have ever been written." Having resigned from the Canadian Players, where she had given Toronto "some of our finest theatre last season,"[127] Charlesworth was presently without a professional home. With the Canadian Players on hiatus and the Crest Theatre on the brink of collapse, questions were arising in the mid-1960s about the sustainability of professional theatre in Toronto.[128]

Some reviews of Alumnae's production of *Three Sisters* slighted the "amateur actors"[129] while simultaneously commending Charlesworth's professional direction. Even Whittaker, Alumnae's great cheerleader, slipped towards this professional distinction, writing that "Miss Charlesworth is a good enough director to manipulate her University Alumnae actors fairly logically across the little platform."[130] Cohen slipped even further. For him, the production "seldom conveys the sustained double dimensions of tears and laughter simultaneously experienced by its characters and the audience. On the other hand, as directed by Marigold Charlesworth, the production is consistently sympathetic to the Chekhov spirit and to the evocation of the right atmosphere." Where the actors did not find the style, Charlesworth found consistency and atmosphere. All of this points to the decade's emerging preoccupation with defining "professional" against "amateur." Playing the two off each other while allowing the contradictions to linger, as when the amateur actors miss the style while the professional director finds the spirit and atmosphere, was becoming standard shorthand in critical discourse. Thus, Cohen's assessment of the actors was lukewarm: Don Bryn was "substantially convincing," Patricia Grant had the "outline of a satisfactory characterization," and Janet Gladdis was "touching"; overall, despite the "weakness of most of the acting, the play holds."[131] Ron Evans's assessment in the *Telegram* was more divided: Charlesworth "makes a marvelous try at it with a company of earnest tyros," while she

> struggles to recreate … the pre-revolutionary Russian bourgeoisie, if not through the limited expression of her players, at least through the mechanics of authentic setting, [costumes, music, sound, and] sensitive lighting. And there she achieves really astounding success considering the resources at hand … But ultimately the success of production must rest on the quality of individual performances and that's where all efforts go awry."

Thus, although Evans applauded Charlesworth for her casting choices of the three sisters, who were "of striking resemblance; being all fairly tall, gaunt and devitalized," he faulted the actors' "aptitude" in the roles. He then left knowledge of Alumnae behind, declaring that the sisters, played by Elizabeth Mascall, Margaret Hogarth, and Janet Gladish, "understandably, with their underdeveloped skills and lack of time and opportunity for real study … can come no closer than nodding distance to these so specific ladies from a time and place light-years outside their ken."[132] It would, of course, be impossible to accuse Alumnae president Mascall of lacking experience in the way Evans recites; Hogarth, while away from Toronto for eight years, had studied with the renowned French instructor Étienne

Decroux; and Gladish had been an assistant stage manager at the Shaw Festival the previous summer, according to a company press release. Moreover, Patricia Grant, as Natasha, was a graduate of London's Central School of Speech and Drama and had played at the Red Barn at Jackson's Point the summer before. There were many professional credits attached to the ensemble's names, for those counting, leaving one to search for accuracy in Evans's argument. Here the critic, in seeking to make sense of a mixed production, reductively bestowed its successes on the professional director and its shortcomings of the amateur performers.

But Urjo Kareda, now lead theatre critic in his second year with the *Varsity* (a few years before leaving for England to pursue a doctorate focused on Chekhov and the theatre of the absurd), evidently saw through the transparent professional distinction clung to by Whittaker, Cohen, and Evans. Although he agreed that an "autumnal sadness is to be felt both outside and inside the Coach House Theatre," he attributed *Three Sisters*' failure that fall to Charlesworth's "series of misjudgments. The play's tempo is erratically grasped, and the fluidity of emotional expression is not always clear." Moreover, Charlesworth "miscast, by reason of age, physique or dramatic ability," her actors and "misjudged her theatre" by having her actors "overact and overproject."[133] Kareda neither pandered to professionalization nor blamed nonprofessionalization for the production's failure. Whether it was Alumnae or Charlesworth that failed Chekhov's writing, the production clearly did not succeed artistically in the eyes of the critics. Nevertheless, Alumnae declared in a subsequent press release that *Three Sisters* played to 84 per cent houses and reported that it "yielded a net profit of approximately $1600."[134] They concluded that their association with Charlesworth had been "enriching and instructive."[135] Although Alumnae's productions were generally regarded as among the best nonprofessionalizing theatre in Toronto, with the growth of professional theatre the public's perception of nonprofessionalizing theatre generally was changing, and there was less patience for time wasted in darkened spaces.

Actors' Equity in the House

As professional theatre practitioners' formal representatives, Actors' Equity associations emerged in the early twentieth century in the United States (1913), England (1931), and Canada (1976, although Canadians could be members of the American branch as of 1955, a change spurred by the inauguration of Stratford Festival two years earlier). Equity's expanding influence across Canada's theatre ecology restructured not only the opportunities and working conditions of its members, but collaterally those of nonprofessionalizing theatre practitioners as well. Alumnae's relationship with Actors' Equity is direct when the company retains Equity members as actors or directors: it fills out the requisite contracts and pays Equity's prescribed fees to the artist through Equity.

From the 1950s on, Equity members were generally required to present Equity paperwork to the producing amateur company; the company then paid the Equity artist at the prescribed reduced amateur rate. Equity artists who were also Alumnae members would sometimes choose to donate some or all of their income back to Alumnae. The arrangement benefited both Alumnae, which could cast the talent they wished, and Equity members, who were eager to play roles they might not find elsewhere. This loose arrangement proceeded with only a handful of difficulties (discussed below) until the 1990s, when it became clear that Alumnae were spending more and more money to engage Equity and, later, Alliance of Canadian Cinema, Television, and Radio Artists (ACTRA) members – who were often (but not always) Alumnae members – in an effort to compete for audience and critical attention (even if it meant budget deficits) and in order to raise Alumnae's profile by capitalizing on artists' professional renown. Alumnae eventually came to terms with the idea that they need not employ Equity and ACTRA members so often. This "soul searching" sapped a great deal of collective energy from Alumnae's leaders, especially during the 1990s, when they often reworked policies to respond to both budget shortfalls and "astonished"[136] members. This decades-long back and forth between Alumnae and Equity provides insight into the changing nature of nonprofessionalizing theatre practice in the professionalizing theatre era.

The professionalization of mid-century Canadian theatre artists was a matter of public interest, and the *Globe and Mail*'s Herbert Whittaker, as already shown, was paying close attention. In October 1956, Canadian Equity sent what Whittaker termed a "milestone" letter to its membership reminding them of a regulation – up to then rarely enforced, he noted – that Equity members could not participate in amateur productions unless they received a $25 fee. Although American Equity had been adhering to such a rule for years, Canada Equity did not strictly enforce it, in order to "suit the tender growth of professional theatre here" (so Whittaker explained). Whittaker's article, titled "Equity splits theatre in vote of confidence," described what he viewed as a watershed moment for the professionalization of theatre in the country and an "expression of bounding optimism on the part of Actors' Equity Association in Canada." He expected at the time that the move "may do more harm than good," in that Equity estimated that only seventy-five to one hundred Canadian members were employed in a country where only Toronto, Montreal, Vancouver, and "sporadically" Ottawa had professionalizing theatre communities. Said Whittaker, the "rest of the country still depends on the amateur or academic theatre" to develop talent where there are "more actors than opportunities." He noted that American Equity "once registered a 90 per cent unemployment at one period" and warned that making the fee mandatory could move Canada towards that number. Actors might find other work in radio, television or film, but that would not "improve them as stage actors." Moreover, "experience of any kind is valuable, under conditions less than perfect or less than professional." Whittaker was adamant that as along as an actor was not being exploited for profit, he should be allowed to participate in a not-for-profit theatre company if he could be cast in a role he might not be elsewhere, for the benefit of himself as well as members of the nonprofessionalizing group, who would learn from his experience. He listed past Alumnae guest actors John Colicos, Richard Easton, Ted Follows, Williams Needles, David Gardner, Ron Hartman, and Suzanne Finlay as examples of actors who had "advanced their careers in such productions." He concluded by saying that "such arbitrary divisions between professional and amateur acting besmack of snobbism" and that while Equity must protect its members from "exploitation," it must not shield them from "earning an experience."[137] Under early professionalization, the career-building elements of income and experience were at odds. Whittaker was describing the tensions in navigating them.

Some Alumnae members had been Equity members since the early days of Actors' Equity in Canada. The number of Equity members cast in Alumnae shows occasionally swelled through the mid-1960s as more actors signed on to Equity while still seeking the high-quality, high-profile stage experience Alumnae could provide. But as Actors' Equity began to push its members to sign contracts when engaging with nonprofessionalizing companies, Alumnae began to enforce these regulations more stringently as well. Member Margaret Spence recounts of the 1960s that

> back on Huron Street we had to have a general meeting to decide that we actually had to have that person and had to budget for it … It wasn't an expectation, it was a devout hope [that

> they would donate their fee back]. And some of the actresses couldn't afford to give it back. A couple of the actresses would be members ... There were certain members you could count on [who] would give it back. Some actors couldn't afford it, I mean quite frankly ... It was always done *quasi-sub rosa*. *Quasi*-nobody-had-to-acknowledge this [*laughs*]: Equity contract; the money went over ... It was probably just a part [for which] we didn't have a member that was equal to it. Sometimes men. Sometimes women. But we just looked over the membership list and the people who applied to read the part. And there just wasn't anyone that we felt was adequate or suitable. And at that point we would have to go to Equity. Which was sometimes better and sometimes not [in terms of] acting ability ...
>
> By and large they were justified. It was somebody [for whom] they felt the part was extraordinary and they would have to go to an Equity person and we bankrolled it.[138]

When the issue drew the attention of Alumnae's executive in the winter of 1965, they ruled that the number of Equity members "used in any production must be curtailed," that following Equity's edict "no more than two such members may be used," and that this "should be made clear at [audition] readings in the future."[139] They announced to the membership that it was up to the producer or stage manager attending casting readings to "find out which actors belong to Equity." Moreover, Alumnae underscored that from their position, "considering the restrictions and complications imposed by Equity, it is unreasonable to use an Equity member unless absolutely necessary. The legal limit [imposed by Equity] is two per show. A check with the president [of Alumnae] should be made before casting."[140] Clearly, Alumnae's leadership took Equity's policies seriously and took measures not to run afoul of them.

The issue of retaining Equity members resurfaced regularly, until by the late 1980s it was beginning to consume the company. Alumnae's August 1987 newsletter reported to the membership that the "use of Equity actors was discussed with some heat;"[141] it had been decided that Alumnae members (including those who were members of Equity) should be given casting priority over non-Alumnae members (including those who were members of Equity). In November 1991, Alumnae's board of directors, under financial and disciplinary pressure as a result of casting (and paying) Equity actors and retaining Equity directors, voted to disallow "auditioning an Equity actor unless the actor is a member in good standing of the Alumnae Theatre Company." Board member Ruth Pincoe, absent from the meeting, wrote a strong objection to that decision:

> Our impressive history, to which we constantly refer, is deeply integrated with the professional and semi-professional theatrical community. Times have changed, but perhaps more than we think. If there is to be a place for us in the years to come, if we are not to become another ordinary community theatre group, if we are to continue to provide the high quality shows of which we are so proud, we must come to realistic terms with the professional theatre community. We can't just pretend it doesn't exist.[142]

Alumnae members generally wanted the opportunity to cast trained professional actors. A number of Equity members were drawn to Alumnae by the camaraderie with other women and the opportunity to be cast in challenging roles. Alumnae directors were willing to work under Equity's restrictions concerning how many Equity members could work on an Alumnae show; in return, some Equity members, of their own volition, continued to donate part or all of their fees back to Alumnae.

During the recession of the early 1990s, which struck freelance artists particularly hard, this generous gesture became less forthcoming, until the habit was all but history. Treasurer Carol Palmer set the issue in stark relief at the 1998 annual general meeting: Alumnae's loss for the 1997–98 season was $16,000, $9,000 of which had been spent on Equity actors and directors.[143] Echoing the bureaucratic creep that had pulled members into silos across the company since they began managing the Firehall in the early 1970s, Palmer stressed that "we cannot only look at our own particular wishes and gratifications; we have to consider the well being of the Company as a whole. I am sure that will be done."[144] Alumnae's Equity committee set out to address the matter, asking the membership to decide "whether Alumnae is a club, a community theatre or a professional theatre, or something else in-between"[145] with the purpose of finding a suitable arrangement with Equity. By the turn of the twenty-first century, Alumnae's long-standing members Francess Halpenny and Helen Dunlop were referring to Alumnae as an "active, semi-professional producing theatre."[146] The change in terminology from "amateur" reflected not only the broad degradation of the term "amateur" over the decades, but also the defining effect that Actors' Equity was exerting on the company's personnel choices and budgets.

A number of Equity members among Alumnae's ranks wished to act with Alumnae, but because the company was faced with a deficit, it was becoming more and more difficult to argue that even one or two members of the cast, or the director, could be paid nearly $1,000 for an eighteen-show Studio run and nearly $700 for a thirteen-show Mainstage run.[147] Although it was never Alumnae's formal policy to ask Equity members to return part, or all, of their Equity fee,[148] the practice was still not uncommon. It came under scrutiny by the board of directors. Before the fall of 1999, Alumnae's board passed the motion that "there be no more than one Equity member per show, including the director, and no more than one Equity member per New Ideas week, with first consideration being given to casting Alumnae Equity members."[149] Aware of the conversation when it arose at the 1999 spring annual general meeting, but perhaps unaware of the motion, Pamela Terry wrote to the board that fall showing expense numbers from the previous season's productions that included Equity actors that were, to her, "plainly unacceptable." She added that the "Alum is, and always has been, scrupulous in its dealings with [Equity]," but that the theatre should not expect, even "unspoken," Equity members to return any or all of their fees.[150] She concluded that Alumnae "can't continue to be vague and feel uncomfortable, and often harassed, about individual [Equity] members' decisions to overrule its legitimate wishes that earnings be donated, then a tax receipt issued."[151] In September 2000, board members Jennifer Parr and Margaret Lamarre volunteered to research the history between Alumnae and Equity before meeting with Equity to discuss a "special status"[152] for Alumnae's Equity members. When Equity denied this request for special status, Alumnae's board raised further concerns that returning fees might violate agreements with Revenue Canada regarding taxation and the City of Toronto.[153] The relative ease with which Equity members participated in Alumnae productions during the Coach House years was in stark contrast to twenty-first-century concerns at the Firehall Theatre.[154]

For Alumnae, the problem was compounded when ACTRA entered into a joint agreement with Equity. It meant that Alumnae members who were also ACTRA members (but not necessarily Equity members) would need to be paid the Equity fee as well[155] and that they would be included in the ratio that determined how many Equity/ACTRA members could be cast in a show. The board noted that by 2001, "many" Alumnae members were

Equity or ACTRA members or both and that the company had "already lost many of our members because of past restrictions about using Equity members" and now was "bound to lose many more valuable members unless we can arrange a new agreement with Equity/ ACTRA." Alumnae thus considered a Fringe Festival–inspired solution on a trial basis for the New Ideas Festival in which 80 per cent of the profits would be split among all participants, whether Equity/ACTRA members or not.[156] They were stuck between existing as a not-for-profit club and one that had some members who were also members of a professional association that governed the activities they hoped to pursue in the club. Parr acknowledged that because of the Equity/ACTRA decision, there was a "resulting narrowing of the pool of talent from which we normally draw." She tried to put it in a positive light: "Now is our chance to move forward and take the Alumnae into the 21st century with our flags flying high."[157] She also asked,

> Is our mandate now the same as the original mandate? How can we define or adapt it to take us into the future? Why did we all join the Alumnae? Why do we stay? The original mandate from the research I have done, was twofold: first – to provide opportunities for women to work in all aspects of the theatre, opportunities that were not available to them elsewhere; and second – to present productions of professional quality of cutting edge plays from the existing and new international repertoire. The Alumnae has such potential to be a focal point in the city for "women-driven theatre" whether women playwrights, directors, designers, technicians or actors.[158]

Professionalization in the theatre was ever-expanding and continued to infringe on Alumnae's practices, as it had since the Second World War. In a notice that a special members' meeting would be held to discuss the issue, the question was posed: "How shall we define ourselves for the future? Do we redefine ourselves as more than a community theatre? Do we need a new definition? What would that new definition look like?"[159] Alumnae had reached a crucial moment. For the June 2002 annual general meeting, PJ Hammond put it this way: "Equity issue is not our fight. It concerns the rules of that union. And we're not union."[160] By 2010, Alumnae's policy had been refined to say that "participation by union actors be limited to members in good standing of our club, and for those roles that are very difficult to cast."[161]

Beyond the views of critics and the emergence of Actors' Equity, the emergence of professional opportunities in theatre, radio, and television had a defining effect on Alumnae's membership. On the one hand, it gave many the hope that by working with Alumnae, they might gain experience that would launch them towards a professional career; on the other, it necessarily altered members' views of Alumnae's value to the local and national performance ecologies. This dynamic, bifurcated view was also noticed by theatre-goers, thus moulding the company's reputation.

At their annual meeting in June 1956, having described recent production successes and thanked standout members, president Eleanor Beecroft spoke perceptively about Alumnae's changing place in light of an emerging profession:

> The policy of the UADC as an amateur group has been to put on a show that is worthy of being done by us to the best of our ability; to try and make an artistic contribution to the living Canadian theatre; to raise the standards each year a little higher – if we can; to work together successfully as a unit and not competitively.

> Now with greater opportunities arising in TV and radio as well as live theatre, I feel that we as a Club have a duty to give young actresses – and actors too – a chance to move on and up in the professional field. This will mean that they may not be with us very long as active members, but their sojourn with us will be beneficial to all of us – and to them. For who knows but someday they may realize that this group of strong-minded women [brought] together by one love – the theatre – has taught them the value of working together in harmony. And we who are left behind to battle with the same problems year after year will be enriched from having known their companionship for even a short time.[162]

Professionalization meant that some of Alumnae's members and male guests were leaving the company for professional work, impacting Alumnae's ability to maintain a core of experienced participants. But Beecroft articulated Alumnae's "duty" to have a positive impact on participants' aspirations. Her words provide clear evidence of how Alumnae saw themselves in the early years of Canadian theatre's professional era. It is hardly surprising that a company so deeply ingrained in its city's theatre ecology would show such a self-awareness of its value to community and country.

Conclusions

And here they had all this success. They had a pattern to follow, like you're not reinventing the wheel every time. But then they move into this building and this whole wave of theatre all over the country starts and they're like, "Oh, who are we going to be now?" ... And I thought, how terrifying that must have been. Me worrying about sales on this show is so small scale compared to, "What do we do now in the middle of that tsunami of theatre?" And it really put in perspective what I was struggling with in a different way ... In the 60s they very clearly had an identity before they moved into this building. And then they're faced with Tarragon, Factory ...[1]

– PJ Hammond

Today's Alumnae Theatre Company looks very different from the group that produced *The Bluestockings* in 1918. Wrote Francess Halpenny in 1968, "in adaptation to changes in the theatre in Toronto with the passing years [Alumnae have found the] stamina for surviving in the inveterately ephemeral world of the theatre."[2] Alumnae's willingness to adapt their programming, sometimes radically, without shifting away from an all-female membership, is what separates them from other companies and defines their success in theatre. For much of their history, they have sought to produce plays that other companies will not or cannot. At the heart of their culture is this notion of alterity, even when it is in debate. In the 1920s and 1930s they provided an alternative to British and Amcrican touring shows by producing recent plays from Europe during the rise of Canada's Little Theatre Movement; from the 1930s through the 1960s they frequently met, and even set, a high bar during the rise of the Dominion Drama Festival; from the 1940s through the 1960s they maintained programming that included the classics when no one else could afford to do so; in the 1950s and 1960s they provided a venue for avant-garde European plays, new Canadian plays, and new translations when other companies would not; in the 1960s they offered radical and political programming when only a handful of other companies would; since the 1970s they have pivoted explicitly towards work by and about women, counterbalanced by commercial fare; and since the late 1980s they have emphasized new play development. Like other long-standing nonprofessionalizing theatre groups, Alumnae are both rooted and fluid, connected to their past by membership and audience, flexible enough to pivot with the times, and they often lead with programming innovation and new play production. In these ways, they have maintained an intense belonging to their city while being positioned as outsiders and women leaders in a field in which men often lead. They are members of a nonprofessionalizing theatre in a professionalizing era.

Other long-standing nonprofessionalizing companies such as Ottawa Little Theatre, Regina Little Theatre, Victoria's Langham Court Theatre, and Halifax's Theatre Arts Guild are not women-only groups (although OLT was formed at an open meeting of the multi-institutional University Women's Club in 1913[3]). Yet these companies have often been run by women. Historically, the reasons for this may be similar to Alumnae's reasons for remaining *all*-women. In their early decades, women involved in these companies were often university-educated, viewing their participation as a leisure pursuit focused on reading, and educating each other about, dramatic literature. Moreover, they were unlikely to be their household's primary wage earners, and this allowed them to focus their time on organizing and performing theatre. To a less overt extent, these companies sometimes organized philanthropic events in their cities. All achieved notable success at the Dominion Drama Festival, which encouraged them to compare their work to that of other nonprofessionalizing artists across the country. Each dealt with the onset of professionalization in unique ways that befitted their locales. The strong impact of the professionalization of Toronto's theatre ecology eventually affected companies across the country. When professionalizing theatre took root in Edmonton when Joseph Schocter founded the Citadel Theatre in 1965, Edmonton's nonprofessionalizing company, Walterdale Theatre Associates, began producing edgier fare – accomplished, of course, by local theatre artists.[4] As with Alumnae, these companies featured participants at all points of their lives, from school age to "9-5ers" to retirees. As *Edmonton Journal* theatre critic Liz Nicholls put it in 1983, "Walterdale's membership roster runs from students and secretaries to dentists, doctors, oil company execs, truck drivers and carpenters, some of them highly trained actors"[5] – many of them putting their professional skills to use in nonprofessionalizing theatre as carpenters, electricians, architects, educators, and even lawyers revising company constitutions.[6]

Alumnae's members are professionals in their salaried jobs, freelance work, and "gig" economy jobs. They are professionals with post-secondary degrees, career "9-to-5ers," stay-at-home moms, and retirees. They are professionalizing and nonprofessionalizing actors, directors, designers, choreographers, musical directors, and theatre administrators. They are using their professional training from theatre schools and they are using Alumnae's stages and workshops for training and experience. They are university age, they are young adults, they are middle-aged, and they are seniors. They were, and are, educated, ambitious, and often active in theatre and committee work as current and past undergraduates. Their company's longevity is a result of members' education, connections, work ethic, dedication to theatre as a participatory activity, and position within, and outside of, the women's liberation and feminist movements of the day. Since the 1970s, Alumnae members have been career women, women in the process of gaining theatre experience with a view to becoming professional artists, and professional artists wishing to be part of a club dedicated to women's interests in a theatre that provides challenging opportunities for onstage and backstage practices. This extraordinary variety of lifestage and lifestyle positioning gives the company an energy, relevance, and alterity not possible in professionalizing practices.

Alumnae's marginality as a group of women largely uninterested in generating personal income from theatre is not encumbering, but rather, perhaps paradoxically, enabling. Their founders came from families that could afford to send their daughters to university. Their earned accreditations as university alumnae afforded them the educational capital and status to attract audiences to their shows and donors to their philanthropy. After the Second World War, members parlayed this notoriety into a list of subscribers who were curious about new and little-known modern plays, and into attracting donors to help them purchase a new experimental theatre. They in turn parlayed this real estate experience into convincing municipal officials to place a historic building with a long-term lease in their capable hands. All of these property and programming successes were complicated by the fact that they were navigating this century of intellectual and capital expansion as women who were not expected to guide the big moves, figuratively or literally, of a theatre company. At a time when men were more conservative in their programming because they were seeking to professionalize their companies to create careers, Alumnae's women, who often held busy full-time jobs, repeatedly positioned the company as alternative. Alumnae's longevity is largely due to their enigmatic, intersectional positioning as privileged and underprivileged, legitimate and illegitimate, historic and contemporary.

Studies on women in Canadian professional theatre over the past forty years reveal gender disparity in leadership positions. The first of these studies, Rina Fraticelli's *The Status of Women in the Canadian Theatre*, found that in 1982, only 11 per cent of artistic directors in Canadian professional theatres were women;[7] by 2006, Rebecca Burton found that the number had risen, but only to 33 per cent;[8] in 2010, PACT found that the number had dropped slightly to 28 per cent.[9] Men usually lead the larger theatres, whereas women are found in greater numbers leading smaller companies. Burton's study notes that in 2006 the mean average of women board members at professional Canadian theatres was 56 per cent.[10] Clearly, these percentages were lower for women in the decades before Fraticelli's report. When these numbers across the decades are taken as partial context for Alumnae's first century, the company's unique contribution to theatre in Canada is easier to grasp. What is also apparent throughout this study is that many of Alumnae's prominent leaders were involved for decades in running the company; they included Agatha Leonard, Francess Halpenny, Molly Thom, Pamela Terry, and Margaret Spence. Their consistent involvement has been a significant factor in the company's longevity. Alumnae's choice to remain all-female has carved out a unique niche. Their position of gendered alterity facilitated Alumnae's programming alterity over their first century.

Programming Alterity

It would be a challenge to reconcile the philanthropic circumstances under which Alumnae formed with the rhetoric associated with today's reasons for producing theatre. For the post-war nonprofessionalizing practitioner, the combination of familiar drawing room comedies and societal patronage in a drama-in-education setting could draw hundreds of scholars, students, and the "upper crust" to a night of theatre while contributing significantly to campus causes. The sort of theatre Alumnae practised in their first two decades was not aimed at strengthening a profession or creating employment for consecrated (and consecrating) artists; it was practised because the campus and city needed the monetary and social rewards the group offered. This was a world of patronage, public acts of charity, personal development of theatre and elocution skills, and patriotism, as well as institutional support and recruitment into all of these loci of cultural activity.

Alumnae's income then turned to benefiting the group itself when they began managing their own theatre buildings. When their programming turned back to social awareness in the late 1960s and 1970s, it was in the radical, politically aware sense of that generation.

In recent years, scholars have begun to examine the potential for resistance, experimentation, and even revolution inherent in nonprofessionalizing practices, even as these practices often contain within them, seemingly paradoxically, aspects of traditionalism and reactionism. Nadine Holdsworth and colleagues delineate certain forms of amateur theatre practice as a "facilitating space of alterity, aesthetically or political, that becomes quickly absorbed into the cultural mainstream as innovation." Other forms are part of their country's national agenda, and still others entail being "expert guardians of traditional forms."[11] Alumnae have encompassed each of these cultural practices, at times producing radical political plays, at other times participating in the DDF's nationalizing agenda, and at other times still producing the classics when other companies would not. By manufacturing alterity out of programming and fiscal flexibility, nonprofessionalizing theatres in Canada have often defined their work as progressive, radical, and separate from the profession of the day. Going further, Ben Walters moves his argument for the impacts of nonprofessionalizing theatre practices from alterity to the potential for radical cultural disruption, asserting that

> amateurs have more fun. Rather than connoting failure or delusion, the figure of the amateur can generatively engage the refusal of normative productivity, the distinctive expression of marginalized subjectivities and the embrace of pleasure. These attributes, I argue, can in turn build empathy, relationality and hope on self-defined terms. A focus on the DIY functionality of the amateur – rather than, say, the relation of the amateur to broader understandings of public reception or normatively validated achievement – can align amateur practice with the value of autonomy in anarchist thinking.[12]

Walters has in mind nonprofessionalizing theatre's potential to contribute to queer performance in the UK, but the sentiment might well be applied to Alumnae's contributions to play programming in Toronto. Alumnae are a regenerative group of women. Their refusal to play within those structures of twentieth-century theatre leadership that have been the traditional domain of men has echoes in Walter's description of refusing normative productivity from a marginalized position. Alumnae's work also responds to Kristina Huneault's provocations when she asks in her introduction to *Rethinking Professionalism* whether women artists in Canada have historically defied a male-led "dominant professional paradigm."[13] Working outside the male-led emerging theatre profession, yet working with professionalism, Alumnae's women most certainly have done so.

The terms "nonprofessionalizing" and "amateur" hold meaning in modern usage under industrial capitalism, where one is expected to work for a living. This is important to remember because discussions about nonprofessionalizing theatre practices are impossible without considering how one's time is valued, commodified, and spent. Alumnae's alterity is largely a result of remarkable flexibility, moving within and around what Helen Nicholson and colleagues term the twentieth century's "commodification of creativity"[14] under capitalism. Along these lines, Nicholas Ridout offers what may be the most pressing argument to date for studying nonprofessionalizing theatre practices: he sees "the amateur" as a "crucial figure for understanding the appearances of romantic anticapitalism in theatre," because the amateur is "someone who interrupts his or her work in order to make theatre, rather than making theatre his or her work." Ridout contends that the "most important of capitalism's 'defining qualities' is its organization of all human life around wage labor, in which human activity and creative capacity are primarily valued for what they can contribute to the accumulation of capital, and in which life is measured out in units of productive time." Theatre's "division of labor" is performed "right where people go looking for something very different."[15] Nonprofessionalizing performance is a radical performance of the interruption of capitalism, even if the material and economic necessities of theatre dictate that it is only the illusion of the interruption; it may, in fact, be the rehearsal for the interruption. By choosing to conduct unwaged labour for the purpose of theatre creation rather than personal income, and by involving practitioners from across income brackets, Alumnae engage in, and publicly perform, a creative practice that is partly set off from capitalism's core tenet that labour transfers capital vertically.

Nicholson and colleagues posit four types of responses to the commodification of creativity by nonprofessionalizing theatre companies: the amateur as "counter-cultural figure," the amateur as found in the "wider public," the amateur in the "digital age," and the amateur in "diverse settings."[16] Each of these responses paints the practitioner of nonprofessionalizing theatre, however illusorily, as outside the lines drawn by the capitalist market in terms of income, gifting, expertise, sociability, aesthetics, and the objectives of production and consumption. This flexible, radical, social alterity (Ridout calls it "communist potential"[17]) reminds us that art and its receptions can be in the hands of everyone, accomplished under the utopian haven of egalitarian production and consumption. For Alumnae, this formulation of radical practice was most concentrated during their late Coach House years and early Firehall years. Even in its most naturalistic forms, all theatre has at its core escapism, including, at least momentarily, from capitalism. The study of a nonprofessionalizing company like Alumnae shows that doing theatre, for all its grounding in material trappings and financial volatility, is an escapist act. Nonprofessionalizing theatre offers opportunities to rehearse and perform as an escape from one's day-to-day labour.

Alumnae's alterity was brought to the fore most profoundly in 1972, not because of their own programming, but because other theatres began offering the sort of alternative programming for which Alumnae had become known. While Alumnae were moving into the Firehall and preparing a season featuring plays by Dubliner Seán O'Casey, Quebecker Anne Hébert, Americans Clare Booth Luce and Edward Albee, and Russian Maxim Gorky, Toronto was famously entering its theatre renaissance. The year was a watershed for those companies that Urjo Kareda termed "alternate theatres."[18] Often aided by federal youth employment grants and "baby boom" university graduates entering the workforce with income to spend on cultural pursuits, professionalizing companies like Tarragon Theatre, Toronto Free Theatre, Theatre Passe Muraille, Factory Lab Theatre, the Global Village, the Bathurst Street Theatre, the Poor Alex Theatre, the New Theatre, Toronto Arts Productions, and Creation 2[19] featured local young talent and new Canadian plays at affordable ticket prices, sometimes in predictable venues.[20] The idea of hiring local actors, directors, crew, and administrators was normalizing. In defining this renaissance, Kareda wrote that "new Canadian plays have found productions much more swiftly than new plays from England or the United States"[21] and that "alternative theatre carries hope for the future."[22] As professionalizing companies publicized and commodified alterity, alterity could no longer be the unique purview of nonprofessionalizing companies like Alumnae. That which Nathan Cohen had celebrated in Alumnae just a few years earlier, Kareda now celebrated in the new alternative professionalizing theatres. In the early days of Toronto's alternative theatre boom, critics and audiences viewed Alumnae as being part of, yet separate from, Toronto's emerging alternative theatres.

Despite public fanfare at the time, the achievements of Alumnae's women before and during this period have largely been forgotten in the male-dominated myth-making discourse that consumed Toronto theatre in the early 1970s. Even long-time member Molly Thom describes Alumnae's relationship to the alternative theatres as "almost nonexistent even though Toronto Free was just down the street. They were doing their thing, we were doing ours. We were doing it first but we didn't have the risk because the money wasn't an issue."[23] Some understood Alumnae's relationship as an enabling precursor to this growth with phrases like "Toronto's original alternate theatre."[24] Critics were changing their tone towards Alumnae's productions as local talent were able to find paid work. The rise in prominence of these companies, like the rise of the city's first professional theatres fifteen years earlier, redefined Alumnae. Among many definitive moments in Alumnae's history, the rise of professionalizing companies bent on alterity stands as having had the greatest transformative impact on Alumnae's positioning in Toronto's theatre ecology.

For most of the twentieth century, critics applauded Alumnae's innovative and proactive approach to play production. Their educated members stayed ahead of Toronto's, and Canada's, theatre trends while gradually attaining autonomy over their material assets, making them the envy of their peers and the recipients of lifelong gratitude from theatre artists and audiences. They are their city's most persistent nonprofessionalizing group, and their productions have often been viewed as meeting or exceeding the city's professional standards. They have not simply played reactionary witness to Canada's landmark theatre movements; from one decade to the next they set the pace. As a theatre group created decades before a Canadian theatre profession emerged, they have been active participants, and at times catalysts, in redefining local theatre programming, sometimes inspired by, and inspiring with, foreign plays, other times producing premieres, several of them award-winning. They produced the classics when they were available only to be read, and they produced modern works before anyone else in the country dared to take the risk. With moments of remarkable foresight, Alumnae shifted their public identity to adapt to the needs of theatre programming in their city.

Much of this book has been occupied with an analysis of Alumnae's play programming because programming ultimately defines a theatre's value to its audiences and milieu. Nicholson and colleagues argue in the UK context that the "accumulated wealth of amateur theatre performances inflects and contributes to the forming of a national theatrical repertoire in ways that have not been fully appreciated." This includes the fact that nonprofessionalizing theatre programming on a wide scale can generate a "familiarity" with certain plays among audiences that is a "pre-condition" for recognizing the exceptionalism attributed to innovative works that enter the "canon."[25] In Canada, the shared repertoire of nonprofessionalizing companies like Alumnae in the interwar and DDF years expanded awareness of European, and to a lesser extent American and Canadian, plays. But since the 1970s, as professionalization has taken root, this influence has diminished. Moreover, in Canada, the notion of a shared "national theatrical repertoire" shifted from a state-sponsored goal eagerly adopted in the early and mid-twentieth century to a racialized goal by the late twentieth century. Efforts to encourage new plays by introducing European writing to Canadian stages were increasingly questioned as theatre-makers noted that Indigenous and racialized voices were perceived to be always already under threat by the white settler-colonizer writing represented by European texts, and those they inspired. This has led some nonprofessionalizing companies to pivot their programming, and the membership that chooses it, towards diversity and community outreach. Among scholars in Canada, the very notion of a "national theatrical repertoire" is increasingly viewed as an agent of colonization. In practice, the impulse for nonprofessionalizing companies to change their programming must come from their constitutive membership and the audiences to which they are beholden.

Nostalgia Houses: Making Theatre History

Directly following Alumnae's annual meeting on 15 June 1968, at which president Elizabeth Mascall outlined the club's then-fifty-year history, early member Marion Squair Hunter, Alumnae's illustrious event host for many years, arrived for supper. The minutes record that she "told the members that they must not be complacent, we owe a great deal to the Founders and the people who helped the Club grow. Any reputation we have today we owe to the tradition we inherited." Mascall moved a "motion of appreciation to the Founders and older members of the Club," which was seconded by Margaret Spence, still today an active costume designer for Alumnae. As recorded, Francess Halpenny then added that the "strength of the club was found in its ability to adapt to new ideas; the enthusiasm, energy and ideas of new members being tempered with the experience of the older ones."[26] Hunter's and Halpenny's words, taken together, reflect the ways in which Alumnae have found longevity and programming success over the years. These successes are, in turn, singular and instructive for an understanding of Canadian theatre and performance practices as they emerged in the early twentieth century.

As Alumnae moved into a historic firehall, their historicity came to the fore. The press fused Alumnae's long history of theatre production with their new venue's long history to establish a narrative of cultural longevity that connected ethereal plays with material bricks and mortar. With so many new theatres run by young men appearing around the city in the 1970s, Alumnae were easily perceived as history personified. Alumnae members a generation or two removed from the company's founders began to reflect on their secret to "survival." This emergence of generational distance enabled from within the company a nostalgia that set its present operational ethos in the light of the past. One company document attributed Alumnae's longevity to two factors, beyond exclusively the "ability and enthusiasm" of the founders:

> The first was their generosity in attracting, welcoming, absorbing, and developing new members, so that full use could be made of their capacities. This is more unusual than it sounds. No one was ever refused membership because of any personal characteristic, peculiarity, or idiosyncrasy, but somehow, the club managed to utilize such apparent drawbacks, and transmute them from idiosyncrasies to assets, which enriched and strengthened the club.
>
> The second is that their roots were firmly established at a season when the theatrical climate in Toronto was encouraging – for amateurs, and a few small professional groups.[27]

This positivity among members in welcoming new talent in a nonprofessionalzing theatre atmosphere was, in turn, reproduced outwardly to the public and reviewers of the day. Generally positive media attention in their first fifty years resulted in excellent word-of-mouth publicity and, reciprocally, confidence among company members.

We want to learn from thriving organizations because they can teach us lessons about what choices found success at certain times. But theatre organizations hold particular challenges when we try to trace their histories. When dealing with popular history, memories

Figure 9.1. Alumnae's longest-serving member during their first century, Francess Halpenny, is seen here with Alumnae production photographs on display at the company's 100th Anniversary Gala in October 2017. Halpenny joined Alumnae in 1939 before appearing on stage for them for the first time in 1941. She would go on to become one of the company's strongest guiding voices until her death two months after the Gala on Christmas Day 2017 at the age of ninety-eight. Photo Credit: Bruce Peters. Courtesy of Alumnae Theatre Company.

can be short, incomplete, or prone to emotional memory that privileges enjoyable processes over great challenges and even failures. This is due, in part, to the fact that theatre trades constantly with the present. Its participants must live in the present in rehearsal, on stage, and in administration. To what degree does theatre's constant focus on presence enable historical knowledge to become contested terrain, or even targeted, or weaponized? Past board member PJ Hammond reflects on a relatively recent moment in time that, in her view, could augur trouble for the future of companies like Alumnae:

> The problem with a volunteer organization is that institutional knowledge is lost. So whatever I contributed is gone. It's gone. Or if it was my contribution I'm not credited with it in any way. I'm going to give you an example. It's actually horrible. A few years ago, [we] were cleaning in the basement because a rack of lumber storage and little things have fallen off … and probably haven't moved in years. And [one of us] squeezed in behind and dragged out all of this lumber and we were going to get a big disposal bin. But in the meantime we were stacking it in garbage bins. And I picked up a piece of wood and it was heavier than anything else. And I looked at it and it's the original oak paneling that has been stored in this lumber rack … from the lockers and wainscoting. All of the stuff that got torn up and didn't get used in the [1971]

renovation is all there in the basement. And we make a stack of what was this original oak paneling. [Another] renovation was coming up. If we could tell people we had this we could get it built into the design! At the very least, if we want to make extra cash we have oak paneling from a 1904 building with a pedigree we could assure. So [we] separated it all and we stack it all together underneath the workbench in the basement.

And then a couple of years later they did a cleanup in the building and they threw it all in the garbage. They threw it all in the garbage. And that's what's happening. That's what is happening to everything. It's like you walk into a room and you think nobody's ever been in this room before. Or you think that nobody's had this idea before. The people that are doing things right now think they're the first ones to have any idea. And it's terribly disheartening when I have loved this place for so long [*cries*] … They're going to break the thing you love and you have to stand back and let them …

The current mentality is, "let's put up a show in the barn" and they're *not* honouring the 100-year-old history of brilliant stuff that has happened. Even the recent stuff that has been brilliant, they talk about, you know, [Daniel MacIvor's] *You Are Here*, a fantastic show. But they don't put in the work for what is going to be the next fantastic show … [They're] taking initiative to throw out the 100-year-old wood in the basement. [They're] taking initiative without any thought …

The gala is tonight. Why are all of the past presidents you can invite not there?[28]

Hammond's story, hewn from oak, is chilling. And recognizable. It points to an observation that might be transposed onto any moment in any long-running volunteer organization's history. Volunteers, especially in the theatre, rely on social capital for the hard work they accomplish. The feeling of not being recognized for one's work can lead one to despair for the future. But it can also generate the impulse to do more for the collective – or, over time, to walk away. For most of their first century, Alumnae's leaders have tended to respect the company's history and to rally it for inspiration and publicity. This respect has led to concrete ideas that have moved the company forward to reinvent its position in Toronto's theatre ecology. Members recognize, for example, that Alumnae have presented new plays for most of their history, and when the need arises they draw on that tradition to create something new, like the FireWorks Festival in 2013. Particularly ambitious members compensate for periods of scarcity in volunteerism, although they invariably burn out and a new group of members emerges to guide the theatre again.

As nonprofessionalizing theatres faded from the national stage in the late twentieth century, professional theatre strengthened, disciplining the field and redefining it as vocational. As Holdsworth and colleagues acknowledge in the UK context, "many national cultural policies privilege professional cultural activity."[29] Eating its own tale, the narrative could then confirm that nonprofessionalizing practices were inferior because they were no longer deserving of national attention (and funding). In Canada, this extended to the logic of a maturing nation intent on nationalizing and professionalizing its artistic practices. Influential voices like Vincent Massey and Robertson Davies viewed the Little Theatre Movement in Canada as a stepping stone towards a professionalized national theatre that would perform the nation back to itself with home-grown plays and talent. This rhetoric quickly cemented the notion that a mature and autonomous nation must have a mature and autonomous professional theatre: the proof was before us in live performance.[30] In mid-twentieth-century Canada, if the nation and its stories were to be performed, those who were professionalizing would have to perform it. A nationalizing country must be seen as a professionalizing country.

The dominance that nonprofessionalizing theatres held before the Second World War had diminished by the end of it. The Little Theatre Movement was over in Canada, and only a handful of groups from that era were still together, or reorganized after a hiatus. Alumnae played a leading role in rebuilding Toronto's theatre ecology by giving experience to theatre artists and offering important plays to audiences. When Alumnae chose to expand their membership beyond the university, they took with them educational capital that served their play programming and armed them in avoiding commercial fare. As Francess Halpenny put it, "standards of performance and presentation were firmly raised"[31] as professionalizing companies emerged.[32] Professionalizing discourse intensified, eventually engulfing and disciplining the space of theatre practice in Canada.

This study has traced human activity that contributed to defining and building a profession while creating space for participatory creation beyond the periphery of the profession, and did so in a way that echoed far beyond the spaces of those who generated it. This is the space in which to view Alumnae Theatre Company as generative survivors. May their accomplished path provide fair warning to scholars and practitioners alike to take for granted neither the nonprofessionalizing practices of past, present, and future, nor their documented traces; may we learn from Alumnae's long history of success and struggle as savvy producers and documenters of ephemeral performance.

Selected Biographies of Alumnae's Early Women

The following are brief biographies of influential founding and early members of Alumnae Theatre Company, originally called the Dramatic Club of the University College Alumnae Association. They have been chosen because the members' work with Alumnae falls within the company's first dozen years and because they returned to work with Alumnae, sometimes for decades. All were graduates of the University of Toronto's University College (UC). As UC students, most participated in campus clubs, including the University College Women's Dramatic Club (WDC). All helped to define the Club's early operations, programming, and public profile under the auspices of the University College Alumnae Association (UCAA).

Miss Edna Reynolds Bach (Mrs. Arthur Caven Norwich) was a member of Alumnae from *The Bluestockings* in 1918 until the late 1940s, appearing in about sixteen plays and occasionally sitting on the executive until the early years of the Second World War. She brought to Alumnae three years of experience with the WDC (1915–17), playing the part of Beatrice in Shakespeare's *Much Ado About Nothing* "most gracefully," wherein her "teasing-banter and easy movement on the stage was quite delightful."[1] In her final year she was WDC president, graduating in 1917. She also sat on the UC second-year executive (1914–15) in the curiously titled position of "Prophetess" and was treasurer of the UC Permanent Executive.[2]

Edna was the daughter of Dr. James S. Bach, a Toronto physician who was president of the Ontario Association of Osteopathy[3] in 1912 and a member of the Association for Psychic Research of Canada in 1919.[4] Upon graduation, Edna took a position on the editorial staff at the *Toronto Daily Star*.[5] In a "war wedding"[6] five months after *The Bluestockings*, she "quietly"[7] married Lieutenant Arthur Caven Norwich, R.A.M.C., a physician "recently returned from Mesopotamia and India, on sick leave."[8] In 1922, he and Edna had a daughter, Marion,[9] two years later a second daughter, Joan,[10] and in 1936 a son, Joseph.[11] Edna's theatre work was centred on Alumnae, but Francess Halpenny later wrote that Edna became "very well-known in Little Theatre circles."[12] She acted with other groups, including in a Dr. Rudolph Uren play called *Salvage: A Drama in Modern Life* with Betty Mitchell, produced by Emmett Lewis and Ralph Millard.[13] After the Second World War, Edna and her family moved to White Rock, British Columbia,[14] at which point she dropped her membership in Alumnae.

Even before she entered university to focus on Modern History, **Eleanor Agnes Barton (Mrs. Moffatt St. Andrew Woodside)** was known in the papers for her accomplishments in both acting and the increasingly popular sport of competitive figure skating, through the Toronto Skating Club, as she would be for years after graduating in 1929. Among early Alumnae members, she was probably the most actively involved in undergraduate leadership, even while staying focused enough on her studies to be nominated for a scholarship. At UC she sat on a number of undergraduate committees, often as secretary. Those committees included the relatively new UC Players' Guild executive (three times, including as vice-president in her graduating year) in the years that Raymond Card was their director, as well as the UC 2T9 Women's Executive (1926–27). In 1928, she served as secretary of the UC Women's Undergraduate Association, and in 1928–29, her graduating year, as its president, which also placed her on the Joint Executive of Students' Administrative Council and the Women's Students' Administrative Council that year. That June, she frequently represented her UC graduating class at well-attended (and photographed) receptions and other functions. From her second year on she was also a member of the Alpha Phi sorority. In her graduating year, Eleanor was interviewed by the *Varsity* about the value of co-education at the university, and offered her view that although she had not experienced any other type of education, men "certainly did make college more lively."[15] She also successfully organized an event called "Mile of Nickels," in which students donated a line of coins on the sidewalk on campus in aid of the women's residence building fund; the event raised $150.[16] For years, she maintained strong ties with UCAA, attending graduations and garden parties. During and after her undergraduate days she acted, skated (including at Toronto's annual Carnival, which she organized in 1937,[17] as well as nationally), and even played competitive golf, in addition to frequenting golf tournaments,[18] debutant balls, coming-out parties, dances, and teas.

Her multitude of social functions and administrative duties were surely inspired by her father, Toronto-area Judge Thomas Herbert Barton, K.C. Eleanor was born in 1907 to Judge Barton and Jean Ethel Barton (née Jardine). Following "many charming parties,"[19] in 1933 she married fellow thespian, classmate,[20] 1928 UC Classics graduate, and Varsity Rhodes scholar Moffatt St. Andrew Woodside in "one of the most interesting weddings of the summer season."[21] Moffatt taught at UC and then Victoria College before pursing an administrative route at the university, becoming Professor of Ancient History and Registrar at Victoria College, Dean of Arts for U of T (1952), acting president of the university (1957-58), Principal of UC (1959–63), Vice-President academic (1963-68), and Provost (1965-68). Together they had three children.

Eleanor was appointed secretary for Hart House Theatre a year after graduating, while continuing to act with that company and beginning to act with Alumnae. By the summer of 1931, she was a "well-known player of Hart House Theatre," leaving for a month to train in New York at the American Academy of Dramatic Art.[22] She eventually became "very well-known in Little Theatre circles,"[23] frequently appearing in Alumnae, Hart House Theatre, and Dickens Fellowship productions. With Alumnae, Eleanor acted in nearly a dozen plays between 1930 and 1952, occasionally serving on the executive, and remaining a member until 1966. She died suddenly in August 1984 in Muskoka, Ontario, while vacationing; her obituary asked for donations to be sent to the Varsity Fund / University College in her memory.[24]

The graduating yearbook entry for **Miss Margaret Boyle (Mrs. Walter Harold Martin)** quoted *The Iliad*: "Persuasive speech … and eloquence of eyes."[25] Born to Mr. and Mrs.

John Boyle, she graduated from UC with a BA in English Literature and History in 1915, having been extremely active in a number of student leadership roles. She does not appear to have acted in the WDC, but she was vice-president of the UC Permanent Executive in 1914–15[26] and the UC Women's Literature Society in 1914–15,[27] a judge for the UC Women's Literary Society's annual Oratorical Contest in 1917,[28] and a member of the Polity Club and the intercollegiate debating team.[29] She appeared in the casts of *The Far-Away Princess*, *The Bluestockings*, and, a month later, the Conservatory School of Expression's production of Edmond Rostand's *The Romancers*.[30] She went on to perform in most of Alumnae's productions until at least 1930, and in other dramatic performances around campus.[31] Besides directing at least three plays for Alumnae, Margaret was Alumnae's inaugural president from 1918 until Elspeth Wilson took over the role in 1924, and then again in 1929–30.

Less than a year after *The Bluestockings*, Margaret began teaching English and History at Toronto's Technical School[32] (now Central Technical School), before teaching at Oakwood Collegiate Institute,[33] where she remained until she married Walter H. Martin in 1930.[34] They had a daughter (Mary Eleanor) the following year,[35] at which point Margaret seems to have stopped participating in Alumnae,[36] although she remained a member until at least 1948.

As reported on the society pages, before she married, Margaret routinely attended a range of local events, from the School of Expression and the Heliconian Club to the Dickens Fellowship and the St. Andrews Society. Among her notable public accomplishments was her work as founding "organizing secretary" of the Ontario Women's Liberal Association, a position she took on in the spring of her graduating year, at a time when that organization anticipated changes because of the war and politics generally.[37] A decade later, she gave a talk for the Toronto Women's Liberal Association on "The Development of Responsible Government."[38] She was also an active member of the University Women's Club and the Women's Art Association, whose interests periodically intersected with Alumnae's interests.

In 1915, **Miss Mary Elizabeth Buckley (Mrs. Harry Van Wyck Laughton)** was just the seventh woman in Ontario to become a lawyer. In 1919, she helped found the Women's Law Association of Ontario.[39] In what was possibly the first article written by a female Canadian lawyer,[40] Mary wrote in *Maclean's* in 1920 that the woman lawyer is "looked upon with admiration not unmixed with awe and she is expected to be a leader of resource and initiative."[41] Mary graduated from UC in 1912, but was a WDC member from 1910 to 1913, remaining with the club during her first year at law school and sitting as president, vice-president, and secretary. Her "Class Horoscope" said that her "Characteristic" was "Light and airy" and that her "Aim in Life" was to "be a prima donna."[42]

Born in 1890, Mary wedded lawyer Harry Laughton (both grew up in Parkhill, Ontario) while studying law at Osgoode Hall.[43] She passed her examinations in 1915, was called to the bar the same year, and worked as a junior solicitor in Clara Brett Martin's office, but did not practise there. Instead, she took a social service course at the university[44] and then practised law with her husband.[45] She worked at Toronto's Juvenile Court as General Secretary of the Big Sisters Association[46] from 1917 until leaving that position due to ill health in 1921.[47] She made a career of advocating for the mentally ill,[48] particularly women,[49] and for boarding houses and vocational training for girls in the city.[50] She also publicly encouraged more women to enter law.[51] In August 1920, the *Globe* listed her among the patrons of a screening at Massey Hall of the American Social Hygiene Association's silent film *The*

End of the Road.[52] Older than most of her fellow cast members in *The Bluestockings*, Mary acted with Alumnae from 1918 until the 1926–27 season, appearing in two more productions: *Trelawny of the Wells* and, *apropos* of her social work, *The Charity That Began at Home*.[53] She died in November 1966.[54]

Miss Christina Charlton Cooper (Mrs. Gilbert Templeton) was not in the cast of *The Bluestockings*, but from Alumnae's 1919 production of Pinero's *Trelawny of the Wells* until their 1966 production of Chekhov's *Three Sisters*, she was one of their most active members onstage and off. In 1908, Christina's father, Rev. W. Barnett Cooper, moved the family from Bristol, England, to Toronto, where he served as General Secretary of the Canadian Bible Society,[55] leading efforts to provide bilingual Bibles (in English and their own language) to all new immigrants to Canada.[56] Christina's mother had artistic inclinations[57] and was active with the Toronto Travel Club.[58] Christina attended Havergal College before graduating from UC in 1916 in Modern Languages. She did not participate in WDC productions but remained selectively active each year, sitting on the *Varsity* board of directors (1913–14), then becoming second vice-president of the Modern Language Club executive (1914-15) and, in her graduating year (1915–16), vice-president of the UC Women's Literary Society. In 1925, she married Gilbert George Gilmour Templeton at Knox College Chapel with three Alumnae friends, Erskine Keyes, Marion Squair, and Margaret Tytler, as ushers.[59] She died in 1969, as announced in an obituary that stated donations could be made to the Canadian Bible Society or UNICEF.[60] Christina's nephew Mark briefly acted for Alumnae in the late 1980s, and her daughter, Phoebe Cleverley, managed subscriptions for Alumnae for a couple of years in the 1990s.

Miss Alison Ewart (Mrs. Albert William Blackburn Hewitt) began with Alumnae in December 1927 by acting in a "dramatic fairy tale"[61] at the Women's Union called *The Rim of the World*. That year her lyrical "biography" read:

> In an attempt to ferret out ability
> Tradition says one first should play a maid,
> Thus, each starts her career in true humility,
> And slowly, step by step, she makes the grade.
> But, in this instance, what do we behold?
> No humble servant of a modest mien;
> This maiden used her wiles and made so bold,
> That in the end we find her crowned a queen!

This was followed by two decades of onstage appearances with Alumnae, as well as executive duties (including as president). She also stored the company's costumes in her attic. She occasionally appeared in plays produced by other groups, such as the Shakespeare Society,[62] the Playwrights Studio Group,[63] the Dickens Fellowship,[64] and the Westminster Central Church.[65] During the Second World War, Alison and Agatha Leonard performed their own skit, *A Day in May*, for various functions, including the CODL revue *Well of All Things*, the Pedagogues' Wives' Auxiliary, and the St. Hilda's College Alumnae Bridge.[66] She was also one of the Alumnae members who performed in the famed touring *Merry-Go-Round* troupe show.

Alison's father, Captain John Ewart, was a sea captain whose work frequently found him travelling overseas. She spent summers with her parents on his ship until she was eighteen,[67] and in February 1914 she travelled to Bermuda.[68] She graduated with honours from Glen Mawr Girls' School (where U of T's graduate residence now stands) in 1918[69] and entered UC when she was sixteen.[70] She joined the Sigma Chapter of the Kappa Alpha Theta Sorority ("Thetas") and remained a member for decades.[71] She was perhaps more focused on academics and sorority life than on clubs; her only club activity on record was reading a term paper on J.M. Barrie during her second year for the UC Women's Literary Society.[72] Under her graduation photograph in 1922, Alison quotes from Shakespeare's *Romeo and Juliet*: "'Tis not so deep as a well, nor so wide as a church-door; but 'tis enough, 'twill serve," followed by her description: "It has been deep enough to sound the depths of English and History. It has been wide enough to leave room for Burns, Barrie and bicycling. I think 'twill serve to take her to Oxford, and carry her through life."[73] Ewart stayed closely connected to UC, attending graduation-related events organized by the UCAA (she was their president in the early 1930s[74]) and assisting in organizing events at the University Women's Club.

At UC, Alison earned a Master's degree and worked in the Department of History. Alison's 1926 article "The Personnel of the Family Compact, 1791–1841,"[75] which she co-wrote with Julia Jarvis, is one of several of her important publications on Canadian history. Having given "valuable assistance to the Editor of the *Canadian Historical Review*,"[76] Alison was appointed general editor of all University of Toronto Press publications in 1932. She "established its editorial department" and hired fellow Alumnae member and future influential editor Francess Halpenny as a junior editor in 1941.[77] For the *University of Toronto Quarterly*, Alison assisted editor A.S.P. Woodhouse in developing the first iteration of the influential survey of Canadian culture and letters, "Letters in Canada: 1935."[78] In particular, she collected the survey's series of bibliographies with, according to the university's board of governors, "conspicuous success."[79]

In June 1940, Alison married Albert William Blackburn Hewitt, a commercial artist who painted much of the calligraphy signage around the university campus at the time. In 1945, when they adopted their daughter Shelagh, Alison left her job,[80] as social norms of the time dictated, but became busy with artistic organizations throughout the city, including the CODL executive. After five years, Alison returned to work, this time with fellow Alumnae member Agatha Leonard, in the university library system; together, they boosted the library's Canadiana holdings and improved acquisitions. She retired in 1966. Shelagh today describes her mother as a "really really strong feminist," a stance that only solidified after Alison was required to leave her position at the press for five years.[81] Alison and her husband Albert died within two weeks of each other in 1987.[82]

Alison sometimes brought Shelagh to Alumnae's rehearsals,[83] inspiring the latter's interest in theatre in general and Alumnae in particular. Shelagh, who married *Star* theatre critic and Tarragon Theatre artistic director Urjo Kareda, appeared in Günther Grass's *Mister, Mister* and directed two Lanford Wilson plays for Alumnae. She also engaged in several years of key administrative work on the club's executive as publicist and on playreading committees as they moved into and maintained the firehall in the early 1970s.

Miss Erskine Keys was born into the "comfortable but not elite"[84] Toronto family of David Keys and his wife (also) Erskine. Her parents had met while studying abroad in Leipzig, Germany. Heather Murray, in her joint biography of David and his sister Florence, writes that the couple attended the first performance of *Siegfried* staged outside of Bayreuth. David was among a set of "pioneering" English professors at the University of Toronto. He also maintained a hectic social life in Toronto, with engagements "seemingly every night of the week," Her father shared a maternal grandmother with the influential philanthropist and arts supporter Margaret Eaton (of the Eaton's department store family), which meant she was Margaret's younger cousin, with family invitations to the Eatons' "city and country homes." Like her sociable and artistically inclined father, Erskine was a "joiner,"[85] appearing in a WDC production in her graduating year of 1917 (Sheridan's *A School for Scandal*, in which her Benjamin Backbite was "at times deliciously droll"[86]), serving as president of the UC Women's Literary Society in 1916–17, and playing basketball with the UC Women's Athletic Association. In 1922–23, she returned to UC as the Players' Guild executive's honorary president. Between her performances in *The Far-Away Princess* and *The Bluestockings* (1942), she acted in most of Alumnae's productions, occasionally sitting on their executive. She remained an Alumnae member until the 1953–54 season. A social worker,[87] Erskine worked for many years in Toronto with the Children's Aid Society.

For decades Erskine and her sister Jean (somewhat infamously) refused to sell their Avenue Road home, which had been owned by their family since 1897,[88] to developers who had "hacked" it in half in 1954 to build an adjoining hotel. A *Globe and Mail* article described them in 1974 as "two little old ladies, both under five feet, over 75, unmarried, happy. They are sisters and they have beautiful faces. Jean has a limp and Erskine stoops. Erskine talks more and worries more. They like animals. They don't eat much" and live "below what is usually regarded as the subsistence level in Canada." They repeatedly refused the developer's offers to purchase their house and felt "identically about needing the house and the cats and God, and not needing money or men."[89] Erskine died in 1984, ten years to the week after the *Globe and Mail* interview.[90] A few months later, a notice to creditors appeared in the paper regarding "claims against the estate of Erskine Keys," "spinster."[91]

Miss Agatha Leonard's 1949 biography in Alumnae's *Autumn Crocus* program reads: "While Agatha Leonard is not one of the original members of the Club she has been its devoted slave for a great many years. It would be impossible to list here the number of Club plays in which she has taken part." Leonard would prove to be one of Alumnae's long-time administrative anchors from the 1920s through to the 1980s. Her leadership included sitting on at least fourteen Alumnae executives between 1923 and 1971, when she helped lead the club as a member of the first Alumnae executive in the firehall. In the early 1960s, she was part of Alumnae's building fund committee as they sought a new space. Her Alumnae acting credits stretched from *A Single Man* in 1923 to the third instalment of their Moderns reading series in the fall of 1961, where she read for Martha in Michel de Ghelderode's *The Women at the Tomb*. She was active with other groups as well, as when she appeared in Hart House Theatre productions such as Herman Voaden's symphonic Expressionist piece *Ascend as the Sun*, a performance the *Globe and Mail*'s Hector Charlesworth described a "magnetic."[92] During the Second World War, she was a frequent performer on the homefront in revues for Alumnae and Hart House Theatre, and she was a performer and organizer for the famed *Merry-Go-Round* troop show.[93]

Agatha was born in 1899. In the early twentieth century, her father, Charles J. Leonard, was a "well-known citizen" of Toronto as a prominent trust company lawyer. He was also the skip for a national champion lawn bowling team, an avid curler, an ardent horseracing follower, and an international whist player.[94] Among Agatha's five siblings, one of whom died in the First World War, Thomas D'Arcy Leonard served as a lawyer and president of the National War Finance Committee during the Second World War before accepting a Senate appointment for Toronto-Rosedale in 1955.

Agatha graduated from UC in 1921 after a notably active undergraduate career in theatre with the WDC, the UC Modern Language Club, and the UC Women's Literary Society. She also sat on the UC Third Year Executive as "Poetess"[95] and was the first secretary-treasurer of the university's newly formed Women's Press Association.[96] Building on these student leadership experiences, she frequently sat on various society committees in Toronto. She maintained a long association with the UCAA, attending UC garden parties, teas, and dinners for all occasions, often as a member of the executive. Following the war in 1946, she sat as the only female member on the "revived" Hart House Theatre Board of Syndics when it reconvened after a nine-year hiatus[97] and Robert Gill was brought in as Hart House Theatre's new director. Agatha's name appeared frequently in the dailies from the 1920s through the 1960s, not only for her well-known work on stage, but also for her seemingly endless appearances at social engagements, both theatre-related and otherwise. Off-campus, she appeared at social gatherings: for the Mississauga Horse cavalry regiment (with "multi-coloured and handsome frocks of the ladies, the dazzling uniforms of scarlet and gold of the officers"[98]) and the Royal Canadian Yacht Club,[99] at ladies' night dances and bridge parties at the Freemasons' Zetland Lodge,[100] and at the Seigniory Club in Montebello, Quebec, the Royal Ontario Museum (on the occasion of its 1933 expansion),[101] a display and subsequent supper party by the Women's League of Health and Beauty,[102] a recital at the Heliconian Club,[103] and a luncheon for the Opera and Concert Committee of the Royal Conservatory of Music.[104] She often hosted events at her family's home on Heathdale Road for Alumnae members and other friends, as listed in the dailies.

For thirty-six years, Agatha was on the library staff at the University of Toronto. She became head librarian[105] for the university's medical library and, later, head of the library acquisitions department for thirteen years.[106] She was, at one time, president of the Toronto branch of the Special Libraries Association, and she presented papers on the history of Ontario's special libraries[107] and statistical methods in medical school.[108] Agatha's extensive efforts in retaining Alumnae's early production records made much of this study possible. She died in 1991 at the age of 91.[109]

Miss Agnes Isobel Muldrew (Mrs. Edgar Stone), "singularly gifted"[110] as an actor, was Alumnae's most renowned performer during the club's first two decades and one of the city's most significant performers in the early years of the Little Theatre movement. Her work with nonprofessionalizing theatres, particularly Alumnae and Hart House Theatre, made her "one of Toronto's leading amateur actresses," including in "prize-winning"[111] Dominion Drama Festival productions. She often worked under acclaimed director Edgar Stone, whom she married in 1930.

Agnes was born in Gravenhurst, Ontario, to influential parents whose names appeared regularly in the dailies, especially her mother Jean, who was a schoolteacher and "active in social work."[112] Jean became Director of the Home Branch of the Soldier Settlement Board (later the Land Settlement Board) of Canada, which had been founded to help war brides settle in Canada after the First World War. In this capacity, she helped inaugurate Canada's first short courses in Home Economics, initially for the benefit of settled war brides.[113] Jean was also Convener of the National Council of Women and Honorary Regent of an Imperial Order Daughters of the Empire (IODE) chapter.[114] Agnes's father, Dr. William Hawthorne Muldrew, was a principal at Gravenhurst's first high school; in 1903, he was appointed the first Dean of the Ontario Agricultural College's first residence, before dying suddenly in

1904. Muldrew Lake, southwest of Gravenhurst, is named after him for his tourism work in the late nineteenth century.

As a UC student, Agnes was active in the WDC from 1914 to 1918 (in Sheridan's *School for Scandal* she reportedly "became quite impassioned"[115] as Sir Peter). She also frequently appeared in UC Women's Literary Society plays, including giving a "spirited interpretation"[116] of Gregory Smirnov in Chekov's *The Bear*. Soon after, she played Charles Roche in J.M. Barrie's *Rosalind.*[117] For the Women's Lit, she performed with other recent UC graduates Adeline Lobb, Marion Squair, and Mabel Child in Shaw's *The Man of Destiny* in the 1918–19 school year, and then again with Lobb and Squair in a presentation of Dunsany's one-act play *Fame and the Poet* in December 1919[118] (this may explain why she did not appear in Alumnae's *The Bluestockings* that year). Future governor general Vincent Massey reportedly directed Agnes at some point during her undergraduate degree.[119] She held executive positions with the WDC, the YWCA (president), and the UC Women's Undergraduate Association (as YWCA representative) and was active in the Kappa Alpha Theta sorority, the Forest Hill Village Home and School Club, and the Red Cross, to which she gave blood throughout her life. In 1918, a year after finishing her BA in Household Science, and while pursuing her MA in Biochemistry at the university (which she completed in 1919), she acted with the WDC in Sheridan's *The Rivals*. Agnes's humour is evident under her yearbook graduation photograph, which begins with a citation from *Twelfth Night*: "'*The knave counterfeits well.*' A notable case is leaving the University Hospital this April, having come through a severe attack of Household Science which was complicated by chronic attacks of the dread disease, Dramatics, *The Critic*, *The Pigeon*, *The School of Scandal*. The patient also underwent the Presidency of the YWCA. Remarkable vitality carried her through."[120]

With Alumnae, Agnes was an actor and director from 1922, when the *Globe* published a photograph of her in advance of playing a "leading part"[121] as Melisande in A.A. Milne's *The Romantic Age*, until the 1943–44 season, when she sat as Alumnae's vice-president. She was also active with Hart House Theatre, occasionally appearing in new plays presented there,[122] often directed by her husband Edgar Stone. She also acted with other local companies, including the Dickens Fellowship,[123] the New Theatre of the Margaret Eaton School,[124] the Playwrights' Studio Group,[125] and the Arts and Letters Club.[126] The dailies' critics consistently praised her talents.

Agnes was "engaged in bio-chemistry for some years"[127] and was secretary[128] at the Radium Institute,[129] a private clinic for X-ray and radium cancer treatment run in Toronto by Dr. Williams Aikins, until he died in 1924.[130] The clinic treated more than 3,000 patients from across the country.[131] She also may have worked at the new Radium Institute established in Toronto in 1930.[132] After a "ripening"[133] romance over several years, in October 1930 Agnes married Hart House Theatre director Edgar Stone in a "pretty and interesting wedding" at Hart House Chapel. Frequent Hart House Theatre and Alumnae actor Ivor Lewis was best man.[134] Reported the *Varsity*, "so secret were the arrangements and so quiet the ceremony that even the secretary of Hart House Theatre, Miss Eleanor Barton, was not aware of it until afterwards."[135] There had been engagement notices in the daily papers a few weeks earlier, as well as an announcement the day before, but the wedding's actual location must have been kept extraordinarily under wraps, given that Muldrew and Barton were preparing to rehearse together, under Stone's direction, for Alumnae's fall Hart House Theatre production (the Toronto premiere of Milne's *To Have the Honour*). The family of Alumnae's Marion Squair hosted the wedding reception for "immediate relatives and friends."[136] Agnes and Edgar had a son, Richard, in 1932 and a daughter, Elizabeth, in 1934.

After an illness of several months,[137] on Friday, 15 February 1946, Agnes died in her fifties at Toronto's Queen Elizabeth Hospital, her death "such a grievous loss"[138] to Alumnae.

As evidence of a larger-than-life personality, an Alumnae "biography" of Agnes, typed and pasted into the Club's 1927–28 minute book, reads poetically:

> The voice that split a thousand tubes
> The awful majesty that fussed us;
> As, poisoning scales or sugar cubes,
> She poured out tea or justice.
> Her courts have infinite extent,
> They reach from president to president.
> Her S.A. spans the footlights glare.
> And slays the hundreds watching there;
> Full often too she treads the boards
> Of robes and roles creator;
> Who can she be, this prodigy?
> Not God, but our DICTATOR!

In the 1960s, **Eleanor Chambers Norton (Mrs. Julian Balfour Beecroft, Mrs. Charles D. Stewart)** was one of the busiest "familiar faces"[139] on southern Ontario's professional stages, but she had her start four decades earlier with Alumnae. Her stage appearances with major professional theatres such as the Shaw Festival,[140] the St. Lawrence Centre, and Centre Stage,[141] summer stock theatres like the Straw Hat Players, and nonprofessionalizing theatres like Alumnae, spanned seven decades. She appeared in some of Alumnae's most important productions between 1928 and 1961, including the world premiere of Alumnae member Katherine Anglin's *Boomerang* in 1935, *Yerma* in 1948 (for which she won CODL's best supporting actress award), and, in 1956 (while she was Alumnae's president), the Canadian premiere of Patricia Joudry's *Teach Me How to Cry*. The latter won the DDF's Calvert Trophy, and the prize money from that award allowed Alumnae to rent their first theatre. In the 1950s, Eleanor found herself playing leading roles across Toronto, and the papers invariably selected her name when printing a show's abbreviated cast list. She began acting with the CBC in 1958.[142] Her film appearances included the Canadian-made 1961 3D horror film *The Mask*; the 1961 film *One Plus One* with Kate Reid, Barbara Hamilton, and Douglas Rain, based on a radio play about the Kinsey Report; the 1980 horror film *Funeral Home*; and the 1980 crime film *Atlantic City* with Burt Lancaster and Susan Sarandon. A profile of her life aired on the Vision network in 1994.[143] Well into her nineties, Eleanor continued to perform with fellow residents at Toronto's Performing Arts Lodge (PAL),[144] a "living, working breathing building that has a theatrical bent,"[145] which she co-founded and moved into in 1993.[146] By 2001 she was ninety-five, and PAL's oldest resident.[147]

Eleanor was born in London, Ontario, in 1906, the only daughter of Eleanor May McLaughlin and Andrew Christie Norton. When Eleanor was five, the family moved to Toronto, where she attended Parkdale Collegiate.[148] She entered UC in 1924, studied Modern Languages, and was the first-year representative for the Modern Language Club.[149] She developed an interest in theatre, attending touring productions as they visited the city; she later called these years the "most exciting times culturally."[150] She also started acting. In her third year, she appeared in Hart House Theatre's Canadian premiere of C.K.

Munro's *At Mrs. Beam's*, and in her fourth year she appeared in Hart House Theatre's *Alice in Wonderland* with Agnes Muldrew. Across all four undergraduate years, Eleanor acted with the UC Players' Guild. In her graduating year of 1927–28 she was the UC Players' Guild's treasurer; she also performed as Dona Laura in the Italian-Spanish Club's production of Serafín and Joaquín Alvarez Quintero's *Mañana de Sol.*[151] Upon graduation in 1928, she worked with her father at the Timothy Eaton Company[152] while continuing to perform at Hart House Theatre, often with other Alumnae members. Her first productions with Alumnae were two one-act plays in 1935 at the Women's Union. She acted in Babette Hughes's two-hander *Three Players, a Fop and a Duchess*, alongside future CBC radio personality Andrew Allan; and she directed Gordon Bottomley's *Sisters* for the same evening. She trained as an actor under E.G. Sterndale Bennett at his Canadian Theatre School near Bay and College streets,[153] while becoming increasing familiar to the city's Little Theatre audiences through Alumnae and Hart House Theatre.

In 1931, Eleanor "very quietly"[154] married Julian Balfour Beecroft – a one-time pianist (until he lost three fingers in a woodworking accident), machinist, and inventor (notably of the world's first wire-and-tape voice recorders[155] – at her parents' home on Gormley Avenue and moved to Brooklin, near Whitby, Ontario, where Julian's father resided at the famed residence The Grange. Between 1936 and 1949, she fell off of Alumnae's membership list and out of the daily papers as she raised their five children.[156] Julian built aircraft machine parts in Barrie, Ontario, during the Second World War.[157] In 1947, her marriage with Julian ended, and in 1950 she returned to the stage, directing two Alumnae productions and appearing in more than a dozen others with the club until 1961, by which point her professional acting career, at middle age, was taking her across the province. In 1958, Eleanor began acting on CBC radio and television. Then, with her daughters Norma and Jane and her son Stuart, she established a "small dynasty" at CBC with Norma as a music producer, Jane a freelance writer, Stuart a videotape technician, and Eleanor, a "tousle-haired blonde who doesn't look her 60 years,"[158] an actor.

In 1972, Eleanor married Supreme Court of Ontario Justice Charles D. Stewart, who was an amateur artist, Arts and Letters Club member, and, formerly, a DDF board member.[159] But five months later he died, and, as reported in the *Toronto Star* years later, with the "immeasurable strength that had helped her get her through a life that was often cruel, she picked herself up and carried on with her career."[160] In 1981, Eleanor became president-elect of the Heliconian Club.[161] She died in Toronto in 2007 at 102,[162] having led a decidedly remarkable life.

Miss Mary Wallace Smart, not to be confused with the popular music teacher and founder of Toronto's Heliconian Society, Mary Smart, began acting with Alumnae in 1921 in Sheridan's *A Trip to Scarborough.* She performed in about a dozen Alumnae plays until 1954 and served on about half a dozen Alumnae executives during the 1940s and 1950s. Mary was one of four children of Lieutenant-Colonel Robert Wallace Smart and Georgianna Adelaide Cooper Smart. At UC, she did not act with the WDC, but was "business manager of plays" for the UC Modern Language Club (1918–19), which presumably means she had a hand in organizing the two plays they presented that year: a Spanish play by Marcial Dorado and a French play by Marivaux.[163] She was vice-president of the UC Women's Literary Society when graduates Agnes Muldrew, Adeline Lobb, Marion Squair, and Mabel Child presented Shaw's *The Man of Destiny.* Mary was also vice-president of the Anglican Women's Club (1917–18). She noted in her 1919 graduation photograph that she was "but five feet high."[164]

Less than a year after graduating from UC, Mary completed her provincial library apprenticeship and examination. Along with six other women, including fellow UC graduate and Alumnae member Doris V. Dignum, she was recommended for a permanent staff position with the Public Library Board. (That day in January 1920 was also notable in the papers because it was the first day that the College Street Public Library had reopened after the epidemic, so the number of checked-out books rose considerably.[165]) In 1927, Mary was elected president of the Toronto Public Library Association. Although she was not as involved as some of her contemporaries in Alumnae social functions, she was active in UCAA garden parties and other entertainments, as well as in Toronto Public Library events; for example, she acted in their Dramatic Association's productions of *Pride and Prejudice*[166] and *Told in a Garden* in the spring of 1922. The latter also involved Dignum.[167] She was present when a "short musicale was held" in the St. George Street public library branch's new auditorium in March 1931, an auditorium in which Alumnae would stage several plays over the next forty years as the Central Library Theatre. Mary died in 1962.[168]

Miss Marion R. Squair (Mrs. Harold S. Hunter), among early Alumnae members, led a notably public life, not only onstage with Alumnae but with other public organizations as well. She was known as a popular "mistress of ceremonies" and hostess for various social events citywide, often alongside her mother, including at their home.

As a young woman, Marion was listed in the *Globe* as an usher for a popular Stephen Leacock lecture in 1915 at the Royal Alexandra Theatre.[169] Marion's father was UC French professor John Squair, himself a graduate of UC and first president of the UC Modern Language Club, which he founded in 1881.[170] When her father gave a lecture for the tercentenary celebration of Molière's birth at Hart House in 1922, Marion and her UC classmates performed *Les Prècieuses ridicules*. Throughout her undergraduate career, she was active on campus with the WDC and the Modern Language Club as an actor (her Sir Oliver in *A School for Scandal* was rendered "exceptionally well"[171]), director, and executive member (the latter, in her father's footsteps). According to the caption under Marion's graduate photograph, she loved a "puck and stick on good keen ice."[172] Marion was also a Kappa Alpha Theta member. For some years after graduation, she remained active with that sorority and as a performer with the UC Women's Literary Society. While a student, she volunteered for the Franco-British Aid Society with Erskine Keys and Agnus Muldrew when it presented arts events for the war effort, and she helped arrange for WDC proceeds to go to that organization as well. In 1917, she worked for the war effort as a Farmerette in the Niagara District with other early Alumnae members, including Alison Ewart, and wrote about that experience in a piece published by her daughter in which Marion described organizing an elected committee to air grievances with the farmers as well as a variety show to entertain the locals.[173] She was active in raising funds for the UC women's building, apart from Alumnae, as early as 1920, when she hosted a tea at her mother's house.[174]

Following her graduation in 1918, Marion was highly active in events hosted by the UCAA, the Women's Art Association (from which Alumnae would rent space), the Shakespeare Society, the Heliconian Club, and the Glen Mawr Old Girls' Association. She earned an MA in French and was appointed lecturer in UC's French department from 1927 to 1930.[175] An avid theatre and concert goer, Marion performed in Roy Mitchell's famed provocatively modern production of *Love's Labour's Lost* at Hart House Theatre in June 1920.[176] She also acted in about a dozen Alumnae shows, from Milne's *The Romantic Age* in 1922 to Rachel Field's *The Londonderry Air* in 1940, while also, somewhat famously, serving as mistress of ceremonies for Alumnae's skits and one-acts, particularly during the early years of the Second World War. In 1929, the year after her father died, Marion married Harold S. Hunter, and the two frequently attended public events together. They appeared onstage together in two Alumnae productions: Maugham's *Caesar's Wife* a year before their marriage, and a short play produced by Alumnae in June 1939 titled *Mistaken Identity*. She remained an Alumnae member until 1942.

Between 1921 and 1961, **Miss Margaret "Peggy" Tytler** appeared in about thirty Alumnae productions. She was among their most consistently active members both on and off stage, as both actor and director and, in their first two decades, in various executive positions.

Margaret was born in 1894 to Jennie and John Tytler. Her father was a lawyer and then, from 1921 until he retired in 1934, a York County judge.[177] He was active with the Toronto-based Sons of Scotland Benevolent Association.[178] An actor from an early age, Margaret appeared in the Harbord Street Collegiate Institute's production of Shakespeare's *The Merchant of Venice*[179]. While she was a BA student from 1913 to 1917, she was active with the WDC as an executive member and as an actor in one Sheridan and three Shakespeare comedies; her Mrs. Candour was reportedly "ebulliently vivacious,"[180] and her Dogberry was a "triumph. Delightfully stupid, pompous and good natured, she kept the audience in roars of laughter with her torrents of eloquence."[181] She also acted with the UC Women's Literary Society and sat on the UC Women's Athletic Executive in 1916–17, at a time when fellow Alumnae member Erskine Keys was on the UC basketball team.[182] Margaret's "biography," typed and pasted into Alumnae's 1927–28 minutes book, reads poetically with reference to her presidency that year:

> She's never better than in Scottish haunts,
> For who could e're forget her Highland Mary?
> When Archie Campbell threatened her with taunts,
> Of biting curses she was far from chary.
> This year she has had much to try her mettle,
> She had the full command behind the scenes;
> 'Tis well her Gaelic fury did not settle
> Upon the household of the Considines.

Along with Agnes Muldrew, Margaret was one of Toronto's most "well known"[183] Little Theatre performers, directors, and organizers, working not only with Alumnae but also with other groups at Hart House Theatre and the Margaret Eaton Theatre, as well as the Civic Theatre Association, the Shakespeare Society, and the Playwrights Studio Group. Between the DDF's inaugural year in 1933 and its suspension for the war in 1939, Peggy and Alumnae's Alison Ewart were among the few people who participated in every CODL festival.[184] Notably, she featured in world and Canadian premieres produced in years when these were rare.[185] Her last Alumnae appearance was a fall 1961 reading of Mrs. Rooney in Beckett's *All That Fall*, as part of the club's second in a set of three modern play readings. Lawrence Stone called her reading a "dynamic performance within the limited means she had to work with. She was a comic and yet pathetic figure of wizened self-pity, and her good facial expressions transformed a mere script-reading into an interesting demonstration of exaggerated suffering, the characteristic of Mrs. Rooney."[186] Margaret passed away at her cottage at Buck Lake, Muskoka, in 1968.

Miss Katherine (Kay) Baswick Wells (Mrs. Robert Edmund Anglin) was an early and active actor and executive member with Alumnae, having a hand in two significant moments in the company's history: her play *Boomerang* in 1935 was the first world premiere produced by Alumnae (she directed it as well); and as president of Alumnae during the Second World War, she led the club's formal departure from University College. A vocal exponent of new playwriting from the 1930s on, she once wrote a letter to the *Globe and Mail* questioning how a particular new play that had been "held up to public ridicule"[187] could have received the honour of best one-act play by the adjudicator at the Eastern Ontario Drama League festival. (The production's director later responded by agreeing that the adjudicator apparently disliked the play but appreciated the production.)[188]

Katherine was born in 1903 to Mary Barwick and architect and inventor Arthur E. Wells. She did not participate in the WDC but was increasingly active on campus with the Women's Undergraduate Association (1920–21), the Anglican Club (recording secretary 1921–22), the first UC Players' Guild (wardrobe mistress 1922–23 with Erskine Keys as honorary president and playwright W.S. Milne as master electrician; and 1923–24 as vice-president and wardrobe mistress), the UC Women's Literary Society (vice-president 1923–24), and the *Varsity* staff (associate editor 1923–24, with W.S. Milne as drama editor). Prefiguring both her playwriting and the impact of her leadership on Alumnae, Katherine's graduation photograph in 1924 reads:

> *Her pen's her tongue and faithfully doth serve her.*
> If she says she will, she will,
> And there's an end on it,
> What'er the task may be,
> 'Tis done, depend on it.
> Plays, costumes, teas, "Lit."
> Or *Varsity*, she'll do her bit,
> And loves a good time too!
> Oh yes, we think she'll do![189]

Katherine appeared in Hubert Henry Davies's *A Single Man* for Alumnae in 1923, while still a student, and again the next year in Fenn and Pryce's *'Op-o'-Me Thumb* as an Alumnae member, going on to appear in a number of Alumnae productions until 1927, and to sit on the executive several times between 1925 and 1949. In 1928, she married lawyer Robert Edmund Anglin, who had acted in Alumnae's *The Evil Doers of Good* in 1925. Although she does not appear to have frequented Toronto social gatherings as much as some of her Alumnae contemporaries, she did attend Havergal College events. She died in 1983 and is buried with her parents in Toronto.

Miss (Jessie) Elspeth Wilson was born in Niagara Falls, Ontario, in 1892 and came to UC in 1908 when her father James Wilson, the Superintendent of Parks for the Village of Niagara Falls, moved to Toronto to become Toronto Parks Commissioner, a position he held until his death in 1911. Likely occupied with dealing with her father's death and internment in Niagara Falls, Elspeth took some time away from college, before returning to focus on drama with the WDC, for which she was secretary in her graduating year of 1912–13 (in that year, her Olivia in WDC's production of Shakespeare's *Twelfth Night* was deemed to be "stately and dignified, though perhaps a little lacking in force and passion"[190]). She wrote beside her graduation photograph, perhaps a little rebelliously, that her "personality, however, has not been submerged in the madding crowd, but has localized its interest in the Dramatic Club."[191]

Following graduation, Elspeth took up work at the Canadian Bank of Commerce as private secretary to the Bank's Staff Inspector, C.L. Foster, notably contributing editorial skills to the publication of wartime pamphlets titled "Letters from the Front," which recorded enlistments, promotions, activities, and casualties among officers who had worked at the bank, for the benefit of the bank's staff.[192] Her writing can be found publicly in various publications, as when she wrote a curious letter to the *Globe* in 1917, concerned about dogs roaming the streets in towns and villages ("Their name is legion and their habits not commendable"). "With food prices high and soaring," she wrote, money could be spent feeding a "working-man's family"[193] instead of the stray dogs. In the *Farmers' Magazine* she wrote of the injustice of farmers' "Fowl-less dinner tables"[194] in Sarnia on Christmas Day 1918 due to the appointment of a price committee on farm produce in that city and the lack of respect for farmers among the townspeople.[195]

Elspeth was the second president of Alumnae, taking over for Margaret Boyle in 1924–25 and returning to the executive in 1943–44 for two years as recording, and then corresponding, secretary. She first performed in an Alumnae production in April 1924 (St. John Hankin's *The Charity That Began at Home*) and acted with Alumnae until 1942, remaining a member most years until 1957. Like many of her fellow Alumnae members, she volunteered for and organized UCAA and University Women's Club events, sitting on the latter's executive in the 1930s, including as financial officer at the national level.[196] She was also active annually in balls put on by the Canadian Bank of Commerce Athletic Association and the Canadian Army Medical Corps in both Toronto and the Niagara region, where she had grown up (one of her brothers, Hugh, was a lieutenant-colonel, and her other brother, Malcolm, was a lieutenant-colonel and physician who served in the First World War and, later, in Mesopotamia before returning to Toronto to practise medicine and teach at the university[197]). Although she lived in Toronto most of her life, Elspeth died in 1965 in Sault Ste. Marie, Ontario, and was interred where she had grown up, in Niagara Falls.

Appendix II

Alumnae Production History Pre-Firehall

Run Dates	Show	Writer	Play Dates	Director	Venue	Premiere	Style	Festivals	Cast
15–16 Feb. 1918 (Fri., Sat., 8:00pm)	*The Bluestockings (Les Femmes Savantes)*	Molière	1672 prem. late-1800s or 1908 trans.	Dr. Frank Home Kirkpatrick	Conservatory Music Hall, Toronto Conservatory of Music (SW Corner of College St. and University Ave.)		Period (Comedy)		Miss Isobel Cassidy, Mrs. M.E. Laughton [was Mary Buckley] Miss Mona E. Clark, Miss Edna Bach [Norwich], Miss Marjorie J.F. Fraser, Miss Isabel Jones, Miss Margaret Boyle, Miss Erskine Keys, Miss Jessica Reid, Miss Helen Stewart, Miss Norma Mortimer
27–8 Mar. 1919 (Thu., Fri.)	*Trelawny of the Wells*	Arthur Wing Pinero	1898 prem.	Dr. Frank Home Kirkpatrick	Conservatory Music Hall, Toronto Conservatory of Music (SW Corner of College St. and University Ave.)		Period (Comedy)		Mrs. Laughton (Rose Trelawney), Mrs. Arthur C. Norwich (Avonia Bunn), Miss Chirstina Cooper (Miss Trafalger Gower), Miss Margaret Boyle (Ferdinand Gadd), Miss Mabel Child (Tom Wrench), Miss Erskine Keys (James Telfer)
No productions in 1919–20 season									
15–16 Apr. 1921 (Fri. eve., Sat. 2:30 p.m., Sat. eve.)	*A Trip to Scarborough*	Richard Brinsley Sheridan	1777 prem.	Directed by the cast	Hart House Theatre		Period (Comedy)		Marguerite Phillips (Lord Foppington), Mabel Child (Sir Tunbelly Clumsy), Margaret Wilson (Colonel Townly), Margaret Boyle (Loveless), Erskine Keys (Tom Fashion), Edith Lambert (La Varole), Freda Waldon (Lory), Winnifred Simpson (Probe), Margaret Austin (Mendlegs), Freda Stanbury (Jeweler, Servant), Jessie MacGowan (Shoemaker), Olive Cale (Tailor), Marie Peterkin (Post-boy), Christina Cooper (Amanda), Margaret Tytler, (Berinthia), Alice Lewis (Miss Hoyden), Mary Smart, (Mrs. Coupler), Grace Messervy (Nurse), Vera Robinson (Seamstress), Margaret Shorthill (Servant), Clare Millar (Servant)
28–9 Apr. 1922 (Fri., Sat.)	*The Romantic Age, A Comedy in Three Acts*	A.A. Milne	1920 prem., 1921 publ.	A. Monro Grier	Hart House Theatre	Toronto	Modern (comedy)		Mr. James (Jim) J. Craig, Miss Margaret Boyle, Miss Margaret (Peggy) Tytler, Mr. A. Monro Grier, Miss Christina Cooper, Miss Marion Squair [Hunter], Mr. Ivor R. Lewis (played Gentleman Susan), Mr. Henry Button, Agnes Muldrew [Stone]

(Fri. eve., Sat. mat., Sat. eve.)	*and Original Comedy in Four Acts*	Davies	1914 publ.		Theatre	(Comedy)	Worthington), Raymond Card (Henry Worthington), Margaret Tytler (Henry's wife), Harcourt Brown (Dicky), Agnes Muldrew (strong-minded Lady Cotterill), Marion R. Squair [Hunter] ('the romp'), Edna Norwich (sympathetic Miss Heseltine), Christina Cooper (Louise Parker the would-be 'yamp'), Katherine Wells [Anglin] (Bertha Simms), Margaret Boyle (servant), Audrey Young (servant), Agatha Leonard (servant)
17 Apr. 1923 (Tues.)	*The Romantic Age* (Act -)	A.A. Milne		None on record.	University Women's Club (80 Bloor St. W.)	Modern (comedy)	Maragert Boyle, Marion Squair [Hunter], Margaret Tytler, Chirstine Cooper
25 Oct. 1923 (Thurs.)	*Rosalind* (one-act)	Sir James (J.M.) Barrie	1910 prem	Margaret Boyle	Women's Union (79 St. George St.) (This new Women's Union opened Jan. 1923)	Modern (comedy)	Mrs. Arthur Norwich (Beatrice), Miss Doris Dignum (The Landlady), Mr. Robert Finch (Charles)
1 Feb. 1924 (Sat.)	Three Short Plays:				Women's Union (79 St. George St.)		
	• *The Twelve-Pound Look*	Sir James (J.M.) Barrie	1910 prem., 1914 publ., 1920 film	None on record.		Modern (Comedy)	F.H. Coombs, Audrey Young, Adeline Lobb
	• *The Green Scarf [An Artifical Comedy in One Act]*	K.S. [Kenneth Sawyer] Goodman	1920 prem.	None on record.		Modern (comedy)	Margaret Boyle, F.J. Mallett
	• *The Stronger*	August Strindberg	1889 prem.	None on record.		Modern	Agnes Muldrew, Christina Cooper, Doris Dignum
4–5 Apr. 1924 (Fri. eve., Sat. mat. and eve.)	*The Charity that Began at Home* [A comedy in Four Acts] "A comedy for philanthropists" in program]	St. John Hankin	1906 prem.	Margaret Boyle	Hart House Theatre	Modern (comedy)	Mrs. H.V. (Mary) Laughton, Dr. Edith Gordon, Miss Dorothy Stacey, Miss Agnes Muldrew, Miss Elspeth Wilson, Major John Mood, Mr. F.J. Mallett, Mr. Leslie Reid, Mr. F.W. Hawkes, Mr. J.W. MacDonald, Margaret Tytler
12 May 1924 (Mon.)	*Balm*	Merrill Denison	1923 prem., 1926 publ.	Miss M.E. Allen	Women's Union (79 St. George St.)	Modern (comedy)	No cast found.

(*Continued*)

Run Dates	Show	Writer	Play Dates	Director	Venue	Premiere	Style	Festivals	Cast
23 Oct. 1924 (Thurs.)	*'Op-o'-Me Thumb* (one-act)	Frederick Fenn and Richard Pryce	1906 (dir. by André Antoine at Théâtre Antoine)	None on record.	Women's Union (79 St. George St.)		Modern		Doris Dignum, Erskine Keys, Katherine Wells, Adeline Lobb, Marion Squair [Hunter], Mr. Raymond Card
3 Dec. 1924 (Wed.)	*Three one-act plays:*				Women's Union (79 St. George St.)				Raymond Card and Miss Elspeth Wilson announced each play and presided; casts in the three plays included: Miss Margaret Boyle, Miss Agatha Leonard, Miss Lena Cooper
	• *The Storm*	John Drinkwater	1915 publ.	None on record.			Modern		
	• *Hiatus*	Eden Phillpotts	1912 publ. 1913 prem.	None on record.			Modern		
	• *Augustus Does His Bit*	George Bernard Shaw	1917 prem.	None on record.			Modern		
10–11 Feb. 1925 (Tues., Wed.)	*The Evil Doers of Good* (*Los Malhechores del Bien*) [A Satire of Manners]	Jacinto Benavente, trans. J. G. Underhill	1905 prem., 1923 trans.	Wallace House	Hart House Theatre	Toronto	Modern (comedy)		Mr. H.E. Hitchman (Don Helio Doro), Miss Marion Squair [Hunter], Miss Agnes Muldrew, Miss Dorothy Stacey, Mr. Ramsey Duff, Mr. Leslie Reid, Margaret Boyle, Mr. William Scott, Elspeth Wilson, W.S. Milne, Agatha Leonard, Robert Anglin, G.R. Hatton
23 Apr. 1925 (Thurs.)	"An evening of drama and song"				Women's Union (79 St. George St.)		Variety		No cast found.
20–1 Jan. 1926 (Wed-Thurs.)	Three One Act Plays:				Women's Union (79 St. George St.)				
	• *Spring*	Colin Campbell Clements	1924 publ.	None on record.			Modern (drama)		W.R. Turner, Ramsay Duff, Muriel Smith
	• *Campbell of Kilmhor*	J.A. Ferguson	1921 publ., 1939 film	None on record.			Modern (drama)		Prof. E.A. Dale, Margaret Tytler, W.S. Milne, Emmy Lou Carter, F.J. Mallett, Alex McLure, Ramsay Duff, W.R. Turner
	• *Overruled*	George Bernard Shaw	1912 prem.	None on record.			Modern (comedy)		Mr. F.J. Mallet, Elspeth Wilson, A.F. Stephenson, Margaret Boyle
27 Jan. 1927 (Thurs.)	Three Short Plays:				Women's Union (79 St. George St.)				
	• *A Marriage Has Been Arranged*	Alfred Sutro	1904 prem.	Miss Margaret Boyle			Modern		Emmie Lou Carter, Raymond Card
	• *Mrs. Pat and the Law*	Mary Aldis	1923 publ.	Miss Agnes Muldrew			Modern		Miss Marion Squair [Hunter], Dr. Edith Gordon, Miss Mary Smart, Col. Patterson, Mr. R. Macdonald

			story	[Margaret] Tytler			Norwich, Miss Margaret McCready, Mr. H.B. Fennell
28 Jan. 1927 (Fri.)	Three Short Plays:				Women's Art Association (23 Prince Arthur Ave.)		
	• *A Marriage Has Been Arranged*	Alfred Sutro	1904 prem	Miss Margaret Boyle		Modern	Same as 27 Jan. 1927
	• *Mrs. Pat and the Law*	Mary Aldis	1923 pub	Miss Agnes Muldrew		Modern	Same as 27 Jan. 1927
	• *Dorinda Dares*	Angela Morris	1909 short story	Miss Peggy [Margaret] Tytler		Modern	Same as 27 Jan. 1927
11–12 Mar. 1927 (Fri, Sat)	*Getting Married: A Disquisitory Play*	George Bernard Shaw	1908 prem.	H.E. Hitchman	Hart House Theatre	Modern (comedy)	Agnes Muldrew, Arthur Cox, Dorothy Stacey, Desmond Preston, Mr. F.J. Mallet, Margaret Tytler, Mr. F.H. Coombs, Edgar Stone, Margaret Boyle, Doris Dignum, A. Monro Grier, John Brockie, H.J.C. Ireton
1 Nov. 1927 (Tues.)	Three Short Plays:				Women's Union (79 St. George St.)		Presumably similar casts as 23 Nov. 1927.
	• *Fourteen*	Alice Gerstenberg	1919 prem., 1920 publ.	None on record.		Modern (farce)	
	• *Will-o'-the-Wisp: A Fantasy in One Act*	Doris Halman	1924 prod.	None on record.		Modern (fantasy)	
	• *The Dear Departed*	Stanley Houghton	1908 prem., 1910 publ.	None on record.		Modern (comedy)	
23 Nov. 1927 (Wed.)	Three Short Plays:				First Unitarian Church (216 Jarvis St.)		
	• *Fourteen*	Alice Gerstenberg	1919 prem., 1920 publ.	None on record.			Margaret Boyle (Mrs. Pringle), Muriel Smith (Eileen Pringle), F.J. Mallet (The Butler "Dunnham")
	• *Will-o'-the-Wisp*	Doris Halman	1924 prod.	None on record.			Agnes Muldrew (The Old Woman), Doris Dignum (Waif), Elspeth Wilson (Servant Maid), Edna Norwich (Poet's Wife)
	• *The Dear Departed*	Stanley Houghton	1908 prem., 1910 publ.	None on record.			Margaret Tytler (Mrs. Henry Slater), Agatha Leonard (Victoria, her daughter), J.W. Chester (Henry, her husband), F.L. Newton (Mr. Ben Jordan), Marion Squair [Hunter] (Mrs. Jordon), Frank T. Rostance (Abel Merryweather)

(*Continued*)

Run Dates	Show	Writer	Play Dates	Director	Venue	Premiere	Style	Festivals	Cast
11 Dec. 1927 (Sun.)	*The Rim of the World*	Floyd Dell	1915 prem.	None on record.	Women's Union (79 St. George St.)		Modern (fantasy)		Miss Agatha Leonard, Miss Alison Ewart, Miss Peggy Tytler, Mr. Edgar Stone, Mr. Ramsay Duff
9–10 Mar 1928 (Fri., Sat. eve., Sat. mat.)	*Mary, Mary, Quite Contrary*	St. John Ervine	1923 publ.	H.E. Hitchman (director and producer)	Hart House Theatre		Modern (comedy)		George Patton, F. Mallett, W. Ward Price, Edgar Stone, H.E. Hitchman, Edna Norwich, Agatha Leonard, Agnes Muldrew, Edith Cosens, Erskine Keys
23–4 Nov. 1928 (Fri., twice Sat.)	*Caesar's Wife* [A Comedy in Three Acts]	W. Somerset Maugham	1919 prem., 1922 publ.	H.E. Hitchman	Hart House Theatre		Modern (comedy)		F.J. Mallett, Robert Finch, Murray Bonnycastle, Harold S. Hunter, Lambert Dusseau, Agnes Muldrew, Alison Ewart, Margaret Tytler, Marion Squair [Hunter], Eric Stangroom, G. Alexander Fee, Gordon MacNamara
28 Feb. 1929 (Thu)	*Three Short Plays:*				Women's Union (79 St. George St.)				No casts found.
	• *Seven Women*	Sir James (J.M.) Barrie	1917 prem.	None on record.			Modern		
	• *The Only Jealousy of Emer*	W.B. Yeats	1922 prem.	None on record.			Modern (lyrical)		
	• *The Florist Shop [A Comedy in One Act]*	Winifred Hawkridge	1915 prem.	None on record.			Modern (comedy)		
19 Nov. 1929 (Tues.)	• Two one-act plays:				Women's Union (79 St. George St.)				
	• *The Fourth Mrs. Phillips*	Carl Glick	1913 prem.	None on record.			Modern (comedy)		Pearl Gray, Erskine Keys
	• *Three Players, a Fop and a Duchess*	Babette Hughes	1928 prem., *circa*	None on record.			Modern (comedy)		Miss Eleanor Norton, Mr. Andrew Allan
5–8 Feb. 1930 (Wed-Sat eve + Sat mat).	*Pomander Walk*	Louis N. Parker	1910 prem.	Edgar Stone	Hart House Theatre		Modern (comedy)		Ivor Lewis, Mr. H.E. Hitchman, Everard Nash, Miss Pearl Gray, Margaret Boyle [Martin] and Eleanor Norton [Beecroft], Andrew Allan (Dr. Sternroyd), Eleanor [Barton] Woodside, Agnes Muldrew Stone, Mary Smart, Nora Turnbull, Doris Shiell [Stacey]
7–8 Nov. 1930 (Fri., Sat.)	*To Have the Honour* [A Comedy in Three Acts]	A.A. Milne	1924 prem.	Edgar Stone	Hart House Theatre	Toronto	Modern (comedy)		Brendon Mulholand, H.E. Hitchman, F.J. Mallet, John Patton, Ray Purdie, Agnes Muldrew, Alison Ewart, Eleanor Barton, Margaret Tytler, Constance Shiell

(Fri.)					(79 St. George St.)		
	• *A Matter of Husbands*	Franz Molnar (Ferenc Molnár)	1920s prem., *circa*	None on record.		Modern (comedy)	
	• Trifles	Susan Glaspell	1916 prem.	None on record.		Modern (drama)	
	• *The Shepherd in the Distance [A Pantomime in Three Scenes]*	Holland Hudson	1915 prem.	None on record.		Modern (pantomime)	
27 Nov. 1931 (Fri.)	[Three Plays]				Parish Hall, Christ Church, Deer Park (1570 Yonge St.)		
	• *Joint Owners in Spain*	Alice Brown [program says Olive Brown]	1914 prem.	None on record.		Modern (comedy)	Erskine Keys (Mrs. Mitchell), Doris Dignum (Miss Fullerton), Edith Gordon (Miss Dyer), Marion Hunter [Squair] (Mrs. Blair)
	• *The Valiant*	Holworthy Hall and Robert Middlemass	1920 prem.	None on record.		Modern (mystery)	Stewart Reburn (The Warden), Melville Keay (Father Daly), Jack Williamson (The Attendant), Arthur Fitzgerald (James Dyke), Nora Turnbull (Josephine Paris)
	• *Dorinda Dares*	Angela Morris [program says Angeline Morris]	1909 short story	None on record.			Andrew Allan (Lord Bobingbrooke), J.A. Romeyn (Saunders, his servant), Helen Anderson (Doris Desborough), Isabel Cleland (Kitty Kymanston) F. Keeling – stage manager)
11–12 Mar. 1932 (Fri., Sat.)	*The Young Idea*	Noël Coward	1923 prem.	Edgar Stone	Hart House Theatre	Modern (comedy)	Florence Mathews, Edna Norwich, Lucille MacLeod, Isabel Cleland, Agatha Leonard, Doris Dignum, Margaret Tytler, with Ross Millard, Stewart Reburn, Arthur Fitzgerald, Gontran Rochereau de la Sablière, B. Ward Price, F.G. Venables, Percy Schutte
9 Dec. 1932 (Fri.)	*Nine Till Six* (3rd act)	Aimée and Phillip Stuart	1930 prem., 1930 publ., 1932 film	None on record.	Women's Union (79 St. George St.)	Modern (drama)	Cast likely similar to 24 Mar. 1933 CODL entry.

(*Continued*)

Run Dates	Show	Writer	Play Dates	Director	Venue	Premiere	Style	Festivals	Cast
12 Dec. 1932 (Mon.)	*Christmas Tableaux*			None on record.	Women's Union (79 St. George St.)		Christmas Tableaux		No cast found.
16 Mar. 1933 (Thurs.)	*Nine Till Six* (full play)	Aimée and Phillip Stuart		Margaret Tytler ("produced")	Eaton Auditorium (Eaton's College St. store, 444 Yonge St.)				Agatha Leonard (Mrs. Pembroke), Edith Gordon (Miss Roberts), Isabel Cleland (Freda), Alison Ewart (Gracie Abbott), Genevra Campbell (Mrs. Abbott), Eleanor Barton (Clare Pembroke), Doris Dignum (Daisy), Florian Moore (Gwladys), Margaret Donald (Bridget Penarth), Elspeth Wilson (Lady Avonlaye), Nora Turnbull (Violet), Mary Smart (Carrie), Florence Mathews (Beatrice), Katherine McBurney (Judy), Helen Eakin (Helen), Marion Hunter [Squair] (M'selle) Margaret Tytler – producer Edna Norwich – prompter
24 Mar. 1933 (Fri.)	*Nine Till Six* (3rd act)	Aimée and Phillip Stuart		Margaret Tytler ("produced")	Hart House Theatre			Alumnae's entry in CODL1 (DDF)	Agatha Leonard (Mrs. Pembroke), Eleanor Barton (Clare Pembroke), Edith Gordon (Miss Roberts), Isobel Cleland (Freda), Alison Ewart (Gracie Abbot), Genevra Campbell (Mrs. Abbott) Edna Norwich – prompter
1 Apr. 1933 (Sat.)	*Nine Till Six*	Aimée and Phillip Stuart		Margaret Tytler	Hart House Theatre				Cast likely similar to 16 March 1933 full production.
20 Apr. 1933 (Thurs.)	*Sure of a Fourth: A Satirical Comedy in One Act*	Rica McLean Farquharson	1933 prem., 1935 publ.	Margaret Tytler	Women's Union (79 St. George St.)		Modern (comedy)		Mary Smart, Christina Templeton, Alison Ewart, Helen Eakin, Edna Norwich, Murray Bonnycastle
11 Dec. 1933 (Mon.)	Irish Nativity play	Lady Gregory		Eleanor Barton Woodside	Women's Union (79 St. George St.)		Christmas Nativity		No cast found.

(Fri.)		Maria Martinez Sierra (likely recent trans. by Helen and Harley Granville Barker)		Rumball	Theatre		(farce)		Norwich (Regina), Betty Green (Finna), A. Monro Grier (Mr. Turner), Florian Moore (Sussy), Norman Green (Faustino), Murray Bonnycastle (Mario), Eleanor Barton (Astrid), Katherine Anglin (Miss Turner), Lionel Reid (2nd Officer), Alison Ewart (Marcella), Agnes Muldrew (Donna Dolores), Archibald Swan (Don Francesco), Margaret Donald (Margarita), Ross Millard (Milano), Doris Shiell (Lorenza), Margaret Tytler (Juliana), Elspeth Wilson, Margaret Colvin, Peggy McCready (Young ladies on shipboard) Ruth Home – properties Agatha Leonard – prompter Jack Barber – stage manager Murray Bonnycastle painted the portrait in Act II, Canada Steamship Line lent deck chairs and life belts
19 Mar. 1934 (Mon.)	*Smoke Screens*	Harold Brighouse	1932 publ.	Agatha Leonard	Central Library Theatre (then called "Auditorium of the Toronto Public Library") (20 St. George St.)		Modern (comedy)		Florence Mathews, Margaret Tytler, Edna Norwich, Margaret Donald
28 Mar. 1934 (Wed.)	*Smoke Screens*	Harold Brighouse		Agatha Leonard	Hart House Theatre			CODL2	Cast likely similar to 19 March 1934.
10 Dec. 1934 (Mon.)	*The Littlest Shepherd*. Christmas Play (the story of David, the children's shepherd)	Florence Ryerson and Colin Clements	1929 publ.	None on record.	Women's Union (79 St. George St.)		Christmas Nativity		No cast found.
25 Jan. 1935 (Fri.)	Three one-act plays:				Women's Union (79 St. George St.)				
	• *Boomerang*	Katherine Anglin	1935 prem.	Katherine Anglin		World	Modern		Margaret Donald, Elspeth Wilson, Dorothy Batcheller, Mary Smart, Betty Green, Robert Christie, Kenneth Mayall, Robert McCrae

(*Continued*)

Run Dates	Show	Writer	Play Dates	Director	Venue	Premiere	Style	Festivals	Cast
	• *Sisters*	Gordon Bottomley		Agnes Muldrew Stone and Eleanor Norton Beecroft			Modern (poetic)		Agnes Muldrew Stone, Eleanor Norton Beecroft
	• *Villa for Sale*	Sacha Guitry		Margaret Tytler			Modern (comedy)		Margaret Tytler, Florian Moore, Christina Templeton, Agatha Leonard, John Hamilton
30 Mar. 1935 (Sat.)	*As the Tumbrils Pass* (a play in one act)	Ethel Van der Veer and Franklyn Bigelow	1923 publ.	W.S. Milne	Hart House Theatre		Modern (drama)	CODL3	Agatha Leonard, Margaret Tytler, Erskine Keys, Doris Shiell, Alison Ewart, Dorothy Batcheller, Christina Templeton
25–8 Nov. 1935 (Mon.–Thurs.)	*Ladies in Waiting* (a play for women in three acts)	Cyril Campion	1934 publ.	Frank Hemingway	Hart House Theatre	Toronto	Modern (mystery)		Margaret Tytler, Margaret Donald, Christina Templeton, Agatha Leonard, Alison Ewart (Hewitt), Doris Shiell (Stacey), Margaret Tytler, Erskine Keys, Dorothy Batcheller, Agnes Muldrew, Eleanor Barton, Genevra Campbell Florian Moore and Leslie Hunt – properties Edward Lauder – lighting director Erskine Keys – prompter
11 Feb. 1936 (Tues.)	Short Plays				Women's Union (79 St. George St.)				No casts found.
	• *Spinsters of Lush: Comedy in One Act*	Philip Johnson	1930 publ., 1929 perf.	None on record.			Modern (comedy)		
	• *Shanghai*	Winifred Stuckes Raffo	1930 pub	None on record.			Modern		
	• On with the New (from Ne dites pas Fontaine)	Francis de Croisset	1919 publ. Fr., 1933 publ. Eng.	None on record.			Modern (comedy)		
28 Mar. 1936 (Sat.)	*Empurpled Moors*	Oscar W. Firkins	1932 publ.	Frank Hemingway	Hart House Theatre		Modern	CODL4	Sidney B. Watson (Patrick Bronte), Agnes Muldrew (Charlotte Bronte), Dudley Doughty (Patrick Brawnwell Bronte), Dorothy Batcheller (Emily Bronte), Alison Ewart (Anne Bronte), Agatha Leonard (Evelyn Robinson), Christina Templeton (Tabitha 'Tabby') Dama Lumley – prompter Margaret Tytler – properties Norm. Nichol – stage manager Set designed and executed by Edna Starr Thompson, costumes by Katherine (Kay) Anglin,

(Fri.)				Hemingway	Gore Street, Hamilton (Players Guild)				including Christina Templeton, Alison Ewart, Agnes Muldrew, Dorothy Batchellor, Dudley Doughty
2 Oct. 1936 (Fri.)	One Act Plays:				Radio Hall (12 Spadina Rd.)				Mary Smart, Cecylia Long, Edith Cosens, Dorothy Batcheller, Edna Norwich, Helen Eakin, Sheila Tisdall, Doris Sheill, Janet Kennedy, Harriet Clarke, Agatha Leonard, Alison Ewart, Dama Lumley, Geneva Campbell, Mr. Rai Purdy
	• *Poor Henry*	Dorothy Winthrop	1935 publ.	Edgar Stone			Modern (comedy)		
	• *The Illusionist*			Edgar Stone			Modern		
	• *April Shower*	Philip Johnson	1932 publ.	Edgar Stone			Modern (comedy)		
7–14 Dec. 1936 (Sun.-Mon.).	*Charity Begins: A Comedy in Three Acts*	Ireland Wood	1936 publ.	Edgar Stone	Hart House Theatre	Toronto	Modern (comedy)		Erskine Keys, Sheila Tisdall, Christina Templeton, Eleanor Barton, Mary Smart, Agnes Muldrew, Margaret Tytler, F.G. Venables, Dudley Doughty, Stuart Parker
16 Dec. 1936 (Wed.)	Christmas Tableaux			None on record.			Christmas Tableaux		No cast found.
26 Feb. 1937 (Fri.)	*The Cradle Song* (Act I)	Gregorio and María Martínez Sierra, trans. John Garrett Underhill	1922 publ.	Edgar Stone	Hart House Theatre		Modern	CODL5: 3rd place. Top 3 went on to DDF	Agatha Leonard, Agnes Muldrew, Edna Norwich, Margaret Tytler, Alison Ewart, Doris Shiell, Jean Hunnisett, Christina Templeton, Erskine Keys, Katherine Anglin, Margaret Ness, Alice Keys, Elspeth Wilson, Florian Moore, W.E.S. Briggs
20 Apr. 1937 (Tues.)	*The Cradle Song* (Act I)	Gregorio and María Martínez Sierra, trans. John Garrett Underhill		Edgar Stone	Margaret Eaton Hall ("Old YMCA and Association Hall" at 21 McGill St.)				Same cast as 26 Feb. 1937.
1 May 1937 (Sat.)	*The Cradle Song* (Act I)	Gregorio and María Martínez Sierra, trans. John Garrett Underhill		Edgar Stone	Ottawa Little Theatre			DDF5: Festival Plaque (for best presentation in English other than the Festival winner)	Same cast as 26 Feb. 1937.

(Continued)

Run Dates	Show	Writer	Play Dates	Director	Venue	Premiere	Style	Festivals	Cast
22–7 Nov. 1937 (Mon.–Sat.)	*The Family Portrait*	John Coulter		Edgar Stone	Hart House Theatre	World	Modern		Agnes Muldrew, Florian Moore, Edith Gordon, Christina Templton, Margaret Tytler, Mary Smart, Jean Hunnisett, Donald Smith, Arthur Williams, Ivor Lewis, Eric Aldwinckle, H.E. Hitchman, C.A.G. Matthews
12 Dec. 1937 (Sun.)	Christmas Tableaux/ Carols			None on record.	Women's Union (79 St. George St.)		Christmas Tableaux		No cast found.
21 Jan. 1938 (Fri.)	Revue I. *As We Are* II. *The Portrait* III. *After Office Hours* IV. *Solo* V. *Athletics* VI. Monologues VII. *Prompt Corner* INTERMISSION I. *Wrong Numbers* II. *Charlie McCarthy* III. *As Others Hear Us* IV. *Deteur en Vignes* V. Monologue VI. *As We Wish We Were* Reception	Essex Dane wrote *Wrong Numbers* (1919 publ.)		None on record.	Women's Union (79 St. George St.)	World	Revue		Agnes Muldrew Stone, Agatha Leonard, Christina Templeton, Doris Shiell, Dr. Edith Gordon, Elspeth Wilson, Ruth Holm, Peggy Tytler, Jean Hunnisett, Emmie [Mary?] Smart, Florian Moore, Alison Ewart, Florrie Hunt, Jean Dow, Dorothy Batchellor, Margaret Ness
28 Mar. 1938 (Mon.)	*The Old Maid* (episodes from)	Zoë Atkins	1935 pub	Lorna Sheard (Mrs. Terrance Sheard)	Hart House Theatre		Modern (drama)	CODL6	Dorothy Batcheller, Agnes Muldrew, Christina Templeton, Alison Ewart, Jean Dow, Archibald Swan, Robert Chidwick, Donald Smith, Robert McRae
28 May 1938 (Sat.)	Evening of Plays:				Mrs. Mary Evans' (Mrs. Watson Evans) Country Home, Erindale				No casts found.
	• *Unnatural Scene*	Kathleen Davey	1933 perf., 1938 publ.	Lorna Sheard (Mrs. Terance Sheard)			Modern (comedy)		
	• *Slow Curtain: A Play of the Theatre in One Act for Women*	Muriel and Sydney Box	1935 publ.	Agnes Muldrew Stone			Modern		
21–6 Nov. 1938 (Mon.–Sat. 8:30 p.m.)	*Miss Black Sheep: A Comedy in Three Acts*	Brenda Girvin and Monica Cosens	1937 publ.	Edgar Stone	Hart House Theatre	North America	Modern (comedy)		Doris Shiell, Jean Dow, Earl Fisher, Agnes Muldrew, Alison Ewart, Jean Stewart

(Tues.)	*A Comedy in Three Acts*	and Monica Cosens			Guild)				
18 Feb. 1939 (Sat.)	Two one-act plays:				Women's Union (79 St. George St.)				
	• *The Italian Woman*	Wilfred Grantham		Lorna Sheard (Mrs. Terance Sheard)			Modern (history)		Agnes Muldrew (Catherine de Medici), Alison Ewart, Christine Templeton, Jean Dow, Dorothy Batchellor, Jessie Fleming, George Daly
	• *Short Circuit*	Margaret Ness		Rai Purdy		World	Modern (comedy)		Edna Norwich, Margaret Tytler, Florian Moore, Aileen O'Brien, Murray Bonnycastle
17 Mar. 1939 (Fri.)	*Short Circuit*	Margaret Ness		Rai Purdy	Hart House Theatre			CODL7	Edna Norwich, Margaret Tytler, Florian Moore, Aileen O'Brien, Murray Bonnycastle
28 June 1939 (Wed.)	Four Plays and Two Monologues			None on record.	Erindale Community Hall		Revue		
	• *A Slice of Contemporary Life*								Agatha Leonard, Alison Ewart
	• *Outdoor Life*								Earl Foster, Eleanor Woodside, Dorothy Batchellor
	• *Wrong Numbers*	Essex Dane	1919 publ.						Doris Shiell, Florian Moore, Alieen O'Brien
	• *Mistaken Identity*								Gloria VanKoughnett, Marion Hunter [Squair], Harold Hunter
	Monologue 1								
	Monologue 2								
27 Nov. 1939 (Mon.)	Two Plays for the Dickens Fellowship Meeting:				Hart House Theatre				
	• *Anti-Clockwise*	Muriel and Sydney Box		Margaret Tytler			Modern (drama)		Dorothy Batchellor, Aileen O'Brien (Doctor), Jean Stewart, Aileen Maguire
	• *Green Eyes from Romany*	John Kirkpatrick		Dixon Wagner		Toronto	Modern (comedy)		Agatha Leonard (Fanny Meadows), Jean Dow, Agnes Muldrew (Madame Kharavhocci the fortune teller), Christine Templeton (the poor relation), Helen Goulding (Lucy Guilford) [Goulding is the cousin of Raymond Massey], Eleanor Woodside (Emily Prescott), Elspeth Wilson, Ruth Home

(*Continued*)

Run Dates	Show	Writer	Play Dates	Director	Venue	Premiere	Style	Festivals	Cast
14 Dec. 1939 (Thurs.)	Four Short Skits			None on record.	University Women's Club (80 Bloor St. W.)				Master of Ceremonies: Marion Squair [Mrs. Harold Hunter]
	Monologue						Monologue		Agnes Muldrew Stone, Jean Stewart
	Air Raid Troubles	Margaret Tytler and Jean Stewart					Skit		Maragert Tytler, Jean Stewart
	The Charity Bizarre	Eleanor Moffat Woodside and Helen Goulding					Skit		Eleanor Moffat Woodside, Helen Goulding
	The Royal Visit	Agatha Leonard and Alison Ewart					Skit		Agatha Leonard, Aileen O'Brien
13 Jan. 1940 (Sat.)	Second Annual Revue			Edgar Stone ("assisted in producing")	Women's Union (79 St. George St.)		Revue		Mistress of Ceremonies: Marion Hunter [Squair]
	• *Pajamas for the Poles*								
	• *"Baby Snooks"-style skit*	Cast: Eleanor Moffat Woodside							Eleanor Moffat Woodside
	• *Helen of Troy skit*	Cast: Helen Goulding							Helen Goulding
	• *Air raid fashion skit*	Margaret Tytler and Jean Stewart							Margaret Tytler, Jean Stewart
	• *For Amusement Only*								
	• *Bowery girls*								
	• *Song and dance*								Singer: Aileen O'Brien
	• *Why Scots no longer wear kilts*								Margaret Tytler, Genevra Campbell
	• *Mendelssohn's "Spring Song" in dance*								Singer/dancer: Alice Keys
	• *Large crowd cheering King and Queen*								Agatha Leonard, Alison Ewart
	• "Put on Your Old Grey Bonnet"								Singer: Dorothy Batcheller

Feb. 1940 (Mon.–Sat.). Added troop performance 5 Feb. 1940 (Mon.)	CODL revue featuring 22 sketches)			Bennett	Theatre	revue in Toronto		Ivor Lewis *It's Only a Question of Time* cast: Alison Ewart, Agatha Leonard
	• *A Day in May*	Agatha Leonard and Alison Ewart						
12 Feb. 1940 (Mon.)	[Short skits]			None on record.	Moulton College			
	Monologue	Agnes Muldrew Stone					Monologue	Agnes Muldrew Stone
	Monologue	Dorothy Batchellor					Monologue	Dorothy Batchellor
	Skit	Margaret Tytler and Jean Stewart					Skit	Margaret Tytler, Jean Stewart
	Skit	Margaret Tytler and Jean Stewart					Skit	Margaret Tytler, Jean Stewart
	A Day in May (skit)	Alison Ewart and Agatha Leonard	Prem. 1940			World	Skit	Alison Ewart, Agatha Leonard
	A Dance	Alice Lewis (Mrs. Norman Keys)					Dance	Alice Lewis [Mrs. Norman Keys]
12 Mar. 1940 (Tues.)	Three One Act Plays:				Hart House Theatre			
	• *The Londonderry Air*	Rachel Field	1927 publ., 1938 film	E.G. Sterndale Bennett			Modern	Helen Goulding, Marion Hunter [Squair], Willard B. Thomson, James E. Dean.
	• *Love and Learning (orig. Fr. Les jeux de l'amour et de la conférence)*	Romain Coolus		Edgar Stone			Modern (comedy)	Agatha Leonard, Helen Alles, Agnes Muldrew Stone, Janet Kennedy, John Watson, H.E. Hitchman
	• After the Tempest	Geoffrey Trease	1938 publ.	Percy Schutte			Modern	Edna Norwich, Aileen O'Brien, Dorothy Batchellor, Linton Cole, Barry Fitzgerald
9 Apr. 1940 (Tues.)	*A Day in May* (skit)	Alison Ewart and Agatha Leonard		None on record.	St. Hilda's College		Skit	Alison Ewart, Agatha Leonard

(*Continued*)

Run Dates	Show	Writer	Play Dates	Director	Venue	Premiere	Style	Festivals	Cast
18 Apr. 1940 (Thurs.	Two Entertainments			None on record.	St. Hilda's College				
	A Day in May (skit)	Alison Ewart and Agatha Leonard					Skit		Alison Ewart, Agatha Leonard
	Adagio Dance	Constance Vernon					Dance		
31 Jan–1 Feb 1941 (Fri.–Sat.)	Two Plays				Women's Union (79 St. George St.)				
	• *Mr. Sampson*	Charles Lee	1927 prem., 1927 publ., 1938 publ.	Percy Schutte, Margaret (Peggy) Tytler			Modern		Percy Schutte (Mr. Sampson), Jean Stewart, Doris Stacey (Caroline)
	• *Sunday Costs Five Pesos*	Josefina Niggli	1937	Bill [W.S.] Milne			Modern (comedy)		Alison Ewart (Celestina), Florine Hunt (Berta), Francess Halpenny (Tonia), Dorothy Batchellor (Salome), John Bowen (Fidel)
Either 28 Apr. or 5 May 1941 (Sun.)	*Sunday Costs Five Pesos*	Josefina Niggli	1937	Bill [W.S.] Milne	Camp Borden				Alison Ewart (Celestina), Florine Hunt (Berta), Francess Halpenny (Tonia), Dorothy Batchellor (Salome), John Bowen (Fidel)
14 June 1941 (Sun.)	*The Unattainable*	W. Somerset Maugham	1915 writ 1916 perf 1923 pub		Lorne Park, ON		Modern (farce)		No cast found.
7 Feb. 1942 (Sat.)	Three One Act Plays:				Women's Union (79 St. George St.)				
	• *Rehearsal*	Christopher Morley		Francess Halpenny			Modern (Comedy)		Francess Halpenny (played the Director), Agatha Leonard, Doris Stacey, Dorothy Batcheller, Mary Smart, Ruth Home
	• *It May Happen Here*	Winifred Pilcher		Jean Stewart		World	Modern (comedy)		Jean Stewart (Maid), Christina Templeton, Elspeth Wilson, Margaret Ness
	• *The Screen*	Jerry Emerson		Eleanor Barton Woodside			Modern		Eleanor Woodside, Janet Kennedy, Frederic Manning, Peter Mews

(Fri.)	1 *Powder-room* Pow-wow by Mary Bruck and Doris Stacey 2 The Plumber (monologue) by Alice Keys 3 Song by Doris Stacey 4 Sadie Hoards by Francess Halpenny, 5 A pantomime by Billie May Dinsmore and Mary Bruck 6 Cats Cradle by Noël Coward 7 Waiting for a Streetcar by Isabelle Cleland 8 Song by Doris Stacey 9 [untitled] by Margaret Ness			Atkinson	(79 St. George St.)			2 Alice Keys 3 Doris Stacey 4 Francess Halpenny, Billie May Dinsmore, Mary Bruck 5 Agatha Leonard, Alison Hewitt 6 Isabelle Cleland 7 Doris Stacey 8 Jane Mallett and Freddie Manning 9 Margaret Ness
11 Dec. 1942 (Fri.)	*The Babe at the Inn*	Delle Oglesbee Ross	1935 publ.	None on record.	St. Alban's Cathedral parish hall (100 Howland Ave.)		Christmas Nativity	Peggy [Margaret] Tytler, Gertrude McCance (Simian), Jean Stewart (Lady Rebecca), Doris Stacey (Miriam), Elspeth Wilson, Frances MacLennan (Shepherd), Katherine Anglin (Shepherd), Mary Smart (Messenger), Eleanor Woodside (Mary in tableau at end), Erskine Keys (Joseph)
3 June 1944 (Sat.)	Annual Meeting entertainments			None on record.	Alice Key's home (Scarborough)			
	• *Cupid Rampant*	Percy Corry	1939 prem.				Modern	
	• *A new monologue*	Alice Keys					Monologue	Alice Keys
	• *The Picnic*	Alice Keys					Skit	Alice Keys
	• *The Plumber*	Alice Keys					Skit	Alice Keys
2 June 1945 (Sat.)	Annual Meeting entertainments			None on record.	Alice Key's home (Scarborough)			

(*Continued*)

Run Dates	Show	Writer	Play Dates	Director	Venue	Premiere	Style	Festivals	Cast
	• *Thursday Night (sketch)*	Alice Keys	1945 prem.				Skit		Florrie Hunt
	• *The Old Actress (monologue)*	Margaret Tytler	1945 prem.				Monologue		Margaret Tytler
	• *In the Midst of Life*	Jean Stewart and Alison Hewitt (Ewart)	1945 prem.				Skit		Jean Stewart, Alison Hewitt (Ewart)
23 Feb. 1946 (Sat.)	February Frolic:				Women's Union (79 St. George St.)				
	• *Orange Blossoms*	Philip Johnson	1943 publ.	E.G. Sterndale Bennett			Modern (comedy)		Christina Templeton (Mrs. Duckworth), Campbell Munro (Mr. Duckworth), Francess Halpenny (Auntie Lola), Jean Stewart (Auntie Lottie), Ruth Johnson (Gladys Duckworth), Charmian King (Amy Foster), Melwyn Breen (Fred Ashford)
	• *Interlude*	Norman Tytler [or Titler]		None on record.			Interlude		Norman Tytler
	• *The Picnic, a monologue*	Alice Keys		None on record.			Monologue		Alice Keys
	• *A Banner with a Strange Device*	Mary Lowry Ross		None on record.		World	Modern		No cast found.
10 Apr. 1946 (Wed.)	*Orange Blossoms*	Philip Johnson		E.G. Sterndale Bennett	Northern Vocational School Auditorium (851 Mt. Pleasant Rd.)			Civic Drama Festival	Same cast as 23 Feb. 1946. Agatha Leonard – prompter Mary Rose – stage manager Margaret Tytler and Woodside – stage crew Katherine (Kay) B. Anglin – provided costumes
17 Apr. 1946 (Wed.)	*Orange Blossoms*	Philip Johnson		E.G. Sterndale Bennett	Northern Vocational School Auditorium (851 Mt. Pleasant Rd.)			Civic Drama Festival	Same cast as 10 Apr. 1946.
7 Nov. 1946 (Thurs.)	Three Short Plays:			None on record.	Women's Union (79 St. George St.)				No casts found.
	• *A Change of Mind*	R. (Russell) Speirs	1931 publ.				Modern		
	• *Day's End*	A. (Alice) Pieratt	1929 publ.				Modern		
	• *The Happy Journey*	Thornton Wilder	1930 publ., 1931 prem.				Modern		

(Wed.–Fri.)		Joaquin Alvarez Quintero. English Version by Helen and Harley Granville-Barker			Theatre		(comedy)		Halpenny, Agatha Leonard, Margaret Nichol, Margaret Munro, Ruth Johnson, Betty Mustard, A. Campbell Munro, Norman Green, Christopher Taylor, George Gibson, Guy Purser
13 Feb. 1947 (Thurs.)	"Drama Night"			None on record.	Women's Union (79 St. George St.)		Variety		Cast included the UC Glee Club, the Alumnae Dramatic Society, and Jane Mallett "monologuist"
25 Feb. 1947 (Tues.)	*The Happy Journey*	Thornton Wilder		E.G. Sterndale Bennett	Hart House Theatre			CODL8 (revival)	Jean Stewart, Jean Smith, Ruth Johnson, Sydney Collins, Robert Jackson, Sam Telford
20 May 1947 (Tues.)	Evening of Plays:			None on record.	Grace Church-on-the-Hill (300 Lonsdale Rd.)				No casts found.
	• *A Change of Mind*	R. (Russell) Speirs							
	• *Suppressed Desires*	Susan Glaspell	1915 prem., 1917 publ.				Modern (comedy)		
6–7 Nov. 1947 (Thurs.–Fri.)	*Wild Decembers*	Clemence Dane	prem. 1932, publ. 1932	Karen Glahn	Hart House Theatre	Toronto	Modern		Ruth Johnson, Elizabeth Mascall, Marian Jones, Alice Keys, Barbara Allen, Agatha Leonard, Molly Golby, Joy Kennedy, Christina Templeton, Margaret Munro, Melwyn Breen, George Gibson, Norman Green, Lorne Sullivan, Murray Paulin, Sydney Collins, John Conway
18 Mar. 1948 (Thurs.)	*Years Ago* (Act 1)	Ruth Gordon	1946 prem.	John Mantley	Hart House Theatre		Modern	CODL9: Hugh Eayrs Trophy for the best presentation of the Festival; CODL President's Award for best male actor (Alex McKee); runner-up for the Nella Jefferis award for best actress (Barbra Allen).	Christina Templeton, Barbara Allen, Beatrice Ramsey, Elizabeth Rand, Alex McKee, David Gardner Ruth Johnson - prompter Mary Rose - organized costumes Agatha Leonard and Alison Hewitt - properties Katherine Anglin - managed the production. Gordon Drew and Frank Fice - stage crew

(*Continued*)

Run Dates	Show	Writer	Play Dates	Director	Venue	Premiere	Style	Festivals	Cast
30 Apr. 1948 (Fri.)	*Years Ago* (Act 1)	Ruth Gordon		John Mantley	Ottawa Little Theatre			DDF9 entry	Christina Templeton, Barbara Allen, Beatrice Ramsey, Elizabeth Rand, Alex McKee, David Gardner
12 June 1948 (Sat.)	*Dark Brown: A Melodrama in One Act*	Philip Johnson	1946 publ.	Elizabeth Mascall	Alice Keys' home		Modern (melodrama)		Alice Keys (Mrs. Collins), Elizabeth Mascall (Miss Tasker), Elizabeth Rand (Jenny Brown), Ruth Johnson (Bella Crewe), Sidney Collins (Fred Whitworth), Marion Jones (Mrs. Persophelous), Frank Butler (Arthur Brown)
1–4 Nov. 1948 (Mon.–Thurs.)	*Years Ago* (full play)	Ruth Gordon		John Mantley	Hart House Theatre	Canada			Christina Templeton, Barbara Allen [Barnett] (Ruth Gordon), Beatrice Ramsay, Elizabeth Rand, Marion Jones, Alex McKee, David Gardner (Fred Whitmarsh), John Murray, Guy Purser, a cat
27 Jan. 1949 (Thurs.)	Three one-act plays:				The Parish Hall of the Church of the Messiah (240 Avenue Rd.)				
	• *Soldadera: A One-Act Play of the Mexican Revolution*	Josephina Niggli	1936 publ.	Sam Payne			Modern (melodrama)		Michael Ney (the prisoner), Ruth Johnson, Francess Halpenny, Elizabeth Rand
	• *The High-Backed Chair*	Norman Holland	1938 prem.	Ruth Johnson			Modern (drama)		Agatha Leonard (old woman), Stuart Parker (young man)
	• *No Smoking: A Farce in One Act*	Jacinto Benavente	1904 prem., 1919 publ.	Karen Glahn			Modern (comedy)		Murray Paulin (gentleman in railway car), Alice Keyes (mother), Joy Kennedy (daughter)
22 Mar. 1949 (Tues.)	*The High-Backed Chair*	Norman Holland		Karen Glahn	Hart House Theatre			CODL10	Barbara McNabb, Agatha Leonard, Jean Coupe, Stuart Parker
7–9 Nov. 1949 (Mon.–Wed.)	*Autumn Crocus: A Play in Three Acts*	C.L. Anthony (Dodie Smith's pseudonymn)	1931 prem.	William Needles	Hart House Theatre		Modern (drama)		Douglas Nay, Cicely Thomson, Christina Templeton, Elizabeth Mascall, Agatha Leonard, Betty Gray, Harry Stitch, Dixon Wagner, Bob Beale, Francess Halpenny, Elizabeth Rand
28 Mar. 1950 (Tues.)	*Thérèse: A Tragedy in Two Acts*	Thomas Job (from Émile Zola's Thérèse Raquin	1945 prem.	Henry Kaplan	Hart House Theatre		Modern (tragedy)	CODL11	Francess Halpenny, Ruth Johnson, Barbara Allen, Bea Lennard, William Needles, Frank Perry, Norman Green, E.M. Margolese

1950 (Tues.–Sat.)	*Being Earnest*				Theatre		(comedy)		Edith Orde Tuff, Ruth Johnson, Eleanor Beecroft, Michael Kane, William Hutt, John Beckwith, Gus Kristjanson, Peter Francis
5–7 Oct. 1950 (Thurs.–Sat.)	*Kind Lady*	Edward Chodorov	1935 prem.	Henry Kaplan	Hart House Theatre		Modern (thriller)		Barbara Allen, William Needles, David Gardner, Francess Halpenny, Michael Kane, Stuart Parker, Margaret Munro, Edith Orde Tuff, Christina Templeton, Elizabeth Rand, Gus Kristjanson, Joyce Bocknek
16 Dec. 1950 (Sat.)	Two Plays:				Hart House Theatre				
	• *Possession: A Peep Show in Paradise*	Laurence Housman	1921 pub	Francess Halpenny			Modern (drama)		Eleanor Beecroft, Elizabeth Gray, Eleanor Woodside, Elizabeth Rand, Cecily Thomson, George Robertson, Lawrence Heisey
	• *Dona Clarines*	Serafin and Joaquin Alvarez Quintero		E.G. Wanger			Modern (comedy)		Sheila Craig, Kathleen Knox, Agatha Leonard, Joyce Bocknek, Douglas Ney, William Hutt, Donald Sinclair
27 Feb. 1951 (Tues.)	*In Good King Charles's Golden Days: A True History that Never Happened*	George Bernard Shaw	1939 prem.	Herbert Whittaker	The Arts and Letters Club (14 Elm St.)	Canada	Modern (history)		Christina Templeton, Edith Orde Tuff, Sheila Craig, Marian Jones, Ruth Norris, Francess Halpenny, Ted Follows, John Colicos, Ron Poffenroth, Norman Moore, William Needles
15 Mar. 1951 (Thurs.)	*In Good King Charles's Golden Days: A True History that Never Happened*	George Bernard Shaw		Herbert Whittaker	Hart House Theatre			CODL12: Hugh Eayrs Trophy for Best Play; Best Actor (John Colicos);Best visual presentation	Same cast as 27 Feb. 1951.
2–7 Apr. 1951 (Mon.–Sat.)	*In Good King Charles's Golden Days. A True History that Never Happened*	George Bernard Shaw		Herbert Whittaker	Forest Hill Collegiate Auditorium (730 Eglinton Ave. W.)				Same cast as 27 Feb. 1951.
21 Apr. 1951 (Sat.)	*Possession: A Peep Show in Paradise*	Laurence Housman		Francess Halpenny	Hart House Theatre			CODL One-Act Festival	Possibly same cast as 16 Dec. 1950.

(*Continued*)

Run Dates	Show	Writer	Play Dates	Director	Venue	Premiere	Style	Festivals	Cast
18 May 1951 (Fri.)	*In Good King Charles's Golden Days: A True History that Never Happened*	George Bernard Shaw		Herbert Whittaker	Grand Theatre (London, ON)			DDF12: Le Trophee de Merites Louis Jouvett for best directed play (Whittaker, tied). Henry Osborne Challenge Trophy for best male performance (Colicos); Colicos also received a "memento" from Mrs. L.T. White of Ottawa.	Same cast as 27 Feb. 1951.
16–18 Oct. 1951 (Tues.-Thurs.)	*Dear Octopus*	Dodie Smith (C.L. Anthony)	1938 prem.	William Needles	Hart House Theatre		Modern (Comedy)		Christina Templeton, Ruth Johsnon, Eleanor Beecroft, Marian Jones, Judy Morris, Michele Landsberg, Francess Halpenny, Elizabeth Gray, Sheila Craig, Edith Orde Tuff, Margaret Munro, Alison Hewitt, W.H. Brodie, Arthur House, Charles K. Winter, Bill Davis, Douglas Ney
8 Dec. 1951 (Sat.)	Christmas Invitational Two One-Act Plays:				Cicely Thomson's home in Richmond Hill				No cast found.
	• *The Queens of France*	Thornton Wilder	1931 publ.	Marian Jones			Modern (comedy)		
	• *Three Mrs. Madderleys*	Gordon Daviot (Josephine Tey)		Eleanor Beecroft			Modern		
10 Mar. 1952 (Mon.)	*Olympia*	Ferenc Molnár	1928 prem	Herbert Whittaker	Hart House Theatre		Modern (comedy)	CODL13: President's award for Best Performance by an Actor (Douglas Ney)	Marian Jones, Francess Halpenny, Barbara Barnett, Frank Lalor, Norman Green, Douglas Ney, Hugh Webster

(Sat.)				Whittaker	Collegiate Auditorium (Eglinton Ave. and Vesta Dr.)				
4 Apr. 1952 (Sat.)	*Olympia*	Ferenc Molnár		Herbert Whittaker	Hart House Theatre				Possibly same cast as 10 Mar. 1952.
3–6 June 1952 (Tues.–Fri.)	*Miranda*	Peter Blackmore	1948 pub	Peter Francis	Hart House Theatre		Modern (Comedy)		Joyce Bocknek, Norma Edwards, Edith Orde Tuff, Ruth Johnson, Christina Templeton, Murray Bonnycastle, Charles Telling, George McCown
13–18 Oct. 1952 (Mon.–Sat.)	*The Heiress*	Ruth and Augustus Goetz, adapted from/suggested by the Henry James novel, *Washington Square*	1947 prem	E.G. Sterndale Bennett	Hart House Theatre	Toronto	Modern (Drama)		Ruth Norris, Eleanor Beecroft, Norma Edwards, Eleanor Woodside, Joyce Bocknek, Ruth Johnson, John Frid, Andrew Body, Douglas Ney
20 Feb. 1953 (Fri.)	*The Family Reunion*	T.S. Eliot	1939 prem.	Herbert Whittaker	The Arts and Letters Club (14 Elm St.)	Toronto	Modern (poetic)		Ruth Johnson, Ruth James, Christina Templeton, Francess Halpenny, Edith Orde Tuff, Norma Edwards, Elizabeth Gray, Renee Eckleberry, Marion Stewart, with Rex Sevenoaks, David Gardner, Richard Easton, Norman Green, W.A. Atkinson, James Armour
20 Mar. 1953 (Fri.)	*The Family Reunion*	T.S. Eliot		Herbert Whittaker	Hart House Theatre			CODL14: (new) Calvert Trophy for Best Play; President's Award for Best Actor (Richard Easton); Best Visual Presentation; Best Direction (Herbert Whittaker)	Probably the same cast as Feb. 20, 1953
17–18 Apr. 1953 (Fri.–Sat.)	*The Family Reunion*	T.S. Eliot		Herbert Whittaker	Hart House Theatre				Probably the same cast as Feb. 20, 1953

(*Continued*)

Run Dates	Show	Writer	Play Dates	Director	Venue	Premiere	Style	Festivals	Cast
21 Apr. 1953 (Tues.)	*The Family Reunion*	T.S. Eliot		Herbert Whittaker	Forest Hill Collegiate Auditorium (Eglinton Ave. and Vesta Dr.)				Probably the same cast as 20 Feb. 1953
6 May 1953 (Wed.)	*The Family Reunion*	T.S. Eliot		Herbert Whittaker	Royal Theatre (Victoria, B.C.)			DDF14 Festival Plaque for Best Presentation in English; ("a close second" behind Dubé's *Zone*, reported Whittaker 11 May 1953); Martha Allan Challenge Trophy for Best Set Design; Louis Jouvet Challenge Trophy for Best Director (Whittaker)	Probably the same cast as 20 Feb. 1953
13–15 Oct. 1953 (Tues.–Thurs.)	*Venus Observed*	Christopher Fry	1950 prem.	E.G. Sterndale Bennett	Hart House Theatre	Toronto	Modern (comedy)		Probably same cast as Nov. 6, 1953.
6 Nov. 1953 (Fri.)	*Venus Observed*	Christopher Fry		E.G. Sterndale Bennett	Central Technical School (725 Bathurst St.)				Pamela Terry (Perpetua), Francess Halpenny, Marian Jones, Ruth James, Rex Sevenoaks, John Lindsey (Hereward), Ted Scott, Peter Benjamin, Peter Stewart, Les Hayter
5 Dec. 1953 (Sat.)	Christmas Invitational [unclear if it ran or not]			None on record.	St. James-Bond United Church (Avenue Rd.)				
	Colombe	Jean Anouilh	1951				Modern		Betty Campbell, Gay Esdale
	Elizabeth Refuses	Margaret MacNamara	1926				Modern (Comedy)		Elizabeth Gray, Barbara McNabb, Eilleen Renée Eckelberry

(Mon.)				Bennett	Theatre		Marian Jones, Ruth James, Rex Sevenoaks, John Lindsey, Ted Scott, Douglas Thomas (replacing Peter Benjamin), Peter Stewart, Les Hayter
29 Mar. 1954 (Mon.)	*The Old Ladies: A Play in Three Acts*	Rodney Ackland, adapted from the novel by Hugh Walpole	1935 prem.	Robert Gill	Etobicoke High School (86 Montgomery Rd.)	Modern (thriller)	Agatha Leonard, Barbara Barnett, Eleanor Beecroft
6–7 Apr. 1954 (Tues., Wed.)	*The Old Ladies: A Play in Three Acts*	Rodney Ackland, adapted from the novel by Hugh Walpole		Robert Gill	Hart House Theatre		Same cast as Mar. 29, 1954.
10 May 1954 (Mon.)	Two One-Act Plays:				St. James-Bond United Church (1066 Avenue Rd.)		
	• *Overlaid*	Robertson Davies	1948 prem.	Christina Wade		Modern (comedy)	Cecily Thompson, Harold Hunter, Russ Waller
	• *The Matron of Ephesus*	Georges Sion	1950–51 prem.	Elizabeth Gray		Modern	Renee Eckelberry, Pamela Beckwith, Donna Rosenberg, Mart Watson, Betty Campbell, John Finley, David Cargill
14–16 Oct. 1954 (Thurs.– Sat.)	*A Woman of No Importance*	Oscar Wilde, new adaptation by Paul Dehn	1893 orig. prem., 1953 adpt. Prem., 1954 adpt. publ. as Acting Edition	Leonard Crainford	Hart House Theatre	Period (comedy)	Christina Templeton, Elizabeth Campbell, Barry Page Knibbs, Ruth James, Rex Sevenoaks, Douglas Thomas, Michael Snow, Edith Orde Tuff, Molly Golby, Russ Waller, Robert Peace, Malcolm Martin, Paul Break, Ruth Johnson, Cicely Thomson
8–9 Mar. 1955 (Tues., Wed.)	*Uncle Vanya: Scenes from Country Life*	Anton Chekov, trans. Marion Fell	1898 publ., 1899 prem.	Herbert Whittaker	Hart House Theatre	Modern (comedy)	Francess Halpenny, Marian Jones, Pamela Terry, Christine Wade, David Gardner, John Hardinge, Ronald Hartmann, Rex Sevenoaks, Harold C. Willettes

(*Continued*)

Run Dates	Show	Writer	Play Dates	Director	Venue	Premiere	Style	Festivals	Cast
31 Mar. 1955 (Thurs.)	*Uncle Vanya: Scenes from Country Life*	Anton Chekov, trans. Marion Fell		Herbert Whittaker	Hart House Theatre			CODL16: Best Visual Presentation, Best Supporting Actor (Rex Sevenoaks); Best Actor (Ronald Hartmann); Best Supporting Actress (Francess Halpenny); Bessborough Trophy for a presentation of unusual merit of a classical play across all regional finals.	Same cast as Mar. 31, 1955.
11–13 Oct. 1955 (Tues.–Thurs.)	*Gigi*	Anita Loos, from Sidonie-Gabrielle Colette's novella	1944 novella 1949, fr. film 1951 play, 1958 Hollywood film	David Gardner	Hart House Theatre	Toronto	Modern (comedy)		Molly Golby, Muriel Cuttell, Cicely Thomson, Christina Templeton, Eileen Williams, Robert Peace, Syd Pattison
13–14 Mar. 1956 (Tues., Wed.)	*Teach Me How to Cry*	Patricia Joudry; musical score by Dr. Richard Johnson, RCM professor	1955 prem., 1956 publ.	Leon Major	Hart House Theatre	Canada	Modern (drama)		Phyllis Malcolm Stewart, Eleanor Beecroft, Suzanne Finlay, Molly Golby, Ray Butryn, Irene Mloszewska, Helen Dunlop, Les Lawrence, Edith Orde Tuff, Hugh Watson, Douglas Ney, George Luscombe, Elizabeth Gray, Elizabeth Beattie Musicians: Ben Rose, Ronald Chandler, Lloyd Orchard

(Fri.)				Theatre	Production; Lieutenant-Governor Award for Best Canadian Play; Samuel French Challenge Trophy for Best Presentation of a Play by a Canadian; Edgar Stone Challenge Trophy for Direction (Leon Major); Best Actress Award (Suzanne Finlay).	1956.
17–21 Apr. 1956 (Tues.–Sat.)	*Teach Me How to Cry*	Patricia Joudry	Leon Major	Hart House Theatre		Same cast as 13 Mar. 1956, except Francess Halpenny replaced Elizabeth Gray
17 May 1956 (Thurs.)	*Teach Me How to Cry*	Patricia Joudry	Leon Major	St. Charles University Auditorium (Sherbrooke, QC)	DDF17: Calvert Trophy	Possibly same cast as 17 Apr. 1956.
4–9 June 1956 (Mon.–Sat.)	*Teach Me How to Cry*	Patricia Joudry	Leon Major	Garden City Theatre, Vineland Festival		Phyllis Malcolm Stewart, Eleanor Beecroft, Irena Mloszewska (replaced Suzanne Finlay), Molly Golby, Ray Butryn, Elizabeth Beattie (replaced Irena Mloszewska), Helen Dunlop, Les Lawrence, Edith Orde Tuff, Hugh Watson, Douglas Ney, George Luscombe, Francess Halpenny Musicians: Ben Rose, Ronald Chandler, Lloyd Orchard

(*Continued*)

Run Dates	Show	Writer	Play Dates	Director	Venue	Premiere	Style	Festivals	Cast
13–14 Nov. 1956 (Tues., Wed.)	*To Ride a Tiger*	Norman Williams (Toronto playwright)	1956 prem.	Herbert Whittaker	Hart House Theatre	World	Modern		Russ Waller, David Bedard, Ivor Jackson, Muriel Cuttell, Wendy Aitken, Saundra Collis, Powell Jones, Antony Parr, Raymond Card, Marian Stewart, Elizabeth Beattie, Rex Southgate, Godfrey Jackman, Douglas Ney, Barbara Walker, Barbara Barnett, Bob Gain, Garry Woolgar, John Richardson, David Thomson, John Horton, Barry Ogg, Peter Stewart. The Boxers were played by students from Leaside High School trained for the play by a phys. ed. instructor at the school: Bob Gain, Garry Woolgar, John Richardson, David Thomson, John Horton, Barry Ogg, Peter Stewart. Music Composed by Richard Johnston
21–3 Nov. 1956 (Wed.–Fri.)	*To Ride a Tiger*	Norman Williams (Toronto playwright)		Herbert Whittaker	Leaside High School (200 Hanna Rd.)				Same cast as 13 Nov. 1956.
8 Jan. 1957 (Tues.)	*To Ride a Tiger*	Norman Williams (Toronto playwright)		Herbert Whittaker	Hart House Theatre			CODL18: Lieutenant Governor's Award for best Canadian play (Norman Williams); Samuel French Challenge Trophy for best presentation of a Canadian play; L.C. Tobias award for Best Supporting Actor (Rex Southgate); DDF executive committee	Same cast as 13 Nov. 1956.

								play written by a Canadian in all the Regional Festivals (Norman Williams); Sir Barry Jackson Trophy for the best presentation of a Canadian play in all the Regional Festivals	
26–31 Mar. 1957 (Tues.–Sun.)	*John Gabriel Borkman*	Henrik Ibsen	1896 writ.	Christina Wade	Coach House Theatre (16 Huntley St.)		Modern		Pamela Terry, Doris Stacey, Edith Orde Tuff, Elizabeth Beattie, Lorna Rogers, Rex Southgate, David Bedard, Antony Parr
9 Apr. 1957 (Tues.)	*The Skin of Our Teeth* (act one)	Thornton Wilder	1942 prem.	Francess Halpenny	Hart House Theatre		Modern (comedy)	CODL One–Act Festival	Molly Golby, Barbara Walker, Margaret Thomas, Elizabeth Thomas, Elizabeth Beattie, Helen Dunlop, Powell Jones, Bob Huber, Ivor Jackson. Various Alumnae members and their friends played the refugees
18–23, 24 June 1957 (Tues.–Sun., Mon. holdover)	*Ardèle ou la Marguerite* (*The Cry of the Peacock* in English translation)	Jean Anouilh	1948 Fr. prem.	Gordon Johnson	Coach House Theatre (16 Huntley St.)	Canada	Modern (comedy)		Francess Halpenny, Elizabeth Mascall, Molly Golby, Maureen Fitzgerald, Catherine Thompson, Rex Southgate, Russ Waller, Douglas Ney, Robert Huber, Powell Jones (June 22–24), Guy Bannerman
16–20, 23–6 Oct. 1957 (Wed.–Sun., Wed.–Sat.)	*A Dream Play*	August Strindberg, trans. Elizabeth Spriggs	1901 writ., 1907 prem.	Elizabeth Gray	Coach House Theatre (16 Huntley St.)		Modern		Elizabeth Beattie, Peggy [Margaret] Tytler, Frances Jackson, Doris Stacey, Elaine McNichol, Eileen Williams, Joyce Kamins, Bruce Evoy, Roy Passano, Robert Peace, Maurice Evans, Leslie Whittaker, Don Sutherland (Lawyer), Erwin Biener, David Stewart, Robert Huber, Reg Barnes,

(*Continued*)

Run Dates	Show	Writer	Play Dates	Director	Venue	Premiere	Style	Festivals	Cast
6–10, 13–17, 20–2 Nov. 1957 (Wed.–Sun., Wed.–Sun., Wed.–Fri.)	*Waiting for Godot*	Samuel Beckett	1952 Fr. publ., 1953 Fr. prem., 1954 Eng. pub., 1955 Engl. Prem.	Pamela [Beckwith] Terry	Coach House Theatre (16 Huntley St.)	Toronto (Canadian premiere at UBC June–July 1957)	Modern (Theatre of the Absurd)		Fred Euringer, Kenneth Wickes, Powell Jones, Ivor Jackson, Reg Barnes
15–19, 22–6 Jan. 1958 (Wed.–Sun., Wed.–Sun.)	*The Lion and the Unicorn*	Norman Newton	1958 prem.	Helen Dunlop	Coach House Theatre (16 Huntley St.)	World	Modern (drama)		Edith Orde Tuff, Leslie Whittaker, Pamela Terry, Kenneth Wickes, Rita Ubrisco, Maurice Evans, Russ Waller, Norman Young, Kenneth Shorey, Alan Toff, George Appleby, Ed Simenup
27 Mar. 1958 (Thurs.)	*Waiting for Godot*	Samuel Beckett		Pamela [Beckwith] Terry	Hart House Theatre			CODL19: Challenge Trophy for best play; Edgar Stone Trophy for Best Director (Pamela [Beckwith] Terry); Honourable Mention for best actor (Fred Euringer); honourable mention for best supporting actor (Powell Jones); runner–up for best production but was selected to compete at the DDF	Same cast as 6 Nov. 1957.
8–12 Apr. 1958 (Tues.–Sat.)	*Waiting for Godot*	Samuel Beckett		Pamela [Beckwith] Terry	Hart House Theatre				Same cast as 6 Nov. 1957.

(Thurs.)				[Beckwith] Terry	High School Auditorium, Halifax NS			Festival Plaque for the best production in English other than the winner of the Calvert Trophy; Henry Osborne Trophy for best actor in a leading role (Kenneth Wickes)	
17–21, 24–7 June 1958 (Tues.–Sat., Tues.–Fri.)	*A Scrap of Paper*	Victorien Sardou	1860 Fr. prem.	Gordon Johnson	Coach House Theatre (200 Bedford Rd.)		Period (comedy)		Leith Macdonald (Suzanne), Douglas Ney, Kenneth Wickes, Eleanor Beecroft, Helen Dunlop, Marian Stewart, Eileen Williams, Ruth Ubriaco, Maurice Evans, David Bedard, John Peowrie, Don Guyatt, Gordon Johnson
1–5, 8–12, held over 16–17 Oct. 1958 (Wed.–Sun., Wed.–Sun., Thurs.–Fri.)	*The Beaux' Stratagem*	George Farquhar	1707 prem.	Molly Golby [Thom]	Coach House Theatre (200 Bedford Rd.)		Period (comedy)		Judith Teague, Pamela Terry, Powell Jones, Cicely Thomson, Christina Templeton, Sue Cousland, Carol Purvis, Ivor Jackson replacing Rex Sevonoaks, Kenneth Wickes, Michael Tait, Ivan Thornley-Hall, Martin Hunter, Allen Chandler, James Cunningham
7–9, 12–16, 19–20 Nov. 1958 (Fri.–Sun., Wed.–Sun., Wed.–Thurs.)	*As You Desire Me*	Luigi Pirandello	1930 publ., 1932 film	Elizabeth Gray	Coach House Theatre (200 Bedford Rd.)		Modern		Ann Weldon, Marian Stewart, Eleanor Beecroft, Jacqueline White, Pamela Thayer, Ivor Jackson, Jim Mulligan, Alan Toff, Abe Roytenberg, Roy Passano, Kenneth Pogue, Alan Toff
3–7, 10–14 Dec. 1958 (Wed.–Sun., Wed.–Sun.)	*Yerma*	Federico Garcia Lorca	1934 prem.	Francess Halpenny	Coach House Theatre (200 Bedford Rd.)	Toronto	Modern (tragedy)		Elizabeth Mascall, Eleanor Beecroft, Judith Teague, Margaret Tytler, Doris Stacey, Eileen Williams, Eleanor Stewart, Barbara Barnett, Molly Golby, Helen Dunlop, Judith Hunter, Ruth Rashkis, Muriel Cuttell, Kathy Totton, Peggy Sherriff, Powell Jones, Ivor Jackson, Martin Hunter, Kenneth Pogue, Alan Toff, Hamish White. Recorded guitar by John Beckwith

(*Continued*)

Run Dates	Show	Writer	Play Dates	Director	Venue	Premiere	Style	Festivals	Cast
7 Jan. 1959 (Wed.)	*Yerma*	Federico Garcia Lorca		Francess Halpenny	Hart House Theatre			CODL20: Best Supporting Actress (Eleanor Beecroft).	Same cast as 3 Dec. 1958.
11–15, 18–22, held over 25–28 Mar. 1959 (Wed.–Sun., Wed.–Sun.)	*The Alchemist*	Ben Jonson	1610 prem.	Pamela [Beckwith] Terry	Coach House Theatre (200 Bedford Rd.)		Modern (comedy)		Michael Tait, James Mainprize, Patricia Carroll Brown, Rex Southgate, Christopher Sealy, Alan Toff, David White [Renton], Peter Stewart, Abe Roytenberg, Anne Weldon [Tait], James Manser, James MacDougall
22–6, 29–30 April, 1–3 May 1959 (Wed.–Sun., Wed.–Sun., Fri.–Sat.)	Two One-Act Plays:				Coach House Theatre (200 Bedford Rd.)				
	• *The Bald Soprano*	Eugene Ionesco	1950 Fr. prem.	Gordon Johnson			Modern (Theatre of the Absurd)		Muriel Cuttell, Abe Roytenberg, Pamela Terry, Lynn Orr, Douglas Ney, Kenneth Wickes
	• *The Lesson*	Eugene Ionesco	1951 Fr. prem.	Gordon Johnson			Modern (Theatre of the Absurd)		Powell Jones, Joanna Richardson, Francess Halpenny
2 May 1959 (Sat.)	*The Lesson*	Eugene Ionesco		Gordon Johnson	Eastwood Collegiate Auditorium, Kitchener, ON			Ontario One-Act Play Festival: "Best performance" ($100); best actor (Powell Jones); best supporting actress (Joanna Richardson)	
18 May 1959 (Mon.)	*The Lesson*	Eugene Ionesco		Gordon Johnson	Hunting Room of the King Edward Hotel (37 King St. E.)				Powell Jones, Francess Halpenny, Joanna Richardson
Week of 25 May 1959, no day recorded	*The Lesson*	Eugene Ionesco		Gordon Johnson	Coach House Theatre (200 Bedford Rd.)				Probably the same cast as 18 May 1959.

June 1959 (Thurs.–Sun., Wed.–Sun.)	*Husband: A Modern Reconstruction of the Myth of Tythonus and Aurora*			Macdonald	Theatre (200 Bedford Rd.)		(fantasy)		Elizabeth Parr, Joseph Maher, Michael Tait, Maurice Evans
21–5 Oct., 28 Oct.–1 Nov. 1959 (Wed.–Sun., Wed.–Sun.)	*A Month in the Country*	Ivan Turgenev, adapted into English by Emlyn Williams		Blanche Hogg	Coach House Theatre (200 Bedford Rd.)		Modern (comedy)		Marian Stewart, Francess Halpenny, Doris Stacey, Molly Golby, Jacqueline White, Rex Southgate, Roy Passano, Bob Zawydiwski, David White, Kenneth Post, Maurice Evans, James Manser, Robert Peace
1–6, 8–13, 15, 16 Dec. 1959 (Tues.–Sun., Tues.–Sun.)	*Endgame*	Samuel Beckett	1957 Fr. prem.	Herbert Whittaker	Coach House Theatre (200 Bedford Rd.)		Modern (Theatre of the Absurd)		Uriel Luft (Hamm), Kenneth Pauli (Clov), Ken Wickes, Jacqueline White
13–17, 20–4, held over 28–31, Jan. 1960 (Wed.–Sun., Wed.–Sun., held over Thurs.–Sun.)	*The Killdeer: A Comedy*	James Reaney	1960 prem., 1962 publ.	Pamela [Beckwith] Terry	Coach House Theatre (200 Bedford Rd.)	World	Modern		Francess Halpenny, Muriell Cuttell, Eleanor Beecroft, Virginia McLeod, Jayne Ford, Robin Smith, Margaret Shotton, Ivor Jackson, Kenneth Poste, Don Bryn, Robert Huber, Don Richards (later replaced by James Mainprize), George Hayward, John Dolphin (later replaced by Russ Waller)
24–8 Feb., 2–6, 9–13 Mar. 1960 (Wed.–Sun., Wed.–Sun., Wed.–Sun.) (heldover twice, played 17 nights)	*The Way of the World: A Comedy*	William Congreve	1700 prem.	Molly Golby [Thom]	Coach House Theatre (200 Bedford Rd.)		Period (comedy)		James Mainprize, Norman Edmondson, David White, Rex Southgate, William Innes, Don Lewis, Judith Teague, Francess Halpenny, Patricia Brown, Barbara Barnett, Joan Shaw, Joanna Richardson, Daron Egan, Joan Morcom
2 Apr. 1960 (Sat.)	*The Killdeer: A Comedy*	James Reaney		Pamela [Beckwith] Terry	Hart House Theatre			CODL21: Calvert Trophy for best play; Edgar Stone Challenge Trophy for best direction (Pamela Terry), Samuel French Trophy	Possibly same as 18 May 1960.

(Continued)

Run Dates	Show	Writer	Play Dates	Director	Venue	Premiere	Style	Festivals	Cast
								for best presentation of a Canadian play; Hugh Eayrs Trophy for best visual presentation	
5–7 May 1960 (Thurs.–Sat.)	*The Killdeer: A Comedy*	James Reaney		Pamela [Beckwith] Terry	Hart House Theatre				Possibly same as May 18, 1960.
18 May 1960 (Wed.)	*The Killdeer: A Comedy*	James Reaney		Pamela [Beckwith] Terry	Queen Elizabeth Theatre, Vancouver			DDF21: Sir Barry Jackson Trophy for best production of a Canadian play; Louis Jouvet Trophy for best direction (Terry); Martha Allan Trophy for best set design (Martha Mann); new Massey award for best playwright (Reaney); Saturday Night plaque for best supporting actress (Virginia MacLeod)	Francess Halpenny, Muriel Cuttell, Virginia MacLeod, Jayne Ford, Robin Smith, Margaret Shotton, Eleanor Beecroft, Don Bryn, Ivor Jackson, Robert Huber, Kenneth Poste, James Mainprize, George Hayward, Russ Waller
28–30 Apr., 3–7 May 1960 (Thurs.–Sat. Tues.–Sat.)	*Queen after Death*	Henri de Motherlant's	1942 Fr. prem.	Elizabeth Gray	Coach House Theatre (200 Bedford Rd.)	Toronto	Modern		Lead roles: Ann Weldon, Molly Golby, David White, Harold Burke
13–15 Oct. 1960 (Thurs.–Sat.)	*The Way of the World*	William Congreve		Molly Golby [Thom]	Hart House Theatre				James Mainprize, Norman Edmondson, David White, Rex Southgate, William Innes, Don Lewis, Gary Files, Francess Halpenny, Judith Teague, Patricia Brown, Barbara Barnett, Joan Shaw, Joanna Richardson, Dawn Egan, Joan Morcom

Dec. 1960 (Thurs.–Sat., Wed.–Sat.)					Theatre (20 St. George St.)		(comedy)		Dennis, Marilyn Turner, Margaret Surrey, Helen Winters, Kenneth Wickes, George Harrison, Sean O'Ceallaigh, Abe Roytenberg, Derrick Crawley, Don Ward, Alan Stebbings
2–4, 7–11 Mar. 1961 (Thurs.–Sat., Tues.–Sat.)	*The Queen and the Rebels*	Ugo Betti	1951 prem., 1951 publ., 1956 trans.	Pamela [Beckwith] Terry	Central Library Theatre (20 St. George St.)	Canada	Modern		Patricia Carroll Brown, Margaret Heery, Eileen Williams, Shirley Sims, Peter Brockington (Equity), Leonard Freiser, Edward Semenuk, Ivor Jackson, Don Ward, Allen Chandler, Dennis Lee, Raymond Duplain, Simon Beckwith
21 Mar. 1961 (Tues.s)	*The Way of the World*	William Congreve		Molly Golby [Thom]	Hart House Theatre			CODL22	Kenneth Pogue (Fainall), Norman Edmondson (Mirabell), Maurice Evans (Witwoud), John Saxton (Petulant), Rex Sevenoaks (Sir Wilfull Witwoud), Lewis Gordon (Waitwell), Francess Halpenny (Lady Wishfort), Judith Teague (Mrs. Millamant), Patricia Brown (Mrs Marwood), Barbara Barnett (Mrs. Fainall), Joan Shaw (Foible), Suzanne Cousland (Mincing), Dawn Egan (Betty), Mary Robson (Peg)
1, 4–8, 12–15 Apr. 1961 (Sat., Tues.–Sat., Wed.–Sat.)	Two Fascinating Modern Dramatic Satires:				Central Library Theatre (20 St. George St.)				
	• *The Chairs*	Eugene Ionesco	1952 prem	Fred Euringer		Toronto	Modern (Theatre of the Absurd)		Lewis Gordon, Virginia MacLeod, Roy Passano
	• *The Sandbox*	Edward Albee	1959 writ., 1960 prem.	Fred Euringer		Toronto	Modern (Theatre of the Absurd)		Muriel Cuttell, Jayne Ford, Rex Southgate, Robert Peace, Ron Pollock
4 Oct. 1961 (Wed.)	Three Moderns: ("Seven Moderns" Series I) Readings				Trinity College's Convocation Hall (6 Hoskin Ave.)				
	• *Dock Brief*	John Mortimer	1958 writ.	Francess Halpenny			Reading (modern)		David Renton (Mr. Morgenhall, the lawyer) and John Mew (Mr. Fowle, the prisoner)

(*Continued*)

Run Dates	Show	Writer	Play Dates	Director	Venue	Premiere	Style	Festivals	Cast
	• *Three Sketches:*								
	> *Applicant*	Harold Pinter	1959 writ., 1961 publ., 1964 radio	Juliana Saxton			Reading (modern)		Joan Shaw (Piffs), Robert Peace (Lamb, the applicant)
	> *The Black and White*	Harold Pinter	1959 prem.	Juliana Saxton			Reading (modern)		Agatha Leonard (First Old Woman), Christina Templeton (Second Old Woman)
	> *Gladly Otherwise*	N.F. Simpson	1959 prem.	Juliana Saxton			Reading (modern)		Tilda Stevens, John Mew, Robert Peace
	• I Spy	John Mortimer	1958 publ., 1959 prem.	Anne Weldon			Reading (Mmdern)		Derrick Crawley (Mr. Fruit), Vivian Smith (Mrs. Morgan), Maurice Evans (Captain Morgan), Michael Tait (The lawyer), Tilda Stevens (Gladys)
25 Oct. 1961 (Wed.)	"Seven Moderns" Series II Readings				Trinity College's Convocation Hall (6 Hoskin Ave.)				
	• *All That Fall*	Samuel Beckett	1956 writ., 1957 radio, 1963 Fr. TV, 1966 stage	Molly Golby [Thom]			Reading (modern)		Margaret Tytler (Mrs. Rooney, a lady in her seventies), Manuel Erikson (Christy, a carter), John Mew (Mr. Tyler, a retired bill-broker), Robert Peace (Mr. Slocum, Clerk of the Racecourse), Garry Applegath (Tommy, a porter), Donald Brun (Mr. Barrell, a station master), Judith Hunter (Miss Fitt, a lady in her thirties), Charlotte Holmes (Dolly's mother), Shirley Sims (Dolly, a small girl), Harold Burke (Mr. Rooney, Mrs. Rooney's husband), Brian Silversides (Jerry, a small boy).
	• *Last to Go*	Harold Pinter	1959	Judith Ramsey			Reading (modern)		Dennis Thatcher (a Barman), Rex Sevenoaks (Newspaper Seller)
	• *Embers*	Samuel Beckett	1957 writ., 1959 radio, 1957 stage	Robert Brodie			Reading (modern)		John Cantelon (Henry), Shriley Sims (Ada)
15 Nov. 1961 (Wed.)	"Seven Moderns" Series III Readings				Trinity College's Convocation Hall (6 Hoskin Ave.)				
	• *The Maids*	Jean Genet	1957 prem.	Martin Hunter			Reading (modern)		Alison Cunningham, Barbara Walker
	• *The Flowered Suit*	Don Bryn	1961 prem.	Helen Dunlop		World	Reading		Eleanor Beecroft, Judith Hunter,

	Tomb	Ghelderode		Beecroft			(modern)		Francess Halpenny, Eleanor Stewart, Virginia MacLeod, Evelyn McDermid, Jacqueline White, Robin Smith, Joyce Bocknek, Edith Orde Tuff, Ruth Rashkis, Richard King
6 Dec. 1961 (Wed.)	*Les Femmes Savantes (The Blue Stockings)*	Molière, translated by Eleanor Stewart (Alumnae member)	1672 prem.	Leith Macdonald	Art Gallery of Toronto Sculpture Court (317 Dundas St. W.)		Period (comedy)		ChristinaTempleton, Eleanor Beecroft (mother), Mary Jameson, Marilyn Turner, Jane Carnwath, Robert Peace, Kenneth Poste, John Cantelon, Gary Applegath, Glenn Gilmar, Dick King, Richard Robinson, George Hayward
2–5 May 1962 (Wed.–Sat.)	"An Evening of Modern Theatre":				The Grenville Street Playhouse (23 Grenville St.)			no CODL entry in 1962	
	• *What Shall We Tell Caroline*	John Mortimer	1958 publ., 1958 prem., 1958 TV	Pamela [Beckwith] Terry			Modern		Kenneth Pogue (Equity), Mary Jameson, Dennis St. John, Margaret Hamilton
	• *The Babies: A Study in Misconception*	Anna Lippman (Can.)	1962 prem.	Francess Halpenny		World	Modern		Virginia MacLeod, Ivor Jackson
2 Nov. 1962 (Fri.)	*The Easter Egg*	James Reaney	1962 prem.	Pamela [Beckwith] Terry	Physical Sciences Auditorium at McMaster University	World	Modern		Probably the same cast as 9 Nov. 1962.
9–11, 13–18 Nov. 1962 (Fri.–Sun. for "patrons," Tues.–Sun.)	*The Easter Egg*	James Reaney	1962 prem.	Pamela [Beckwith] Terry	Coach House Theatre (151 Huron St.)				Glenna Davis, Margaret Hamilton, Peter Peer, Ivor Jackson, Lewis Gordon
12–13 Dec. 1962 (Wed.–Thurs.)	A mystery play Christmas production			Eileen Williams	University Women's Club (80 Bloor St. W.)		Christmas Mystery Play		No cast found.
16 Jan.–2, 7–9 Feb. 1963 (Wed.–Sat., Wed.–Sat., held over Thurs.–Sat.)	*The Duchess of Malfi*	John Webster	1613 prem.	Gordon C. Johnson	Coach House Theatre (151 Huron St.)		Period (Tragedy)	no CODL entry in 1963	Molly Golby, Mary Jameson, Patricia Carroll Brown (Equity), Marilyn Turner, Bruce Envoy, Douglas Ney, John Watts, Thomas Shandel, Roy Passano, Sol Mandlsohn, Keith Melville, Ronald Kivinen, Gary Shallenberg, Allan Connolly, Ivor Jackson
13–17 and 20–4 Mar. 1963 (Wed.–Sun.)	Two Plays:				Coach House Theatre (151 Huron St.)				

(Continued)

Run Dates	Show	Writer	Play Dates	Director	Venue	Premiere	Style	Festivals	Cast
	• *The Hole*	N.F. Simpson	1957 prem.	Herbert Whittaker		Toronto	Modern (Theatre of the Absurd)		Jackie White, Glenna Davis, Gino Empry, Alex Eftimoff, Donald Bryn, John Watts, David O. Charles, Garnet Traux
	• *The Room*	Harold Pinter	1957 prem.	Herbert Whittaker		Toronto	Modern (Theatre of the Absurd)		Nan Dobson, Tilly Crawley, Edward Kelly, Donald Ewer (Equity), John Burgess, Howard Mathew
1–12 May 1963 (Wed.–Sun.)	*The Trial of Corporal Adam: A Comedy in Verse*	Wilfred Watson	1963	Michael Tait	Coach House Theatre (151 Huron St.)	World	Modern		Anne Weldon, Kay Martin, Tilly Crawley, Donna Wilkins, Robin Ward, John Watts, Ivor Jackson, Edward Kelly, Graham Fugle, Robert Graham, James Peddie (Equity), Derrick Crawley, Gary Schallenberg, James Dickinson, Peter Peer, Garnet Traux, Abe Roytenberg, Kenneth Pogue (Equity), William Manson
29 May–9 June 1963 (Wed.–Sun.)	*Gallows Humour*	Jack Richardson	1963	Wilf Pegg	Coach House Theatre (151 Huron St.)	World	Modern (comedy)		Part I: Muriel Cuttell, John W. McMullan, Robert Coutts; Part II: Virginia MacLeod (Actors Equity), John W. McMullan, Don Bryn
15–26 Oct. 1963 (Tues.–Sat.)	*Major Barbara*	George Bernard Shaw	1905 writ. 1905 prem., 1907 publ.	Pamela [Beckwith] Terry	Coach House Theatre (151 Huron St.)		Modern		Barbara Armitage, Mary Jameson, Patricia Fairman, Tilly Crawley, Patricia Craig, Celia Armitage, Ian Gibson, Allen Farrell, Ronald Decent, Garnet Truax, Peter Court, Peter Peer, John W. McMullen, Kenneth Pogue (Equity)
29–30 Nov., 3–7, 10–14 Dec. 1963 (Fri.–Sat., Tues.–Sat., Tues.–Sat.)	*The Double Dealer*	William Congreve	1693 prem	Peter Brockington	Coach House Theatre (151 Huron St.)		Period (comedy)		Patricia Carroll Brown, Harold Burke, Patricia Craig, John Crawford, Albert Downs, Thomas Hoisveen, Charlotte Homes, Ivor Jackson, Edward J. Kelly, William Manson, Robert Osborne, Alan Stebbings, Gwen Thomas, Dan Claus
31 Jan.–1, 4–8, 11–15 Feb. 1964 (Fri.–Sat., Tues.–Sat., Tues.–Sat.)	*Count Oederland*	Max Frisch	1951 prem.	Patricia Carroll Brown	Coach House Theatre (151 Huron St.)	Canada	Modern	no CODL entry in 1964	Valli Lama, Suzanne Bryant, Eileen Williams, Pat Carson, Ken Pogue (Equity), Alfred Ludwig, Eric Kosky, Alan Stebbings, Don Ward, Roy Passano, Ken Hewitt, Sol Medelson, Garnett Truax, Ivor Jackson, Ron Kivenen, Bill Manson, Gino Empry, Len Doncheff, Ron Gilmore, Ken Hewiit,

3–7, 10–14, Mar. 1964 (Fri.–Sat., Tues.–Sat., Tues.–Sat.)			1960 publ.	Whittaker	Theatre (151 Huron St.)		(Theatre of the Absurd)		Barton [Polley]
1, 2, 7–10, 13–17 May 1964 (Fri., Sat. cancelled for illness, Thurs.–Sun., Wed.–Sun.)	*The Gibbet (Le Gibet)*	Jacques Languirand, trans Albert Bermel	1964 Fr. prem., 1964 Eng. prem.	Anne Weldon (Tait)	Coach House Theatre (151 Huron St.)	World (in English)	Modern (comedy)		Raynold Gideon (Equity), Guy Sanvido (Equity), Mary Barton (Equity) Muriel Cuttell, Diane Buchan [Polley], Helen Carscallen, Bruce Armstrong, Allan Sherwood-Anderson, James Hunter, David Beard, James Dickenson, Robert Graham, Donald Prout, Raymond Bellow
20–Nov.–1 Oct. 1964 (Tues.–Sun.)	*The Emperor* (a new English adapation of *Enrico IV* [*Henry IV*]	Luigi Pirandello, trans Eric Bentley	1921 Ital. writ., 1922 Ital. prem.	Gordon C. Johnson	Coach House Theatre (151 Huron St.)		Modern		Valli Lama, Merrilee Houston, Ron Kivinen, Bruce Armstrong (Equity), William Mockridge, Keith Melville, John Ruta (Equity), Bob Mumford, Poy Passano, David Beard, Rex Southgate (Equity)
27–8 Nov., 1–5, 8–12, Dec. 1964 (Fri.–Sat., Tues.–Sat., Tues.–Sat.)	*Doctors of Philosophy*	Muriel Spark	1962 prem.	Cicely Thomson	Coach House Theatre (151 Huron St.)	Toronto	Modern (comedy)		Helen Dunlop, Mary Fitzpatrick, Muriel Cuttell, Joann Noyes, Rita Merkelis, Christina Templeton, Gordon Jocelyn, Robert Graham, David Thomson
5–6, 9–20 Feb. 1965 (Fri.–Sat., Tues.–Sat., Tues.–Sat.)	*Next Time I'll Sing to You*	James Saunders	1962 prem.	Pamela [Beckwith] Terry	Coach House Theatre (151 Huron St.)		Modern	no CODL entry in 1965	Jean McCall, David Thomson, Les Hayter (Equity), Don Ward (Equity), Allen Farrell
19–20, 23–7, 30–1 Mar., 1–3 Apr. 1965 (Fri.–Sat., Tues.–Sat., Tues.–Sat.)	*A Touch of the Poet*	Eugene O'Neill	1958 prem.	Herbert Whittaker	Coach House Theatre (151 Huron St.)	Toronto	Modern (drama)		Diane Buchan [Polley], Helen Carscallen, Molly Thom [Golby], Don Ward (Equity), Michael Tregenza [Polley] (Equity), Kenneth Pogue (Equity), Ronald Kivinen, David Thomson, Patrick Fairbairn, David Beard
30 Apr., 1, 4–8, 11–15 May 1965 (Fri.–Sat., Tues.–Sat., Tues.–Sat.)	*The Good Woman of Setzuan*	Bertolt Brecht (English adaptation, Eric Bentley)	1941 writ., 1943 prem.	Patricia Carroll Brown	Coach House Theatre (151 Huron St.)		Modern		No cast found.

(*Continued*)

Run Dates	Show	Writer	Play Dates	Director	Venue	Premiere	Style	Festivals	Cast
19–23, 26–30 Oct. 1965 (Tues.–Sat., Tues.–Sat.); 15–16 Oct. (Fri.–Sat.) cancelled due to death	*The Condemned of Altona*	Jean-Paul Sartre, trans. from the French by Sylvia and George Leeson	1959 prem.	Adam Ludwig	Coach House Theatre (151 Huron St.)	North America	Modern		Adam Ludwig, John Jowsey, Michael Tregenza [Michael Barton Polley] (Equity), Rita Roy, Diane Buchan [Polley], Clark Wallace, Terry Shaw, Muriel Cuttell
17 Oct. 1965 (Sun.)	*The Flowered Suit*	Don Bryn	1961 prem.	Glenna Davis	Colonnade Theatre (131 Bloor St. W.)		Modern	CODL's Canadian One-Act Play Workshop	Muriel Cuttell, Kay Martin, Glenna Davis, Dan Calinescu
19–20, 23–7, 30 Nov., 4 Dec. 1965 (Fri.–Sat., Tues.–Sat., Tues.–Sat.)	*Love for Love*	William Congreve	1695 prem	Harold Burke	Coach House Theatre (151 Huron St.)		Period (comedy)		Christina Templeton, Eileen Williams, Norma Clark, Frances Jackson, Merrilee Houston, Marie Wreford, Paul J. Johnson, Heinar Piller, Ron Booker, Ron Gilmore, Bernard Thorp, David Battle, David Thomson, Ian Brooke, Franz Robinow
28–9 Jan., 1–12 Feb. 1966 (Fri., Sat., Tues.–Sat., Tues.–Sat.)	*The Deadly Game*	James Yaffe (adapted from the novel *Trapps* by Friedrich Dürrenmatt)	1960 prem.	Martin Hunter	Coach House Theatre (151 Huron St.)	Toronto	Modern	no CODL entry in 1966	Glenna Davis, Douglas Ney, Ivor Jackson, Garnet Truax, Tom Britton, Earl Bennett, Marshall Bruce Envoy
16 Feb. 1966 (Wed.)	*The Deadly Game*	James Yaffe (adapted from the novel *Trapps* by Friedrich Dürrenmatt)		Martin Hunter	McMaster University				Probably same cast as 28 Jan. 1966.
18–19, 22 Mar.–2 Apr. 1966 (Fri.–Sat., Tues.–Sat., Tues.–Sat.)	*A Country Scandal (Platonov)*	Anton Chekhov, trans. and adapted by Alex Szogyi.	1878 writ., 1923 publ.	Brian Meeson	Coach House Theatre (151 Huron St.)	Toronto (Canada?)	Modern (comedy)		Rita Roy, Virginia McLeod (Equity), Kay Martin, Donna Wilkins, Tilly Stevens, Geza Kovacs, Sol Mandlsohn, Ron Vivenen, Charles Hayter (Equity), Bill Butler, George Fraser, Garnet Traux, Ernest Luwich, Ian Brooks
3–15 May 1966 (Tues.–Sun., Tues.–Sun.)	Three from Ottawa:			Herbert Whittaker, Associate Director Martin Hunter	Coach House Theatre (151 Huron St.)				Original music composed by Andrew A. Melzer, courtesy of B.M.I. Canada Ltd.

							(Theatre of the Absurd)	Perkins (Equity)
	• *The Year of the Lemmings*	George G. Blackburn	1966			World	Modern	Muriel Cuttell, Merrilee Houston, Barbara MacCallum, Christina Templeton, Francess Halpenny, Marilyn Nixon, Harold Burke, George Fraser, Ivor Jackson, Rob Gilmore, Terry Noble, Bill Butler, Alan Stebbings, Peter Peer, Sol Mandlsohn
	• *The Rest Room, or Just a Song at Twilight*	Russell MacCallum	1966			World	Modern (farce)	Muriel Cuttell, Merrilee Houston, Barbara MacCallum, Christina Templeton, Donna Wilkins, George Fraser, Ivor Jackson, Terry Noble, Bill Butler, Andrew A. Melzer
12 Sept. 1966 (Mon.)	*The Young Visiters*	Daisy Ashford	1890 novel	Molly [Golby] Thom	Coach House Theatre (151 Huron St.)	World (reading)	Reading (period)	Molly Thom, Helen Carscallen, Tilly Crawley, Ruth Elizabeth McLellan
18–22, 25–9 Oct., 1–5 Nov. 1966 (Tues.–Sat., Tues.–Sat., Tues.–Sat.)	*The Three Sisters*	Anton Chekhov	1901 prem	Marigold Charlesworth	Coach House Theatre (151 Huron St.)		Modern (comedy)	Elizabeth Mascall, Margaret Hogarth, Janet Gladish, Patricia Grant, Christina Templeton, Miranda Davies, Bill Butler, David Rowe, Lee Norgate, Ron Kivinen, Ron Gilmore, Don Bryn, Allan Duncan, Zane Boyd, Garnet Truax
9 Nov. 1966 (Wed.)	*Daisy Miller*	Henry James	1878 story, 1884 play	Joan Shaw	Rosedale Home of Alison Roach		Reading (period)	Joan Shaw, Barbara Walker, Kay Martin, Charlotte Holmes, Jackie White, Miranda Davies
25 Nov.–10 Dec. 1966 (Fri.–Sat., Tues.–Sat., Tues.–Sat.)	*The Wings of the Dove*	Christopher Taylor, from the novel by Henry James	1963 prem., 1964 publ	Martin Hunter	Coach House Theatre (151 Huron St.)	North America	Modern	Barbara Jean Friend, Cecil Thomson, Jean Graham, Pat Carson, Frank Spezzano, Keith Melville, Christopher Goulding
9 Jan. 1967 (Mon.)	An Excursion into Jacobean Theatre			Judy Ramsay, assisted by Ming Tsow	Rosedale Home of Lorna F. Rogers			Janet Gladish, Meg Griffiths, Ruth James, Barbara MacCallum, Judy Ramsay, Ming Tsow, Barbara Walker
		Samuel Johnson					Reading (period)	
		John Webster					Reading (period)	
		Francis Beaumont and John Fletcher					Reading (period)	

(Continued)

Run Dates	Show	Writer	Play Dates	Director	Venue	Premiere	Style	Festivals	Cast
24 Feb.–11 Mar. 1967 (Fri.–Sat., Tues.–Sat., Tues.–Sat.)	*Women Beware Women*	Thomas Middleton	1612–1627 writ., 1657 publ.	Brian Meeson	Coach House Theatre (151 Huron St.)	North America	Period (tragedy)		Davena Turvey, Judith Darragh, Barbara Collier, Ruth James, True Knabe, Patricia Chicoine, Sue Taylor, Christian Grotrian, Bill Butler, Frank Gallagher, Ron Solloway, Louis Thompson (Equity), Ernest Luwish, Michael Tregenza [Polley] (Equity), Kingsley Owen, Peter Jason, Phillip Smith, Mark Czarnecki, Douglas Shaw, Nicholas Pawley
17 Mar. 1967 (Thurs.)	*Daily News from the Whole World*	Rae Davis	1967 prem.	Pamela [Beckwith] Terry	Hart House Theatre	World	Modern (avant-garde)	CODL28	No cast found.
2 Apr. 1967 (Sun.)	*A Centennial Tribute to the Ladies of the Canadian Frontier*				Coach House Theatre (151 Huron St.)				
	• *Part 1. The Gentle-women of Upper Canada*	Susanna Moodie, Catherine Parr Traill, Anna Jameson, Anne Langton. Prepared by Molly [Golby] Thom	1967	Molly [Golby] Thom		World (reading)	Reading (modern)		Charlotte Holmes, Janet Gladish, Joan Shaw, Meg Hogarth
	• *Part 2. Excerpts from the Life and Works of Sarah Binks, Sweet Songstress of Saskatchewan*	Paul Hiebert (by the kind permission of Oxford University Press)	1967	Elizabeth Mascall		World (reading)	Reading (modern)		Francess Halpenny, Eileen Williams, Ivor Jackson
28 Apr., 2–13, 16–20 May 1967 (Fri., Tues.–Sat.. Tues.–Fri., held over Tues.–Fri.)	*The Circle*	W. Somerset Maugham	1921 prem.	Maurice Evans	Coach House Theatre (151 Huron St.)		Modern (comedy)		Dorothy Spencer (Equity), Barbara Friend, Eileen Williams, George Friend, Andrew Bassett-Spiers, Al Hand, Adrian Poole, Keith Melville
13–28 Oct. 1967 (Fri., Tues.–Sat.)	*The Eccentricities of a Nightingale* (a revision of *Summer and Smoke*)	Tennessee Williams	1951 writ., 1962 publ., 1976 Broadway prem.	Martin Hunter	Coach House Theatre (151 Huron St.)	North American	Modern		Maureen Fox, Eileen Williams, Francess Halpenny, Robin Smith, Donna Wilkens, Marshall Bruce Evoy, Geza Kovacs, Peter Stead, Ron Kivinen, Gary Shallenburg

1967 (Fri., Tues.–Sat.)		trans. Eric Bentley	1911 Germ. prem., 1957 Eng. publ.		Theatre (151 Huron St.)		(comedy)	Bill Butler, David Rowe, Keith Melville, Paul Dutton
26 Nov., 3 and 10 Dec. 1967 (Sun. evenings)	*This Beggarly Wooden Country: A Centennial Tribute*				Coach House Theatre (151 Huron St.)			
	• *Part 1: The Gentle-women of Upper Canada*	Susanna Moodie, Catherine Parr Traill, Anna Jameson, Anne Langton. Prepared by Molly [Golby] Thom		Molly [Golby] Thom			Reading (modern)	Charlotte Holmes, Joan Shaw, Margaret MacAulay, Meg Hogarth Songs: Deirdre Blades
	• *Part 2: Highlights from the Life and Works of Sarah Binks, Sweet Songstress of Saskatchewan*	Paul Hiebert (by the kind permission of Oxford University Press)		Elizabeth Mascall			Reading (modern)	Eileen Williams, Francess Halpenny, Ivor Jackson (playing seven male parts)
18 Feb. 1968	*This Beggarly Wooden Country: A Centennial Tribute*	Susanna Moodie, Catherine Parr Traill, Anna Jameson, Anne Langton. Prepared by Molly [Golby] Thom and Paul Hiebert (by the kind permission of Oxford University Press)		Molly [Golby] Thom and Elzabeth Mascall	Catharine Parr Traill College, Trent University		Reading (modern)	Charlotte Holmes, Joan Shaw, Margaret MacAulay, Meg Hogarth, Eileen Williams, Francess Halpenny, Ivor Jackson (playing seven male parts)
22 Feb.–9 Mar. 1968 (Fri., Tues.–Sat.)	*Aperitif*	Jack Cunningham	1968 prem.	Herbert Whittaker	Coach House Theatre (151 Huron St.)	World	Modern (drama)	Albert Hand (Alf), Elizabeth Ward (Bea), Robert [R.H.] Thomson (Jamie), Gary Shallenberg (Jerry), Beverley Paul (Janice)
17, 24 Mar. 1968 (Sun. eves)	*Folksongs of Canada* (5 themes)	Various songwriters		Miranda Davies (Producer)	Coach House Theatre (151 Huron St.)		Folksongs	Miranda Davies

(Continued)

Run Dates	Show	Writer	Play Dates	Director	Venue	Premiere	Style	Festivals	Cast
3 Apr. 1968 (Wed.)	*Shelley, or The Idealist: A Tragicomedy*	Ann Jellicoe	1965 prem., 1966 publ.	Helen Boychuk	Coach House Theatre (151 Huron St.)	World (reading)	Reading (modern)		Maggie Bassett, Gloria Hutchinson, Trude Knabe, Penny Perfect
18 Apr.–11 May 1968 (Fri., Tues.–Sat.)	*Little Malcolm and His Struggle against the Eunuchs*	David Halliwell	1965 prem., 6 hr. version	Brian Meeson	Coach House Theatre (151 Huron St.)	Canada	Modern (radical)		Pamela Campion, Robert McKenna, Peter Stead, Michael Polley (Equity), John Astington
22–3 May 1968 (Wed., Thurs.)	*The Matter of Arthur: A Panorama of the Great King whom the Centuries Would Not Willingly Let Die*	Francess Halpenny (after Tennyson, Mallory, and Spenser)	1968	Francess Halpenny	Coach House Theatre (151 Huron St.)	World (reading)	Reading (modern)		No cast found.
17 Oct.–2 Nov. 1968 (Thurs., Fri., Tues.–Sat.; invitation preview Wed., 16 Oct.)	*Viet Rock (A Folk War Movie)*	Megan Terry	1966 prem., 1966 publ.	Molly [Golby] Thom	Coach House Theatre (151 Huron St.)	Toronto	Modern (radical)		Phyllis Benvenuto, Susan Devore, Rita Moonilak, Beverley Paul, Joan Shaw, David Clement (Equity), Jeff Cohen, Wayne Laurence, David Rotenburg, Garry Shallenberg
20–7 Oct. 3 Nov. 1968 (Sunday evenings)	*The Matter of Arthur: A Panorama of the Great King whom the Centuries would Not Willingly Let Die*	Francess Halpenny (prepared), Tennyson, T.H. White.		Francess Halpenny	Coach House Theatre (151 Huron St.)				Wendy Butler, Norma Clark, Maureen Fox, Elizabeth Mascall
28 Nov.–14 Dec. 1968 (Thurs.–Sat., Tues.–Sat., Tues.–Sat.)	*The Promise*	Aleksei Arbuzov; trans. Ariadne Nicolaeff	1965 Rus. written., 1966 Eng. prem.	Wendy Butler	Coach House Theatre (151 Huron St.)	Toronto (possibly Canada?)	Modern		Lorna Wilson (Lika), Robert Thomason (Marat), John Astington (Leonidik)
1, 8, 15 Dec. 1968 (Sundays)	*So Great a Sweetness: Yeats and Maud Gonne: A Dramatic Reading*	Anne Tait		Anne Tait (prepared and directed)	Coach House Theatre (151 Huron St.)	World (reading)	Reading (modern)		Elisabeth Mascall, Maureen Fox (Maud), Meg Hogarth, Tresa O'Driscoll, Michael Tait (as Yeats), Robert O'Driscoll
23 Jan.–8 Feb. 1969 (Tues.–Sat., Thurs.–Sat., Thurs.–Sat.)	*The Birthday Party*	Harold Pinter	1958 prem., 1959 publ.	Herbert Whittaker	Coach House Theatre (151 Huron St.)		Modern (Theatre of the Absurd)		Jacqueline White, Pamela Campion, Ian Orr, Robert McKenna, Neville Dawkins, Michael Polley (Equity)
26 Jan., 2 and 9 Feb. 1969 (Sundays)	*Many Mothers: An evening of dramatic readings from poetry, prose, plays, about [Many Mothers]*			Helen Dunlop and Norma Clark (prepared by)	Coach House Theatre (151 Huron St.)	World (reading)	Reading (modern)		Francess Halpenny, Ruth James, Joan Shaw, Phyllis Benvenuto, Barbara Collier
11 Mar. 1969 (Tues.)	*Mary Stewart, Queen of Scots*	Friederich Schiller / Maxwell	1800 prem., 1936 prem.	Phyllis Benvenuto	Home of Agatha Leonard (Heathdale Rd.)		Reading (period)		Meg Griffiths, Molly Thom

Apr. 1969 (Thurs.–Sat., Tues.–Sat., Tues.–Sat.)			prem.		Theatre (151 Huron St.)		(comedy)	Beckwith, Shelagh Hewitt, Muriell Cuttell, Peter Stead, Jerry Lupien, Norma Clark (Equity).
23, 30 Mar. 1969 (Sundays)	*So Great a Sweetness: Yeats and Maud Gonne: A Dramatic Reading*	Anne Tait		Anne Tait			Reading (modern)	Maureen Fox, Judith Hunter, Elizabeth Mascall, Michael Tait, Ian Orr
19, 26 Oct., 2 Nov. 1969 (Sundays)	*Sir Gawain and the Green Knight*	Anne Tait		Anne Tait (prepared and directed)	Coach House Theatre (10 Maplewood Ave.)	World (reading)	Reading (modern)	Norma Clark, Barbara Collier, Michael Tait, Rex Southgate, Skip Shand
9, 16, 23 Nov. 1969 (Sundays)	*The Song Is Far Away:* "A Dramatic Reading of a New Play"	Michael B. Polley		Elizabeth Mascall	Coach House Theatre (10 Maplewood Ave.)	World (reading)	Reading (Radical)	Gordon Jocelyn, Harold Burke, Tom Talaba, Mary Anne Coles, Jeremy Hole, Ivor Jackson, Lorna Wilson
12–22 Nov. 1969 (Wed.–Sat., Tues.–Sat.)	*The Ecstasy of Rita Joe*	George Ryga	1967 prem.	Herbert Whittaker	Central Library Theatre (20 St. George St.)	Toronto	Modern	Alan Bleviss (Equity), Molly Thom, Duke Redbird, Sheila MacDonald, Ian Orr, Sol Mandlsohn, Jacqueline White, Neville Dawkins, Keith Melville, Peter Melville, Vic Stanton, John McCormick, Rein Ristmagi, John Mason, Douglas Donald, Florence Cook, Ted Pilkington (musician) Mallory Gilbert – lighting operator and producer Michael Spence – set construction assistant
30 Nov. 1969 (Sun.)	*Improvisation*	Alumnae Workshop		Joan Shaw (director); Martin Hunter (dramaturge)	Coach House Theatre (10 Maplewood Ave.)	World (improv)	Improv	Phyllis Benvenuto, Deborah Clipperton, Mavis Hayman, Jennifer Mascall, Beverly Miller, Sally Wente, Jonathan Beckwith, Jim Wente, Jack Zimmerman; several teenagers including Sandy Mayzel, Timothy Brook, Tim Jocelyn, Jeffrey Cohen, David Rotenberg.
18, 25 Jan., 1 Feb. 1970 (Sundays)	*Mine of Souls (The Making of a Poet)*	Laurie Lee and Francess Halpenny		Francess Halpenny (prepared and directed)	Coach House Theatre (10 Maplewood Ave.)	World (reading)	Reading (modern)	Blair Mascall, Mavis Hayman, Barbara Collier, Stephanie Bonar, Francess Halpenny
8, 15, 22 Feb. 1970 (Sundays)	*Collision Course (5 short plays)*		1968 publ.		Coach House Theatre (10 Maplewood Ave.)			

(Continued)

Run Dates	Show	Writer	Play Dates	Director	Venue	Premiere	Style	Festivals	Cast
	• *Camera Obscura*	Robert Patrick	1969 prem.	Joan Shaw			Modern (radical)		Blair Mascall (Man), Beverly Miller (Woman), Robert Morgan (Male voice), Betty Mascall (Female voice)
	• *Tour*	Terrence McNally	1967 prem.	Joan Shaw			Modern (radical)		Beverly Miller (Mrs. Wilson), Robert Morgan (Mr. Wilson), Jeffrey Cohen (Chauffeur), David Rotenberg, Blair Mascall (Monks)
	• *The Unexpurgated Memoirs of Bernard Mergendeiler*	Jules Feiffer	1959 publ.	Joan Shaw			Modern (radical)		Sandy Mayzel (Naomi), Jeffrey Cohen (Bernard)
	• *Momma as She Became – But Not as She Was*	John Rechy	1968 publ.	Joan Shaw			Modern (radical)		Betty Mascall (Momma), Jennifer Mascall (Daughter), Blair Mascall (Son)
	• *Rats*	Israel Horowitz	1968 publ.	Joan Shaw			Modern (radical)		David Rotenberg (Jebbie), Jeffrey Cohen (Bobby), Blair Mascall (Baby)
12–21 Mar. 1970 (Thurs.–Sat.)	*America Hurrah*	Jean-Claude van Itallie	1966 prem.	Phyllis Benvenuto	Central Library Theatre (20 St. George St.)	Toronto	Modern (radical)		Micki Moore, Jacqueline White, Ruth Green, Marion Swadron, Walter Bolton, Ian Warner, Timothy Brook, Ian Orr
5, 12, 19 Apr. 1970 (Sundays)	*Shelley, or The Idealist: A Tragicomedy*	Ann Jellicoe		Cicely Thomson	Coach House Theatre (10 Maplewood Ave.)		Reading (modern)		Barry Pearson (Shelley), Bob Morgan (Hogg, Telawny), Garnet Traux (Coplestone, Godwin, Lord Eldon), Ivor Jackson (Walker, Westbrook, Baliff), Keith Melville (Master, Edward Williams, Moneylender, Clerk), Randy McLeod (Moneylender), Mary Ann Coles (Mary Godwin, Miss Ferney), Peggy Larkin (Harriet Westbrook), Cathy Larkin (Miss Pubus, Eliza Westbrook), Anne Bridel (Hellen Shelley, Mrs. Godwin), Valerie Grabove (Miss Meeks, Jane Williams, Clare Claremont)
25 Oct., 1, 8 Nov. 1970 (Sundays)	*Mine of Souls (The Making of a Poet)*	Laurie Lee and Francess Halpenny		Francess Halpenny (prepared and directed)	Coach House Theatre (10 Maplewood Ave.)		Reading (modern)		No cast found.
	Two Plays:				Central Library Theatre (20 St. George St.)				

24–7, Feb., 6 Mar. 1971 (Thurs.–Sat., Wed.–Sat., Wed.–Sat.) preview 17 Feb. (Wed.)	*Holroyd: A Drama in Three Acts*		1914 pub., 1966 publ.				(drama)	Elizabeth Adams, Mary Solovew, Ruth James, Dennis Mills, Nicholas Bacon, Jonathan Bryant, Peter Stead, Ron Kivinen, Les Japp, Andrew Gillanders
21–3, 28 Feb. 28, 1,2 Mar. 1971 (Sat.–Tues., Sat.–Tues.)	*D.H. Lawrence: Man and Demon*	Anne Tait	1971 prem	Anne Tait		World (reading)	Reading (modern)	Mavis Hayman, Molly Thom, Pamella Campion, Ilene Cummings, Andrea Rosnick, with Michael Polley, David Humphries, John Cartwright, Alan Toff
21 Oct.–6 Nov. 1971 (Thurs.–Sat., Tues.–Sat., Tues.–Sat.)	Two Plays:				Coach House Theatre (10 Maplewood Ave.)			
	• *Creditors*	August Strindberg	1888 writ. 1889 publ., 1890 Swed. prem.	Adam Ludwig			Modern	Pamella Campion, Harold Burke, Adam Ludwig
	• *One Man Masque*	James Reaney	1960 prem.	Pamela [Terry] Beckwith			Modern	Robert Morgan
24, 31 Oct., 7 Nov. 1971 (Sundays)	*Pablo Neruda: Lives of the Poet*	Compiled and directed by Lina Ladron de Guevara. Trans. by Prof. Keith Ellis (Hispanic Studies Dept. U of T) and Lina Landron de Guevera.	1971 prem.	Lina Ladron de Guevara; Assistant Director Elizabeth Mascall	Coach House Theatre (10 Maplewood Ave.)	World (reading in English)	Reading (modern)	Jenifer Mascall, Pat Futterer, Patricia Evans, Howard Cole, Michael Polley (Equity), Michael Powicke, John W. Hughes, John Taylor
25 Nov.–11 Dec. 1971 (Thurs.–Sat., Tues.–Sat., Tues.–Sat.)	*Tonight: Bert Brecht* *Part I: The Art of Non-Tolerance* • *Introduction* • *Does Man Help His Fellow Man?* • *"What Keeps a Man Alive?"* • "Of Poor B.B	Bertolt Brecht, adapted by Anne Tait	1971 prem.	Anne Tait with Beverly Miller	Coach House Theatre (10 Maplewood Ave.)	World	Revue	Patricia Carroll Brown, Judy Darragh, Rod Beattie, Dan Calinescu, Ron Kivinen, Michael B. Polley, Michael Evans, Simon Waegemakers

(*Continued*)

Run Dates	Show	Writer	Play Dates	Director	Venue	Premiere	Style	Festivals	Cast
	• *"If Sharks Were People"* • *"Mac the Knife"* *<u>Part II: Change the World; It Needs It</u>* • *"On God"* • *"The Love Market* • *"I cast my lot with the common people"* • *"On the Infanticide, Marie Farrar* • *poems on the theatre from Brecht's Der Messingkauf* • *The Measures Taken* *<u>Part III: Can this Disease Not be Curable</u>?* • *"The Parable of the Burning House"* • *The Jewish Wife* • *"Written on the Wall" from A German Primer for War* • *"The German Miserere"* • *"The Ballad of the Dead Solider"* • *"The Marked Man"* • *"The Soldier of La Ciotat"* • *"Mother Courage lives off the war"* • *"Ein Vaterland"* • *"In Flight from my Countrymen"* • *Brecht in America.*								

	Contradictions Are Our Only Hope • pieces on the Berliner Ensemble and the importance of a passport • "The Solution" • "My Teacher"; • an excerpt from The Caucasian Chalk Circle • "To the Next Generation" • "Should the World Be Changed" • "Happy Ending" • "A Tombstone"						
3–19 Feb. 1972 (Thurs.–Sat., Tues.–Sat., Tues.–Sat.)	*Mixed Doubles: An Entertainment on Marriage: 8 Playlets*	Various authors including Owen, Saunders, Pinter, Bowen, etc. (File available at Alumnae)	1969 prem., 1970 publ.	Molly [Golby] Thom	Coach House Theatre (10 Maplewood Ave.)	Modern (comedy)	Produced by Anna Ferguson; SM: Susan Higgonson; ASM: Mallory Gilbert, Ena Brown; Props: Margaret Spence, Stephanie Bonar, Lillian Burke; Costumes: Margaret Edgar, Judith Friendman; Lights designed by Les Japp; Operated by Shelagh Kareda, Barbara Seaman; Prompters: Jackie White, Frances Schaefer, Barba MacCallum, Patty Proctor; House Manager: Ruth Miller; Publicity: Shelagh Kareda; Set construction by Les Japp
	• *Man's Best Friend*	James Saunders					Anne McKenna (Bride), Harry Lane (Groom)
	• *Score*	Lyndon Brook					Ian Orr (Harry), Joy Thwaite (Sheila)
	• *Norma*	Alun Owen					Anne McKenna (She), Harry Lane (He)
	• *Night*	Harold Pinter					Joy Thwaite (The Woman), Ian Orr (The Man)
	• *Permanence*	Fay Weldon					Anne McKenna (Helen), Harry Lane (Peter)
	• *Countdown*	Alan Aykbourn					Ian Orr (Husband), Joy Thwaite (Wife)

(*Continued*)

Run Dates	Show	Writer	Play Dates	Director	Venue	Premiere	Style	Festivals	Cast
	• *Silver Wedding*	John Bowen							Anne McKenna (Audrey), Harry Lane (Julian)
	• *Resting Place*	David Compton							Joy Thwaite (Old Woman), Ian Orr (Old Man)
6, 13, 20 Feb. 1972 (Sundays)	*The Trial of the Catonsville Nine*	Daniel Berrigan	1971 prem.	Diane Polley	Coach House Theatre (10 Maplewood Ave.)	Toronto (Reading)	Reading (modern)		Muriel Cuttell, Jane Carnwath, Marianne Coles, Michael Polley (Equity), Harold Burke (Equity), Dan Calinescu, Ron Kivinen, Kurt Jacobs, Bill Butler, Jim Irving, Stephen Moyer, Nigel Spencer, Dion McHugh Michael Tait and Geoffrey Stead provided voices on tape. Shelagh Kareda provided publicity
9–25 Mar. 1972 Thurs.–Sat., Tues.–Sat., Tues.–Sat.); 8 Mar. preview	Two Plays:			Urjo Kareda	Coach House Theatre (10 Maplewood Ave.)				
	Landscape	Harold Pinter	1968 radio prem., 1969 prem.			Toronto	Modern (Theatre of the Absurd)		Barbara Collier, Ian Orr
	Silence	Harold Pinter	1969 prem.			Toronto	Modern (Theatre of the Absurd)		Mavis Hayman, Peter Stead, Skip Shand

Appendix III

Alumnae Production History Firehall

Run Dates	Show	Writer	Play Dates	Director	Venue	Premiere	Style	Cast
19 Oct.–4 Nov. 1972 (Thurs. to Sat.)	*The Plough and the Stars*	Sean O'Casey	1926 prem.	Patricia Carroll Brown	Firehall Theatre (70 Berkeley Street)		Modern (drama)	Mavis Hayman, Doris Cowan (Equity), Morna Wales (Equity), Robin Beckwith, Donna Yazzolino, Jane Reynolds, Anthony Hayman, George Truss, Peter Stead, Peter Higginson, Terance Belleville, Ted Brock, Anthony E. Jones, Ron Kivinen, Bob Wilkinson, William Scott, Less Japp
23 Nov.–9 Dec. 1972	*Le Temps Sauvage*	Anne Hébert, trans. Elizabeth Mascall	1966 prem. (Fr), 1972 prem. (Eng.)	John Van Burek	Firehall Theatre	World (in English)	Modern (drama)	Anna Ferguson, Susan Morgan, Judy Darragh, Mary Vaughn, Melleny Brown, Allegra Fulton, Ian Orr, John Turnbull, Jean-Marc Amyot
5–7, 12–14 Jan. 1973	*Sir Gawain and the Green Knight*	Unknown author. Trans. and dramatized by Anne Tait	1400 orig., 1973 read	Anne Tait	Stage 2 at the Firehall Theatre (Studio)		Reading (adaptation)	Norma Clark (Equity), Barbara Collier, Michael Polley (Equity), Nigel Spencer, Ian Orr
15 Feb.–3 Mar. 1973	*The Women*	Clare Boothe Luce	1936 prem.	Ron Solloway	Firehall Theatre		Modern (comedy)	Robin Beckwith, Kay Cook, Mary Vaughn, Diane Polley, Jacqueline White, Judy Darragh, Heather Cook, Eileen Williams, Sheila MacDonald, Razie Brownstone, Sandra Shuman, Margaret Edgar, Marion Swadron, Sony Freedman, Eleanor Robbins, Lenie Lenz, Susan Darlington, Ilene Cummings
9–11, 16–18 Mar. 1973	*Box* and *Quotations from Chairman Mao Tse-Tung*	Edward Albee	1968 prem.	Pamela [Beckwith] Terry	Stage 2 at the Firehall Theatre (Studio)	Toronto	Modern (Theatre of the Absurd)	Norma Clark, Morna Wales (Equity), Virginia MacLeod (Equity), Peter Stead, William Buyers
29 Mar.–14 Apr. 1973	*The Zykovs*	Maxim Gorky, adapted by Molly [Golby] Thom from David Huntley's translation	1914 writ., 1918 prem.	Molly [Golby] Thom	Firehall Theatre	North America	Modern (adaptation)	Sandra Shuman, Rita Davies, Francess Halpenny, Patsy Nichols, Debra Barton, Ian Orr, David Dowling, Graham Harley, John Norton Smith, David Beard, Allan Whiteley
18 Oct.–3 Nov. 1973	*Kaspar*	Peter Handke. Trans. Michael Roloff	1967 publ., 1969 prem.	Pamela [Beckwith] Terry	Firehall Theatre	Canada (in English; Trinity College said they did it in 1971)	Modern	Diane Brdar, Melleny Brown, Ena Brown, Anne Tait, Terance Belleville, John Illingworth, Allan Whiteley, Steve Woodjetts

29 Nov.–15 Dec. 1973	*Once in a Lifetime*	George S. Kaufman and Moss Hart	1930 prem.	Phyllis Benvenuto	Firehall Theatre		Modern (comedy)	Beverley Miller, Marita Ensio, Sandra Shuman, Kathleen Gould, Barbara Keen, Anna Ferguson, Melleny Brown, Barbara Japp, Ruth Green, Catherine Swing, Gretchen Helbig, Debra Friedman, Robin Henry, Sheila MacDonald, Glenn Gilmar, Ted Brock, Sol Mandlsohn, Ian Orr, Gerry Bryars, Joel Kazman, Colin Parks, Larry Bennett, Charles Holzberg, Keith Melville, Stuart Murray, Peter Hiscocks, Ron Kivinen, Marc Dassas
11–15 Dec. 1973	Two Famous One-Act Plays!				Stage 2 at the Firehall Theatre (Studio)			
	• *Still Life*	Noël Coward	1936 prem.	Barbara Keen			Modern	Penny Gawn, Sylve Germaine, Claire Goren, Betty Leventhal, Barbara Smialey, Raymond Rutitis, Glenn Gilmar, Ian Orr, Keith Melville
	• *A Phoenix Too Frequent*	Christopher Fry	1946 prem.	Barbara Keen			Modern (comedy)	Anna Ferguson, Ilene Cummings, Graeme Ratcliffe
31 Jan.–16 Feb. 1974	*Total Eclipse*	Christopher Hampton	1968 prem.	Anne Tait	Firehall Theatre	Toronto	Modern (historical)	Anna Ferguson (Equity), Linda Stephen, Colleen Wagner, Eileen Williams, Jean Gawn, John Astington, Ray Stancer, John Illingworth, Joseph Erickson, Peter Higginson, Derke Webster, David Beard, Michael G. McKinnon Guitarist: Terry McKenna
22–4 Feb., 1–3 Mar. 1974	*The Young Visiters or, Mr. Salteena's Plan*	Molly [Golby] Thom, from the novel by Daisy Ashford	1919 novel, 1974 prem.	Molly [Golby] Thom	Firehall Theatre (Studio)	World	Modern (adaptation)	Susan Morgan, Catherine Borg, Jane Milne, John Gilbert, Peter Higginson, Harold Burke, John Illingworth, Ian Orr, Richard Selignman
20 Mar.–6 Apr. 1974	*Old Times*	Harold Pinter	1971 prem.	Herbert Whittaker	Firehall Theatre	Toronto	Modern (Theatre of the Absurd)	Sheila MacDonald, Norma Clark (Equity), Michael Polley (Equity)
2–18 May 1974	*Muddy Little York*	Prepared by the company and some non-acting contributors	1974 prem.	Juliana Saxton	Firehall Theatre	World	Docudrama	Diane Brdar, Cheryl Hay, Jeanie Lawrence, Ellen Messing, Joan Shaw, Cicely Thomson, Rick Axon, Tony Gifford, John Illingworth, Jim Irving

(*Continued*)

Run Dates	Show	Writer	Play Dates	Director	Venue	Premiere	Style	Cast
5, 12, 19 May 1974 (Sundays)	*The Rimers of Eldritch*	Lanford Wilson	1966 prem.	Shelagh Hewitt	Stage 2 at the Firehall Theatre (Studio)		Modern	Barbara Parfit, Phyllis Benvenuto, Jackie White, Lillian Burke, Catherine Borg, Daphne McDowell, Cheryl Kramsky, Eileen Williams, Elissa Pane, Diane Polley, Stuart Murray, Ian Orr, Chuck Syme, Gordon Jocelyn, Wade Hampton, Skip Shand, Graeme Ratcliffe
24–6, 31 May, 1–2 June 1974	Two plays:				Stage 2 at the Firehall Theatre (Studio)			
	• *The Day Dumbfounded Got His Pylon*	Henry Livings	1963 radio, 1965 prem., 1967 publ.	Mavis Hayman			Modern (comedy)	Jean Gawn, Margaret Peek, Alan D. Clifton, Peter Stead, Peter Higginson, Anthony Hayman
	• *The Criminals*	José Triana	1967 prem.	Mavis Hayman			Modern	Colleen Wagner, Margaret Edgar, Peter Higginson
17 Oct.–2 Nov. 1974	*Lemon Sky*	Lanford Wilson	1970 prem.	Shelagh Hewitt	Firehall Theatre	Toronto	Contemporary	Joan Shaw, Cheryl Kramsky, Jean Melusky, Chris Britton (Equity), Gordon Jocelyn, Lawrence Beckwith, Douglas Legg
21 Nov.–7 Dec. 1974	*Shelter*	Carol Bolt	1974 prem.	Eric Steiner	Firehall Theatre	World	Contemporary (comedy)	Diane Polley, Pixie Bigelow, Collen Wagner, Phyllis Benvenuto, Helen Carscallen
6–22 Feb. 1975	*The Power of Darkness*	Molly Thom's adaptation of Leo Tolstoy play	1886 writ., 1902 prem.	Molly [Golby] Thom	Firehall Theatre	World (adaptation)	Period (drama)	Margaret Edgar, Joan Caldarera, Vickie Fagen, Francess Halpenny, Alix Arnett, Razie Brownstone, Jane McGahey, John Gilbert, Peter Kunder (Equity), Walter Bolton, Ian Orr, John W., Tomas Guzman, Chris Walat
20 Mar.–15 Apr. 1975	*Forget-Me-Not Lane*	Peter Nichols	1971 prem.	Mavis Hayman	Firehall Theatre	Toronto	Contemporary (drama)	Mary Harrison, Sheila MacDonald, Martha Jocelyn, Anne Coakley (Equity), Gerry Crack, Peter Higginson, Graeme Ratcliffe, Jonathan Beckwith, Peter Stead; voices of Frank's children on tape by Emma Higginson, Jeremy Burke, Graeme Ratcliffe
6–17 May 1975	*The Marriage of Figaro: Or the Follies of a Day*	Pierre-Augustin Caron de Beaumarchais	1776 writ., 1784 prem.	Phyllis Benvenuto (in the program, but advertised as Pamela Terry)	Firehall Theatre		Period (comedy)	Jane Carnwath, Alix Arnett, Geraldine Diver, Betty Leventhal, Anna Leventhal, Barbara Japp, Tova Rapoport, Harold Burke (Equity), Allen Farrell, Peter Stead, Bruce Wall, Herb Field, Gerald Smith, John Ward, Keith Melville, Neil Davies, Derek Webster, Mark Manchester, Derek Webster, Ronald Kivinen

9–25 Oct. 1975	*Hippolytos*	Euripedes. Trans. Robert Bragg	428 BCE prem.	Juliana Saxton	Firehall Theatre		Period (tragedy)	Phyllis Benevenuto, Eileen Williams, Betty Leventhal, Barbara Smialey, Barbara Japp, Jane Carnwath, Judy Darragh, Deirdre Bowen, Michael Kopsa, Andrew Leech, Dominic Hogan, (Equity), Lawrence Sheffit
2, 9, 16, 30 Nov. 1975; 11, 18, 25 Jan., 8, 15, 22, 29 Feb. 1976	*Women Writers Speak: A Series of Sunday Evening Talks and Readings at the Firehall Theatre*	Margaret Atwood Marie-Claire Blais Nicole Brossard Marian Engel Gwendolyn MacEwen Travis Lane Phyllis Gotlieb Judith Merril Joy Kogawa Janis Rappoport Jackie Crossland Carol Bolt Dorothy Livesay Molly Thom's *This Beggarly Wooden Country*	*various*	–	Firehall Theatre		Readings	Margaret Atwood, Marie-Claire Blais, Nicole Brossard, Marian Engel, Gwendolyn MacEwen, Travis Lane, Molly Thom's *This Beggarly Wooden Country*, Phyllis Gotlieb, Judith Merril, Joy Kogawa, Janis Rappoport, Jackie Crossland, Carol Bolt, Dorothy Livesay
27 Nov.–13 Dec. 1975	*Crabdance*	Beverley Simons	1969 prem.	Mavis Hayman	Firehall Theatre	Toronto	Contemporary (tragicomedy)	Margaret Edgar, William Deacon, Ian Orr, Peter Stead, John Ward, Garnet Fraser, Neil Davies, Blair Mascall (Equity)
7, 14 Dec. 1975	*This Beggarly Wooden Country*	Molly [Golby] Thom	1969 prem. reading	Molly [Golby] Thom	Stage 2 at the Firehall Theatre (Studio)		Reading	Charlotte Norcop, Margaret MacAulay, Joan Shaw, Meg Hogarth, Jane Carnwath
5–21 Feb. 1976	*The Unexpected Guest*	Agatha Christie	1958 prem.	Cicely Thomson	Firehall Theatre		Modern (mystery)	Olwyn Millington, Esther Hockin, Maggie Bassett, Ian Orr, Bruce Wall, Hugh Graham, John Cummings, Ray Stancer, John Illingworth
16–21 Mar. 1976	*"The admirable history of a penitent woman MADELEINE": An instance of Daemonic Possession in Seventeenth Century France*	W.H. Rockett	1971 writ., 1972 radio, 1976 prem.	Jean Bartels	Firehall Theatre (Studio)	World (adapted for stage)	Modern (thriller)	Kay Griffin, Mavis Hayman, Lyn Green, Barbara Japp, Betty Leventhal, Anna Leventhal, Geoff Blackman (Equity), Peter Kunder (Equity), John Pepper (Equity), Jonathan Beckwith, Denny Hollows, Gary Myers

(*Continued*)

Run Dates	Show	Writer	Play Dates	Director	Venue	Premiere	Style	Cast
1–17 Apr. 1976	*The Rover or The Banish't Cavaliers: A Comedy of Intrigue*	Aphra Behn, adapted "slightly" by Molly [Golby] Thom	1677 prem.	Molly [Golby] Thom	Firehall Theatre		Period (comedy)	Sally Jay, Barbara Collier, Patricia Hodgins, Eileen Williams, Beverley Miller, Juliana Saxton, Danielle Pascall, Elizabeth Young, Peter Higginson, Michael Polley (Equity), Ian Large, John Offen, Blair Mascall (Equity), Peter Noy, Graham Stimpson, Paul McConvey, Mike Parker, Bill X. Carson
20 May–5 June 1976	*The House of Blue Leaves*	John Guare	1971 prem.	Phyllis Benvenuto	Firehall Theatre		Contemporary (comedy)	June Hammerschlag, Anna Ferguson (Equity), Janet Davies, Elissa Pane, Kathleen Gould, Shelley Ashbury, James B. Douglas (Equity), Bill X. Carson, Barry D. Minshull, Doug Downie, Dennis Gingrich, Kenneth Golby
7–23 Oct. 1976	*Murder on the Nile*	Agatha Christie	1944 prem.	Pamela [Beckwith] Terry	Firehall Theatre		Modern (mystery)	Kay Griffin, Lyn Green, Nola Morgan-Wade, Margaret Milne, Jacqueline Swartz, Joseph Grosso, James MacLachlan, Dirk McLean, Peter Higginson, Richard Allon, Keith Melville, Bertram Schwarzschild, Peter Brodie-Brown, Joseph Grosso
14–16, 21–3 Jan. 1977	*Pocket Full of Promises* (one-act)	Nan (Nancy) Brien	1977 prem.	Diane Wilkinson	Stage 2 at the Firehall Theatre (Studio)	World	Contemporary (Commedia dell'arte style)	Barbara Burt, Jane Hamara, Ken Stern, Ian Murdoch, Allan Whiteley, Brian Sewell, Kurt Jacob, Don Johnston
10–26 Feb. 1977	*The Children's Hour*	Lillian Hellman	1934 prem.	Mavis Hayman	Firehall Theatre		Modern (drama)	Laurie Brown, Sarah Carnwath, Allison Diver, Maggie Milne, Miriam Bloomenfeld, Tracy Edgar, Helen Wedge, Penny Kluger, Angela Winter, Barbara Collier, Maggie Bassett, Cicley Thomson, Peter Higginson, John Buchan [Diane Polley's son]
15–20 Mar. 1977	*Ivona, Princess of Burgundia*	Witold Gombrowicz	1938 writ., 1957 prem.	Pamela [Beckwith] Terry	Firehall Theatre (Studio)		Modern (comedy)	Barbara Keen, Gail Ricci, Eileen Williams, Esther Hockin, Ilene Cummings, Maria McEvenue, Betty Leventhal, Charles Foster (Equity), Dan Bradley, Dirk McLean, Keigh Melville, Jonathan Hartman, Don Payne, Dirk McLean, Shawn O'Grady, Don Payne
31 Mar.–16 Apr. 1977	Two Farces by Tom Stoppard				Firehall Theatre			

	• *The Real Inspector Hound*	Tom Stoppard	1962 writ., 1968 prem.	Molly [Golby] Thom			Modern (Theatre of the Absurd)	Kay Griffin, Deborah Jarvis, Sandra Shuman, Susan Morgan (Equity), Ian Orr, Eric Kosky, Peter Kunder, Ian McHaffie, John Illingworth, Bill Carson
	• *After Magritte*	Tom Stoppard	1970 writ., 1972 prem.	Molly [Golby] Thom			Modern (Theatre of the Absurd)	Nola Wale, Danda Humphreys, John Illingworth, Harold Burke (Equity), Brian Sewell
3–7 May 1977	*Our Own Particular Jane: A piece of theatre based on the Life, Letters and Literature of Jane Austen*	Joan Mason Hurley	1975 publ.	Cicely Thomson	Stage 2 at the Firehall Theatre (Studio)		Contemporary (drama)	Margaret MacAulay, Olwyn Millington, Jane Reynolds, Esther Hockin, Ilene Cummings, Donald Richards, Gordon Jocelyn
19 May–4 June 1977	*He Who Gets Slapped: A Play in Four Acts*	Leonid Andreyev	1922 prem.	Frank Canino	Firehall Theatre		Modern (melodrama)	Barbara Japp, Mavis Hayman, Jane Carnwath, Rhonda Krish, Debra Anderson, Karin Tari, Carolyn White, Lisa Weisbrod, Allan M. Whiteley, Ronald Kivinen, Dennis Hayes (Equity), Bob McCormack, Dirk McLean, Robert Galbraith (Equity), Richard Seligman, Alexander B. Millar, Drew Webb, Terry Blumenstein
1 Oct. 1977 (Sat.)	*The Trial before Caiaphas* (part of UofT PLS's *The York Cycle of Mystery Plays*)	Unknown	1300s, 1548 previous perf.	Virginia Reh	U of T's Convocation Hall (planned to be outside at U of T's King's College Circle)		Period (medieval cycle)	Jean Gawn, Bruce Mason, Dirk McLean, Dan Godin, Howie Slapcoff, Dave Satterfield, Bob McCormack, Brian Kaulback, Glenn Geb, Garnet Traux (Ben Gunter replaced Traux the day– of when the performance had to start several hours late and moved indoors because of rain)
6–22 Oct. 1977	*Absurd Person Singular*	Alan Ayckbourn	1972 prem.	Marie Hopps	Firehall Theatre		Contemporary (comedy)	Danda Humphreys, Morna Wales (Equity), Barbara Collier, Eric Kosky, John Illingworth, Peter Higginson
1–17 Dec. 1977	*The Schoolmistress*	Arthur Wing Pinero	1886 prem.	Cicely Thomson	Firehall Theatre		Period (farce)	Deborah Lobban, Penny Kluger, Jacqueline Mann, Elizabeth Paddon, Becky Trenton, Margaret Edgar, Mavis Hayman, Michael Holton, Bertram Schwarzschild, Kim Hansen, John Brodych, Bill Carson, Brian Sewell, John Guest, Bob McCormack

(*Continued*)

Run Dates	Show	Writer	Play Dates	Director	Venue	Premiere	Style	Cast
9–25 Feb. 1978	*Light Up the Sky*	Moss Hart	1948 prem.	Robert D. Vogel	Firehall Theatre		Modern (comedy)	Judith Abraham, Barbara Japp, Fran Handman, Sandra Shuman, Gerry Cooper, Richard Seligman, Danny Chushing, Derek Webster, David Vaughan, Jerry Painting, John Moore
30 Mar.–15 Apr. 1978	*When Did You Last See My Mother?*	Christopher Hampton	1964 writ., 1966 prem., 1967 pub	Anne Tait	Firehall Theatre		Modern (drama)	Rose Mary Sowby, Deborah Jarvis, Christopher Barry, Larry Lewis (Equity), Carl Ritchie
18 May–3 June 1978	*Tango*	Slawomir Mrozek. Trans. Nicholas Bethell and Tom Stoppard	1965 prem.	Pamela [Beckwith] Terry	Firehall Theatre		Modern (drama)	Mavis Hayman, Barbara Keen, Judith Abraham, Charles Foster (Equity), Peter Higginson, Michael Kopsa, Jack Zimmerman
12–28 Oct. 1978	*The Beaux' Stratagem*	George Farquhar	1707 prem.	Molly [Golby] Thom	Alumnae Theatre (Mainstage)		Period (comedy)	Maggie Milne, Pamela Redfern, Barbara Michalak, Esther Hockin, Deirdre Bowen, Rosalie Shackleton, Maggie Milne, David Lippett, Peter Kunder (Equity), Geoffrey Blackman (Equity), Harold Burke (Equity), Bertram Schwarzschild, Ian Orr, Brian Sexsmith, John Kenny
31 Oct.– 5 Nov. 1978	*Pablo Neruda: Lives of the Poet*	Lina Ladron de Guevara assembled the material	1971 prem.	Joan Shaw	Alumnae Theatre (Studio)		Reading (modern)	Diane Polley (Equity), Jane Reynolds, Michael Connolly, Michael Polley (Equity), Gerry Crack, Richard Bronskill, Mark Irwin
16 Nov.–2 Dec. 1978	Two plays:				Alumnae Theatre (Mainstage)			Mavis Hayman, Joyce Seeley, Toby Ciglen, Mary Illman, Francess Halpenny, Molly Thom, Cicley Thomson, Garry Hunt, Nic Labriola, Red Southgate (Equity), Jeffery Edgar, Michael Polley (Equity), John Alexis, John Kenny, Brian Kowalchuk, Gary Malott, Robert MacLeod, Christopher Barry, Duncan McIntosh (Equity), Gary Malott, John Illingworth, John Alexis
	• *A Life in the Sun: Thornton Wilder's The Alcestiad*	Thornton Wilder	1955 prem.	Herbert Whittaker		Canada	Modern	
	• *The Drunken Sisters (a satire play)*	Thornton Wilder	1955 prem.	Herbert Whittaker		Canada	Modern (satire)	

5–10 Dec. 1978	*The Women of Margaret Laurence: A Dramatic Anthology based on "The Manawaka Novels"*	Norma Edwards in collaboration with Juliana Saxton	1978 prem.	Francess Halpenny	Alumnae Theatre (Studio)	World	Contemporary (drama)	Norma Edwards
9–21 Jan. 1979 (Tues.–Sat.)	*La nef des sorcières / A Clash of Symbols*	Marie-Claire Blais, Nicole Brossard, Odette Gagnon, France Theoret, Marthe Blackburn, Pol Pelletier, Luse Guilbeault. Trans. Linda Gaboriau.	1976 prem. (Fr.)., 1979 prem. (Eng.)	Molly [Golby] Thom	Alumnae Theatre (Studio)	World (in English)	Contemporary (drama)	Judith Darragh, Joan Shaw, Barbara Michalak, Juliana Saxton, Nola Wale, Cicely Thomson
1–17 Feb. 1979	*Can You See Me Yet?*	Timothy Findley	1976 prem.	Mavis Hayman	Alumnae Theatre (Mainstage)	Toronto	Contemporary (drama)	Mary Solovew, Esther Hockin, Celeste Freed, Michele, Fansett, Jane Reynolds, Ilene Cummings, Dirk McLean, Robert Yacknin, Peter van Wart
22 Mar.–7 Apr. 1979	*The Increased Difficulty of Concentration*	Wraclav (Václav) Havel	1969 prem.	Pamela [Beckwith] Terry	Alumnae Theatre (Mainstage)	Toronto	Contemporary (farce)	Jane Carnwath, Sally Jay, Judy Shiner, Eileen Williams, Ian Orr, Michael Lambert, John Guest, Wayne Brine
23–8 Apr. 1979	*Celebrations: A springtime cabaret of silly sketches & musical merriment*	Charlotte Blunt, Peter Gray, Ron Hindle, Pat Hume, Anton Leo, Steve Lowy, Mavor Moore, Paul Perlove, Michael Polley, Morna Wales, Nip 'n Tuck	1979 prem.	Anne Tait	Alumnae Theatre (Studio)	World	Cabaret	Michele Fansett, Jazzmin Lausanne, Sandy Shuman, John George, Steve Lowy, Jim Tuck; Jamie Pearl at the piano
11–27 Oct. 1979 (Tues.–Sat.)	*Sqrieux-de-Dieu: A Comedy*	Betty Lambert	1975 prem.	Mavis Hayman	Alumnae Theatre (Mainstage)	Toronto	Contemporary (comedy)	Judith Abraham, Barbara Keen, Mary Solovew, Yvonne, Burnett, Diane Polley (Equity), Peter Higginson, Rob Fairley, Richard Bronskill
30 Oct.–4 Nov. 1979 (Tues.–Sat.)	*Emily Carr in Words: An Interpretation for the Theatre*	Francess Halpenny and Juliana Saxton from published works by Emily Carr	1979 prem.	Norma Edwards, assisted by Helen Dunlop and Juliana Saxton	Alumnae Theatre (Studio)	World (reading)	Contemporary (adaptation; staged reading)	Francess Halpenny, Ilene Cummings, Ian Orr

(*Continued*)

Run Dates	Show	Writer	Play Dates	Director	Venue	Premiere	Style	Cast
13–18 Nov. 1979	*Cider with Rosie*	Francess Halpenny adapted Laurie Lee's autobiography	1979 prem.	Joan Shaw	Alumnae Theatre (Studio)	World	Contemporary (adaptation; staged reading)	Mavis Hayman, Jo-Anne Martino, Susan Seagrove, Thomas Rickert, Ian Orr, Laurence Stevenson
22 Nov.–8 Dec. 1979	*La Nef des Sorcières / A Clash of Symbols*	Marie-Claire Blais, Nicole Brossard, Odette Gagnon, France Theoret, Marthe Blackburn, Pol Pelletier, Luse Guilbeault. Trans. Linda Gaboriau.	1976 prem. (Fr.) 1979, prem. (Eng.)		Alumnae Theatre (Mainstage)		Contemporary (drama)	Possibly same as 9 Jan. 1979.
31 Jan.–16 Feb. 1980	*The House of Bernarda Alba*	Garcia Lorca	1945 prem.	Virginia Reh (Equity)	Alumnae Theatre (Mainstage)		Modern (drama)	Catherine Beecraft, Eileen Williams, Razie Brownstone, Arwen Chenery, Margaret McCarthy, Helen Barron, Rosaleen Heller, Carole Chabot, Catherine Porter, Ayesha Young, Barbara Japp, Diane Swallowell (Equity), Christa Jacobs, Nancy Kee, Jane Carnwath, Ilene Cummings
26 Feb.–2 Mar. 1980	Two plays:				Alumnae Theatre (Studio)			
	• *Counting the Ways*	Edward Albee	1976 prem.	Helen Dunlop			Contemporary (comedy)	Norma Clark (Equity), John Illingworth
	• *All That Fall*	Samuel Beckett	1956 writ., 1957 radio, 1957 publ.	Molly Thom			Modern (Theatre of the Absurd)	Helen Carscallen (Equity), Rosemary Sowby, Margaret MacAulay, Ian Orr, Glenn Gilmar, John Illingworth, Ken McAuliffe, Ian Orr, Harold Burke (Equity), Adam Thom Alex Taylor – sound effects
13–23 Mar. 1980	*The Secret of the Spyglass: A Melodrama*	William Pendergrast	1973 prem., 1973 publ.	Cicely Thomson	Alumnae Theatre (Mainstage)		Contemporary (melodrama)	Penny Kluger, Karen Dickie, Rosalie Shackleton, Esther Hockin, Margaret Milne, Jane Leduc, Aida Jordaõ, Esther Hockin, Gary Malott, Ross Marchildon, Kim Hansen (Equity), Gordon Jocelyn, Jack Zimmerman John Illingworth, John Curtis, Jack Zimmerman
23–8 Sept. 1980	*The First Night of Pygmalion*	Richard Huggett	1968 prem.	Rex Southgate	Alumnae Theatre (Studio)		Contemporary (comedy)	Rose Mary Sowby, Margaret MacAulay, Harold Burke (Equity), Bermot Grice (Equity)

9–25 Oct. 1980	*The Right Honourable Gentleman*	Michael Dyne	1964 prem.	Cicely Thomson	Alumnae Theatre (Mainstage)		Modern (drama)	Anne Malton, Jacqueline Tarne, Ronalda Jones, Keith Melville, Catherine Beecraft, Morna Wales (Equity), Roberta Hutchinson, Maggie Milne, Richard Bronskill, John Illingworth, Laurence Prance, Peter Malton, Keith Melville, Steve Moreland, Gary Furlong
4–9 Nov. 1980	*Happy Days*	Samuel Beckett	1961 prem., 1961 writ., 1961 publ.	Anne Tait	Alumnae Theatre (Studio)		Modern (Theatre of the Absurd)	Esther Hockin, Willie Jack Zimmerman
13 Nov. 1980	*The Heart of Rosedale*	Wayne Carley	1980 prem.	Lewis Baumander	Hart House Theatre	World	Contemporary (comedy)	Barbara Barnett, Sandi Ross (Equity), Nola Wale, Gordon Jocelyn, Ian Orr, Harold Burke (Equity), Andrew Bassett-Spiers, Robert Craig
26 Nov.– 6 Dec. 1980	*The Heart of Rosedale*	Wayne Carley		Lewis Baumander	Alumnae Theatre (Mainstage)			Same cast as 13 Nov. 1980.
21 Jan.–1 Feb. 1981	Two Comedies:				Alumnae Theatre (Studio)			
	• *The Private Ear*	Peter Shaffer	1962 prem., 1962 publ.	Mavis Hayman			Modern (comedy)	Rosalie Shackleton, Bob Sherman, Christopher Barry (Equity)
	• *The Public Eye*	Peter Shaffer	1962 prem., 1962 publ.	Mavis Hayman			Modern (Comedy)	Laurie Waller (Equity), Peter Raffo, Eric Kosky
12–28 Feb. 1981	*Gossip*	George F. Walker	1977 prem.	Nola Morgan Wale, Molly [Golby] Thom	Alumnae Theatre (Mainstage)		Contemporary (film noir)	Lee Bristow, Margaret Milne, Heather Dick (Equity), Sharon Tranmer, Ian Orr, Bruce Girard, Allan Whiteley, Bruce Deller
10–15 Mar. 1981	*Media Memories: A Play on Words All about Memory*	Various	1981 prem.	Norma Edwards	Alumnae Theatre (Studio)	World	Contemporary	Deborah Lobban, Joan Shaw, Jacqueline White, Quintino Bordonali, Neil Gordon, Alan Toff, William Yurick; Announcer: Christopher Saxton
2–18 Apr. 1981	*School for Scandal*	Richard Brinsley Sheridan	1777 prem.	Araby Lockhart, assisted by Francess Halpenny	Alumnae Theatre (Mainstage)		Period (comedy)	Jo Skilton, Eleanor Aylesworth, Michelle Lionel, Mary Solovew, Carol Chabot, Jane Garbutt, James Mainprize, Ian McHaffie, Hal Eisen (Equity), Kenneth Stern, Gordon Jocelyn, Terrence Bryant, George Harrison, Stephen Moreland, Ray Bradford, Derek Johnston, Richard Carter, Andrei Pauzer, Russell Ferrier

(*Continued*)

Run Dates	Show	Writer	Play Dates	Director	Venue	Premiere	Style	Cast
8–24 Oct. 1981	*A Lovely Sunday for Creve Coeur* (one–act)	Tennessee Williams	1976 writ., 1979 prem.	Morna Wales	Alumnae Theatre (Mainstage)		Contemporary (drama)	Marie Stillin, Bernice Quiggan, Anne Tait, Toby Ciglen (Equity)
10–22 Nov. 1981	*Extraordinary People: A Comedy in Two Acts.*	Peter Raffo	1981 prem., 1981 publ.	Mavis Hayman	Alumnae Theatre (Studio)	World	Contemporary (comedy)	Esther Hockin, Maggie Milne, Margaret Edgar, Marsha Field, Jane Carnwath, Chipper Thompson, Gerry Crack, Stephen Moreland, Hadley Sandiford, David Griffith
26 Nov.–12 Dec. 1981	*A Woman of No Importance*	Oscar Wilde	1893 prem.	Cicely Thomson	Alumnae Theatre (Mainstage)		Period (comedy)	Betty Harris, Susan Gillatt (Equity), Helen Bell (Equity), Christine Lieber, Michelle Lionel, Jacqueline Tarne, Rosaleen Heller, Hereward Pooley, Robert Nemeth, Andrew Malton, Roger Hell, Peter Malton, Bill Walker, Ian McHaffie
4–21 Feb. 1982	*Come as You Are*	John Mortimer	1970 prem., 1971 publ.	Nola Morgan Wale, Associate Director: Donald H. Ford	Alumnae Theatre (Mainstage)		Contemporary (farce)	Mavis Hayman, Danda Humphreys, Ian Orr, Bill Boyle
9–14 Mar. 1982	*But This Is Our War*	Francess Halpenny, from writing by Grace Morris Craig	1982 prem.	Francess Halpenny	Alumnae Theatre (Studio)	World (reading)	Reading (contemporary adaptation)	Norma Syme, Nancy Kelly, Ilene Cummings, Susan Caradine, Cecilia Buy, Karen Dickey, Steve Kerwin, Ross Fraser, Stan Jensen, Craig Williams, David-Alan Love
25 Mar.–10 Apr. 1982	*The Cocktail Party*	T.S. Eliot	1948 writ., 1949 prem.	Herbert Whittaker	Alumnae Theatre (Mainstage)		Modern	Shirley Josephs, Jo Skilton, Jane Carnwath, Barbara Japp, Ian Orr, G. Neill Kennedy, Hereward Pooley, Michael Tait (Equity), Stan Dalton
20 Apr.–1 May 1982	*The Club*	Eve Merriam	1976 prem.	B.J. Castleman. Music Director Chip Thompson	Alumnae Theatre (Studio)		Contemporary (musical revue)	No cast found.
24–5 Sept. 1982	*But This Is Our War*	Francess Halpenny, from writing by Grace Morris Craig	1982 prem.	Francess Halpenny	Pembrooke, Ontario		Contemporary (adaptation)	Norma Syme, Cathy Smith, Ilene Cummings, Cecilia Buy, Karen Dickie, Steve Kerwin, Ross Frasser, Stan Jensen, Craig Williams, David-Alan Love
7–23 Oct. 1982	*Poor Murderer*	Pavel Kahout	1976 prem.	B.J. Castleman	Alumnae Theatre (Mainstage)		Contemporary (drama)	Sheila Palka, Karen Scanlan (Equity), Michelle Lionel, Catherine Beecraft, G. Neill Kennedy, Bill Zaget (Equoty), Robert Galbraith (Equity), Keith Melville, Douglas Stone, Ron Kivinen, Kenneth McKenzie

26–31 Oct. 1982	*Confusions*	Alan Ayckbourn	1974 prem.	Nan Hirst	Alumnae Theatre (Studio)		Contemporary (comedy)	Deborah Radbourne, Jane Forbes-Roberts, Nadra Muzaffar, Rosalie Shackleton, Norma Sym, Virginia Reh (Equity), Mary Wentz, Steve Ness, John Cummings, John Park, Ross Fraser, John Cummings
25 Nov.–11 Dec. 1982	*The Little Foxes*	Lillian Hellman	1938 prem.	Peter Hart	Alumnae Theatre (Mainstage)		Modern (drama)	Peta Coffeng, Esther Hockin, Norma Harrs (Equity), Karen Scanlan (Equity), with Lloyd Bartholomew, Ted Brock, Simon Joynes, Alex Dixon, Reg Dreger, Kurt Jacob
23–30 Jan. 1983	Fragments: Three One-Act Plays by Canadian Authors				Alumnae Theatre (Studio)			
	• *What Do Bakers Die Of?*	Gerry and Gordon Diver	1983 prem.	Nola Wale		World		No cast found.
	• *The Hoax*	Jill Gowland	1982 prem.	Nola Wale		Toronto		No cast found.
	• *Bedpan Deadpan*	Tony de Santis	1982 prem.	Nola Wale		Toronto		No cast found.
3–19 Feb. 1983	*A Delicate Balance*	Edward Albee	1966 prem.	Mavis Hayman	Alumnae Theatre (Mainstage)		Modern (Theatre of the Absurd)	Katherine Guselle, Esther Hockin, Eleanor Yeoman, Heather-Lynne Meacock, with B.J. Castleman, Ron Kivinen
1–6 Mar. 1983	*Alice Munro's Lives of Girls and Women* (in program); *The Women of Alice Munro* (in season brochure)	Francess Halpenny and Helen Dunlop adapted the novel for staged reading	1983 prem.	Francess Halpenny	Alumnae Theatre (Studio)	World (reading)	Reading (contemporary adaptation)	Norma Clark (Equity), Eleanor Aylesworth, Ilene Cummings, Beverley Couse, Joan Shaw
17 Mar.– 2 Apr. 1983	*The Mumberley Inheritance*	Warren Graves	1971 prem.	Cicely Thomson	Alumnae Theatre (Mainstage)		Contemporary (melodrama)	Rosalie Shackelton, Jane Forbes-Roberts, Jamie Orr, John Illingworth, Stephen Clifford, Peter Murray, Roger Kell; pianists: Katherine Guselle, Patricia Mearns
6–22 Oct. 1983	*Absent Friends*	Alan Ayckbourn	1974 prem.	Nan Hirst	Alumnae Theatre (Mainstage)		Contemporary (comedy)	Dawn Ritchie, Angela Pool, Mavis Hayman, Jerry Painting, Roger Kell, John Cummings

(*Continued*)

Run Dates	Show	Writer	Play Dates	Director	Venue	Premiere	Style	Cast
24 Nov.–10 Dec. 1983	*The Cherry Orchard*	Anton Chekov. Trans. John Gielgud	1903 writ., 1904 prem.	Herbert Whittaker	Alumnae Theatre (Mainstage)		Modern (comedy)	Beverley Couse, Judith Edmondson, Delora Harvey, Rosalind Goldsmith, Molly Thom, Barbara Japp, Tauni Mallett, Michael Polley (Equity), James Ridyard, William Shelden, Rex Southgate (Equity), Ian Orr, Robert Galbraith (Equity), David Fry, Aaron Henderson
24–9 Jan. 1984	*Dogg's Hamlet & Cahoots Macbeth*	Tom Stoppard	1979 prem., 1979 publ.	Dorothy Kelleher	Alumnae Theatre (Studio)		Contemporary (comedy)	Nancy Kee, Catherine MacDougall, Patricia Medwid, Cathy Smith, Marcus Bruce, Chris Downham, James Kee, Robert Leeming, Joe Madziak, Richard Seligman, Peter Stead, Douglas Sutherland
9–25 Feb. 1984	*Knuckle*	David Hare	1974 prem.	Mavis Hayman	Alumnae Theatre (Mainstage)		Contemporary (mystery satire)	Rosalind Goldsmith, Barbara Collier, Bill Zaget (Equity), John Illingworth, Walter Scherzer, Ron Kivinen
22 Mar.– 7 Apr. 1984	*Ah, Wilderness!*	Eugene O'Neill	1933 prem.	Cicely Thomson	Alumnae Theatre (Mainstage)		Modern (comedy)	Esther Hockin, Brooke Johnson, Ilene Cummings, Jane Forbes-Roberts, Karen Scanlan (Equity), Patricia Medwid, Eric Thomson Sigurdson, David King, Christopher O'Toole, Frank Ouinlan, James Kee, Walter Bolton (Equity), Ross Marchildon, Chris Downham, Alan Washbrook
10–15 Apr. 1984	*84, Charing Cross Road*	Helen Hanff, adapted for the stage by James Roose–Evans	1970 novel 1982 prem.	Francess Halpenny and Helen Dunlop	Alumnae Theatre (Studio)		Contemporary (adaptation)	No cast found.
11–27 Oct. 1984	*The Barretts of Wimpole Street*	Rudolf Besier	1930 prem.	Nan Hirst	Alumnae Theatre (Mainstage)		Modern (drama)	Judy Zarowny, Cicely Thomson, Melanie Scarr, Jennifer Brittain, Morghynn Karenn, George Neill Kennedy, Chris Ogden, Nicholas Bacon, Adrian Parker, Mark Hitchman, Eric James, Richard Allen, Jamie Mainprize, George Neill Kennedy, Peter Timmerman, Eric James, Hereward Pooley
8–17 Nov. 1984	*The Last Real Summer: A Memory Play*	Warren Graves	1981 prem.	Laurie Steven	Elizabeth Mascall Studio		Contemporary	Jane Reynolds, Alison Galt, Ruth Maltese, Nadine Liberto, Adrian Parker, Mary Ellen Fenwick, Bob Mifflin, Adrian Parker, Ian Orr, Eugene Cipparone
29 Nov.–15 Dec. 1984	*The Suicide*	Nicholai Erdman, adapted and translated by Eileen Thalenberg and Alan [illegible]	1928 writ., Rus. 1979, prem. Eng.	Brian Longstaff	Alumnae Theatre (Mainstage)		Contemporary (adaptation)	Miriam Laurence, Esther Hockin, Fernne Kane, Lorraine Pace, Michelle H. Wilsdon, Norma Syme, Doug Bentham, Art Austin (Equity), David Savoy, David Sepejak, Michael Kohut, Steve Adams, George King

24 Jan.–2 Feb. 1985 (Thurs.–Sat. 8 p.m.; Sat. 3 p.m.)	*Don Juan Returns from the War*	Ödön von Horváth, trans. by Christopher Hampton	1936 writ., 1952 prem.	Pamela [Beckwith] Terry	Elizabeth Mascall Studio		Modern	No cast found.
14 Feb.–2 Mar. 1985	*Enter a Free Man*	Tom Stoppard	1968 prem.	Dorothy Kelleher	Alumnae Theatre (Mainstage)		Modern (comedy)	Norma Syme, Jane Miller, Lisa Bunting, Peter Higginson, James Lukie, Ron Kivinen, Ed Clements, Alan Thomas
14–23 Mar. 1985	*Sea Marks*	Gardner McKay	1981 prem.	Mel Tuck	Elizabeth Mascall Studio		Contemporary (drama)	Catherine Marshall, Sean O'Hara (Equity)
4–20 Apr. 1985	*The Coarse Acting Show* [From *The Coarse Acting Show 2*]	Michael Green	1980 publ.		Alumnae Theatre (Mainstage)		Contemporary (comedy)	Lyla Bendsen, Norma (Clark) Crawford (Equity), June Garba, Mavis Hayman, Maggie Milne, Barbara Japp, John Cummings, David Fry, Peter Hart, John Illingworth, Ian Orr, Bruce Smith, Ed Clements
	• *The Cherry Sisters*			Molly [Golby] Thom				
	• *Moby Dick*			Molly [Golby] Thom				
	• *All's Well that Ends As You Like It*			Molly [Golby] Thom				
	• *Il Fornicazione*			Harold Burke				
	• *Streuth*			Harold Burke				
10–26 Oct. 1985	*Ten Times Table*	Alan Ayckbourn	1977 prem.	Robert Buck	Alumnae Theatre (Mainstage)		Contemporary (comedy)	Nancy Kee, Heather Mann, Anne Cartwright, Debra Mitchell, Peter Timmerman, Peter Stead, Brian Kelly (Equity), Reg Dreger (Equity), John Shepherd (Equity), Earl Mallia
7–16 Nov. 1985	*Painting Churches*	Tina Howe	1983 prem.	Virginia Reh	Alumnae Theatre (Studio)		Contemporary (drama)	Betty Harris, Jill Kinsella, Daniel Hyatt (Equity)
28 Nov.–14 Dec. 1985	*Full Circle*	Erich Maria Remarque. Adapted by Peter Stone	1956 writ., 1973 prem., 1974 publ.	Cicely Thomson	Alumnae Theatre (Mainstage)		Modern (drama)	Sheila Palka, Judy Zarowny, Walter Scherzer, Craig Williams, Alec Dixon, Chris Rowland, Ed Clement, Joe Danese, Richard Nester
23 Jan.–1 Feb. 1986	Catch Me I'm Falling	Denis Caslon	1986 prem.	Anne Tait	Alumnae Theatre (Studio)	World	Contemporary (comedy)	Karen Scanlan (Equity), Peter Timmerman, James D. Morris, Tom Melissis

(Continued)

Run Dates	Show	Writer	Play Dates	Director	Venue	Premiere	Style	Cast
13 Feb.–1 Mar. 1986	*Queen Christina*	Pam Gems	1977 prem.	Molly [Golby] Thom	Alumnae Theatre (Mainstage)	Canada	Contemporary	Anna Brown, Lori Lansens, Lorraine Pace, Nadine Roth, Harold Burke, Joe Danese, Derek Demierre, George King, Ian Orr, David Sepejak, John Woodhill
13–22 Mar. 1986	*One Writer's Beginning*	Francess Halpenny dramatized writings by Eudora Welty	1986 prem.	Francess Halpenny	Alumnae Theatre (Studio)	World (reading)	Reading (contemporary adaptation)	Ellen Litvak, Barbara Barnett, Mary-Ellen Scott-Fenwick, Toby Ciglen, Glenn Gilmar
17 Apr.–3 May 1986	*To Grandmother's House We Go*	Joanna McClelland Glass	1980 prem., 1981 publ	Mavis Hayman	Alumnae Theatre (Mainstage)	Canada	Contemporary (comedy)	Esther Hockin, Morag Sinkins, Ruth James, Helen Carscallen (Equity), Victor Sutton (Equity), D.J. Jestadt (Equity), Diane Polley (Equity), Susanne Gillies Smith, Keram Malicki–Sánchez
23 Oct.–8 Nov. 1986	*Ring around the Moon*	Chirstopher Fry's adaptation of Jean Anouilh *L'invitation au Chateau*	1947 prem. (Fr.), 1950 prem. (Eng.)	Theresa Sears	Alumnae Theatre (Mainstage)		Modern (drama)	Lucinda Nielsen, Linda Findlay, Patricia Delves, Ruth James, Emma Davey, Mavis, Hayman, John Ladell, Richard Thornton, Glen White (Equity), James Battersby, Peter Hart
20–9 Nov. 1986	*Talking With …*	Jane Martin	1982 prem.	Rita Spannbauer	Alumnae Theatre (Studio)		Contemporary (drama)	Kay Montgomery, Julia Tait, Susan Stiege, Naomi Thomson, Hilary Taylor, Elizabeth Bone, Marilyn Stone, Dawn Mari McCaugherty, Lisa Hitch, Emma Darcy, Anna Menelaus Brown
22 Jan.–7 Feb. 1987	*Fen*	Caryl Churchill	1983 prem.	Molly [Golby] Thom	Alumnae Theatre (Mainstage)	Canada	Contemporary (drama)	Gail Webster, Barbara Hanna, Rosalie Shackleton, Betty Harris (Equity), Mona el Baroudi, Susan Kerr, Hereward Pooley
19–28 Feb. 1987	*A Beckett Celebration for His 80th Birthday*:			Pamela [Beckwith] Terry	Alumnae Theatre (Studio)			
	• *Come and Go*	Samuel Beckett	1965 writ. (Eng) 1966 prem., (Germ) 1968 prem. (Eng)				Modern (Theatre of the Absurd)	Eileen Williams (Flo), Mavis Hayman (Vi), Rose Dyson (Ru)
	• *Ohio Impromptu*	Samuel Beckett	1980 writ., 1981 prem.				Modern (Theatre of the Absurd)	John Cummings (Reader), Ron Kivinen (Listener)
	• *Catastrophe*	Samuel Beckett	1982 writ., (Fr) 1982 prem. (Fr)				Modern (Theatre of the Absurd)	John Cummings (Protagonist), Ron Kivinen (The Director), Dawn Mari McCaugherty (The Assistant), Catherine Spence (Pat)

	• *Play*	Samuel Beckett	1963 writ., 1963 prem., (Germ. 1964 prem. (Eng.)				Modern (Theatre of the Absurd)	Esther Hockin (First Woman), Kay Montgomery (Second Woman), Peter Hart (Man)
12–28 Mar. 1987	*Filumena*	Eduardo de Filippo	1946 writ. 1946 prem. (Spanish) 1950 musical (Spanish) 1977 prem. (Eng.)	Harold Burke	Alumnae Theatre (Mainstage)		Modern	Diane Polley (Equity), Beth Robinson (Equity), Heather Mann, Janet Miller, Liz Gordon, Michael Polley (Equity), Chris Rowland, Franco de Francesco, Kimball Fox, Joe Danese, Kurt Jacob, Alan Mozes
31 Mar. 1987	*An Evening of FASHIONS from hobbles and stays to sensual skins*	–	–	–	Alumnae Theatre		Fashion Show	Models: Barbara Barnett, Barbara Hanna, Judith Darragh, Beverley Milligan, Margaret Garrison, Jayme Moss, Elizabeth Kee, Stephanie Kee
9–18 Apr. 1987	*Glimpse of Paradise: D.H. Lawrence and Frieda at Love and War*	Michael Tait	1987 prem., 1987 radio	Anne Weldon Tait	Alumnae Theatre (Studio)	World	Contemporary (drama)	Vanessa Dylyn, Cali Gold (Equity), Robert McKenna (Equity), Robert Latimer (Equity)
30 Apr.–16 May 1987	*The Art of Dining*	Tina Howe	1979 prem.	Jane Carnwath	Alumnae Theatre (Mainstage)		Contemporary (comedy)	Margaret Edgar, Liz Gordon, Jill Kinsella (Equity), Molly Thom, Judith Darragh, Leah Black, Chip Thompson, Harvey Levkoe, Dennis Hayes (Equity)
22 Oct.–7 Nov. 1987	*Morning's at Seven*	Paul Osborn	1939 prem.	Mavis Hayman	Alumnae Theatre (Mainstage)		Modern (comedy)	Esther Hockin, Betty Harris (Equity), Eileen Williams, Colleen Williams, Laura Newland, Kurt Jacob, Jack Zimmerman, Ron Kivinen, Trevor Cobain
19 Nov.–5 Dec. 1987	*Rose*	Andrew Davies	1981 prem.	Rita Spannbauer	Alumnae Theatre (Studio)		Contemporary (comedy)	Carol Hay, Mavis Hayman, Patricia Delves, Barbara Hanna, Alison Galt, G. Peter O'Neil, Peter Stead
21 Jan.–6 Feb. 1988	*Special Occasions*	Bernard Slade	1982 prem.	Joan Shaw	Alumnae Theatre (Studio)	Canada	Contemporary (comedy)	Dona Hird, Robert Bidaman; Voices: Joan Armstrong, Christa Weber, Andrew Richards, Rodger McLennan
18 Feb.–5 Mar. 1988	*Tom and Viv: T.S. Eliot's First Marriage*	Michael Hastings	1984 prem.	Jane Carnwath	Alumnae Theatre (Mainstage)	Canada	Contemporary	Madeleine Atkinson, Nancy Carter, Barbara Hanna, Trygve Bratteteig, Paul Larocque (Equity), Ian Orr, Christopher Sinclair

(*Continued*)

Run Dates	Show	Writer	Play Dates	Director	Venue	Premiere	Style	Cast
17 Mar.–12 Apr. 1988	*Gertrude Stein and a Companion*	Win Wills	1985 prem.	Pamela [Beckwith] Terry	Alumnae Theatre (Studio)	Canada	Contemporary (drama)	Susan Kerr, Ilene Cummings
14–30 Apr. 1988	*Lydie Breeze*	John Guare	1982 prem.	Molly [Golby] Thom	Alumnae Theatre (Mainstage)	Canada	Contemporary	Gail Webster, Deanne Dougherty, Valerie Planche, Ian Orr, Chris Owens, Mark Cleverley (Equity), Chip Thompson
12–21 May 1988	*New Ideas [1st]*	Various		Various	Alumnae Theatre (Studio)	World (festival)	New and Experimental Play Festival	
29 Sept.–15 Oct. 1988	*A Month of Sundays*	Bob Larbey	1985 prem.	Mavis Hayman	Alumnae Theatre (Studio)	Canada	Contemporary (comedy)	Susan Steige, Colleen Williams, Madeleine Atkinson, John Woodhill, George Harrison, Ron Kivinen
3–19 Nov. 1988	*The Late Blumer (one-act)*	John Lazarus (Can)	1984 prem., 1987 publ.	Sherry Wells	Alumnae Theatre (Mainstage)	Toronto	Contemporary (comedy)	Lesley Kelly, Sandra Shuman (Equity), John Gazey, Arthur Corber, Hereward Pooley
1–17 Dec. 1988	*Beyond Therapy*	Christopher Durang	1981 prem.	Kerri Macdonald	Alumnae Theatre (Studio)		Contemporary (comedy)	Wendy Krekeler, Margaret Lamarre, Kevin Haxell, Costin Manu, Ken Burton, Jonathan Tanner
19 Jan.–4 Feb. 1989	*Letters Home*	Rose Leiman Goldemberg	1979 prem., 1980 publ.	Colleen Williams	Alumnae Theatre (Studio)		Contemporary (drama)	Mary Land, Joan Heney (Equity)
16 Feb.–4 Mar. 1989	*The Madwoman of Chaillot*	Jean Giraudoux, adpated by Maurice Valency	1943 writ., 1945 perf. (Fr.) 1948, prem. (Eng.) 1958, trans. (Eng.)	Jane Carnwath	Alumnae Theatre (Mainstage)		Modern	Marcia Johnson, Elswyth Fryer, Tania Leil, Claire de Auer, Andrea Burck, Naomi Thomson, Gina Clayton (Equity), Esther Hockin, Barbara Barnett, Susan Kerr, Molly Thom, Marcia Johnson, Gina Clayton (Equity), Richard Matthews, Jodi Racicot, William Edwards, John Woodhill, Gerry Honrado, Hereward Pooley, A.P. Cappuccitti, Jonathan Seglins, Paul Figueiredo, Henry Longstaff, Karl Jason, Sandy MacMaster, Ivan Shaver, John Woodhill
13–29 Apr. 1989	*Gone to Glory*	Suzanne Finlay	1986 prem.	Pamela [Beckwith] Terry	Alumnae Theatre (Mainstage)	Toronto	Contemporary	Esther Hockin, Betty Heron, Margaret A. Lamarre (Equity), Naomi Thomson, Lawrence Beckwtih, Harvey Levkoe
11–17 May 1989	*New Ideas [2nd]*	Various		Various	Alumnae Theatre (Studio)	World (festival)	New and Experimental Play Festival	

12–28 Oct. 1989	*Stepping Out*	Richard Harris	1984 prem.	Mavis Hayman	Alumnae Theatre (Mainstage)		Contemporary	Karen Anthony, Darlene MacLeod, Wendy Krekeler, Anne Craig, Brenda Somers, Morghynn Karenn, Colleen Reynolds, Connie Neil, Kay Montgomery, John Cummings
14 Nov.–2 Dec. 1989	*Largo Desolato*	Václav Havel, adapted by Tom Stoppard	1984 writ., 1985 publ., 1986 prem. (Engl)	Pamela [Beckwith] Terry	Alumnae Theatre (Studio)		Contemporary (drama)	Margaret Lamarre (Equity), Sydney Clark, Jennifer Armstrong, Ian Orr, Harvey Levkoe, Richard Matthews, Wayne McNamara, Anthony Cappuccitti, Ron Kivinen, Colin Wallace
18 Jan.–3 Feb. 1990	*Three by Tenn:*				Alumnae Theatre (Studio)			
	• *The Lady of Larkspur Lotion*	Tennessee Williams	1948 prem.	Hereward Pooley			Modern (drama)	Margaret Lamarre (Equity), Esther Hockin, Kerri MacDonald
	• *Hello from Bertha*	Tennessee Williams	1946 prem., 1961 TV	Sally Han			Modern (drama)	Denise Ryan, Jo Ann Peritz, Crescence Crueger, Tina Lamarre
	• *Something Unspoken*	Tennessee Williams	1958 prem.	Peter Lloyd			Modern (drama)	Bonita Beach (Equity), Ilene Cummings
22 Feb.–10 Mar. 1990	*Camille*	Pam Gems, a new version of Alexandre Dumas's *La Dame aux Camelias*	1984 prem.	Molly [Golby] Thom	Alumnae Theatre (Mainstage)		Contemporary (adaptation)	Kaya McGregor, Susan Kerr, Aura Ostrowski, Wendy Krekeler, Kirsten Kieferle, Judy England, Lane White (Equity), Chalres Kerr (Equity), Walter Scherzer, Hereward Pooley, David Phillips, John Woodhill, Kurt Jacob, Ralf Joneikies, Jodi Racicot, Colin Wallace, Jeffrey England
22 Mar.– 7 Apr. 1990	*Red Emma: Queen of the Anarchists*	Carol Bolt	1974 prem., 1974 publ.	Kerri MacDonald	Alumnae Theatre (Mainstage)		Contemporary	Colleen Lanki, Jennifer Armstrong, Bridget Donovan, Antonia Berlingeri, David Sinclair, Benson Simmons (Equity), Brad Loghrin, Patrick Noonan, Gordon Jocelyn (Equity)
26 Apr.– 12 May 1990	*Reckless* (co-produced with Eclectic Theatre Productions)	Craig Lucas	1983 prem.	Jordan Merkur	Alumnae Theatre (Mainstage)	Canada	Contemporary (comedy)	Wendy Krekeler, Alison Smiley, Molly Thom, Patricia Delves, Richard Sali (Equity), Kevin Hicks (Equity), Stephen Flett
No record found.	*New Ideas*	Various		Various	Alumnae Theatre (Studio)	World (festival)	New and Experimental Play Festival	No cast found.
18 Oct.– 3 Nov. 1990	*Two One Act Plays.*				Alumnae Theatre (Mainstage)			

(*Continued*)

Run Dates	Show	Writer	Play Dates	Director	Venue	Premiere	Style	Cast
	• *The Actor's Nightmare*	Christopher Durang	1981 prem.	Kerri MacDonald			Contemporary (comedy)	Carol Badger (Equity), Wendy Krekeler, Bonita Beach (Equity), Jody Racicot, Victor Sutton (Equity), Mark Caspi
	• *'Dentity Crisis*	Christopher Durang	1978 prem.	Kerri MacDonald			Contemporary (comedy)	Carol Badger (Equity), Bonita Beach (Equity), Wendy Krekeler, Jody Racicot, Victor Sutton (Equity)
15 Nov.–1 Dec. 1990	*Real Estate*	Louise Page	1987 prem.	Molly [Golby] Thom	Alumnae Theatre (Studio)	Canada	Contemporary (drama)	Sheila MacDonald, Esther Hockin, Ian Orr, David Phillips
16 Jan.–2 Feb. 1991	*New Ideas Program 1*	Various		Various	Alumnae Theatre (Studio)	World (festival)	New and Experimental Play Festival	
21 Feb.–9 Mar. 1991	*Wild Honey*	Michael Frayne's translation and adaptation of Anton Chekhov's *Platonov*	1878 writ., Rus 1984 prem. Eng	Jane Carnwath	Alumnae Theatre (Mainstage)		Contemporary (adaptation)	Aura Ostrowski, Colleen Williams, Karen Ivany, Heidimarie Guggi, Hereward Pooley, John Izod, David C. Phillips, Noah Heney, Kurt Jacob, John Woodhill, Nicu Branzea, Ricahrd Matthews, Dale Landry, Gary Baker
13–30 Mar. 1991	*New Ideas Programs 1, 2, 3*	Various		Various	Alumnae Theatre (Studio)	World (festival)	New and Experimental Play Festival	
16 Apr.–11 May 1991 (opening night Apr. 18)	*Bloody Poetry (co-produced with Eclectic Theatre Productions)*	Howard Brenton	1984 prem.	Jordon Merkur	Alumnae Theatre (Mainstage)	Canada	Contemporary	Martha Burns (Equity), Robyn Stevan (Equity), Julie Donoahue, Brent Carver (Equity), Peter Spences (Equity), Ralf Joneikies
24 Oct.–9 Nov. 1991	*You Can't Take It With You*	Moss Hart and George S. Kaufman	1936 prem.	David Savoy	Alumnae Theatre (Mainstage)		Modern (comedy)	Kay Montgomery, Geraldine Ronan, Esther Hockin, Rebecca Nile, Rose Dyson, Gloria Surage, Wendy Merck, Chris Edmondson, Joseph van Veen, Allen Farrell, Jack Zimmerman, Michael Proudfoot, Justin Hay, Horace Walter, Randall Vickerson, Joel Kaiser
28 Nov.–14 Dec. 1991	*Eleemosynary*	Lee Blessing	1985 prem.	Jane Carnwath	Alumnae Theatre (Mainstage)	Toronto	Contemporary	Catriona Murphy, Judith Orban (Equity), Tricia Brioux
15 Jan.–1 Feb. 1992	*New Ideas Series 1*	Various		Various	Alumnae Theatre (Studio)	World (festival)	New and Experimental Play Festival	

20 Feb.–7 Mar. 1992	*The Love of the Nightingale*	Timberlake Wertenbaker's adaptation of the Ancient Greek myth	1988 prem.	Molly [Golby] Thom	Alumnae Theatre (Mainstage)	Toronto	Contemporary (adaptation)	Gail Webster, Eileen Pedde, Rosallie Shackleton, Margaret Gobie, Sherrie Johnson, Rebecca Schwarz, Krysta Sluda, Beverley Miller, Moyra Hewlett, Diane Dale, Susan Vance, Andrew Batten, William Beddoe, Ian Orr, David W. Sinclair, David Young, Peter Van Wart (Equity), Sandy MacMaster, J.R. Willis
18 Mar.–4 Apr. 1992	*New Ideas Series 2*	Various		Various	Alumnae Theatre (Studio)	World (festival)	New and Experimental Play Festival	
23 Apr.–9 May 1992	*The Shadow Walkers* (formerly *A Spider in the House*)	Brian Tremblay	1984 prem	Rita Spannbauer	Alumnae Theatre (Mainstage)	Toronto	Contemporary	Claire Winterton, Sandra Kay, Holly Stevenson, Susan Vance, Amanda Tapping, Michael Proudfoot, Sten Eirik (Equity), Sammy
15–31 Oct. 1992	*The Sea*	Edward Bond	1973 prem.	Diana Kolpak	Alumnae Theatre (Mainstage)		Contemporary (comedy)	Kay Montgomery, Patricia Baergen, Susan Vance, Dinah Watts, Monica Gretton, Costin Manu (Equity), Terrance Bryant, David W. Sinclair, Donald Haddad, Mark Hondroyanis, Peter Reitzel, Robert Dow
19 Nov.–5 Dec. 1992	*Sarah Binks and Friends*				Alumnae Theatre (Studio)			
	• *Part 1: This Beggarly Wooden Country*	Susanna Moodie, Catharine Parr Traill, Anne Langton, and Anna Jameson exerpted. "Additions and alterations to the original text have been made for this production by Jeffery Aarles" (program)	1967 prem.	Jeffrey Aarles, Colleen Williams (co-director)			Modern	Rosalie Shackleton, Margaret Gobie, Rhona Buchan, Marie Bridget Dundon (Equity)
	• *Part 2: Sara Binks, Sweet Songstress of Saskatchewan*	Paul Hiebert's novel adapted by Elizabeth Mascall	1967 prem.	John McKillop			Modern	Rai Fisher, Sheila Russell, Victor Sutton (Equity), Michael Proudfoot

(*Continued*)

Run Dates	Show	Writer	Play Dates	Director	Venue	Premiere	Style	Cast
27 Jan.–13 Feb. 1993	*New Ideas Programs 1, 2, 3*	Various		Various	Alumnae Theatre (Studio)	World (festival)	New and Experimental Play Festival	
11–27 Mar. 1993	*The Trojan Women*	Euripides, adapted by Gwendolyn MacEwan	1978 prem.	Jeannette Lambermong	Alumnae Theatre (Mainstage)		Contemporary (adaptation)	Merle Matheson (Equity), Shauna Black, Karen Waddell (Equity), Alexandra Thomson, Mary Culmone, Morgonn Ewen, Wendy Krekeler, Anne Marie Loder, Jackie McKeown, Caitriona Murphy, Christine Oddy, Molly Thom, Lisa Walter, Caludette Williams, Olivier L'Ecuyer, Jamie Williams, Andrew Batten, Raffael Pacitti, James Robert Woods
21 Apr. 1993	*New Ideas Programs 4, 5, 6*	Various		Various	Alumnae Theatre (Studio)	World (festival)	New and Experimental Play Festival	
10–26 June 1993	*Cloud Nine*	Caryl Churchill	1978 prem.	Victoria Dawe	Alumnae Theatre (Mainstage)		Contemporary (drama)	Tricia Brioux, Kay Montgomery, Dinah Watts, Ben Carlson, Christopher Edmondson, David Roddis, Steve Ross
7–23 Oct. 1993	*Mystery of the Rose Bouquet*	Manuel Puig	1987 prem.	David Savoy	Alumnae Theatre (Studio)	Canada	Contemporary	Joan Heney (Equity), Sheila MacDonald
26 Nov.–11 Dec. 1993	*Masterpieces*	Sarah Daniels	1983 prem.	Elizabeth Shepherd	Alumnae Theatre (Mainstage)	Canada		Jean McNeil (Equity), Rai Fisher, Lorraine Pace, Caitriona Murphy, Lindsay Empringham, Monica Gretton, Dinah Watt, Wendy Krekeler, Jonathan Tanner (Equity), Tom Bradshaw, Hereward Pooley, Peter Higginson, Scott Bell, Phil Arnold, Michael Hermiston
26 Jan.–12 Feb. 1994	*New Ideas 1*	Various		Various	Alumnae Theatre (Studio)	World (festival)	New and Experimental Play Festival	
3–19 Mar. 1994	*Les Belles Soeurs*	Michel Tremblay, trans. John Van Burek and Bill Glassco	1965 writ., 1968 prem. Fr. 1973 prem. Eng.	Sue Miner	Alumnae Theatre (Mainstage)		Contemporary (drama)	Susan Hagen, Liz Gordon (Equity), Christine Manning, Maggie Shaw, Margaret LaMarre (Equity), Ilene Cummings, Molly Thom, Sara Armstrong, Marilyn Wallis, Razie Brownstone, Dietre Courchesne, Tracy Carroll, Esther Hockin, Barbara Barnett, Tricia Brioux
6–16 Apr. 1994	*New Ideas 2*	Various		Various	Alumnae Theatre (Studio)	World (festival)	New and Experimental Play Festival	

5–21 May 1994	*Under Milk Wood*	Dylan Thomas	1953 read 1954 radio 1954 prem., 1972 film	Josephine Le Grice	Alumnae Theatre (Mainstage)		Modern	Sarah Weatherwax, Holly Lee Dwyer, Anne Harper, Anne Hoselton Maargaret Lamarre (Equity), Tina Lamarre, Lindsey Lomax, Laura Manarich, Glenna Sims, Sandy MacMaster, Rick Bland, Rod Carruthers, Ian Chaprin, Alan Clifton, Jerry Getty, David Roddis
6–22 Oct. 1994	*Blood Relations*	Sharon Pollock	1980 prem.	Lynda Hill	Alumnae Theatre (Mainstage)		Contemporary (mystery)	Ilene Cummings, Esther Hockin, Lynn Woodman, Don Ciaschini, Mark Hondroyanis, Joel Rinzler
24 Nov.–10 Dec. 1994	*Happy End*	Bertolt Brecht, Kurt Weill	1929 prem. (Germ) 1977 prem. (Eng)	Rebecca Cann	Alumnae Theatre (Mainstage)		Musical (comedy)	Valerie Sing Turner, Linda Ballantyne, Sarah Evans, Christine Oddy, Naomi Snieckus, Wendy Krekeler, Caitriona Murphy, Martha Spence, Marcia Walker, Scott Bell, Gil Rivera Blas (Equity), Mark Brownell (Equity), A.J. Pittis, Drew Leavy, Timothy Luginbuhl
9–25 Feb. 1995	*The Rivals*	Richard Brinsley Sheridan	1775 prem.	Margaret Gobie	Alumnae Theatre (Mainstage)		Period (comedy)	Elizabeth Allen, Stacie Clark, Morgonn Ewen, Agatha Marinakis, Dinah Watts, Paul Babiak, Gregory Cooke, Mark Ellis, Christopher Goebel, Troy MacPhail, Harry Nye, Jason Sweeney
15 Mar.–8 Apr. 1995	*New Ideas Festival 95*	Various		Various	Alumnae Theatre (Studio)	World (festival)	New and Experimental Play Festival	
27 Apr.–13 May 1995	*Thirteen Hands*	Carol Shields	1993 prem. 1993 publ.	Molly [Golby] Thom	Alumnae Theatre (Mainstage)	Toronto	Contemporary	Barbara Barnett, Judy Darragh, Anne Harper, Esther Hockin, Sheri Astorino, Lindsay Empringham, Tita Griffin, Chantale Groulx, Tracy Carroll, Esther Jaciuk, Shannon Rowe, Danielle Saul
19 Oct.–4 Nov. 1995	*Six Characters in Search of an Author*	Luigi Pirandello, trans. Eric Bentley	1921 prem. Ital 1922 prem. Eng	Linda Matassa	Alumnae Theatre (Mainstage)		Modern	Nancy R. Bond, Paula Caplan, Annelies McConnachie-Howarth, Claudette Williams, Ada Balon, Joanne D'Angelo, Leah Davidson, Marie-Christine Gagné, Cynthia Mantel, Tracy Rankin, Ann Shisko, Paul Babiak, David Beecraft, Chad Bruce, Peter Hart, Deepak Jain, Tony DiMito, Brad Holland, Edward Morysiak, Nicolas Sanford, Norman Stinson (Equity), Al Syrelle
30 Nov.–16 Dec. 1995	*On the Verge*	Eric Overmyer	1985 prem.	Jane Carnwath	Alumnae Theatre (Mainstage)		Contemporary	Included: Dinah Watts, Andrew Pifko

(*Continued*)

Run Dates	Show	Writer	Play Dates	Director	Venue	Premiere	Style	Cast
25 Jan.–10 Feb. 1996	*Getting Out*	Marsha Norman	1978 prem.	Mary Dwyer	Alumnae Theatre (Mainstage)	Toronto	Contemporary (drama)	Marie-Christine Gagné, Elisa Moolecherry, Rai Fisher, Paula Caplan, Jennifer Douglas, Karen Anthony, Wendy Krekeier, Tony DiMito, Ian Orr, Brad Robertson, Glenn O'Brien
20–3 Mar. 1996	*New Ideas Festival 96*	Various		Various	Alumnae Theatre (Studio)	World (festival)	New and Experimental Play Festival	
25 Apr.–11 May 1996	*An Italian Straw Hat*	Eugene Labiche, trans. Thomas Walton, adapted by David Savoy	1851 prem.	David Savoy	Alumnae Theatre (Mainstage)		Period (comedy)	Jennifer Hall, Chantale Groulx, Shelly Cass, Brigitte Solem, Jennifer Douglas, Andrea Lyons, Corrina Hodgson, Sam Kalalia, Marcus Hamer, Howard Davis, Robert Shipman (Equity), Peter Tebbutt, Rob McDowell, Jason Sweeney, Tom Bradshaw, John Sweet, Ted Powers, Robert Ouellette (Equity), Gary Allan, Robert Ouellette
17 Oct.–2 Nov. 1996	*Departures and Arrivals*	Carol Shields	1984 prem., 1990 publ.	Tracy Caroll	Alumnae Theatre (Mainstage)		Contemporary (comedy)	Jocelyn Drainie, Anne Harper, Pamela Redfern (Equity), Siu Ta, Tracey Schiebel, Samantha Faye Tyler, John Kalangis, Martin Moreau, Gordon Sheppard
28 Nov.–14 Dec. 1996	*Top Girls*	Caryl Churchill	1982 prem.	Molly [Golby] Thom	Alumnae Theatre (Studio)		Contemporary	Rai Fisher, Corrina Hodgson, Margaret Lamarre (Equity), Tina Lamarre, Barbara Larose, Elaine Martyn, Pamela Redfern (Equity), Valerie Reinis, Shannon Rowe, Joanne Towgood
13 Feb.–1 Mar. 1997	*The Seagull*	Anton Chekhov, trans. David French	1895 writ., 1896 prem. Rus 1909 prem. Eng 1977 trans. Eng D.F.	Jennifer Brewin	Alumnae Theatre (Mainstage)		Modern (comedy)	Becky Blake, Severn Thompson, Margaret Lamarre (Equity), Dinah Watts, Adela Rodriguez, Chantale Groulx, Patrick McManus, Ian Orr, Mariusz Sibiga, Peter Higginson, Blair Williams (Equity), Ron Kivinen, Eugen Zborovsky
12–29 Mar. 1997	*New Ideas Festival 97*	Various		Various	Alumnae Theatre (Studio)	World (festival)	New and Experimental Play Festival	
24 Apr.–10 May 1997	*Andorra, A model*	Max Frisch, trans. Michael Bullock	1961 writ., 1961 prem. Ger 1964 pub Eng	Guillaume Bernardi	Alumnae Theatre (Mainstage)		Modern	Wendy Akerboom, Cécile Lasserre, Christine Marano, Katie Brigid O. Murphy, Gail Naipaul (Equity), Lisa Pijuan, Jarvey Levin, Ted Powers, Bryan Taylor, Doug Wilson

16 Oct.–8 Nov. 1997 (extended run)	*The Gut Girls*	Sarah Daniels	1988 prem., 1989 publ.	Jane Carnwath	Alumnae Theatre (Studio)		Contemporary (drama)	Ruth Barrett, Lori Dixon, Mary Gordon, Aimée Lococo, Renate Pohl, Tara Kapeluch, Catherine Bruce (Equity), Lindsay Empringham, Rai Fisher, Stephen A. Coombs (Equity), Peter Hart, Martin Kalin, Christopher McNally
27 Nov.–13 Dec. 1997	*The Visit: A Tragicomedy*	Friedrich Dürrenmatt, trans. Patrick Bowles	1956 prem. (Ger.)	Kelly Thornton	Alumnae Theatre (Mainstage)		Modern (tragicomedy)	Wendy Akerboom, Ariel Balevi, Linda Brokenshire, Razie Brownstone, Jeanie Calleja, Fiona Carver, Sarah Carver, Monica Côté, Anna Ferguson, Tanya Henley, Veronika Hurnik, Anna Kowalchuk, Tina McCulloch, Natasha Priest, Kate Story, Edith Tankus, Anne Van Wijk, Brad Brackenridge, Deitre Courchesne, Brian Cram, Blake Howard, Geoffrey Link, Dan Luff, Ryan McViddle, Colin Miller (Equity), Robin Pittis, Simon Story, Paul Tedeschini, Michael Weinberg, Jon Wichelow
5–21 Feb. 1998	*Better Living*	George F. Walker	1987 prem.	Victoria Dawe	Alumnae Theatre (Mainstage)		Contemporary (comedy)	Wendy Krekeler, Margaret Lamarre (Equity), Sophia Tsouluhas, Karen Tufts, with Robert Graham, Dennis Hayes (Equity), Dan Luff
18 Mar.–4 Apr. 1998	*New Ideas Festival 98*	Various		Various	Alumnae Theatre (Studio)	World (festival)	New and Experimental Play Festival	
23 Apr.–9 May 1998	*The Sisters Rosensweig*	Wendy Wasserstein	1992 prem.	Barbara Larose	Alumnae Theatre (Mainstage)		Contemporary	Ruth Barrett, Shelley Goldstein (Equity), Lori Nancy Kalamanski, Elaine Martyn, Warren Coughlin, Peter Higginson, Michael Posthumus, Alan Rosenthal (Equity)
16 Oct.–1 Nov. 1998 (Fri. eve.–Sat. mat.)	*Dancing at Lughnasa*	Brian Friel	1990 prem.	Kerri L. MacDonald	Alumnae Theatre (Mainstage)		Contemporary (drama)	Lindsay Empringham, Ingrid Heming, Vanessa Hunt, Mary Francis Moore, Isolde O Neill (Equity), Nicholas Banks, Jeff Miller (Equity), Hereward Pooley
27 Nov.–13 Dec. 1998	*Bag Babies: A Comedy of (Bad) Manners*	Allan Stratton	1990 prem., 1991 publ.	Wendy Thatcher	Alumnae Theatre (Mainstage)		Contemporary (comedy)	Alexis Butler, Kirklynne Barrett, Pamela Redfern (Equity), Pam Nepszy, Erin Archer, Renee Hillier, David Archambault, Kevin Hammond, Darryl Pring
5–28 Feb. 1999	*The Progress of Love*	Alice Munro short story adapted by Guillaume Bernardi	1999 prem.	Guillaume Bernardi	Alumnae Theatre (Studio)	World	Contemporary (adaptation)	Vanessa AvRuskin, Anna Drblik, Yashoda Ranganathan, Gregory Thomas

(Continued)

Run Dates	Show	Writer	Play Dates	Director	Venue	Premiere	Style	Cast
22 Feb. 1999 (Mon.)	*The Progress of Love*	Alice Munro short story adapted by Guillaume Bernardi		Guillaume Bernardi	Arts and Letters Club			Same cast as 5 Feb. 1999.
24 Mar.–10 Apr. 1999	*New Ideas Festival 1999*	Various		Various	Alumnae Theatre (Studio)	World (festival)	New and Experimental Play Festival	
5–21 May 1999	*The Illusion*	Tony Kushner, adapted from Pierre Corneille's play *L'Illusion Comique*	1634 prem. (Fr.), 1994 publ. (Eng.) T.K.	Rebecca Cann	Alumnae Theatre (Mainstage)		Contemporary (adaptation)	Included: Walter Young, Pedro Guevara Mann, Warren Coughlin
12–28 Nov. 1999	*Les Liaisons Dangereuses*	Christopher Hampton, from the novel by Pierre Choderlos de Laclos	1782 novel, 1985 prem.	Jennifer Parr	Alumnae Theatre (Mainstage)		Contemporary (adaptation)	Françoise Balthazar (Equity), Elaine Lindo, Melissa Haller, Ilene Cummings, Jennifer Gauthier, Mara Marini, Stephanie Thorpe, Michael Boisvert, Steven Burley, Stephen Lobo, Peter Jull, Peter Witz
28 Jan.–13 Feb. 2000	*A View from the Roof*	Dave Carley, based on the stories of Helen Weinzweig	1996 prem.	Jane Carnwath	Alumnae Theatre (Mainstage)		Contemporary (adaptation)	Lindsay Empringham, Risa Gitelman, Sheila Tait, Patti Kazmer, Hereward Pooley, Scott McLaren, Ron Kivinen, Pedro Guevara Mann
8–25 Mar. 2000	*New Ideas Festival 2000*	Various		Various	Alumnae Theatre (Studio)	World (festival)	New and Experimental Play Festival	
14–30 Apr. 2000	*The Real Thing*	Tom Stoppard	1982 prem.	David Savoy	Alumnae Theatre (Mainstage)		Contemporary (comedy)	Alison Burn, Iona MacKay, Jamie Levak, Peter Tebbutt, Andy Rhodes, John Blakey, David Cook
12 May–4 June 2000	*Under the Skin*	Betty Lambert	1985 prem.	Sarah Sked	Alumnae Theatre (Studio)		Contemporary (drama)	Tricia Brioux, Kelly Fanson (Equity), John Healy (Equity)
20 Oct.–12 Nov. 2000	*Talley's Folly*	Lanford Wilson	1980 prem.	PJ Hammond	Alumnae Theatre (Studio)		Contemporary (drama)	Tabitha Keast, Paul Babiak
26 Jan.–11 Feb. 2001	*Ten Lost Years*	Toronto Workshop Productions collective creation dramaturged by Cedric Smith and Jack Winter	1974 prem.	Jill Frappier	Alumnae Theatre (Mainstage)		Contemporary (drama)	Natalie Maclean Ackers, Alison Dalwhinnie Burn (Equity), Elswyth Fryer, Janet Gigliotti, Naomi Priddle Hunter, Pat McCarthy, Tina McCulloch, Sean Curran, Alastair Love, Mike Lummis, Peter Prystanski (Equity), Andrew Welch

14–31 Mar. 2001	*New Ideas Festival 2001*	Various		Various	Alumnae Theatre (Studio)	World (festival)	New and Experimental Play Festival	
20 Apr.–6 May 2001	*Moo*	Sally Clark	1988 prem.	Kristen Scheiner	Alumnae Theatre (Studio)		Contemporary (comedy)	Danielle Brett (Equity), Stefanie Drummond, Susanne Egier, Heather Ferguson, Risa Gitelman, Kathleen Killen, Brandon Barré, Stephen Chambers, Darren Stewart-Jones
	Presentation of Staged Readings from New Ideas Festival 2001	Various		None on record.	Alumnae Theatre (Studio)			
17–20 May 2001	• *Feelers*	Paul Babiak	2001 read				Reading (contemporary)	
17–20 May 2001	• *I Love You … Just Kidding*	Kynn Kavanaugh	2001 read				Reading (contemporary)	
24–7 May 2001	• *China, 1938*	Diane Forrest	2001 read				Reading (contemporary)	
24–7 May 2001	*Paths to Forgetting*	Matt McLennan	2001 read				Reading (contemporary)	
26 Oct.–10 Nov. 2001	*The Pear is Ripe*	Shirley Barrie	1995 prem.	Molly [Golby] Thom	Alumnae Theatre (Mainstage)	Toronto	Contemporary (drama)	Mary Durkan (Equity), Lindsay Empringham, Elisabeth Feltaous, Jane Magregor, Colleen McKay, Paul Babiak, Sean Curran, Adam Revesz, Aaron Willis
23 Nov.–15 Dec. 2001	*The Attic, the Pearls and Three Fine Girls*	Jennifer Brewin, Leah Cherniak, Ann–Marie MacDonald, Alisa Palmer and Martha Ross	1995 prem.	PJ Hammond	Alumnae Theatre (Studio)		Contemporary (comedy)	Jill Morrison, Erin Shields, Tina-Yeung-Moore
25 Jan.–9 Feb 2002	*Orpheus Descending*	Tennessee Williams	1957 prem.	Rita Spannbauer	Alumnae Theatre (Studio)		Modern (drama)	Elaine Lindo, Ryanne Chisholm, Nike Abbott, Heather Middlestadt, Bonnie Gray, Gloria Lambert, Sandy Kellerman, Lucy DiPucchio, Tracy Rankin (Equity), Sandi Ross (Equity), Anne Harper, Tricia Brioux, Jan Fine, Steve Burley, Hugh Barnett, Sean Curran, Paul Soren, Martyn Wolfman

(*Continued*)

Run Dates	Show	Writer	Play Dates	Director	Venue	Premiere	Style	Cast
1–23 Mar. 2002	*New Ideas Festival 2002*	Various		Various	Alumnae Theatre (Studio)	World (festival)	New and Experimental Play Festival	
26 Apr.–11 May 2002	*Woman in Mind*	Alan Ayckbourn	1985 prem.	Warren Coughlin	Alumnae Theatre (Mainstage)		Contemporary (tragicomedy)	Andy Rhodes, Loretta Walsh, Lindsay Empringham, Karie Richards, Toby Steel, John Blakey (Equity), Peter Church, Paul Babiak (Equity), Steven Burley
27 Sept.–12 Oct. 2002	*Beautiful City*	George F. Walker	1987 prem.	Angela Finlay	Alumnae Theatre (Mainstage)		Contemporary (comedy)	Barbara Larose, Eve Wylden, Mary Claire Thompson, Tricia Brioux, Zachary Bennett (Equity), Chris Owens (Equity), Stephen Near, Jason Gautreau, J. Danlen Moore
15 Nov.–7 Dec. 2002	*Collected Stories*	Donald Margulies	1996 prem.	Nicole Arends	Alumnae Theatre (Studio)		Contemporary (drama)	Patti Kazmer (Equity), Claire Calnan
24 Jan.–8 Feb. 2003	*Amy's View*	David Hare	1997 prem.	Rosemary Doyle	Alumnae Theatre (Mainstage)		Contemporary (tragicomedy)	Kelly Bolt, Razie Brownstone, Jane Carnwath (Equity), Vincent de Tourdonnet, John Illingworth, Jake Willet
12–29 Mar. 2003	*New Ideas Festival 2003*	Various		Various	Alumnae Theatre (Studio)	World (festival)	New and Experimental Play Festival	
25 Apr.–10 May 2003	*Lettice and Lovage*	Peter Shaffer	1987 prem.	Rita Spannbauer	Alumnae Theatre (Mainstage)		Contemporary (comedy)	No cast found.
26 Sept.–11 Oct. 2003	*Summer & Smoke*	Tennessee Williams	1948 prem.	Victoria Shepherd	Alumnae Theatre (Mainstage)		Modern (drama)	Gloria Lambert, Elaine Lindo, Tina McCulloch, Karie Richards, Emily Sanford, Emily Wurts, Jason Gautreau, J. Danlen Moore, Neal Murphy, Peter Nelson, Ian Orr, Paul Soren
21 Nov.–6 Dec. 2003	*The Real World?*	Michel Tremblay	1987 prem.	Barbara Larose	Alumnae Theatre (Studio)		Contemporary (drama)	Dinah Watts (Equity), Adrienne Rogers, Sharon Marquez, Andy Fraser Rhodes, Josh Healy (Equity), David Austin
23 Jan.–7 Feb. 2004	*A Lie of the Mind*	Sam Shepard	1985 prem.	Paul Hardy	Alumnae Theatre (Mainstage)		Contemporary (drama)	No cast found.
10–27 Mar. 2004	New Ideas Festival 2004	Various		Various	Alumnae Theatre (Studio)	World (festival)	New and Experimental Play Festival	
23 Apr.–8 May 2004	*Absurd Person Singular*	Alan Ayckbourn	1972 prem.	Brad Lepp	Alumnae Theatre (Mainstage)		Contemporary (comedy)	No cast found.

24 Sept.–9 Oct. 2004	*Who's Afraid of Virginia Woolf*	Edward Albee	1962 prem.	Barbara Larose	Alumnae Theatre (Mainstage)		Modern (drama)	Tricia Brioux (Equity), Karie Richards, Mark Whelan, Jason Gautreau (Equity)
19 Nov.–4 Dec. 2004	*Criminal Hearts*	Jane Martin	1992 prem., 1992 publ.	PJ Hammond	Alumnae Theatre (Studio)		Contemporary (comedy)	No cast found.
21 Jan.–5 Feb. 2005	*After You*	Dave Carley	1995 prem	Jane Carnwath	Alumnae Theatre (Mainstage)	Toronto	Contemporary (drama)	Meg Hogarth (Equity), Margaret Evans, Elva Mai Hoover (Equity), Alicia Flaherty, Aaron Hutchinson
9–26 Mar. 2005	*17th Annual New Ideas Festival*	Various		Various	Alumnae Theatre (Studio)	World (festival)	New and Experimental Play Festival	
22 Apr.–7 May 2005	Two Plays:				Alumnae Theatre (Mainstage)			
	• *Problem Child*	George F. Walker	1997 prem.	Brad Lepp			Contemporary (comedy)	No cast found.
	• *Criminal Genius*	George F. Walker	1997 prem.	Brad Lepp			Contemporary (comedy)	No cast found.
23 Sept.–8 Oct. 2005	*She Stoops to Conquer*	Oliver Goldsmith	1773 prem.	None on record.	Alumnae Theatre (Mainstage)		Period (comedy)	No cast found.
18 Nov.–3 Dec. 2005	Two One-Act Plays				Alumnae Theatre (Studio)			
	• *Ashes to Ashes*	Harold Pinter	1996 prem.	Natasha Mytnowych			Contemporary	Dinah Watts (Equity), James Lukie
	• *This Is a Play*	Daniel MacIvor	1992 prem.	Margaret Gobie			Contemporary (comedy)	Greta Kerasia, Tricia Brioux (Equity), Neal Murphy, Chris Kozak
20 Jan.–4 Feb. 2006	*Homeward Bound*	Elliott Hayes	1991 prem.	Jane Carnwath	Alumnae Theatre (Mainstage)		Contemporary (drama)	Elva Mai Hoover, Tabitha Keast, Joe Boyd, Zvi Gilbert, John Illingworth, Lee Poulin
8–25 Mar. 2006	*The 18th Annual New Ideas Festival*	Various		Various	Alumnae Theatre (Studio)	World (festival)	New and Experimental Play Festival	
21 Apr.–6 May 2006	*Moonlight and Valentino*	Ellen Simon	1989 prem.	Dinah Watts	Alumnae Theatre (The Main Stage)		Contemporary (dramady)	Rachel Wilson (Equity), Natalie Forcier, Andrea Irwin, Andy Fraser, Chris Lang

(*Continued*)

Run Dates	Show	Writer	Play Dates	Director	Venue	Premiere	Style	Cast
22 Sept.–7 Oct. 2006	*Baby with the Bathwater*	Christopher Durang	1983 prem.	Dinah Watts	Alumnae Theatre (The Main Stage)		Contemporary (comedy)	Julie Burris, Natalie Colalillo
17 Nov.–2 Dec. 2006	*Perfect Pie*	Judith Thompson	2000 prem.	Paul Hardy	Alumnae Theatre (The Studio)		Contemporary (drama)	No cast found.
19 Jan.–3 Feb. 2007	*Lady Windermere's Fan*	Oscar Wilde	1892 prem.	Barbara Larose	Alumnae Theatre (The Main Stage)		Period (comedy)	Cathy McKim, Heather Couch, Dinah Watts, Tina McCulloch, Tennille Read, Trician Brioux, Carol McLennan, Gloria Lambert, Gina Hetland, Stephen Flett, Andrew Batten, Tim Braddock, Conor O'Hegarty, Patrick Brown, David Simor
7–24 Mar. 2007	*New Ideas Festival (19th)*	Various		Various	Alumnae Theatre (Studio)	World (festival)	New and Experimental Play Festival	
20 Apr.–5 May 2007	*If We Are Women*	Joanna McClelland Glass	1993 prem.	Rita Spannbauer	Alumnae Theatre (The Main Stage)		Contemporary (drama)	Rosemary Doyle, Jane Carnwath, Pat McCarthy, Gina Rae
28 Sept.–13 Oct. 2007	*The Memory of Water*	Shelagh Stephenson	1996 prem.	Barbara Larose	Alumnae Theatre (The Main Stage)		Contemporary (comedy)	Tabitha Keast (Equity), Chantale Groulx, Andy Fraser, Andrea Romaldi, Andrew Batten, Connor O'Hegarty
16 Nov.–1 Dec. 2007	*For the Pleasure of Seeing Her Again*	Michel Tremblay	1998 prem. Eng.	Lee Poulin	Alumnae Theatre (The Studio)		Contemporary	Included: Darlene Spencer, Paul Hardy
18 Jan.–2 Feb. 2008	*Private Lives*	Noël Coward	1930 prem.	Ed Rosing	Alumnae Theatre (The Main Stage)		Modern (comedy)	Michelle Alexander, Ruth Miller, Dinah Watts (Equity), Scott Clarkson, Derek Perks
5–22 Mar. 2008	*The 20th Annual New Ideas Festival*	Various		Various	Alumnae Theatre (Studio)	World (festival)	New and Experimental Play Festival	
18 Apr.–3 May 2008	*Daughter of the House*	Lucy Brennan	2008 prem., 2008 publ.	Jane Carnwath	Alumnae Theatre (The Main Stage)	World	Contemporary	Julie Burris, Nonnie Griffin, Maureen Lukie, Adrianna Prosser, Liam Doherty, Derek Perks, Chris Reid, Jason Winther
26 Sept.–11 Oct. 2008	*Wit*	Margaret Edson	1995 prem.	Barbara Larose	Alumnae Theatre (The Main Stage)		Contemporary (drama)	Dinah Watts (Equity), Cathy McKim, Lindsay Empringham, Sarah Naomi Campbell, Sarah Illiatovitch-Goldman, Idil Mussa, Richard Jones, Adam Brooks, Dave Norman
14–29 Nov. 2008	*Talking Heads*	Alan Bennett	1991 prem.	Mat Howard	Alumnae Theatre (The Studio)		Contemporary	Dia Frid, Chantale Groulx, Nonnie Griffin (Equity)

16–31 Jan. 2009	*Pride & Prejudice*	Jane Austen's novel adapted by Christina Calvit	1985 writ., 1986 prem.	Jane Carnwath	Alumnae Theatre (The Main Stage)		Contemporary (adaptation)	Razie Brownstone, Suzanne Courtney (Equity), Carolyn Hall, Naomi Priddle Hunter, Lara Johnson, Maureen Lukie, Leslie McBay, Tina McCulloch, Amy Pearson, Tennille Read, Charlene Rockwell, Brenda Somers, Alanna Stone, Ryan Browne, Hugh Buller, Steven Burley, Dave Casey, Scott Clarkson, Richard Jones (Equity), James Lukie, Maureen Lukie, Jake Michaels
11–14 Mar. 2009	*The New Ideas Festival 2009*	Various		Various	Alumnae Theatre (Studio)	World (festival)	New and Experimental Play Festival	
17 Apr.–2 May 2009	*Closer*	Patrick Marber	1997 prem.	Laura Roald	Alumnae Theatre (The Main Stage)		Contemporary (drama)	Laura Vincent, Tabitha Keast, Dave Lapsley, Steven Burley
25 Sept.–10 Oct. 2009	*A Delicate Balance*	Edward Albee	1966 writ., 1966 prem.	Barbara Larose	Alumnae Theatre (Mainstage)		Modern (Theatre of the Absurd)	Dinah Watts (Equity), Tricia Brioux (Equity), Carol McLennan, Patricia Hammond, Mark Whelan (Equity), Rob Candy
13–28 Nov. 2009	*Palace of the End*	Judith Thompson	2007 prem., 2007 publ.	Jason Maghanoy	Alumnae Theatre (The Studio)		Contemporary (docudrama)	Laura Vincent, Sochi Fried, Christopher Kelk
15–30 Jan. 2010	*Hay Fever*	Noël Coward	1924 writ., 1925 prem.	Kevin John McDonald	Alumnae Theatre (Mainstage)		Modern (comedy)	Tamara Lubek, Anne Harper, Dinah Watts (Equity), Tina Sterling, Kaitly Riordan, Ken MacAlpine, Hereward Pooley, Leete Stetson, Jonathan Thomas
10–27 Mar. 2010	*New Ideas Festival*	Various		Various	Alumnae Theatre (Studio)	World (festival)	New and Experimental Play Festival	
16 Apr.–1 May 2010	*The Queens*	Normand Chaurette, trans. Linda Gaboriau	1990 prem. (Fr.), 1992 prem. (Eng.), 1992 publ.	Mat Howard	Alumnae Theatre (The Main Stage)		Contemporary (drama)	Elaine Lindo, Jessica Moss, Janice Tate, Meghan McNicole, Nonnie Griffin (Equity), Patricia Hammond, Danniele Capretti, Kat Lai, Kat Letwin
20 June 2010 (Sat.)	*The Abortion Monologues* (staged reading)	Jane Cawthorne	2009 prem.		Alumnae Theatre (Studio)	Toronto (reading)	Contemporary Reading	No cast found.
24 Sept.–9 Oct. 2010	*You Are Here*	Daniel MacIvor	2000 prem., 2002 pub	Paul Hardy	Alumnae Theatre (The Main Stage)		Contemporary	Tabitha Keast (Equity), Seema Lakhani, Alyssa Quart, Michael Vitorovich, Joseph Cochrane, Cameron Johnston, Will O'Hare, Jamieson Child

(*Continued*)

Run Dates	Show	Writer	Play Dates	Director	Venue	Premiere	Style	Cast
12–27 Nov. 2010	*Hedda Gabler*	Henrik Ibsen, trans. and adapted by Judith Thompson	1891 prem. (Danish), 1991 prem. (Eng.)	Jane Carnwath	Alumnae Theatre (Studio)		Period (drama)	Ilene Cummings, Jane Reynolds, Sochi Fried, Leslie McBay, James Harbeck, Andrew Batten, Malcolm Taylor
21 Jan.–5 Feb. 2011	Two plays:			Ellen Green and Barbara Larose	Alumnae Theatre (The Main Stage)			
	• *The Real Inspector Hound*	Tom Stoppard	1962 writ., 1968 prem.				Modern (Theatre of the Absurd)	Brenda Somers, Laura Vincent, Richard Jones (Equity), Scott Moore, John Fleming, Leeman Kessler, Andy Frasser, Rob Candy, Derek Perks
	• *After Magritte*	Tom Stoppard	1970 writ., 1972 prem.				Modern (Theatre of the Absurd)	Andrea Brown (Equity), Susan Q Wilson, Patrick Brown, Rob Candy, Adrian Yearwood
No dates found.	*New Ideas Festival*	Various		Various	Alumnae Theatre (Studio)	World (festival)	New and Experimental Play Festival	
15–30 Apr. 2011	*Guinea Pigging*	Catherine Frid	2011 prem.	Molly [Golby] Thom	Alumnae Theatre (Mainstage)	World	Contemporary (comedy)	Laura Vincent, Krista Marchand, Chantale Groulx, Arfina Abdourahime, Michael Vitorovich, Chris Reid, Tim Walker, Lionel Boodlal
23 Sept.–7 Oct. 2011	*After Mrs. Rochester*	Polly Teale	2003 prem., 2003 publ.	Laura Roald	Alumnae Theatre (Mainstage)	Canada	Contemporary (drama)	Susan Q Wilson, Laura Jabalee, Tina McCulloch, Jessica Rose (Equity), Julie Burris, Kanika Ambrose, Laine Newman, Tabitha Keast (Equity)
11–26 Nov. 2011	*Sylvia*	A.R. Gurney	1995 prem.		Alumnae Theatre (Studio)		Contemporary (comedy)	No cast found.
20 Jan.–4 Feb. 2012	*The Trojan Women*	Euripides, trans. by Gwendolyn MacEwen	415 BCE prem. Ancient Greek 1981, Eng. trans. Gwendolyn MacEwen	Alexandra Seay	Alumnae Theatre (Mainstage)		Period (tragedy; Adaptation)	Molly Thom, Sochi Fried, Susan Q Wilson, Andrea Blakey, Suzette McCanny, Anne Shepherd, Stephanie Carpanini, Katie Ribout, Carys Lewis, Nicole St. Martin (Equity), Tara Zacharias, Andrew P. McMaster (Equity), Scott Moore
14–31 Mar. 2012	*New Ideas Festival 2012*	Various		Various	Alumnae Theatre (Studio)	World (festival)	New and Experimental Play Festival	
13–28 Apr. 2012	*Cosi*	Louis Nowra	1992 prem.	Jane Carnwath	Alumnae Theatre (Main Stage)		Contemporary (drama)	Joanne Sarazen, Patricia Hammond, Tina McCulloch, Laura Vincent, Jamieson Child, Ryan Kotack, Michael Vitorovich, Sean Speake, Matt Brioux, Christopher Kelk (Equity), James Warner

21 Sept.–6 Oct. 2012	*February*	Lisa Moore, based on her novel	2009 novel, 2012 prem.	Michelle Alexander	Alumnae Theatre Mainstage	World	Contemporary	Victoria Fuller, Lavetta Friffin, Kathlen Jackson Allamby, Trevor Cartiledge, Justin Skye Conley (Equity), John Fray, Steve Switzman
16 Nov. –1 Dec., 2012	*Drowning Girls*	Beth Graham, Charlie Tomlinson, Daniela Vlaskalic	1999 writ., 1999 prem.	Taryn Jorgenson	Alumnae Theatre (Studio Theatre)		Contemporary	Tennille Read, Jennifer Neales, Emily Opal Smith
25 Jan.–9 Feb. 2013	*A Woman of No Importance*	Oscar Wilde	1893 prem.	Paul Hardy	Alumnae Theatre Mainstage		Period (comedy)	Gillian English, Sophia Fabiilli, Andy Fraser (Equity), Áine Magennis, Kathleen Pollard, Paula Schultz, Amy Zuch, Andrew Batten, James Graham, Nicholas Porteous, Daniel Staseff, Jason Thompson, Michael Vitorovich
6–24 Mar. 2013	*New Ideas Festival (25th)*	Various		Various	Alumnae Theatre (Studio)	World (festival)	New and Experimental Play Festival	
12–27 Apr. 2013	*The Killdeer*	James Reaney	1960 prem., 1962 publ.	Barbara Larose	Alumnae Theatre Mainstage		Modern	Tricia Brioux (Equity), Marie Carrière Gleason, Blythe Haynes, Tina McCulloch, Joanne Sarazen, Anne Shepherd, Naomi Vondell, Matt Brioux, Rob Candy, Paul Hardy (Equity), Peter Higginson, Michael Vitorovich
13 Nov.–1 Dec. 2013	*FireWorks [1st]*	Various			Alumnae Theatre (Studio)			
	• *Measure of the World*	Shirley Barrie	2013 prem.	Molly [Golby] Thom		World	Contemporary	No cast found.
	• *Gloria's Guy*	Joan Burrows	2013 prem.	Anne Harper		World	Contemporary	No cast found.
	• *Theory*	Norman Yeung	2013 prem.	Joanne Williams		World	Contemporary	No cast found.
24 Jan.–18 Feb. 2014	*The Lady's Not for Burning*	Christopher Fry	1948 prem.	Jane Carnwath	Alumnae Theatre Mainstage		Modern (comedy)	No cast found.
No record	*New Ideas Festival 2014*	Various		Various	Alumnae Theatre (Studio)	World (festival)	New and Experimental Play Festival	
11–26 Apr. 2014	*Rabbit Hole*	David Lindsay-Abaire	2006 prem.	Paul Hardy	Alumnae Theatre Mainstage		Contemporary Tragedy	Paula Schultz, Joanne Sarazen, Sheila Russell, Cameron Johnston, Christopher Manousos

(*Continued*)

Run Dates	Show	Writer	Play Dates	Director	Venue	Premiere	Style	Cast
26 Sept.–11 Oct. 2014	*Escape from Happiness*	George F. Walker	1991 prem.	Andrea Wasserman	Alumnae Theatre Mainstage		Contemporary (comedy)	Andrea Brown (Equity), Renée Haché, Heli Kivilaht, Leslie Robertson, Joanne Sarazen, David Cairns, Maxwell King, Colin McDonald, Ryan Seeley, Robert Skanes (Equity)
13–19 Nov. 2014	*FireWorks! [2nd]*				Alumnae Theatre (Studio)			
	• *Burying Toni*	Catherine Frid	2014 prem.	Ginette Mohr		World		Natalie Kulesza, Glenda Romano, Jillian Welsh
	• *You Have to Earn It*	Ramona Baillie and Mari Popoff	2014 prem.	Jennifer Radford		World		Kathleen Jackson Allamby, Jill Kooymans, Kelly–Marie Murtha, Tim Nussey, Paul Stafford, Steven Arran, Allan Yates
23 Jan.–7 Feb. 2015	*Blood Relations*	Sharon Pollock	1980 prem.	Barbara Larose	Alumnae Theatre Mainstage		Contemporary (mystery)	Marisa King, Andrea Brown (Equity), Kathleen Jackson-Allamby, Sheila Russell, Steven Burley, Rob Candy, Thomas Gough
11–29 Mar. 2015	*New Ideas Festival 2015 (27th)*	Various		Various	Alumnae Theatre (Studio)	World (festival)	New and Experimental Play Festival	
10–25 Apr. 2015	*I Am Marguerite*	Shirley Barrie	1990 radio 2015 prem.	Molly Thom	Alumnae Theatre Mainstage	World	Contemporary	Daniela Pagliarello, Heli Kivilaht, Sara Price, Chris Coculuzzi, Christopher Oszwald
18 Sept.–3 Oct. 2015	*Antigone*	Jean Anouilh, adapted by Lewis Galantiere	1942 prem. (Fr.), 1948 prem. (Eng.)	Janet Kish	Alumnae Theatre Mainstage		Modern (tragedy)	Amanda Cordner, Kaya Bucholc, Carly Telford, Christina Leonard, Sara Stahmer (Equity), Renee Awotwi, Martha Breen, Christopher Oszwald, Scott Moore, Erik Mrakovcic, Patrick Fowler
4–22 Nov. 2015	*FireWorks! 2015 [3rd]*				Alumnae Theatre (Studio)			
	• *Divine Wrecks*	Chloë Whitehorn	2015 prem.	Pamela Redfern		World	Contemporary	Fleur Jacobs, Annelise Hawrylak, Megan O'Kelly, Hugh Ritchie, Michael Pearson, Luis Guillermo Villar
	• *Radical*	Charles Hayter	2015 prem.	Neil Affleck		World	Contemporary	Helly Chester, Kelly-Marie Murtha, Anne Shepherd, Rob Candy, Feerass Ellid
	• *Cottage Radio*	Taylor Marie Graham	2015 prem.	Julia Haist		World	Contemporary	Madeline Leon, Amanda Pereira, Dave Martin, Jean-Phillipe Allamby
22 Jan.–6 Feb. 2016	*Stepping Out*	Richard Harris	1984 prem.	Brenda Darling	Alumnae Theatre Mainstage		Contemporary	Alyssa Quart Cartlidge Jeanette Dagger (Equity), Linette Doherty (Equity), Robecca Grenier, Lisa Kovack, Kay Randewich, Felicia Simone Mish Tam, Jessica Westerman (Equity), Scott Turner

9–27 Mar. 2016	*New Ideas Festival 2016*	Various		Various	Alumnae Theatre (Studio)	World (festival)	New and Experimental Play Festival	
8–23 Apr. 2016	*August: Osage County*	Tracy Letts	2007 prem.	Victoria Shepherd	Alumnae Theatre Mainstage		Contemporary (tragicomedy)	Kathleen Jackson Allamby, Marie Carriere Gleason (Equity), Melinda Jordan, Andrea Lyons, Carol McLennan, Kelly-Marie Murtha, Pearl Ho, Andrew Batten, Neil Cameron, Rob Candy, Paul Cotton, Thomas Gough, Chris Peterson
16 Sept.–1 Oct. 2016	*This*	Melissa James Gibson	2009 prem.	Rebecca Ballarin	Alumnae Theatre Mainstage		Contemporary (comedy)	Amanda Jane Smith, Audra Gray (Equity), Andrew Batten, Michael Harvey, Christian Martel
9–27 Nov. 2016	*FireWorks! 2016*				Alumnae Theatre (Studio Theatre)			
	• *The Creases in My Sari*	Sindhuri Nandhakumar	2016 prem.	Kimberley Radmacher		World	Contemporary	Brittany Miranda, Jasmine D'Costa (Equity), Suchiththa Wickremesooriya, Lionel Boodlal (Equity), Vivek Hariharan, Anjali Rai
	• *Inked Heart*	D.J. Sylvis	2016 prem.	Pamela Redfern (Equity)		World	Contemporary	Amanda McKnight, Liz Wigderson, Britt Wilen, Zachary McKendrick, Andrew Gaunce
	• *Motherland*	Kristine Greenaway	2016 prem.	Andreja Kovac		World	Contemporary	Krys Potapaczyk, Konstantina Mantelos, Erik Mrakovcic, James Hyett
20 Jan.–4 Feb. 2017	*The Gut Girls*	Sarah Daniels	1988 prem., 1989 publ.	Maya Rabinovitch	Alumnae Theatre Mainstage		Contemporary (drama)	Claire Keating, Kaya Bucholc, Sarah Thorpe (Equity), Alexandra Augustine, Tasia Loeffler–Vulpe, Nicole Arends, Mike Hogan, Brendan O'Reilly
8–26 Mar. 2017	*New Ideas Festival 2017*	Various		Various	Alumnae Theatre (Studio)	World (festival)	Contemporary (Festival)	
7–22 Apr. 2017	*The Clean House*	Sarah Ruhl	2004 prem.	Ali Joy Richardson	Alumnae Theatre Mainstage		Contemporary (comedy)	Andrea Irwin (Equity), Lilia Leon, Marin Moreira, Annemieke Wade, Neil Silcox
20 Oct.–4 Nov. 2017	*Thirteen Hands*	Carol Shields	1993 prem., 1993 publ.	Claren Grosz	Alumnae Theatre Mainstage		Contemporary	Andrea Massoud, Jesselle Laurén, Kelly-Marie Murtha, Lawrie Hopkinson, Mahlet Tesfu, Marlo Alcock, Maureen Murray, Olivia Croft, Sandi Globerman

(*Continued*)

Run Dates	Show	Writer	Play Dates	Director	Venue	Premiere	Style	Cast
8–28 Nov. 2017	*FireWorks 2017: Three New Plays*	Various			Alumnae Theatre (Studio)			
	• *This Will Be Our Last Transmission*	Natalie Frijia	2017 prem.	Ara Glenn-Johanson		World	Contemporary	Melanie Leon, Megan Miles, Alexandra Milne, Rouvan Silogix
	• *Surrender, Dorothy*	Liz Best	2017 prem.	Joan Burrows		World	Contemporary	Mary Claire Thompson, Lisa Kovack, Barbara Clifford, Alysa Golden
	• *Gash*	Caitie Graham	2017 prem.	Madeleine Jullian		World	Contemporary	Caitie Graham, Meara Khanna, Blake Murray
9 Jan.–3 Feb. 2018	*Omission*	Alice Abracen	2018 prem.	Anne Harper	Alumnae Theatre Mainstage	World	Contemporary	Gillian Reed, Andrea Irwin, Lawrence Aronovitch, Thomas O'Neill
7–25 Mar. 2018	*New Ideas Festival 2018: Three Weeks of New Works*	Various		Various	Alumnae Theatre (Studio)	World (festival)	New and Experimental Play Festival	
13–28 Apr. 2018	*Queen Marie*	Shirley Barrie	2012 prem., 2013 publ.	Rosemary Doyle	Alumnae Theatre Mainstage		Contemporary	Jessica Bowmer, Fallon Brown, Katherine Cappellacci, Michel Dodick, Siena Dolinski, Nance Gibson, Tess Keery, Katrina Koenig, Gabriella Kosmidis, Stella Kulagowski, Indira Layne, Naomi Peltz, Catherine Ratusny, Leslie Rennie, Seira Saeki, Nina Tischhauser, Paula Wilkie, Adam Bonney, Paul Comeau, Rick Jones, Conor Ling, James Phelan

Notes

AAGM Alumnae annual general meeting minutes, various dates.
ABM Alumnae board meeting minutes, various dates.
AEM Alumnae executive meeting minutes, various dates.
AMM Alumnae meeting minutes, various dates.
ASGM Alumnae special general meeting minutes, various dates.

Preface

1 Brenda Darling, "President's Report for the 100th Season of Alumnae Theatre Company," Alumnae Annual General Meeting (minutes), 24 June 2018.
2 Since 1 January 2019, Alumnae have required all productions in the firehall's Mainstage and Studio theatres, including rentals, to play a recorded Land Acknowledgment: "We acknowledge that the land on which we gather at Alumnae Theatre has been a site of human activity for thousands of years and is the traditional territory of the Anishnaabe Nation, the Haudenosaunee Confederacy, the Wendat-Huron Nation, and most recently, the Mississaugas of the New Credit First Nation. We recognize with gratitude the enduring presence of Indigenous people on this land as the original keepers of this land. Megwich." Alumnae, "Alumnae Theatre Rentals: Frequently Asked Questions," 1 January 2019. Web.
3 Darling, "President's Report for the 100th Season."
4 Thom, Letter to Sid Adilman, 29 June 1972.
5 Ahsan, "She stoops to conquer," *National Post*, 3 August 2019, WP6.
6 Shelia MacDonald Tait, "History of the Alumnae Theatre Project," Alumnae newsletter, 15 May 1996.
7 Alumnae Board of Directors Meeting (minutes), 5 May 1997.
8 ABM, 2 October 2000.
9 ABM, 1 May 2001.
10 ABM, 4 June 2001.
11 Halpenny, Prospectus, "The Alumnae Theatre."
12 AMM, 9 June 2002.
13 Helen I. Dunlop, Report of the History Project Committee, AAGM, 9 June 2002.
14 AAGM, 9 June 2002.

Introduction

1 "Debut of New Dramatic Club," *Toronto Telegram*, 12 February 1918. In addition to the ten women listed in the *Telegram*, Isabel Jones was in the cast of eleven.
2 "You Can't Afford to Miss *Bluestockings*," *Varsity*, 15 February 1981, 1.
3 "Notices to Women," *Globe*, 9 February 1918, 10.
4 "You Can't Afford to Miss *Bluestockings*," *Varsity*, 15 February 1981, 1.
5 "*The Bluestockings* staged by Alumnae of University Coll.," *Varsity*, 13 February 1918, 1, 4.
6 "You can't afford to miss *Bluestockings*," *Varsity*, 15 February 1918, 1.
7 "*Blue Stockings* played," *Globe*, 16 February 1918, 10.
8 "*The Bluestockings* staged."
9 "*Blue Stockings* played."
10 "U.C. Alumnae score distinct success," *Varsity*, 18 February 1918, 1, 4.
11 "*Blue Stockings* Played." Unless appearing in the Women's section as a social function, *Globe* theatre and music reviews between 1898 and 1924 were authored by E.R. Parkhurst and were, arguably, intended for that paper's "audience of educated and influential Torontonians." Ross Stuart argues that in reviews of the day, "critical insight" was less apparent than the "popular pleasures and prejudices of [the] time." [E.] Ross Stuart, "The Critic as Reviewer: E.R. Parkhurst at the Toronto *Mail* and *Globe*, 1876–1924," in Anton Wagner, ed. *Establishing Our Boundaries*, 95.
12 "U.C. Alumnae score distinct success."
13 "You Can't Afford to Miss *Bluestockings*."
14 "U.C. Alumnae score distinct success."
15 "Alumnae of U.C. will stage play Feb. 15 & 16," *Varsity*, 14 February 1918, 1. Several cast members of *The Bluestockings* who had acted with the undergraduate UC Women's Dramatic Club (WDC) before graduating had been accustomed to working with Kirkpatrick since his first WDC show in 1912. In fact, two weeks before *The Bluestockings* opened, Kirkpatrick had directed WDC students in Sheridan's complex restoration comedy, *The Rivals*. His leadership in advance of *The Bluestockings*' opening night was acknowledged by the *Varsity* when it referred to his "able management [under which] the play promises to be a great success." "You Can't Afford to Miss *Bluestockings*."

Dr. Frank Home Kirkpatrick arrived in Toronto in 1905 from Ohio's University of Wooster (now College of Wooster) to take the position of Principal of the Toronto Conservatory School of Expression, a position he held for fourteen years. In 1912, he took over the direction of WDC productions from Emma Scott Raff and the WDC moved its annual productions from the Eaton School to U of T's Convocation Hall. This brought a larger, city-wide audience to the WDC as when, in 1912, more than 1,200 people attended their one-night performance of *Much Ado About Nothing*. Indeed, under Kirkpatrick's leadership during the war, the WDC became the "dominant dramatic group on campus." Averill, *Dramatis Personae*, 6. Each winter between 1912 and 1916 he directed the WDC in a Shakespearean comedy performed at U of T's Convocation Hall. These were followed by two Kirkpatrick-directed Sheridan comedies in 1917 and 1918 at the Toronto (now Royal) Conservatory's Music Hall. The Alumnae and the WDC retained Kirkpatrick until he left Toronto in the summer of 1919 to teach at Columbia University's post-graduate department. "Prof. F.H. Kirkpatrick," *Globe*, 13 March 1919, 8, provides evidence of their appreciation of his eight years of leadership.

As an oratory educator, Kirkpatrick had contributed a section called "Hints" to Donald G. French's *Standard Canadian Reciter* in 1918. Kirkpatrick would later write the oratory book

How to Speak in Public in 1923. For more on Kirkpatrick, Emma Scott Raff, and their influence on the WDC, see R. Whittaker, "'Entirely Free of Any Amateurishness'"; and Murray, "Making the Modern."

16 Molière, *The Learned Ladies*, 9, 10.

17 "The Women's Literary Society of University College," *Torontonensis 1920*, 41.

18 "The Women's Athletic Association of University College," *Torontonensis 1917*, 180.

19 Purser, "The Homemaker," 17.

20 Halpenny, Prospectus.

21 Bird, *Redressing the Past*, 13.

22 Pritchard, Gillian, "Down from the pedestal: On the eve of its 60th birthday, the 'Alum' is shedding its elitist image. There'll be some changes made," *Scene Changes*, September 1978, 10, 19, 27.

23 For studies on the status of women in the Canadian theatre profession, see MacArthur, *Achieving Equity in Canadian Theatre*; Burton, *Adding It Up*; Fraticelli, *The Status of Women in the Canadian Theatre*; and "Any Black Crippled Woman Can!," *Room of One's Own* 8, no. 2 (July 1983): 7–18.

24 The Canterbury Old Stagers in England claim to be the world's "oldest surviving amateur dramatic company." "The Old Stagers history," Web. They were founded in 1842 by the Hon. Frederick Ponsonby, later the third Earl of Bessborough. Interest in drama was reborn with at least one of his successors, Vera Brabazon Ponsonby, the ninth Earl of Bessborough and fourteenth Governor General of Canada, who founded the Dominion Drama Festival in Ottawa in 1933.

25 "Women university grads buy a theatre," *Paper Doll*, 12 November 1962; UADC, "History," 1963, 3; Alumnae, Press Release for *Next Time I'll Sing to You*, February 1965; Alumnae, Press Release to Beth Slainey, 17 November 1966.

26 Halpenny, "University Alumnae Dramatic Club," 574.

27 Hood, "Seven Decades of Dedication," 14–15.

28 Halpenny, "Shall we join the ladies?"

29 Holdsworth, Milling, and Nicholson, "Theatre, Performance, and the Amateur Turn," 11.

30 Halpenny, "History of the University Alumnae Dramatic Club," 6–7.

31 Spence, interview with Whittaker, 21 October 2017.

32 Holdsworth, Milling, and Nicholson, "Theatre, Performance, and the Amateur Turn," 12.

33 Hammond, interview with Whittaker, 20 October 2017.

34 Carnwath, interview with Whittaker, 19 October 2017.

35 Chansky, *Composing Ourselves*, 152.

36 MacArthur, "Historiographing a Feminist Utopia," 163–4.

37 Carstairs and Janovicek, "Introduction," 6.

38 Gidney, "Feminist Ideals and Everyday Life," 110.

39 Forestell, "Mrs. Canada Goes Global," 13.

40 See Scott, *Nightwood Theatre*.

41 Linda Gordon flags "consciousness raising" as a "new method of organizing," including among second-wave feminists, under the civil rights movement. Gordon, "Socialist Feminism," 23.

42 Linda Gordon notes that the "majority of U.S. women identified with" second wave feminism and that it lasted "unusually long as far as social movements go" (Gordon, "Socialist Feminism,'" 21). In Canada, as Janine Brodie has articulated, second-wave feminism found its political effects as a result of the federal government's construction of the welfare state in the

1950s and early 1960s and the appointment of the Royal Commission on the Status of Women (RCSW) in 1967. Brodie, "We Are All Equal Now," 151–2.

43 MacArthur, "Re-viewing Reception," 4, 6.

44 "About Us," *Alumnae Theatre Company*. Web.

45 "Alumnae Theatre," on Facebook.

46 Prominent examples are found in 1957, when Alumnae famously produced Canada's second production of Samuel Beckett's *Waiting for Godot* (see chapter on festivals), and in 1964, when they produced the Toronto premiere of Harold Pinter's *The Caretaker*. Neither play features acting roles for women (see chapter on Coach House).

47 Darling, Report of the Executive Producer, 12 June 2016.

48 Aitken, "Between You and Me," *Toronto Telegram*, 9 April 1953.

49 Andrew Allen acted in three Alumnae productions between 1929 and 1931 before embarking on his famed radio career at Toronto's CFRB radio in 1933 and then CBC radio.

50 W.E.S. Briggs's part in Alumnae's 1937 production of *The Cradle Song* preceded his notoriety with CBC radio.

51 W.S. Milne was a noted Canadian playwright. As a University College student he was also a campus contemporary of several Alumnae founders.

52 Nicholson et al., *The Ecologies of Amateur Theatre*, 81.

53 Nicholson et al., *The Ecologies of Amateur Theatre*, 284.

54 Dobson, *Shakespeare and Amateur Performance*, 7–8.

55 Some members emphatically, and variously, qualify the term "community theatre" when they apply it to Alumnae. Says Jane Carnwath, "We were doing T.S. Eliot, the Russians, things that you wouldn't normally see on a playbill, certainly not for a community theatre" (Carnwath, interview with Whittaker, 19 October 2017). PJ Hammond says, "Alumnae is bizarre even in the community theatre community … The reasons I choose Alumnae over any other community theatre: because we're better" (Hammond, interview with Whittaker, 20 October 2017). Others reject the term altogether. Says Margaret Spence, "It's not a community theatre. Whatever the papers may say, we're not a community theatre. It's a semi-professional theatre in Toronto. And I think it's worth being listed along with [professional companies]." Spence, interview with Whittaker, 20 October 2017.

56 Bell and Newby, *Community Studies*, 15, 22.

57 "Amateur," *Oxford English Dictionary*. Web.

58 Nicholson et al., *The Ecologies of Amateur Theatre*, 11, 6.

59 Gilbert et al., "On Amateurs," 9.

60 Knott, "Fancy Dress as an Amateur Craft," 9, 99.

61 Le Cercle Molière (founded in 1925, professionalized in the 1970s) and London Little Theatre (founded in 1936, professionalized in 1971) began as nonprofessional groups.

62 Nicholson et al., *The Ecologies of Amateur Theatre*, 672–4.

63 Criterion Research Corp., "Live Theatre Attendance in Edmonton."

64 Holdsworth, Milling, and Nicholson, "Theatre, Performance, and the Amateur Turn," 9.

65 Halpenny, "University Alumnae Dramatic Club."

66 Saddlemyer and Plant, eds., *Later Stages*.

67 Sperdakos, *Dora Mavor Moore*, 213.

68 Friedland, *The University of Toronto: A History*.

69 Various publications trace individual histories of several of Canada's amateur theatres, including Ottawa Little Theatre, Edmonton's Walterdale Playhouse, Kingston's Domino Theatre, and London's amateur-turned-professional Grand Theatre. They include: Winston, *Staging*

a Legend; Arthurson, *For Love Not Money*; Weston and Beharriell, *The Domino Affair*; and Johnston, *Let's Go to The Grand!*

70 Holdsworth, Milling, and Nicholson. "Theatre, Performance, and the Amateur Turn," 6.

71 Nicholson et al., *The Ecologies of Amateur Theatre*; Dobson, *Shakespeare and Amateur Performance*; and Ridout, *Passionate Amateurs.*

72 *Nineteenth Century Theatre and Film* 38, no. 2 (2011); *Theatre, Performance, and the Amateur Turn* 27, no. 1 (2017); *Performance Research* 25, no. 1 (2020).

73 Gilbert et al., "On Amateurs," 2.

74 Dobson, *Shakespeare and Amateur Performance*, 8.

75 Nicholson et al., *The Ecologies of Amateur Theatre*, 238.

76 Nicholson et al., *The Ecologies of Amateur Theatre*, 239.

77 On 23 March 2023, Canada's Theatre Museum announced a "new home located in the Elgin and Winter Garden Theatre Centre" "Canada's Theatre Museum Announces Its New Home." *Theatre Museum Canada*. Web.

78 Nicholson et al., *The Ecologies of Amateur Theatre*, 242.

79 Alumnae participate in the annual event Doors Open Toronto, for which they provide tours of their historic firehall-turned-theatre as part of a weekend of open house events across the city.

80 Nicholson et al., *The Ecologies of Amateur Theatre*, 248.

81 On their website, Alumnae maintain a production blog, a common means of disseminating what Helen Nicholson and colleagues call "thick description and emotionality that may be lost if not captured in the immediate and informal language of blogging." Nicholson et al., *The Ecologies of Amateur Theatre*, 273.

82 Gilbert et al., "On Amateurs," 8.

83 Spiegel, "Amateur Performance," 122, 124.

84 Nicholson et al., *The Ecologies of Amateur Theatre*, 8.

85 Bliss, "The Amateur Spirit," in *The Amateur Spirit*. Freeport: Books for Libraries, 1969 (1904), 1–34, 27, 26, 28, 31.

86 Burton and Lane, *New Directions*, 21.

87 Kuftinec, *Staging America*, 23.

88 Holdsworth, Milling, and Nicholson, "Theatre, Performance, and the Amateur Turn," 10.

89 Nicholson et al., *The Ecologies of Amateur Theatre*, 95.

90 Holdsworth, Milling, and Nicholson, "Theatre, Performance, and the Amateur Turn," 13.

91 Nicholson et al., *The Ecologies of Amateur Theatre*, 157.

92 Gilbert et al., "On Amateurs," 6.

93 Holdsworth, Milling, and Nicholson, "Theatre, Performance, and the Amateur Turn," 8.

94 Cochrane, "The Pervasiveness of the Commonplace," 233–4.

95 Dobson, *Shakespeare and Amateur Performance*, 10.

96 Gilbert et al., "On Amateurs," 6.

97 Pitches, "High Culture," 31.

98 Gilbert et al., "On Amateurs," 5.

99 Robert A. Stebbins has written voluminously on his concept of "serious leisure" as the "systematic pursuit of an amateur, hobbyist, or volunteer activity that is sufficiently substantial and interesting for the participant to find a career there in the acquisition and expression of its special skills and knowledge" (3). Stebbins, *Amateurs, Professionals, and Serious Leisure*, 3.

100 Hutchison and Feist, *Amateur Arts in the UK*, xiii, 9, 10.

101 In framing the professionalization of the discipline of history in English Canada, Donald Wright defines a profession's characteristics as "including prolonged training in a definable

body of knowledge, a credential system, a code of ethics, self-government, and legislated access to a particular labour market. Professionalization, then, refers to the acquisition of these characteristics over time." Wright, *The Professionalization of History in English Canada*, 4.

102 Dobson, *Shakespeare and Amateur Performance*, 9.

103 "Amateur," *Oxford English Dictionary*.

104 Hawley, "Dilettante Theatricals," 70.

105 "Amateur dramatic," *Oxford English Dictionary*.

106 Wickham, *The Medieval Theatre*, 179, 181–2, 189.

107 Wickham, *The Medieval Theatre*, 187.

108 Dobson, *Shakespeare and Amateur Performance*, 3.

109 Hawley, "Dilettante Theatricals," 68.

110 See R. Whittaker, "'Entirely Free of Any Amateurishness.'"

111 Alumnae, "How has the U.A.D.C. managed to survive and flourish for sixty years?"

112 For an extended discussion of these professional touring companies and the Toronto venues they visited, see Scott, "Professional Performers and Companies," 15–16.

113 Alumnae, "How has the U.A.D.C. managed?"

114 Beecroft, quoted in Bennett, "Twenties follies roar again."

115 This historical narrative is interrupted when, as Alan Filewod discusses, the Canadian National Exhibition's annual grandstand pageants (1887–1943) "disturb the historian's traditional acceptance of canonical dramas as indexes of theatrical 'maturity.'" Filewod, "Erect Sons and Dutiful Daughters, 60.

116 In Ottawa, members of the University Women's Club formed the Society for the Study and Production of Dramatic Art in May 1913, the first Canadian branch of the Drama League of America, which became the Ottawa Drama League by year's end. Since 1951 it has been known as the Ottawa Little Theatre, after the building it has run since 1928. Winston, *Staging a Legend*.

117 Nicholson et al., *The Ecologies of Amateur Theatre*, 25, 29, 34–5, 36, 38.

118 Masthead, *Varsity*, 19 February 1920, 2.

119 Alumnae, "How has the U.A.D.C. managed?"

120 Chansky, *Composing Ourselves*, 149, 150, 151.

Chapter 1

1 "Lady graduates organize," *Mail and Empire*, 29 November 1898; "*Blue Stockings* Played," *Globe*, 16 February 1918, 10.

2 "Professor Kennedy at Queen's Hall," *Varsity*, 26 Januaary 1916, 1.

3 "U.C. Alumnae score distinct success," *Varsity*, 18 February 2018, 1, 4.

4 "Drama in the University," *Varsity*, 22 January 1915, 2.

5 For more on Emma Scott Raff and the Margaret Eaton School of Literature Expression, see Murray, "Making the Modern"; and Fischlin, "The Margaret Eaton School."

6 *Torontonensis 1917*.

7 "Proceeds of Play," *Mail*. [No date recorded]

8 "*Much Ado about Nothing* to be a clever production," *Varsity*, 9 February 1916, 1.

9 "Proceeds of play given to C.O.T.C.," *Varsity*, 22 January 1915, 1.

10 *Torontonensis 1918*.

11 "A review of the dramatic situation," *Varsity*, 5 March 1917, 2. Between 1913 and 1918, the WDC presented six annual comedies, each directed by Dr. Frank Home Kirkpatrick:

Shakespeare's *Twelfth Night* (February 1913), *As You Like It* (February 1914), *A Midsummer Night's Dream* (February 1915), and *Much Ado About Nothing* (February 1916) at Convocation Hall; and Sheridan's *A School for Scandal* (January 1917) and *The Rivals* (January 1918) at the Toronto Conservatory Musical Hall. At least seventeen future UC Alumnae Dramatic Club members acted in these WDC productions: Margaret Tytler, Agnes Muldrew, Erskine Keys, Marion Squair (Hunter), Marjorie Fraser, Isobel Cassidy, Elspeth Wilson, Helen Kirby, Edna Bach, Mabel Child, Mona Clark, Alice Lewis, Margaret Phillips, Adeline Lobb, Helen Stewart, Freda Waldon, and Clare Millar. The plays were chosen for their suitability as teaching devices for elocution, poetry, and literature as well as for their popularity. Also, the fact that they are period "costume" comedies facilitated the women playing male characters while the men were at war.

The undergraduate members of the WDC used theatre to raise money for social causes, including the war effort. Women had been allowed to enrol in University of Toronto courses in 1884, often pursuing Bachelor of Arts degrees in languages and literature. Parallel to the introduction of co-education at the University of Toronto was the emergence of elocution schools, among the most prominent of which was the Margaret Eaton School of Literature and Expression and the Toronto Conservatory School of Expression, where young women learned and publicly demonstrated elocution skills through the study and performance of dramatic texts. From its founding in 1905, the WDC nurtured ties with the Margaret Eaton School through its founding "instructress" Mrs. Emma Scott Raff, who directed their publically acclaimed, sold-out annual Shakespeare productions. As Paula Sperdakos notes, this made the WDC one of the first clubs on the continent to link its course work with theatrical performance. It is arguable that without Scott Raff, and later Dr. Frank Home Kirkpatrick, the student members of the WDC who would go on to found Alumnae would not have had the artistic leadership to mount large performances of canonical plays for large audiences and future fundraising projects.

The fact that these were multi-talented women working at a time when public ambition was normally reserved for men was not entirely overlooked. Of the WDC's production of *Twelfth Night* in February 1913 at Convocation Hall, where there were no stage curtains, the *Varsity* reported that "much amusement was caused by the occasional changes of scenery made in front of the audience. Apparently we have the suffragette stage carpenter with us also" ("*Twelfth Night* presented on Friday," *Varsity*, 24 February 1913, 2). Apparently a motivating factor in the WDC production's move from Convocation Hall to the Conservatory's Hall in January 1917 was that when the group began producing Sheridan plays they required a "drop-curtain" for scene changes. "Women's Dramatic Club give *School for Scandal*," *Varsity*, 15 January 1917, 1.

Other intramural groups also raised money and awareness for causes on campus before and during the First World War. For example, at Convocation Hall on the evening of Wednesday, 12 December 1917, a group of female students from University College, Victoria University, and St. Hilda's "under the auspices" of the University Women's Administrative Council offered a "unique and enlivening entertainment [in which] life in the various fruit camps was cleverly portrayed." Among these "farmerettes" was future Alumnae member Erskine Keys. The *Globe* reported that "excellent moving pictures showing girls at work in field and orchard were shown." "University Fruit Pickers," *Globe*, 13 December 1917, 10; Kechnie, "'I'd give anything to come home,'" 27. For more on the WDC, see Whittaker, "'Entirely Free of Any Amateurishness.'"

12 "Social Events," *Globe*, 13 November 1917, 12.

13 Beatrice Embree was later known for her 1920 boarding school novel *The Girls of Miss Clevelands'* and her work at the Ottawa Little Theatre.

14 "U.C. Women's Lit," *Varsity*, 5 January 1918, 1.
15 "UC grads. provide interesting program," *Varsity*, 7 January 1918, 1.
16 Halpenny, "History of the University Alumnae Dramatic Club," 1945, 5.
17 "Assisting returned soldier students," *Toronto Star*, 3 March 1919.
18 "Club History," *Newsletter*, UADC, c. 1954.
19 "Club History."
20 "U.C. Alumnae score distinct success," *Varsity*, 18 February 1918, 1, 4.
21 "*The Bluestockings* staged by Alumnae of University Coll.," *Varsity*, 13 February 1918, 1, 4; "*Blue Stockings* played," *Globe*, 16 February 1918, 10.
22 Pinero's play had premiered in 1898 at London's Royal Court Theatre, receiving subsequent revivals in London and New York (performances in 1911 featured Ethel Barrymore as Rose Trelawny), but a silent film version released in 1916 had kept the clever "actor's life" comedy in the public imagination.
23 "University Alumnae," *Varsity*, 24 March 1919, 2.
24 The initial idea, to memorialize the "university men who have made the supreme sacrifice in the war" ("Alumni prepare to erect memorial in honour of Varsity's soldiers," *Varsity*, 29 November 1918, 1), was unanimously approved at a meeting of the university's joint alumni and alumnae associations two weeks after Armistice Day.
25 "Social Events," *Globe*, 26 March 1919, 10; "On Dit," *Mail and Empire*, 26 March 1919, 10; "What Women Are Doing," *Evening Telegram*, 27 March 1919, 12.
26 "*Trelawney of the Wells* by University Alumnae," *Globe*, 28 March 1919, 8.
27 "What Women Are Doing," *Evening Telegram*, 28 March 1919, 4. Mabel Child and Erskine Keys in particular had had a busy winter as two months earlier they had acted in plays at the Margaret Eaton School, produced by the Couchiching Camper's Club, alongside recent UC graduates Agnes Muldrew, Marion Squair, Adeline Lobb, and Alice Ball. "Dramatic caste recalls old U.C. Literary Society," *Varsity*, 24 January 1919, 1.
28 "What Women Are Doing."
29 Quoted in Whittaker, "Ambitious Winnipeg seeks subscribers," *Globe and Mail*, 27 July 1961, 8.
30 "Prof. F.H. Kirkpatrick," *Globe*, 13 March 1919, 8.
31 "Art and Culture," *Varsity*, 8 December 1919, 2.
32 [Untitled], *Varsity*, 2 February 1920, 4.
33 *The P.B.I.* ran at Hart House Theatre in March 1920, as did a discussion about how to be a critic. The play is printed in Filewod, *Reliving the Trenches*. For more on *The P.B.I.*, see chapter 3 of Filewod's *Committing Theatre*.
34 "Flu stops all lectures for past three days in social service dept," *Varsity*, 6 February 1920, 1.
35 "Ban on social functions to be lifted in week," *Varsity*, 27 February 1920, 1.
36 "No Theatre Night this year," *Varsity*, 23 February 1920, 1.
37 "University College enrollment now well over thousand mark," *Varsity*, 17 November 1919, 1.
38 "The alumnae and the memorial," *Varsity*, 16 Decembeer 1918, 1.
39 "Hart House and University College," *The Rebel* 3, no. 5 (March 1919), 193.
40 "First meeting of U.C. Alumnae Association," *Varsity*, 20 October 1919, 1.
41 "First meeting of U.C. Alumnae Association."
42 "Co-education and U.C.," *Varsity*, 28 November 1919, 2.
43 "U.C. women lay plans for coming campaign," *Varsity*, 20 February 1920, 1.
44 "New women's building seems assured fact," *Mail*, 22 April 1920.
45 "U.C. Women lay plans for coming campaign."
46 "Women to hear of professions open to college grads," *Varsity*, 9 February 1920, 1.

47 "Co-education and U.C."
48 "Another Campaign," *Varsity*, 16 February 1920, 2.
49 "The Building Fund objective is passed," *Varsity*, 17 March 1920, 1.
50 "*The Romantic Age* – 1922 [...] Expenses," Early Account Book 1, 29 April 1922.
51 "New Buildings for U.C. women," *Varsity*, 14 March 1919, 1 ; "Alumnae open," *Mail*, 4 April 1920; "University College Women's," *Toronto Star*, 8 April 1920; "U.C. Alumnae hold," *Monthly*, May 1922.
52 In January 1926, an editorial in the *Varsity* titled "The oft recurring protest" (21 January, 2) returned to, and fuelled, the gendered space deficit. It asserted a *status quo* segregationist stance, stating that for events at Hart House, "there is no reason why women should be granted admission." But it added that, "unquestionably, there is at present a serious demand for a Women's Building which will answer the purposes of Hart House, if on a considerably less ambitious scale, in view of limited funds."
53 Whitney Hall was named after E.C. Whitney, an Ottawa lumberman and the brother of Ontario Premier Sir James Whitney. E.C. bequeathed a sum of money to the University of Toronto, which used $450,000 to build Whitney Hall ("New university women's residence Whitney Hall formally dedicated," *Varsity*, 5 October 1931, 1). In *The University of Toronto: A History*, Martin L. Friedland clarifies a popular confusion that it was James after whom the building is named, stating that it was in fact E.C. (although he states that the sum E.C. bequeathed was $300,000) (200).
54 "Alumnae gift brings library to Whitney Hall," *Varsity*, 2 December 1932, 1.
55 "Women's residences will be completed sometime next year," *Varsity*, 28 January 1930, 1, 2.
56 "Dreams near realization," *Varsity*, 7 October 1930, 1, 4.
57 "Whitney Hall opens portals to University College women," *Varsity*, 1 October 1931, 1, 7; "$25,000 donation gift of Alumnae," *Varsity*, 9 February 1931; "Dreams near realization."
58 The UC Women's Undergraduate Association contributed a further $2,500 to purchase three pianos for each of the residence's three houses. "New University women's residence Whitney Hall."
59 "City's needy made happy by University Settlement," *Varsity*, 14 March 1941, 27.
60 Cathy L. James, "Practical Diversions and Educational Amusements: Evangelia House and the Advent of Canada's Settlement Movement, 1902-09," *Historical Studies in Education / Revue d'histoire de l'éducation* 10, nos. 1/2 (1998), 57.
61 James, "Practical Diversions," 54.
62 James emphasizes the "important parallels to Western imperialist colonization" (50n9) in the language and structure of settlements, even as they elude precise description: "Settlements resist definition, partly because of their insistence on remaining responsive to the needs of their local clientele. Generally speaking, the settlement was part middle-class residence, part social welfare agency, part recreation centre, and part cultural outpost in the slums. The residential aspect of the settlement house was its most unique characteristic; movement leaders insisted that at least some 'settlers' had actually to live in or near the premises in order for an institution to be considered a settlement. Settlement workers had to be neighbours, not merely visitors, in 'neglected' districts." James, "Practical Diversions," 50.
63 "The Alumnae Association...," *Toronto Telegram*, 12 December 1927.
64 "Social Events," *Globe*, 12 December 1927, 15.
65 Alumnae meeting minutes [hereafter AMM], 30 December 1936.
66 Francess Crowther, Letter to Mrs. Stone (Agnes Muldrew), 16 January 1939.

67 "University College: *Well of All Things…!*," *University Monthly*, February 1940.
68 AMM, 5 February 1940.
69 Francess Crowther (University Settlement), letter to Agatha Leonard, 27 March 1940. Alumnae Theatre Company collection.
70 One night in 1914, students infamously rioted at the Royal Alexandra Theatre, throwing paper streamers, confetti, and, even more egregiously, "small bags of flour," rice, wheat, iron bolts, coins, beans, peas, "heavy paper darts," and rolls of paper. See Mr. Solman, quoted in "Pre-war theatre night to be revived in near future," *Varsity*, 27 January 1919, 1. After the war, for a decade starting in 1919, student administrative councils struggled in vain to sign contracts with these professional theatres to bring back the Theatre Nights that had been so popular before the war. Theatres refused to reserve clusters of tickets or to discount their tickets below the regular price (around $3.50 at the time), making large-group student ticketing impossible.
71 "*Miss Black Sheep* to be dramatized," *Toronto Telegram*, 15 November 1938.
72 Along with the Toronto Flying Club, Old St. Andrew's Church, the Toronto branch of the Special Libraries Association, and, after the war, the UCAA itself, Alumnae sold Theatre Nights to women's groups, including the Zonta Cub, the Canadian Business and Professional Women's Club, the Lyceum Women's Art Association, the Margaret Scott Circle of the Big Sisters' Association, the Toronto branch of the Canadian Women's Press Club, the General B.L. Montgomery Chapter of the IODE, and the Humber Valley Women's Progressive Conservative Association. They also sold Theatre Nights to medical groups such as the Private Duty Nurses of Toronto General Hospital, the Toronto branch of the Ontario Society of Occupational Therapy (in aid of the Curative Workshop), the Nurse's Alumnae of Toronto East General Hospital, the Toronto General Hospital Alumnae Association, and the Toronto Hospital Occupational Therapists Association (THOTA). Other Theatre Nights went to schools, school associations, and alumni groups such as Moulton College, the Bishop Strachan School Association, the Toronto Home and School Association, U. of T.'s Alumni Federation, the Branksome Hall alumnae, and U of T's Library School alumni. Theatre Nights were also sold to an abecedary of fraternities, including Kappa Kappa Gamma, Kappa Alpha Theta, Phi Gamma Delta, and Pi Beta Phi, or their alumnae clubs.
73 "Social Events," *Globe*, 26 November 1935, 8.
74 Bridle, "U.C. Alumnae present clever mystery play," *Toronto Star*, 26 November 1935.
75 "Toronto Flying Club holds theatre night," *Toronto Star*, 25 November 1935.
76 "Moulton alumnae hold theatre night," *Star*, 28 November 1935.
77 Halpenny, "Shall we join the ladies?"
78 Enthusiastically pitching a Theatre Night for the Club's November 1948 production of Gordon's *Years Ago*, president Ruth Johnson wrote to the Zonta Club about the production's DDF regional festival win eight months earlier: "'I laughed my fool head off!' – that's what [adjudicator] Robert Speaight said when he awarded first place" (letter from Johnson to the Secretary of the Zonta Club of Toronto, 27 September 1948). Although the Zonta Club did not buy a *Years Ago* Theatre Night, three other groups did, including the Bishop Strachan School Association, of which club actor Barbara Allen was an "old girl," and to which the club contributed annually to the scholarship fund ("Bishop Strachan Alumnae to aid," *Globe and Mail*, 27 October 1948, 14; see also "Raise Fund through play," *Toronto Telegram*, 26 October 1948.) The Bishop Strachan School Association Theatre Night was the Tuesday. The Wednesday performance was a "Half Theatre Night" for the Toronto Branch of the Canadian Women's Press Club. And the Thursday performance was a Theatre Night for the UCAA, hearkening back to the days that the club raised funds directly for their founding organization.

79 Halpenny, "History of the University Alumnae Dramatic Club," 4–5; UADC *Newsletter*. 1.
80 Bourdieu, *Distinction*, 4.
81 Chansky, *Composing Ourselves*, 14.
82 Halpenny, Prospectus, "The Alumnae Theatre: A History."
83 MacKay, *The Little Theatre in the United States*, 3–4, 18, 20, 21.
84 Murray, "Making the Modern," 39.
85 Gardner, "Little Theatre Movement," 16 December 2013. Web.
86 Nicholson and colleagues note that in the UK, as in Canada, the number of women directors in nonprofessionalizing theatre puts the professional theatres to shame. Nicholson et al., *The Ecologies of Amateur Theatre*, 19.
87 Club membership more than doubled, from sixteen during the 1924–25 season to thirty-eight during the 1935–36 season. By 1935, meetings' details were being summarized in minutes. Those summaries provide insights into the club's activities and the impulses behind them, and sometimes also into the members' social lives. For example, at an August 1951 meeting held shortly after the wedding of new club president Barbara Barnett, they retired to "partake of the bride's delicious sponge cake and sandwiches." AMM, 2 August 1951.
88 AMM, 21 September 1935.
89 AMM, 28 May 1938.
90 AAGM, 3 June 1944.
91 Jones, "The 'oldest and proudest' Toronto theatrical company," *Toronto Star*, 23 September 1989, M4.
92 Halpenny, "Shall we join the ladies?"
93 "The University Alumnae Dramatic Club," 1956, 3.
94 UADC, "Building Fund Appeal," 1961, 1.
95 Francess Halpenny, "Shall we join the ladies?"
96 Bridle, "U.C. Alumnae present clever mystery play."
97 Certainly, few people had the technical knowledge to understand the complicated lighting machinery required to realize productions at Hart House Theatre at the time. The artistic director then, Bertram Forsyth, "was not a technical man," and this created challenges for him in his job. "Bertram Forsyth," in *Hart House Theatre*.
98 All of these directors fluidly moved between theatre groups in the interwar years. An unfortunate outcome of this cross-pollination is that chroniclers of these years often credit Alumnae's annual productions to Hart House Theatre itself. Robertson Davies's various recounts of early theatre in Canada provide evidence to answer the question of why Alumnae's early years have heretofore been lost to time, as when he recalls Parker's *Pomander Walk* but does not note that it was Alumnae's production. Davies, "Fifty Years of Theatre in Canada," 72. See also Davies, "Robertson Davies on the Young Vincent Massey," 98.
99 AMM, 2 September 1935.
100 W.A. (Bill) Atkinson later moved to Ottawa, where, according to Francess Halpenny, he had the "Ottawa Little Theatre audiences eating out of his hand." Halpenny, "History of the University Alumnae Dramatic Club," 2.
101 AMM, 21 June 1935.
102 Readings were given at the meeting from Rutherford Mayne's one-act Irish tragedy *Red Turf* and Hart House Theatre's first play of the next season, Moss Hart and George S. Kaufman's satirical comedy *Once in a Lifetime*. Nancy Pyper invited Alumnae members to audition for the latter. Then, "over coffee," the club considered a "very long list of plays for our coming Hart House production." AMM, 21 June 1935.

103 AMM, 27 September 1935.
104 AMM, 10 October 1935.
105 AMM, 20 April 1936.
106 Among the campus clubs making use of the new UC Women's Union auditorium was the new UC Players' Guild. With heavy publicity in the *Varsity* and the *Globe*, and dozens signing on as members in the preceding months, the UC Players' Guild opened as UC's only co-ed, non-departmental dramatic society in December 1922, beginning productions at the Women's Union in January 1923. Viewed from the outset as an undergraduate alternative to Hart House Theatre's "amateur repertory theatre" group the Players Club (Massey, *What's Past Is Prologue*, 60), the UC Players' Guild adopted a similar policy of not only producing plays but also developing "student interest in the theatre and everything connected with it" ("Players' Guild," *Torontonensis 1925*, 320). The guild had inherited operating funds from the WDC, which, having inspired Alumnae's founding daughters to pursue theatre, had collapsed two years earlier with the departure from Toronto of Roy Mitchell, their last director, and before him Dr. Frank Home Kirkpatrick. Alumnae members Erskine Keys and Katherine Anglin, along with playwright W.S. Milne, sat on the UC Players' Guild inaugural executive ("Players' Guild of University College Executive, 1922–23," *Torontonensis 1923*, 35). The UC Players' Guild kept close ties with Alumnae, including providing backstage crew for their early Hart House Theatre shows (Alumnae program for *Mary, Mary, Quite Contrary*. March 1923) and, for decades, giving early theatre experience to future Alumnae members like Francess Halpenny (who served on the UC Players' Guild's executive for three years). "University College Players Guild," *Torontonensis 1938*, 254; *1939*, 257; *1940*, 269. "U.C. Players Form"; "This column"; "U.C. Players' Club; "Folk"; "Players Guild"; "U.C. Players Guild"; "The Players' Club."
107 "New Women's Union building opens," *Varsity*, 10 January 1923, 4; "Alumnae's fund," *Mail*, 18 July 1922.
108 "Art, Music and Drama," *Varsity*, 31 October 1923.
109 "Opening meeting," *Toronto Telegram*, 2 February 1924.
110 K.B.W., "Alumnae Plays," *Varsity*, 5 February 1924, 2.
111 *Balm* premiered at Hart House Theatre in August 1923 ("Hart House Theatre Production History," *Hart House Theatre*, 2013. Web). In 1927, *Balm* found its way into Vincent Massey's two-volume collection *Canadian Plays from Hart House*, one of the country's most influential Little Theatre play publications.
112 *Calendar [...] 1904–1905*, 67; University of Toronto Alumni Association, *University Monthly* 16 (1915–16).
113 Averill, *Dramatis Personae*, 9.
114 Stacey, "U.C. Alumnae Dramatics," *Varsity*, 21 January 1926.
115 Murray, "Making the Modern," 54n5.
116 When Alumnae produced George Bernard Shaw's 1917 war play *Augustus Does His Bit* in 1924, *Varsity* noted the "present enthusiasm" for Shaw in a campus year (1924–25) that saw no fewer than five of his plays that were "not often produced." "Misalliance," *Varsity*, 15 December 1924, 2.
117 "Alumni Plays," *Varsity*, 31 January 1927, 4.
118 [No title recorded] *Telegram*, 28 January 1927.
119 [No title recorded] *Mail*, 29 January 1927.
120 Masthead, *Varsity*, 11 November 1930, 2.
121 Beamish, "U.C.A.A. Production," *Varsity*, 20 November 1929, 2.

122 "Christmas party features carols," *Varsity*, 9 December 1932, 1.
123 "Christmas party great success," *Varsity*, 12 December 1933, 1, 4.
124 "The Bulletin Board," *Varsity*, 14 March 1924, 3; "Witty Comedy Well Done," *Toronto Telegram*, 10 March 1928.
125 "Hart House Theatre will link Toronto with Little Theatre Movement," *Varsity*, 27 October 1919, 2.
126 Ford, *A Path Not Strewn with Roses*, 67.
127 "A splendid gift," *Varsity*, 4 March 1910.
128 "New Hart House a marvel in art of building," *Varsity*, 5 March 1913, 1.
129 Mitchell, quoted in "Hart House Theatre." *Varsity*, 31 October 1919, 1.
130 When the Massey estate made public their plans to erect a memorial building for Vincent's late grandfather Hart A. Massey in March 1910, students and faculty expected the building to be the "most magnificently appointed clubhouse on the American continent" ("Finest club house on the continent," *Globe*, 18 April 1912, 9). In 1913, Vincent and his colleagues created Hart House's resident theatre company, the Players Club, with the purpose of presenting "some of the best dramatic work of all countries and ages, specializing exclusively upon plays whose nature makes them unsuited to performances in the down-town theatres" ("Reorganization of Players Club," *Varsity*, 15 October 1919, 1). But by October 1914, under the pressure of total war, the Massey family and the federal government had repurposed the nearly complete building for military service. The Players Club suspended its activities as the war "swept away the membership of the club" ("Reorganization," 1). The building was soon placed under the control of the Military Hospitals Commission for use as the University of Toronto Base Hospital ("Hart House now for re-education: Restore men to normal," *Globe*, 10 May 1917, 9; "*Blue Stockings* Played," *Globe*, 16 February 1918, 10). During the five years preceding its opening, Hart House remained "occupied by the military authorities." "Governor-General coming to university to open art House officially," *Varsity*, 6 October 1919, 1.

When the war concluded, the university renovated the firing range into a 470-seat "little underground auditorium." Boasted the *Varsity*, "a most efficient and modern system will provide the latest scenic effects. There are but two theatres in America with lighting equipment comparable to that which has been installed in this theatre. Water effects including fountains and rain storms will be used, besides imitations of other natural phenomena, including fog, smoke and fire. The state-of-the-art electrical system, "entailing a fabulous cost," was to be run by third-year students (all male) from the university's School of Practical Science. "Hart House Theatre will link Toronto with Little Theatre Movement," *Varsity*, 27 October 1919, 2.

The rejuvenated Players Club, now under Roy Mitchell's direction, was the resident company. It produced its own season of plays while making the theatre and the building's other halls available for lectures on drama and other subjects, as well as for use by a variety of campus groups like Alumnae (R.B., "The Players Club, Hart House Theatre and the University," *The Rebel* 4, no. 2: 80–2). There were some questions as to whether the Players Club had been granted too much authority over the state-of-the-art theatre at the expense of the affiliated colleges' dramatic societies, but the expressed intention was much grander: Hart House Theatre was "to link up the Players Club of the University with the 'Little Theatre' movement now having such a pronounced artistic success in the bigger centres of the United States" ("Hart House Theatre will link Toronto"). By the time of the official opening of Hart House, there was great anticipation for a campus-wide revival of dramatics, with Hart House Theatre as its epicentre. Hart House Theatre's first season offered eight productions, including plays by Dunsany, Jonson, Euripides, and Shakespeare. The second season was equally ambitious and included Merrill Denison's *Brothers in Arms*, the first of many Canadian works to premiere there.

Within a few years of its official opening, the Board of Syndics that governed Hart House Theatre clarified to students who were complaining that they did not have the access they should to the new state-of-the-art performance space, that "Hart House Theatre has no connection with Hart House." Moreover, the Syndics operated the theatre and were responsible to the Governors of the University, and the theatre was understood to be in the first place an "Art Theatre in the University, existing to promote the interests of dramatic art in the widest sense," art that was "intelligently produced." As such, "all other considerations must be subordinate" to the production of the Hart House Theatre season and of a "standard [that] must be kept as high as possible, and therefore the most competent assistants, both amateur and professional, must be found whether in the University or outside." "Theatre syndics issue statement," *Varsity*, 23 February 1923, 1, 6.

But the following fall, as chair of the Board of Syndics while running his family's agricultural equipment company, Massey-Harris, Vincent Massey told *Varsity* that student tickets for Hart House Theatre shows were to be reduced from $1.00 to 75¢ and that student rental rates for the theatre were to be "substantially reduced." Along with a reorganization of the resident Players Club constitution and the addition of a library and reading room featuring books on stage craft, these changes, the *Varsity* declared, were aimed at a "reawakening of undergraduate interest" in the theatre, one that would "inaugurate a new era of useful activity" there. Massey may well have been playing politics with student interest by reducing financial pressures and increasing benefits to appease their ire about being kept from the stage. "The Theatre and the undergraduate," *Varsity*, 12 October 1923, 2.

The educational and material philosophies built into the burgeoning Little Theatre Movement had an early influence on the university's alumni and students. In less than two years, Hart House Theatre was part of a remarkable campus-wide expansion of theatre activity, which ballooned to more than one hundred shows crewed by fewer than twenty men ("Faculty nights allotted for use of the theatre," *Varsity*, 13 March 1923, 1). The colleges and departments of UC, Trinity, St. Michael's, and Victoria were also involved in this increase.

One prominent member of the Women's Dramatic Club of Victoria College was Elizabeth Sterling (graduated 1920), who served as president of that group while participating in various performances and readings throughout the year, before acting at Hart House Theatre in its first season and moving to Edmonton, Alberta, in 1922, where she contributed considerably to that province's theatre. Edmonton's annual theatre awards are named in her honour. "Vic. Dramatic Club appoints executive for coming year," *Varsity*, 8 October 1919, 1.

131 Friedland, *The University of Toronto: A History*, 273.

132 "Hart House Theatre will link Toronto."

133 During the building's first few months, women could walk through Hart House. But a brief article in one of the dailies around the time that Alumnae produced *A Trip to Scarborough* there signalled some of the gender politics at play in relation to the "men's union" building: "Varsity women are really almost as interested in the splendid new 'union' for the men students as the members of Hart House are themselves. And for the first few days of the term, little groups of feminity [*sic*] might often be seen exploring the long corridors and admiring this or that special feature of the place … But now these are forbidden delights. A stern notice, to the effect that 'women are admitted only at such (infrequent) times as may be specially announced,' is posted at the various entrances. Hart House is 'out of bounds' for women … Of course, there are women secretaries in different offices in the building, who come and go as they will, but apart from these, and the inevitable reporter, the male element has undisputed possession." "Forbidden," *Telegram*[?], n.d.

134 "Announcements," *Globe*, 16 April 1921, 17.
135 "Social Events," *Globe*, 11 April 1921, 8.
136 "Social Events," *Globe*, 16 April 1921, 17.
137 Waldon, "Recollections of University Dramatics" [Letter to the Editor *of The Homemaker*], *Globe and Mail*, 29 December 1949, 8.
138 Waldon, "Recollections."
139 Day, "Treading the Arduous Road to Eleusis," 191.
140 Duchesne, "Critical Introduction," in Mitchell, *Creative Theatre*, xxii, xvi, xxxiv.
141 For example, see Gardner, "Little Theatre and Amateur Theatre," 303; and Day, "Treading the Arduous Road to Eleusis."
142 Duchesne, "Critical Introduction," xii, xvi, xxiv.
143 Moira Day has written about Roy Mitchell's interest in staging ancient Greek theatre (Euripides's *The Trojan Women* during Hart House Theatre's first season), as well as the impact this choice may have had on the campus and perhaps on the city and Canada generally. Whichever companies may have received this influence, Alumnae was not one. They did not produce a play from Greek antiquity until well into their firehall years (although some members made up part of the cast of Robert Gill's notable production of *The Trojan Women* at Hart House Theatre in 1958). Nor did they apparently share the society- and nation-building ethos that Day argues informed Mitchell's theosophist views and his art. Day, "Treading the Arduous Road to Eleusis."
144 Duchesne, "Critical Introduction," xxvi.
145 Card, "Drama in Toronto," 69.
146 Usmiani, "Roy Mitchell: Prophet in Our Past," 154.
147 Among Alumnae's modern plays produced at Hart House Theatre were several premieres, including two world (Coulter's *The Family Portrait* and Williams's *To Ride a Tiger*), one North American (Girvin and Cosen's *Miss Black Sheep*), three Canadian (Sierra's *Take Two from One*, Gordon's *Years Ago*, and Jourdry's *Teach Me How to Cry*), and eleven Toronto (A.A. Milne's *The Romantic Age* and *To Have the Honour*, Benavente's *The Evil Doers of Good*, Campion's *Ladies in Waitin,* Wood's *Charity Begins*, Alvarez's *A Hundred Years Ago*, Clemence Dane's *Wild Decembers*, Goetz's *The Heiress*, Eliot's *The Family Reunion*, Fry's *Venus Observed*, and Loos's *Gigi*).
148 "*Romantic Age* charming play," *Globe*, 29 April 1922, 17.
149 Hector Charlesworth, "The third comedy …," *Saturday Night*. 6 May 1922.
150 Mona Purser, "The Homemaker: Alumnae Dramatic Club to present *Autumn Crocus*," *Globe and Mail*, 24 October 1949, 17.
151 *University of Toronto Monthly* 23 (June 1922), 383, 420.
152 Halpenny, "Shall we join the ladies?"
153 Ontario's Lieutenant-Governor Henry Cockshutt and his wife attended the production. "Play *Romantic Age*," *Globe*, 21 April 1922, 17. The show's financial ledger indicates that tickets cost $1.00 each across the Friday evening and two Saturday performances (notably up from the 25¢ and 50¢ prices for their inaugural production of *The Bluestockings* in 1918). Expenses included $75.00 for the rental of Hart House Theatre, $71.21 for Milne's royalty, $40.20 for the war tax (still in place for larger businesses to cover the country's expenses from the war), $56.75 for postage, and $1.50 for "smokes" (the cost of about 100 cigarettes at the time). "Player's Navy Cut Cigarettes" [advertisement], *Varsity*, 21 February 1923, 2.
154 Charlesworth, "The third comedy …" *Saturday Night*, 6 May 1922.
155 Charlesworth, "The third comedy …" *Saturday Night*, 6 May 1922.

156 "*Romantic Age* charming play."
157 Charlesworth, "The third comedy …"
158 "*Romantic Age* charming play."
159 Charlesworth, "The third comedy …"
160 "*Romantic Age* charming play."
161 Charlesworth, "The third comedy …"
162 Halpenny, "History of the University Alumnae Dramatic Club," 2.
163 Purser, "The Homemaker," 17.
164 "Social Events," *Globe*, 3 March 1923, 29.
165 "*A Single Man*," *Varsity*, 5 March 1923, 2.
166 "Engagements," *Mail*, 6 October 1930.
167 "*A Single Man*."
168 With *A Single Man*, the Club netted $62.08 above paying Hart House Theatre $125.00, $75.16 for royalties, $10.00 for plants, and $2.00 for "smokes."
169 Hankin, *The Charity That Began at Home*, 1907, 33.
170 The production cost $100.00 to rent Hart House Theatre and $70.29 in royalties. It sold $621.50 in tickets that went for $1.00 during the two evenings and 75¢ for the matinee.
171 Chansky, *Composing Ourselves*, 9.
172 *Mail*, 14 January 1925.
173 "University College Alumnae Dramatic Club presents *The Evil Doers of Good*" [advertisement], *Globe*, 24 January 1925, 2.
174 "Appearing at Hart House Next Week," *Varsity*, 6 February 1925, 1.
175 N.P.H.B., "*Getting Married*," *Varsity*, 15 March 1927, 2.
176 "*Getting Married* is well presented," *Globe*, 12 March 1927, 35.
177 "Social Events." *Globe*. 12 March 1927, 38.
178 N.P.H.B., "*Getting Married*."
179 Charles P. Stacey, "*Getting Married*," *Varsity*, 8 March 1927, 2.
180 "*Getting Married* is well presented."
181 "Theatre and Concert Hall: Brief Comment," *Globe*, 5 March 1927, 20.
182 "*Getting Married* is well presented."
183 N.P.H.B., "*Getting Married*."
184 Jones, "The 'oldest and proudest' Toronto theatrical company."
185 Maugham, *Caesar's Wife*. London: William Heinemann, 1922, 2.
186 Agatha Leonard had entertained the cast on a Tuesday a month earlier at her Heathdale Road home, as published in the Social Events section of the *Globe* ("Social Events," *Globe*, 26 October 1928, 20). Expenses for *Caesar's Wife* included the $125.00 royalty fee, Hitchman's $75.02 director's fee, the $100.00 rental of Hart House Theatre, and $4.00 for the set's palms.
187 P.A. Gardner (P.A.G.), "U.C. Alumnae dramatics," *Varsity*, 15 March 1932, 2.
188 *The Young Idea* featured a few stalwart members returning to the stage, a large number of newcomers to the club, and male guests who included figure skater Stewart Reburn (Halpenny later noted that figure skating "eclipsed his other talents," as well as Gontran Rochereau de la Sablière (whose lengthy name Gardner reprimanded in his review), Percy Schutte (whom Halpenny called a "loyal and good friend of the Club"), and W.E. Milne. Halpenny, "History of the University Alumnae Dramatic Club." Tickets were $1.00, although a notice went out in the *Varsity* that students could pay 50¢ for the Friday performance. "Women's Dramatic Club," *Varsity*, 11 March 1932, 4.
189 The prompt book and rehearsal schedule for Alumnae's production of *Take Two from One* is held in their collection; it is their earliest extant prompt book.

190 Lorna G. Rumball was not listed as an Alumnae member but had attended the Ontario Ladies' College in Whitby, where she excelled in Drama and Expression and graduated in 1923. *Vox Collegii*, Ontario Ladies College, Whitby, vol. 32 (June 1923), 8.
191 Three stage assistants were paid $3.00 each to support the production, which made $278.05 at the door covering $206.92 in expenses with tickets reserved at $1.00 (plus tax) and 55¢ at the door.
192 Halpenny, "History of the University Alumnae Dramatic Club," 4.
193 Alumnae meeting notes, 24 November 1935.
194 Augustus Bridle, "U.C. Alumnae present clever mystery play," *Toronto Star*, 26 November 1935.
195 Bridle, "U.C. Alumnae present clever mystery play."
196 M.K.H., "Arts, Music and Drama," *Varsity*, 28 November 1935, 2.
197 Bridle, "U.C. Alumnae present clever mystery play."
198 M.K.H. "Arts, Music and Drama."
199 Bridle, "U.C. Alumnae present clever mystery play."
200 A great deal of detail about Alumnae's production of *Ladies in Waiting* can be gleaned from extant archival sources. Hemingway held auditions and chose a tentative cast at an Alumnae meeting at past-president Doris Shiell's Rosedale neighbourhood home on Thursday, 10 October 1935. They rehearsed three times a week, with line rehearsals held in members' homes and subsequent rehearsals held at the UC Women's Union, their storage barn on Lonsdale Rd., and Radio Hall, the latter of which was arranged by Edgar Stone. The first dress rehearsal was held at Radio Hall on Saturday, 23 November, and the second at Hart House Theatre the following day.

Alumnae increased their publicity expenditures by advertising with *Curtain Call* and several other outlets. They printed 2,000 flyers, some of which were handed out in person "to loved ones and friends" as well as "players they knew" (AEM, 18 October 1935). Ten posters were ordered, with additional ones to be copied. And a write-up was sent to *University Monthly*. This advertising blitz worked, and the whole run was sold out through publicity and Theatre Night sales.

For the closing Thursday performance, which was open to the public, the financial statements show in detail that many individual Alumnae members were active in selling tickets. Anglin sold 40 tickets, the most of anyone. The open Thursday evening grossed $374.00 from 488 seats sold at 50¢ and $1.00 plus tax (there were also eleven complimentary tickets given out for the Thursday). An additional $2.60 was made across the three theatre nights from a sausage bar, totalling a gross income of $826.60. Expenditures for the production totalled $500.00 and included the $50.00 per night rental of Hart House Theatre; $15.00 royalty per performance; $33.43 for poster, program, and ticket printing; and $2.00 for cigarettes for the volunteer stage crew. In addition, "at the last moment, two négligées were bought for the play. Alison Ewart agreed to purchase one. The other was raffled at 25 cents a ticket to defray its expense." Alumnae meeting minutes, 5 December 1935. A $100.00 payment was made to Hemingway for directing and $12.00 to the Hart House Theatre stage manager. The profit for the production was $326.33, of which $256.60 went to the University Settlement and an additional $25.00 "bonus" to Hemingway as director. All told, the club "retained as profit" $44.73 for the week.

Chapter 2

1 AMM, 7 September 1939.
2 Between the 1939–40 season and the 1944–45 season, club membership steadily plummeted from 34 to 11. As soon as the war ended, membership immediately jumped to 28 and rose to 50 in the decade before they moved off-campus.

3 Young, "Rambling with Roly," *Globe and Mail*, 29 October 1945, 25.
4 AMM, 26 September 1939.
5 AMM, 2 October 1939.
6 Tippett, *Making Culture:* 156.
7 B.N.P., "Dickens club is entertained by two plays," *Toronto Telegram*, 28 November 1939.
8 Wagner, Letter to Agatha Leonard.
9 "Variety program presented at University Women's Club Christmas Party Thursday," *Globe and Mail*, 15 December 1939, 15.
10 "Variety program presented."
11 "University College: Dramatic Club entertains," *University Monthly*, January 1940.
12 "War-time revue features galaxy of stage stars aided by radio artists," *Varsity*, 19 January 1940, 1.
13 Thelma Craig, "Wartime revue proves full of pep and punch," *Globe and Mail*, 30 January 1940, 4.
14 "Little Theatre groups will present revue," *Globe and Mail*, 20 January 1940, 9.
15 "Little Theatre leaders here query his right to sit as a judge: Challenge issued," *Globe and Mail*, 29 January 1940, 3.
16 "*Well of All Things* begins war revue at Hart House," *Varsity*, 30 January 1940, 1, 4.
17 "Royal Canadian Air Force Chapter sponsors Hart House event Monday," *Globe and Mail*, 23 January 1940, 9.
18 Craig, "Wartime revue proves full of pep and punch."
19 Rose MacDonald, "Revue's 'Punch' refutes crack at 'Little Theatre,'" *Toronto Telegram*, 30 January 1940.
20 "University College: *Well of All Things …*!," *University Monthly*, February 1940.
21 "*Well of All Things* proceeds for war holds Hart House stage next week," *Globe and Mail*, 25 January 1940, 9.
22 "Society Notes," *Globe and Mail*, 24 January 1940, 8.
23 "*Well of All Things* proceeds for war holds Hart House stage next week," *Globe and Mail*, 25 Jan 1940, 9.
24 "*Well of All Things* proceeds for war."
25 "University College: *Well of All Things…*!"
26 Brock Brace, "*Well, of All Things*," *Varsity*, 30 January 1940, 2.
27 Brace, "*Well, of All Things*."
28 AMM, 16 January 1940.
29 "University College: *Well of All Things …*!"
30 *Gossip*, 5 February 1940.
31 MacDonald, "Revue's 'punch' refutes crack at 'Little Theatre.'"
32 *Gossip*, 5 February 1940.
33 "University College: *Well of All Things…*!"
34 The opening evening also featured a range of non-Alumnae talent. This included the "excruciating clowning" of Conny Vernon; the ballet of Boris Volkoff and Janet Volkoff; the music-hall foursome of Rupert Lucas, Frederic Foy, Frank Rostance, and George Patton; and the "exotic Spanish dance-rhythms of Conchita Triana" (Brace, "*Well, of All Things*"), who danced with "vigourous grace and brilliant skill." MacDonald, "Revue's 'punch' refutes crack at 'Little Theatre.'"

As reported by Brock Brace in *Varsity*, future Canadian radio, theatre, and film icon Jane Mallett, with "adroit timing and ability to wait for laughs," performed a "pert monologue in a beer-parlour," written by Murray Bonnycastle. After the break, a piece called *Dreary Drama* by the Town Tonics "proved that Festival Players can still laugh at themselves and had the first-nighters in stitches." Peggy and Lawrence Lester performed an "appealing little song-and-dance"; they were followed by Elizabeth Johnston, formerly of the Trudi Schoop Ballet, who gave a "nimbly graceful acrobatic turn." Lucas returned for a "sly" offering of *Play the Game – You Cads!* "Tuneful, singable music" was provided by Crawford, Aldwinckle, and Woodland-Tisdale. Throughout, Charles Woodland-Tisdale and Dennis Vaughan provided "running commentary on two pianos." Other talents included Rai Purdy, Jack Maclaren, Frederic Manning, Napier Moore, W.A. Atkinson, Zoe Christie, and Elizabeth Forgie. In *Varsity*, Brace concluded of the opening night that the "performance had some rough spots, but Mr. Bennett's infallible touch will smooth them out. The show clicks." Brace, "*Well, of All Things.*"

35 Claire Wallace, "Your handshake reveals your character …" *Star*. [No date recorded]

36 The *Londonderry Air* featured Goulding and Hunter with Willard B. Thomson and James E. Dean, while Patrick McClory played the "Londonderry Air" song. *Love and Learning* featured Agatha Leonard as a learned lady supported by her mother (Muldrew) in giving a feminist lecture assisted by her prompter and fiancé (John Watson), who is distracted by the learned lady's sister (Helen Alles), while her father (H.E. Hitchman) and their maid Marie (Janet Kennedy) deal with them. *After the Tempest* featured Edna Norwich, Dorothy Batchellor, and Aileen O'Brien, with Linton Cole and Barry Fitzgerald.

37 AMM, four meetings, April and May 1940.

38 AAGM, 8 June 1940.

39 AMM, 4 November 1940.

40 AMM, 11 September 1940.

41 AMM, 6 May 1941.

42 W.S. Milne, letter to Edna Norwich, 8 February 1941.

43 The cast featured Alumnae members Alison Hewitt as Celestina, Florrie Hunt as Berta, Dorothy Batchellor as Salome, and Francess Halpenny as Tonia, with guest John Bowen as Fidel. For the Women's Union performance, Margaret Tytler and Percy Schutte also directed Charles Lee's English West Country play *Mr. Sampson*, featuring Jean Stewart and Doris Stacey as spinster sisters wooed by their next-door tenant Mr. Sampson, played by Schutte.

44 AMM, 19 September 1939.

45 AMM, 26 September 1939.

46 AMM, 6 May 1941; emphasis in original.

47 AMM, Fall 1941. Reginald Denham's 1940 Broadway play *Ladies in Retirement* was considered, with Arthur Burroughs and Gordon Alderson discussed as possible directors; the former declined and the latter felt the play could not be accomplished at the Women's Union. Although Alderson and Alumnae examined other plays, the idea was ultimately scrapped, and Alderson was paid $5 for his reading time. One of the plays Alderson pondered was Robert Ardrey's *Thunder Rock*, which had just premiered on Broadway in 1939 and became a symbol of British resistance in wartime London after it transferred to the Globe Theatre with funding from the Exchequer. Other plays they read included Joseph A. Fields and Jerome Chodorov's American comedy *My Sister Eileen*, John Van Druten's Broadway comedy *Old Acquaintance*, and Maugham's three-act farce *The Unattainable*. Ultimately, they turned their attention to programming at the Women's Union: an evening of short plays for the UCAA in February and a series of skits in April 1942.

48 AMM, 10 February 1942.

49 Bowring, curator, "Dancer, Director, Collaborator, 1930s." Web.

50 AMM, March 1942.
51 Alumnae minutes book, note about skits presented on 24 April 1942.
52 AMM, March 1942.
53 AMM, 24 April 1942.
54 AAGM, 30 May 1942; emphasis in original.
55 AAGM, 30 May 1942. The skits featured Phoebe Templeton (member Christina's daughter) and her young friend giving a guest presentation; Doris Stacey and Francess Halpenny reading a skit adapted by the latter from the *Powder-Room Pow-Pow* skit presented at the Women's Union in April 1942 (Halpenny's first playwriting experience on record with Alumnae); Edna Norwich, Eleanor Woodside, Margaret Tytler, and Florian Moore (Florie Hunt) giving a "very amusing burlesque of a woman's executive meeting"; members reading a skit by Katherine Anglin about "casting problems"; Agnes Muldrew doing an Irish monologue; and Eleanor Stewart and Doris Stacey reading "very effectively" (AAM, 30 May 1942); and the Armenian-American dramatist William Saroyan's 1939 comedy *My Heart's in the Highlands.*
56 AMM, 21 September 1942.
57 The plays read at meetings in the fall of 1942 were Mabel Constanduros and Howard Agg's *The Shadow Passes* (read 28 September); the Introduction to Maxwell Anderson's *Candle in the Wind* (12 October), which, they recorded, "contains some very interesting ideas on the nature and purpose of the drama and the influence of the theatre on society"; Acts I and II of Joseph Kesselring's *Arsenic and Old Lace* (12 October); Acts I and II of Noël Coward's *Blythe Spirit* (26 October); Dell Oglesbee Ross's *The Babe at the Inn* (26 October), which they presented at St. Alban's Cathedral parish hall on Howland Avenue that December; Maxwell Anderson's *Miracle on the Danube*; and Act I of Mark Reed's *Yes, My Darling Daughter* (26 October).

In January and February, only one play was read at each sitting. They were notably more political and timely: Arch Obelor's 1924 radio play *Chicago, Germany* (18 January); Act I of a third Maxwell Anderson play, *Wingless Victory* (26 January), although it was "not wholeheartedly endorsed"; Frederick Hazlitt Brennan's *The Wookey*, about the people of England's attempts to thwart Hitler (8 February); and Archibald McGleich's *Fall of the City* (22 February). Starting on 8 March, Alumnae's notes say that members edited the plays before reading them. These plays were Anderson's *Candle in the Wind* again (8 March), which had been pre-read by the group and cut by Agnes Muldrew for the meeting; Clifford Odets's *Golden Boy* (22 March) and *Till the Day I Die* (5 April); Acts I and III of Thornton Wilder's *By the Skin of Our Teeth* (19 April) at a meeting at the Women's Union; Chekhov's *The Cherry Orchard* (3 May); Patrick Hamilton's *Angel Street* (17 May); and a fifth Maxwell Anderson play, *Eve of St. Mark* (21 June).
58 AMM, 13 October 1945.
59 AMM, 2 November 1942.
60 AMM, 9 November 1942.
61 AMM, 18 January 1943.
62 AMM, 26 January 1943, 8 February 1943, 22 March 1943, and 5 and 19 April 1943.
63 AMM, 8 March 1943.
64 AMM, 22 January 1943.
65 AMM, 9 November 1942.
66 Panofsky, *Toronto Trailblazers*, 72.
67 AMM, 13 October 1942; Panofsky, *Toronto Trailblazers*, 72.
68 AMM, 13 October 1942.

69 AMM, 18 January 1943.

70 "Introduction: Information, Propaganda, Censorship, and the Newspapers," Canadian War Museum, 7 July 2018. Web.

71 AMM, 8 November 1943.

72 Alumnae's meeting on Monday, 4 October 1943 attracted nine members: Tytler, Woodside, Hunt, Templeton, Stewart, Muldrew, Leonard, Wilson, and Home. Here they read John Van Druten and Lloyd Morris's 1942 play *The Damask Cheek*, cut for reading by Woodside, soliciting the club's conclusion: "promising material" (AMM, 4 October 1943). At a meeting on Monday, 19 October 1943, they read *Distant Point*, a modern (1935) Russian play by Aleksandr Afinogenov, the only Russian play that would be produced by a Canadian theatre during the war (by the Montreal Repertory Theatre in 1943; see Clayton, "Bears and Beavers." A subsequent meeting in November was attended by seven members – Tytler, Muldrew, Hewitt, Woodside, Templeton, Anglin, and Wilson – who read three short plays: Philip Johnson's one-act comedy *Hullabaloo* (from J.W. Marriott's *Best One-Act Plays of 1941*); *The Courting of Marie Jenvrin: A Comedy of the Far North* by Gwen Pharis Ringwood (from Margaret Mayorga's *Best One-Act Plays of 1942*); and the morality play *Miracle at Blaise* by Josephina Niggli, which the group concluded would be "difficult to do" (AMM, 8 November 1943). Further plays read that fall were a play in choral speech (6 November) and F. Sladen-Smith's 1929 one-act play *The Man Who Wouldn't Go to Heaven* (6 November). At their next meeting, with a "large turnout of the club," they decided to attend the Toronto premiere of Noël Coward's *Blithe Spirit* the following Monday, 22 November, at the Royal Alexandra Theatre (AMM, 15 November 1943). They also read Florence Ryerson and Colin Campbell Clements's play *Harriet* (15 November and 13 December), based on the life of abolitionist Harriet Beecher Stowe, synopsized by Muldrew, with the club drawing the conclusion that it was a "very strong play."

In the winter, Margaret Ness reviewed for the club Kurt Weill and Ira Gershwin's psychological play with music from 1941, *Lady in the Dark* (16 January 1944); Christina Templeton "slightly reviewed" Seán O'Casey's 1943 *Red Roses for Me*, which, they decided, was made of "many scenes, loosely put together, but some very good dialogue and characterization [that] might play better than it reads [and] much depends on lighting effects" (AMM, 31 January 1944); Templeton reviewed Arnaud D'Usseau and James Gow's 1943 Broadway play *Tomorrow the World* (14 February); "as part of a study of earlier famous plays" (AMM, 13 March 1944), they read Eugene O'Neill's *Emperor Jones* (13 March); Richard Brinsley Sheridan's *The Critic* (27 March); Eugene O'Neill's *Ah, Wilderness!* (17 April); and A.G. Macdonell's *The Fur Coat*, summarized by Mary Smart (1 May).

73 AMM, 1944–45.

74 AMM, 19 October 1943.

75 AMM, September 1943.

76 AMM, 1944–45.

77 The plays read in 1944–45 were John William Van Druten's 1943 Broadway comedy *The Voice of the Turtle*, about being single in New York during the war; Shakespeare's *Antony and Cleopatra* and *King Lear*; Stephen Vincent Benét's 1938 one-act play *The Devil and Daniel Webster*, based on Benét's Faustian short story; Lynn Rigg's 1930 Broadway play *Green Grow the Lilacs*, on which the 1943 musical *Oklahoma!* was based; S.N. Behrman's 1944 Broadway comedy *Jacobowsky and the Colonel*, which was currently playing at New York's Martin Beck Theatre; and Ruth Gordon's 1944 Broadway comedy *Over 21*, which was turned into a movie with the same name in August 1945. AMM, 1944–45.

78 Roly Young, "Rambling with Roly," *Globe and Mail*, 29 October 1945, 25.
79 Herb Wood, "Agatha Leonard: Danseuse, librarian in six languages," *Varsity*, 31 January 1949, 1, 3.
80 "*Merry-Go-Round* show brings breezy variety," *Globe and Mail*, 26 January 1944, 8
81 Halpenny, "Shall we join the ladies?"
82 "*Merry-Go-Round* show brings breezy variety."
83 Wood, "Agatha Leonard."
84 "*Merry-Go-Round* show brings breezy variety."
85 Young, "Rambling with Roly," 29 October 1945.
86 Wood, "Agatha Leonard."
87 Young, "Rambling with Roly."
88 Wood, "Agatha Leonard."
89 Wood, "Agatha Leonard."
90 AAGM, 2 June 1945.
91 AMM, 1944–45.
92 AAGM, 2 June 1945.
93 AMM, 1944–45.
94 AAGM, 2 June 1945.
95 Only 7 of the 28 registered members were present: Agatha Leonard, Agnes Muldrew Stone, Elspeth Wilson, Margaret Tytler, Christina Templeton, Edna Norwich (listed as "inactive"), and Margret Ness. AMM, 18 September 1945.
96 Srigley, *Breadwinning Daughters*, 127.
97 AMM, 14 October 1936.
98 AMM, 16 October 1936.
99 AMM, 6 November 1936.
100 AMM, May 1942.
101 AAGM, 30 May 1942.
102 AAGM, 30 May 1942.
103 Katherine B. Anglin, letter (draft) to H.J. Cody, 16 May 1942, Alumnae Theatre Company collections.
104 H.J. Cody, letter to Katherine Anglin (Mrs. R.E. Anglin), 25 June 1942, Alumnae Theatre Company collections.
105 Halpenny, "Shall we join the ladies?"
106 AMM, 21 September 1942.
107 In 1963, Alumnae president Molly Thom announced: "Those eligible are: graduates of any university, those connected with a university but not graduates, graduates of any other institutes of high learning" (AAGM. 5 November 1963).
108 AMM, 28 September 1942.
109 Halpenny, "History of the University Alumnae Dramatic Club," 6.
110 AMM, 26 October 1951.
111 AMM, 23 November 1942.
112 Enid Marion Walker, letter to Members of the U.C. Dramatic Society, n.d., Alumnae Theatre Company collection.
113 Walker, letter to Members of the U.C. Dramatic Society.
114 AMM, 13 October 1942.
115 "Personal Notes," *Globe and Mail*, 12 February 1947, 12.
116 Halpenny, "History of the University Alumnae Dramatic Club."

117 Sabiston, “17 play groups active, “17 play groups active; world music reviving,” *Globe and Mail*, 5 October 1946, 18.
118 “To enter play,” *Globe and Mail*, 21 November 1949, 15.
119 CODL, Newsletter, September 1954, 1.
120 AMM, 26 October 1951.
121 “Summary of Year’s Activities. 1947–48.”
122 “Summary of Year’s Activities. 1947–48.” Perhaps coincidentally, the Centre Island Little Theatre group, the Showshop, produced *Dark Brown* the following weekend. Roly Young, “Rambling with Roly: Homecoming,” *Globe and Mail*, 12 June 1948, 11.
123 AMM, 21 November 1951.
124 AMM, 16 January 1952.
125 “Social and Personal Notes,” *Globe and Mail*, 29 May 1950, 16.
126 For example, for September 1952 they had read Lorca’s *The House of Bernarda Alba*; Lillo’s *The London Merchant*; Eliot’s *The Family Reunion* (which they would later produce); van Druten’s *Bell, Book, and Candle*; Storm’s *Black Chiffon*; Bagnold’s *Lottie Dundas*; and Raphelson’s *Hilda Crane* – although the last two were not approved for further consideration. AMM, 18 September 1952.
127 AMM, June 1952.
128 AAGM, 29 May 1954. By January 1954, Alumnae were considering several plays for the next fall, including Wynyard Browne’s *The Holly and the Ivy*; Emily Williams’s *Trespass*; Lillain Hellman’s *Autumn Garden* (possibly as a festival entry); Oscar Wilde’s *A Woman of No Importance* (which they later approved as the next fall’s show; AAGM, 29 May 1954); Sommerset Maugham’s *Home and Beauty*; and Anton Chekov’s *Three Sisters* (which they would not produce until the fall of 1966; AMM, 27 January 1954). Katherine Anglin had also “sent word that she had access to new one-act Canadian plays which we might try” (AMM, 27 January 1954).

In April, a refreshed reading committee was set with Halpenny as convener, Anglin offering her home, and Eleanor Beecroft attending. Hart House Theatre’s Robert Gill recommended John Colton and Miles Carlton’s tragedy *#9 Pine Street* “as an opening show.” AMM, April 1954. They also considered Charles Morgan’s 1953 play *The River Line* (based on his own novel of the same name, although the rights were not yet available); Margery Sharpe’s *The Foolish Gentlewoman*, which they called “a type like Dodie Smith’s, playable and castable”; and Anita Loos’s *Gigi*, which they said was “well liked but not too suitable for theatre night audiences,” although they would produce it in October 1955. They also found Jean Anouilh’s *Colombe* “very provocative – possibly a festival entry – a director would be very important.” At the end of the season, after producing Rodney Ackland’s *The Old Ladies*, the committee “decided to move away from poetic drama and thriller-type [plays] which we have just done” (AAGM, 29 May 1954).
129 “Prize dramatists give *Octopus* for 3 evenings,” *Varsity*, 10 October 1951, 2.
130 “English comedy by Alumnae club,” *Globe and Mail*, 22 September 1951, 8.
131 “Versatile director,” *Globe and Mail*, 6 October 1951, 8.
132 AMM, 2 August 1951.
133 After Whittaker, Needles was Alumnae’s choice to direct, although several other names were also discussed, including Henry Kaplan, John Lindsay, and Bob Christie. AMM, 2 August 1951.
134 E.G. Wanger, “Polite English comedy played at Hart House,” *Globe and Mail*, 17 October 1951, 22.

135 Wanger, "Polite English comedy."
136 Malcolm MacKinnon, "Mahogany around the Bath," *Varsity*, 18 October 1951, 5.
137 Wanger, "Polite English comedy." Alumnae had had some difficulty sourcing numerous properties and furniture for the show. For example, they had to figure out what an "epergne" was (an ornamental table centrepiece) and where one might be found (AMM, 11 October 1951).
138 AMM, 2 August 1951.
139 Wanger, "Polite English comedy."
140 MacKinnon, "Mahogany around the Bath."
141 AMM, 26 October 1951. Media outlets sought reviewers to cover the increasing number of theatre productions going on in cities across the country, while seeking to manage possible conflicts of interest. To that end, reporters were sometimes transferred from the news, crime, or sports pages to review, or report on, the theatre and the other arts.
142 AMM, 21 November 1951.
143 AMM, 19 May 1952.
144 Whittaker, "A lifetime in the cause of theatre," *Globe and Mail*, 2 June 1956, 10.
145 "Lefevre's tour: 57 full plays, 18 playlets," *Globe and Mail*, 1 March 1952, 8.
146 "Bennett directs Alumnae's first," *Globe and Mail*, 20 September 1952, 10.
147 Whittaker, "Show Business," *Globe and Mail*, 22 September 1952, 14.
148 MacKinnon, "*Ars Gloria Artis*," 10 November 1952, 5.
149 AMM, 30 October 1952.
150 AMM, 4 September 1952.
151 "Costumer claims boning vital for Victoria part," *Globe and Mail*, 6 October 1952, 19.
152 Rose MacDonald, "Dramatic club most adept in *The Heiress*," *Toronto Telegram*, 14 October 1952.
153 Hugh Thomson, "Alumnae drama club fine in *The Heiress*," *Toronto Star*, 14 October 1952.
154 Whittaker, "Show Business," *Globe and Mail*, 15 October 1952, 47.
155 Malcolm MacKinnon, "Anna & *The Heiress*," *Varsity*, 20 October 1952, 3.
156 MacDonald, "Dramatic club most adept."
157 Thomson, "Alumnae drama club fine in *The Heiress*."
158 Whittaker, "Show Business," 15 October 1952.
159 MacKinnon, "Anna & *The Heiress*."
160 Whittaker, "Show Business," 15 October 1952.
161 MacKinnon, "Anna & *The Heiress*."
162 Whittaker, "Show Business," 15 October 1952.
163 AMM, 30 October 1952. Among the show's props was a hundred-year-old backgammon board borrowed from Mary Smart (AMM, 4 September 1952). A photograph of the board ran in the *Telegram* in advance of the show, with actors Eleanor Beecroft and Douglas Ney in mid-game ("University club rehearses play," *Toronto Telegram*, n.d.).
164 "The University Alumnae Dramatic Club," 1956, 4.
165 Whittaker, "Showbusiness," *Globe and Mail*, 15 October 1954, 9.
166 Malcolm MacKinnon, *CJBC Views the Shows*, n.d.
167 Alumnae, "University Alumnae Dramatic Club," 1956, 2.
168 AAGM, 4 June 1955. Crainford, who was British, but whose wife was Canadian, had been the general manager of the Stratford-Upon-Avon Memorial Theatre. Alumnae approached him in May to direct their fall show and immediately asked him to cast the show the first week of June and to rehearse it before he left for England in the summer (AAGM, 29 May 1954). Jupiter Theatre had brought Crainford to Canada from England the previous season "to handle

its administration [but he] was left to forage for himself when that organization suffered severe reverses and suspended operations." Thus stuck in Toronto, he became very busy. He did some parts on radio, performed in one television drama, participated in several television panel shows, and was a "talent adjudicator" for CBC-TV, the Stratford drama critic for England's *The Stage* publication, and "even a disc-jockey on a program beamed to the United Kingdom." Within a few months, he was also hired to a permanent position on the production end of CBC television and agreed to direct Wilde's play for Alumnae and another play for the Trinity College Dramatic Society (Whittaker, "Showbusiness," *Globe and Mail*, 7 July 1954, 8). He also "screened" plays to be accepted into the 1955 CODL Festival (Whittaker, "Showbusiness," *Globe and Mail*, 8 February 1955, 19). Clearly there was no shortage of work for the British actor-director in Toronto. But apparently, as Beecroft later reported, there was some question as to whether Crainford would return to Canada at the end of the summer. AAGM, 4 June 1955.

169 AAGM, 4 June 1955.
170 AAGM, 2 June 1956.

Chapter 3

1 Blair Mascall, "The Alumnae Theatre Company" [Speech], 6 April 2002.
2 Halpenny, "Shall we join the ladies,"
3 Hunter, *Still Hunting*.
4 Johnston, "Bill Glassco and Tarragon Theatre," 18–19; Johnston, *Up the Mainstream*, 153.
5 Johnston, "Bill Glassco and Tarragon Theatre"; Johnston, *Up the Mainstream*.
6 "Coach House Theatre: Happy in factory," *Toronto Star*, 14 March 1959.
7 Rogers, New Members Report, 13 June 1964.
8 UADC, "Building Fund Appeal," July 1961, 1.
9 UADC, "Building Fund Appeal," July 1961, 2.
10 Halpenny, "Shall we join the ladies?"
11 AMM, 5 November 1963.
12 AMM, 11 September 1963.
13 AMM, 10 January 1968.
14 Hunter, *Still Hunting*.
15 AAGM, 10 June 1967.
16 AMM, 23 May 1963.
17 AEM, 12 January 1965.
18 AEM, 7 July 1965.
19 AMM, 23 May 1963.
20 Alumnae, "Building Fund Appeal," 2.
21 Molly Thom, interview with Whittaker, 25 October 2017.
22 Martha Mann Southgate, interview with Whittaker, 25 October 2017.
23 Margaret MacAulay, letter to DDF Professional Direction Committee, 1 April 1969.
24 Karr, "Alive or dead, "Alive or dead? Royal Alex only Toronto theatre with season set," *Toronto Star*, c. fall 1957.
25 Pamela Terry, letter to W.P. Rowley, 23 May 1964.
26 Helen Dunlop, quoted in Janice Tyrwhitt, "Amateur theatre's cast of thousands," *Maclean's*, 6 January 1962, 54.
27 Alumnae, "Building Fund Appeal," July 1961, 1.

28 Alumnae, "University Alumnae Dramatic Club," 1956, copied from original by L. Burke in 1980.
29 Quoted in Terry, "Report of the Playreading Committee," 1.
30 Johnston, "Bill Glassco and Tarragon Theatre"; Johnston, *Up the Mainstream*, 153.
31 Whittaker, "Alumnae Dramatic Club presents wry comedy of love," *Globe and Mail*, 19 June 1957, 10.
32 "Less master," *Varsity*, 23 October 1957, 3.
33 Curiously, Alumnae lore maintains that Donald Sutherland played the character of God in the play, but the program and reviews indicate that he played the Lawyer (Whittaker, "Showbusiness," *Globe and Mail*, 18 October 1957, 8). In fact, Sutherland was unable to make all of the performances in the middle of the run and Russ Waller was needed as a "last-minute substitution," which meant, according to John Douglas in the *Varsity*, that, "one missed the sullen power of [Sutherland] at his best" (John Douglas, "Less Master," *Varsity*, 23 October 1957, 3). Sutherland was foregrounded in *A Dream Play*'s preview publicity with Robert Pease and Robert Huber ("Alumnae launches season," *Toronto Star*, 5 October 1957, 20; "Coach House Theatre," *Globe and Mail*, 5 October 1957, 14). Whittaker said that among the play's large cast, Sutherland's work was the "most successful of the 33 performances [because] it creates its own reality" (Whittaker, "Mews Strindberg," *Globe and Mail*, 18 October 1957, 8). Shortly after working with Alumnae, Sutherland left for England to study at the London Academy of Music and Dramatic Art. Born in Saint John, New Brunswick, he had also studied engineering and drama at U of T's Victoria College. His successful campus engagments included UC Follies and, at Hart House, the UC Literary and Athletic Society's musical *Katy Cruel*, lauded in the *Varsity* as the "best college musical this university has seen in a long time" ("Theatre," *Varsity*, 15 January 1960, 5).
34 Rose MacDonald, "Festival winnings furnish theatre," *Toronto Telegram*, 27 March 1957, 26.
35 Whittaker, "Showbusiness," *Globe and Mail*, 28 March 1957, 13.
36 "Anouilh play extends run," *Toronto Telegram*, 22 June 1957.
37 Rose MacDonald, "Glorious absurdities," *Toronto Telegram*, 25 April 1959.
38 Rose MacDonald, "University Alumnae offer Anouilh play," *Globe and Mail*, 19 June 1957, 31.
39 MacDonald, "University Alumnae offer Anouilh play."
40 Halpenny, "Shall we join the ladies?"
41 Nathan Cohen, "Life to Anouilh plainly futile not to say funny," *Sunday Telegram*, 23 June 1957.
42 Whittaker, "Alumnae Dramatic Club presents wry comedy of love."
43 MacDonald, "University Alumnae offer Anouilh play."
44 Whittaker, "Alumnae Dramatic Club presents wry comedy of love."
45 Rose MacDonald, "University Alumnae offer Anouilh play," *Globe and Mail*, 19 June 1957, 31.
46 Whittaker, "Alumnae Dramatic Club presents wry comedy of love."
47 Cohen's dense and lengthy piece mused about Anouilh's plays and the "hardships" they endure when translated into English (Cohen, "Life to Anouilh plainly futile not to say funny").
48 "Coach House Theatre: Happy in factory," *Toronto Star*, 14 March 1959.
49 "Old Coach house is new playhouse for dramatic club," *Toronto Star*, 23 March 1957.
50 MacDonald, "University Alumnae offer Anouilh play."
51 UADC [history document], 1960, 3.
52 Whittaker, "Notes on things," *Globe and Mail*, 26 March 1957, 11.

53 "*Beaux Stratagem*," *Varsity*, 16 October 1958, 5.
54 Cohen, "Life to Anouilh plainly futile not to say funny."
55 Whittaker, "Alumnae Dramatic Club presents wry comedy of love."
56 MacDonald, "University Alumnae offer Anouilh play."
57 UADC, Fiftieth anniversary season pamphlet.
58 Johnston, "Bill Glassco and Tarragon Theatre"; Johnston, *Up the Mainstream*, 153.
59 Francess Halpenny, "Shall we join the ladies?"
60 Halpenny, "Shall we join the ladies?"
61 Alumnae, "University Alumnae Dramatic Club," Summer 1960, 4–5
62 Martha Mann Southgate, interview with Whittaker, 25 October 2017.
63 Terry, "Report of the Playreading Committee," AAGM, 9 June 1962, 4. During the 1961–62 season, along with Wilfred Watson's *Cockcrow and the Gulls* and *Corporal Adam*, Alumnae considered several other modern plays, including three one-acts by Norman Williams, Andreyev's *He Who Gets Slapped*, Beckett's *Happy Days*, Pinter's *Slight Ache* and *The Room*, Richardson's *Gallows Humor*, Ibsen's *Rosmersholm*, Pirandello's *Henry IV*, Farquar's *The Recruiting Officer*, Congreve's *The Double Dealer*, and Webster's *The Duchess of Malfi*. They were also planning to read Simpson's *The Hole*, an adaptation of Frisch's plays called *The Aspern Papers*, O'Neill's *A Touch of the Poet*, Weinstein's *The Red Eye of Love*, and Arrabal's *The Automobile Graveyard*. The modern plays were all recent and cutting-edge; Alumnae would later produce *The Double Dealer* and *The Recruiting Officer*.

When a theatre company becomes more involved in building procurement and management, it often begins to see its core activities of choosing and producing plays in an altered light. The 1961 playreading committee report recommended that the committee's name be changed to the more authoritative "programming committee" because "it is no longer a group of ladies reading plays for their own entertainment" (Molly Golby, "Report of the Playreading Committee," AAGM, June 1961, 4). Whether or not past chairwomen like Francess Halpenny viewed it in that way, the new name made sense to the membership, and the motion carried, although the choice was not always adhered to.
64 Terry, "Report of the Playreading Committee," AAGM, 15 June 1963. While she was playreading committee chair in 1962, Terry explained that Coach House programming consisted of "contemporary works, including Canadian, plus a lively delve into the classics, mostly English" (Terry, "Report of the Playreading Committee," AAGM, 9 June 1962, 1).
65 Halpenny, "Shall we join the ladies?"
66 Alumnae. "Building Fund Appeal," July 1961, 1.
67 The exact days of the weeks changed slightly from one season to the next, but in September 1963 the club decided to shift production runs to Tuesday through Saturday in order to free up underattended Sundays (AAGM, 11 September 1963). These Sundays were eventually filled with their popular evening reading series.
68 Golby, "Report of the Playreading Committee," AAGM, June 1961, 1–2.
69 Whittaker, "Notes on things," *Globe and Mail*, 26 March 1957, 12.
70 UADC "History," 1963, 2.
71 Whittaker, "The Bluestockings have a blueprint," *Globe and Mail*, 22 July 1961, 11.
72 Whittaker, "Toronto's Little Theatres Find Their Place Together," *Globe and Mail*, 17 November 1962, 13.
73 "UADC [history document], 1968, 3.
74 Alumnae, "In 1918 a group of women with a common love …" [History document], October 1963.

75 "Pioneering Bluestockings launch Toronto's next theatre," *Ocean Times*, 5 December 1961.
76 Ralph Thomas, "Alumnae Players Finally Find a Home," *Toronto Star*, 2 November 1962.
77 Whittaker, "Showbusiness," *Globe and Mail*, 31 July 1957, 9.
78 Lorna F. Rogers, Publicity Report, AAGM, 9 June 1962, 3.
79 AAGM, 13 June 1964.
80 Harry Bruce, "Home at last," *Maclean's*, 17 November 1962, 97.
81 Whittaker, "The Bluestockings have a blueprint."
82 Nathan Cohen, "At last a home for the UADC," *Toronto Star*, 14 November 1962.
83 Cohen, "At last a home for the UADC."
84 Nathan Cohen, "Each time I read …," *Toronto Star*, week of 14 December 1963, 42.
85 "UADC [history document] 1968, 2.
86 Halpenny, "Shall we join the ladies?" In 1963, Cohen even "reprimanded them when they did not meet his programming expectations of producing enough plays by Pinter and Frisch" (Pamela Terry Beckwith, letter to Nathan Cohen. 8 March 1963). When Pamela Terry wrote to him noting that they had already been attempting to secure the amateur rights for several of their plays, Cohen replied, "You see, you again prove my point of the enterprise and initiative of the University Alumnae. Here I thought I was bringing something to your attention, and once again the Alumnae was ahead of me. That is one of the reasons why the Alumnae is such a favoured dramatic group of mine" (Cohen, letter to Pamela Terry Beckwith, 12 March 1963).
87 Molly Thom, "From Coach House to Firehall. DRAFT," note to Robin C. Whittaker, 23 August 2009.
88 MacDonald, "Glorious absurdities,".
89 Whittaker, "Showbusiness: Ionesco available," *Globe and Mail*, 1 May 1959, 11.
90 "Ionescu the rage on stage," *Globe and Mail*, 18 April 1959, 13.
91 MacDonald, "Glorious absurdities."
92 "Ionescu the rage on stage."
93 Whittaker, "Showbusiness: Ionesco available."
94 MacDonald, "Glorious absurdities."
95 Whittaker, "Showbusiness: Ionesco available."
96 David Peddie, *CJBC Views the Shows*, 3 May 1959, 2.
97 Whittaker, "Showbusiness: Ionesco available."
98 Peddie, *CJBC Views the Shows*, 3 May 1959.
99 Nathan Cohen, "A disturbing double bill," *Star*, 23 April 1959.
100 Cohen, "A disturbing double bill."
101 Peddie, *CJBC Views the Shows*, 3 May 1959.
102 Whittaker, "Showbusiness: Ionesco available."
103 Whittaker, "Ionesco provides destructive study," *Globe and Mail*, 9 May 1959, 13.
104 Peddie, *CJBC Views the Shows*, 3 May 1959.
105 Martin, *Still Hunting*.
106 Warren Wilson, "Give me a pain-killer," *Varsity*, 2 December 1959, 5.
107 Even Wilson admitted that Whittaker's design was "admirable, although the lighting was too warm to adequately suggest the bleakness of the scene" Ever helpful, he added, "Perhaps it would have been more effective if the lights had been dimmed right out of the final scene, rather than closing with so abrupt a curtain" (Wilson, "Give me a pain-killer"). Wilson's own play *Endgame Revisited* was given a reading in a "dark, dilapidated barn-house on Asquith Ave. [where] a respectable cross section of campus literati […] launched a popular form of

entertainment – a vocal magazine" (Elmo Ciprietti, "Top drawer at the first floor," *Varsity*, 9 March 1960, 4–5).

108 Wilson, "Give me a pain-killer."

109 Whittaker, "Theatre Guild seeking Robertson Davies play," *Globe and Mail*, 23 November 1959, 25.

110 D.M., "Poet Reaney turns playwright," *Varsity*, 13 January 1960, 3.

111 Antony Ferry, "*Endgame*'s writer dispenser of gloom," *Toronto Star*, 3 December 1959.

112 Ferry, "*Endgame*'s writer dispenser of gloom."

113 Kirstie Bosanquet, "Two views of Beckett's *Endgame*," *Globe and Mail*, 9 December 1959, 6.

114 Ferry, "Two views of Beckett's *Endgame*," *Globe and Mail*, 9 December 1959, 6.

115 Bosanquet, "Two views of Beckett's *Endgame*," *Globe and Mail*, 9 December 1959, 6.

116 Lotta Dempsey, "Last four on earth intruiging subject," *Toronto Star*, 21 December 1959.

117 Whittaker reported a decade later that Samuel Zacks, a Toronto art collector and friend of Samuel Beckett, wrote to Beckett in reference to Whittaker's direction of *Endgame*, saying that the "first play I saw of yours was *Endgame*. It made a great impression on me and for days I kept wondering if you were a positivist or a negativist, because it gave me a feeling that nothing really mattered but why do we continue and I think you have communicated this message on many fronts to thousands of people who have read or seen your plays" (Whittaker, "Beckett, Zacks: a friendship eased painful months," *Globe and Mail*, 14 November 1970, 29).

118 Virginia Conner, "Crest climbs right out of the trough with Albee and Beckett," *Varsity Weekend Review*, 13 October 1961, 4–5.

119 "*Intimate Relations* embarrassing," *Varsity Weekend Review*, 1 December 1961, 4.

120 Warren Wilson, "*Rhinoceros* at Civic Square," *Varsity Weekend Review*, 1 December 1961, 4–5.

121 Ralph Thomas, "Wilson returns to Hart House with excellent *Pantagleize*," *Varsity*, 2 February 1961, 6.

122 Tony Robinow, "Three interesting moderns presented by the Coach House Theatre," *Varsity Weekend Review*, 17 November 1961, 4.

123 Warren Wilson, "*Rhinoceros* at Civic Square," *Varsity Weekend Review*, 1 December 1961, 4–5.

124 Peter Halsall and William Mitchell, "Ionesco's *Amédée* good farce, but what does it mean?," *Varsity Weekend Review*, 1 December 1961, 5.

125 Rose MacDonald, "*Caretaker* pleases at Coach House," *Toronto Telegram*, n.d.

126 Ralph Hicklin, "A bum's career is well evoked," *Globe and Mail*, 29 February 1964, 16.

127 Alumnae, "Theatre Listings" [press release for *Old Times*], March 1974.

128 Morriss, "The Critics Say," *Globe and Mail*, 4 July 1964, 14.

129 Helen Carscallen, Theatre Manager's Report, 13 June 1964.

130 Arnold Rockman, "A masterpiece of nonsense," *Toronto Star*, n.d.

131 Michael Barton (Polley) would later marry Diana McMillan and raise the actor and filmmaker Sarah Polley, whose film about her parents offers a brief glimpse of the set of this production of *The Caretaker*.

132 Don Ward's children Robin and Lynn were part of the folk group the Allen-Ward Trio. "Actor's death delays opening at Coach House," *Globe and Mail*, 13 October 1965, 1.

133 Hicklin, "A bum's career is well evoked."

134 Tony Advokaat, "Alumnae shows versatility with Pinter," *Varsity*, 6 March 1964, R9.

135 Hicklin, "A bum's career is well evoked."

136 Advokaat, "Alumnae shows versatility with Pinter."

137 The reason for Gielgud's attendance at Alumnae's *The Caretaker*, according to a press release, was that Ewer had met Gielgud during the Second World War and Gielgud had encouraged him to apply for a scholarship at the Royal Academy of Dramatic Art in London, which he did, successfully. Clearly, the forty-one-year-old star was still on the rise. As reported at one Alumnae meeting, Ewer held the professional rights to produce *The Caretaker* and "he insists that he will stage a rival production unless he is [a] paid star of ours. Molly [Thom] is to offer him an $80 gratuity for the run" (AMM, 22 January 1964). Alumnae noted in another release that two backers of the film version of *The Caretaker*, Richard Burton and Elizabeth Taylor, were in Toronto at the time to see Anouilh's *Becket* at the University Theatre (Whittaker, "*Guardian*'s critic to be adjudicator," *Globe and Mail*, 25 February 1964. 12). It is not know whether they attended Alumnae's production.
138 AAGM, 13 June 1964. With that fiscal year's income totalling $6,763.12 and expenditures totaling $6,669.90, Alumnae netted $93.22 over the year. Added to their existing balance of $235.31, the Club finished the season with $328.52 in the bank.
139 Whittaker, "New theatre, play will open Friday," *Globe and Mail*, 1 April 1964, 14; "Floating stage drops anchor," *Globe and Mail*, 17 October 1964, 13.
140 AAGM, 19 June 1965.
141 Halpenny, Prospectus, "The Alumnae Theatre."
142 AAGM, 19 June 1965.
143 AEM, 7 July 1965.
144 AEM, 10 June 1967.
145 Because the production of Jean-Claude Van Itallie's *America Hurrah* required an unusually high number of set and prop pieces, the crew was provided with a seven-page handwritten set of instructions for obtaining, verifying, and dealing with furniture and props. It noted that furniture and props usually came from members' houses unless there was a specific rental budget for them and that these pieces should not be brought into the theatre unless the director and designer had approved it, and not before the first technical rehearsal. If any pieces were borrowed from a shop, the proprietor would receive two complimentary tickets and program credit.
146 "Actor's death delays opening at Coach House."
147 Whittaker, "Opening of play honours performer," *Globe and Mail*, 20 October 1965, 15.
148 AEM, 9 December 1965.
149 Golby, "Report of the Playreading Committee," AAGM, June 1961, 3.
150 Golby, letter to Emanuel Wax, 26 October 1960.
151 Golby, letter to Emanuel Wax, 22 September 1961.
152 Golby, letter to Emanuel Wax, 22 September 1961.
153 Rogers, Publicity Report, AAGM, 9 June 1962, 1.
154 Rose MacDonald, "Three gems of satire," *Toronto Telegram*, 6 October 1961.
155 Rogers, Publicity Report, AAGM, 9 June 1962, 1.
156 Tony Robinow [Robineau], "Coach House theatre for few," *Varsity Weekend Reviewed*, 6 November 1961, 5.
157 MacDonald, "Three gems of satire."
158 Robinow, "Coach House theatre for few."
159 David C. Humphreys, "Beckett revived by Coach House," *Varsity Weekend Review*, 27 October 1961, 4.
160 Lawrence Stone, "One reading found pleasing, other boring," *Globe and Mail*, 26 October 1961, 34.
161 Stone, "One reading found pleasing, other boring."

162 Humphreys, "Beckett revived by Coach House."
163 Jack Winter, "New play included in drama reading," *Toronto Star*, 16 November 1961.
164 Whittaker, "Library, stage, theatre, play make news," *Globe and Mail*, 16 November 1961, 31.
165 Tony Robinow, [Robineau], "Three interesting moderns presented by the Coach House Theatre," *Varsity Weekend Review*, 17 November 1961, 4.
166 Robinow, [Robineau], "Three interesting moderns presented by the Coach House Theatre."
167 AMM, 27 November 1961.
168 Rogers, Publicity Report, 9 June 1962, 2.
169 AMM, 12 September 1966. Thom later adapted Ashford's novel for production at Alumnae's Firehall Studio in winter 1974, calling it *The Young Visters or, Mr. Salteena's Play*.
170 AAGM, 15 June 1968.
171 AAGM, 10 June 1967.
172 AMM, 9 November 1966.
173 AAGM, 10 June 1967.
174 Urjo Kareda, "University dramatic club far below usual standard," *Toronto Star*, 22 October 1971.
175 The mailout included a poem in homage to Percy Bysshe Shelley: "To Our Shelley / Hail to thee, Bysshe Shelley! / So honour'd never wert – / At Maplewood shalt hear it / Alumnae taking part / In profound scenes of thy domesticated art. / [...] / "Better than all measures / Of delightful sound, / Better than all treasures / That in books are found," / Our skills to Shelley's words three Sundays shall compound."
176 Urjo Kareda, "*Mixed Doubles* playlets welcome change in revues," *Toronto Star*, 5 February 1972, 50.
177 Urjo Kareda, "*Catonsville Nine* an exceptional testament," *Toronto Star*, 7 February 1972.
178 Kareda, "*Mixed Doubles* playlets welcome change in revues."
179 CODL newsletter, June 1958.
180 "Sardou play will open new Alumnae Coach House," *Globe and Mail*, 14 June 1958, 13.
181 CODL newsletter, June 1958.
182 Thom, "From Coach House to Firehall. DRAFT." Martha Mann's father Fred Mann, a prominent Toronto amateur actor, had introduced her to Alumnae, and when they heard she wanted to design and could paint she began an active association with the club as designer, executive member, and playreading committee member throughout the Coach House years (Mann Southgate, interview with Whittaker, 25 October 2017). She also designed many shows with Hart House Theatre and the Grand Theatre in London, Ontario.
183 Whittaker, "Showbusiness," *Globe and Mail*, 18 June 1958, 21.
184 Rose MacDonald, "'Merry evening' staged by Alumnae players," *Toronto Telegram*, 3 October 1958, 47.
185 "Alumnae open with comedy," *Toronto Telegram*, 1 October 1958, 18.
186 Douglas, "Restoration comedy, *Varsity*, 6 October 1958, 5.
187 Arthur Brydon, "Coach House plays good fun to watch," *Globe and Mail*, 9 October 1958, 33.
188 MacDonald, "'Merry evening' staged by Alumnae players."
189 Brydon, "Coach House plays good fun to watch."
190 MacDonald, "'Merry evening' staged by Alumnae players."
191 Douglas, "Restoration comedy."
192 Brydon, "Coach House plays good fun to watch."
193 MacDonald, "'Merry evening' staged by Alumnae players."
194 Rogers, Publicity Report, AMM, 9 June 1962, 2.

195 AMM, 27 November 1961.
196 Whittaker, "Gallery Molière," *Globe and Mail*, 6 December 1961, 11.
197 AAGM, 10 June 1967.
198 Quoted in Whittaker, "Going half a century, drama club optimistic," *Globe and Mail*, 16 October, 196. 12.
199 Along with *Viet Rock*, Alumnae had considered two other "very contemporary" plays created by New York's off-off Broadway group Café La Mama, founded in 1961: Jean-Claude-van Itallie's *America Hurrah* and another play called *U.S.* (AMM, 3 April 1968). But they had set their sights on Jon Gay's *The Beggars' Opera* as a "jubilee special" to open the season before concluding they could not afford it (Agatha Leonard, Report of the Programme Committee, 7 June 1969).
200 Margaret MacAulay, letter to DDF Professional Direction Committee, 1 April 1969.
201 Whittaker, "The Weekend: Things to see and do in Toronto," *Globe and Mail*, 25 October 1968, 14.
202 Terry, "Production Notes," *Viet Rock*, 21–2.
203 Whittaker, "Numbers game by city's most 'in' group," *Globe and Mail*, 7 October 1968, 16.
204 Whittaker, "The Weekend," *Globe and Mail*, 25 October 1968, 14.
205 Whittaker, "The Weekend," *Globe and Mail*, 18 October 1968, 11
206 Whittaker, "The Weekend," *Globe and Mail*, 25 October 1968, 14.
207 Whittaker, "The Weekend," *Globe and Mail*, 18 October 1968, 11.
208 Kaspars Dzeguze, "primates progress … crimea to viet nam," *Varsity*, 1 November 1968, R10.
209 Whittaker, "*Viet Rock*: beautifully integrated," 18 October 1968, 13.
210 Don Rubin, "A curiosity piece for the avant-garde – that's *Viet Rock*," *Toronto Star*, n.d.
211 R.H. (Ralph Hicklin), "*Viet Rock*" strikes no sparks for Alumnae," *Toronto Telegram*, 25 October 1968.
212 Whittaker, "*Viet Rock*: beautifully integrated."
213 Whittaker, "*Viet Rock*: beautifully integrated."
214 Herman Surkis, "*Viet Rock*," *Excalibur* [York University], 31 October 1968.
215 Surkis, "*Viet Rock*."
216 Whittaker, "*Viet Rock*: beautifully integrated."
217 R.H., "*Viet Rock*" strikes no sparks for Alumnae."
218 Whittaker, "*Viet Rock*: beautifully integrated."
219 Rubin, "A curiosity piece for the avant-garde – that's *Viet Rock*."
220 R.H., "*Viet Rock*" strikes no sparks for Alumnae."
221 Wasserman, "George Ryga," 24.
222 Kaspars Dzeguze, "The irony of Rita Joe fails to project," *Globe and Mail*, 13 Noember 1969, 11.
223 Jamie Portman, "Ecstasy of Rita Joe still manages to shock and scourge," *Vancouver Province*, 12 April 1976, 10.
224 Martin Stone (Oscar Ryan), "Theatre Review," *Canadian Tribune*, 19 November 1969, 10.
225 Lorne Fienberg, "Ugh!," *Varsity*, 21 November 1969, R10.
226 Nathan Cohen, "*The Ecstasy of Rita Joe* is ridiculously inept," *Toronto Star*, 13 November 1969, 34. In a colonial voice, Cohen added this was in the context of Quebec sovereignty "steadily gathering in pressure and momentum." He called the fact of Alumnae's *Rita Joe* opening on the same day as the chiefs' demand a "regrettable coincidence" despite the "worthy intentions" of Ryga's script. The review goes on to outline the bitter and growing divide between Indigenous people and the Canadian government before comparing the flashbacks in

Ryga's script to the "worst excesses of the Norman Corwin era on American TV and the *Stage* series on the CBC."

227 Cohen, "*The Ecstasy of Rita Joe* is ridiculously inept."

228 Dzeguze, "The irony of *Rita Joe* fails to project."

229 Quoted in Kaspars Dzeguze, "Indian Duke Redbird turns to the soft, cerebral sell," *Globe and Mail*, 10 November 1969, 15.

230 Dzeguze, "The irony of *Rita Joe* fails to project."

231 Cohen, "*The Ecstasy of Rita Joe* is ridiculously inept." Owing to the importance of the play's Toronto premiere, cast biographies were included in the program, an unusual occurrence for Alumnae programs at the time. The cast featured several names of note. Jacqueline White, a CBC radio and TV actor who had played the voice of Howdy Doody, played the School Teacher (Alumnae, "Jacqueline White [School Teacher]," Biography, November 1969). Alan Bleviss, as the Magistrate, was a University of Alberta and National Theatre School graduate who had worked at Neptune Theatre, the Manitoba Theatre Centre, and CBC radio and television, as well as other professional theatres. Sheila MacDonald, then a high school history theatre arts teacher, played Rita's sister. And Sol Mandlsohn as Mr. Homer and Ian Orr as the Priest had both accrued a good deal of nonprofessionalizing theatre credits over the years, including with Alumnae.

232 Dzeguze, "The irony of *Rita Joe* fails to project."

233 Stone, "Theatre Review."

234 Fienberg, "Ugh!"

235 Dzeguze, "The irony of *Rita Joe* fails to project."

236 Kay Martin's stage manager prompt book for Alumnae's production of *The Ecstasy Rita Joe*, typed on legal paper, is extant in Alumnae's collection. The second page bears typed "Staging" and "Opening" notes that resemble those published in Wasserman's *Modern Canadian Plays*, vol. 1, anthology. Twenty years to the week after Alumnae's production, in November 1989, the McGilligan Group produced *Rita Joe* at Hart House Theatre; the advertising called this the "Professional Toronto Premiere of a Canadian Classic." They had already presented it as an Equity Showcase production at Toronto's Harbourfront Studio Theatre, 19–29 April 1989. Judith McGilligan directed both the Equity Showcase and the public production, the latter of which was billed as the "first time the play has been staged with a Native cast." ("The Professional Toronto Premiere of a Canadian Classic: *The Ecstasy of Rita Joe*," postcard flyer, November 1989.) However, referring to a Prairie Theatre Exchange production in Winnipeg, Wasserman writes that the play was produced in 1981 with "Native performers in all the Native roles" (Wasserman, *Modern Canadian Plays*, vol. 1, 24).

237 "The Anti-Defamation League of B'nai B'rith," *ADL Intercom*, December–January 1971, 6.

238 Terry, Report of the Programming and Play Reading Committee, 15 June 1963.

239 Agatha Leonard, Report of the Programme Committee, 15 June 1968. Securing the rights to produce the plays they wanted was often a struggle. At the September 1966 general meeting it was reported that the programming committee was running into challenges with securing rights for plays with "casts of thousands" and plays that would be "star vehicles [with] 15 walk-ons" (AAGM, 12 September 1966). By the end of the season, committee chair Agatha Leonard reported that they could not secure rights to the American and British plays the committee had selected. They "seriously considered" O'Neill's *Mourning Becomes Electra* as a Centennial project, but Mrs. O'Neill, they reported, had "permanently withdrawn all performing rights for non-professional groups" (AAGM, 10 June 1967).

240 Leonard, Report of the Programme Committee, 7 June 1969.

241 AAGM, 10 January 1968.
242 Halpenny, "Shall we join the ladies?"
243 Gordon Jocelyn, "*Little Malcolm and His Struggle* fascinates Toronto," *Montreal Gazette*, 11 May 1968, 17.
244 Molly Thom quoted in Whittaker, "Going half a century, drama club optimistic," *Globe and Mail*, 16 October 1968, 12.
245 Margaret MacAulay, letter to membership, 8 October 1968.
246 Alumnae, 7 June 1969 annual meeting announcement, n.d.

Chapter 4

1 Urjo Kareda, "Our most creative theatre group opens in a new home Thursday," *Toronto Star*, 14 October 1972.
2 Deborah Hodgkinson, "Women's theatre alive at Firehall," *Ryersonian*, 31 January 1975, 11.
3 Quoted in Liane Heller, "'Inspired madwomen' produced stars," *Toronto Star*, 30 April 1984, D2.
4 Carol Palmer, Treasurer's Report, AAGM, 17 June 1995.
5 Palmer, Treasurer's Report, AAGM, 21 June 1998.
6 Kareda, "Our most creative theatre group opens in a new home Thursday."
7 Molly Thom, letter to Sid Adilman, 29 June 1972.
8 Alumnae, "Firehall Theatre Renamed" [Press Release], 10 July 1978.
9 Alumnae, AMM, June 1978.
10 Alumnae. "Firehall Theatre Renamed."
11 AEM, 25 May 1987.
12 Kay Montgomery, letter to City Director of Real Estate, 10 September 1991.
13 Alumnae, "Alumnae Theatre Company," Draft, 20 May 1996.
14 Leonard, "Alumnae Theatre: The Women Speak," July 2007, reposted on *The Alumnae Theatre Company's Blog*, 5 January 2012.
15 Sharma, *In the Meantime*, 148.
16 Heller, "'Inspired madwomen' produced stars."
17 Shaw, Program Committee Report, 17 June 1995.
18 Joan Shaw, Program Committee Report for Alumnae annual general meeting, 17 June 1995.
19 Barbara Larose, "Mainstage Programming Committee," In AAGM, 24 June 2018.
20 Kee, "The Alumnae Theatre," c. 1981.
21 Heller, "'Inspired madwomen' produced stars."
22 Hodgkinson, "Women's theatre alive at Firehall."
23 Urjo Kareda, "Toronto's theatre signpost is pointing closer to home," *Toronto Star*, c. September 1974.
24 Urjo Kareda, "Alternative theatre offers hope for the future." *Toronto Star*, 16 September 1972, 63.
25 Quoted in Heller, "'Inspired madwomen' produced stars."
26 Vit Wagner, "Duo borrows big from Smothers Brothers' style," *Toronto Star*, 27 November 1987, D12.
27 Wagner, "Duo borrows big from Smothers Brothers' style."
28 Tina McCulloch, Publicity/Marketing Report, AAGM, 9 June 2002.
29 Nan Hirst (program director), letter to membership, August 1985.
30 On the second Sunday during the run of their production of Aphra Behn's *The Rover* in April 1976, Alumnae celebrated the twenty-fifth anniversary of Whittaker's direction of his first

Alumnae show, Shaw's *In Good King Charles's Golden Days*, with actors John Colicos and Ron Hartmann returning to honour him and his "long a fruitful association" with the club (Alumnae, Press Release, April 1976). When Whittaker left his position at the *Globe and Mail* in September 1975 after twenty-six years, the article announcing his retirement quoted him attributing Canadian theatre's choice to (finally) eschew "transplanted American culture" to the Vietnam War, the Nixon administration, and government subsidies, no doubt referring to the federal Local Initiative Program grants that supported Canada's professionalizing alternative theatres in their early years ("Whittaker retires, Fraser and O'Toole to write on drama and dance," *Globe and Mail*, 13 September 1975, 23). But Whittaker knew that nationalistic professional theatre did not entirely define the field. Never again would Alumnae benefit from criticism like his, Cohen's, or Kareda's.

31 "Professional Director's Award Goes to Jordan Merkur," *Toronto Tonight*, 10–24 May 1990.

32 ASGM, 9 July 1990. Initially, there were concerns, especially at the board level, where support was split (3 for, 3 against, 3 abstained) as to whether the directing award should exist at all (ABMM, 11 June 1990). Would the initiative draw Alumnae too far into "professional theatre," and would the audiences they attract simply "follow the director" elsewhere? Would the director simply "treat members as 'amateurs'"? (ASGM, 9 July 1990). Although some directors had been receiving a $200 to $500 dollar honorarium before the honorarium was removed completely (ABMM, 5 May 1997), some asked whether the act of giving money to a particular group might "cause division in the Company" (ASGM, 9 July 1990). Would giving the award to a man defeat their mandate of fostering female talent? Would outside money "come with strings attached" that could compromise Alumnae's "autonomy" and even affect their charitable status? Would this affect Alumnae's relationship with Equity? After "some debate," the motion carried in a vote of 27 to 20 "that the Alumnae Theatre Company approve an award to be given regularly, preferably annually, to a promising director, preferably female, to direct a play in the Company's regular season and that funding be secured from outside sources" (ASGM, 9 July 1990). A committee was struck to move forward with the idea.

33 Genevieve Kierans, "The old with the new," *Toronto Tonight*, 26 April–10 May 1990.

34 Alumnae, "Director's Award Guidelines," ABMM, 3 September 1991.

35 In 1996–97 and 1997–98, the Bickell Foundation provided $5,000 across both seasons for the director's award (ABMM, 12 February 1996), and again funded it in 1998–99 (ABMM, 13 January 1998) before denying the request for 2000–1 (ABMM, 17 October 2001).

36 ABMM, 11 September 2000.

37 Sarah Hood, "Seven decades of dedication: Alumnae Theatre continues to thrive through nearly seventy years of transformation and acclaimed productions," *Toronto Theatre*, Spring 1988, 14–15.

38 Alumnae had sought the royalties a year earlier without success.

39 Bryan Johnson, "Theatre," *Globe and Mail*, 12 October 1977, A8.

40 Bryan Johnson, "Ayckbourn goes lethal, loses humor," *Globe and Mail*, 20 September 1977, 15.

41 "Theatre," *Varsity*, 21 October 1977, 14.

42 Ray Conlogue, "Tobacco gets into the arts," *Globe and Mail*, 27 March 1982, E11.

43 "Theatre," *Varsity*, 24 March 1982, 24.

44 Ray Conlogue, "*Kicking Inside* inconsistent," *Globe and Mail*, 6 April 1985, E13.

45 Conlogue, "*Kicking Inside* inconsistent."

46 AAGM, Report from the publicity chairman, 14 June 1986.

47 Ann Sargent, quoted in Hood, "Seven decades of dedication," 14-15.

48 Pat Fisher, Production Report for *The Last Real Summer*, 19 November 1984.

49 Pat McCarthy (Alumnae president), letter to *Now Magazine*, 5 December 2000.
50 Michael Hollet (*Now Magazine* editor/publisher), form email to Suzanne Courtney (Alumnae secretary), 7 December 2000.
51 PJ Hammond, Executive Producer's Report, AGMM, 9 June 2002.
52 Marci McDonald, "The arts are rescuing a gray old hobo of a street," *Toronto Star*, 22 July 1972, 37.
53 Zena Cherry, "O'Casey played in the firehall," *Globe and Mail*, 19 October 1972, W2.
54 Donald Jones, "The 'oldest and proudest' Toronto theatrical company," *Toronto Star*, 23 September 1989, M4.
55 Cherry, "O'Casey played in the firehall."
56 McKenzie Porter, "The Rev. Harry S. D. Robinson …" *Toronto Telegram*, 20 October 1969.
57 John Palmer, letter to Molly Thom, 23 October 1972.
58 Frank Michael, "A new barn cannot stimulate creative juices of sacred cow," *Canadian Jewish News*, 3 November 1972.
59 Whittaker, "Unofficial Moliére festival at Hart House," *Globe and Mail*, 16 October 1972, 23.
60 Martin Stone (Oscar Ryan), "Red stars for Dublin," *Canadian Tribune*. c. October 1972.
61 Stone, "Red stars for Dublin."
62 Urjo Kareda, "Firehall Theatre launched," *Toronto Star*, 20 October 1972.
63 Nigel Spencer, "*The Plough and the Stars*," *Toronto Theatre*, 3 November 1972.
64 Kareda, "Firehall Theatre launched."
65 Whittaker, "O'Casey play makes timely fare," *Globe and Mail*, 20 October 1972, 14.
66 Whittaker, "Around Toronto this week," *Globe and Mail*, 27 October 1972, T2.
67 Anne Weldon Tait, an Honours English graduate from U of T's Victoria College, started her work with Alumnae in Pirandello's *As You Desire Me* as an actor, having been lured to the company by classmate Molly Thom. Tait appeared in and directed several Alumnae plays in the early 1960s. On staff at CBC television, first in children's programming (*The Canadian Howdy Doody Show*) and then in drama, Tait returned to Alumnae in the late 1960s to write and direct several readings at the Maplewood Avenue Coach House and then the Firehall Studio while pursuing her Masters degree in English at U of T (Weldon Tait, interview with Whittaker, 19 October 2017).
68 Whittaker, "An Arthurian legend in platform reading," *Globe and Mail*, 8 January 1973, 14.
69 Anne Tait, email to Robin C. Whittaker, 10 March 2018.
70 Murray Pomerance, "We turned up later …," *Walrus*, 26 February 1973.
71 Urjo Kareda, "New theatre is lovely but first play isn't," *Toronto Star*, 6 January 1973, 76.
72 Pomerance, "We turned up later …"
73 Member Elizabeth Mascall translated the world premiere in English of Anne Hébert's influential Québécois play *Le Temps Sauvage* for the Mainstage; it ran in November 1972. The production featured Margaret Spence's warm, rustic costume designs, which complimented Hébert's oppressive rural atmosphere (see Robin C. Whittaker, "Un/Disciplined Re/Collections"). CBC radio producer Ron Solloway directed Clare Boothe Luce's 1936 "barbed comedy" *The Women* with an eighteen-woman cast by which, according to the *Toronto Star*'s Harvey Chusid, "Women's Lib was dealt a severe blow" (Chusid, "*The Women*: Unabashed attack on 'weaker sex,'" *Toronto Star*, 16 February 1973, 33). Pamela Terry returned to Alumnae to direct Edward Albee's "most adventurous experiment with form," an attempt to simulate the effect of a musical structure. This 1968 work linked *Box* and *Quotations from Chairman Mao Tse-Tung*. Kareda described it as "well planned and thoughtful, quite good though not good enough to ward off the boredom" (Urjo Kareda, "Two theatres experimenting with abstracts," *Toronto Star*, 13 March 1973).

74 Whittaker, "Gorki drama strains actors' skills," *Globe and Mail*, 30 March 1973, 14.
75 Urjo Kareda, "Play moves in right direction," *Toronto Star*, 30 March 1973.
76 Urjo Kareda, "An amazing theatre piece at Firehall," *Toronto Star*, 19 October 1973, E8.
77 At the time, the Trinity College Dramatic Society (TCDS) wrote to *Varsity* to dispute the claim that Alumnae had staged the English-language Canadian premiere of *Kaspar*. *Varsity*'s "Watsup" entertainment-listings editor wrote that "it has been rather vehemently brought to my attention that in the Spring of 1971, the TCDS put on a full production of *Kaspar* in Cartwright Hall. Hesitating to get into distinctions between amateur and professional productions (ones you have to pay for) here the issue may rest – Watsup having been partially absolved of unfair spotlighting. A larger point emerges in that the *Varsity* would very much like to cover the diverse range of theatrical activities now operating on campus, if those concerned would advise us of SHOWTIME, DATE AND PLACE" ("Theatre," *Varsity*, 26 October 1973).
78 Although this definition of professional is thin given that Alumnae and TCDS were both nonprofessionalizing companies, it may be that TCDS did not publicize the production widely enough. I could find no evidence, even in *Varsity*, that *Kaspar* was produced in Toronto before Alumnae offered it.
79 "Theatre," *Toronto Life*, October 1973.
80 Kareda, "An amazing theatre piece at Firehall."
81 David McCaughna, "*Kaspar*," *Toronto Citizen*, 9–22 November 1973.
82 Kareda, "An amazing theatre piece at Firehall."
83 McCaughna, "*Kaspar.*"
84 Kareda, "An amazing theatre piece at Firehall."
85 Whittaker, "*Kaspar*: Shadings of meaning," *Globe and Mail*, 19 October 1973, 14.
86 Allan M. Gould, Letter to the Editor, "*Kaspar*," *Globe and Mail*, 20 October 1973, 7.
87 Gould, Letter to the Editor, "*Kaspar*."
88 Whittaker, "*Kaspar*: Shadings of meaning."
89 Kareda, "An amazing theatre piece at Firehall."
90 "Terry, Pamela Anne (Beckwith)" [Obituary], *Times Colonist*, 28 November 2006.
91 "*Old Times*," *Toronto Calendar*, n.d.
92 Urjo Kareda, "Pinter's *Old Times* is an intriguing play," *Toronto Star*, 22 March 1974, E12.
93 Urjo Kareda, "Champion Pinter," *Toronto Star*, 19 March 1974; David McCaughna, "Pinter's *Old Times* is a superb play," *Toronto Citizen*, n.d.
94 Kareda, "Champion Pinter."
95 Byron Laviolette, "*Wit*," *eye weekly*, 29 September 2008.
96 Ray Conlogue, "Meet me in another theatre," *Globe and Mail*, 7 December 1989, C9.
97 Conlogue, "Meet me in another theatre."
98 Alumnae's *Largo Desolato* files include a stack of dramaturgical press material covering daily developments in Czechoslovakia in 1989, including highlighted passages about Havel's involvement and the December 1989 issue of *Maclean's* with the cover proclaiming "Prague's Autumn Revolt." The play appeared on the PBS television series *Great Performances* the following May (television listings, *Globe and Mail*, 5 May 1990, 33).
99 "Arts & Entertainment across Canada," *Globe and Mail*, 21 March 1990, C12.
100 Robert Everett-Green, "New operas tackle a poet, a god, and Emma Goldman," *Globe and Mail*, 13 January 1990, C1, C3.
101 Brian Davis, "The raw power of *Red Emma*," *Canadian Tribune*, 2 April 1990, 10.
102 Davis, "The raw power of *Red Emma*."
103 Carol Bolt, Letter To Whom It May Concern [at Alumnae Theatre Company], 17 June 1990.

104 Bolt, Letter To Whom It May Concern," 17 June 1990.
105 Ray Conlogue, "An elegant, whimsical fable," *Globe and Mail*, 28 April 1990, C8.
106 Genevieve Kierans, "The old with the new," *Toronto Tonight*, 26 April–10 May 1990.
107 Kierans, "The old with the new."
108 Margaret Edgar, Production Report for *Reckless*, ABMM, 11 June 1990.
109 Jon Kaplan, "Flashes of beauty glimmer in *Jewel*," *Now Magazine*, 10–16 May 1990.
110 Patterson, Alex. "*Reckless* wears out welcome," *Metropolis*, 3 May 1990, 3.
111 Molly Thom, "*Thirteen Hands* report by Molly Thom (director)," *Alumination*, May 1995.
112 Christopher Winsor, "A novel approach: Acclaimed CanLit queen Carol Shields' *Thirteen Hands*," *eye weekly*, 4 May 1995, 37.
113 Carol Palmer, Treasurers Report, AAGM, 17 June 1995.
114 Vit Wagner, "Esther Hockin trumps in Carol Shields play," *Toronto Star*, 28 April 1995.
115 Molly Thom, Audience Development Report, AAGM, 17 June 1995.
116 Alumnae board meeting minutes. 23 January 1995.
117 Richard Ouzounian, "*Thirteen Hands* by Carol Shields (Alumnae Theatre)," CBC, 28 April 1995.
118 Jon Kaplan, "Strong suit," *Now Magazine*, 4–10 May 1995, 61.
119 Winsor, "A novel approach."
120 Ouzounian, "*Thirteen Hands* by Carol Shields."
121 Winsor, "A novel approach."
122 Wagner, "Esther Hockin trumps in Carol Shields play."
123 Therese Beaupre, "Difficulties overcome in massive production," *Varsity*, 7 October 1977, 13.
124 Martin Stevens, "The York Cycle: From Procession to Play," *Leeds Studies in English*, n.s. 6 (1972), 55.
125 Stevens, "The York Cycle," 55.
126 Beaupre, "Difficulties overcome in massive production."
127 Barbara Palmer et al., "The York Cycle in Performance: Toronto and York," *Early Theatre* vol. 1 (1998), 164.
128 ABMM, 1 April 1997.
129 Cherry, "O'Casey played in the firehall."
130 AEM, 4 November 1974.
131 Kareda, "Our most creative theatre group opens in a new home Thursday."
132 Margaret Edgar, Report on Subscriptions, AAGM, 20 June 1987.
133 Jane Carnwath, interview with Whittaker, 19 October 2017.
134 Gillian Pritchard, "Down from the pedestal: On the eve of its 60th birthday, the 'Alum' is shedding its elitist image. There'll be some changes made," *Scene Changes*, September 1978, 10, 19, 27.
135 Nicholson et al., *The Ecologies of Amateur Theatre*, 158.
136 This view might be further adjusted in the digital age to include not only leisure time consumption but also leisure time production of Web content (both non-monetized and monetized), thus increasing the urgency of the question about what is being produced and how it serves the capitalist model. See Anderson, *The Long Tail*.
137 Nicholson et al., *The Ecologies of Amateur Theatre*, 157.
138 Pritchard, "Down from the pedestal."
139 AEM, 4 November 1974.
140 Pritchard, "Down from the pedestal," 10.
141 Quoted in Pritchard, "Down from the pedestal."

142 Kee, "The Alumnae Theatre," c. 1981.
143 Deirdre Bennison, Membership Report, AAGM, 21 June 1998.
144 Margaret Edgar, letter to Alumnae membership, October or November 1974.
145 "More about women on Firehall stage."
146 Edgar, letter to Alumnae membership, October or November 1974.
147 Roz Heller, letter to Alumnae membership, 20 August 1986; emphasis in original.
148 AEM, 12 January 1987.
149 Quoted in Wagner, "Duo borrows big from Smothers Brothers style."
150 PJ Hammond, Executive Producer's Report, AGMM, 9 June 2002.
151 PJ Hammond, interview with Whittaker, 20 October 2017.
152 Nicholson et al., *The Ecologies of Amateur Theatre*, 186.
153 Molly Thom, quoted in Sadaf Ahsan, "She stoops to conquer," *National Post*, 3 August 2019, WP6.
154 Catherine Spence, interview with Whittaker, 21 October 2017.
155 Nicholson et al., *The Ecologies of Amateur Theatre*, 186.
156 Sharma, *In the Meantime*, 148.
157 Ives, *Sure Thing*.
158 Carnwath, interview with Whittaker, 19 October 2017.
159 ABMM, 16 November 2000.
160 Hammond, interview with Whittaker, 20 October 2017.
161 ABMM, 16 November 2000.
162 ABMM, 7 January 2001.
163 ABMM, 5 September 2001.
164 ABMM, 26 November 2001.
165 Spence, interview with Whittaker, 21 October 2017.
166 Nicholson et al., *The Ecologies of Amateur Theatre*, 220, 222.
167 Barry Freeman examines Toronto's Czech and Slovak *Nové divadlo* (New Theatre) as one example of a Toronto immigrant community theatre that has, for decades, produced resonant nonprofessionalizing theatre. See Freeman, *Staging Strangers*, 28; and Filewod, "Erasing History Difference."
168 Liz Best, "Report on the Vice President Membership," AAGM, 24 June 2018.
169 "Annual party skit," June 1974.
170 *The Towering Darkness* script. Spring 1975.
171 Invitation to 8 June 1974 annual meeting.
172 Invitation to Alumnae annual general meeting on 18 June 1988.
173 ABMM, 22 May 2000.

Chapter 5

1 "Hart House Theatre will link Toronto with Little Theatre Movement," *Varsity*, 27 October 1919, 2.
2 Urjo Kareda, "Firehall Theatre launched," *Toronto Star*, 20 October 1972.
3 McKinnie, *City Stages*, 75.
4 Alumnae would return to the Women's Art Association during the 1990s to hold their annual general meetings when the firehall theatre spaces were unavailable due to June rentals. ABMM, 23 January 1995.
5 Toronto Public Library, "Forty-Seventh Annual Report," 32, 33.

6 AMM, 3 March 1953. The 1878-built Staff House (see *Toronto and Early Canada*, 16, Web), to the west of the Reference Library on College St., west of St. George St., had been the home of the late Dr. Charles McKenna until the library acquired it as an "experimental enterprise" in 1928 and used it until it was demolished in 1964. Staff House gave library staff a space to commune and the Library Board a complete "block of property." Renovations to the house created "permanent quarters for the staff, with cafeteria, rest rooms, club-rooms, *etc.*" *Toronto and Early Canada*, 16; Toronto Public Library, "Forty-Seventh Annual Report," 33, 6.
7 AAGM, 29 May 1954.
8 AMM, 14 June 1954.
9 It seems that at the time, the Cumberland location was behind a home occupied by a part-time lecturer in Mechanical Engineering at the university. *University of Toronto Academic Divisions Calendar, 1953–54*, 14.
10 UADC Newsletter, June 1954; AMM, 20 April 1936.
11 AMM, 18 January 1943.
12 Shelagh Kareda, interview with Whittaker, 20 October 2017.
13 AMM, 20 February 1939.
14 Kareda, interview with Whittaker, 20 October 2017.
15 AMM, 18 January 1943.
16 AMM, 26 January 1943.
17 AMM, 18 January 1944–45.
18 AMM, September 1951.
19 AMM, 11 October 1951.
20 AMM, 26 October 1951.
21 AMM, 4 December 1951.
22 AMM, 30 October 1952.
23 AMM, 27 January 1954.
24 AMM, 27 January 1954.
25 UADC Newsletter, June 1954.
26 Lotta Dempsey, "Person to Person," *Globe and Mail*, 13 November 1954, 21.
27 Dempsey, "Person to Person."
28 AMM, 25 October 1954.
29 For example, one group asked to rent the set from Alumnae's production of *Dear Octopus* for $40 along with a fireplace that Alumnae had in storage, to which members agreed (AMM, November 1951). Alumnae discussed another request to rent flats for a production of *The Snow Queen*; they decided to rent them for $10 (AMM, 21 November 1951). Subsequently, owing to a request from Trinity College and Whittaker, who was directing that group's production of Moliére's *Tartuffe*, the club passed a motion that rentals would be at the discretion of the executive and that a fee charged should include a deposit and be determined in consideration of the cost of cleaning, the article in question, and the group to which it was being rented (AMM, 7 February 1952). The rental determined in this case was $25.
30 AMM, 14 September 1953.
31 AMM, 28 September 1953.
32 The plays Alumnae considered included Godefroy's *Fail Not Our Feast* and the proposal scene from *Pride and Prejudice*, "On the Train" (Alumnae meeting minutes. 26 Oct 1953). By November, president Christina Templeton announced that the experimental theatre evening at St. James-Bond church would be Saturday, December 5, 1953 at 8:30pm, with two plays to be presented: one (presumably a portion of) Jean Anouilh's 1951 four-act play *Colombe*,

featuring Betty Campbell and Gay Esdale, and the other Margaret MacNamara's Jane-Austin-inspired 1926 comedy *Elizabeth Refuses* (Alumnae meeting minutes. 30 Nov 1953).

33 AAGM, 29 May 1954.
34 Thom, "From Coach House to Firehall."
35 UADC, "History," 1963, 2.
36 AAGM, 4 June 1955.
37 Molly Thom, interview with Whittaker, 19 October 2017.
38 AMM, 21 April 1955.
39 Thom, "From Coach House to Firehall."
40 CODL Newsletter, January 1957.
41 AMM, 1 June 1955.
42 AAGM, 4 June 1955.
43 Ralph Thomas, "Alumnae Players Finally Find a Home," *Toronto Star*, 2 November 1962.
44 CODL Newsletter, January 1957.
45 Thomas, "Alumnae Players Finally Find a Home."
46 Thom, "From Coach House to Firehall."
47 Rose MacDonald, "Festival winnings furnish theatre," *Toronto Telegram*, 27 March 1957, 26. Alumnae designer Martha Mann Southgate recalls that the ceiling height was nine feet, still not high enough to hang lights. Martha Mann Southgate, interview with Whittaker, 20 October 2017.
48 Thom, "From Coach House to Firehall."
49 AAM, 2 June 1956.
50 Alumnae, "The University Alumnae Dramatic Club," 1956, 4.
51 AMM, 8 September 1956.
52 Whittaker, now beginning to prefer robust plot synopses to thorough acting critiques, felt that although the exposition-filled first act did not need the "immediacy of gloom which it received" from Wade, because "there is time for that to come" in the play, she deserved "only admiration" for her handling of the script. Whittaker, "Small Ibsen spell," *Globe and Mail*, 28 March 1957, 13. The eight-person cast included Pamela Terry, who, according to Rose MacDonald, played with "strongly disciplined" emotions, alongside an "elegant" Doris Stacey as the twin sisters; Edith Orde Tuff was "pretty and animated," although falling short of suggesting the "experienced cosmopolitan Fanny Wilton." MacDonald, "Festival winnings furnish theatre."
53 MacDonald, "Festival winnings furnish theatre."
54 Christina Templeton, Rosemary Hodgins, and Frances McNeil created stage effects, Elizabeth Beattie ran sound, and Lorna Rogers managed properties.
55 Mann Southgate, interview with Whittaker, 20 October 2017.
56 Alumnae, "University Alumnae Dramatic Club," Summer 1960, 3.
57 Thom, "From Coach House to Firehall."
58 Alumnae, "University Alumnae Dramatic Club," Summer 1960, 3–4.
59 Halpenny, "Shall we join the ladies?"
60 Thom, "From Coach House to Firehall."
61 Alumnae, "University Alumnae Dramatic Club," Summer 1960, 4.
62 "Coach House Theatre: Happy in factory," *Toronto Star*, 14 March 1959.
63 Rose MacDonald, "World premiere here for *Lion and Unicorn*," *Toronto Telegram*, 29 January 1958, 25; Whittaker, "Show Business," *Globe and Mail*, 24 January 1958, 8.
64 Whittaker, "Show Business," 24 January 1958, 8.

65 Halpenny, Francess. “Shall we join the ladies?”
66 Whittaker, “Show Business,” *Globe and Mail*, 18 June 1958, 21.
67 “Alumnae find a new theatre,” *Globe and Mail*, 24 May 1958, 16.
68 Whittaker, “Showbusiness,” *Globe and Mail*, 18 June 1958, 21.
69 Molly Golby, quoted in “Coach House Theatre: Happy in factory.” Anne Tait recalls being told by Martha Mann Southgate to purchase red curtains for the building’s front window. But with fabric being too expensive, she heard that red burlap would work. After struggling to cut the material, she put up the curtains for opening night and realized that the theatre now “smelled like a barnyard.” Anne Weldon Tait, interview with Whittaker, 19 October 2017.
70 “Coach House Theatre: Happy in factory.”
71 Jack Winter, “Amateur,” *Canadian Forum*, November 1960.
72 “Alumnae drama club seeks own playhouse.” *Globe and Mail*, 24 Septeeber 1960, 13.
73 Whittaker, “Lunts answer critics, star in serious play,” *Globe and Mail*, 25 February 1960, 11.
74 Thomas, “Alumnae Players Finally Find a Home.”
75 Halpenny, “Shall we join the ladies?”
76 Thom, “From Coach House to Firehall.”
77 Alumnae, “Building Fund Appeal,” July 1961, 2.
78 Alumnae, “University Alumnae Dramatic Club,” 1, 5.
79 Whittaker, “The Bluestockings have a blueprint,” *Globe and Mail*, 22 July 1961, 11.
80 Alumnae, “Building Fund Appeal,” 2.
81 Kathryn Horler, “Their plays pave a way to theatre of their own,” *Toronto Telegram*, 14 October 1960, 49; Alumnae, “Building Fund Appeal,” 2.
82 Alumnae, “Building Fund Appeal,” 2.
83 UADC, “About the Coach House Theatre,” c. November 1962.
84 Whittaker, “The Bluestockings have a blueprint.”.
85 Thom, “From Coach House to Firehall.”
86 Alumnae, “University Alumnae Dramatic Club,” 5.
87 Alumnae, “Building Fund Appeal,” 2.
88 Vida Peene had been Commandant of the Food Administration Section of the Red Cross Corps in Toronto and was a lifelong fundraiser for the arts. See Ontario Arts Council. “Vida Peene Fund,” Web.
89 Alumnae, “University Alumnae Dramatic Club: Coach House Theatre,” 1; Whittaker, “The Bluestockings have a blueprint.”
90 Halpenny, “Shall we join the ladies?”
91 Other fundraising committee members were the Hon. Mr. Justice Carl D. Stewart, Mrs. D.W. McGibbon, Mrs. James Milner, Mrs. W. Hewitt Bayley, and Arthur Gelber. “Alumnae drama club seeks own playhouse.”
92 Alumnae, “University Alumnae Dramatic Club,” 1.
93 Alumnae, “Building Fund Appeal,” 2.
94 Whittaker, “The Bluestockings Have a Blueprint.”
95 Halpenny, “Shall we join the ladies?”
96 Whittaker, “The Bluestockings Have a Blueprint.”
97 Alumnae, “University Alumnae Dramatic Club,” 5.
98 AAGM, 9 June 1962.
99 AAGM, 27 November 1961.
100 AAGM, 14 September 1961.
101 AAGM, 7 September 1961.

102 AEM, 7 September 1961.
103 AAGM, 27 November 1961.
104 Molly Golby, Theatre Manager's Report, AAM, 9 June 1962, 1.
105 UADC, "History," 1963, 3.
106 Golby, Theatre Manager's Report, 9 June 1962, 1.
107 Pamela Terry, "Report of the Playreading Committee," AAM, 9 June 1962, 2.
108 Terry, "Report of the Playreading Committee," 9 June 1962, 2.
109 Executive, memorandum to members of the UADC, 30 July 1962; Thomas, "Alumnae Players Finally Find a Home."
110 AEM, 7 January 1962.
111 Golby, Theatre Manager's Report, 9 June 1962, 1.
112 Nathan Cohen, "At Last a Home for the UADC," *Toronto Star*, 14 November 1962.
113 AMM, 15 March 1962.
114 AMM, c. April 1962.
115 Eileen Williams, letter to fellow members, 30 May 1962, 1.
116 AMM, 15 March 1962.
117 AMM, c. April 1962.
118 Terry, "Report of the Playreading Committee," 9 June 1962, 2.
119 Lorna F. Rogers, Publicity Report, AAM, 9 June 1962, 3.
120 AEM, 9 May 1962. Unpaid membership fees would become a theme in the years to come, with the executive soon deciding that "no notices should be sent to new members until fees have been received by the secretary." Alumnae executive meeting minutes, 7 July 1965.
121 Williams, letter to fellow members, 2.
122 AAGM, 16 May 1962.
123 Williams, letter to fellow members, 1.
124 Golby, Theatre Manager's Report, 1, 2.
125 Williams, letter to fellow members, 2, 3.
126 Golby, Theatre Manager's Report, 1.
127 AMM, 5 September 1962.
128 AMM, 23 January 1961.
129 Alumnae notice of special resolution and application for Supplementary Letters Patent of incorporation, 19 July 1962.
130 AMM, 15 June 1968.
131 Alumnae were not the first nonprofessionalizing theatre in Toronto to own their own theatre. The York Community Theatre owned its own studio theatre on La Plante Ave. shortly before Alumnae staged their first play at the Huntley St. Coach House Theatre. (CODL Newsletter, January 1957).
132 Executive, memorandum to members of the UADC, 30 July 1962.
133 AMM, 5 September 1962.
134 AMM, 5 December 1962.
135 By fall 1962, the Birch Ave. property was still not sold. This was a "problem to be solved quickly, as money would be needed to pay contractors" (AMM, 5 September 1962). When the membership met in October 1962, they discovered that their financial situation was "worse than expected" because of the contractor's very high bill, which left them to find "about $13,000 more!" They sought to negotiate a $6,000 bank loan and approached the Atkinson Foundation (named after former *Toronto Star* publisher and philanthropist Joseph E. Atkinson) for $3,000 for lighting and a lighting board. Further donations were encouraged, a "Club

Levy" was discussed without resolution, and it was urged that each show should earn $1,000, so the Club "*must* get people to attend" (AMM, 24 October 1962; emphasis in original). As a result of the construction bill, in December 1962, for the first time in their history, Alumnae reported that they were in debt. More than ever, it was "imperative we do well with our shows" (Alumnae meeting minutes. 5 December 1962).

The new year found a number of financial worries addressed, albeit in some worrying ways. They were still unable to pay the contractor, and there was talk of litigation. It was reported that president Williams, who was ill and could not attend the February 1963 meeting, had lent Alumnae $2,000 of the $4,000 they owed. Alumnae sought to pay the rest by June (AMM, 14 February 1963); as it turned out, their debt would not be paid off until May 1964. The debt to Williams, which was without interest, would take longer to pay back (Mascall, Financial Statement, AAGM, 13 June 1964). In February 1963 the Birch Ave. property sold for $6,175, including $3,000 cash. The $3,000 went toward playing off half of their bank loan (AMM, 14 February 1963).

136 Perin, *The Many Rooms of This House: Diversity in Toronto's Places of Worship Since 1840*. Toronto: U Toronto P., 2017. 137.
137 Perin, *The Many Rooms of This House*, 335.
138 "R'Moshe Langner of Kozowa-Strettin," *Geni*, 16 May 2019.
139 Perin, *The Many Rooms of This House*, 138, 335.
140 Thom, "From Coach House to Firehall."
141 Whittaker, "Drama club to use synagogue," *Globe and Mail*, 15 August 1962, 8.
142 AMM, 23 January 1961.
143 AMM, 4 February 1962.
144 AMM, 23 January 1961.
145 Alumnae, "About the Coach House Theatre," c. 9 November 1962.
146 Thomas, "Alumnae players finally find a home," *Toronto Star*, 2 November 1962.
147 Joan Reid, "Alumni [*sic*] players need to speed production," *Globe and Mail*, 16 October 1963, 36.
148 Alumnae, "About the Coach House Theatre." Long-time members recall an incident during their run of *The Duchess of Malfi* in the winter of 1963 when the set's giant crucifix was left uncovered on the stage on Friday night. They received a flustered call on Sunday from the Rabbi, who discovered it when he arrived Saturday morning for *shul*. It may have been the last time synagogue services were held in the Coach House Theatre. Thom, interview with Whittaker, 19 October 2017; Tait, interview with Whittaker, 19 October 2017; Margaret and Michael Spence, interview with Whittaker, 21 October 2017.
149 Thomas, "Alumnae players finally find a home."
150 AMM, 23 January 1961.
151 Cohen, "At last a home for the UADC."
152 "Women university grads buy a theatre," *Paper Doll*, November 1962.
153 Cohen, "At last a home for the UADC."
154 Thomas, "Alumnae players finally find a home."
155 Cohen, "At last a home for the UADC."
156 Alumnae, "About the Coach House Theatre."
157 AMM, 24 October 1962.
158 UADC, "About the Coach House Theatre"; AMM, 24 October 1962.
159 AMM, 24 October 1962.
160 Alumnae, "About the Coach House Theatre."

161 Williams, letter to fellow members, 30 May 1962, 1.
162 Cohen, "At last a home for the UADC."
163 AMM, 5 December 1962.
164 Alumnae. "About the Coach House Theatre."
165 Thomas, "Alumnae players finally find a home"; AEM, 4 February 1962.
166 Halpenny, "Shall we join the ladies?"
167 Alumnae. "About the Coach House Theatre."
168 Thom, "From Coach House to Firehall."
169 AEM, 4 February 1962.
170 Williams, letter to fellow members, 1.
171 Executive, memorandum to members of the UADC, 30 July 1962.
172 Eileen Williams, letter to friend of the Coach House Theatre, 7 September 1962. Alumnae, "About the Coach House Theatre." The labour was extensive. By the start of September 1962, the contractors had put in a "new ceiling, more power, new staircases, and various carpentry and plastering. The heating [and] some plumbing remained to be finished" (AMM, 5 September 1962). A "plan of operation" (executive, memorandum, 30 July 1962) was put in place, with volunteer members and supportive men listed as department heads for costumes, painting, cleaning, and so forth. They kept a "Men's Work List" with thirty-four men's names, all "male actors, husbands and friends" (Alumnae, "About the Coach House Theatre"), with phone numbers, noting "supervisors" and "carpenters." Anne Tait, as assistant manager, kept a list of duties with the names in charge and their phone numbers. Among the names were fifteen female supervisors and nine male supervisors organizing eighteen departments: washrooms, stage building, seating, lobby construction, painting interior, floors, draperies, house lighting, stage lighting, dressing rooms, basement cleanup, equipment storage, costume storage, painting exterior, bricklaying boulevard, signs and graphic material, courtyard cleanup, and theatre cleaning and equipment. Ken Poste and Arthur Davies (also the club's lawyer) set to building the stage and installing the lighting, respectively (executive, memorandum, 30 July 1962). Many of the male volunteers were actors like Douglas Ney, Ivor Jackson, Ken Pogue, Bob (Robert) Peace, Rex Sevenoaks, and Jamie Mainprize. Members commended their theatre manager, Molly Golby, for "having done a wonderful job" (AMM, 5 Septmber 1962) organizing volunteer members and workmen (executive, memorandum, 30 July 1962).
173 AMM, 23 January 1961.
174 Thom, "From Coach House to Firehall."
175 AMM, 24 October 1962.
176 F.E. Wellwood, letter to University Alumnae Dramatic Club, 14 November 1962.
177 Wellwood, letter to University Alumnae Dramatic Club.
178 AEM, 21 November 1962.
179 Shirley Sims, Property Management Report, AAGM, 15 June 1963.
180 AAGM, 9 June 1962.
181 Golby, Theatre Manager's Report, 9 June 1962, 2.
182 Michael Spence arrived in Toronto to work at Ontario Hydro and trained in lighting design under Robert Gill (Alumnae, *Homeward Bound* cast bios, 20 Janauary 2006). In 1968, he became president of the Central Ontario Drama League. Alumnae president Elizabeth Mascall "extended special good wishes" to him as a "great strength" while leading set construction crews (AAGM, 15 June 1968). He would later be Alumnae's building manager at the Firehall Theatre.
183 Golby, Theatre Manager's Report, AAGM, 15 June 1963.

184 AMM, 24 October 1962.
185 AAGM, 15 June 1963.
186 "Women university grads buy a theatre."
187 UADC, "History," 4.
188 Quoted in Thomas, "Alumnae players finally find a home."
189 AMM, 24 October 1962.
190 Alumnae, "About the Coach House Theatre."
191 AMM, 24 October 1962.
192 Whittaker, "An odd egg is opened in an odd eggcup," *Globe and Mail*, 14 November 1962, 9.
193 Cohen, "At last a home for the UADC."
194 Nathan Cohen, "How the Canada Council can help playwrights," *Toronto Star*, 4 September 1962, 18.
195 Nathan Cohen, "A question of theatres," *Toronto Star*, 24 November 1962, 22.
196 Whittaker, "Toronto's little theatres find their place together," *Globe and Mail*, 17 November 1962, 13.
197 Golby, Theatre Manager's Report, 15 June 1963.
198 Rogers, Publicity Report, 15 June 1963.
199 Alumnae, "In 1918 a group of women with a common love …," History document, October 1963.
200 AMM, 11 September 1963.
201 AMM, 10 November 1964.
202 Helen Carscallen, Theatre Manager's Report, 13 June 1964.
203 Carscallen, Theatre Manager's Report, 13 June 1964.
204 AMM, 10 November 1964.
205 AAGM, 19 June 1965.
206 Margaret Spence, Theatre Manager's Report, AAGM, 19 June 1965.
207 Carscallen, Theatre Manager's Report, 13 June 1964.
208 AMM, 11 September 1963.
209 AMM, 11 September 1963. Over the first twelve months of productions at the synagogue Coach House, it was reported that the total loss on the theatre and the house was $844 (AMM, 11 September 1963); by November 1963 they had a bank balance of just $595 with a mortgage payment of $314 due. To increase income, the budget for each show was set at $400 with the aim of netting $500 per show (AMM, 5 November 1963). Student ticket prices were set at $1 for Tuesdays to Thursdays and $1.50 for the better-attended Fridays and Saturdays (AMM, 11 September 1963). By the end of the season, they were forced to raise admission to $2 on Friday and Saturday evenings (AMM, 9 March 1964). A new rental fee structure for the theatre was decided on in which groups could rent rehearsal space for $10 to $15 per night and $25 per night for a "performance with use of lighting." Costume rentals were set at $5 for a "complete costume for a week" and $1.00 extra for "shoes, hats, cloaks, properties" (AMM, 11 September 1963), to be advertised to high school and university drama groups. Use of platforms and flats was $50 (Alumnae general meeting minutes, 22 January 1964). Their first rental under these new terms was to CODL for a workshop on 9 and 10 November 1963 (AMM, 5 November 1963). Along with a CODL rental, a student group rented the Coach House for two nights through a member. Alumnae reported that "both proved successful and lucrative" (Carscallen, Theatre Manager's Report, 13 June 1964). Fortunately, they received $1,000 from their Atkinson Foundation application to purchase lighting equipment, although this fell short of the $3,000 they had asked for (AMM, 19 March 1964). An anonymous club

member donated an additional $500. Alumnae purchased a lighting board with "8 autotransformer type dimmers each of 2500 watt capacity with interlocking handles and one master handle plus 18 lights and 5 barn door attachments." The balance owing, it was reported, "will be less than our rental of lights from Strand Electric" (Carscallen, Theatre Manager's Report, 13 June 1964).

210 AAGM, 19 June 1965.
211 AMM, 14 January 1964.
212 AMM, 5 November 1963.
213 Carscallen, Theatre Manager's Report, 13 June 1964.
214 AMM, 5 November 1963.
215 Carscallen, Theatre Manager's Report, 13 June 1964. By June 1965, with the technical demands of their productions increasing, they resolved to "purchase permanent sound equipment from Mandlsohn, including a good quality stereo tape recorder and a second hand amplifier, the whole to be enclosed in a cupboard which will lock" (AAGM, 19 June 1965). Mandlsohn would "design the system and donate five or six speakers which will be permanently located in various positions around the theatre." The system would be mounted in a "permanent location with a locking case and enclosure" (Spence, House Manager Report. AAGM, 19 June 1965). However, by July it was clear that Alumnae "cannot commit ourselves to spending money immediately for sound equipment" and should continue to borrow from Mandlsohn for the time being (AEM, minutes, 7 July 1965).
216 "Floating stage drops anchor," *Globe and Mail*, 17 October 1964, 13.
217 AAGM, 13 June 1964.
218 Carscallen, Theatre Manager's Report, 13 June 1964.
219 AAGM, 13 June 1964.
220 AMM, 15 September 1964.
221 "Floating stage drops anchor."
222 Whittaker, "Coach House stage suits the Emperor," *Globe and Mail*, 21 October 1964, 12.
223 "Floating stage drops anchor."
224 Nathan Cohen, "At the awkward stage," *Toronto Star*, n.d.
225 AAGM, 13 June 1964.
226 "Floating stage drops anchor."
227 AMM, 15 September 1964.
228 AEM, 2 November 1964.
229 AAGM, 19 June 1965.
230 AEM, 2 November 1964.
231 Molly Thom, Note to Alumnae membership, 1964.
232 "Floating stage drops anchor."
233 Whittaker, "Coach House stage suits the Emperor."
234 AEM, 2 November 1964.
235 Glenna Davis, letter to Cicely Thomson. 16 January 1965.
236 AEM, 2 November 1964.
237 Alumnae mailout announcement in advance of the 15 February 1965 general meeting.
238 AEM, 12 January 1965.
239 Alumnae mailout announcement in advance of the 15 February 1965 general meeting.
240 AAGM, 19 June 1965.
241 Sims, Rental Property Report, AAGM, 13 June 1964.
242 Johnston, "Bill Glassco and Tarragon Theatre" [originally published in *Canadian Drama*], 3.

243 Glenna Davis, Secretary's Report, AAGM, 13 June 1964.
244 AMM, 9 March 1964.
245 Glenna Davis, Secretary's Report, AAGM, 13 June 1964; Johnston, "Bill Glassco and Tarragon Theatre," 3.
246 AMM, 9 March 1964; Carscallen, Theatre Manager's Report, 13 June 1964.
247 AMM, 15 September 1964.
248 AEM, August 1964.
249 Rogers, Property Manager Report, AAGM, 19 June 1965.
250 AAGM, 19 June 1965.
251 Rogers, Property Manager Report, AAGM, 19 June 1965.
252 Rogers, Annual Report of Property Manager, 11 June 1966.
253 Rogers, Property Manager Report, AAGM, 19 June 1965.
254 Rogers, Annual Report of Property Manager, 11 June 1966.
255 Michael and Margaret Spence, interview with Whittaker, 21 October 2017.
256 AMM, 12 September 1966.
257 AMM, 9 November 1966.
258 AMM, 9 November, 12 September 1966.
259 AMM, 9 November 1966.
260 Alumnae general meeting, 9 November 1966.
261 AMM, 15 June 1968.
262 AMM, 3 April 1968.
263 Toronto Police Service, "Proud of Our Past, Confident of Our Future" [Brochure], 4.
264 AMM, 3 April 1968.
265 AMM, 15 June 1968.
266 MacAulay, letter to friend of the Coach House, 11 March 1969.
267 Alumnae, 11 March 1969 general meeting announcement, n.d.
268 MacAulay, letter to friend of the Coach House, 11 March 1969.
269 Alumnae, "Subscription Series 1969–70" [Flyer], Fall 1969.
270 City Property Commissioner, Report to City of Toronto Executive Committee, 26 August 1970.
271 Michael Spence, interview with Whittaker, 21 October 2017.
272 Alumnae, 22 April 1969 general meeting announcement, n.d.
273 Thom, "From Coach House to Firehall."
274 Michael Spence, interview with Whittaker, 21 October 2017.
275 Alumnae, report on the general meeting, 11 December 1969.
276 Urjo Kareda, "University dramatic club far below usual standard," *Toronto Star*, 22 October 1971; Michael Spence, interview with Whittaker, 21 October 2017.
277 Alumnae notice of general meeting on 10 February 1970, 23 January 1970.
278 Alumnae letter to membership "re the Enoch Turner Schoolhouse" in advance of general meeting on 11 December 1969.
279 Lillian Burke, letter to Norma Clark, 18 November 1971.
280 "Ladies - re the Enoch Turner Schoolhouse," Alumnae letter to membership in advance of general meeting on 11 December 1969.
281 Burke, letter to Norma Clark, 18 November 1971.
282 Kareda, "University dramatic club far below usual standard."
283 Alumnae general meeting announcement on 25 September 1969.
284 Thom, "From Coach House to Firehall. DRAFT."

285 DuBarry Campau, "Oldest school crumbling," *Toronto Telegram*, 29 June 1967, 10.
286 Corporation of Trinity Church signatories, letter to R.B. Apted, 10 September 1969.
287 McKenzie Porter, "The Rev. Harry S.D. Robinson ..." *Toronto Telegram*, 29 June 1967, 10.
288 Alumnae notice of general meeting on 20 April 1970.
289 Thom, "From Coach House to Firehall."
290 Alumnae notice of general meeting on 20 April 1970. Molly Thom, Norma Clark, and Francess Halpenny attended an "open meeting" to discuss the future of the schoolhouse. The church offered a twenty-year lease on the schoolhouse for their "normal rent" of $100 per year plus the design and cost of interior renovations, upkeep of the building, and all heating, plumbing, and electrical costs. Alumnae would have "sole possession of the property" and discretion of choice of programming. With this in mind, the executive wrote to members asking several pertinent questions, including whether they would go to that area of the city to work, whether the schoolhouse was easy for them to reach, whether twenty years was suitable knowing that they would have the "responsibilities of ownership," although the property would not be Alumnae's after that date because the "diocese has ruled that there can be no sale," and whether members would take part in a search for a different location if they did not approve of the schoolhouse (Alumnae letter to membership "re the Enoch Turner Schoolhouse" in advance of general meeting on 11 December 1969). Reciprocally, members raised concerns about the "character" of the area, the difficulty in reaching it, the possibility the building would be demolished during the lease (although the building was being somewhat protected by a pending historical designation), and the length of time for urban renewal in the area to take hold and make it a "'smart' district." Further concerns were about the agreement: while Alumnae's reputation might work in favour of them continuing past the twenty years, or finding a new place before then, a lease would be "playing false" with those who had donated to purchase a property. It was noted that although present members' had contributed the legwork, they were still indebted to the "efforts of those who came before us, and we have, therefore, an obligation to those who will follow." Detailed consideration of show income and annual expenses led to the conclusion that the shows would pay for the expenses most years, and that renting Maplewood too, instead of selling it, would require a caretaker. There was also some discussion of staying only with the Maplewood location, but it was generally agreed that if the Club wanted to "continue in the future as a group producing a full season of plays in our own theatre, larger premises must be found as quickly as possible." Halpenny moved that the "executive be empowered to choose three members of the Club to discuss with our legal representatives the lease for the Enoch Turner Schoolhouse; such terms to be presented to the membership of the Club for a Deciding vote"; Halpenny's motion passed with one dissenting vote (Alumnae report on the general meeting 11 December 1969).
291 Thom, "From Coach House to Firehall."
292 Whittaker, "A pair of new theatres spring from Toronto's past," *Globe and Mail*, 10 June 1972, 29.
293 Thom, "From Coach House to Firehall."
294 Ron Thom had eyed the old gasworks for Alumnae as a potential "centre for restaurants, boutiques, offices and a theatre," but a "developer thwarted this scheme." Toronto Free had thought they would have to work out of Hart House Theatre before they approached the developer of the gasworks. With their own renovations under way, Toronto Free crews dug up a corpse in the cellar. They were able to start previews of their first show, the world premiere of Larry Fineberg's *Hope*, on 13 June 1972. Whittaker, "A pair of new theatres spring from Toronto's past."

295 Thom, "From Coach House to Firehall."
296 McDonald, "The arts are rescuing a gray old hobo of a street," 37.
297 S.C., "Watsup: Theatre," *Varsity*, 12 February 1971, 12.
298 Alumnae, "The University Alumnae Dramatic Club acquires the Berkeley Street Firehall" [Press Release], Fall 1971.
299 Thom, "From Coach House to Firehall."
300 George Ono, [no headline], *Ryersonian*, 25 January 1972.
301 Alumnae note, "Former use Number 4 Fire Station," n.d.
302 Alumnae, "For Toronto Walking Guide: The Firehall Theatre, No. 70 Berkeley Street" [Draft].
303 "Lombard Street Central Fire Hall," *Lively Legacy of Lombard Street*, 3 March 1918. Web.
304 Ono, [no headline], *Ryersonian*.
305 Alumnae. "The University Alumnae Dramatic Club acquires the Berkeley Street Firehall."
306 City Property Commissioner, Report to City of Toronto Executive Committee, 26 August 1970.
307 Alumnae, "The University Alumnae Dramatic Club acquires the Berkeley Street Firehall."
308 Halpenny, Prospectus. "The Alumnae Theatre: A History 1919-1999," in Alumnae board of directors meeting minutes, 4 June 2001.
309 City Property Commissioner, Report to City of Toronto Executive Committee, 5 February 1970.
310 Alumnae, "The University Alumnae Dramatic Club acquires the Berkeley Street Firehall."
311 Thom, "From Coach House to Firehall."
312 Thom, "From Coach House to Firehall."
313 City Property Commissioner, Report, 26 August 1970.
314 Alumnae, "The University Alumnae Dramatic Club acquires the Berkeley Street Firehall."
315 City Property Commissioner, Report, 5 February 1970.
316 French, "Toronto's architectural heritage sacrificed to parking lots."
317 Alumnae, "The University Alumnae Dramatic Club acquires the Berkeley Street Firehall."
318 Clair M. Lavier (president, Industrial Interiors Ltd.), letter to Mrs. R. Thom, 11 September 1970.
319 Alumnae, "The University Alumnae Dramatic Club acquires the Berkeley Street Firehall."
320 Shinan Govani, "Klaus Nienkamper conquered Canada by design," *Toronto Star*, 30 June 2018.
321 Alumnae, draft letter to Committee on Parks and Recreation, c. Summer–Fall 1970.
322 Alumnae, "The University Alumnae Dramatic Club acquires the Berkeley Street Firehall."
323 Nicholson et al., *The Ecologies of Amateur Theatre*, 113.
324 Urjo Kareda, "An ideal home for our oldest theatrical group," *Toronto Star*, 5 November 1971, 25.
325 Alumnae, "The University Alumnae Dramatic Club acquires the Berkeley Street Firehall."
326 Quoted in "Club wants fire hall to be used as theatre," *Globe and Mail*, 23 July 1970, 11.
327 "Club wants fire hall to be used as theatre," *Globe and Mail*, 23 July 1970, 11.
328 City Property Commissioner, Report, 26 August 1970.
329 Thom, "From Coach House to Firehall."
330 "The park thieves" [editorial], *Globe and Mail*, 24 July 1970, 6.
331 W.K., "Two nice fire halls are o.k.," Parks and Recreation, October 1970.
332 Karl Jaffary, Letter to the Editor, *Globe and Mail*, 29 July 1970, 6.
333 Jaffary, Letter to the Editor.
334 Morna Wales, Letter to the Editor, *Globe and Mail*, 29 July 1970, 6.

335 Henry S. Rosenberg, "The need for parks," Letter to the Editor, *Globe and Mail*, 29 July 1970, 6; Kathleen Young, "The need for parks," Letter to the Editor,' *Globe and Mail*, 31 July 1970.
336 W.K. "Two nice fire halls are o.k."
337 City Property Commissioner, Report, 5 February 1970.
338 Donald Wallace, letter to Commissioner of Parks and Recreation, 29 September 1970.
339 Pamela Campion, unaddressed letter to "Dear Sir," 19 September 1970.
340 Lavier, letter to Mrs. R. Thom, 11 September 1970.
341 Campion, unaddressed letter to "Dear Sir."
342 Lavier, letter to Mrs. R. Thom.
343 W.K. "Two nice fire halls are o.k."
344 Campion, unaddressed letter to "Dear Sir," 19 September 1970.
345 Campion, unaddressed letter to "Dear Sir," 19 September 1970.
346 W.K. "Two nice fire halls are o.k." Parks and Recreation. October 1970.
347 Claire L. McLaughlin, letter to Committee on Parks and Recreation, 20 September 1930.
348 City Clerk, Report to the City of Toronto Executive Committee, 2 October 1970.
349 W.K., "Two nice fire halls are o.k."
350 "Theatre in a firehall," *Toronto Telegram*, 2 October 1970.
351 James Acland, (president, Architectural Conservancy of Ontario), letter to City Property Commissioner, 10 October 1970.
352 Alumnae, Agenda for 27 October 1970 general meeting.
353 City of Toronto Executive Committee Report No. 31, c. March 1971.
354 Molly Thom, letter to Alderman David Rotenberg, 27 April 1971.
355 Molly Thom, letter to Alderman Thomas Wardle, 28 April 1971.
356 Thom, letter to Wardle.
357 Alumnae, "The University Alumnae Dramatic Club acquires the Berkeley Street Firehall."
358 Corporation of the City of Toronto By-Law No. 191-71, 5 August 1971.
359 Alumnae, "The University Alumnae Dramatic Club acquires the Berkeley Street Firehall."
360 Whittaker, "A pair of new theatres spring from Toronto's past."
361 Kareda, "An ideal home for our oldest theatrical group."
362 Ono, [no headline], *Ryersonian*.
363 Kareda, "An ideal home for our oldest theatrical group."
364 "Mayor William Dennison …," Photo caption, *Toronto Sun*, 5 November 1971, 11.
365 Pritchard, "Down from the pedestal." Alumnae had to raise their renovation and restoration investment promise to $101,000 because more steel was needed to secure the tower, the "original drywall contractor has gone broke," and there was an issue with the third-floor toilet (AEM, 18 January 1972). They eventually applied for and received a Local Initiatives Project grant of $25,857 to pay for nine months of renovations because they qualified as a "winter works project" (Susan Goldenberg, "Saving the flavour of an earlier Toronto can also save cash," *Globe and Mail*, 22 September 1972, 17).
366 Alumnae, "The University Alumnae Dramatic Club acquires the Berkeley Street Firehall."
367 The club publicly thanked a number of aldermen who had supported their efforts, including John Sewell (the other alderman for Alumnae's Ward 7, along with Jaffary), William Kilbourn, Fred Beavis, David Rotenberg, and "one of the Club's most enthusiastic supporters in this matter, Alderman Horace Brown" (Alumnae, "The University Alumnae Dramatic Club acquires the Berkeley Street Firehall"; Kareda, "An ideal home for our oldest theatrical group").
368 Kareda, "An ideal home for our oldest theatrical group."
369 Thom, "Architectural Program."

370 Thom, "Architectural Program."
371 Alumnae. "The University Alumnae Dramatic Club acquires the Berkeley Street Firehall."
372 Alumnae note, "Former use Number 4 Fire Station," n.d.
373 Alumnae, "The University Alumnae Dramatic Club acquires the Berkeley Street Firehall"; Alumnae, "For Toronto Walking Guide."
374 Alumnae, "The University Alumnae Dramatic Club acquires the Berkeley Street Firehall."
375 Alumnae, "For Toronto Walking Guide."
376 Thom, "From Coach House to Firehall."
377 A large wooden bell-tower extension had been added at one time, like the one on Toronto's notable College St. and Bellevue Ave. firehall, but it may have been removed around 1952 because of deterioration (Alumnae note, "Former use Number 4 Fire Station").
378 Alumnae note, "Former use Number 4 Fire Station."
379 Alumnae, "For Toronto Walking Guide."
380 Alumnae note, "Former use Number 4 Fire Station."
381 Thom, "From Coach House to Firehall."
382 Alumnae note, "Former use Number 4 Fire Station."
383 UADC, membership flyer. c. 1980; Donald Jones, "The 'oldest and proudest' Toronto theatrical company," *Toronto Star*, 23 September 1989, M4.
384 Jones, "The 'oldest and proudest' Toronto theatrical company."
385 Alumnae, "For Toronto Walking Guide."
386 Alumnae note, "Former use Number 4 Fire Station."
387 Ono, [no headline], *Ryersonian*.
388 "In View: A selections of events and places to go, from what's doing this month," *Toronto Calendar Magazine*, 29 September 1972, 14.
389 Goldenberg, "Saving the flavour of an earlier Toronto can also save cash."
390 Alumnae notice for 10 June 1972 annual meeting; Whittaker, "A pair of new theatres spring from Toronto's past."
391 It is remarkable that during these two years of securing and renovating the firehall, Alumnae were able to maintain productions at the Central Library and Maplewood Ave. In fact, deep into the firehall renovations, they still had not finished with Maplewood. Like the unused Birch Ave. location, Maplewood proved to be a challenge to sell. But in the spring of 1972, just months before Alumnae opened their first Firehall Theatre production, Maplewood was sold to the First United Church of Jesus Christ Apostolic for $27,500 (Alumnae, "Motion re 10 Maplewood," n.d.; Alumnae notice for 10 June 1972 annual meeting).
392 Whittaker, "A pair of new theatres spring from Toronto's past."
393 Alumnae notice for 10 June 1972 annual meeting.
394 McDonald, "The arts are rescuing a gray old hobo of a street."
395 Florida, *The Rise of the Creative Class*.
396 Alumnae publicized their inaugural season at the Firehall Theatre at the same time that Tom Hendry and John Palmer announced Toronto Free Theatre's inaugural productions (Urjo Kareda, "A new flourish," *Toronto Star*, 5 June 1972), although, reportedly, neither was aware of the other's planned theatres (Whittaker, "A pair of new theatres spring from Toronto's past").
397 Nicholson et al., *The Ecologies of Amateur Theatre*, 116.
398 Two months later, Susan Goldenberg wrote a feature piece in the *Globe and Mail*'s "Friday Real Estate" section about renovating old buildings into workspaces. She included Alumnae's

and Toronto Free's new theatres among buildings that were helping to repurpose and revitalize the city's derelict neighbourhoods. She grouped Alumnae's new theatre and Toronto Free Threatre with the former home of Hart Massey (Vincent Massey's grandfather and the namesake of the theatre in which Alumnae originally made their mark), Lyndhurst Lodge (originally the home of Woolworth's president Ralph Connable and later converted into a post-war rehabilitation hospital), the former Borden Dairy plant (which was purchased by the University of Toronto), the CNR railway station, and the Lombard St. firehall (Goldenberg, "Saving the flavor of an earlier Toronto can also save cash").

399 Mark McAllister, "Unpolished performers weaken impact of O'Casey's topical play," *Varsity*, 27 October 1972, 21.

400 McAllister, "Unpolished performers weaken impact of O'Casey's topical play."

401 Kareda, "Firehall Theatre launched."

402 Kareda, "New theatre is lovely but first play isn't."

403 Whittaker, An Arthurian legend in platform reading."

404 Nicholson et al., *The Ecologies of Amateur Theatre*, 28.

405 Francess Halpenny, Prospectus, "The Alumnae Theatre," In ABMM, 4 June 2001.

406 City of Toronto By-Law No. 191-71.

407 Robinowitz, letter to Mayor John Sewell, copied to Alumnae, 16 October 1979.

408 Agreement between University Alumnae Dramatic Club and the Corporation of the City of Toronto, 8 July 1971.

409 AEM, 14 April 1982.

410 Michael Spence, interview with Whittaker, 21 October 2017.

411 AEM, 12 January 1987.

412 AEM, 12 January 1987; Alumnae Board of Management meeting minutes, 30 March 1987.

413 These amendments cover the definitions of membership, annual fees, meetings, voting, Alumnae directors and their duties and responsibilities, subcommittees, and finances (Alumnae, UADC By-laws, 17 June 1987).

414 Nola Wale, "Thoughts on the Rental Policy of the Alumnae Theatre," in AEM, 21 November 1985.

415 AEM, 4 November 1974.

416 AMM, 1 October 1979.

417 AMM, 1 October 1985.

418 Wale, "Thoughts on the Rental Policy of the Alumnae Theatre."

419 Angela Finlay, Rentals Report, AAGM, 9 June 2002.

420 Liane Heller, "'Inspired madwomen' produced stars," *Toronto Star*, 30 April 1984, D2.

421 Other Alumnae committees have overseen various activities and initiatives, including committees that oversee wardrobe cleanings, anniversary celebrations, and other one-off public events. (AEM, 14 April 1982.

422 Margaret Edgar (executive producers), "Everything you wanted to know about the theatre – and were afraid to ask …," August 1985.

423 Letter to executive, 3 September 1985.

424 Leonard, for Alumnae, "A Manual of Production Procedures for the University Alumnae Dramatic Club," 1970.

425 By the fall of 1985, while in the process of purchasing a new lighting board (for which there is a framed recognition certificate for Ruth E. Pincoe and others who helped install the Strand Mantrix 2S lighting system), Alumnae were considering hiring a theatre technician paid for by rental fees (AEM, 5 November 1985).

Chapter 6

1 "Amateur festival 'art democracy,'" *Toronto Telegram*, 25 March 1939.
2 Pearl McCarthy, "Drama Festival," In "Rambling 'Round with Roly," *Toronto Star*, c. March 1936.
3 Nicholson et al., *The Ecologies of Amateur Theatre*, 257.
4 Halpenny, Prospectus, "The Alumnae Theatre."
5 Whittaker, "Showbusiness," *Globe and Mail*, 21 May 1956, 14.
6 David Gilbert et al., "On Amateurs," 4.
7 Quoted in Lee, *Love and Whisky*, 96.
8 "Dominion Drama Festival," *Globe*, 18 February 1933, 14.
9 Lee, *Love and Whisky*, 96.
10 "Dominion Drama Festival."
11 Quoted in "Governor-General plans 'Dominion Drama Festival,'" *Varsity*, 1 November 1932, 1, 4.
12 "Dramatic festival heartily endorsed by undergraduates," *Varsity*, 2 November 1932, 1, 3.
13 Norah Bowers, quoted in "Dramatic festival heartily endorsed by undergraduates," *Varsity*, 2 November 1932, 1, 3.
14 Lawrence Mason, "Festival awards: Prize-winners named by adjudicator," *Globe*, 30 March 1936, 12.
15 Pearl McCarthy, "Arts and Letters Win Play Award," *Toronto Star*, c. March 1936. This was the same hope stated in the 1936 regional festival program by the DDF's founding patron, the Earl of Bessborough: "A Renaissance of the Drama is taking place in Canada. As the success of the Dominion Drama Festival testifies, it is a widely national movement, attended by the most promising developments and by the many good auguries of the future; its value as a permanent institution in the cultural life of this country will, I am confident, become more and more apparent in each succeeding year." Inciting a nationally connected discourse about theatre would be Bessborough's great legacy in Canada.
16 By way of an extended botanical metaphor, Pearl McCarthy wrote, "few could have guessed that, in a short time, the project would have taken root, seeded itself in all kinds of ground and appeared everywhere as such a lusty and astonishing growth. It is anything but a hothouse plant now." She reported Wade's warning to theatre companies "against frittering time on poor plays" and that a "national movement is a thing too big to be taken carelessly. It seems to follow logically that such encouragement as can be given to Canadian playwrights is well-advised." McCarthy, "Drama Festival."
17 Pearl McCarthy suggested that "different types of entries" might better stream participant groups so that groups in rural areas would be given better opportunity to compete and improve, "for nobody can tell where talent will blossom, and the finding of it involves only a little less gamble than staking a mining claim." McCarthy, "Drama Festival."
18 Roly Young, "Festivaluation," In "Rambling 'Round with Roly," *Toronto Star*, c. March 1936.
19 Young, "Festivaluation."
20 "The Drama, Feast or Festival," *Varsity*, 1 March 1937, 2. From the moment the inaugural regional competition schedule was publicized in February 1933, it was clear that because the Central Ontario regional festival dates were so close to university exams, undergraduate dramatic clubs could not compete. This campus conflict would persist for decades, usually leaving Hart House Theatre and Alumnae to represent the university ("Dominion Drama Festival"). For the *Varsity* to claim that the UC Players' Guild, for example, would have placed

higher than the Toronto Masquers, the Theatre of Action, or Alumnae was a bold claim given the relative prominence of these three local theatres. But given the good-quality training these students were receiving at the time, it was not inconceivable.

21 "The Drama, Feast or Festival."

22 Nancy Pyper, "Among the amateurs," *Saturday Night*, n.d.

23 Martha Mann Southgate, interview with Whittaker, 20 October 2017.

24 In her 1935 Central Ontario regional festival recap, *Globe* arts writer Pearl McCarthy amusingly compared the competition's environment to a sports venue, complete with recreational betting: "The fun was high on Saturday night. Plays entered might be deathly serious, but the competition itself took on the aspect of cultural sport. The bets were varied and amusing. Boxes of cigarettes, handkerchiefs, gloves and sweepstakes of small amounts at stake made merry comment in the last intermission. As was noted by the adjudicator, the stage work was eminently earnest and sincere, but almost everybody took the competitive element with good nature and not a little cheer." (McCarthy, "Edgar Stone play wins first place in drama festival," *Toronto Star*, 1 April 1935)

25 In her scholarship on British women playwrights of the 1920s and 1930s, Maggie B. Gale underscores *Nine Till Six*'s significance, concluding that it was "clearly a play about a *woman*'s world of work, which places questions about women's working methods, class interaction, and women's relationship to the economy in the public arena." Gale, "Women's playwrights of the 1920s and 1930s," 29; italics in original.

26 The *Globe*'s reviewer wrote that he regretted missing the December production of *Nine Till Six*'s third act, among several other nonprofessionalizing productions, in a busy week of theatre. Other shows that week included those produced by Hart House Theatre, the Trinity College Dramatic Society, the teachers of Northern Vocational School, and the Little Theatre Club of Upper Canada College. "Theatre and Concert Hall: Brief Comment," *Globe*, 10 December 1932, 5.

27 Now known as the Carlu Auditorium, the space had opened only two years earlier and, for the next half-century, would go on to host internationally renowned musicians. The auditorium was on the seventh floor of Eaton's College St. store (now known as College Park), reportedly the largest furniture store in the British Empire at the time. Fittingly, Timothy Eaton Co. provided the furniture, stage properties, and furs to furnish the play's setting: a London millinery and dressmaking shop. The University of Toronto's Victoria University Orchestra provided musical accompaniment. Proceeds went in aid of the Student Employment Bureau of the university, which, according to the program, "each year sends many hundreds of undergraduates and graduates to part-time, vacation and permanent employment." Certainly, *Nine Till Six*, about women in the workforce, staged atop Toronto's premier furniture store, was a topical choice to raise funds for student employment.

28 DDF entry rules stipulated that all groups must be amateur. The definition of who was an "amateur" and therefore eligible to participate in DDF competitions, and who was not, was fraught from the start. As Betty Lee describes, DDF vice-chairman and honorary director Colonel Henry Osborne responded this way to eligibility queries: "There is no objection to the employment of a professional director by a group. As to the players, there would be an objection to a professional actor who is temporarily out of employment and who proposes to resume in the future. On the other hand, there is no objection to a person who has abandoned his profession permanently and is now engaged in another occupation (Lee, *Love and Whisky*, 103).

It was understood that professional make-up and costume expertise might be sought. As long as its actors were not in the midst of a professional career, a group could compete, thus providing for the DDF a desirable quantity of willing participants. Across Canada, an astounding ninety English and twenty French plays were entered in the first iteration of the regional competitions in 1933 (Lee, *Love and Whisky*, 108). The rules also stipulated that scenes or one-acts must be self-contained, run between twenty and forty-five minutes, be played in front of a curtain with only necessary properties and indicative scenery, and have both literary and acting merit. Judging was divided the same way in the regionals as in the finals: 50 marks for acting ("characterization, audibility of speech, variation in tone, emphasis, gesture and movement," as described in the festival program), 35 marks for production ("the interpretation of the spirit and meaning of the scene"), and 15 marks for costumes and make-up ("stage setting, properties, lighting, costumes and make-up"). The other two adjudicators were E.G. Sterndale Bennett, who had moved to Toronto that year after twenty-five years of producing theatre in Lethbridge, Alberta (outside of his job as an engineer) and Lieutenant-Colonel H.R. Alley, who just finished three years commanding the Third Battalion, C.E.F. Toronto Regiment. Their comments on Alumnae's performance echoed the Little Theatre philosophy: "judges will favour average smooth performance with good team-work, rather than brilliant individual effort." "Dominion Drama Festival."

29 "Business women's club arranges theatre night," *Mail*, 30 March 1933; "Social Events," *Globe*, 30 March 1933, 11.

30 The groups were: Alumnae; The Theatre Arts Group; Toronto Public Library Dramatic Club; Ontario College of Education Dramatic Guild; Canadian Drama League; St. Chad's Church's Anglican Young People's Association (AYPA); the Beaches Library Drama League; two groups from the Central High School of Commerce Evening Class in Dramatic Literature (one presenting Morrow's *The Catalogue* and the other presenting iconoclastic "symphonic expressionism" playwright Herman Voaden's *Rocks*); and three groups from the Hart House Players (Group A presented selections from Shakespeare's *Twelfth Night* with erstwhile Alumnae actor H.E. Hitchman as Sir Toby Belch, Group B presented John Masefield's *Campden Wonder* with Alumnae stalwart and Stone's wife of two years Agnes Muldrew in the cast alongside a young Ivor Lewis, and Group C presented Pinero's *Thunderbolt*, which included occasional Alumnae participants A. Monro Grier and F.J. Mallett). In *Love and Whisky*, Betty Lee cites the *Globe*'s Lawrence Mason's description of the Central Ontario Region adjudicators' assessment, or lack there of, of Voaden's *Rocks*, "which wholly discards standard realist methods of production in favour of the most modernistic art-of-the-theatre" and was therefore "simply ruled out by the adjudicators because, as they frankly stated to the audience, there was absolutely no provision in the marking system for properly evaluating a presentation of this kind" (Lee, *Love and Whisky*, 121).

31 Lawrence Mason, "Third Drama Program: Ontario regional tourney approaches conclusion at Hart House," *Globe*, 25 March 1933, 2.

32 The *Globe*'s Lawrence Mason noted the adjudicators' concern that Alumnae's program notes "injudiciously lessened the suspense of the plot by giving away the point of the third Act in advance." Mason, "Third Drama Program."

At the DDF finals in Ottawa, Rupert Harvey adjudicated the twenty-four plays representing their respective regions: eighteen in English and six in French. Only two of the twelve plays competing at the first Central Ontario Drama Festival were to go on to the DDF finals in Ottawa. But when Hart House Theatre's three entries (*Twelfth Night*, *Campden Wonder*, and *The Thunderbolt*), each directed by Edgar Stone, placed in the top three, including a third-place tie with the Beaches Library's *Dear Brutus*, the optics were not good.

As initiator of both Hart House Theatre and the DDF, Massey was anxious to avoid the appearance of impropriety under the name of the Queen's own representative, Lord Bessborough.

Stone himself must have been a little nervous, given that not only was he the chairman of a competition with three of his company's own plays in the top three, including one that he had directed, but his wife was in the cast of one of them too. Stone and Sterndale Bennett, Lee informs us, "sat up one night and thrashed out the question of the Toronto invitations" (Lee, *Love and Whisky*, 111), to little conclusion. The problem, or at least the optics of the problem, found conclusion when a winner from Victoria, BC, could not make the trip across the country, opening a third spot for the Beaches Library (and certainly not the third Hart House production). Sending two Hart House Players and one Beaches Library team seemed the most reasonable option under the circumstances. The winning *Twelfth Night* scene from Hart House Group A was the letter-reading sequence from Acts II and III, and featured active Alumnae performers Jane Mallet and H.E. Hitchman (Lawrence Mason, "Drama festival ends," *Globe*, 27 March 1933, 11). The introduction of an official competition between these local groups must have impacted, even strained, their relationships given the crossover of actors between them.

33 Wagner, "Infinite Variety or a Canadian 'National' Theatre," 191–2.

34 On his official adjudication form for *As the Tumbrils Pass*, which is extant in Alumnae's collections, London, England's Morley remarked that overall the "performance was straight forward. The characters played to themselves more than to the others on the stage. Individually their work was good – the team spirit was not always evident inasmuch as the characters did not listen well to each other. Set and costumes fairly good." He wrote that Agatha Leonard's Manon Moreau was "well characterized – needed expansion," Alison Ewart's Gervaise was "fairly good though rather over-declamatory," Doris Shiell's Gobemouche was "interesting," Christina Templeton's "La Vicomtesse was "very fair – too placid in the situation," Marion Hunter's Citizeness Jurevant was "satisfactory," and Dorothy Batcheller as Citizeness Clapart and Margaret Tytler as La Tripère gave "strong performances." Mason in the *Globe* further reported that the "'noises off' were well done" and that Milne "built up tension and atmosphere effectively except for one pivotal weakness: the Vicomtesse failed to 'register'" (Lawrence Mason, "*The Poacher* wins: Arts and Letters Club entry takes first place at Hart House," *Globe*, 1 April 1935, 10). With a revised marking rubric in which Production and Stage Presentation were now combined, the performance received a notably low Acting mark of 27/50 and a Production and Stage Presentation mark of 36/50. Although Alumnae did not go on to the finals, Alumnae member Agnes Muldrew did, as an actor in the Arts and Letter's Club's production of J.O. Francis's *The Poacher*, directed by her husband Edgar Stone, whose direction had won the region's first three festivals. Muldrew's trip to the finals surely provided Alumnae with insight into approaches towards their future entries. *As the Tumbrils Pass* is the first Alumnae festival play to have a photograph extant in their collections.

35 Alumnae's books indicate that *Empurpled Moors* cost the group $151.59, including $10.15 for the royalties, $25.00 for the festival entrance fee, $60.00 for Hemingway to direct, $9.75 for the costumes, and $17.14 for the set; it made Alumnae $62.40.

36 Twenty plays (up from fifteen the year before and fourteen the year before that) from eighteen groups were entered in the festival, and for the first time several more were declined entry owing to burgeoning interest. "Our own drama festival," *Globe*, 21 March 1936, 10.

An information booklet sent to all competing groups gave a glimpse into the production conditions of the festival. The handbook described the Hart House Theatre stage's proscenium opening as 28 feet wide and 24 feet deep, "narrowing quickly toward the back," with a masked height at the proscenium of 10.5 feet (18.5 feet from stage to pulleys). No cycloramic curtains were used, but there were three curtains behind the main curtain, the first of which was "peacock-green"; the other two were "black velour." The back wall of the stage was "pale blue-green tinted plaster to give sky effect." The internationally renowned lighting equipment, explained the booklet, "is modern and flexible and is adequate for all needs," including footlights. "Acoustics – good." "Dressing room accommodation is adequate." Groups sent their stage plan, complete list of props, lighting plot, and cue sheets to the Festival Stage Manager in advance of the festival week. Each group arrived at the festival with its own stage manager, electrician, and stage crew. Performance slots were timed precisely to the length of the play, between thirty and forty-five minutes, with just ten minutes between plays and no curtain calls. The first of three or four shows (depending on the schedule) started promptly at 8:15 p.m. and the last concluded as late as 11:25 p.m. Each group received a two-hour rehearsal slot between 4:00 p.m. and midnight in advance of the festival as well as an optional hour for a lighting and props rehearsal on the afternoon of their performance. The festival ran 23–28 March 1936, with tickets for the first five evenings priced at 75¢ and the final Saturday evening at $1.00 (plus tax). A "series ticket" at a reduced price was available before single tickets were sold. Competing groups were able to purchase reduced tickets to resell at regular prices, which helped offset group production costs. By this point, twenty-five "rules and regulations" governed the festival's shows and adjudication. These included a marking rubric that encouraged groups to avoid "plays that are hackneyed, trivial or uninteresting." Sets should tend towards "indicative scenery only as is necessary for the adequate presentation of the play" and should avoid flats and "undue expenditure of money" because the latter is "outside the spirit of the Festival." The groups that won their respective regional festivals were required to pay their way to the Ottawa finals. However, they could request to be billeted to avoid expenses for board and lodging, and the clear expectation was that ticket income earned at the regional festival would pay for most of the travel expenses for the winning groups. "1936 Festival of The Central Ontario Region of the Dominion Drama Festival" [Information booklet], March 1936.

37 Adjudicator Allan Wade was a British actor who, while in his twenties before the war, had worked as playreader and assistant to famed theatre director and thinker Harley Granville Barker.

38 Quoted in "Arts and Letters Players adjudged best in region," *Toronto Telegram*, c. 30 March 1936.

39 "Arts and Letters Players adjudged best in region." In his official report, adjudicator Allan Wade wrote: "A very good play of its kind and most interesting production. I thought that the three sisters were the most successful in achieving the 'Brontë' atmosphere … I would have liked more attention given to pauses and hesitations, to bring out the underlying unspoken emotion in the play, and I felt that Branwell in particular gave too much of thin surface value only to his lines. The grouping and movements were very good throughout, and the pictorial effect of the costumes and setting was a very valuable asset to the production." Wade, Adjudicator's Report for *Empurpled Moors*.

In his public comments, Wade said of Alison Ewart's Anne, Agnes Muldrew's Charlotte, and Dorothy Batcheller's Emily that the "three sisters were almost perfect; the timid, self effacing Anne; the more masterful Charlotte; the enigmatic Emily who has always been a puzzle to everybody … I could quite believe these actually were the Brontës come to life and playing before us" ("Arts and Letters Players adjudged best in region"). He added that Christina Templeton gave a "very clever little performance" of Tabby (Wade, Adjudicator's Report for *Empurpled Moors*). Wade "thought that with the exception of some minor directorial defects, this more than satisfactory exposition of mid-Victorian inhibitions and repressions was an excellent and courageous bit of workmanship. The differentiation of voice and the costuming of the play were deservedly praised" (Mason, "Festival awards"). The marking rubric had shifted again, with Alumnae earning 32/40 for Acting, 18/25 for Production, 12/16 for Stage

Presentation, 6/10 for Diction and Audibility, and 5/10 for Dramatic Enterprise. With a total mark of 73/100, once again Alumnae did not rank in the top three, and therefore did not progress to the national finals.

Instead of Alumnae, the previous year's DDF winner, the Arts and Letters Club, and its production of MacKaye's *Napoleon Crossing the Rockies*, also directed by Hemingway, went on to Ottawa to be adjudicated by Harley Granville Barker himself. The Beaches Library Drama League also went on to Ottawa for Shaw's *Overruled*, as did the Playwrights' Studio Group with an original farce called *Nellie McNabb* by Lois Reynolds, who was a member of the *Globe*'s editorial staff. Mason, "Festival awards."

In April 1936, invited by the Players Guild of Hamilton, Alumnae presented *Empurpled Moors* at the I.O.O.F. (Independent Order of Odd Fellows) Temple on Gore St. in Hamilton, Ontario, as part of a bill of "Three Festival Plays." Also, the Players Guild presented its regional entry that had gone on to compete in Ottawa, Mary Plowman's all-women drama *Come Out of Your Cage*, while the Toronto Masquers offered their entry, Leonard J. Hines and Frank King's *Calling the Tune*, directed by Sterndale Bennett.

40 Thelma Craig, "Play about Ireland best Canadian drama at regional finals," *Globe and Mail*, 1 March 1937, 4.

41 First place went to the Toronto Masquers for John Coulter's play *The House in the Quiet Glen*, directed by Sterndale Bennett; second place went to Theatre of Action's *Bury the Dead*, produced by David Pressman; and third place went to Alumnae. Nancy Pyper's *This Mad World* was also recommended to go to Ottawa by regional adjudicator George de Warfaz, a Belgian-born British playwright, actor, and producer who taught at the Institut Français du Royaume-Uni in London, and whom Bridle in his column called "caustic" after the first five evenings (Augustus Bridle, "Festival plays reach week's highest level," *Toronto Star*, 27 February 1937). This was the first time that the Central Ontario Region offered a physical trophy to the winner, a silver cup donated by festival president Hugh S. Eayrs. The trophy would remain with the winning group for a year, at which point they received a replica to keep – unless a group won three years in a row, in which case they would keep the original and a new one would be made. Lawrence Mason, "Music in the Home, Concerts, the Drama," *Globe and Mail*, 30 January 1937, 10.

42 Halpenny, "History of the University Alumnae Dramatic Club," 1945, 2.

43 The only man in the cast of *The Cradle Song*, W.E.S. Briggs, played the doctor. He would go on to be a Governor of the DDF. The cast received dramaturgical assistance from Rev. Father Joseph L. O'Donnell, a professor at the university's St. Michael's College, regarding "all music and matters connected with ritual and service." They also received several costume pieces and advice regarding "details of apparel" (*Ottawa Paper*, 3 May 1937, 1–3) from the Sisterhoods of Toronto, to which Alumnae gifted a pair of candlesticks that were, according to a thank you letter, placed "near Our Divine Lord on our High Altar" (Letter from Monastery of Our Lady of Charity to Agatha Leonard, 1 June 1937). The production made $171.32 in ticket sales, but company expenses totaled $360.36, generating a notable loss.

44 Bridle, "Festival plays reach week's highest level."

45 Thelma Craig, "High level reached with play program," *Globe and Mail*, 27 February 1937.

46 Craig, "High level reached with play program."

47 Rose MacDonald, "Adjudicator gives roses, commends three plays," *Toronto Evening Telegram*, 27 February 1937.

48 Lew Weingarten, "Drama Festival," *Varsity*, 1 March 1937, 2.

49 Craig, "High level reached with play program."

50 MacDonald, "Adjudicator gives roses, commends three plays."
51 Craig, "High level reached with play program."
52 MacDonald, "Adjudicator gives roses, commends three plays." In contrast to earlier superlatives lauding the improved quality of productions, Warfaz deemed the 1937 productions to be disappointing.
53 AMM, 19 March 1937. On Tuesday, 20 April 1937, Alumnae remounted Act I of *The Cradle Song* at the Margaret Eaton Hall theatre as part of a presentation of the three winning plays at the Central Ontario Region festival, "in reverse order of their original adjudication," according to the program. Here, Alumnae made a profit of $165.37, leaving a deficit across the two performances of $20.67, before heading to Ottawa the following week. The now merged *Globe and Mail* reported that there was "considerable social activity" around the three plays during their Margaret Eaton Theatre run, listing several dinners before and after the performance. "Mrs. Allen Neilson is hostess at large tea this afternoon at her home on Warren Road," *Globe and Mail*, 15 April 1937, 14.
54 AMM, 9 June 1936.
55 The Toronto Masquers won the Bessborough Trophy for best play in either language for Coulter's *The House in the Quiet Glen*, notable in that it was an original Canadian play. This was the second time in a row that a new Canadian play won the DDF. (The London Little Theatre's production of *Twenty-Five Cents* by Sarnia's W.E.M. Harris won the previous year.)
56 Saint-Denis, "*The Cradle Song*. M. St.-Denis, Saturday Night adjudication," Adjudicator's Report, 1 May 1937, 1. The first French DDF adjudicator, Michel Saint-Denis was co-founder and managing director of the London Theatre Studio and, later, a major consulting voice in the establishment of the National Theatre School of Canada.
57 Saint-Denis, "*The Cradle Song*."
58 Quoted in "Bessborough trophy won by Toronto entry in original Canadian play," *Ottawa Citizen*, 3 May 1937, 1, 16.
59 Sandwell, [no title recorded] *Saturday Night*, 15 May 1937.
60 AMM, 2 May 1937.
61 AMM, 5 May 1937.
62 "Complimentary dinner for festival players, directors and author," *Globe and Mail*, 4 May 1937, 10.
63 "Alumnae Association enjoy original revue," *Varsity*, 24 January 1938, 1.
64 AMM, 12 January 1938.
65 "U.C. Alumnae," *University Monthly*, May 1937.
66 Halpenny, "History of the University Alumnae Dramatic Club," 1945, 3.
67 "U.C. Alumnae," *University Monthly*, May 1937.
68 At a meeting of the club executive in early April 1938, the matter arose that adjudicator Malcolm Morley had received an "anonymous letter" that was "attributed to one of our members." Although there is no record of the contents of that letter or the reason it had been sent to Morley, the situation was serious enough that a motion was passed that Agatha Leonard and president Florrie Hunt would compose a response on behalf of the club to the Festival Committee "disclaiming all responsibility" for the letter (AEM, 5 April 1938). Whether someone had expressed disapproval of Morley's adjudication of *The Old Maid* is unclear. But Alumnae's executive, it was clear, would not stand for unprofessional activity in their name. At a club meeting three days later, Hunt read the proposed letter to be sent to the Festival Committee, the Club voted that it should be sent, and, as noted in the same paragraph in the minutes, a motion passed that club member Doris Dignum's resignation from the club be

accepted (AMM, 8 April 1938). Although she had not been involved in *The Old Maid*, Dignum had been one of the club's most consistently active members since appearing in their production of the one-act *Rosalind* in 1923. By the following month, letters had been received from the Festival Committee and Morley (AMM, 13 May 1938). The matter was not mentioned again.

69 "Six groups offer plays by Canadians," *Globe and Mail*, 27 February 1939, 9.

70 As the festival rules had changed again, this time allowing both one-act and full-length plays to compete, this was also the first festival at which a full-length Canadian play was presented: H. Campbell Duncan's *Dark Orchard* ("Six groups offer plays by Canadians"). In her festival announcement, festival director Nella Jefferis commented that "this is a hopeful sign. It was an indication that the Canadian playwright has arrived. It should be a definite stimulus to Canadian playwriting and should begin to make us feel the possibilities of a really Canadian theatre movement" (quoted in "Six groups offer plays by Canadians"). For the occasion, Ness entertained at tea at the Eaton's Round Room in honour of the director and cast of her play, and on other occasions that week at the home of Katherine Anglin, at a "waffle party" hosted by Club president Mary Evans, and, on the Festival's opening night, at the Women's Union.

This latter event at the Women's Union included the presence of several members of the cast of *The Importance of Being Earnest* on their dark night at the Royal Alexandra Theatre. This notably high number of publicized events surrounding Ness's play may have been, at least in part, filling a void left when the DDF's Central Ontario Region committee did not plan its usual pre-festival events owing to the recent death of its past president, "dear friend and inspiring leader" Albert H. Robson (Margaret Aitken, "Festival Plans," in "Between You and Me," *Toronto Telegram*, n.d.), whose influence as a literary and art critic as well as vice-president of the Toronto Art Gallery had earned him Lord Bessborough's nod as one of the original governors of the DDF ("A. H. Robson, prominent Canadian critic, dies," *Varsity*, 8 March 1939, 1).

71 "Amateur festival 'art democracy,'" *Toronto Telegram*, 25 March 1939.

72 "Central Ontario Drama Festival" [Program], February 1947, 1.

73 "Amateur festival 'art democracy.'"

74 Roly Young, "Rambling 'Round with Roly," *Globe and Mail*, 25 February 1947, 9.

75 AMM, 1944–45.

76 AAGM, 2 June 1945.

77 AMM, 18 September 1945. In September 1945, Agatha Leonard reported that she had attended a meeting of the CTA and, having consulted previously with Kay Anglin, Eleanor Woodside, and Mary (Emmy) Smart, who attended the CTA with her, recommended that the club join the CTA by paying the $25 fee entitling Alumnae to two members on the CTA council. Members present at the Alumnae meeting voted in favour of joining: Agatha Leonard, Agnes Muldrew Stone, Elspeth Wilson, Margaret Tytler, Christina Templeton, Edna Norwich, and Margaret Ness (Secretary *pro tem*). Leonard and Templeton agreed to be representatives on the CTA council.

78 "Civilians enjoy soldiers' revue," *Globe and Mail*, 2 November 1945, 23.

79 As Anton Wagner notes, the inaugural issue of Roly Young's *Civic Theatre Magazine* listed the following charter members: Belmont Players, Canada Players, Canadian Ballet, Canadian Mastersigners, Comedy Theatre Players, Community Players, Plaquest Drama Group, Toronto Children's Theatre, Village Players, the Players Guild of Hamilton, and the Woodstock Dramatic Society (Roly Young, "What is the Civic Theatre Association?," *Civic Theatre Magazine* [October 1945], 7.) A subsequent *Globe and Mail* article added to this list the Academy of Ballet, Toronto Caravan Players, University Alumnae Dramatic Club, and the

Playwrights Studio Group, but omitted the Toronto Children's Theatre and the Village Players ("The Civic Theatre Association," *Globe and Mail*, 13 September 1945, 6.). See Wagner, "Infinite Variety or a Canadian 'National' Theatre," 188n17.

80 Wagner, "Infinite Variety or a Canadian 'National' Theatre," 174.

81 Roly Young, "Rambling with Roly," *Globe and Mail*, 3 April 1946, 9.

82 Roly Young, quoted in Helen Beattie, "Drama Festival," *Globe and Mail*, 11 April 1946, 8.

83 Young, quoted in Helen Beattie, "Drama Festival."

84 The CTA chose eight adjudicators for the festival, four of whom judged each performance at a time. Among them were names familiar to Toronto theatre before the war, like Edgar Stone, Herman Voaden, Lt.-Col. Rai Purdy, Prof. Robert Finch, Mary Lowery Ross, Dora MacMillan, and James Dean. The "guest chairman" of the adjudicators was *Maclean*'s magazine editor H. Napier Moore (Roly Young, "Rambling with Roly," *Globe and Mail*, 10 April 1946, 17). Born in Newcastle upon Tyne, Moore was an anglophile of the first order; some saw him as a relic of the Commonwealth past and adversary of Canadian content. He was an avid contributor to the Arts and Letter Club variety review, and a theatre lover (McKillop, *Pierre Berton: A Biography*, 222–3). His opening remarks linked the CTA Drama Festival to the on-hiatus DDF and its local feeder, the Central Ontario Region festival, observing a "general satisfaction over the revival of the drama festival movement" (H. Nappier Moore, quoted in Helen Beattie, "Drama Festival"). Moore's "imperial disposition" (McKillop, *Pierre Berton: A Biography*, 222) may have endeared him to Philip Johnson's *Orange Blossoms*.

85 Roly Young, quoted in Beattie, "Drama Festival."

86 W.A.D., "Drama Festival Trophy Awarded to Belmont Group," *Globe and Mail*, 18 April 1946, 29.

87 The CODL adjudicator was Mr. Esse W. Ljungh, who was a student dramatist, producer, and director in Sweden before he moved to Winnipeg in 1927 to work as a journalist and then as a practitioner at the Winnipeg Little Theatre and the Winnipeg Radio Players. He then became the director of drama for CBC for the prairie region before transferring to the CBC's Toronto offices in June 1946 ("Central Ontario Drama Festival" [Program], February 1947, 1–2). The ten productions competing at CODL that year included two plays by Pirandello and one by Clifford Odets by companies that included the Newmarket Dramatic Club, the Trinity College Dramatic Society (featuring William Hutt), the Caravan Players (twice, featuring William Needles), the University College Players' Guild, the Civic Theatre (Young's initiative was participating twice, including with one production featuring Eric House), the Arts and Letters Club, and the Toronto Conservatory Players. Alumnae's *The Happy Journey* featured Jean Stewart and Sam Telford as Ma and Pa Kirby and Robert Jackson and Jean Smith as their children; the four drive from Newark to Camden to visit their daughter Beulah (Ruth Johnson); the Stage Manager character (Sydney Collins) spoke lines from the minor characters.

88 E.G. Sterndale Bennett, letter to Mary Wallace Smart, 30 April 1947.

89 Ruth Johnson, letter from to the Secretary of the Zonta Club of Toronto, 27 September 1948.

90 E.G. Wanger, "Varsity Alumnae dramatists shine in *Years Ago*," *Globe and Mail*, 2 November 1948, 25. Alumnae encountered challenges in mounting the production. They initially had difficulty finding a director, as evidenced in a letter from the CODL festival committee secretary Julia Jarvis to Alumnae president Francess Halpenny, stating: "I hear from Agatha [Leonard] that you have chosen a play, but have had bad luck with the director so far. I hope things will straighten out soon, as we simply couldn't have a Festival without your help! I think things are going along very well so far, and we hope to have a good week" (Jarvis, letter to Frances Halpenny, 16 January 1948). Alumnae finally retained John Mantley, who had done radio and stage acting and stage directing in Toronto and Pasedena, California, having graduated from

Victoria College in 1942 (Elizabeth Mascall, "Drama festival winners to present *Years Ago*," *Varsity*, 1 November 1948, 1). There were also wardrobe issues, as reported by Margaret Aitken in her *Telegram* column "Between You and Me," as two pairs of high button boots were not forthcoming. Instead, they found two pairs of skating boots of appropriately different sizes and asked a cobbler to dye one pair brown and one pair black. However, as Aitken described it, "the cobbler made a mistake. He dyed two shoes black and two brown, all right, but not the matching two." As a result, Barbara Allen and Elizabeth Rand wore shoes that matched in colour, but not in size (Aitken, "Pinched," *Toronto Telegram*, 13 March 1948).

91 Robert Stuart came from Scotland, having had a career in Lancashire and London before joining the Royal Air Force. On D-Day his plane was shot down and he broke his back and was unconscious for four days ("Central Ontario Drama Festival" [Program], March 1948, 2). The *Globe and Mail*'s Colin Sabiston drew attention to Stuart's judgments as being of a "man not only professionally conversant with every phase of theatrical activity, but also of one who is keenly conscious of the right of an audience to expect good value from those who undertake its entertainment." Colin Sabiston, "Alumnae Club, Winnifred Pilcher given festival awards at Hart House," *Globe and Mail*, 22 March 1948, 3.

92 Quoted in Colin Sabiston, "Two festival evenings enjoyed by audiences," *Globe and Mail*, 20 March 1948, 10. On his form, Stuart remarked that the "fresh spontaneity that this group put into their playing was so invigorating as to make one forget it is not an excellent play. Their attack and sensitiveness to the audience response was quite professional. Very well done indeed" (Robert Stuart, Adjudicator's form, CODL, 18 March 2019). He Awarded *Years Ago* 78/100 with 8's for Team Work, Interpretation, Tempo, Grouping, Climax, and Variation; 8's for Properties and Costumes; and 7's for Setting (which he said was "Well done but dull") and Lighting.

93 Chapman, *"Who's in the Goose Tonight?,"* 231.

94 Roly Young, "Bergner play postponed; the wildest of Wilder; Alumni [*sic*] does *Years Ago*," *Globe and Mail*, 16 October 1948, 8.

95 Sabiston, "Two festival evenings enjoyed by audiences."

96 "14 plays chosen for Dominion Drama Festival," *Globe and Mail*, 22 March 1948, 3.

97 "Central Ontario Drama Festival" [Program], March 1948, 9, 2.

98 Rose MacDonald, "Alumnae cast wins trophy as best in drama festival," *Evening Telegram*, 22 March 1948.

99 Sabiston, "Alumnae Club, Winnifred Pilcher."

100 MacDonald, "Alumnae cast wins trophy as best in drama festival."

101 Four full-length and six one-act plays competed, including two Canadian plays (Mona Purser, "Drama festival week contest of fine talent," *Globe and Mail*, 12 March 1948, 13). In all, 72 productions competed across all regionals that year ("14 plays chosen for Dominion Drama Festival"), featuring nearly 500 actors ("The Dominion Drama Festival" [Program], April 1948, 3). In his concluding remarks, Stuart added that he hoped the Toronto regional festival would someday present only Canadian plays (Sabiston, "Alumnae Club, Winnifred Pilcher given festival awards at Hart House," *Globe and Mail*, 22 March 1948, 3). On Friday, 2 April 1948, Alumnae member Ruth Johnson entertained the cast, crew, and members of past productions at her home in honour of their CODL-winning play ("Personal Notes," *Globe and Mail*, 2 April 1948, 12).

102 Kay Rex, "Theatre hopefuls ready for drama fete," *Globe and Mail*, 26 April 1948, 12.

103 The DDF's British adjudicator Robert Speaight was an actor, producer, author, critic, and BBC broadcaster who had practised theatre in Liverpool and London before founding the Summer School of Drama at the University of Notre Dame, Indiana ("Dominion Drama Festival" [Program], April 1948, 7).

104 Quoted in “Comedy, tragedy share Dominion Drama Festival,” *Globe and Mail*, 1 May 1948, 10.
105 “Comedy, tragedy share Dominion Drama Festival.”
106 Quoted in “Comedy, tragedy share Dominion Drama Festival.”
107 “Comedy, tragedy share Dominion Drama Festival.”
108 Kay Rex, “London Little Theatre in Shaw’s *Saint Joan* judged festival’s best,” *Globe and Mail*, 3 May 1948, 3.
109 Alumnae, *Autumn Crocus* program, November 1949, 7.
110 “*Years Ago* in Hart House Theatre November. 1, 2, 3, and 4,” *Toronto Telegram*, 16 October 1948.
111 John Mantley, CP telegraph to Katherine Anglin, 28 April 1948.
112 “Dramatic club seek aspidistra for Friday play,” *Ottawa Citizen*, 30 April 1948.
113 “Dramatic club seek aspidistra for Friday play.”
114 Michael Meiklejohn, “Serial Letter,” n.d.
115 Even after it arrived back in Toronto, production difficulties revisited *Years Ago*. It was reported in the *Star* that the “ancient and valuable telescope” they had borrowed for the play had a broken glass: “Gloom settled over the company as they tried to calculate how many weeks, at how much per week, it would take them to pay for the damage. Home again, they confessed the breakage and promised to make amends. ‘Oh, that’s all right,’ said the owner cheerfully, ‘It’s been broken for years’” (“*Years Ago*,” *Star*, 22 October 1948). Other unusual props sourced by Agatha Leonard for the play included one whale’s tooth used as a doorstop, a Dresden china spittoon, ancient lamps, and a corset cover.

The other thirteen groups competing at the DDF finals were the Vancouver Little Theatre, Edmonton Community Theatre, Workshop 14 (Calgary), Little Theatre Club of Saskatoon, London Little Theatre, two groups from the Ottawa Drama League, Le Caveau (Ottawa), the Montreal Repertory Theatre, Les Compagnons (Montreal), the Theatre Guild of Saint John, the University of Manitoba Dramatic Society, and Le Cercle Molière (Winnipeg), which was the only professional group (Kay Rex, “Theatre hopefuls ready for drama fete,” *Globe and Mail*, 26 April 1948, 12). Many of these groups were already, or would become, influential theatre-makers in their respective cities.
116 Rose MacDonald, “Witty comedy on Irish life features bill,” *Toronto Telegram*, 28 January 1949.
117 “*Mighty Mr. Sampson* tops drama offerings,” *Globe and Mail*, 23 March 1949, 4.
118 Quoted in Jack Karr, “Expert, graphic description *Jericho* fine foreign film,” *Toronto Star*, 23 March 1949.
119 “Drama festival brings two new Canadian plays,” *Globe and Mail*, 25 March 1950, 28.
120 The festival adjudicator, Maxwell Wray, was a British actor experienced on stage at the Old Vic Theatre before becoming director of Sir Barry Jackson’s Birmingham Repertory Theatre.
121 Rose MacDonald, “Audibility is emphasized first ‘must’ for actors,” *Toronto Telegram*, n.d.
122 Quoted in MacDonald, “Audibility is emphasized first ‘must’ for actors.”
123 Nathan Cohen, *The Critic* 1, no. 2 (April 1950).
124 Whittaker, *Setting the Stage*, 1999, 165.
125 Whittaker enumerated the tendencies of Robert Speaight, the year’s regional adjudicator, as he had observed them in the past, including that although his favourites had been “widely varied,” he tended to go “directly to the axis of a play for his final judgment. On which character or characters does the axis rest? Are these roles sufficiently well-played to carry the whole weight of the drama’s resolution? If they are, then the play might be accounted successful in its most important aspect.” Whittaker also noted that because Speaight was an actor, he “is less likely

to be impressed by good direction than by good acting. He has remarked that for him the actor must take precedence above the director, the designer, or even the playwright." Also, "he has rewarded worthy Canadian plays," an important aspect to the DDF's ongoing mission to nationalize the country's theatre. And Speaight had rewarded good ensemble acting and also designers who "triumphed over the limitations of stage facilities." These "few remarks" were intended to be of some last-minute help to the theatre groups competing that year, although he quipped, "no guarantee is offered, however, no entrance fees refunded." Whittaker thus signalled that he was more knowledgeable about the national theatre scene than any Toronto theatre critic who had come before. Whittaker, "Original Canadian plays enthuse festival judge," *Globe and Mail*, 19 March 1949. 12.

126 Whittaker, "Show Business," *Globe and Mail*, 3 April 1950, 9. Taking a post-war interest in encouraging cultural growth and artistic professions in the country, Prime Minister Louis St.-Laurent appointed the Royal Commission on National Development in the Arts, Letters and Sciences in April 1949. Known as the Massey Commission because it was chaired by Vincent Massey, now the University of Toronto's Chancellor, its members travelled the country meeting professional and amateur artists, scholars, and other experts in their fields to determine how to best found and encourage cultural activity. The commission was driven in part by concern that American influence could neutralize "Canadian" arts and culture. The resulting Massey Report laid the groundwork for many cultural initiatives across the country, not the least of which was for a "national theatre." The report ultimately recommended state-funded support for this arts; this led to the creation of the Canada Council for the Arts in 1957.

127 Whittaker, "Show Business," *Globe and Mail*, 22 February 1951, 9.

128 Lotta Dempsey, "Person to Person," *Globe and Mail*, 27 February 1951, 12; "Shaw work club's entry in festival," *Globe and Mail*, 24 February 1951, 8.

129 Alex Barris, "Sylvia Paige, John Colicos, judged best actors," *Globe and Mail*, 19 March 1951, 19.

130 Halpenny, "Shall we join the ladies?"

131 Whittaker, "Agonies of suspense – but festivals thrive on rivalry," *Globe and Mail*, 10 March 1951, 10.

132 "Shaw very weak, sleeps deep sleep of a tired man," *Globe and Mail*, 1 November 1950, 1.

133 UADC, "Fifth Concert and Theatre Series," Forest Hill Collegiate Auditorium Program for *In Good King Charles's Golden Days*, 2–7 April 1951, 2.

134 "University club play praised by adjudicator," *London Free Press*, 19 May 1951.

135 Lotta Dempsey, "Person to Person." *Globe and Mail*, 27 February 1951, 12.

136 Dempsey, "Person to Person," 27 February 1951.

137 Regarding Alumnae's Canadian premiere of the play, David Peddie in the *Varsity* concluded, ambivalently, that the characters "hold the attention of the audience and maintain their interest in spite of the speech making." Peddie said that Colicos, who was already working for Andrew Allan and Esse Ljungh "in top CBC productions," was "splendid as the Merry Monarch, charming, urbane, witty, and in the last Act combined his charm with the serious disappointment of a man of great intelligence into perfect harmony." Poffenroth and Needles were "outstanding," although Follows as Newton was "uneven" because he took Newton too seriously and seemed out of keeping with the rest of the group" (Peddie, "*Good King Charles*," *Varsity*, 1 March 1951, 6). Rose MacDonald faulted Follows for his "light voice," but praised Francess Halpenny for her "excellent and curiously touching Katherine" (MacDonald, "Alumnae shine in Shaw play for festival," *Toronto Telegram*, 28 February 1951).

138 Nathan Cohen described adjudicator Robert G. Newton, a British actor, producer, writer, and critic, as a "small man of intense and good-humoured sensitivity. He's an extraordinarily active man. How engaging he was, as he scuttled about the stage making his points with his whole body, like some darting and benevolent spider! He put himself completely in the spirit of the festival. He kept it much more festive than competitive." Nathan Cohen, *CJBC Views the Shows* [Transcript], CJBC, 18 March 1951, 3.
139 Barris, "Sylvia Paige, John Colicos, judged best actors."
140 Nathan Cohen, *CJBC Views the Shows* [Transcript], CJBC, 18 March 1951, 1.
141 Quoted in Grant Roberts, "Presentation of GBS work highly praised," *Globe and Mail*, 16 March 1951, 12; and quoted in Barris, "Sylvia Paige, John Colicos, judged best actors."
142 Quoted in Barris, "Sylvia Paige, John Colicos, judged best actors."
143 Quoted in "University Alumnae club is praised at festival," *Toronto Star*, 16 March 1951, 8.
144 "University Alumnae club is praised at festival."
145 Whittaker had directed the twenty-two-year-old Colicos several times in Montreal and, remarkably, Colicos had played Hamlet the night before the CODL performance in a CBC broadcast (Barris, "Sylvia Paige, John Colicos, judged best actors"). Cohen said on CJBC: "I don't think I'll forget for a long time Mr. Colicos's graciousness, his warmth, the poetry of his gestures, the music of his voice. I belong to the 'dancing on one's hat for joy' school of criticism and Mr. Colicos made me do just that ... Well, if you could see John Colicos in the flesh you'd find that he has a figure and gracefulness to match his voice and you would, as we all did, agree that he was the happy choice, the only choice for the best." Cohen, *CJBC Views the Shows*, 18 March 1951.

Speaking of Colicos at CODL afforded Cohen the opportunity to remark on the relationship between professional and amateur theatre in 1951: "The distinction between amateur and professional is very fine, quite often. A clever definition – which isn't originally mine – is that what the amateur may sometimes do through happy inspiration, the professional does as a matter of course. The distinction also has to do with stage presence, the ease that suggests one is to the manner born. And that's what there is about Mr. Colicos: he is to the manner born. You can learn this ease: it depends on one's experience, of course; and it also depends on one's confidence in the director, in one's fellow players and in the play itself. Mr. Colicos has all these to make him professional. But he has something that's beyond professionalism. Hazlitt says somewhere that a great actor is great the first time he steps upon a stage. You can learn to be a good actor, an excellent actor; but you cannot learn to be a great one, anymore than you can learn to be a great preacher. I have scarcely the courage to admit that there's greatness in Mr. Colicos's acting; but I think that there's something of this." Cohen, *CJBC Views the Shows*, 18 March 1951, 2.

Like Colicos, Needles had a busy twenty-four hours, playing the role of John in the CBC serial *John and Judy* "less than half an hour before walking onto the stage" as Kneller. "Fifth Concert and Theatre Series," Forest Hill Collegiate Auditorium Program, 2.
146 Quoted in "University Alumnae club is praised at festival."
147 "University Alumnae club is praised at festival."
148 Lotta Dempsey, "Person to Person," *Globe and Mail*, 17 March 1951, 15.
149 Barris, "Sylvia Paige, John Colicos, judged best actors."
150 Whittaker, "Show Business," *Globe and Mail*, 19 March 1951, 29.
151 Roberts, "Presentation of GBS work highly praised."
152 Quoted in "Presentation of GBS work highly praised."
153 Roberts, "Presentation of GBS work highly praised."

154 "Gala night opens drama tests," *London Free Press*, 15 May 1951, 1.

155 Lenore Crawford, "Best English play award for Welland," *London Free Press*, 21 May 1951, 1.

156 Jose Ruben, the French-born and American-employed DDF adjudicator, was known for directing musicals and operas as well as for teaching theatre on the American west coast. He also occasionally took a sabbatical year as a director of amateur societies, including the Comedy Club and the Snarks in New York. Beatrice F. Taylor, "Drama festival adjudicator, N.Y. expert lauds amateurs," *London Free Press*, 14 May 1951.

157 Kay Rex, "Toronto Alumnae club praised for handling Shaw play well," *Globe and Mail*, 19 May 1951, 10.

158 Nathan Cohen, *CJBC Views the Shows* [Transcript], 20 May 1951.

159 Whittaker, "John Colicos, 23, wins award for best actor," *Globe and Mail*, 21 May 1951, 21.

160 Jack Karr, "Showplace," *Toronto Star*, n.d. Montreal's Les Compagnons de St.-Laurent won the festival's top prize for their production of the Flemish comedy *Les Gueux au Paradis*, receiving the red-, gold-, and blue-illuminated Bessborough Trophy on Sunday, the day after festival concluded. Crawford, "Best English play award for Welland."

161 Cohen, *CJBC Views the Shows* [Transcript], 20 May 1951.

162 Alumnae's March 1952 CODL entry, Ferenc Molnár's three-act political satire *Olympia*, did not fare as well. Directed by Whittaker with a set co-designed by Whittaker and Roy Jackson, the choice was part of a "Molnár trend" (Whittaker, "Show Business," *Globe and Mail*, 29 February 1952, 25). Andrew Allan's *Stage '52* radio drama series ran *The Captain of St. Margaret's* the same week, the Ottawa Repertory Theatre produced *The Play's the Thing* that season, and Hart House Theatre produced *Liliom* the following season. For *Olympia*, Douglas Ney received the best actor award for his "outstandingly good" work as Kovacs (quoted in Cecil J. Young, "Top drama festival award goes to *Golden Boy*," *Globe and Mail*, 17 March 1952, 3). Adjudicator Pierre Lefevre, a New York-born Frenchman who had acting experience in the West End and the Old Vic as well as broadcast experience during the war, commended Whittaker's pacing and Halpenny's "deep understanding of the play, the period, and the style of the writer." But he declared that he had to choose between *Olympia* and the upstart Actors Company production of Odets's *Golden Boy*, selecting the latter because it had fewer "unexplained" moments (quoted in Young, "Top drama festival award goes to *Golden Boy*"; and in "*Golden Boy* hits hard, takes title," *Globe and Mail*, 17 March 1952, 3). The Saturday before the CODL festival week, the *Globe and Mail* ran an illustration featuring a whimsical sketch of each of the seven competing plays.

Lefevre faulted the production's "partial failure to present more strongly the seriousness of the love between Olympia and Kovacs" and a lack of "intellectual argument," although the "comedy was excellent" ("Drama festival: Adjudicator finds *Olympia* amusing and distinguished opening presentation," *Globe and Mail*, 11 March 1952, 8). Rose MacDonald reported that he singled out Halpenny with his highest compliments for "having a very good sense of period and poise" and because "she dared to use her face" (MacDonald, "Sharp wit in *Olympia* fine drama week start," *Toronto Telegram*, 11 March 1952). Although they were not selected to go to the DDF finals in Saint John, New Brunswick, they did produce *Olympia* twice more to raise funds in the event that the winning group, the Actors Company, could not travel (Whittaker, "Show Business," 28 March 1952, 12). Alumnae sent the Actors Company a telegram while they were competing at the DDF finals wishing them well (AMM, 1 May 1952).

163 AMM, 4 December 1951.

164 AMM, 16 January 1952.

165 AMM, June 1952.

166 Malcolm MacKinnon, "The family furies," *Varsity*, 24 February 1953, 7.
167 Rose MacDonald, "Alumnae cast plays difficult drama by Eliot," *Toronto Telegram*, 21 February 1953.
168 AMM. 27 November 1952.
169 "This is the T.S. Eliot season," *Globe and Mail*, 14 February 1953, 10. Back in June, Ruth Francis had suggested Enid Bagnold's three-act play *Lottie Dundas* as a possible festival show. Discussion ensued with Francess Halpenny's suggestion that before the group submitted a show to CODL, that show should have a previous production planned with a performance space secured. Katherine Anglin agreed to chair a committee to find a suitable location. They had also considered Fry's 1950 *Ring Round the Moon*, an adaptation of Jean Anouilh's 1947 *Invitation to the Castle*. At the end of October, Alumnae voted to look into its availability and to ask Whittaker to direct it, noting that if it could not be done, *The Family Reunion* was a second option (AMM, 27 November 1952). Within a month, Whittaker cast *The Family Reunion*, having learned that the Vic Dramatic Club would be doing *Ring Round the Moon* in December, leading him to throw the "weight of his opinion for *The Family Reunion*" (AMM, 27 November 1952). There was also the question of where they would present *The Family Reunion* before the CODL festival. Initially they planned for a two-night run at the Unitarian Church with a seating capacity of 350, but they ultimately chose the Arts and Letters Club (AMM, 19 January 1953), which proved to be advantageous because it "cost less than the average show" (AMM, 3 Mar 1953). Rehearsals began on 1 December.
170 MacKinnon, "The family furies." E.G. Wanger called the production a "rich and thought-provoking experience," but also "often disappointing" owing to a "persistent and arbitrary reoccurrence of dimming and brightening of lights without logical motivation, only to underline mood" (Wanger, "Preview of festival entry thought provoking experience," *Globe and Mail*, 21 February 1953, 10). Rose MacDonald called Whittaker's direction "thoughtful if perhaps controversial" when dealing with Eliot's challenging poetic text (MacDonald, "Alumnae cast plays difficult drama by Eliot"). Malcolm MacKinnon said Ruth Johnson's Amy "subsides in quiet frailty" while Francess Halpenny "leaves Agatha an unexplained paradox, but delivers her lines with a faultless sense of timing and vigorous rhythm" (MacKinnon, "The family furies"), although, said Wanger, "her tragedy remains largely superficial" (Wanger, "Preview of festival entry thought provoking experience"). The "very young, but talented" (MacDonald, "Alumnae cast plays difficult drama by Eliot") Richard Easton gave a "richness of attack and clarity of vision [to] establish Harry as the dominant figure" (MacKinnon, "The family furies"), giving his "lines with an appreciation of the sonority of their content" (MacDonald, "Alumnae cast plays difficult drama by Eliot"). His was a "strong and rich interpretation" by "an actor of keen intelligence and a tremendous flair for dramatic highlights. Apart from occasional lapses into flamboyant oration, he gives a most compact and poignant performance" (Wanger, "Preview of festival entry thought provoking experience").
171 MacKinnon, "The family furies."
172 Wanger, "Preview of festival entry thought provoking experience."
173 "*Family Reunion* chosen with seven other plays for Dominion finals," *Globe and Mail*, 6 April 1953, 5.
174 Filming the production would cost "$9.00 a reel for a five minute film, and about $20.00 for the filming and processing," AMM, 3 March 1953.
175 Alex Barris, "Adjudicator liked play itself but vague about performance," *Globe and Mail*, 21 March 1953, 10.
176 Barris, "Adjudicator liked play itself but vague about performance."

177 Quoted in Barris, "Adjudicator liked play itself but vague about performance."
178 Whittaker, "Bessborough – Father of the Drama Festival," *Globe and Mail*, 17 March 1956, 14.
179 "Frances Tobias, R. Easton are two best performers," *Toronto Star*, n.d.
180 Richard Easton was a former Montrealer ("Frances Tobias, R. Easton are two best performers") who had already played in "professional or semi-professional theatre" in Canada and would perform in the Stratford Festival's inaugural season that summer. MacDonald, "Alumnae cast plays difficult drama by Eliot."
181 Barris, "Adjudicator chooses Alumnae club players over six other groups."
182 Margaret Aitken, "Between You and Me," *Toronto Telegram*, 9 April 1953. Whittaker and James E. Dean, an active member of CODL, were also given awards separate from the festival "for outstanding service in the interests of Canadian drama." "Frances Tobias, R. Easton are two best performers," *Star*.
183 Aitken, "Between You and Me," 9 April 1953.
184 AMM, 9 April 1953.
185 Beyond raising funds, Ruth Johnson needed to find both a sitter for her children and a substitute for her role in the radio program *Kindergarten of the Air*. Lotta Dempsey, "Person to Person," *Globe and Mail*, 10 April 1953, 1.
186 Whittaker, "Show Business," *Globe and Mail*, 13 May 1953, 13.
187 AMM, 9 April 1953.
188 "*Family Reunion* chosen with seven other plays for Dominion finals."
189 "Toronto cast wins praise at festival," *Star*, 7 May 1953.
190 Quoted in "Toronto cast wins praise at festival."
191 Quoted in Ray Baines, "Toronto drama bid given high praise," *Victoria Daily Colonist*, 7 May 1953.
192 Quoted in "Toronto cast wins praise at festival."
193 Audrey St. Denys Johnson, "Eliot play praised by festival judge," *Victoria Daily Times*, 7 May 1953, 16.
194 Quoted in Baines, "Toronto drama bid given high praise."
195 Whittaker, "Show Business," *Globe and Mail*, 13 May 1953.
196 Whittaker, Letter to Margret Spence, 25 March 1999.
197 "Sculptured memento," *Globe and Mail*, 10 June 1953, 10; "Presentation of new drama trophy," *North Toronto Herald*, 16 October 1953. Thirteen brand-new trophies were handed out to the festival's various winners, each sculpted in wood by leading Canadian artists Frances Loring, Florence Wyle, and Sylvia Daoust. The trophies were gathered together and displayed at the Art Gallery of Toronto (now the Art Gallery of Ontario) throughout June 1953. "Presentation of new drama trophy," *North Toronto Herald*, 16 October 1953; Whittaker, "Show Business," *Globe and Mail*, 17 June 1953, 12.
198 Whittaker, "Show Business," *Globe and Mail*, 11 May 1953, 18.
199 Quoted in Whittaker, "Show Business," 11 May 1953.
200 Quoted in Whittaker, "'Future of Canadian theatre is now' – adjudicator Lefevre," *Globe and Mail*, 9 May 1953, 14. Lefevre acknowledged that he himself had played the role of Downing, Harry's servant, on the London stage. Baines, "Toronto drama bid given high praise."
201 Whittaker, "Show Business," *Globe and Mail*, 17 June 1953, 12.
202 AAGM, 30 June 1953.
203 The minutes added, "Then the Club discovered yet another of Dave Gardner's talents when he showed the colour shots he had taken during the trip to Victoria." AAGM, 30 June 1953.

204 Whittaker, "Show Business," *Globe and Mail*, 8 May 1953, 14.

205 In response to Lefevre's critique of the show's lighting, Whittaker wrote parenthetically: "(How one longed to tell him at this point that the fuses had blown no less than five times during the production. Here was lack of subtlety indeed. But in a festival as with any other performance, alibis have no value nor have good intentions)." Whittaker, "Show Business," 8 May 1953).

206 Whittaker, "Show Business," 8 May 1953.

207 The awkward tongue-in-cheek column began with the question, "Tell me, my dear sir, how you feel about the directorial honour conferred upon you?" "Pleased but frustrated" was the answer, and Whittaker-the-director went on from there, eventually concluding that "I am naturally proud and happy about winning the Louis Jouvet Trophy. I am also well aware that I owe the honour to a great many people." He concluded: "Yes, I see what you mean, Mr. Whittaker. And I hope you will always be able to retain your humility." Whittaker, "Jouvet Trophy for direction is honor that must be shared," "Showbusiness," *Globe and Mail*, 16 May 1953, 12.

208 AMM, 30 June 1953.

209 Across all five of its iterations – at the Arts and Letters Club, CODL at Hart House, Hart House again, Forest Hill, and the DDF in Victoria – *The Family Reunion* had cost Alumnae $4,054.00, while they received $3,179.20, meaning they need to defray costs of $874.80 (AMM, 25 May 1953). It was decided to pay Whittaker another $50 to "supplement his director fees" (AMM, 25 May 1953). Back in April, Alumnae were in conversation with the Manitoba Drama League about remounting *The Family Reunion* in Winnipeg ("CODL winners go to Hart House," *Globe and Mail*, 4 April 1953, 10) "on their return from Victoria" (AMM, 9 April 1953), but the invitation was later "withdrawn" (AMM, 9 April 1953).

210 Whittaker, letter to Margret Spence, 25 March 1999.

211 Quoted in Alex Barris, "*Venus Observed* draws praise of adjudicator," *Globe and Mail*, 12 January 1954, 20.

212 Jack Karr, "On-Stage," *Star*, 5 March 1955, 11.

213 Whittaker, "Showbusiness." *Globe and Mail*, 5 April 1955, 9.

214 Rose MacDonald, "Playcraftsmen gain Dominion Festival bid," *Toronto Telegram*, 5 April 1955; Whittaker, "Showbusiness," *Globe and Mail*, 5 April 1955, 9.

215 Whittaker, "Playwrights are setting Canada on world's stage," *Globe and Mail*, 9 April 1955, 11.

216 Whittaker, "Bessborough – Father of the Drama Festival."

217 Whittaker, "Our stage has turrets; now for a broad base," *Globe and Mail*, 10 March 1956, 14.

218 Whittaker, "Our stage has turrets; now for a broad base."

219 To call the director Leon Major "promising," Dave Dunsmuir wrote in *Varsity*, "seems a little inadequate by now." He took Joudry's "heavy-handed piece of modern theatre" and "utilized the methods of split-level staging and split-second, non-representational emotional exchanges" to create a "clever presentation." Moreover, "Major's staging has neatly avoided a sense of moony introspection, scene succeeding on scene with a satisfying rapidity, from multi-purpose plateau to one (and occasionally both) of the downstage domestic locales." Dave Dunsmuir, "Real Canadian theatre," *Varsity*, 16 March 1956, 12.

220 Jack Karr, "Varsity group captures 5 drama festival prizes," *Toronto Star*, 9 May 1956.

221 Jack Karr, "Showplace," *Toronto Star*, 14 March 1956.

222 "Delayed premiere," *Toronto Star*, 3 March 1956.

223 The Garden Centre Theatre in Vineland, in the Niagara region, planned to give the play its Canadian premiere, but the plan had fallen through by July 1955, presumably because it could

not be cast (Whittaker, "Showbusiness," *Globe and Mail*, 23 May 1955, 30). Agatha Leonard entertained Alumnae members at her house on Sunday, 19 February 1956, to celebrate the forthcoming production ("Social and Personal Notes," *Globe and Mail*, 21 February 1956, 13).

224 "Delayed premiere."

225 Quoted in Whittaker, "Our stage has turrets; now for a broad base."

226 Whittaker, "Our stage has turrets; now for a broad base."

227 Whittaker, "Showbusiness," *Globe and Mail*, 14 March 1956, 11.

228 Rose MacDonald, "Fine production of Joudry play," *Toronto Telegram*, 14 March 1956.

229 Jack Karr, "Showplace," *Toronto Star*, 14 March 1956.

230 Rose MacDonald, "Fine production of Joudry play," *Toronto Telegram*, 14 March 1956.

231 Karr, "Showplace," 14 March 1956.

232 MacDonald, "Fine production of Joudry play."

233 Karr, "Showplace," 14 March 1956.

234 Whittaker, "Showbusiness," *Globe and Mail*, 2 August 1956, 27.

235 Whittaker, "Showbusiness," *Globe and Mail*, 29 March 1956, 10.

236 Karr, "Showplace," 14 March 1956.

237 Whittaker, "Showbusiness," *Globe and Mail*, 6 April 1956. 9.

238 "One of the properties," *Globe and Mail*, 5 April 1956.

239 Whittaker, "Alumnae entry wins praise of adjudicator," *Globe and Mail*, 7 April 1956, 4.

240 Quoted in Whittaker, "Alumnae entry wins praise of adjudicator," *Globe and Mail*, 7 April 1956. 4.

241 Whittaker, "Alumnae entry wins praise of adjudicator," *Globe and Mail*, 7 April 1956, 4.

242 Quoted in Whittaker, "Alumnae entry wins praise of adjudicator."

243 Quoted in Karr, "Varsity group captures 5 drama festival prizes."

244 Whittaker, "Alumnae entry wins praise of adjudicator."

245 Quoted in Whittaker, "Alumnae entry wins praise of adjudicator."

246 At the request of CODL, Alumnae ran *Teach Me How to Cry* for five evenings at Hart House Theatre to defray the costs of the Sherbrooke trip (Karr, "Varsity group captures 5 drama festival prizes"). But on one evening, Lawrence was unable to perform because of the "press of university work" (Whittaker, "Showbusiness," *Globe and Mail*, 18 April 1956, 9), so Major took over, making that performance "something of a collectors item," in Whittaker's words Whittaker, "Showbusiness," *Globe and Mail*, 18 April 1956, 9.

Of note, playwright J.B. Priestley, in town to promote his new novel, attended a rehearsal for *Teach Me How to Cry*, as well as the Crest's production of Noël Coward's *Present Laughter*, before embarking on a cross-Canada tour with Robertson Davies for the Canadian Association for Adult Education "in an examination of mass media and the expression of individualism." Whittaker, "Showbusiness," 18 April 1956, 9.

247 Whittaker, "Alumnae tops festival with *Teach Me How to Cry*," *Globe and Mail*, 9 May 1956, 15.

248 Karr, "Varsity group captures 5 drama festival prizes."

249 Quoted in Karr, "Varsity group captures 5 drama festival prizes."

250 Quoted in Whittaker, "Our drama festival needs a self-diagnosis," *Globe and Mail*, 14 April 1956, 12.

251 Whittaker, "Our drama festival needs a self-diagnosis."

252 Whittaker, "Our drama festival needs a self-diagnosis."

253 UADC, letter (draft) to musicians' union re: musicians for the 17–21 April 1956 run of *Teach Me How to Cry*, n.d.

254 Whittaker, "Showbusiness," *Globe and Mail*, 19 April 1956, 34. The three musicians were Johnston's Royal Conservatory of Music students: Ben Rose (trumpet), Ronald Chandler (first clarinet), and Lloyd Orchard (second clarinet).
255 "The Alumnae win a festival," *CODL Newsletter*, June 1956, 1.
256 Whittaker, "Showbusiness," *Globe and Mail*, 18 May 1956, 9.
257 Quoted in Rose MacDonald, "Joudry play moving, pleasing," *Toronto Telegram*, 18 May 1956.
258 Whittaker, "Let the stars shine – and experts adjudicate," *Globe and Mail*, 26 May 1956, 18.
259 Rose MacDonald, "Calvert trophy to Toronto," *Toronto Telegram*, 22 May 1956, 34.
260 "Toronto players win with *Teach Me How to Cry*," *Toronto Star*, 22 May 1956.
261 Whittaker, "Showbusiness," *Globe and Mail*, 21 May 1956, 14.
262 MacDonald, "Calvert trophy to Toronto."
263 Whittaker, "Showbusiness," *Globe and Mail*, 4 June 1956, 33.
264 Whittaker, "Showbusiness," 25 May 1956.
265 E.H. Lampard, "Raucous audience helps destroy effect of first Vineland play," *St. Catherine's Standard*, 5 June 1956.
266 Rose MacDonald, "New Melinda in role in Pat Joudry Play," *Toronto Telegram*, 6 June 1956.
267 Whittaker, "Showbusiness," *Globe and Mail*, 6 June 1956, 17.
268 "City honours drama group," *Toronto Telegram*, 6 July 1956, 16.
269 *"Teach Me How to Cry," Bizstore Books*, https://store.bizbooks.net/teachmehowtocry.aspx
270 Whittaker, "Showbusines," *Globe and Mail*, 17 June 1958, 9.
271 Accompanied by Canadian music, text from the play was read at the university's Convocation Hall in December 1956 ("Canadian works make bow," *Globe and Mail*, 8 December 1956, 8; John Kraglund, "Music in Toronto," *Globe and Mail*, 14 December 1956, 10). Joudry's next play, *Three Rings for Michelle*, ran at Toronto's Avenue Theatre with "over $3000 worth of seats" selling before rehearsals even began. Whittaker, "Showbusiness," *Globe and Mail*, 19 October 1956, 14.
272 AAGM, 2 June 1956.
273 Doris N. Stacey, letter to Dramatists' Play Service, 27 June 1957.
274 Stacey, letter to Dramatists' Play Service.
275 Andrew J. Loeffler (Dramatists Play Service Inc.), letter to Doris N. Stacey, 2 July 1957. As was usual at the forty-seat Coach House, admission was by invitation only ("Theatre's grain market: Finances, xenophilia hamper output of British playwrights," *Globe and Mail*, 21 September 1957, 23) and by "contribution taken in lieu of a regular admission," a point that convinced Dramatists Play Service to reduce the royalties "drastically" (Loeffler, Letter to Doris N. Stacey).
276 "Showbusiness," *Globe and Mail*, 31 December 1957, 4.
277 Molly Thom, "From Coach House to Firehall. DRAFT," note to Robin C. Whittaker, 23 August 2009.
278 Whittaker, "Alumnae Dramatic Club presents controversial *Waiting for Godot*," *Globe and Mail*, 9 November 1957, 17.
279 Program for Samuel Beckett's *Waiting for Godot* at the Frederic Wood Theatre, Vancouver [Playbill], 28, 29 June and 2–6, July 1957. Photograph of 1957 production in program for Samuel Beckett's *Waiting for Godot* at the Frederic Wood Theatre, Vancouver, 21 September–3 October 1983. 15. Both in UBC Library Open Collections online. The production is also noted in David Spurgeon, "Gadgets add to hobby so brush is good gift," *Globe and Mail*, 22 June 1957, 19. Many Alumnae members believe their production to have been the Canadian premiere. But in her curriculum vitae from the early 2000s, Pamela Terry listed

her Alumnae *Waiting for Godot* production, adding, "which I now find, for sure, was not a Canadian premiere as UBC staged it before UADC."

280 Whittaker, "Alumnae Dramatic Club presents controversial *Waiting for Godot*."

281 Rose MacDonald, "Nobody walked out on this varsity *Godot*," *Toronto Telegram*, 7 November 1957, 52.

282 Thom, "From Coach House to Firehall."

283 Whittaker, "Showbusiness," 15 November 1957, 11; "Curtain Club plans comedy on Bigamy," *Globe and Mail*, 16 November 1957, 15; "*Godot* held over," *Toronto Star*, 16 November 1957, 13.

284 Halpenny, Prospectus, "The Alumnae Theatre: A History 1919-1999," In ABMM, 4 June 2001.

285 Beckwith, ed., *Unheard of*, 323.

286 Mary Jukes, "Once over lightly," *Globe and Mail*, 14 April 1958, 19.

287 Quoted in Jukes, "Once over lightly."

288 Quoted in Maurice Cutler, "Toronto actors praised at Halifax festival," *Toronto Telegram*, 16 May 1958.

289 Beckwith, ed., *Unheard of*, 324, 323.

290 "*Venus Observed* stars Miss Terry," *Globe and Mail*, 26 September 1953, 10.

291 Halpenny, "Shall we join the ladies?"

292 Rose MacDonald, "Nobody walked out on this varsity *Godot*," *Telegram*, 7 November 1957, 52. Beckett, and since his death his estate, has famously shut down performances of his work that are not staged to the letter, including maintaining the gender restrictions that the actors in *Waiting for Godot* must be men, leading to various court cases. These restriction led the London, England clown-based group Silent Faces, made up of female and non-binary performers, to create their show *Godot is a Woman*. Kate Wyver, "Not waiting for Godot: new show tackles Beckett's ban on women," *The Guardian*, 18 October 2020.

293 MacDonald, "Nobody walked out on this varsity *Godot*."

294 PJ Hammond, interview with Whittaker, 20 October 2017.

295 Beckwith, ed., *Unheard of*, 323.

296 Helen Parmelee, "Two full-time jobs on her hands," *Toronto Telegram*, 31 December 1960.

297 "The play keeps coming back," *Toronto Telegram*, n.d.

298 Whittaker, "Alumnae Dramatic Club presents controversial *Waiting for Godot*."

299 MacDonald, "Nobody walked out on this varsity *Godot*."

300 Cathie Breslin, "Waiting waiting waiting," *Varsity*, 7 November 1957, 4.

301 MacDonald, "Nobody walked out on this varsity *Godot*."

302 Denis W. Johnston notes that Fred Euringer provided "inspirational leadership" to Theatre Passe Muraille founder Jim Garrard while Euringer taught him at Queen's University. Johnston, *Up the Mainstream*, 31.

303 Breslin, "Waiting waiting waiting."

304 Ronald Johnson, "Moving with the movies," *Globe and Mail*, 10 April 1958, 8.

305 MacDonald, "Nobody walked out on this varsity *Godot*."

306 Breslin, "Waiting waiting waiting."

307 E.W., "Toronto players score smash hit," *Halifax Mail-Star*, 16 May 1958, 2, 6.

308 Whittaker, "Showbusiness," *Globe and Mail*, 15 November 1957, 11.

309 MacDonald, "Nobody walked out on this varsity *Godot*."

310 Breslin, "Waiting waiting waiting."

311 Whittaker, "Showbusiness," *Globe and Mail*, 24 October 1957, 8.

312 Whittaker, "Showbusiness," *Globe and Mail*, 1 November 1957, 8.

313 Whittaker, "Alumnae tackle Beckett's Godot," *Globe and Mail*, 2 November 1957, 13.
314 MacDonald, "Nobody walked out on this varsity *Godot*."
315 Whittaker, "*Waiting for Godot* evokes varying interpretations," *Globe and Mail*, 11 April 1958, 8.
316 Whittaker, "Showbusiness," *Globe and Mail*, 31 December 1957, 4.
317 Jukes, "Once over lightly."
318 "Five Toronto groups in '58 drama festival," *Toronto Star*, 22 March 1958.
319 Quoted in Rose MacDonald, "Irish charm, whimsy in *Waiting for Godot*," *Toronto Telegram*, 28 March 1958.
320 R.C.M., "'Bombshell' returns to Hart House" [No newspaper, n.d.].
321 MacDonald, "Irish charm, whimsy in *Waiting for Godot*."
322 Quoted in Whittaker, "Showbusiness," *Globe and Mail*, 28 March 1958, 10.
323 Whittaker, "University Alumnae win top honour at Drama Festival," *Globe and Mail*, 31 March 1958, 14.
324 Jukes, "Once over lightly."
325 Quoted in Jukes, "Once over lightly."
326 Jukes, "Once over lightly."
327 Quoted in Jukes, "Once over lightly.".
328 Quoted in Jukes, "Once over lightly."
329 Parmelee, "Two full-time jobs on her hands."
330 Jukes, "Once over lightly."
331 Alumnae, Press Release for *The Increased Difficulty of Concentration*, 17 March 1979.
332 "*Venus Observed* stars Miss Terry"; Jukes, "Once over lightly"; Parmelee, "Two full-time jobs on her hands." Pamela Terry's curriculum vitae from the 1990s indicates that while touring with the US Army of Occupation, Special Services Branch, as an actress in Austria, southern Germany, and Trieste, she performed in the 1947 Broadway play by Norman Krasna, *John Loves Mary* (Ronald Reagan starred in the 1949 film version) and in the 1937 farce by Allen Boretz and John Murray, *Room Services* (Jack Lemmon starred in the New York premiere).
333 "*Venus Observed* stars Miss Terry"; Jukes, "Once over lightly."
334 "AM&D Calendar," *Varsity*, 9 December 1958, 5.
335 Whittaker, "University Alumnae win top honour at Drama Festival."
336 Whittaker, "*Waiting for Godot* evokes varying interpretations."
337 Whittaker, "University Alumnae win top honour at Drama Festival."
338 Whittaker, "*Waiting for Godot* evokes varying interpretations."
339 "*Now* we tell you," *CODL Newsletter*, April 1958, 8–9.
340 Now a seasoned theatre critic with the *Manchester Guardian*, *Time and Tide* magazine, and the BBC, Hope-Wallace was president-elect of the Critics Circle of Great Britain. Whittaker, "Showbusiness," *Globe and Mail*, 15 April 1958, 13.
341 This amount, the DDF's invitation explained, was part of $10,000 distributed to the eight regional winners invited to compete, $7,000 of which came from the Canada Council. The amount was decided upon based on distance travelled to the finals and number of members in the cast, their stage managers, and directors. R. MacDonald, letter to Mrs. John Beckwith, 22 April 1958.
342 Cutler, "Toronto actors praised at Halifax festival."
343 CN telegraph to the cast (*Waiting for Godot*), 15 May 1958.
344 Barbara Barnett, CN telegraph to *Waiting for Godot*, 15 May 1958.
345 Alumn, CN telegraph to The Cast (*Waiting for Godot*), 15 May 1958.

346 Kenneth Levinson, CP telegram to Mrs. Pamela Beckwith, 15 May 1958.
347 Kay, CP telegram to Ivor Jackson, 15 May 1958.
348 E.W., "Toronto players score smash hit."
349 Quoted in E.W., "Toronto players score smash hit."
350 Quoted in Joe Dupuis, "Toronto play and actor win festival honours," *Toronto Telegram*, 20 May 1958, 35.
351 E.W., "Toronto players score smash hit."
352 Quoted in E.W., "Toronto players score smash hit."
353 E.W., "Toronto players score smash hit."
354 Quoted in Cutler, "Toronto actors praised at Halifax festival," *Toronto Telegram*, 16 May 1958.
355 Quoted in E.W., "Toronto players score smash hit."
356 Whittaker, "Praise is cautious for Alumnae's *Godot*," *Globe and Mail*, 16 May 1958, 12.
357 Whittaker, "B.C. players win top awards at festival; director sold pies to pay rent for hall," *Globe and Mail*, 19 May 1958, 1.
358 Ed Simon, "He's prepared to like what he sees: Drama adjudicator Hope-Wallace on way," *Globe and Mail*, 3 May 1958, 13.
359 "*Now* we tell you," 9.
360 Whittaker, "Lorca play here," *Globe and Mail*, 8 December 1958, 25.
361 Whittaker, "DDF chain reaction touched off tonight," *Globe and Mail*, 7 January 1959.
362 In a moment that became part of CODL lore, on the festival's last night a voice from the auditorium, Russ Waller's, interrupted a production of *Mrs. McThing* to say, "Stage manager, there's a fire on stage!" "Beat it out with your broom" said another voice to the actress playing the Ugly Witch. She did, while two crew members tried to rip off the fabric covering the burning scenery. With the fire extinguished, the play went on – and went on to win best visual presentation. The fire, it was reported, had been caused by the smoke-flash effect that accompanied the witch's entrance. The tense moment afforded Whittaker the opportunity to report that "even if the place burned down, evidently nobody could get too excited by this year's regional Festival." Whittaker, "Richmond Hill Club wins top festival awards," *Globe and Mail*, 12 January 1959, 10; "Hart House witch fights stage fire," *Toronto Star*, 11 January 1959.

Whittaker noted that the growing dissatisfaction around the festival was not as evident in less populated regions of Canada, where "professional theatre is not yet so well established in those centres that the non-professional efforts can be spurned." He added the distinction that in Montreal, the "other professional (and somewhat healthier) centre," "ambitious professional groups" were using the DDF as a stepping-stone. But in Toronto the "split between devoted amateur and aspiring professional is more marked" and the "Toronto regional, therefore, has changed in character. The standards are higher, competing for audiences against the professionals, as the amateur groups must do. The entries are fewer." Whittaker, "DDF chain reaction touched off tonight."

A year, later in a preview piece written while Alumnae prepared to travel to the DDF finals with James Reaney's new play *The Killdeer* in May 1960 (see New Play Chapter), Whittaker, a DDF governor and executive committee member, asked whether the twenty-seven-year-old festival had "kept up with the country in the advances made since the end of the war," advances that included the proliferation of television, the opening of the Stratford Festival, the funding schemes from the Canada Council, and the "huge new auditoriums which dot the land." He also wondered whether the "advance of professional theatre" would mean that the DDF festival had served its purpose, although he offered that even if professional theatre advanced in "more than two or three centres across the country, and more firmly marked than it is at present, there would be no end to the need of the Festival." He concluded by arguing that a "closer bond must be established between the existing, community-rooted Little Theatres and the tiny visionary professional and semi-professional projects now thrusting their heads above ground." In effect, Whittaker was arguing for nonprofessionalizing companies like Alumnae to help establish a profession, with the DDF as a catalyst. Whittaker, "Westward ho actors go," *Globe and Mail*, 14 May 1960, 13.

363 Quoted in Rose MacDonald. "Toronto group wins four victories," *Toronto Telegram*, 4 May 1959, 12.
364 MacDonald, "Toronto group wins four victories."
365 Whittaker, "Special showing," *Globe and Mail*, 14 May 1959.
366 Nathan Cohen, "Five down, three to go," *Toronto Star*, 22 May 1959.
367 Whittaker, "Mr. Congreve's play," *Globe and Mail*, 29 February 1960, 28.
368 "Congreve revived," *Globe and Mail*, 8 October 1960, 16.
369 Antony Ferry, "Coach House team score in comedy," *Toronto Star*, 25 February 1960.
370 Whittaker, "Mr. Congreve's play."
371 Ferry, "Coach House team score in comedy."
372 Whittaker, "Mr. Congreve's play."
373 "*Boy Friend* returns to local speakeasy," *Globe and Mail*, 17 September 1960, 18.
374 Whittaker, "Remember amateurs? They're still around," *Globe and Mail*, 14 October 1960, 32.
375 Whittaker, "Remember amateurs? They're still around"; Rose MacDonald, "Comedy of 3 centuries ago 'sold out' today," *Toronto Telegram*, 14 October 1960.
376 MacDonald, "Comedy of 3 centuries ago 'sold out' today."
377 Whittaker, "Well-advised British rejection," *Globe and Mail*, 22 March 1961, 30.
378 Quoted in Whittaker, "Well-advised British rejection."
379 Whittaker, "Adjudicator's wife gets directing award," *Globe and Mail*, 27 March 1961, 27.
380 Quoted in Whittaker, "Adjudicator's wife gets directing award."
381 Whittaker, "Adjudicator's wife gets directing award," The Drao Players went on to win best production at the DDF finals that year. Janice Tyrwhitt, "Amateur theatre's cast of thousands," *Maclean's*, 6 January 1962.
382 Alumnae, "Building Fund Appeal," July 1961, 1.
383 AMM, 14 September 1961.
384 AMM, 23 January 1961.
385 "Markyta wins again," *Globe and Mail*, 14 April 1962, 13.
386 AMM, 23 January 1961.
387 AMM, 14 September 1961.
388 In October 1965, after Alumnae returned to CODL membership, they offered in the "Canadian One-Act Play Workshop" Don Bryn's thirty-minute play *The Flowered Suit*, directed by Glenna Davis, at the then new, but now demolished, Colonnade Theatre at 131 Bloor St. W. Alumnae had introduced Bryn's play as part of their series of modern readings four years earlier. Ron Hartmann provided responses for the non-adjudicated "workshop." AEM, 8 September 1965.
389 "Cure for shyness saved money too," *Toronto Star*, 16 September 1967, 81.
390 Beckwith, ed., *Unheard of*, 326.
391 Hunter, *Still Hunting*. Web.
392 Whittaker, "What's all this fuss next week about Canadian plays and playwrights?," *Globe and Mail*, 11 March 1967, 25. Other regions offered Norman Williams's *Line of Vision* (East), Martin Hunter's *Out Flew the Web and Floated Wide* (North), and Aviva Ravel's *The Adventures of Mendel Fish* (West).

393 Quoted in Whittaker, "What's all this fuss next week … ?"
394 Whittaker, "Hunter big winner in CODL finals," *Globe and Mail*, 20 March 1967, 15.
395 Beckwith, ed., *Unheard of*, 325.
396 Whittaker, "Impressions of electronic life charm audience," *Globe and Mail*, 18 March 1967, 21.
397 Whittaker, "Hunter big winner in CODL finals."
398 Theatre Ontario membership certificate for UADC, 1972.

Chapter 7

1 Tony Robinow, "Three interesting moderns presented by the Coach House Theatre," *Varsity Weekend Review*, 17 November 1961, 4.
2 Nancy Kee (Alumnae publicity), "The Alumnae Theatre," c. 1981.
3 Pamela Terry Beckwith, letter to Peter M. Dwyer (Canada Council), 25 June 1963.
4 See Robin C.Whittaker, *Hot Thespian Action!*, 2008.
5 Jane Carnwath, interview with Whittaker, 19 October 2017.
6 Carnwath, interview with Whittaker.
7 Wagner, "Introduction: Establishing Our Boundaries," 3.
8 Barton, "Introduction: Creating Spaces," ix.
9 Dora Smith Conover, in O'Neill, "The Playwrights Studio Group," 90.
10 Lois Reynolds Kerr, "The Playwrights Studio Group, 1932–1941," 35. Like many Little Theatre playwrights, the Playwrights Studio Group founders were journalists (Chansky, *Composing Ourselves*, 13) – and in their case, members of the Canadian Women's Press Club. They had approached Hart House Theatre artistic director Edgar Stone for feedback on their plays and were granted a minimal production slot two or three times a year. Most of the group's members were women, and most of their plays were comedies, inspired by the popular playwright Noël Coward, to make people laugh during the Depression. Group co-founder Dora Smith Conover noted that there were men who had plays produced by the group, but said they did not help and that the plays "proved feeble and blatantly crude and the men did not come along with us any more … We didn't set up to be a women's group, it just happened. No men cared to work. We'd have welcomed men writers." Quoted in O'Neill, "The Playwrights Studio Group," 92.
11 Kerr, "The Playwrights Studio Group, 1932–1941."
12 Alumnae produced plays by group members Rica McLean Farquarson – *Sure of a Fourth*, directed by Margaret Tytler for Alumnae and likely for its world premiere at Hart House Theatre too – and Winifred Pilcher – *It May Happen Here*, directed by Jean Stewart. Farquarson was herself from a family of journalists: she was editor of the *Canadian Home Journal*, her husband Bob became managing editor of the *Globe and Mail*, and her son Duart, born two years later, became a respected foreign correspondent ("Newsman a consummate pro," *Edmonton Journal*, 2 April 2011). Group member Dora Smith Conover later recalled that "our sweet tenacious" Leonora McNeilly "cajoled, bullied and practically forced" Stone into producing their first set of plays at Hart House Theatre. Between 1932 and 1941, group members remained active playwrights and CODL festival competitors, producing dozens of full-length and one-act plays, revues, skits, and songs, often at Hart House Theatre, two or three times a year. O'Neill, "The Playwrights Studio Group," 90.
13 "Alumnae presents three plays." *University Monthly*. February 1935.
14 Alongside Anglin's play that evening, Margaret Tytler directed Sacha Guitry's *Villa for Sale*, a "sparkling comedy excellently translated," while Agnes Muldrew Stone directed and acted

in Gordon Bottomley's *Sisters*, a "poetic interlude skillfully produced and acted." "Alumnae presents three plays," February 1935.

15 AMM, 10 July 1935.

16 Augustus Bridle, "U.C. Alumnae present clever mystery play," *Toronto Star*, 26 November 1935.

17 At their January 1936 meeting, accompanied by Frank Hemingway and "unusually delicious sandwiches and cakes, not to mention the customary coffee," the club passed a motion "with astonishing unanimity," according to Genevre Campbell's minutes, to produce Oscar W. Firkins's *Empurpled Moors* for the regional festival instead of a work-in-progress by Anglin. AMM, 3 January 1936.

18 "Drama in Canada," *Globe and Mail*, 26 June 1937, 24.

19 AMM, 19 September 1937.

20 John Coulter's star was already on the rise. He had moved to Canada from Ireland in June 1936 ("Just off the press," *Globe and Mail*, 8 May 1937, 28), and the next year his play *The House in the Quiet Glen* won the DDF award for best Canadian play. The Abbey Theatre Players in Dublin produced *The Folks in Brickfield Street* that year and had already agreed to acquire the rights to produce *The Family Portrait*. Augustus Bridle noted that it would be the "first Belfast play ever taken by the Dublin company" (Bridle, "Amateur cast stars in new Coulter play," *Toronto Star*, n.d.). One daily reported that "rumour has it that New York scouts are to be in Toronto this week to look it over" (unattributed clipping in Alumnae Theatre Company collection, Toronto), while another daily noted that Coulter had accepted an invitation from Michel Saint-Denis to join him in London next January at his theatre ("Abbey Players will perform Toronto play," *Toronto Telegram*, n.d.). An advertisement in the program noted *The Family Portrait*'s publication "in two editions" by Macmillan of Canada, one in separate paper cover for 75¢ and the other for $1.75 in cloth combined with *The House in the Quiet Glen*. The publication was given a "Presentation" a week before the production ("Book fair news," *Globe and Mail*, 5 November 1937, 26). Receptions were held in Coulter's honour after the Tuesday and Thursday performances, with member Dorothy Batchelor as convenor ("Society Notes," *Globe and Mail*, 15 November 1937, 12).

21 Rose MacDonald, "College group presents play at Hart House," *Toronto Telegram*, c. November 1937, n.pag.

22 "Theatre and Concert Hall: Brief Comment," *Globe and Mail*, 4 December 1937, 5.

23 MacDonald, "College group presents play at Hart House."

24 Augustus Bridle, "Amateur cast stars in new Coulter play," *Toronto Star*, n.d.

25 MacDonald, "College group presents play at Hart House."

26 Bridle, "Amateur cast stars in new Coulter play."

27 MacDonald, "College group presents play at Hart House."

28 Eric Alwinckle became a war artist of note. Francess Halpenny, "History of the University Alumnae Dramatic Club," 1945, 2.

29 MacDonald, "College group presents play at Hart House."

30 Deputy Assistant Secretary to the Governor General, letters to Mrs. Leslie Hunt, 3, 5, 6, 10, 15, 18 November 1937. Alumnae Theatre Company collection, Toronto.

31 Halpenny, "History of the University Alumnae Dramatic Club," 3–4.

32 AMM, 4 November 1937.

33 Joan (Mrs. George) Pape, letter to Alumnae Dramatic Club, 27 November 1937, Alumnae Theatre Company collection, Toronto.

34 "Alumnae Association enjoy original revue," *Varsity*, 24 January 1938, 1.

35 AMM, 2 December 1938.

36 Margaret Ness's *Enter the Prince* was published in *Curtain Call* (Toronto, DDF's official magazine) in January 1938.

37 "Graduate writes festival entry," *Varsity*, 8 March 1939, 1.

38 Kerr, "The Playwrights Studio Group, 1932–1941."

39 AMM, 8 September 1938.

40 "Alumnae Dramatic Club," *University Monthly*, March 1939. Ness had had difficulty researching an important historical date for her play. In order to know what sort of flowers to decorate the set with, she needed to find out the month that the Pulitzer Prize would have been awarded to one of her characters – answers apparently had ranged from "summer" to "September" until she learned it was May. Margaret Aitken, "Festival Plans" and "On Her Toes," *Toronto Telegram*, n.d.

Alumnae had no less difficulty confirming the other one-act. Once they had secured as director Arthur Vogel, the director of the communist group Theatre of Action, they changed the play from his choice, James Wallace Bell's *Symphony in Illusion*, to Grantham's *The Italian Women*, at which point Vogel pulled out because, according to Alumnae's notes, "he did not feel capable of directing" it (AMM, 28 December 1938). According to the program, *The Italian Woman*, set in Catherine de Medici's bedchamber on a snowy night in AD 1588, concerns Catherine, who is "wracked with pain and tortured by ghosts" while the Council of France meets with the Duke of Guise across the courtyard and Henry III awaits the deliberations. Lorna Sheard directed it instead.

41 AMM, 20 February 1939.

42 "Alumnae Dramatic Club," March 1939. Also noted in Aitken, "Growing Up."

43 Thelma Craig, "Dramatic fare of wide range at festival," *Globe and Mail*, 18 March 1939, 4.

44 Craig, "Dramatic fare of wide range at festival."

45 Paraphrased in Craig, "Dramatic fare of wide range at festival."

46 Craig, "Dramatic fare of wide range at festival."

47 "Alumnae Dramatic Club," March 1939.

48 Thelma Craig, "Best Canadian play, *Dark Orchard*, also takes top honours of festival," *Globe and Mail*, 20 March 1939, 17.

49 Craig, "Best Canadian play, *Dark Orchard*, also takes top honours of festival."

50 "University women honour Margaret Ness," *Globe and Mail*, 20 November 1939, 11.

51 *University of Toronto Quarterly* 9, no. 3 (April 1940), 348–91.

52 Said adjudicator George Skillan, ominously, on the last day of the 1939 regional festival, "I have now come to the end of ten weeks' work. I hope, when I sit within the comfort of my bomb-proof shelter in England and look back behind my gas mask, to see shadows of pleasant memories of my days in Canada" (Craig, "Best Canadian play, *Dark Orchard*).

53 Kerr, "'The Playwrights Studio Group, 1932–1941.'"

54 "University College: Dramatic Club night," *University Weekly*, February 1942.

55 "University College Alumnae dramatists appear tonight," *Globe and Mail*, 7 February 1942, 12.

56 "University College: Dramatic Club night." During the war, Chorley Park in Toronto's affluent Rosedale neighbourhood was used by the military as a hospital and convalescent home for soldiers. Today it is the official home of the Lieutenant Governor of Ontario. It has suffered a series of controversies in recent years. Jamie Bradburn, "Historicst: The Saga of Chorley Park," *Torontoist*, 9 August 2008. Web.

The evening's other two plays were Christopher Morley's *Rehearsal*, directed by Francess Halpenny (her directorial debut with Alumnae) and Jerry Emerson's *The Screen*, directed by

Eleanor Woodside. Two UC undergraduates, George Bolus on violin and James MacDonald on piano, accompanied the performances, playing "two groups of numbers which earned loud and long applause from the audience." "University College: Dramatic Club night," February 1942.

In Morley's play about backstage antics during an amateur theatre rehearsal, Halpenny featured in the role of the director in the play with a "recalcitrant crew." *The Screen* featured Eleanor Woodside as the "fluffy and quite empty-headed wife" of a husband (Frederic Manning of the comedy troupe Town Tonics, which also featured Jane Mallett) who is "deceived and bewildered" by a man played by Peter Mews ("University College: Dramatic Club night," February 1942). Mews would be among the actors in the Stratford Festival's first season. For her script, Alumnae paid Pilcher a $2 royalty. They also agreed to pay half of the show's expenses and included a "strong recommendation to the president to express our dissatisfaction with the food arrangements" (AMM, 10 February 1942).

Alumnae's first production after the war was a multi-event evening featuring a new play and a new monologue by Alumnae members. After what proved to be a two-year hiatus from public performances, they co-produced "February Frolic" with the UC Alumni Association at the UC Women's Union in February 1946. The evening included three events and an interlude. The program featured prolific British playwright Philip Johnson's 1943-published *Orange Blossoms*, directed by E.G. Sterndale Bennett. Norman Tytler hosted the interlude by presenting prizes and, according to the program, providing a distraction from "particular noises backstage [that] merely indicate scene-shifting!" Following the interlude, Alice Keys presented her monologue *The Picnic*, which she had performed at Alumnae's 1944 annual meeting, and Mary Lowry Ross presented her play *A Banner with a Strange Device*. The one-page program thanked the "gentlemen of the cast for playing with us this evening." Alumnae's "Summary of Year's Activities 1945–46" indicates that the royalty paid for *Orange Blossom* was $5.00. Alumnae ran the play again with the Civic Theatre Association three months later.

57 AAGM, June 1953. In 1932, Lois Reynolds Kerr had founded Toronto's Playwrights Studio Group, one of the first organizations in the country focused on playwriting, with which Margaret Tytler worked as a director. She was active with Hart House Theatre and the DDF until 1941. Reynolds Kerr, "Lois Reynolds Kerr Recalls the Playwrights Studio Group 1932–1941," 98.

58 CODL Newsletter, September 1956, 1.

59 E.G. Wanger, "Author's first, tiger presented by Alumnae," *Globe and Mail*, 14 November 1956, 20.

60 Quoted in Rose MacDonald, "Nervous? Who, me? It's actor's problem," *Toronto Telegram*, 3 November 1956.

61 The 1956 CODL one-act festival featured ten Canadian plays among the eighteen entered ("The one-act plans and their players," *Globe and Mail*, 28 April 1956, 10). Norman Williams's *The King Decides* and *The Mountain* appeared in the 1956 one-act CODL festival and *Battle of Wits* at the 1955 one-act festival ("Earl Haig group is judged best," *Globe and Mail*, 7 May 1956, 13). Williams had taken a playwriting course from "symphonic expressionism" playwright Herman Voaden in 1955. On the evening of 21 March 1956 he sat on a CODL-sponsored playwriting panel at the Haliconian Club, chaired by Whittaker, with Voaden, Patricia Joudry, and CODL executive member Howard Lacey, titled "Where Are Our Canadian playwrights?" (Whittaker, "Show Business," *Globe and Mail*, 16 March 1956, 15; "Coming Events," *Globe and Mail*, 17 March 1956, 9). It seems the answer was "working with Alumnae."

62 E.G. Wanger, "Author's first, tiger presented by Alumnae," *Globe and Mail*, 14 November 1956, 20.
63 Klinck, ed., *Literary History of Canada*, vol. 2, 154.
64 Margaret Aitken, "Between You and Me," *Toronto Telegram*, 30 October 1956, 26.
65 Lotta Dempsey, "New Play for Toronto," *Globe and Mail*, 27 October 1936, 11.
66 Quoted in Lotta Dempsey, "New Play for Toronto," *Globe and Mail*, 27 October 1936, 11.
67 Dempsey, "New Play for Toronto."
68 Quoted in Lotta Dempsey, "New Play for Toronto."
69 Whittaker, "Show Business," *Globe and Mail*, 25 October 1956, 10. Williams had produced several television scripts and CBC and Columbia Workshop radio dramas (the latter out of New York). He had also won three awards ("Hart House premiere," *Globe and Mail*, 9 October 1956, 31) for each of his three CODL-acclaimed plays through the Ottawa Little Theatre's playwriting competition. *Worlds Apart*, for which Whittaker had written the preface, already hinted at Williams's interest in diverse settings; in his plays *Battle of Wits* and *Protest* in which he had "manipulate[d] the non-illusionistic devices of the Chinese theatre with ease and originality" (Klinck, ed., *Literary History of Canada*, 154). An advertisement in the *Globe and Mail* at the time pitched the collection as having "settings ranging from ancient China, through the world of Hollywood and the Negro [*sic*] of the deep south to the blustering exuberance of Alexander's Macedonia." The *Montreal Star*'s Sydney Johnson said the collection offered a "careful balance of the stark with the colourful, the tragic with the compassionate, the cynical with the sincere, together with a remarkable gift for dialogue" ("Six Prize-Winning Plays: *World Apart*" [Advertisement], *Globe and Mail*, 14 April 1956, 10).
70 MacDonald, "Nervous? Who, me?," *Toronto Telegram*, 3 November 1956.
71 Peter Growski [possibly Gzowski], "Says *To Ride a Tiger* marvelous experience," *Toronto Telegram*, 9 January 1957.
72 Dempsey, "New Play for Toronto,"
73 MacDonald, "Nervous? Who, me?"
74 Wanger, "Author's first, tiger presented by Alumnae."
75 Rose MacDonald, "Ruthless empress relives in new play," *Toronto Telegram*, 15 November 1956.
76 Jack Karr, "Showplace," *Toronto Star*, 15 November 1956.
77 "Remnants transformed into colourful costumes," *Globe and Mail*, 20 November 1956, 14.
78 MacDonald, "Nervous? Who, me?" MacDonald wrote that Elizabeth Gray's process included studying Chinese dress at the Royal Ontario Museum and blending the basic original dress patterns with the "theatricalism and simplicity needed" for the costumes, resulting in a "display of shimmering colour, carefully selected with an eye to harmony," "one exception … the imperial yellow worn by the royal characters is deliberately keyed to stand out, to jar a bit." The team found bargain fabrics and remnants and then "stenciled and painted Chinese butterflies, dragons, orchids and phoenix, and highlighted them with sequins and gold and silver braid." Barbara McNabb created headdresses from "artificial flowers, Christmas tree ornaments, buckram and unlikely bits and pieces."
79 Wanger, "Author's first, tiger presented by Alumnae."
80 J.M., "Successful tiger-riding," *Varsity*, 16 November 1956, 5.
81 David Peddie, *CJBC Views the Shows*, 25 November 1956, 1.
82 Wanger, "Author's first, tiger presented by Alumnae."
83 Alex Barris, "Casting About with Barris," *Globe and Mail*, 2 November 1956, 11.

84 Stan Helleur, "You Can Quote Me," *Toronto Telegram*, 9 November 1956, 33. David Peddie, in particular, seemed ready for a fight, saying Williams would "probably smile with oriental inscrutability at my interpretation of his play saying that I don't understand the Chinese Theatre. However, I don't care about the Chinese theatre, and Mr. Williams doesn't seem to know about the English-speaking Theatre." Peddie then used this set-up to say that Williams "does not appear to respect" his audience because "it would be better to imitate these writers who successfully use the techniques of English drama than to drag out a tradition that is as outmoded and as alien as the Manchu Dynasty." David Peddie, *CJBC Views the Shows*, 25 November 1956, 2.

Although reviewers concluded that the play is a "theatrical curiosity, bordering on the esoteric" (Karr, "Showplace"), they were kinder to the twenty-three-person cast, which included students from Leaside High School, who played the Boxers and were "trained for the play by a physical education instructor at the school" (MacDonald, "Ruthless empress relives in new play"). Wrote E.G. Wanger, the "large and hard-working cast carries itself with proud distinction and brings off a few pieces of sound acting between inevitable stretches of hollowness and irrelevance" (Wanger, "Author's first, tiger presented by Alumnae").

Marian Stewart showed "strength and majesty" (Wanger, "Author's first, tiger presented by Alumnae") as well as a "vigourous and flexible voice" (J.M., "Successful tiger-riding"), with a "strength and vitality that carried the heavy weight of the show," although was also "monotonous" (Peddie, *CJBC Views the Shows*). Wendy Aitken was "suitably, but rather uninterestingly heroic" as the "brave concubine." And Powell Jones was "pleasantly decadent" as the emperor (Wanger, "Author's first, tiger presented by Alumnae"). The student Boxers "added considerably to the vigour and colour of the play" (MacDonald, "Ruthless empress relives in new play").

On closing night, Christina Templeton hosted an "after-performance party in honour of [the play]" ("Social Notes," *Globe and Mail*, 14 November 1956, 10). A week later, Alumnae ran *To Ride a Tiger* at Leaside High School, at Bayview and Eglinton Avenues, with the same cast. The Leaside Rotary Club sponsored the production, with proceeds going to celiac research at the Hospital for Sick Children (Whittaker, "Play contests show there's need for more," *Globe and Mail*, 24 November 1956, 22).

Lotta Dempsey noted that within a month, Whittaker would be involved with directing no fewer than three productions at once, including another *Globe and Mail* writer's, Mary Juke's, play *Every Bed Is Narrow* for the Crest Theatre and Giraudoux's *Electra* for Victoria College Dramatic Club, along with *To Ride a Tiger* for Alumnae at the festival. Around the same time, he received an invitation to become a member of the American Council of Drama Judges for his theatre criticism. He was already the only Canadian to hold membership in the British Guild of Drama Adjudicators, and he currently sat as CODL's vice-president and as a member of the DDF executive. Lotta Dempsey estimated that by this point Whittaker had directed around 100 plays "since his art student days at the École de Beaux Arts in Montreal" (Dempsey, "Our man on the aisle recognized," *Globe and Mail*, 8 December 1956, 27).

85 The Calvert Trophy was won by the Playcraftsmen for Osborne's *On Borrowed Time*.

86 Adjudicator Cecil Bellamy was a British producer and actor educated in France and known, in part, for producing Ancient Greek plays in their original language. *To Ride a Tiger* was one of only five CODL festival entries that year, all from Toronto (along with the West End Players, the Playcraftsmen, the York Community Theatre, and the Norvoc Players). The festival ran first among the thirteen regionals, presenting a total of fifty-five plays (E.G. Wanger, "Adjudicator praises opening festival play," *Globe and Mail*, 9 January 1957, 10).

87 Quoted in Karr, "Showplace."

88 Growski [possibly Gzowski], "Says *To Ride a Tiger* marvelous experience."

89 Wanger, "Adjudicator praises opening festival play."
90 Quoted in Karr, "Showplace."
91 Whittaker, "Major honours taken by the Playcraftsmen," *Globe and Mail*, 14 January 1957, 7.
92 "Toronto players win place in drama finals," *Globe and Mail*, 15 April 1957, 17.
93 "One-act play festival has eight entries," *Globe and Mail*, 30 March 1957, 18.
94 Mavor Moore, "This play may become part of our history," *Toronto Telegram*, 27 January 1960.
95 Rose MacDonald, "Too many people in new play," *Toronto Telegram*, January 1960, n.d.
96 Mavor Moore, "A short-sighted proposition," *Toronto Telegram*, week of 5 May 1960.
97 Moore, "This play may become part of our history."
98 "Reaney play to premiere," *Toronto Star*, [n.d.] January 1960.
99 John Robert Colombo, "Antichrist as a child," *Varsity*, 18 January 1960, 4.
100 Moore, "This play may become part of our history."
101 Firehall Theatre, formerly the Coach House, Letter to the Editor, *Toronto Star*, 25 November 1973, 1–2 (emphasis in original).
102 Firehall Theatre, Letter to the Editor, 25 November 1973.
103 Colombo, "Antichrist as a child," 5.
104 Moore, "This play may become part of our history."
105 Whittaker, "*The Killdeer*," *Globe and Mail*, 14 January 1960, 35.
106 MacDonald, "Too many people in new play."
107 Nathan Cohen, "Mr. Reaney writes a play," *Toronto Star*, 14 January 1960.
108 Whittaker, "*The Killdeer*."
109 Cohen, "Mr. Reaney writes a play." Howard Adelman reported in the *Varsity* that despite being billed as *The Killdeer: A Comedy*, the "funniest incident of the evening occurred when Nathan Cohen abandoned the magazine he was reading during the last act, and impolitely bent over to groan silently into the palms of his hands" (Adelman, "Canadian killer: An evening with the birds," *Varsity*, 15 January 1960, 4). Reaney later corroborated Adelman's observation, saying Cohen "picked his nose and read the New Yorker all through it … I couldn't get anything out of his criticism to build better plays. He was a theatre personality. It's good to have those around" (quoted in John Wilson, "Articulate and witty Can Lit," *Varsity*, 4 November 1977, 8).
110 P.S., "Theatre," *Varsity*, 28 January 1960. 8.
111 Adelman, "Canadian killer: An evening with the birds."
112 Wilson, "Articulate and witty Can Lit."
113 D.J. Knight, "A re-review," *Varsity*, 22 January 1960, 5.
114 Whittaker, "*The Killdeer*."
115 Moore, "This play may become part of our history."
116 Whittaker, "Women's group wins top festival honours," *Globe and Mail*, 4 April 1960, 5.
117 Whittaker, "Toronto performers help world's victims," *Globe and Mail*, 6 May 1960, 28.
118 For the first time, eight Canadian judges examined the fourteen regions "under a new zoning system." Whittaker, "Westward ho actors go," *Globe and Mail*, 14 May 1960, 13.
119 Quoted in Rose MacDonald, "Honours for university group," *Telegram*, 4 April 1960, 29.
120 MacDonald, "Honours for university group."
121 Quoted in MacDonald, "Honours for university group."
122 Quoted in Whittaker, "Women's group wins top festival honours."
123 Whittaker, "Women's group wins top festival honours."
124 Unlike in previous years, there was no qualification mentioned this time that the award was specifically supposed to encourage new directors.

125 Whittaker, "Women's group wins top festival honours."

126 The *Star* compared the CODL festival to the Stanley Cup finals, in which the Toronto Maple Leafs were about to play the Montreal Canadiens (the Leafs were swept in four games): "The crowd was only a fraction of the one encouraging the Maple Leafs to victory. But the enthusiasm more than equaled that of the most violent Leaf supporter. Reason obviously was that these were participants cheering fellow actors on their own teams. Each time the adjudicator, Dr. Betty Mitchell announced a winner, her words were greeted by an enormous gasp, a cheer, then powerful applause." "University Alumnae win drama awards," *Toronto Star*, 4 April 1960. Alumnae fared much better than their Toronto hockey counterparts that year.

127 Antony Ferry, "*Killdeer* to set Vancouver festival on its ear," *Toronto Star*, 6 May 1960, 27.

128 Whittaker, "Toronto performers help world's victims."

129 Moore, "A short-sighted proposition."

130 John Coulter, "*The Killdeer* and the fantastic," *Globe and Mail*, 12 May 1960, 6.

131 Ferry, "*Killdeer* to set Vancouver festival on its ear."

132 Numerous telegrams poured forth offering the group best wishes. From Martha Mann and Rex Southgate: "Here's hoping Calvert exists on a flight of killdeers good luck to all"; Gordon Johnson: "This birdwatcher predicts auspicious day for *Killdeer* with high flight and happy landing"; Helen Dunlop's Oakwood Collegiate colleagues wrote, "The play's the thing good luck"; Betty Mitchell wrote, "Every possible success to my dear Ba's"; CODL head Blanch Hogg wrote, "Fingers crossed and thumbs up for *Killdeer*. CODL wishes its contender good luck and success. Keep up your own high standards and we will be proud of you"; her husband Frank wrote, "*Killdeer* tonight kill fatted calf Saturday."

133 Ben Metcalfe, "Canadian authors score at festival," *Vancouver Province*, 19 May 1960.

134 Quoted in Metcalfe, "Canadian authors score at festival."

135 Metcalfe, "Canadian authors score at festival."

136 Quoted in Louise Bresky, "London Theatre Festival winner," *Toronto Star*, 24 May 1960, 22.

137 Quoted in Whittaker, "Plays revise mistaken notion," *Globe and Mail*, 20 May 1960, 8.

138 Martha Mann Southgate, interview with Whittaker, 20 October 2017.

139 Mann Southgate, interview with Whittaker. Actor Don Bryn was a runner-up for an apprentice engagement at the Stratford Festival. Of note, for the first time the Quebec government offered a $3,000 award, more than the $1,000 award for the top production prize, to the most promising French-language actor. And during the festival the Canada Council announced that $2,000 would go to four Canadian playwrights and the theatre groups that performed their plays in the regional festival, with $400 going to the group and $100 to the playwrights, one of which was Reaney. "*Killdeer* players get $400," *Toronto Star*, 19 May 1960.

140 Mann Southgate, interview with Whittaker.

141 Margaret Gayfer. "Opera to watch: All about a Stratford flower" [no magazine recorded; n.d.].

142 Quoted in Ralph Thomas, "Alumnae Players Finally Find a Home," *Toronto Star*, 2 November 1962.

143 Quoted in Thomas, "Alumnae Players Finally Find a Home."

144 Nathan Cohen, "How the Canada Council can help playwrights," *Toronto Star*, 4 September 1962, 18.

145 Quoted in Harry Bruce, "Home at last," *Maclean's*, 17 November 1962, 97.

146 Margaret Aitken, "Between You and Me," *Toronto Telegram*, 30 October 1956, 26.

147 Suggestions included the professional group the Questers (Pamela Terry, letter to W.P. Rowley, 23 May 1964) and CBC television, when a member of the CBC staff was on the playreading committee (Terry, letter to Catherine Wilbraham, 17 August 1962).

148 Nathan Cohen, "Canadian theatre 'imitation fireplace,'" 30 March 1964.
149 Donald Jack, quoted in Cohen, "Canadian theatre 'imitation fireplace.'"
150 Jack, quoted in Cohen, "Canadian theatre 'imitation fireplace.'"
151 Pamela Terry Beckwith, letter to Nathan Cohen, 1 April 1964.
152 Molly Golby, "Report of the Playreading Committee," AAGM, June 1961, 2.
153 "Two theatre openings ...," no newspaper recorded, n.d.
154 Whittaker, "Lavish theatre on the page," *Globe and Mail*, 2 September 1972, 28.
155 UADC, "History," 1963, 3; "Women university grads buy a theatre," *Paper Doll*, November 1962.
156 Pamela Terry, "Report of the Playreading Committee," AAGM, 9 June 1962, 3. Copies of *The Killdeer and Other Plays*, which was published that week, were sold in the lobby during the run. Lorna F. Rogers, Publicity Report, AAGM, 15 June 1963.
157 Whittaker, "An odd egg is opened in an odd eggcup," *Globe and Mail*, 14 November 1962, 9.
158 Stewart Brown, "*Easter Egg* lays no egg as arts festival opens," *Hamilton Spectator*, 3 November 1963.
159 Alumnae, "About the Coach House Theatre," c. 9 November 1962.
160 Bill Mathie, letter to Francess Halpenny, 21 August 1962.
161 Stewart Brown, "*Easter Egg* lays no egg as arts festival opens," *Hamilton Spectator*, 3 November 1963.
162 Brown, "*Easter Egg* lays no egg as arts festival opens."
163 Whittaker, "Irish play from U.S. has Toronto actors," *Globe and Mail*, 27 September 1962, 36.
164 Whittaker, "An odd egg is opened in an odd eggcup."
165 Ronald Evans, "Things have definitely ...," *Toronto Telegram*, n.d. According to Whittaker, as the stepson, Peter Peer fashioned a "believable image of a creature awaiting birth, then achieving it," while Glenna Davis as the stepmother "stirred us to something like pitch, having to create one of Mr. Reaney's Ontario witches, and to something like admiration for her gallantry." Margaret Hamilton was "most sympathetic but not too sweet" as the stepdaughter. Whittaker, "An odd egg is opened in an odd eggcup."
166 Whittaker, "Lavish theatre on the page."
167 James Reaney, letter to Shelagh Kareda, 19 January 1973.
168 In early 1973, Alumnae wrote to Reaney asking to read a play of his called *Donnelly*. He replied that he was already looking to work on it with a group of actors in Halifax and that another version of the script was in Lennoxville (Reaney, letter to Kareda). This correspondence refers, of course, to Reaney's now famous trilogy *The Donnellys*, the first play of which, *Sticks and Stones*, opened later that year in November 1973 at the Tarragon Theatre. Instead, Reaney offered, "I would love something to write indirectly about the American takeover of our universities, the whole colonial situation Atwood gets at in *Survival*, but it needs something like a commission, also an investigation of what actors are good at what, in other words work with the director (Pamela Terry is my favourite) and the whole organization a great deal beforehand before putting pen to paper." Reaney, letter to Kareda. Reaney's letter, on letterhead from his employment at the University of Western Ontario, is remarkable as it indicates a step in Reaney's process for one of his landmark plays, particularly his interest in working for a third time with Alumnae, a theatre that had introduced his first play thirteen years to the month earlier with Terry as director.

Alumnae's records indicate the University of Toronto Press, through Halpenny's connection on the editorial staff, was paid to print the dodgers and programs and that Reaney paid back his $90 royalty fee to Alumnae. *The Easter Egg* grossed $950, just shy of Alumnae's $1,000 per show target. AEM, 21 November 1962.

169 Pamela Terry Beckwith, letter to Wilfred Watson, 29 June 1962.
170 Terry, "Report of the Playreading Committee," AAGM, 9 June 1962, 3.
171 Terry Beckwith, letter to Watson, 29 June 1962.
172 Wilfred Watson, letter to Pamela Beckwith, 7 September 1962.
173 As producers, Alumnae had also applied to the Canada Council for a $1,200 grant to stage both Watson's and Reaney's plays that season (Coach House Theatre, letter to Peter Dwyer, n.d.), citing the recent high costs incurred in procuring the synagogue and their extraordinary success at the DDF, particularly with new plays. But that grant application was turned down because of the Canada Council's "policy of giving no direct help to individual amateur groups." Reported Alumnae, this "meant even more penny pinching for us" (AMM, 5 September 1962). The rejection led Nathan Cohen to write that it was "regrettable" and "bewildering" that the Canada Council would say that it would not fund Canadian plays premiered by amateur theatre companies, but would fund the amateur DDF, just as it would not fund George Luscombe's Toronto Workshop Productions, although it would fund Luscombe himself. Cohen concluded that both companies were "doing infinitely more than the formally professional organizations in the cause of the Canadian playwright" (Nathan Cohen, "Reginald Rose coming for Crest opening," *Toronto Star*, 6 September 1962, 22). It was Alumnae's first of a very few attempts at securing Canada Council grants. They decided to write again, "informally," the following summer, encouraged by Robert Weaver's piece in the *Tamarack Review* that suggested, in Alumnae's words, that the Canada Council might preferably give a grant "to help production of new Canadian plays – perhaps to us?" (AAGM, 15 June 1963.) Weaver had specifically named Alumnae as an influential producer of new Canadian plays, and Alumnae saw this, along with their successful grant for Watson, as giving them a "toe in the door" with the Canada Council (Terry Beckwith, letter to Wilfred Watson, 2 August 1963). However, they would, again, be "politely, but firmly, turned down" (Pamela Terry, Programme and Playreading Committee Report, AAGM, 13 June 1964). The following summer they also decided to "investigate possibilities of the new Ontario Government's Arts Council" (AAGM, 15 June 1963). Despite this brief flurry of grant writing, Alumnae would rarely seek operating grants again.
174 Watson, letter to Pamela Terry Beckwith, 29 December 1962.
175 Whittaker, "The Critics Say," *Globe and Mail*, 11 May 1963, 16.
176 Whittaker, "Praises treatment of medieval mystery," *Globe and Mail*, 2 May 1963, 4.
177 Wendy Michener, "New play mere web of words." *Toronto Star*, 2 May 1963.
178 Michener, "New play mere web of words."
179 Ronald Evans, "A solemn cannonade," *Toronto Telegram*, 2 May 1963. 39.
180 Ronald Evans, "Another newcomer …," *Toronto Telegram*, 25 June 1963.
181 Ronald. "A solemn cannonade."
182 Charlotte Holmes, letter to Ron Evans, 25 June 1963.
183 Watson, letter to Pamela Terry Beckwith, 27 February 1963; Whittaker, "Praises treatment of medieval mystery."
184 Whittaker, "Stratford casts join Bard's birthday lineup," *Globe and Mail*, 24 April 1963, 11.
185 "The Gallimaufry," *Toronto Telegraph*, 23 April 1963.
186 "Illness in the cast …," *Toronto Star*, 23 April 1963.
187 Whittaker, "Robarts launches bill creating Arts Council," *Globe and Mail*, 23 April 1963, 11.
188 "Lead role again changed in *Trial of Corporal Adam*," *Globe and Mail*, 27 April 1963, 16.
189 Pamela Terry Beckwith, letter to Peter M. Dwyer (Canada Council), 31 May 1963.
190 Terry Beckwith, letter to Dwyer, 31 May 1963.

191 "Lead role again changed in *Trial of Corporal Adam*."
192 Watson, letter to Pamela Beckwith, 14 July 1963.
193 Watson, *Plays at the Iron Bridge*, 1989.
194 Dennis Sweeting, "*Year of the Lemmings piece de resistance*," *Globe and Mail*, 4 May 1966, 15.
195 Whittaker, "What's all this fuss next week about Canadian plays and playwrights?," *Globe and Mail*, 11 March 1967, 25.
196 Beckwith, ed., *Unheard of*, 325.
197 Sternberg, "Rae Davis: Four Decades of Invention."
198 For more on Rae Davis, see Sternberg, "Rae Davis."
199 Quoted in Whittaker, "What's all this fuss next week …?"
200 Whittaker, "Impressions of electronic life charm audience," *Globe and Mail*, 18 March 1967, 21.
201 Agatha Leonard (programme committee chair), letter to Rae Davis, 15 May 1967.
202 Leonard, letter to Rae Davis.
203 Rae Davis, Letter to Agatha Leonard, 19 May 1967.
204 Jim McPherson, "Leftovers from the bitter belt," *Toronto Telegram*, 23 February 1968.
205 AMM, 11 April 1967.
206 Elizabeth (Mrs. David) Mascall, letter to Jack Cunningham, 6 September 1967.
207 Jack Cunningham, letter to Agatha Leonard, 13 June 1967.
208 Mascall, letter to Cunningham.
209 AAGM, 14 September 1967.
210 Cunningham, letter to Leonard.
211 Cunningham's play survived the usual juried machinations within Alumnae. Once it reached their top set of choices, correspondence went through the DDF's executive secretary Laurier Melanson. One particularly disgruntled playwright whose play Alumnae rejected wrote back to Melanson: "I am sorry that there was not enough script in my play, to make up three acts taking one hour and fifteen minutes [¶] I suppose that you did not notice that there was an Indian [*sic*] War Dance, two Hyms [*sp*], a number of folk songs, and an original final song, which would complete the one hour and fifteen minutes of play time, but were not included in the Script [¶] I am returning the "Play" in case it is still possible that you can include it in your programming [¶] The play time is quite flexible as more songs can be added to make up the hour and fifteen minutes, or courses [*sic*] repeated. [¶] Trusting to hear from you...?" (Harold J. Lippert, letter to Laurier Melanson, 19 April 1967).

Having read the playwright's letter, Mascall responded to Melanson that she had returned the play "some time ago" because "what with the Indian War Dance and the log cabin burning down on stage – not to mention some other drawbacks – we felt it was not quite what we had in mind!" She added that "most of the other scripts we received in our search for a new Canadian play were of somewhat higher calibre" and that they had arrived at four that are "certainly worth doing, though in need of some revision" (Mascall, letter to Laurier Melanson, 25 July 1967). There is, perhaps, some suggestion here that Alumnae were not totally thrilled with the overall quality of new Canadian plays they had read, but that they could certainly make do. Alumnae and Whittaker were no strangers to new play development, and they sought to maintain their standards, particularly when presented with unseemly content disguised as nationalistic bravado.

212 "University Alumnae Dramatic Club" [Advertisement], *Varsity*, 29 September 1967, 20.
213 Laurier Melanson, letter to Mascall, 8 September 1967.

214 Whittaker, letter to Margaret Spence, 25 September 1967.

215 Cunningham had originally titled it *Aperitif*, but by 11 September, possibly on Whittaker's advice, he had changed it to *Weekend Design*, and by the end of the month to the more dynamic, if less erudite, *The Hearth-Fire Burning*. With that title, less the definite article, Alumnae described *Hearth-Fire Burning* in the December casting notice as a "modern Canadian domestic – a family reunion in Toronto." By the New Year, Cunningham had changed the title back to *Aperitif*. Jacques Languirand, whose play *The Gibbet* Alumnae had premiered in translation three years earlier, had already considered *Aperitif* for production at Le Centre Culturel de Vieux Montréal, where Cunningham was assistant artistic director. However, Languirand cleared the way for Alumnae's production by giving theirs "priority" and thus world premiere status. Mascall, letter to Melanson, 6 September 1967.

216 AMM, 14 September 1967.

217 Margaret MacAulay, letter to DDF Professional Direction Committee, 1 April 1969.

218 MacAulay, letter to DDF Professional Direction Committee.

219 AMM, 3 April 1968.

220 Lawrence Stone, "Coach House *Aperitif* is too slight in content," *Globe and Mail*, 23 February 1968, 12.

221 McPherson, "Leftovers from the bitter belt."

222 Nathan Cohen, "*Aperitif*: Just call it games people play," *Toronto Star*, 23 February 1967.

223 Gordon Jocelyn, "Two Canadian plays presented in Toronto," *Montreal Gazette*, 23 March 1968.

224 Jocelyn, "Two Canadian plays presented in Toronto."

225 K.K., "More dullness," *Varsity*, 1 March 1968.

226 Stone, "Coach House *Aperitif* is too slight in content."

227 Jocelyn, "Two Canadian plays presented in Toronto."

228 McPherson, "Leftovers from the bitter belt."

229 Jocelyn, "Two Canadian plays presented in Toronto."

230 K.K., "More dullness."

231 Cohen, "*Aperitif*: Just call it games people play."

232 Stone, "Coach House *Aperitif* is too slight in content." A "charming and interesting person," according to an Alumnae press release, Elizabeth Ward was "forced to re-examine her life and try to carry on" when her husband Don Ward died while rehearsing an earlier Alumnae production. She decided to return to acting at the Children's Theatre, where Molly Thom had worked. Her children Lynn and Robin, at one time two thirds of the Allan-Ward trio, also decided to focus on acting.

233 Stone, "Coach House *Aperitif* is too slight in content."

234 McPherson, "Leftovers from the bitter belt."

235 Cohen, "*Aperitif*: Just call it games people play."

236 Jocelyn, "Two Canadian plays presented in Toronto."

237 AMM, 3 April 1968.

238 AMM, 15 June 1968.

239 Urjo Kareda, "Bert Brecht all together," *Toronto Star*, 26 November 1971.

240 Robinow, "Three interesting moderns presented by the Coach House Theatre."

241 Helen Dunlop directed Don Bryn's *The Flowered Suit* as part of Alumnae's "Seven Moderns" Series III. As it was "virtually a monologue," Eleanor Beecroft "easily walked off with the acting honours of the evening" (Whittaker, "Library, stage, theatre, play make news"). Reviewers noted that it was derivative of Mary Chase's *Harvey* (James Thurber's short story, titled *The*

Secret Life of Walter Mitty) and "other inconsequential classics" (Winter, "New play included in drama reading"), with a character reminiscent of Edward Albee's *The American Dream*. Bryn's writing style was "pleasant and easy; *The Flowered Suit* was well worth doing, and seeing; and one hopes he will write more plays." Robinow, "Three interesting moderns presented by the Coach House Theatre."

242 Winter, "New play included in drama reading."

243 AAGM, 11 June 1966.

244 Molly Thom prepared and directed Part One, called *The Gentlewomen of Upper Canada*, featuring excerpts from works by four historically significant nineteenth-century women who wrote in great detail about their experiences in Upper Canada; each of the four was presented by an Alumnae member. Charlotte Holmes read from Susanna Moodie's memoir *Roughing It in the Bush* (1852); Janet Gladish read from artist Anne Langton's posthumous collection of letters and journals, *A Gentlewoman in Upper Canada* (1950); Joan Shaw read from author Catharine Parr Traill's collection of letters and journals *Backwoods of Canada* (1836); and Meg Hogarth read from art historian Anna Jameson's *Winter Studies and Summer Rambles in Canada* (1838). Elizabeth Mascall prepared and directed Part Two, which featured excerpts from Paul Hiebert's writing about the fictitious Sarah Binks, "sweet songstress of Saskatchewan," narrated by Francess Halpenny, Eileen Williams, Ivor Jackson, and Sarah Binks "herself." Binks proved to be a popular topic in theatre circles. The following February 1968, another adaption of Paul Hiebert's Sarah Binks, this time a mini-musical by Donald Harron called *Here Lies Sarah Binks*, ran at the Central Library Theatre. Jocelyn, "Two Canadian plays presented in Toronto."

245 Deirdre Blades provided songs for Thom's *The Gentlewomen of Upper Canada*; Barbara Walker provided sound for both Thom's piece and Mascall's *Highlights from the Life and Works of Sarah Binks, Sweet Songstress of Saskatchewan*. Two months later, the cast travelled to Trent University in Peterborough, when the Fine Arts Committee of Catharine Parr Traill College picked up the two-part program with a showing in February 1968. Reported Alumnae, the college had a "vested interest in the pioneer ladies … and a student body keen indeed on Sarah Binks. It had all been very well received and had netted us a fee of $50." AMM, 3 April 1968.

246 Halpenny initially planned the readings for March, but she was unable to do those dates "due to her out of town trips copious to the extreme." AMM, 3 April 1968.

247 In June, Halpenny reported that both *The Matter of Arthur* and *This Beggarly Wooden Country* had received paid invitations to be read at the University of Guelph and that *The Matter of Arthur* had also received an invitation from York University (AAGM, 15 June 1968). Halpenny's *The Matter of Arthur* reappeared five months later as the next season's first "Sunday Night at the Coach House" reading during the October to November 1968 run of *Viet Rock*. The "informal entertainment" was open to subscribing members and featured readers Norma Clark, Elizabeth Mascall, Maureen Fox, and Wendy Butler. It was followed by "coffee and conversation with the Company."

248 AAGM, 15 June 1968.

249 Nathan Cohen, "McLuhan knows his Irish letters," *Toronto Star*, 28 November 1968, 46.

250 Nathan Cohen, "Boomet of interest in Yeats continues," *Toronto Star*, 2 December 1968, 20.

251 Cohen, "McLuhan knows his Irish letters."

252 Whittaker, "Ireland, USSR on stage," *Globe and Mail*, 2 December 1968, 14.

253 Cohen, "McLuhan knows his Irish letters."

254 CBC Radio, "*CBC Tuesday Night*: Yeats and Thomas," 13–19 December 1969, 6.

255 Stan Fefferman, “Willie’s Irish blues,” *Toronto Telegram*, 7 December 1968, 8.

256 CBC Radio, “*CBC Tuesday Night*: Yeats and Thomas.”

257 Nathan Cohen wrote that Robert O’Driscoll “formed the Irish Theatre Society last year and is chairman of the conference organizing committee” that brought the artistic director of the Abbey Theatre, Tomás MacAnna, to Toronto that week. Cohen, “McLuhan knows his Irish letters.”

258 Fefferman, “Willie’s Irish blues.”

259 Cohen, “McLuhan knows his Irish letters.”

260 Fefferman, “Willie’s Irish blues.”

261 Cohen, “Boomet of interest in Yeats continues.”

262 Fefferman, “Willie’s Irish blues.”

263 Tait’s script found further life. Alumnae gave *So Great a Sweetness* another set of readings on three Sundays in March 1969. It was then read the following 16 December 1969 in an “edited version” on the radio series *CBC Tuesday Night* by a new cast (CBC Radio, “*CBC Tuesday Night*: Yeats and Thomas”). Tait then travelled to Ireland on a Canada Council grant (Weldon Tait, interview with Whittaker, 19 October 2017) for the purpose of “preparing her script” for a reading at the Abbey Theatre in August 1970 (Whittaker, “Baltimore-born actor gets Othello role in Vancouver, *Toronto Star*, 16 December 1970, 15). MacAnna had attended Alumnae’s December 1968 reading and “afterwards expressed his interest in producing it in Dublin” at the Abbey Theatre (CBC Radio, “*CBC Tuesday Night*: Yeats and Thomas”). Tait recounts that while in Ireland, a relative of two of the play’s characters objected to putting words in her mother’s mouth, so Tait cut them from Act II, saying, “it was better in the long run” (Weldon Tait, interview with Whittaker, 19 October 2017). Seven years later the play was given what “one hesitates to call a play, but rather a dramatized reading” (John J. Dunne, “The love of W.B., the fire of Maud,” *Irish Times*, 1 October 1975) by Nora Lever Productions at the Long Hall of Castletown House, Celbridge, as part of the Dublin Theatre Festival in the fall of 1975 (Desmond Rushe, “Poet’s torture well portrayed,” *Irish Press*, 2 October 1975). John Finegan in the *Irish Press* said the play did a “splendid job in creating the leading figures from their letters and published writings. For the first time on stage the story is told in some detail of the consuming passion which Yeats had for the beautiful Maud Gonne” (John Finegan, “The hopeless love of the poet Yeats,” *Irish Press*, 2 October 1975). Desmond Rushe, like Finegan writing in the *Irish Times*, agreed that the Easter Rising portion was the “weakest in the show which, otherwise, is full of engrossing insights into a remarkable relationship and a stirring period in history” (Rushe, “Poet’s torture well portrayed”). Tait’s revised and abridged 1982 script is extant in Alumnae’s collections with the title *So Great a Sweetness: The Love of W.B. Yeats for Maud Gonne* and a casting change note on the cover saying “No Lady Gregory, less K[atherine] Tynan, 1 all-purpose male.”

264 Anne Kewley, “watsUP: Theatre,” *Varsity*, 24 October 1969, R16.

265 Kewley, “watsUP: Theatre.”

266 Paul Carson, “Universities urged to adopt ‘Counter-Violence,’” *Varsity*, 22 September 1969, 1.

267 Among recent disruptions on the U of T campus were “firecrackers and loud questions” at the otherwise formal “annual University College freshman banquet” at Hart House (Susan Reisler, “UC head table refuses to answer radicals,’” *Varsity*, 22 Sepember 1969, 11) and the disruption of a PoliSci 101 class that came to blows (“SAC rejects motion to investigate Thorson disruption,” *Varsity*, 5 December 1969, 1).

268 “I’m like a dinosaur…,” *Varsity*, 14 November 1969, 1.

269 Reisler, “UC head table refuses to answer radicals.’”

270 Whittaker, Herbert. "D.H. Lawrence double bill proof club fills special role," *Globe and Mail*, 25 February 1971, 11.
271 "D.H. Lawrence on exhibit," *Toronto Citizen*, 25 February 1971.
272 Whittaker, "D.H. Lawrence double bill proof club fills special role," *Globe and Mail*, 25 February 1971, 11.
273 Nathan Cohen, "This puffery won't benefit the theatre," *Toronto Star*, 22 February 1971, 20.
274 Whittaker, "D.H. Lawrence double bill proof club fills special role."
275 "D.H. Lawrence on exhibit," *Toronto Citizen*, 25 February 1971.
276 Cohen, "This puffery won't benefit the theatre."
277 Whittaker, "D.H. Lawrence double bill proof club fills special role."
278 Margaret MacAulay, letter to John E. Hill, DFF, 12 May 1970.
279 MacAulay, Letter to DDF Professional Direction Committee, 1 April 1969. George Luscombe and Jack Winter had already introduced improvisation-based theatre creation to the city through Luscombe's Toronto Workshop Productions (Whittaker, "Some polishing for Stratford," *Globe and Mail*, 6 October 1969, 15). For a study on the influential Toronto Workshop Productions, see Carson, *Harlequin in Hogtown*; Bush, *Conversations with George Luscombe*; and the anthology of Jack Winter's plays *My TWP Plays*.
280 MacAulay, letter to Hill.
281 MacAulay, letter to DDF Professional Direction Committee.
282 John E. Hill, letter to Margaret MacAulay, 7 July 1969.
283 MacAulay, letter to DDF Professional Direction Committee.
284 MacAulay, letter to Hill, 12 May 1970.
285 Whittaker, "Some polishing for Stratford."
286 MacAulay, letter to Hill, 12 May 1970. As listed on the program, the scene titles were: "A Guy's Gotta Live Doesn't He?" "Maybe They'll All Come Home," "A Night Out," "Trailer," "Poor Little Rich Girl," "Night Games," "Splitsville," "Uncertain Feeling," "It's All Happening at the Laundromat," "I'm All Right, Jack" (featuring local actor Jack Zimmerman), and "Nothing's Forever."
287 MacAulay, letter to Hill, 12 May 1970.
288 MacAulay, letter to Hill, 12 May 1970.
289 Hunter, *Still Hunting*. Web.
290 MacAulay, letter to Hill, 12 May 1970.
291 Hunter, *Still Hunting*. Web.
292 MacAulay, letter to Hill, 12 May 1970.
293 Hunter, *Still Hunting* (Web). *Flowers of Paradise* followed a "bunch of hippie kids who came under the influence of a female faith healer" (Hunter, *Still Hunting*), thus continuing the same "anti-Establishment theme as before," Directed by Hunter with his lyrics set to music by Jeffrey Cohen, it premiered just over a year later in February 1971. Regarding Hunter, who was dramaturge at U of T's Drama Centre, H.K. wrote in the *Globe and Mail* that "improvisationary [*sic*] drama tends to cling to the original self-fueling patterns even when structured. *Flowers of Paradise* is so full of confrontations, that the beat of bleat is almost regular." Jeffrey Cohen's written and sung "series of pertinent song-breaks" helped break up this beat. Hunter's play was now much improved, although according to H.K. it needed more work. Echoing some of the criticism levelled at Alumnae's production of *Viet Rock*, H.K. concluded that the "next step surely is to forget the exercises and get on with the drama." H.K. "*Paradise*'s protests against the system sound thin," *Globe and Mail*, 11 February 1971, 11.
294 Urjo Kareda, "The Firchall Theatre's message gets lost in the medium," *Toronto Star*, n.d.

295 Kareda, "The Firehall Theatre's message gets lost in the medium."
296 Whittaker, "Bits of history are sketchily drawn," *Globe and Mail*, 8 May 1974, 15.
297 Kareda, "The Firehall Theatre's message gets lost in the medium."
298 Whittaker, "Bits of history are sketchily drawn." Alumnae returned to the collective creation format in January 2001, this time not to stage their own but to produce Toronto Workshop Production's 1974 Depression-era docudrama *Ten Lost Years*. Directed by Jill Frappier, it featured the original TWP score and a pay-what-you-can performance that was attended by the original TWP cast as well as by Ed and Anne Mirvish. Ed "paid $50.00 for his ticket and wrote a complimentary note in the comment book" (ABM, 1 March 2001). It read: "We both went through the depression. Thank you for letting people know about it. We never will forget. Moving performance. Congratulations. Naomi [Hunter] – excellent performance – all the cast to be congratulated." Ed and Anne Mirvish, note in Comment Book for *Ten Lost Years*, January 2001.
299 Veronica Van Dijk, "Emily Carr in words," *The Newspaper*, 7 November 1979, 7.
300 Helen Nicholson and colleagues have observed a similar phenomenon in British theatre. Nicholson et al., *The Ecologies of Amateur Theatre*, 97–8.
301 *Le Temps Sauvage* is discussed in detail in Whittaker, "Un/Disciplined Re/Collections."
302 Fiona Poole, "Carol Bolt and *Shelter*," *Varsity*, 29 November 1974, 7.
303 "Firehall show was a real blast," *Toronto Star*, 28 November 1974.
304 Theatre listings, *Toronto Life*, November 1974.
305 As a director, Steiner had helped develop George F. Walker's plays at Factory Lab Theatre (Johnston, *Up the Mainstream*, 85) and had worked at Aries Productions, founded by Alumnae members Norma Clark and Morna Wales.
306 Carol Bolt, note to Colleen Wagner.
307 "Artist who painted famous *Queen on Moose* meets Her Majesty," CBC, *As It Happens*. 25 February 2015.
308 Zena Cherry, "Factory becomes art gallery," *Globe and Mail*, 29 October 1974, 14.
309 Urjo Kareda, "Truly Canadian comedy explodes with wit," *Toronto Star*, 22 November 1974, E7.
310 Cecily Thomson's Producer's Report to the Executive, dated 7 December 1974, describes an audition and a callback date at which two or three pages of each act were available, as opposed to the whole script, serving twenty-nine auditioners for the play's five parts. Of the twenty-six rehearsals, eleven were on the Firehall's main stage and nine were at the St. Lawrence Centre's rehearsal rooms.
311 Barb Shainbaum, "Carol Bolt and *Shelter*," *Varsity*, 29 November 1974, 7.
312 Urjo Kareda, "Another *Red Emma* opening," *Toronto Star*, 6 December 1974.
313 Kareda, "Truly Canadian comedy explodes with wit."
314 Shainbaum, "Carol Bolt and *Shelter*."
315 Bert Cowan, untitled review of *Shelter*, *Offstage Voices*, 23 November 1974.
316 Kareda, "Truly Canadian comedy explodes with wit."
317 McKenzie Porter, "Bolt's farce ranks high," *Toronto Sun*, 24 October 1975, 32.
318 Whittaker, "*Shelter* has blithe political spirit," *Globe and Mail*, 22 November 1974, 15.
319 Kaspars Dzeguze, "*Shelter* adds new colour to the political spectrum," *Toronto Sun*, 26 November 1974.
320 Dzeguze, "*Shelter* adds new colour to the political spectrum."
321 Robert Read, "More girl talk from the Alumnae," *Varsity*, 17 January 1979, 9.
322 Blackburn et al., *A Clash of Symbols (La nef des sorcières)*.

323 Read, "More girl talk from the Alumnae."
324 Christopher Power, "Quebec feminist monologues staged," *The Newspaper*, 24 January 1979, 5.
325 Ray Conlogue, "Monologues too demanding for cast," *Globe and Mail*, 12 January 1979, 13.
326 Alumnae staged the play again eleven months later when they could not secure the rights for a very different play, Simone Benmussa's *The Singular Life of Albert Nobbs. A Clash of Symbols* was published in the first volume of Louise H. Forsyth's *Anthology of Québec Women's Plays in English Translation.* Alumnae have not often returned to Quebec writers since, but their production of Michel Tremblay's *The Real World* in November 2003 in the Firehall's Studio earned praise from the weekly newspapers, with *Now Magazine*'s Jon Kaplan calling it the "best Alumnae production in several years." Jon Kaplan, "Tremblay's trials," *Now Magazine*, 27 November–3 December 2003.
327 Halpenny, Prospectus, "The Alumnae Theatre: A History 1919–1999," in ABM, 4 June 2001.
328 Jon Kaplan (*Now Magazine*), quoted in Lamarre, Parr, and Carnwath, letter to the Canadian Actors' Equity Association's Ontario Advisory Council, 2 January 2001.
329 Thom, "New Ideas – Genesis," *Alumination*, March 2007.
330 Thom, interview with Whittaker, 19 October 2017.
331 Thom, "New Ideas – Genesis."
332 Thom, "New Ideas – Genesis."
333 PJ Hammond, interview with Whittaker, 20 October 2017.
334 Pat McCarthy, New Ideas Festival Producer's Report, 1996.
335 Lamarre, Parr, and Carnwath, letter to the Canadian Actors' Equity Association's Ontario Advisory Council, 2 January 2001.
336 Lamarre, Parr, and Carnwath, letter.
337 Thom, "New Ideas Festival 2018" Report, in AAGM, 24 June 2018.
338 Lamarre, Parr, and Carnwath, letter.
339 Thom, "New Ideas – Genesis."
340 ABM, 11 September 2000.
341 ABM, 7 May 2000.
342 ABM, 16 November 2000.
343 Thom, email to Pat McCarthy (Alumnae president) and others, 23 February 2001, in ABM, 1 March 2001.
344 ABM, 1 March 2001, 11 April 2001; and appended letter to members and subscribers, 11 April 2001.
345 Hammond, interview with Whittaker.
346 ABM, 4 June 2001; Hammond, interview with Whittaker.
347 Jane Carnwath, The New Play Development Group Report, 12 June 2011.
348 Carnwath, The New Play Development Group Report.
349 Mary Barnes Amoroso, New Play Development (NPD) Group, in AAGM, 24 June 2018.
350 Barbara Larose, "FireWorks Discussion and Motion – Overview," in AAGM, 12 June 2016.

Chapter 8

1 Nathan Cohen, "An indispensable company," *Toronto Star*, 20 October 1965.
2 Halpenny, "Responsibilities in the Amateur Theatre" [Speech], n.d. (c. Coach House years).
3 "Witty Comedy Well Done," *Toronto Telegram*, 10 March 1928.
4 See Belasco and Winter, *Plays Produced under the Stage Direction of David Belasco*, 33.

5 "Witty Comedy Well Done."
6 Halpenny, "History of the University Alumnae Dramatic Club," 1945, 1.
7 "Grand opera in New York next week," *Globe*, 7 February 1925, 6.
8 See Scott, "Professional Performers and Companies."
9 Trevor Tremain-Garstang went on to work at the Royal Alexandra Theatre before touring across Canada as a stage manager with the Maurice Colbourne Company to "broaden theatrical tastes" for modern theatre, for example, with plays by George Bernard Shaw. He also acted on the British stage and in films under the name Launce Maraschal. See Scott, "Professional Performers and Companies," 33.
10 "Varied programme at alumni reunion," *Varsity*, 27 October 1930, 5.
11 In *To Have the Honour*, Mr. and Mrs. Brown meet again five years after separating, having taken on new lives as Prince Michael and the widow of a "mythical General Bulger," respectively. Clearly, this play about renewing past relations was keenly chosen by Alumnae for the homecoming crowd.
12 "Theatre and Concert Hall: Brief Comment," *Globe*, 15 November 1930, 15.
13 Davies, "Foreword," in Lee, *Love and Whisky*, x.
14 Jose Ruben, quoted in F. Beatrice Taylor, "Drama festival adjudicator, N.Y. expert lauds amateurs," *London Free Press*, 14 May 1951.
15 Ruben, quoted in F. Beatrice Taylor, "Vancouver cast lauded; choice of play courageous," 15 May 1951.
16 "Gala night opens drama tests," *London Free Press*, 15 May 1951, 1.
17 Taylor, "Vancouver cast lauded."
18 Quoted in F. Beatrice Taylor, "Professional theatre forecast," *London Free Press*, 21 May 1951, 18. When Taylor interviewed George Freedley, the creator of the New York Public Library's theatre collection, during the festival, Freedley commented that "professional theatre is a healthy thing for any community [and] the local players do better if there is a professional company to match themselves against." Freedley also described how the American National Theatre and Academy (ANTA), chartered by the U.S. Congress in 1935, "is the fairy Godmother of the living community theatre in the United States." Said Freedley, "When we think of a national theatre we do not have in mind a marble building in Washington or even a building off Broadway though I am thankful to say we have one of the latter now." Instead, the "national theatre concept, then, was a national theatre in each state fulfilling ANTA's aim, more theatre and better theatre for more people." So Taylor paraphrased Freedley. This system was surely influencing Vincent Massey and his royal commission, which would draft recommendations for what would become Canada's professional regional theatre system. Taylor, "'Living Theatre' across border moving into Canadian regions," *London Free Press*, n.d.
19 "Little Theatre salvation of the stage" [Editorial], *London Free Press*, 15 May 1951, 4.
20 Filewod, "Naming the Movement," 228.
21 AMM, 11 October 1951. The Jupiter Theatre, dedicated from the outset to advancing Canadian plays in a professional context, lasted only three seasons, or as Richard Partington puts it, two seasons sandwiched between two half seasons. Partington, "The Jupiter Theatre's Canadian Content and the Critics, 1951–1954," 61.
22 AMM, 11 October 1951.
23 AMM, November 1951.
24 Whittaker, letter to Margret Spence, 25 March 1999.
25 AMM, 27 November 1952.

26 A few months earlier it was reported that when a London columnist criticized Alec Guinness for going to Canada to help start the Stratford Festival, Guinness responded: "I do not consider accepting an invitation to go to Canada to play in a Theatre-in-the-Round, not yet built, in a town with a population of only 18,000, a program quite impossible to present commercially in the West End (*Richard III* and *All's Well that Ends Well*) as entirely unadventurous. The possibilities of disaster are quite formidable." Margaret Aitken, "Between You and Me," *Toronto Telegram*, 9 April 1953.
27 "The University Alumnae Dramatic Club," 1956, 3.
28 Whittaker, "Three professional companies promise healthy competition," *Globe and Mail*, 5 September 1953, 10.
29 Whittaker, "Show Business," *Globe and Mail*, 6 April 1954, 23.
30 AAGM, 19 June 1965.
31 AMM, 14 September 1953.
32 "Venus observed – by two Toronto groups," *Globe and Mail*, 20 October 1953, 12.
33 As with the previous year's fall production of Ruth and Augustus Goetz's *The Heiress*, Alumnae rehearsed the play at Sterndale Bennett's Canadian Theatre School.
34 Rose MacDonald, "Plot of *Venus Observed* fine mirror of our lives," *Toronto Telegram*, 14 October 1953.
35 Whittaker, "Show Business," *Globe and Mail*, 8 October 1953, 10.
36 Whittaker, "'2-week rep' meets dilemma of theatre's hardest school," *Globe and Mail*, 21 February 1953, 10.
37 Whittaker, "Show Business," *Globe and Mail*, 15 April 1953, 8.
38 Iris Winston, *Staging a Legend*. 107.
39 William Arthur Deacon, "The Fly Leaf," *Globe and Mail*, 10 January 1953, 7; "*The Lady's Not for Burning*" [Advertisement], *Globe and Mail*, 17 January 1953, 23.
40 Whittaker, "Show Business," *Globe and Mail*, 8 October 1953, 10.
41 Sperdakos, *Dora Mavor Moore*, 213, 211.
42 Whittaker, "Show Business," *Globe and Mail*, 14 September 1953, 14.
43 Whittaker, "Three professional companies promise healthy competition"; "Alumnae players in *Venus Observed*," *Globe and Mail*, 5 September 1953, 10.
44 Whittaker, "Show Business," *Globe and Mail*, 2 October 1953, 32. This was Guy Verney's third time directing the play. Mona Purser, "The Homemaker: Dr. MacMurchy's career one of true devotion," *Globe and Mail*, 19 October 1953, 21.
45 "*Venus Observed*" [Advertisement], *Globe and Mail*, 13 October 1953, 33.
46 Whittaker, "Show Business," *Globe and Mail*, 19 October 1953, 18.
47 AMM, 2 August 1951.
48 AMM, 11 October 1951.
49 AMM, 3 March 1953.
50 AMM, 9 April 1953.
51 AMM, 25 May 1953.
52 AAGM, 30 June 1953.
53 Sperdakos, *Dora Mavor Moore*, 207–8.
54 "*Venus Observed*," *Globe and Mail*, 18 July 1953, 12.
55 MacDonald, "Plot of *Venus Observed* fine mirror of our lives."
56 "The Callboard," *Varsity*, 2 October 1953, 5.
57 Quoted in Whittaker, "How should plays be picked? Three theatres, three replies," *Globe and Mail*, 30 January 1954, 14.

58 Whittaker, "How should plays be picked?"
59 AMM, 3 March 1953; 14 September 1953.
60 AAGM, 30 June 1953.
61 Mary Jukes, "Stylized costumes made by Alumnae designers," *Globe and Mail*, 12 October 1953, 19. In the play, the Duke of Altair seeks love in his later years and invites three of his favourites to witness a solar eclipse, asking his son to choose the woman for him. But when Perpetua appears, the Duke turns his attention to her, as does his son.
62 "*Venus Observed* stars Miss Terry," *Globe and Mail*, 26 September 1953, 10. Lotta Dempsey wrote in her "Person to Person" column that former music teacher and U of T graduate Marian Jones, playing Hilda, was married to atomic engineer Peter Stewart, playing the butler Reddleman, and that as they drove back and forth from their home in Oakville for rehearsals they took turns giving notes on each other's readings, "driving and reading lines to each other." Dempsey, "Person to Person," *Globe and Mail*, 7 October 1953, 12.
63 MacDonald, "Plot of *Venus Observed* fine mirror of our lives."
64 "*Venus Observed*," *Varsity*, 16 October 1953, 5.
65 Whittaker, "Show Business," *Globe and Mail*, 14 October 1953, 21.
66 "*Venus Observed*," *Varsity*.
67 Whittaker, "Show Business," 14 October 1953.
68 "*Venus Observed*," *Varsity*.
69 MacDonald, "Plot of *Venus Observed* fine mirror of our lives."
70 Whittaker, "Show Business," 14 October 1953.
71 Jukes, "Stylized costumes made by Alumnae designers."
72 Sperdakos, *Dora Mavor Moore*, 213.
73 Nancy S. Donnell, "More astronomy," *Varsity*, 21 October 1953, 2.
74 Donnell, "More astronomy."
75 Sperdakos, *Dora Mavor Moore*, 208.
76 Donnell, "More astronomy."
77 Sperdakos, *Dora Mavor Moore*, 213, 215.
78 AMM, 26 October 1953.
79 AAGM, 29 May 1954.
80 AAGM, 30 June 1953. The new Central Technical School theatre was "supposed to be the best stage in Toronto for amateur productions" (AAGM, 30 June 1953), potentially supplanting Hart House Theatre. The Technical School's new theatre had a seating capacity of 1,130, including the balcony ("Repeat of *Venus Observed*," *Globe and Mail*, 31 October 1953, 12). The rental cost for the dress rehearsal and performance was $75 for three hours; comparatively, Hart House Theatre cost $75 for the whole night (AMM, 14 September 1953). It also had "all kinds of lighting equipment" and a "wider proscenium" (AAGM, 30 June 1953) than Hart House Theatre.
81 AMM, 26 October 1953.
82 Purser, "The Homemaker."
83 Whittaker, "Tax relief signals era of hope and progress," *Globe and Mail*, 12 March 1955, 10.
84 Mark Czarnecki, "The Regional Theatre System," *Contemporary Canadian Theatre: New World Visions*, ed. Anton Wagner (Toronto: Simon and Pierre), 1985, 35–48 at 37.
85 Czarnecki, "The Regional Theatre System," 39.
86 Tippett, *Making Culture*, 186.
87 Whittaker, "Our drama festival needs a self-diagnosis," *Globe and Mail*, 14 April 1956, 12.
88 Whittaker, "Amateurs share fully in a lively season," *Globe and Mail*, 2 October 1954, 12.

89 Whittaker, "Showbusiness," *Globe and Mail*, 7 July 1954, 8.
90 Whittaker, "Amateurs share fully in a lively season."
91 Colin Sabiston, "Alumnae Dramatic Club presents *Wild Decembers*," *Globe and Mail*, 7 November 1947, 12.
92 Eltis, "Reception and Performance History of Wilde's Society Plays," 322.
93 Malcolm MacKinnon, *CJBC Views the Show*, n.d.
94 MacKinnon, *CJBC Views the Show*.
95 Jack Karr, "Those tame Wilde women," *Toronto Star*, 15 October 1954.
96 Whittaker, "Showbusiness," *Globe and Mail*, 14 October 1954, 12.
97 Karr, "Those tame Wilde women."
98 Whittaker, "Showbusiness," *Globe and Mail*, 15 October 1954, 9.
99 Rose MacDonald, "Alumnae players help Wilde have fun," *Toronto Telegram*, 15 October 1954, 23.
100 MacDonald, "Alumnae players help Wilde have fun."
101 Nancy S. Donnell, "*Woman of No Importance*," *Varsity*, 18 October 1954, 5.
102 Nathan Cohen, "Time must have a stop," *Toronto Star*, 12 June 1959.
103 Nathan Cohen, "Thieves' carnival," *Toronto Star*, 12 March 1959, 58.
104 Nathan Cohen, *CJBC Views the Shows*, 15 March 1959.
105 "An evening of 'comedy and hocus-pocus,'" *Toronto Telegram*, 7 March 1959.
106 Whittaker, "Eric House signs for role at Stratford," *Globe and Mail*, 16 March 1959, 14.
107 "An evening of 'comedy and hocus-pocus.'" Whittaker declared that for a "good bawdy evening which demands that you keep on the edge of your upholstered seat, threading your way through a swirl of difficult language, there is nothing to beat it in town."
108 Whittaker, "Remember amateurs? They're still around," *Globe and Mail*, 14 October 1960, 32.
109 Nathan Cohen, "An indispensable company," *Toronto Star*, 20 October 1965.
110 Nathan Cohen, "Directors are …," *Toronto*, 22 November 1965.
111 Cohen, "Directors are …," *Star*.
112 Whittaker, "Old play still a hit on great white way," *Globe and Mail*, 26 November 1965, 15.
113 Whittaker, "Old play still a hit on great white way."
114 Whittaker, "Amateur groups showing lots of life," *Globe and Mail*, 2 Sepember 1975, 15.
115 John Fraser, "*The Rover*: A Restoration curiosity, but nothing more," *Globe and Mail*, 7 April 1976, 15.
116 John Fraser, "*Blue Leaves*: Black humor and savage satire," *Globe and Mail*, 21 May 1976, 17.
117 John Fraser, "Firehall's Christie creaky but fun," *Globe and Mail*, 15 October 1976, 17.
118 John Fraser, "Hellman play timely but overdone," *Globe and Mail*, 11 February 1977, 14.
119 Bryan Johnson, "A madcap night of Stoppard," *Globe and Mail*, 7 April 1977, A10.
120 Gina Mallet, "*Blue Leaves* a brave try by amateurs," *Toronto Star*, 21 May 1976.
121 Gina Mallet, "Pinero asks a great deal," *Toronto Star*, n.d.
122 Jennifer Martin, "*Murder on the Nile*," *Varsity*, 15 October 1976, 8.
123 R. Read, "Rapid pace in *Beaux Stratagem*," *Varsity*, 20 October 1978, 11.
124 Asta Baskevicius, "Moon bays at *Hound*!!," *Varsity*, 6 April 1977, R11.
125 Whittaker, "Director leads club in the training program," *Globe and Mail*, 18 October 1966, 15.
126 AAGM, 10 June 1967.
127 Syd Usprich, "Theatre," *Varsity*, 23 September 1966, R10.
128 Marigold Charlesworth's departure from the Canadian Players "hastened a situation which led to both the Players and the Crest taking a year off" and folding upon their attempted merger. Whittaker quoted Charlesworth as saying that "banning the theatre for a year in Canada would

be good for it." Whittaker added that in Toronto there was now "some examination in depth into the situation. Whittaker, "Director leads club in the training program," *Globe and Mail*, 18 October 1966, 15.

129 Nathan Cohen, "*Three Sisters*: The play still holds," *Toronto Star*, 19 October 1966, 44.
130 Whittaker, "*The Three Sisters* blast their yearnings," *Globe and Mail*, 19 October 1966, 15.
131 Cohen, "*Three Sisters*: The play still holds."
132 Ron Evans, "Why not take the train?," *Toronto Telegram*, 19 October 1966, 62.
133 Urjo Kareda, *Varsity*, 21 October 1966, 12.
134 AMM, 9 November 1966.
135 AAGM, 10 June 1967.
136 Ruth Pincoe, letter to Susan Kerr (president), 22 November 1991.
137 Herbert Whittaker, "Equity splits theatre in vote of confidence," *Globe and Mail*, 3 November 1956, 22.
138 Margaret Spence, interview with Whittaker, 20 October 2017.
139 AEM, 12 January 1965.
140 Alumnae mailout announcement in advance of 15 February 1965 general meeting.
141 Alumnae Newsletter, August 1987.
142 Ruth Pincoe, letter to Susan Kerr (president), 22 November 1991.
143 Carol Palmer, Treasurer's Report, AAGM, 21 June 1998.
144 Palmer, Treasurer's Report, 21 June 1998.
145 "Equity Proposal," *Alumination*, March 2001.
146 Francess Halpenny, Prospectus, "The Alumnae Theatre: A History 1919–1999," in ABM, 4 June 2001.
147 Judy Malkin, email to board of directors "Items for Bd Meeting," in ABM, 11 September 2000.
148 ABM, 7 October 1998.
149 ABM, 4 August 1999.
150 Terry, letter to Barbara Larose, 26 October 1999.
151 Pamela Terry, letter to Barbara Larose appended to ABM, 26 October 1999.
152 ABM, 11 September 2000.
153 ABM, 7 January 2001.
154 Under income tax law, for example, Alumnae's accountants reported that Alumnae executive members could not participate in a show receiving Equity fees and that the law was less clear on whether non-executive members could receive payment in a "profit-sharing production" (ABM, 1 March 2001), like that under consideration with Equity/ACTRA. There was concern that as members of a charitable organization, Alumnae's members could not "directly benefit (in a financial sense) from their participation" (email from Judy Malkin to Alumnae board in ABM, 1 March 2001), but that this was not clear to their accountants on the face of it. After all, Equity members of Alumnae had been paid for their services before.
155 Judy Malkin, email to board of directors, 11 September 2000.
156 Report in ABM, 7 January 2001.
157 Jennifer Parr, email to Molly Thom "re: equity comforts," 15 February 2001, in ABM, 1 March 2001.
158 Andy Rhodes (program committee chair), email to Parr in ABM, 1 March 2001.
159 Alumnae, "Alumnae Theatre – Special Meeting Notice," 23 May 2001.
160 AAGM, 9 June 2002.

161 Alumnae, ABM, 30 October 2010.
162 AAGM, 2 June 1956.

Conclusions

1 PJ Hammond, interview with Whittaker, 20 October 2017.
2 Halpenny, "Shall we join the ladies?"
3 Winston, *Staging a Legend*, 17.
4 Whittaker, *Hot Thespian Action!*, 5.
5 Liz Nicholls, "Well done, Walterdale!," *Edmonton Journal*, 1 October 1983.
6 See Whittaker, "Walterdale Theatre Associates and the In(ter)vention of the Audience," *Canadian Theatre Review* 140 (Fall 2009), 33–9.
7 Rina Fraticelli, *The Status of Women in the Canadian Theatre*.
8 Burton, *Adding It Up*, ii.
9 Cited in MacArthur, *Achieving Equity in Canadian Theatre*, 19.
10 Burton, Rebecca. *Adding It Up*, ii.
11 Holdsworth, Milling, and Nicholson, "Theatre, Performance, and the Amateur Turn," 7.
12 Walters, "Being Among Bluebells," 96.
13 Huneault, "Introduction," in *Rethinking Professionalism*, 4.
14 Nicholson et al., *The Ecologies of Amateur Theatre*, 284.
15 Ridout, *Passionate Amateurs*, 29, 7–8, 9.
16 Nicholson et al., *The Ecologies of Amateur Theatre*, 284, 285, 286.
17 Ridout, *Passionate Amateurs*, 9.
18 Urjo Kareda, "Alternative theatre offers hope for the future," *Toronto Star*, 16 September 1972, 63.
19 Johnston, "Appendix B: Toronto Playlist 1968–1975," 271–3.
20 In May, David French's *Leaving Home* premiered at the Tarragon; in June, Toronto Free Theatre opened its doors for the first time with Tom Hendry's *How Are Things with the Walking Wounded?*; in August, Theatre Passe Muraille's groundbreaking documentary play *The Farm Show* opened in Clinton, Ontario; in September, the Tarragon remounted *Leaving Home* and Theatre Passe Muraille remounted *The Farm Show* in downtown Toronto; and in November, Tarragon produced its first Michel Tremblay translation, *Forever Yours, Marie-Lou*.
21 Urjo Kareda, "Toronto has a theatrical gap to fill," *Toronto Star*, 2 September 1972.
22 Kareda, "Alternative theatre offers hope for the future."
23 Molly Thom, interview with Whittaker, 19 October 2017.
24 Pritchard, "Down from the pedestal."
25 Nicholson et al., *The Ecologies of Amateur Theatre*, 67, 89.
26 AAGM, 15 June 1968.
27 Alumnae, "How has the U.A.D.C. managed to survive and flourish for sixty years?," History document. c. 1978.
28 PJ Hammond, interview with Whittaker, 20 October 2017.
29 Holdsworth, Milling, and Nicholson, "Theatre, Performance, and the Amateur Turn," 9.
30 Alan Filewod exposes the link between Canadian performance history, the "maturation" myth, and state-sponsored nationalism in Filewod, "Erect Sons and Dutiful Daughters."
31 Halpenny, Francess. Prospectus, "The Alumnae Theatre: A History 1919–1999," in ABM, 4 June 2001.
32 Halpenny, "Shall we join the ladies?"

Appendix I

1 "The Women's Dramatic Club." *Torontonensis 1916*, 221.
2 "University College Second Year Executive" [Photograph caption], *Torontonensis 1915*. 57; "E.R. Bach." *Torontonensis 1917*, 14.
3 "Directory of Officers of State Associations," *The Osteopathic Physician*, September 1912, 10.
4 Cook, *The Regenerators*, 250n62.
5 "An interesting war wedding," *Toronto Star*, 23 July 1918.
6 "Norwich-Bach," *Toronto Star*, 23 July 1918.
7 "An interesting war wedding."
8 "Norwich-Bach," *Toronto Star*, 23 July 1918.
9 "Norwich," *Toronto Star*, 25 May 1922; "The Humane Society tag day …," *Toronto Star*, 7 April 1928.
10 "Norwich," *Mail*, 4 September 1924; "The Humane Society tag day …," *Toronto Star*, 7 April 1928.
11 "Norwich," *Mail*, 4 March 1936; "Norwich, Dr. Arthur C.," *Globe and Mail*, 6 February 1965. 39.
12 Francess Halpenny, "History of the University Alumnae Dramatic Club," 1945, 7.
13 "Cast for *Salvage*," *Globe and Mail*, 1 March 1933, 8.
14 "Norwich, Dr. Arthur C."
15 "Co-education helps interest in study and social events," *Varsity*, 31 October 1928.
16 "'Mile of Nickels' day explained," *Varsity*, 3 December 1928; "Co-eds collect 'Mile of Nickels'; forty women protect treasure as 'Silver Walk' is laid on campus," *Globe and Mail*, 6 December 1928, 15.
17 "Six dozen lipsticks to make-up skaters," *Toronto Star*, 12 March 1937.
18 "Great Britain's senior golfers win from Canadians at Toronto," *Globe and Mail*, 4 September 1928, 12.
19 "Social Events," *Globe and Mail*, 14 June 1933, 11.
20 "Name Prof. Woodside U of T Dean of Arts," *Globe and Mail*, 30 May 1952, 4.
21 "Mrs. and Mrs. Moffatt S. Woodside," *Toronto Star*, 19 June 1933.
22 "Social Events," *Globe and Mail*, 10 July 1931, 16, and 10 August 1931, 11.
23 UADC "History," 1945, 7.
24 "Woodside, Eleanor A.," *Globe and Mail*, 15 August 1984, M5.
25 *Torontonensis 1915*, 63.
26 *Torontonensis 1915*, 60.
27 *Torontonensis 1915*, 240.
28 "U.C. Women's Lit will hold oratorical contest," *Varsity*, 24 January 1917.
29 *Torontonensis 1915*, 63.
30 "Series of Plays at Conservatory," *Toronto World*, 17 March 1918.
31 Cordingley, *The Anchora of the Delta Gamma Fraternity*. 473.
32 "Lady graduates receive appointments," *Varsity*, 7 October 1918.
33 "Social Events," *Globe and Mail*, 7 October 1930, 18.
34 "Engagements," *Globe*, 7 October 1930, 18.
35 "Births," *Globe*, 22 September 1931, 14.
36 "Births," *Mail*, 3 May 1933.
37 "Liberal women approve policies of progress," *Globe*, 22 May 1915, 10.
38 "Announcements," *Globe*, 26 February 1924, 8.

39 "Biographies of Early and Exceptional Ontario Lawyers," May 2012.
40 "Celebrating 100 Years of Women's Law Association of Ontario in 2019."
41 Laughton, "Women in Law."
42 "Class Horoscope," *Torontonensis 1912*, 38.
43 "The Boys from Parkhill," laughton.ca.
44 Morgan, "'An embarrassingly and severely masculine atmosphere,'" n131.
45 "Biographies of Early and Exceptional Ontario Lawyers."
46 Neighborhood Workers Association, *Social Services Directory*, Toronto, 1917, 3.
47 "Tenders resignation," *Toronto Star*, 5 May 1921.
48 Hodgins, *Report*, 133.
49 Laughton, "Women in Law."
50 "Court lacking in equipment," *Globe*, 8 February 1919, 9.
51 Laughton, "Women in Law."
52 "Social Events," *Globe*, 30 August 1920, 10.
53 *Journal of Proceeding of the Convocation of benchers*, 1915.
54 "Deaths," *Globe and Mail*, 7 November 1966, 32.
55 "Church work and workers," *Globe*, 22 February 1908, 9.
56 "The forest city: Canadian Bible Society's annual meeting," *Globe*, 13 March 1908, 2.
57 "Artist explains 'Batik' process," *Globe*, 26 February 1921, 31.
58 "News of Women's Organization," *Globe*, 29 October 1930, 16.
59 "Marriages," *Globe*, 24 November 1925, 12.
60 "Deaths," *Globe and Mail*, 30 September 1969, 41.
61 "The Alumnae Association…," *Toronto Telegram*, 12 December 1927.
62 "Theatre and Concert Hall: Brief Comment," *Globe*, 1 April 1933, 5.
63 "Theatre and Concert Hall: Brief Comment," *Globe*, 20 May 1933, 5; "Social Events," *Globe*, 22 October 1934, 8; "Brief Comments," *Globe and Mail*, 15 June 1935, 20.
64 "*When Whirlwind Blows* at Dickens Fellowship," *Globe and Mail*, 24 March 1941, 8.
65 "*Everyman*: Old morality play presented at Westminster Central," *Globe and Mail*, 29 January 1930, 14.
66 "*Well of All Things*, proceeds for war, holds Hart House stage next week," *Globe and Mail*, 25 January 1940, 9; "Pedagogues' wives meet at Moulton," *Globe and Mail*, 13 February 1940, 10; "St. Hilda's College Alumnae Bridge to include *Day in May* and dance on its program," *Globe and Mail*, 18 April 1940, 10.
67 Shelagh Kareda, interview with Whittaker, 12 July 2020.
68 "Social Events," *Globe and Mail*, 11 February 1914, 5.
69 "Social Events," *Globe and Mail*, 12 June 1918, 11.
70 Kareda, interview with Whittaker, 20 October 2017.
71 "Kappa Alpha Theta," *Torontonensis 1950*, 438.
72 "The Women's Literary Society of University College," *Torontonensis 1920*, 41.
73 "Alison Agnes Ewart," *Torontonensis 1922*, 17.
74 "U.C. Alumnae elects Mrs. W. W. Events head," *Globe and Mail*, 26 April 1935, 9.
75 Ewart and Jarvis, "The Personnel of the Family Compact, 1791–1841."
76 Harman, "Founding a University Press."
77 Panofsky, *Toronto Trailblazers*, 71.
78 "University of Toronto Report of the Board of Governors for the Year Ended 30th June 1936," *University of Toronto Quarterly* (1937), 96.
79 "University of Toronto Report," 96.

80 Panofsky, *Toronto Trailblazers*, 72.
81 Kareda, interview with Whittaker.
82 "Hewitt, Agnes Alison," *Globe and Mail*, 23 November 1987, A16; "Hewitt, Albert William Blackburn," *Globe and Mail*, 3 December 1987, A23.
83 Kareda, interview with Whittaker.
84 Heather Murray, "Doubled Lives," 1007.
85 Murray, "Doubled Lives," 1021.
86 "*The School for Scandal*: Presented by the Women's Dramatic Club," *Varsity*, 22 January 1917, 1.
87 Murray, "Doubled Lives," 1021.
88 Robert Stall, "There's a story behind the house beside the big hotel," *Globe and Mail*, *Weekend Magazine*, 19 January 1974, A2.
89 Stall, "There's a story behind the house beside the big hotel," A2.
90 "Keys, Erskine," *Toronto Star*, [Obituary], 22 January 1984.
91 "Notice to creditors and others," *Globe and Mail*, 7 May 1984, B10.
92 Hector Charlesworth, "Story of boy depicted in Hart House drama," *Globe and Mail*, 14 April 1942, 8.
93 "Personal Notes," *Globe and Mail*, 25 February 1943, 14.
94 "Charles J. Leonard barrister, passes," *Globe*, 22 February 1932, 11.
95 "University College Third Year Executive," *Torontonesis 1920*, 33.
96 "Women's Press Association of the University," *Torontonesis 1920*, 255.
97 "Robert Gill new director at Hart House," *Globe and Mail*, 7 September 1946, 8.
98 "Social Events," *Globe and Mail*, 6 February 1926, 15.
99 "Social Events," *Globe and Mail*, 10 December 1926, 16.
100 "Social Events," *Globe and Mail*, 17 January 1931, 16.
101 "President Cody entertains university staff and wives," *Globe*, 28 October 1933, 14.
102 "Society Notes," *Globe and Mail*, 14 May 1940, 10.
103 "Society Notes," *Globe and Mail*, 28 April 1942, 10.
104 "Social Notes," *Globe and Mail*, 5 January 1950, 10.
105 "Social and Personal Notes," *Globe and Mail*, 23 May 1957, 14.
106 "The 1963–64 Office of Education Survey," 348.
107 Leonard, "Special Libraries in Ontario," 137–41.
108 Leonard, "Statistical methods in Medical School Libraries."
109 "Leonard, Agatha," *Globe and Mail*, 5 February 1991, E4.
110 "Singularly gifted in art of stage," *Globe and Mail*, 18 February 1946, 7.
111 "Talented actress Mrs. A. Stone dies," *Toronto Telegram*, 18 February 1946.
112 "Singularly gifted in art of stage," *Globe and Mail*, 18 February 1946, 7.
113 Hilda Ridley, "Pen Portraits of Progressive Women," *Christian Guardian*, 16 March 1931.
114 "Spoke to I.O.D.E.," *Globe*, 12 February 1930, 18.
115 "*The School for Scandal* presented by the Women's Dramatic Club," *Varsity*, 22 January 1917, 1.
116 "U.C. Women's Lit. will stage play: *The Bear*," *Varsity*, 7 February 1917, 4.
117 "Women's Lit. Society meets this evening," *Varsity*, 12 October 1917, 3.
118 "The Women's Literary Society of University College," *Torontonensis 1920*, 39, 41.
119 "Talented actress Mrs. A. Stone dies," *Toronto Telegram*, 18 February 1946.
120 "A.I. Muldrew," *Torontonensis 1917*, 31.
121 "Appears in play at Hart House," *Globe*, 26 April 1922, 13.

122 "Student playwrights present production," *Globe*, 3 April 1923, 16.
123 "When whirlwind blows at Dickens Fellowship," *Globe and Mail*, 14 March 1941, 8.
124 "*The Cherry Orchard* magnificently acted," *Mail*, 20 May 1926.
125 "Theatre and Concert Hall," *Globe*, 2 December 1933, 5.
126 "Winners of drama festival here," *Mail*, 1 April 1935.
127 "Talented actress Mrs. A. Stone dies."
128 *Kappa Alphan Theta Journal* (January 1922), 184.
129 "Singularly gifted in art of stage," *Globe and Mail*, 18 February 1946, 7.
130 Connor, *Doing Good*.
131 Shorter, *Partnership for Excellence*, 502.
132 "Great Radium Institute for cancer treatment forecast for Toronto," *Globe*, 24 September 1930, 1, 2.
133 "Edgar Stone, theatre manager, weds quietly in House Chapel," *Varsity*, 6 October 1930, 1, 4.
134 "Stone-Muldrew." *Globe*. 6 October 1930, 16.
135 "Edgar Stone, theatre manager, weds quietly in House Chapel," *Varsity*, 6 October 1930, 1, 4.
136 "Stone-Muldrew," *Globe*, 6 October 1930, 16.
137 "Singularly gifted in art of stage"; "Talented actress Mrs. A. Stone dies."
138 Alumnae, *Autumn Crocus* program, 7–9 November 1949, 23.
139 John Fraser, "Miller back in vogue with taut *Crucible*," *Globe and Mail*, 7 April 1977, A13.
140 Whittaker," "Jessica Tandy is cast in the Shaw Festival opener," *Globe and Mail*, 30 May 1968, 11.
141 "Experiment in staging in *Sleep My Pretty One*," *Globe and Mail*, 8 April 1961, 13.
142 "CBC's Beecrofts stay together," *Globe and Mail*, 2 December 1967, 27.
143 Television listings, *Globe and Mail*, 9 July 1994, 40.
144 Christopher Winsor, "Theatrical housing for setting stars," *Globe and Mail*, 19 October 1996, C17; "Gathering place: The actors' retirement village," *Globe and Mail*, 28 September 2000, 1, 2; Wallace Immen, "Actors fight plan to build apartment," *Globe and Mail*, 13 June 2001, A17.
145 Bruce Bell, quoted in Winsor, "Theatrical housing for setting stars."
146 "Beecroft-Stewart, Eleanor Chambers (née Norton)," *Toronto Star*, 22 September 2007.
147 Immen, "Actors fight plan to build apartment."
148 "Beecroft-Stewart, Eleanor Chambers (née Norton)."
149 "The Modern Language Club," *Torontonensis 1925*, 300.
150 Beecroft, Eleanor. Quoted in Julia Bennett, "Twenties follies roar again," *Globe and Mail*, 1 March 1997, C8.
151 "University students appear in Italian-Spanish roles," *Globe*, 13 May 1928.
152 "Beecroft-Stewart, Eleanor Chambers (née Norton)."
153 "Honoring Sterndale Bennett," *Globe and Mail*, 23 March 1972, 10.
154 "Engagements." *Globe and Mail*, 10 November 1931, 14.
155 "Julian Beecroft," *Allison Funeral Home*, January 2008.
156 "Beecroft-Stewart, Eleanor Chambers (née Norton)."
157 "Julian Beecroft."
158 "CBC's Beecrofts stay together."
159 Arts and Letters Club, "Monthly Letter," December 1955, 7.
160 "Beecroft-Stewart, Eleanor Chambers (née Norton)."
161 Zena Cherry, "Dinner honors U of T donors," *Globe and Mail*, 22 April 1981, 16.
162 "Eleanor Chambers Beecroft-Stewart," *Globe and Mail*, 22 September 2007, S8.

163 "The Modern Language Club of University College," *Torontonensis 1919*, 47.
164 "Smart, Mary W.," *Torontonensis 1919*, 24.
165 "Rush for books when ban lifts: Big day at College Library after shutdown because of epidemic," *Globe and Mail*, 10 January 1920, 9.
166 "Social Events," *Globe and Mail*, 20 April 1922, 16.
167 "Exceptional treat in amateur drama," *Globe and Mail*, 19 May 1922, 17.
168 "Smart, Mary Wallace."
169 "Social Events," *Globe*, 30 March 1915, 8.
170 C.D. Rouillard et al., "A Golden Age, 1920–1960," *French Studies at the University of Toronto 1853–1993*.
171 "*The School for Scandal*," *Globe*, 20 January 1917, 8.
172 "Squair, Marion R.," *Torontonensis 1918*, 25.
173 Marion Squair Hunter, "World War I from the Berry Patch," late 1960s, posted by Catherine Murno in *Brian Henry's Quick Brown Fox*, 19 March 2020.
174 "Social Events," *Globe and Mail*, 12 April 1920, 10.
175 Rouillard et al., "A Golden Age, 1920–1960."
176 For a discussion of this production, see Badir, "'This Little Academe, Still and Contemplative in Living Art.'"
177 Constance Backhouse and Nancy L. Backhouse, *The Heiress vs the Establishment*, 296n22.
178 "Sons of Scotland meet for 37th Grand Camp, *Globe and Mail*, 28 June 1933, 9.
179 "*The Merchant of Venice*," *Globe*, 17 February 1912, 8.
180 "*The School for Scandal* presented by the Women's Dramatic Club," *Varsity*, January 1917.
181 "*Much Ado about Nothing* presented by Women's Dramatic Club," *Varsity*, 14 February 1916, 2.
182 "The Women's Athletic Association of University College," *Torontonensis 1917*, 180.
183 UADC, "History," 1945, 7
184 Roly Young, "Rambling with Roly," *Globe and Mail*, 25 February 1947, 9.
185 "Hart House Theatre," *Globe and Mail*, 25 March 1927; Lawrence Mason, "Music and the Drama," *Globe and Mail*, 17 May 1927, 14.
186 Lawrence Stone, "One reading found pleasing, the other boring," *Globe and Mail*, 26 October 1961, 34.
187 Kay Anglin, "The play and its production," *Globe and Mail*, 26 February 1955, 6.
188 F.R. Thurston, "The play and its adjudication," *Globe and Mail*, 9 March 1955, 6.
189 "Katherine Barwick Wells," *Torontonensis 1924*, 35.
190 "*Twelfth Night* presented on Friday," *Varsity*, 24 February 1913, 2.
191 "Jessie Elspeth Wilson," *Torontonensis 1913*, 72.
192 C.L. Foster, "Preface," in *Letters from the Front*, vol. 1., ix.
193 Elspeth Wilson, "The Home Forum," *Globe and Mail*, 15 November 1917, 11.
194 Elspeth Wilson, "Fair play," *Farmers' Magazine: Canada's National Farm Magazine*, 15 January 1919, 25.
195 Wilson, "Fair play."
196 "University Women elect Miss Norton," *Globe*, 5 June 1935, 6.
197 "Lt.-Col. M.J. Wilson," *Globe and Mail*, 13 February 1953, 4; "Wilson, Jessie Elspeth," *Globe and Mail*, 28 May 1965, 54.

Works Cited

Archival Material

Frederic Wood Theatre. *Waiting for Godot* [Photograph]. 21 September to 3 October 1983, 15. UBC Library Open Collections. Web.

– *Waiting for Godot* [Playbill]. 28–9 June and 2–6 July 1957. UBC Library Open Collections. Web.

Private Collections

The following primary sources are held at Alumnae Theatre Company's Firehall location, accessed by the author with permission of the theatre's Building Manager and Archivist. This includes internal and public-facing documents, as well as letters, telegrams, and emails originating from, or sent to, Alumnae.

"1936 Festival of The Central Ontario Region of the Dominion Drama Festival." Information Booklet. March 1936.

Agreement between University Alumnae Dramatic Club and the Corporation of the City of Toronto, 8 July 1971.

Alumnae. 11 March 1969 general meeting announcement. Undated notice.

Alumnae. 22 April 1969 general meeting announcement. Undated notice.

Alumnae. general meeting announcement on 25 September 1969.

Alumnae. letter to membership "re the Enoch Turner Schoolhouse" in advance of general meeting on 11 December 1969.

Alumnae mailout announcement in advance of the 15 February 1965 general meeting.

Alumnae management board meeting minutes, 30 March 1987.

Alumnae minutes book. Note about skits presented on 24 April 1942.

Alumnae Newsletter, August 1987.

Alumnae note. "Former use Number 4 Fire Station." n.d.

Alumnae notice for 10 June 1972 annual meeting.

Alumnae notice of general meeting, various dates.

Alumnae program for *Mary, Mary, Quite Contrary*, March 1923.

Alumnae report on the general meeting, 11 December 1969.

Alumnae Special General Meeting minutes, 9 July 1990.

Alumnae. “About the Coach House Theatre,” c. 9 November 1962.
Alumnae. “Alumnae Theatre Company.” Draft. 20 May 1996.
Alumnae. “Alumnae Theatre – Special Meeting Notice.” 23 May 2001.
Alumnae. “Building Fund Appeal.” July 1961.
Alumnae. “Director’s Award Guidelines.” Board Meeting Minutes. 3 September 1991.
Alumnae. “Firehall Theatre Renamed” [Press Release]. 10 July 1978.
Alumnae. “For Toronto Walking Guide: The Firehall Theatre, No. 70 Berkeley Street.” Draft.
Alumnae. “How has the U.A.D.C. managed to survive and flourish for sixty years?” History document. c. 1978.
Alumnae. “In 1918 a group of women with a common love….” [History document]. October 1963.
Alumnae. “Jacqueline White (School Teacher).” Biography. Nov 1969.
Alumnae. “Motion re 10 Maplewood.” n.d.
Alumnae. “Subscription Series 1969–70.” Flyer. Fall 1969.
Alumnae. “The University Alumnae Dramatic Club acquires the Berkeley Street Firehall.” Press Release. Fall 1971.
Alumnae. “Theatre Listings” [Press release] for *Old Times*. March 1974.
Alumnae. “University Alumnae Dramatic Club: Coach House Theatre.” July 1961.
Alumnae. “University Alumnae Dramatic Club.” 1956. Copied from original by L. Burke in 1980.
Alumnae. “University Alumnae Dramatic Club.” Summer 1960.
Alumnae. Agenda for 27 October 1970 general meeting.
Alumnae. *Autumn Crocus* program. 7–9 Nov 1949. 23.
Alumnae. Draft letter to Committee on Parks and Recreation. c. Summer/Fall 1970.
Alumnae. *Homeward Bound* cast bios. 20 January 2006.
Alumnae. Press Release for *Next Time I’ll Sing to You*, February 1965.
Alumnae. Press release for *The Increased Difficulty of Concentration*. 17 Mar 1979.
Alumnae. Press release to Beth Slainey, 17 November 1966.
Alumnae. Press Release. April 1976.
Alumnae. UADC By-laws. 17 June 1987.
Alumnae note, “Former use Number 4 Fire Station,” n.d.
Amoroso, Mary Barnes. “New Play Development (NPD) Group.” AAGM, 24 June 2018.
“Annual party skit.” June 1974.
Autumn Crocus [Program]. November 1949, 7.
Bennison, Deirdre. Membership Report. AAGM, 21 June 1998.
Best, Liz. “Report on the Vice President Membership.” AAGM, 24 June 2018.
Carnwath, Jane. The New Play Development Group Report, 12 June 2011.
Carscallen, Helen. Theatre Manager’s Report, 13 June 1964.
“Central Ontario Festival 1939.” Program. Alumnae Theatre Company collection.
“Club History.” *Newsletter*, UADC, c. 1954.
CODL. Newsletters, September 1954, September 1956, January 1957, June 1958.
Corporation of the City of Toronto By-Law No. 191-71, 5 August 1971.
Darling, Brenda. “President’s Report for the 100th Season of Alumnae Theatre Company.” Alumnae Annual General Meeting (minutes), 24 June 2018.
Darling, Brenda. Report of the Executive Producer. In Alumnae Annual General Meeting (minutes), 12 June 2016.
Davies, Robertson. Secretary’s Report. AAGM, 13 June 1964.
“Dominion Drama Festival.” Program, April 1948, 7.
Edgar, Margaret. Production Report for *Reckless*. ABM, 11 June 1990.

– Report on Subscriptions. AAGM, 20 June 1987.
Finlay, Angela. Rentals Report. AAGM, 9 June 2002.
Fisher, Pat. Production Report for *The Last Real Summer*, 19 November 1984.
Golby, Molly. "Report of the Playreading Committee." AAGM, June 1961, 1–5.
– Theatre Manager's reports, AAGM, 9 June 1962 and 15 June 1963.
Halpenny, Francess. "History of the University Alumnae Dramatic Club." 1945.
– "Responsibilities in the Amateur Theatre." Speech. n.d.
– Prospectus. "The Alumnae Theatre: A History 1919–1999." In ABM, 4 June 2001.
Hammond, PJ Executive Producer's Report. AAGM, 9 June 2002.
Hirst, Nan (program director). Letter to membership, August 1985.
Kee, Nancy, "The Alumnae Theatre." Alumnae publicity, c. 1981.
Larose, Barbara. "FireWorks Discussion and Motion – Overview." AAGM, 12 June 2016.
– "Mainstage Programming Committee." AAGM, 24 June 2018.
Leonard, Agatha. "A Manual of Production Procedures for the University Alumnae Dramatic Club." 1970.
– Reports of the Programme Committee, 15 June 1968 and 7 June 1969.
Mascall, Elizabeth. Financial Statement. Alumnae Annual General Meeting, 13 June 1964.
McCarthy, Pat. New Ideas Festival Producer's Report, 1996.
McCulloch, Tina. Publicity/Marketing Report. AAGM, 9 June 2002.
Palmer, Carol. Treasurer's Reports. AAGM, 17 June 1995 and 21 June 1998.
Report. In Alumnae Board of Directors Meeting (minutes). 7 January 2001.
Rogers, Lorna F. Annual Report of Property Manager, AAGM, 11 June 1966.
– New Members Report. AAGM, 13 June 1964.
– Property Manager Report. AAGM, 19 June 1965.
– Publicity Reports. AAGMs, 9 June 1962 and 15 June 1963.
Shaw, Joan. Program Committee Report for AAGM, 17 June 1995.
Sims, Shirley. Property Management Report. AAGM, 15 June 1963.
– Rental Property Report. AAGM, 13 June 1964.
Spence, Margaret. House Manager Report. AAGM, 19 June 1965.
– Theatre Manager's Report. AAGM, 19 June 1965.
"Summary of Year's Activities, 1947–48." Alumnae Minute Book.
Terry, Pamela. Programme and Playreading Committee Report. AAGM, 13 June 1964.
– Report of the Playreading Committee. AAGM, 9 June 1962.
– Report of the Programming and Play Reading Committee, 15 June 1963.
Thom, Molly. Audience Development Report. AAGM, 17 June 1995.
– "From Coach House to Firehall. DRAFT." Note to Robin C. Whittaker, 23 August 2009.
– "New Ideas Festival 2018." Report. In AAGM, 24 June 2018.
– Note to Alumnae membership, 1964.
Thom, Molly (Building Committee Chair). "Architectural Program: University of Alumnae Dramatic Club – Coach House Theatre," 26 November 1970.
Thomson, Cecily. Producer's Report to the Executive, 7 December 1974.
The Towering Darkness (script), Spring 1975.
UADC, Fiftieth anniversary season pamphlet.
UADC "History," 1963.
UADC [history document], 1960.
UADC [history document], 1968.
University Alumnae Dramatic Club (UADC). "About the Coach House Theatre," c. November 1962.

"University Alumnae Dramatic Club, The." 1956, 1–5.
– "Building Fund Appeal," 1961, 1.
– "Fifth Concert and Theatre Series." Forest Hill Collegiate Auditorium Program for *In Good King Charles's Golden Days*, 2–7 April 1951, 2.
– "History," 1945, 7; 1960; 1963.
– Membership flyer, c. 1980.
– *Newsletter*, June 1954.
Wade, Allan. Adjudicator's Report for *Empurpled Moors*, 26 March 1936.
Wale, Nola. "Thoughts on the Rental Policy of the Alumnae Theatre." In AEM, 21 November 1985.

Letters

All letters were accessed by the author at the collections kept at Alumnae Theatre Company's Firehall location.

Acland, James (President, Architectural Conservancy of Ontario), letter to City Property Commissioner, 10 October.
Bolt, Carol. Note to Colleen Wagner.
Bolt, Carol. Letter To Whom It May Concern [at Alumnae Theatre Company]. 17 June 1990.
Cohen, Nathan. Letter to Pamela Terry Beckwith, 12 March 1963.
Corporation of Trinity Church signatories. Letter to R.B. Apted (Director, Historical Branch, Queen's Park), in application to make Enoch Turner Schoolhouse a historical site. 10 September 1969.
Crowther, Francess (University Settlement). Letter to Agatha Leonard, 27 March 1940, Alumnae Theatre Company collection.
– Letter to Mrs. Stone (Agnes Muldrew), 16 January 1939.
Cunningham, Jack. Letter to Agatha Leonard, 13 June 1967.
Davis, Glenna. Letter to Cicely Thomson, 16 January 1965.
Davis, Rae. Letter to Agatha Leonard, 19 May 1967.
Deputy Assistant Secretary to the Governor-General. Letters to Mrs. Leslie Hunt, 3 5, 6, 10, 15, 18 November 1937.
Davis, Glenna. Letter to Cicely Thomson, 16 January 1965.
Davis, Rae. Letter to Agatha Leonard, 19 May 1967.
Deputy Assistant Secretary to the Governor-General. Letters to Mrs. Leslie Hunt, 3 5, 6, 10, 15, 18 November 1937.
Edgar, Margaret. Letter to Alumnae membership, October or November 1974.
Golby, Molly. Letter to Emanuel Wax (Actact Theatrical and Cinematic Ltd.), 26 October 1960.
– Letters to Emanuel Wax (Actact Theatrical and Cinematic Ltd.), 26 October 1960 and 22 September 1961.
Gould, Allan M. Letter to the Editor, *Globe and Mail*, 20 October 1973, 7.
Heller, Roz. Letter to Alumnae membership, 20 August 1986. [Emphasis in original.]
Hill, John E. Letter to Margaret MacAulay, 7 July 1969.
Holmes, Charlotte. Letter to Ron Evans, 25 June 1963.
Jarvis, Julia. Letter to Frances Halpenny, 16 January 1948.
Johnson, Ruth. Letter to the Secretary of the Zonta Club of Toronto, 27 September 1948.
"Ladies – re the Enoch Turner Schoolhouse." Alumnae letter to membership in advance of general meeting on 11 December 1969.

Lamarre, Margaret, Jennifer Parr, and Jane Carnwath. Letter to the Canadian Actors' Equity Association's Ontario Advisory Council. 2 January 2001.
Leonard, Agatha (program committee chair). Letter to Rae Davis, 15 May 1967.
Letter from Monastery of Our Lady of Charity to Agatha Leonard. 1 June 1937.
Lavier, Clair M. (President, Industrial Interiors Ltd.). Letter to Mrs. R. Thom, 11 September 1970.
Lippert, Harold J. Letter to Laurier Melanson, 19 April 1967.
Loeffler, Andrew J. (Dramatists Play Service). Letters to Doris N. Stacey, 2 and 16 July 1957.
MacAulay, Margaret. Letter to DDF Professional Direction Committee, 1 April 1969.
– Letter to Friend of the Coach House, 11 March 1969.
– Letter to John E. Hill, DFF, 12 May 1970.
– Letter to membership, 8 October 1968.
MacDonald, R. Letter to Mrs. John Beckwith, 22 April 1958.
McCarthy, Pat (Alumnae president). Letter to *Now Magazine*, 5 December 2000.
– New Ideas Festival Producer's Report, 1996.
Mathie, Bill. Letter to Francess Halpenny, 21 August 1962.
McLaughlin, Claire L. Letter to Committee on Parks and Recreation, 20 September 1930.
Meiklejohn, Michael. "Serial Letter" regarding rehearsal and performance information to University Alumnae Dramatic Club, Toronto. n.d.
Melanson, Laurier. Letter to Elizabeth Mascall (Mrs. David), 8 September 1967.
Milne, W.S. Letter to Edna Norwich, 8 February 1941. Alumnae Theatre Company collection.
Montgomery, Kay letter to City Director of Real Estate, 10 September 1991.
Palmer, John. Letter to Molly Thom, 23 October 1972.
Pape, Joan (Mrs. George). Letter to Alumnae Dramatic Club, 27 November 1937.
Pincoe, Ruth. Letter to Susan Kerr (president), 22 November 1991.
Reaney, James. Letter to Shelagh Kareda, 19 January 1973.
Robinowitz, J. (City Auditor). Letter to Mayor John Sewell, copied to Alumnae, 16 October 1979.
Stacey, Doris N. Letter to Dramatists' Play Service, 27 June 1957.
Sterndale Bennett, E.G. Letter to Mary Wallace Smart, 30 April 1947.
Terry, Pamela. Letters: to Barbara Larose, appended to Alumnae Board of Directors Meeting (minutes), 26 October 1999; to Catherine Wilbraham, 17 August 1962; to W.P. Rowley, 23 May 1964.
Terry Beckwith, Pamela. Letters: to Nathan Cohen, 8 March 1963 and 1 April 1964; to Peter M. Dwyer (Canada Council), 31 May 1963 and 25 June 1963; to Wilfred Watson, 29 June 1962 and 2 August 1963.
Thom, Molly. Letters: to Alderman David Rotenberg, 27 April 1971; to Alderman Thomas Wardle, 28 April 1971; to Sid Adilman, 29 June 1972.
Tyrwhitt, Janice. Letter (draft) to musicians' union re: musicians for the 17–21 April 1956 run of *Teach Me How to Cry*. n.d.
Wagner, Dixon. Letter to Agatha Leonard, 9 December 1939. Alumnae Theatre Company Collection.
Walker, Enid Marion. Letter to Members of the UC Dramatic Society. n.d. Alumnae Theatre Company Collection.
Wallace, Donald. Letter to Commissioner of Parks and Recreation, 29 September 1970.
Watson, Wilfred. Letters to Pamela Beckwith, 7 September and 29 December 1962, 27 February and 14 July 1963.
Whittaker, Herbert. Letter to Margaret Spence, 25 March 1999.

– Letters to Margaret Spence, 25 September 1967 and 25 March 1999.
Williams, Eileen. Letter to Fellow Members, 30 May 1962.
– Letter to Friend of the Coach House Theatre. 7 September 1962.

Interviews

Carnwath, Jane. Interview with Robin C. Whittaker, 19 October 2017.
Hammond, PJ. Interview with Robin C. Whittaker, 20 October 2017.
Kareda, Shelagh. Interviews with Robin C. Whittaker, 20 October 2017, 12 July 2020.
Mann Southgate, Martha. Interviews with Robin C. Whittaker, 20 and 25 October 2017.
Spence, Catherine. Interview with Robin C. Whittaker, 21 October 2017.
Spence, Margaret, and Michael Spence. Interview with Robin C. Whittaker, 21 October 2017.
Thom, Molly. Interviews with Robin C. Whittaker, 19 and 25 October 2017.
Weldon Tait, Anne. Interview with Robin C. Whittaker, 19 October 2017.

Telegrams and Emails

Alumn. CN telegraph to The Cast (*Waiting for Godot*), 15 May 1958.
Barnett, Barbara. CN telegraph to *Waiting for Godot*, 15 May 1958.
CN telegraph to The Cast (*Waiting for Godot*), 15 May 1958.
Hollet, Michael. Form email to Suzanne Courtney (Alumnae secretary), 7 December 2000.
Kay. CP telegram to Ivor Jackson, 15 May 1958.
Levinson, Kenneth. CP telegram to Mrs. Pamela Beckwith, 15 May 1958.
Malkin, Judy. Emails to Alumnae board of directors, ABM, 11 September 2000 and 1 March 2001.
Mantley, John. Canadian Pacific telegraph to Katherine Anglin, 28 April 1948.
Parr, Jennifer. Email to Molly Thom "re: equity comforts," 15 February 2001. In Alumnae Board Meeting (minutes), 1 March 2001.
Rhodes, Andy (program committee chair). Email to Jennifer Parr. In Alumnae Board of Directors Meeting (minutes), 1 March 2001.
Tait, Anne. Email to Robin C. Whittaker, 10 March 2018.
Thom, Molly. Email to Pat McCarthy (Alumnae president) and others, 23 February 2001. In Alumnae Board Meeting Minutes, 1 March 2001.
Wellwood, F.E., Commissioner of Buildings. Letter to University Alumnae Dramatic Club, 14 November 1962.

Other Sources

"About Us." *Alumnae Theatre Company*. Web.
"Alumnae Theatre Rentals: Frequently Asked Questions," 1 January 2019. Web.
"A.I. Muldrew." *Torontonensis 1917*, 31.
"Alison Agnes Ewart." *Torontonensis 1922*, 17.
"Alumnae Dramatic Club." *University Monthly*, March 1939.
"Alumnae presents three plays." *University Monthly*, February 1935.
"Alumnae Theatre." Facebook.
Anderson, Chris. *The Long Tail: Why the Future of Business Is Selling Less of More*. New York: Hyperion, 2006.
"The Anti-Defamation League of B'nai B'rith." *ADL Intercom* 1, no. 8 (December–January 1971): 6.
"Any Black Crippled Woman Can!" *Room of One's Own* 8, no. 2 (July 1983): 7–18.

Arthurson, Wayne. *For Love Not Money: 50 Years of Walterdale Playhouse*. Edmonton: self-Published by Walterdale, 2008.

"Artist who painted famous *Queen on Moose* meets Her Majesty." *As It Happens. CBC*, 25 February 2015. Web.

Arts and Letters Club. "Monthly Letter," December 1955, 7.

Averill, Harold A. *Dramatis Personae: An Exhibition of Amateur Theatre at the University of Toronto 1879-1939*. Toronto: Governing Council, University of Toronto, 1992.

Backhouse, Constance, and Nancy L. Backhouse. *The Heiress vs the Establishment: Mrs. Campbell's Campaign for Legal Justice*. Vancouver: UBC Press, 2004.

Badir, Patricia. "'This Little Academe, Still and Contemplative in Living Art': Shakespeare, Modernism, and the Arts and Letters Club of Toronto." *Shakespeare Quarterly* 63, no. 1 (Spring 2012): 77–107.

Barton, Bruce. "Introduction: Creating Spaces." In *Developing Nation: New Play Creation in English-Speaking Canada*, ed. Barton, ix. Toronto: Playwrights Canada Press, 2008.

Beckwith, John, ed. *Unheard of: Memoirs of a Canadian Composer*. Wilfrid Laurier University Press, 2012.

Belasco David, and William Winter. *Plays Produced under the Stage Direction of David Belasco*. New York: n. pub., 1925.

Bell, Colin, and Howard Newby. *Community Studies: An Introduction to the Sociology of the Local Community*. London: Thomas Allen, 1989.

"Bertram Forsyth." In *Hart House Theatre: A Dramatic History*. HIS495Y1: History in the Digital Sphere (U of T course) in cooperation with Hart House Theatre. Web.

"Biographies of Early and Exceptional Ontario Lawyers of Diverse Communities Arranged by Year Called to the Bar, Pt. 1: 1797 to 1940." Law Society of Upper Canada, May 2012.

Bird, Kym. *Redressing the Past: The Politics of Early English-Canadian Women's Drama, 1880–1920*. Kingston and Montreal: McGill–Queen's University Press, 2004.

Blackburn, Marthe, et al. *A Clash of Symbols (La nef des sorcières)*. Toronto: Coach House Press, 1979.

Bourdieu, Pierre. *Distinction: A Social Critique of the Judgment of Taste*. Trans. Richard Nice. Cambridge, MA: Harvard University Press, 1984.

Bowring, Amy, curator. "Dancer, Director, Collaborator, 1930s: 1939 to the Present." *Alison Sutcliffe Exhibition* [2008]. Web. 5 July 2018.

Brodie, Janine. "We Are All Equal Now: Contemporary Gender Politics in Canada." *Feminist Theory* 9, no. 2 (2008): 145–64.

Burton, Peter, and John Lane. *New Directions: Ways of Advance for the Amateur Theatre*. Intro. John Arden. London: MacGibbon and Kee, 1970.

Burton, Rebecca. *Adding It Up: The Status of Women in Canadian Theatre*. Playwrights Guild of Canada. Toronto: Canada Council for the Arts, 2006.

Bush, Stephen. *Conversations with George Luscombe: Stephen Bush in Conversation with the Canadian Theatre Visionary*. Oakville: Mosaic Press, 2012.

Calendar of the University of Toronto for the Year 1904–1905. U of Toronto Press, 1904.

"Canada's Theatre Museum Announces Its New Home within The Elgin and Winter Garden Theatre Centre." *Theatre Museum Canada*. Web.

Card, Raymond. "Drama in Toronto: The Forgotten Years 1919–1938." *English Quarterly* 6, no. 1 (Spring 1973): 67–81.

Carstairs, Catherine, and Nancy Janovicek. "Introduction: Productive Pasts and New Directions." In *Feminist History in Canada: New Essays on Women, Gender, Work, and Nation*, edited by Catherine Carstairs and Nancy Janovicek, 3–20. Vancouver: UBC Press, 2013.

Carson, Neil. *Harlequin in Hogtown: George Luscombe and Toronto Workshop Productions.* Toronto: University of Toronto Press, 1995.

CBC Radio. "CBC Tuesday Night: Yeats and Thomas," 13–19 December 1969, 6.

"Celebrating 100 Years of Women's Law Association of Ontario in 2019." "History." *Women's Law Association of Ontario*, 2019.

"Central Ontario Drama Festival." Programs. February 1947, March 1948.

Chansky, Dorothy. *Composing Ourselves: The Little Theatre Movement and the American Audience.* Carbondale: Southern Illinois University Press, 2004.

Chapman, Vernon. *"Who's in the Goose Tonight?" An Anecdotal History of Canadian Theatre.* Toronto: ECW, 2001.

Charlesworth, Hector. "The third comedy …" *Saturday Night*, 6 May 1922.

City Clerk. Report to the City of Toronto Executive Committee, 2 October 1970.

City of Toronto Executive Committee. Report No. 31, c. March 1971.

City Property Commissioner. Report to City of Toronto Executive Committee, 5 February 1970.

– Report to City of Toronto Executive Committee, 26 August 1970.

"Class Horoscope." *Torontonensis 1912*, 38.

Clayton, J. Douglas. "Bears and Beavers: Canadian Stage Productions of Russian Plays." *Theatre Research in Canada* 3, no. 2 (Fall 1982): 149–63.

Cochrane, Claire. "The Pervasiveness of the Commonplace: The Historian and Amateur Theatre." *Theatre Research International* 26, no. 3 (October 2001): 233–42.

Connor, J.T.H. *Doing Good: The Life of Toronto's General Hospital.* Toronto: U Toronto P, 2000.

Conover, Dora Smith, Patrick O'Neill. "The Playwrights Studio Group: An Interview with Two Women Playwrights of the 1930s." *Atlantis* 8, no. 1 (Fall 1982): 89–96 at 90.

Cook, Ramsay. *The Regenerators: Social Criticism in Late Victorian English Canada*, 2nd ed. Toronto: University of Toronto Press, 2016.

Cordingley, Audrey. *The Anchora of the Delta Gamma Fraternity*, edited by Lambda Chapter. University of Minnesota, May 1923, 473.

Criterion Research Corp. "Live Theatre Attendance in Edmonton: A Research Report." Edmonton: Edmonton Arts Council, August 2001.

Czarnecki, Mark. "The Regional Theatre System." *Contemporary Canadian Theatre: New World Visions*, edited by Anton Wagner, 35–48. Toronto: Simon and Pierre, 1985.

Davies, Robertson. "Fifty Years of Theatre in Canada." *University of Toronto Quarterly* 50, no. 1 (1980): 69–80 at 72.

– "Foreword." In Betty Lee, *Love and Whisky: The Story of the Dominion Drama Festival*, ix–xi. Toronto: McClelland and Stewart, 1973.

– "Robertson Davies on the Young Vincent Massey." *Theatre Research in Canada* 3, no. 1 (Spring 1982): 98.

Day, Moira. "Treading the Arduous Road to Eleusis, Nationalism, and Feminism in Early Post-World War I Canada: Roy Mitchell's 1920 *The Trojan Women*." In *Oxford Handbook of Greek Drama in the Americas*, edited by Kathryn Bosher, Fiona Macintosh, Justine McConnell, and Patrice Rankine, 184–203. Oxford: Oxford University Press, 2015.

"Directory of Officers of State Associations." *The Osteopathic Physician* 22, no. 3 (September 1912): 10.

Dobson, Michael. *Shakespeare and Amateur Performance: A Cultural History.* New York: Cambridge University Press, 2011, 8.

Duchesne, Scott K. "Critical Introduction." In Roy Mitchell, *Creative Theatre.* Ottawa: University of Ottawa Press, 2020.

Eltis, Sos. "Reception and Performance History of Wilde's Society Plays." In *Oscar Wilde in Context*, edited by Kerry Powell and Peter Raby. New York: Cambridge University Press, 2013.

"E.R. Bach." *Torontonensis 1917*, 14.

"Equity Proposal." *Alumination*, March 2001.

Ewart, Alison, and Julia Jarvis. "The Personnel of the Family Compact, 1791–1841." *Canadian Historical Review* 7, no. 3 (September 1926): 209–21.

Filewod, Alan. *Committing Theatre: Theatre Radicalism and Political Intervention in Canada.* Toronto: Between the Lines, 2011.

– "Erasing Historical Difference: The Alternative Theatre Orthodoxy in Canadian Theatre." *Theatre Journal* 42, no. 1 (1989): 201–10.

– "Erect Sons and Dutiful Daughters." In *Imperialism and Theatre*, edited by Ellen Gainor, 56–70. New York: Routledge, 1995.

– "Naming the Movement: Recapitalizing Popular Theatre." In *Performing National Identities: International Perspectives on Contemporary Canadian Theatre*, edited by Sherrill Grace and Albert-Reiner Glaap, 227–43. Vancouver: Talonbooks, 2003.

Filewod, Alan, ed. *Reliving the Trenches: Memory Plays by Veterans of the Great War.* Waterloo: Wilfrid Laurier University Press, 2021.

Firehall Theatre (formerly The Coach House). Letter to the Editor. *Toronto Star*, 25 November 1973, 1–2.

Fischlin, Daniel. "The Margaret Eaton School of Literature and Expression." *Canadian Adaptations of Shakespeare Project*. U of Guelph. Web.

Florida, Richard. *The Rise of the Creative Class: And How It's Transforming Work, Leisure, Community, and Everyday Life*. New York: Basic Books, 2002.

Ford, Anne Rochon. *A Path Not Strewn with Roses: One Hundred Years of Women at the University of Toronto 1884–1984*. Toronto: University of Toronto Press, 1988.

Forestell, Nancy. "Mrs. Canada Goes Global: Canadian First Wave Feminism Revisited," *Atlantis* 30, no. 1 (2005): 7–20.

Foster, C.L. "Preface." *Letters from the Front: Being a Record of the Part Played by Officers of the Bank in the Great War 1914–1919*, vol. 1, ix–xii. Toronto: Canadian Bank of Commerce. Southam Press, 1920.

Fraticelli, Rina. *The Status of Women in the Canadian Theatre*. Report prepared for Status of Women in Canada, June 1982 [excerpts published in "The Invisibility Factor: The Status of Women in Canadian Theatre," *Fuse* 6, no. 3 (September 1982), 112–24.

Freeman, Barry. *Staging Strangers: Theatre and Global Ethics*. Montreal and Kingston: McGill–Queen's UP, 2017.

Friedland, Martin L. *The University of Toronto: A History.* Toronto: University of Toronto Press, 2002.

Gale, Maggie B. "Women's Playwrights of the 1920s and 1930s." In *The Cambridge Companion to Modern British Women Playwrights*, edited by Elaine Aston and Janelle G. Reinelt, 23–37. Cambridge: Cambridge University Press, 2000.

Gardner, David. "Little Theatre Movement." *The Canadian Encyclopedia*, Rev. 16 December 2013. Web.

– "Little Theatre and Amateur Theatre." *The Oxford Companion to Canadian Theatre*. Toronto: Oxford University Press, 1989.

Gayfer, Margaret. "Opera to Watch: All about a Stratford Flower." No magazine recorded. n.d.

Gidney, Catherine. "Feminist Ideals and Everyday Life: Professional Women's Feminism at Victoria College, University of Toronto, 1900–40." In *Feminist History in Canada: New Essays on Women, Gender, Work, and Nation*, edited by Catherine Carstairs and Nancy Janovicek, 96–117. Vancouver: UBC Press, 2013.

Gilbert, David, et al. "On Amateurs." *Performance Research: A Journal of Performing Arts* 25, no. 1 (2020): 2–9.

Gordon, Linda. "Socialist Feminism: The Legacy of the 'Second Wave.'" *New Labor Forum* 22, no. 3 (2013): 21–8.

Halpenny, Francess. "Shall we join the ladies?" *University of Toronto Graduate*, December 1968, 48–51, 102–4, 106.

– "University Alumnae Dramatic Club." In *The Oxford Companion to Canadian Theatre*, edited by Eugene Benson, and L.W. Connolly, 573–74. Toronto: Oxford University Press, 1989.

Hankin, St. John, *The Charity That Began at Home: A Comedy in Four Acts*. New York: Samuel French, 1907.

Harman, Eleanor. "Founding a University Press." In *The University as Publisher*, ed. Eleanor Harmon. Toronto: University of Toronto Press, 1961.

"Hart House and University College." *The Rebel* 3, no. 5 (March 1919): 193.

"Hart House Theatre Production History." *Hart House Theatre*, 2013. Web.

Hawley, Judith. "Dilettante Theatricals: The Elite Amateur in the Georgian Period." *Performance Research* 25, no. 1 (2020): 67–72.

Hodgins, Frank Egerton. *Report on the Care and Control of the Mentally Defective and Feeble-Minded in Ontario*. Toronto: Legislative Assembly, 1919.

Holdsworth, Nadine, Jane Milling, and Helen Nicholson. "Theatre, Performance, and the Amateur Turn." *Contemporary Theatre Review* 27, no. 1 (2017): 4–17.

Hood, Sarah. "Seven Decades of Dedication: Alumnae Theatre Continues to Thrive through Nearly Seventy Years of Transformation and Acclaimed Productions." *Toronto Theatre*. Spring 1988, 14–15.

Huneault, Katrina. "Introduction." In *Rethinking Professionalism: Women and Art in Canada, 1850–1970*, edited by Katrina Huneault and Janice Anderson, 3–52. Montreal and Kingston: McGill–Queen's University Press, 2012.

Hunter, Marion Squair. "World War I from the Berry Patch." Posted by Catherine Murno in *Brian Henry's Quick Brown Fox*, 19 March 2020.

Hunter, Martin. *Still Hunting: A Memoir*. Toronto: ECW Press, 2013.

Hutchison, Robert, and Andrew Feist. *Amateur Arts in the UK*, no. 726. London: Policy Studies Institute, 1991.

"In View: A selection of events and places to go, from what's doing this month." *Toronto Calendar Magazine*, 29 September 1972, 14.

Ives, David. "Sure Thing." In *All in the Timing: Fourteen Plays*. Toronto: Vintage. 2010.

James, Cathy L. "Practical Diversions and Educational Amusements: Evangelia House and the Advent of Canada's Settlement Movement, 1902–09." *Historical Studies in Education / Revue d'histoire de l'éducation* 10, nos. 1–2 (1998).

"Jessie Elspeth Wilson." *Torontonensis 1913*, 72.

Johnston, Denis W. "Appendix B: Toronto Playlist 1968–1975." In *Up the Mainstream: The Rise of Toronto's Alternative Theatres*. Toronto: University of Toronto Press, 1991, 271–3.

– "Bill Glassco and Tarragon Theatre." Toronto: n.p., 1988 [monograph of an article originally published in *Canadian Drama*].

– *Up the Mainstream: The Rise of Toronto's Alternative Theatres*. Toronto: University of Toronto Press, 1991.

Johnston, Sheila M.F. *Let's Go to The Grand! 100 Years of Entertainment at London's Grand Theatre*. Toronto: Natural Heritage Books, 2001.
Journal of Proceeding of the Convocation of benchers of the Law Society of Upper Canada. 1915.
"Julian Beecroft." *Allison Funeral Home*, January 2008. Web.
Kappa Alpha Theta Journal 36, no. 2 (January 1922), 184.
"Kappa Alpha Theta." *Torontonensis 1950*, 438.
"Katherine Barwick Wells." *Torontonensis 1924*, 35.
Kerr, Lois Reynolds. "The Playwrights Studio Group, 1932–1941.'" *Association for Canadian Theatre Research Newsletter* 7, no. 1, 1982.
Klinck, Carl F., ed. *Literary History of Canada: Canadian Literature in English*, 2nd ed., vol. 2. Toronto: University of Toronto Press, 1976.
Knott, Stephen. "Fancy Dress as an Amateur Craft." *Performance Research* 25, no. 1 (2020): 10–17.
Kuftinec, Sonja. *Staging America: Cornerstone and Community-Based Theater*. Carbondale: Southern Illinois University Press, 2003.
Laughton, Mary Elizabeth. "Women in Law." *Maclean's Magazine*, 1 April 1920, 74, 78.
Lee, Betty. *Love and Whisky: The Story of the Dominion Drama Festival*. Toronto: McClelland and Stewart, 1973.
Leonard, Agatha. "Special Libraries in Ontario." *Special Libraries: Official Journal of the Special Libraries Association*. April 1953, 137–41.
– "Statistical Methods in Medical School Libraries." Read at the Annual Meeting of the Medical Library Association, Galveston, Texas, 11 April 1949.
Leonard, Kat. "Alumnae Theatre: The Women Speak." Reposted on *The Alumnae Theatre Company's Blog*, July 2007, reposted 5 January 2012. Web.
"Lombard Street Central Fire Hall." *Lively Legacy of Lombard Street*, 3 March 1918.
MacArthur, Michelle [Laura]. "Re-viewing Reception: Criticism of Feminist Theatre in Montreal and Toronto, 1976 to Present." PhD diss., University of Toronto. 2014.
– *Achieving Equity in Canadian Theatre: A Report with Best Practice Recommendations*. Toronto: Equity in Theatre, 2015.
– "Historiographing a Feminist Utopia: Collective Creation, History, and Feminist Theatre in Canada." In *Women, Collective Creation, and Devised Performance*, ed. Kathryn Mederos Syssoyeva and Scott Proudfit, 161–76. New York: Palgrave Macmillan, 2016.
MacKay, Constance D'Arcy. *The Little Theatre in the United States*. New York: Henry Holt, 1917.
Mail. 14 January 1925 and 29 January 1927.
Makovac, Denise. "Academics and Pandemics: The University of Toronto during the 1918 Spanish Flu." *CIHE Blog*. Centre for the Study of Canadian and International Higher Education, 7 May 2020.
Margaret Ness. *Enter the Prince*. In *Curtain Call*, Toronto, January 1938.
Martin, Jennifer. "*Murder on the Nile*." *Varsity*, 15 October 1976, 8.
Mascall, Blair. "The Alumnae Theatre Company" [Speech]. 6 April 2002.
Mascall, Elizabeth. "Drama festival winners to present *Years Ago*." *Varsity*, 1 November 1948.
Massey, Vincent. *What's Past Is Prologue: The Memoirs of Vincent Massey*. Toronto: Macmillan, 1963.
Mastheads. *Varsity*. 19 February and 11 November 1930.
Maugham, Somerset. *Caesar's Wife*. London: William Heinemann, 1922.
McDonald, Marci. "The arts are rescuing a gray old hobo of a street." *Toronto Star*, 22 July 1972, 37.
McKillop, A.B. *Pierre Berton: A Biography*. Toronto: McClelland and Stewart, 2010.

McKinnie, Michael. *City Stages: Theatre and Urban Space in a Global City*. Toronto: University of Toronto Press, 2007.

Mirvish, Ed and Anne. Note in Comment Book for *Ten Lost Years*, January 2001.

Molière. *The Learned Ladies*. Translated by Curtis Hidden Page. New York: G.P. Putnam's Sons, 1908.

Morgan, Cecilia. "'An embarrassingly and severely masculine atmosphere': Women, Gender, and the Legal Profession at Osgoode Hall, 1920s–1960s." *Canadian Journal of Law and Society* 11, no. 2 (Fall 1996): 19–61.

Murray, Heather. "Doubled Lives: Florence Valentine Keys, David Reid Keys, and the Work of English Studies." *University of Toronto Quarterly* 76, no. 4 (Fall 2007): 1007–39.

– "Making the Modern: Twenty-Five Years of the Margaret Eaton School of Literature and Expression." *Essays in Theatre / Études théâtres* 10, no. 1 (1991): 39–57.

Neighbourhood Workers Association. *Social Services Directory*. Toronto, 1917.

Nicholson, Helen, et al. *The Ecologies of Amateur Theatre*. London: Palgrave, 2018.

Nineteenth Century Theatre and Film 38, no. 2 (Winter 2011).

"*Old Times*." *Toronto Calendar*. n.d.

O'Neill, Patrick. "The Playwrights Studio Group: An Interview with Two Women Playwrights of the 1930s." *Atlantis* 8, no. 1 (Fall 1982): 89–96.

Ontario Arts Council. "Vida Peene Fund."

Ouzounian, Richard. "*Thirteen Hands* by Carol Shields (Alumnae Theatre.)" CBC, 28 April 1995.

Palmer, Barbara, et al. "The York Cycle in Performance: Toronto and York." *Early Theatre* 1 (1998): 139–69.

Panofsky, Ruth. *Toronto Trailblazers: Women in Canadian Publishing*. University of Toronto Press, 2019.

Partington, Richard. "The Jupiter Theatre's Canadian Content and the Critics, 1951–1954." *Theatre Research in Canada* 18, no. 1 (Spring 1997): 59–88.

Performance Research 25, no. 1 (2020).

Perin, Roberto. *The Many Rooms of This House: Diversity in Toronto's Places of Worship Since 1840*. Toronto: University of Toronto Press, 2017.

Perry, Bliss. "The Amateur Spirit." In *The Amateur Spirit* [1904], 1–34. Freeport: Books for Libraries, 1969.

Pitches, Jonathan. "High Culture: Presentations of the Self in Mountain Environments." *Performance Research* 25, no. 1 (2020): 31–8.

"Players' Guild." *Torontonensis 1925*, 320.

"Players' Guild of University College Executive, 1922–23." *Torontonensis 1923*, 35.

Pritchard, Gillian. "Down from the pedestal: On the eve of its 60th birthday, the 'Alum' is shedding its elitist image. There'll be some changes made." *Scene Changes*, September 1978, 10, 19, 27.

Pyper, Nancy. "Among the amateurs." *Saturday Night*, n.d.

Reynolds Kerr, Lois. "Lois Reynolds Kerr Recalls the Playwrights Studio Group 1932–1941." *Theatre Research in Canada* 5, no.1 (Spring 1984): 98–107.

Ridout, Nicholas. *Passionate Amateurs: Theatre, Communism, and Love*. Ann Arbor: University of Michigan Press, 2015.

"*The Romantic Age* – 1922 [...] Expenses." Early Account Book 1, 29 April 1922.

Rouillard, C.D., et al. "A Golden Age, 1920–1960." In *French Studies at the University of Toronto 1853–1993*.

Saddlemyer, Ann, and Richard Plant, eds. *Later Stages: Essays in Ontario Theatre from the First World War to the 1970s*. Toronto: University of Toronto Press, 1997.

Saint-Denis, Michael. "*The Cradle Song*. M. St.-Denis, Saturday Night adjudication." Adjudicator's Report, 1 May 1937.

Sandwell, B.K. [No title recorded]. *Saturday Night*, 15 May 1937.

Sargent, Ann. Quoted in Sarah Hood, "Seven decades of dedication: Alumnae Theatre continues to thrive through nearly seventy years of transformation and acclaimed productions." *Toronto Theatre* (Spring 1988): 14–15.

Scott, Robert B. "Professional Performers and Companies." In *Later Stages: Essays on Ontario Theatre from the First World War to the 1970s*, edited by Ann Saddlemyer and Richard Plant, 13–120. Toronto: University of Toronto Press, 1997.

Scott, Shelley. *Nightwood Theatre: A Woman's Work Is Always Done*. Edmonton: Athabasca University Press, 2010.

Sharma, Sarah. *In the Meantime: Temporality and Cultural Politics*. Durham: Duke University Press, 2014.

Shorter, Edward. *Partnership for Excellence: Medicine at the University of Toronto and Academic Hospitals*. Toronto: University of Toronto Press, 2013.

"Smart, Mary W." *Torontonensis 1919*, 24.

Spencer, Nigel. "*The Plough and the Stars*." *Toronto Theatre*, 3 November 1972.

Sperdakos, Paula. *Dora Mavor Moore: Pioneer of the Canadian Theatre*. Toronto: ECW, 1995.

Spiegel, Jennifer Beth. "Amateur Performance and the Labour of Love or Cultural Reproduction 'after' the Collapse of Capitalism." *Performance Research* 25, no. 1 (2020): 121–4.

"Squair, Marion R." *Torontonensis 1918*, 25.

Srigley, Katrina. *Breadwinning Daughters: Young Working Women in a Depression-Era City, 1929–1939*. Toronto: University of Toronto Press, 2010.

St. Denys Johnson, Audrey. "Eliot play praised by festival judge." *Victoria Daily Times*, 7 May 1953, 16.

Stebbins, Robert A. *Amateurs, Professionals, and Serious Leisure*. Montreal and Kingston: McGill–Queen's University Press, 1992.

Sternberg, Barbara. "Rae Davis: Four Decades of Invention." In *Caught in the Act: An Anthology of Performance Art by Canadian Women*, edited by Tanya Mars and Johanna Householder. Toronto: YYZBOOKS. 2006.

Stevens, Martin. "The York Cycle: From Procession to Play." *Leeds Studies in English* (new series) 6 (1972): 37–61.

Stuart, Robert. Adjudicator's form. CODL, 18 March 2019.

Stuart, [E.] Ross. "The Critic as Reviewer: E.R. Parkhurst at the Toronto *Mail* and *Globe*, 1876–1924," in Anton Wagner, ed. *Establishing Our Boundaries*, 95.

"Teach Me How to Cry." *Bizstore Books*. https://store.bizbooks.net/teachmehowtocry.aspx.

Television listings. *Globe and Mail*, 5 May 1990, 33, and 9 July 1994, 40.

Terence William Goldie, *Canadian Dramatic Literature in English 1919–1939*. PhD diss., Queen's University, 1977.

Terry, Megan. "Production Notes." In *Viet Rock, Comings and Goings, Keep Tightly Closed in a Cool Dry Place, The Gloaming, Oh My Darling: Four Plays by Megan Terry*, 21–3. New York: Simon and Schuster, 1967.

"The 1963–64 Office of Education Survey of College and University Library Statistics." *College and Research Libraries* 25, no. 4 (1964): 348.

"The Boys from Parkhill." Laughton.ca.

"The Dominion Drama Festival." Program, April 1948, 3.

"The Modern Language Club of University College." *Torontonensis 1919*, 47.

"The Modern Language Club." *Torontonensis 1925*, 300.

"The Old Stagers history." *The Old Stagers*. Web.

"The Professional Toronto Premiere of a Canadian Classic: *The Ecstasy of Rita Joe*." Postcard flyer, November 1989.

Theatre Museum Canada. "About Us." Accessed 4 August 2020. Web.
Theatre, Performance, and the Amateur Turn 27, no. 1 (2017).
Thom, Molly. "New Ideas – Genesis." *Alumination*. March 2007.
– "*Thirteen Hands* report by Molly Thom (director)." *Alumination*, May 1995.
Tippett, Maria. *Making Culture: English-Canadian Institutions and the Arts before the Massey Commission*. Toronto: University of Toronto Press, 1990.
Toronto and Early Canada: A Catalogue of the Toronto and Early Canada Picture Collection in the Toronto Public Library. Toronto: Baxter, 1964.
Toronto Life. Theatre Listings, November 1974.
Toronto Police Service. "Proud of Our Past, Confident of Our Future: A History of Policing in Toronto" [Brochure], 4.
Toronto Public Library. "Forty-Seventh Annual Report." Toronto: G.A. Davis, 1930.
Torontonensis 1915, *Torontonensis 1917*, *Torontonensis 1918*.
"Amateur theatre's cast of thousands." *Maclean's*, 6 January 1962, 22–3, 54.
University of Toronto Academic Divisions Calendar, 1953–54.
University of Toronto Alumni Association. *The University Monthly* 16 (1915–16).
University of Toronto Monthly 23 (June 1922), 383, 420.
University of Toronto Quarterly 9, no. 3 (April 1940): 348–91.
"University of Toronto Report of the Board of Governors for the Year Ended 30th June 1936." *University of Toronto Quarterly* 1937, 96.
Usmiani, Renate. "Roy Mitchell: Prophet in Our Past." *Theatre Research in Canada* 8, no. 2 (1987): 147–68.
W.K. "Two nice fire halls are o.k." Toronto Parks and Recreation, October 1970.
Wagner, Anton. "Infinite Variety or a Canadian 'National' Theatre: Roly Young and the Toronto Civic Theatre Association, 1945–1949." *Theatre History in Canada / Histoire du théâtre au Canada* 9, no. 2 (1988): 173–92.
– "Introduction: Establishing Our Boundaries: English-Canadian Theatre Criticism." In *Establishing Our Boundaries: English-Canadian Theatre Criticism*, ed. Wagner, 3–58. University of Toronto Press, 1999.
Wagner, Anton. ed. *Establishing Our Boundaries: English-Canadian Theatre Criticism*. University of Toronto Press, 1999.
Walters, Ben. "Being among Bluebells: Amateurism as Mode of Queer Futurity at Duckie's Slaughterhouse Club." *Performance Research* 25, no. 1 (2020): 96–103.
Wasserman, Jerry, ed. *Modern Canadian Plays*, vol. 1, 4th ed. Vancouver: Talonbooks, 2000.
Wasserman, Jerry. "George Ryga." In *Modern Canadian Plays*, vol. 1, 4th ed., ed. Wasserman, 23–4. Vancouver: Talonbooks, 2000.
Watson, Wilfred. *Plays at the Iron Bridge, or The Autobiography of Tom Horror*, edited by Shirley Neuman. Edmonton: Longspoon/NeWest Press, 1989.
Weston, Ken, and Patricia Beharriell. *The Domino Affair*. Kingston: Domino Theatre, 2002.
Whittaker, Herbert. *Setting the Stage: Montreal Theatre 1920–1949*. Ed. Jonathan Rittenhouse. Montreal and Kingston: McGill–Queen's University Press, 1999.
Whittaker, Robin C. "'Entirely Free of Any Amateurishness': Private Training, Public Taste, and the Women's Dramatic Club of University College, Toronto (1905–21)." *Nineteenth-Century Theatre and Film*. Special Issue: Amateur Theatre in the Long Nineteenth Century. 38, no. 2 (Winter 2011): 51-66.
– *Hot Thespian Action! Ten Premiere Plays from Walterdale Playhouse*. Edmonton: Athabasca University Press, 2008.

– "Un/Disciplined Re/Collections: Toward an Archaeology of Nonprofessionalizing Theatre Practices." In *Canadian Performance Histories and Historiographies*, edited by Heather Davis-Fisch, 161–78. Toronto: Playwrights Canada Press, 2017.

– "Walterdale Theatre Associates and the In(ter)vention of the Audience." *Canadian Theatre Review* 140 (Fall 2009): 33–9.

Wickham, Glynne. *The Medieval Theatre* [1974], 3rd ed. New York: Cambridge UP, 1988.

Winston, Iris. *Staging a Legend: A History of Ottawa Little Theatre*. Carp: Creative Bound, 1997.

Winter, Jack. "Amateur." *Canadian Forum*, November 1960.

Winter, Jack. *My TWP Plays: A Collection Including Ten Lost Years*. Vancouver: Talonbooks, 2013.

"Women university grads buy a theatre." *Paper Doll*, November 1962.

"The Women's Athletic Association of University College." *Torontonensis 1917*.

"The Women's Dramatic Club." *Torontonensis 1916*, 221.

"The Women's Literary Society of University College." *Torontonensis 1919*, *1920*.

Wright, Donald. *The Professionalization of History in English Canada*. Toronto: U of Toronto P, 2005.

Young, Roly. "What Is the Civic Theatre Association?" *Civic Theatre Magazine*, October 1945, 7.

Index

Page numbers in italics refer to figures.